ARY (

ıg scholarly value

Spiritualism and Esoteric Knowledge

Magic, superstition, the occult sciences and esoteric knowledge appear
regularly in the history of ideas alongside more established academic
disciplines such as philosophy, natural history and theology. Particularly
fascinating are periods of rapid scientific advances such as the Renaissance
or the nineteenth century which also see a burgeoning of interest in the
paranormal among the educated elite. This series provides primary texts and
secondary sources for social historians and cultural anthropologists working
in these areas, and all who wish for a wider understanding of the diverse
intellectual and spiritual movements that formed a backdrop to the academic
and political achievements of their day. It ranges from works on Babylonian
and Jewish magic in the ancient world, through studies of sixteenth-century
topics such as Cornelius Agrippa and the rapid spread of Rosicrucianism, to
nineteenth-century publications by Sir Walter Scott and Sir Arthur Conan
Doyle. Subjects include astrology, mesmerism, spiritualism, theosophy,
clairvoyance, and ghost-seeing, as described both by their adherents and by
sceptics.

Phantasms of the Living

This two-volume work, co-authored by Edmund Gurney (1847–1888),
Frederic W. H. Myers (1843–1901) and Frank Podmore (1856–1910),
all leading members of the Society for Psychical Research, was first
published in 1886. It documents over 700 case studies of ghost-seeing, and
aimed to revolutionise thinking about ghosts by proposing a theory that
explained ghost-seeing through the idea of telepathy. Volume 1 includes an
introduction by Myers and an explanation of the analytical methods used in
the study. It then focuses on hypnotism, the telepathic transference of ideas,
mental pictures and emotional impressions, dreams, and hallucinations, and
contains an impressive essay on the history of witchcraft. This pioneering
study is an indispensable source for the history of psychical research. It
provides detailed insights into the Victorian fascination with the occult and
the supernatural, and is still the most extensive collection of ghost-seeing
accounts available.

Cambridge University Press has long been a pioneer in the reissuing of out-of-print titles from its own backlist, producing digital reprints of books that are still sought after by scholars and students but could not be reprinted economically using traditional technology. The Cambridge Library Collection extends this activity to a wider range of books which are still of importance to researchers and professionals, either for the source material they contain, or as landmarks in the history of their academic discipline.

Drawing from the world-renowned collections in the Cambridge University Library, and guided by the advice of experts in each subject area, Cambridge University Press is using state-of-the-art scanning machines in its own Printing House to capture the content of each book selected for inclusion. The files are processed to give a consistently clear, crisp image, and the books finished to the high quality standard for which the Press is recognised around the world. The latest print-on-demand technology ensures that the books will remain available indefinitely, and that orders for single or multiple copies can quickly be supplied.

The Cambridge Library Collection will bring back to life books of enduring scholarly value (including out-of-copyright works originally issued by other publishers) across a wide range of disciplines in the humanities and social sciences and in science and technology.

Phantasms
of the Living

VOLUME 1

EDMUND GURNEY
FREDERIC W. H. MYERS
FRANK PODMORE

CAMBRIDGE
UNIVERSITY PRESS

CAMBRIDGE UNIVERSITY PRESS

Cambridge, New York, Melbourne, Madrid, Cape Town, Singapore,
São Paolo, Delhi, Dubai, Tokyo, Mexico City

Published in the United States of America by Cambridge University Press, New York

www.cambridge.org
Information on this title: www.cambridge.org/9781108027328

This edition first published 1886
This digitally printed version 2011

ISBN 978-1-108-02732-8 Paperback

PHANTASMS OF THE LIVING.

PHANTASMS OF THE LIVING

EDMUND GURNEY, M.A.

LATE FELLOW OF TRINITY COLLEGE, CAMBRIDGE,

FREDERIC W. H. MYERS, M.A.

LATE FELLOW OF TRINITY COLLEGE, CAMBRIDGE,

AND

FRANK PODMORE, M.A.

VOLUME I.

ROOMS OF THE SOCIETY FOR PSYCHICAL RESEARCH,
14, Dean's Yard, S.W.
TRÜBNER AND CO., LUDGATE HILL, E.C.
1886.

The right of translation and reproduction is reserved.

*** In the later copies of this edition, a few mistakes which occurred in the earlier copies have been corrected, and some additions have been made. Of these, by far the most important is the record which appears on pp. lxxxi–iv of this Volume.

PREFACE.

A LARGE part of the material used in this book was sent to the authors as representatives of the Society for Psychical Research; and the book is published with the sanction of the Council of that Society.

The division of authorship has been as follows. As regards the writing and the views expressed,—Mr. Myers is solely responsible for the Introduction, and for the " Note on a Suggested Mode of Psychical Interaction," which immediately precedes the Supplement; and Mr. Gurney is solely responsible for the remainder of the book. But the most difficult and important part of the undertaking—the collection, examination, and appraisal of evidence—has been a joint labour, of which Mr. Podmore has borne so considerable a share that his name could not have been omitted from the title-page.

In the free discussion and criticism which has accompanied the progress of the work, we have enjoyed the constant advice and assistance of Professor and Mrs. Sidgwick,. to each of whom we owe more than can be expressed by any conventional phrases of obligation. Whatever errors of judgment or flaws in argument may remain, such blemishes are certainly fewer than they would have been but for this watchful and ever-ready help. Professor and Mrs. Sidgwick have also devoted some time and trouble, during vacations, to the practical work of interviewing informants and obtaining their personal testimony.

In the acknowledgment of our debts, special mention is due to Professor W. F. Barrett. He was to a great extent the pioneer of the movement which it is hoped that this book may carry forward; and the extent of his services in relation, especially, to the subject of experimental Thought-transference will sufficiently appear in the sequel. Mr. Malcolm Guthrie, Professor Oliver J. Lodge, and M. Charles Richet have been most welcome allies in the same branch of the work. Professor Barrett and M. Richet have also supplied several of the non-experimental cases in our collection. Mr. F. Y. Edgeworth has rendered valuable assistance in points relating to the theory of probabilities, a subject on which he is a recognised authority. Among members of our own Society, our warmest thanks are due to Miss Porter, for her well-directed, patient, and energetic assistance in every department of the work; Mr. C. C. Massey has given us the benefit of his counsel; and Mrs. Walwyn, Mr. Hensleigh Wedgwood, the Rev. A. T. Fryer, of Clerkenwell, the Rev. J. A. Macdonald, of Rhyl, and Mr. Richard Hodgson, have aided us greatly in the collection of evidence. Many other helpers, in this and other countries, we must be content to include in a general expression of gratitude.

Further records of experience will be most welcome, and should be sent to the subjoined address.

14, Dean's Yard, S. W.
June, 1886.

SOCIETY FOR PSYCHICAL RESEARCH.

1886.

PRESIDENT.

PROFESSOR BALFOUR STEWART, F.R.S.

VICE-PRESIDENTS.

THE RIGHT HON. ARTHUR J. BALFOUR, M.P.
PROFESSOR W. F. BARRETT, F.R.S.E.
THE RIGHT REV. THE BISHOP OF CARLISLE.
JOHN R. HOLLOND, M.A.
RICHARD H. HUTTON, M.A., LL.D.
THE HON. RODEN NOEL.
LORD RAYLEIGH, M.A., F.R.S.
THE RIGHT REV. THE BISHOP OF RIPON.
PROFESSOR HENRY SIDGWICK, Lit. D., D.C.L.
W. H. STONE, M.B.
HENSLEIGH WEDGWOOD, M.A.

HONORARY MEMBERS.

J. C. ADAMS, M.A., F.R.S.
WILLIAM CROOKES, F.R.S.
THE RIGHT HON. W. E. GLADSTONE, M.P.
JOHN RUSKIN, LL.D., D.C.L.
LORD TENNYSON.
ALFRED RUSSEL WALLACE, F.R.G.S.
G F. WATTS, R.A.

CORRESPONDING MEMBERS.

COUNCIL.

A. MACALISTER, M.D., F.R.S., Professor of Anatomy, Cambridge
FREDERIC W. H. MYERS, M.A.
FRANK PODMORE, M.A.
LORD RAYLEIGH, M.A., F.R.S.
C. LOCKHART ROBERTSON, M.D.
E. DAWSON ROGERS.
HENRY SIDGWICK, Lit. D., D.C.L., Knightbridge Professor of Moral
   Philosophy, Cambridge.
HENRY A. SMITH, M.A.
J. HERBERT STACK.
BALFOUR STEWART, F.R.S., Professor of Physics, The Owens
   College, Manchester.
J. J. THOMSON, M.A., Professor of Experimental Physics,
   Cambridge.
JAMES VENN, D.Sc., F.R.S.
HENSLEIGH WEDGWOOD, M.A.

HONORARY TREASURER.

HENRY A. SMITH, 1, New Square, Lincoln's Inn, W.C.

HONORARY SECRETARY.

EDMUND GURNEY, 14, Dean's Yard, Westminster, S.W.

In addition to the above, the Society includes over 600 Members and
Associates. The privileges and conditions of membership are thus defined
in the Rules :—

Rule IV.—The Society shall consist of :—

(a) *Members,* who shall contribute not less than two
guineas annually, or a single payment of twenty guineas, and
who shall be entitled to hold any of the offices of the Society ;
to vote in the election of the Governing Council ; to attend all
meetings of the Society ; to use its Reading Room and Library ;
to borrow books from its Library ; and to the free receipt of
any journal, transactions, or periodical publication which may
be issued by the Council.

(b) *Associates,* who shall contribute not less than one
guinea annually, or a single payment of ten guineas, and who
shall be entitled to attend all meetings of the Society, except
such as are convened for business purposes only ; to use its
Reading Room and Library ; and to the free receipt of the
ordinary published. *Proceedings* of the Society, and of the
monthly *Journal.*

Rule V.—All Members and Associates of the Society shall be elected by the Council. Every candidate for admission shall be proposed by two persons who are Members or Associates of the Society, or shall give such references as shall be approved by the Council.

Rule VI.—The subscription shall become due immediately on election, and afterwards in advance on the first day of January in each year. In the case of any Member or Associate elected on or after the 1st October, the subscription then paid shall be accepted as for the following year.

Ladies are eligible either as Members or Associates.

Members and Associates are entitled to purchase copies of all the periodical publications of the Society at half their published price.

The following note appears on the first page of the Society's Constitution :—

" To prevent misconception, it is here expressly stated that Membership of this Society does not imply the acceptance of any particular explanation of the phenomena investigated, nor any belief as to the operation, in the physical world, of forces other than those recognised by physical science."

Reports of investigation, or information relating to any branch of the Society's work, should be addressed to the Hon. Secretary, 14, Dean's Yard, Westminster, S.W.; letters of inquiry, or applications for Membership, should be addressed to the Assistant-Secretary at the same address.

The *Proceedings* of the Society (of which ten parts have been published —the first nine making three bound volumes) may be obtained from all booksellers through Messrs. Trübner and Co., Ludgate Hill, London, E.C.; or on direct application to the Assistant-Secretary, 14, Dean's Yard, Westminster S.W.

SYNOPSIS OF VOLUME I.

INTRODUCTION.

I.

§ 1. The title of this book embraces all transmissions of thought and feeling from one person to another, by other means than through the recognised channels of sense ; and among these cases we shall include apparitions

§ 2. We conceive that the problems here attacked lie in the main track of science

§ 3. The Society for Psychical Research merely aims at the free and exact discussion of the one remaining group of subjects to which such discussion is still refused. Reasons for such refusal .

§ 4. Reasons, on the other hand, for the prosecution of our inquiries may be drawn from the present condition of several contiguous studies. Reasons drawn from the advance of biology

§ 5. Specimens of problems which biology suggests, and on which inquiries like ours may ultimately throw light. Wundt's view of the origination of psychical energy

§ 6. The problems of hypnotism .

§ 7. Hope of aid from the progress of "psycho-physical" inquiries

§ 8. Reasons for psychical research drawn from the *lacunæ* of anthropology

§ 9. Reasons drawn from the study of history, and especially of the comparative history of religions. Instance from the S.P.R.'s investigation of so-called "Theosophy" .

§ 10. In considering the relation of our studies to religion generally, we observe that, since they oblige us to conceive the psychical element in man as having relations which cannot be expressed in terms

CHAPTER I.

PRELIMINARY REMARKS : GROUNDS OF CAUTION.

§ 1. The great test of scientific achievement is often held to be the power to *predict* natural phenomena ; but the test, though an authoritative one in the sciences of *inorganic* nature, has but a limited application to the sciences that deal with *life*, and especially to the department of *mental* phenomena 1–3

§ 2. In dealing with the implications of life and the developments of human faculty, caution needs to be exercised in two directions. The scientist is in danger of forgetting the unstable and unmechanical nature of the material, and of closing the door too dogmatically on phenomena whose relations with established knowledge he cannot trace ; while others take advantage of the fact that the limits of possibility cannot here be scientifically stated, to gratify an uncritical taste for marvels, and to invest their own hasty assumptions with the dignity of laws . 3–5

§ 3. This state of things subjects the study of " psychical " phenomena to peculiar disadvantages, and imposes on the student peculiar obligations 5–6

§ 4. And this should be well recognised by those who advance a conception so new to psychological science as the central conception of this book—to wit, *Telepathy, or the ability of one mind to impress or to be impressed by another mind otherwise than through the recognised channels of sense.* (Of the two persons concerned, the one whose mind *impresses* the other will be called the *agent*, and the one whose mind is *impressed* the *percipient*) 6–7

§ 5. Telepathy will be here studied chiefly as a system of *facts*, theoretical discussion being subordinated to the presentation of evidence. The evidence will be of two sorts—*spontaneous* occurrences, and the results of direct *experiment ;* which latter will have to be carefully distinguished from spurious " thought-reading " exhibitions . 7–9

CHAPTER II.

The Experimental Basis : Thought-Transference.

CHAPTER III.

THE TRANSITION FROM EXPERIMENTAL TO SPONTANEOUS TELEPATHY.

CHAPTER IV.

General Criticism of the Evidence for Spontaneous Telepathy.

§ 1. When we pass to spontaneous exhibitions of telepathy, the nature of the evidence changes ; for the events are described by persons who played their part in them unawares, without any idea that they were matter for scientific observation. The method of inquiry will now have to be the *historical* method, and will involve difficult questions as to the judgment of human testimony, and a complex estimate of probabilities.

§ 2. The most general objection to evidence for phenomena transcending the recognised scope of science is that, in a thickly populated world where mal-observation and exaggeration are easy and common, there is (within certain limits) no marvel for which evidence of a sort may not be obtained. This objection is often enforced by reference to the superstition of *witchcraft*, which in quite modern times was supported by a large array of contemporary evidence . . . .
But when this instance is carefully examined, we find (1) that the direct testimony came exclusively from the uneducated class ; and (2) that, owing to the ignorance which, in the witch-epoch, was universal as to the psychology of various abnormal and morbid states, the hypothesis of unconscious self-deception on the part of the witnesses was never allowed for . . . .

Our present knowledge of hypnotism, hysteria, and hystero-epilepsy, enables us to account for many of the phenomena attributed to demonic possession, as neither fact nor fraud, but as *bonâ fide* hallucinations 117–118
While for the more bizarre and incredible marvels there is absolutely no direct, first-hand, independent testimony 118
The better-attested cases are just those which, if genuine, might be explained as telepathic; but the evidence for them is not strong enough to support any definite conclusion 119

§ 3. The evidence for telepathy in the present work presents a complete contrast to that which has supported the belief in magical occurrences. It comes for the most part from educated persons, who were not predisposed to admit the reality of the phenomena; while the phenomena themselves are not strongly associated with any prevalent beliefs or habits of thought, differing in this respect, *e.g.*, from alleged apparitions of the *dead*. Still we must not, on such grounds as these, assume that the evidence is trustworthy 120–122

§ 4. The errors which may affect it are of various sorts. Error of *observation* may result in a *mistake of identity*. Thus a stranger in the street may be mistaken for a friend, who turns out to have died at that time, and whose phantasm is therefore asserted to have appeared. But it is only to a very small minority of the cases which follow that such a hypothesis could possibly be applied 123–125
Error of *inference* is not a prominent danger; as what concerns the telepathic evidence is simply what the percipient *seemed to himself* to see or hear, not what he inferred therefrom 125–126

§ 5. Of more importance are errors of *narration*, due to the tendency to make an account edifying, or graphic, or startling. In first-hand testimony this tendency may be to some extent counterbalanced by the desire to be believed; which has less influence in cases where the narrator is not personally responsible, as, *e.g.*, in the spurious and sensational anecdotes of anonymous newspaper paragraphs, or of dinner-table gossip. 126–129

§ 6. Errors of *memory* are more insidious. If the witness regards the facts in a particular speculative or emotional light, facts will be apt, in memory, to accommodate themselves to this view, and details will get introduced or dropped out in such a manner as to aid the harmonious effect. Even apart from any special bias, the mere effort to make definite what has become dim may fill in the picture with wrong detail; or the tendency to lighten the burden of retention may invest the whole occurrence with a spurious trenchancy and simplicity of form . . . 129–131

§ 7. We have to consider how these various sources of error may affect the evidence for a case of spontaneous telepathy. Such a case presents a coincidence of a particular kind, with four main points to look to :—(1) A particular state of the agent, *e.g.*, the crisis of death ; (2) a particular experience of the percipient, *e.g.*, the impression of seeing the agent before him in visible form ; (3) the date of (1) ; (4) the date of (2) 131–132

§ 8. The risk of mistake as to the state of the agent is seldom appreciable : his death, for instance, if that is what has befallen him, can usually be proved beyond dispute 132
For the experience of the percipient, on the other hand, we have generally nothing but his own word to depend on. But for what is required, his word is often sufficient. For the evidential point is simply his statement that he has had an impression or sensation of a peculiar kind, which, if he had it, he knew that he had ; and this point is quite independent of his *interpretation* of his experience, which may easily be erroneous, *e.g.*, if he attributes objective reality to what was really a hallucination   133–134
The risk of misrepresentation is smallest if his description of his experience, or a distinct course of action due to his experience, has *preceded* his knowledge of what has happened to the agent . 134–136

§ 9. Where his description of his experience dates from a time *subsequent* to his knowledge of what has happened to the agent, there is a possibility that this knowledge may have made the experience seem more striking and distinctive than it really was. Still, we have not detected definite instances of this sort of inaccuracy. Nor would the fact (often expressly stated by the witness) that the experience did not at the time of its occurrence suggest the agent, by any means destroy— though it would of course weaken—the presumption that it was telepathic 136–138

§ 10. As regards the interval of time which may separate the two events or experiences on the agent's and the percipient's side respectively, an arbitrary limit of 12 hours has been adopted—the coincidence in most cases being very much closer than this ; but no case will be presented as telepathic where the percipient's experience *preceded*, by however short a time, some grave event occurring to the agent, if at the time of the percipient's experience the state of the agent was normal . 138–140

§ 11. It is in the matter of the *dates* that the risk of mis-statement is greatest. The instinct towards simplification and dramatic completeness naturally tends to make the coincidence more exact than the facts warrant 140–142

Note on Witchcraft.

The statement made in Chapter iv. as to the lack of first-hand evidence for the phenomena of magic and witchcraft (except so far as they can be completely accounted for by modern psychological knowledge) may seem a sweeping one. But extensive as is the literature of the subject, the actual records are extraordinarily meagre; and the staple prodigies, which were really nothing more than popular legends, are quoted and re-quoted *ad nauseam.* Examples of the so-called evidence which supported the belief in *lycanthropy*, and in the *nocturnal rides and orgies*

The case of witchcraft, so far from proving (as is sometimes represented) that a more or less imposing array of evidence will be forthcoming for any belief that does not distinctly fly in the face of average public opinion, goes, in fact, rather surprisingly far towards proving the contrary . . . .

This view of the subject is completely opposed to that of Mr. Lecky, whose treatment seems to suffer from the neglect of two important distinctions. He does not distinguish between *evidence*—of which, in respect of the more bizarre marvels, there was next to none ; and *authority*—of which there was abundance, from Homer downwards. Nor does he discriminate the wholly incredible allegations (*e.g.*, as to transportations through the air and transformations into animal forms) from the *pathological* phenomena, which in the eyes of contemporaries were equally supernatural, and for which, as might be expected, the direct evidence was abundant

A most important class of these pathological phenomena were *subjective hallucinations of the senses*, often due to terror or excitement, and some-times probably to hypnotic suggestion, but almost invariably attributed to the direct operation of the devil. Other phenomena—of insensibility, inhibition of utterance, abnormal *rapport*, and the influence of reputed witches on health—were almost certainly hypnotic in character ; " posses-sion " is often simply hystero-epilepsy ; while much may be accounted for by mere hysteria, or by the same sort of faith as produces the modern " mind-cures " . . . .

Learned opinion on the subject of witchcraft went through curious vicissitudes ; the recession to a rational standpoint, which in many ways was of course a sceptical movement, being complicated by the fact that many of the phenomena were too genuine to be doubted. Now that the separation is complete, we see that the exploded part of witchcraft never had any real evidential foundation ; while the part which had a real evidential foundation has been taken up into orthodox physiological and psychological science. With the former part we might contrast, and with the latter compare, the evidential case for telepathy .

CHAPTER V.

SPECIMENS OF THE VARIOUS TYPES OF SPONTANEOUS TELEPATHY.

CHAPTER VI.

TRANSFERENCE OF IDEAS AND MENTAL PICTURES.

CHAPTER VII.·

EMOTIONAL AND MOTOR EFFECTS.

CHAPTER VIII.

DREAMS.

PART I.—THE RELATION OF DREAMS TO THE ARGUMENT FOR TELEPATHY.

The great interest of the distinctly sensory specimens lies in the fundamental resemblance which they offer, and the transition which they form, to the externalised "phantasms of the living" which impress *waking* percipients; the difference being that the dream-percepts are recognised, on reflection, as having been hallucinatory, and unrelated to that part of the external world where the percipient's body is; while the waking phantasmal percepts are apt to be regarded as objective phenomena, which really impressed the eye or the ear from outside   . 296–297

§ 2. But when we examine dreams in respect of their *evidential* value —of the proof which they are capable of affording of a telepathic correspondence with the reality—we find ourselves on doubtful ground. For (1) the details of the reality, when known, will be very apt to be *read back* into the dream, through the general tendency to make vague things distinct; and (2) the great *multitude* of dreams may seem to afford almost limitless scope for *accidental* correspondences of a dream with an actual occurrence resembling the one dreamt of. Any answer to this last objection must depend on statistics which, until lately, there has been no attempt to obtain; and though an answer of a sort can be given, it is not such a one as would justify us in basing a theory of telepathy on the facts of dreams alone   298–300

§ 3. Most of the dreams selected for this work were exceptional in *intensity;* and produced marked distress, or were described, or were in some way acted on, *before* the news of the correspondent experience was known.   In *content*, too, they were mostly of a distinct and unusual kind; while some of them present a considerable amount of true detail . 300–302
And more than half of those selected on the above grounds are dreams of *death*—a fact easy to account for on the hypothesis of telepathy, and difficult to account for on the hypothesis of accident   .   . 303

§ 4. Dreams so definite in content as dreams of death afford an opportunity of ascertaining what their actual frequency is, and so of estimating whether the specimens which have coincided with reality *are* or are *not* more numerous than chance would fairly allow. With a view to such an estimate, a specimen group of 5360 persons, taken at random, have been asked as to their personal experiences; and, according to the result, the persons who have had a vividly distressful dream of the death of a relative or acquaintance, within the 12 years 1874-1885, amount to about 1 in 26 of the population. Taking this datum, it is shown that the number of *coincidences* of the sort in question that, according to the law of chances, ought to have occurred in the 12 years, among a section of the population even larger than that from which we can suppose our telepathic evidence

PART. II.—EXAMPLES OF DREAMS WHICH MAY BE REASONABLY REGARDED AS TELEPATHIC.

CHAPTER IX.

" Borderland " Cases.

CHAPTER X.

HALLUCINATIONS : GENERAL SKETCH.

§ 1. Telepathic phantasms of the externalised sort are a species belonging to the larger genus of *hallucinations ;* and the genus requires some preliminary discussion 457
Hallucinations of the senses are distinguished from other hallucinations by the fact that they do not necessarily imply false belief . . 458
They may be defined as *percepts which lack, but which can only by distinct reflection be recognised as lacking, the objective basis which they suggest :* a definition which marks them off on the one hand from true perceptions, and on the other hand from remembered images or mental pictures 459–460

§ 2. The old method of defining the *ideational* and the *sensory* elements in the phenomena was very unsatisfactory. It is easy to show that the delusive appearances are not merely *imagined,* but are actually *seen* and *heard*—the hallucination differing from an ordinary percept only

in lacking an objective basis ; and this is what is implied in the word
psycho-sensorial, when rightly understood 461–464

§ 3. The question as to the physiological starting-point of hallucinations—whether they are of *central* or of *peripheral* origin—has been warmly
debated, often in a very one-sided manner. The *construction* of them,
which is central and the work of the brain, is quite distinct from the *excitation* or *initiation* of them, which (though often central also) is often
peripheral—*i.e.*, due to some other part of the body that sets the brain to
work 464–468

§ 4. This excitation may even be due to some objective external
cause, some visible point or mark, at or near the place where the
imaginary object is seen ; and in such cases the imaginary object, which
is, so to speak, attached to its point, may follow the course of any optical
illusion (*e.g.*, doubling by a prism, reflection by a mirror) to which that
point is subjected. But such dependence on an external stimulus does
not affect the fact that the actual sensory element of the hallucination, in
these as in all other cases, is imposed from within by the brain 468–470

§ 5. There, are, however, a large number of hallucinations which are
centrally initiated, as well as centrally constructed—the excitation being
due neither to an external point, nor to any morbid disturbance in the sense-
organs themselves. Such, probably, are many visual cases where the
imaginary object is seen in free space, or appears to move independently of
the eye, or is seen in darkness. Such, certainly, are many auditory
hallucinations ; some hallucinations of pain ; many hallucinations which
conform to the course of some more general delusion ; and hallucinations
voluntarily originated 470–480

§ 6. Such also are hallucinations of a particular internal kind common
among mystics, in which the sensory element seems reduced to its lowest
terms ; and which shade by degrees, on the one side into more externalised
forms, and on the other side into a mere feeling of presence, independent
of any sensory affection 480–484

§ 7. A further argument for the central initiation may be drawn from
the fact that *repose* of the sense-organs seems a condition favourable to
hallucinations ; and the psychological identity of waking hallucinations
and dreams cannot be too strongly insisted on . . . 484–485

§ 8. As regards the *construction* of hallucinations—the cerebral
process involved in their having this or that particular form—the question
is whether it takes place in the specific sensory centre concerned, or in
some higher cortical tract 485–488

CHAPTER XI.

TRANSIENT HALLUCINATIONS OF THE SANE: AMBIGUOUS CASES.

CHAPTER XII.

The Development of Telepathic Hallucinations

INTRODUCTION.

καὶ τὸν θεὸν τοιοῦτον ἐξεπίσταμαι,
σοφοῖς μὲν αἰνικτῆρα θεσφάτων ἀεί,
σκαιοῖς δὲ φαῦλον κἂν βραχεῖ διδάσκαλον.

SOPHOCLES.

§ 1. THE subject of this book is one which a brief title is hardly sufficient to explain. For under our heading of " Phantasms of the Living," we propose, in fact, to deal with all classes of cases where there is reason to suppose that the mind of one human being has affected the mind of another, without speech uttered, or word written, or sign made ;—has affected it, that is to say, by other means than through the recognised channels of sense.

To such transmission of thoughts or feelings we have elsewhere given the name of *telepathy* ; and the records of an experimental proof of the reality of telepathy will form a part of the present work. But, for reasons which will be made manifest as we proceed, we have included among telepathic phenomena a vast class of cases which seem at first sight to involve something widely different from a mere transference of thought.

I refer to *apparitions ;* excluding, indeed, the alleged apparitions of the *dead,* but including the apparitions of all persons who are still living, as we know life, though they may be on the very brink and border of physical dissolution. And these apparitions, as will be seen, are themselves extremely various in character ; including not visual phenomena alone, but auditory, tactile, or even purely ideational and emotional impressions. All these we have included under the term *phantasm* ; a word which, though etymologically a mere variant of *phantom,* has been less often used, and has not become so closely identified with *visual* impressions alone.

Such, then, is the meaning of our title ; but something more of explanation is necessary before the tone and purport of the book can

c 2

be correctly apprehended. In a region so novel we could hardly be surprised at any amount of misinterpretation. Some readers, for instance, may fancy that a bulky and methodical treatise on phantoms can be but a half-serious thing. Others may suspect that its inspiration is in the love of paradox, and that a fantastic craving for originality has led the authors along a path where they cannot expect, and can hardly desire, that the sober world should follow them.

§ 2. It is necessary, therefore, to state at once that we have no wish either to mystify or to startle mankind. On the contrary, the conjoint and consultative scheme according to which this book has been compiled is thus arranged mainly with a view to correcting or neutralising individual fancies or exaggerations, of leaving as little as possible to the unchecked idiosyncrasy of any single thinker. And, again, we wish distinctly to say that so far from aiming at any paradoxical reversion of established scientific conclusions, we conceive ourselves to be working (however imperfectly) in the main track of discovery, and assailing a problem which, though strange and hard, does yet stand next in order among the new adventures on which Science must needs set forth, if her methods and her temper are to guide and control the widening curiosity, the expanding capacities of men.

We anticipate, in short, that although it may at first be said of us that we have performed with needless elaboration a foolish and futile task, the ultimate verdict on our work will rather be that we have undertaken—with all too limited a knowledge and capacity—to open an inquiry which was manifestly impending, and to lay the foundation-stone of a study which will loom large in the approaching age.

Our only paradox, then, is the assertion that we are not paradoxical; and that assertion it is the main business of this Introduction to justify.

§ 3. For this purpose two principal heads of exposition will be required. In the first place, since this book (for whose contents we are solely responsible) was undertaken by us at the request of the Council of the Society for Psychical Research, and is largely based on material which that Council has placed at our disposal, it will be necessary to say something as to the scope and object of the Society in question;—its grounds for claiming a valid scientific position, and its points of interconnection with established branches of philosophic inquiry.

And, secondly, it will be needful to indicate the precise position which the theme of this book occupies in the field of our investigations; the reason why we have isolated these special phenomena in a separate group, and have selected them for discussion at this early stage of the Society's labours.

A reader of the programme of the Society will probably feel that although the special topics to which attention is there invited may be unfamiliar, yet its general plea is such as he has often noted in the history of science before. " To approach these various problems without prejudice or prepossession of any kind, and in the same spirit of exact and unimpassioned inquiry which has enabled Science to solve so many problems, once not less obscure nor less hotly debated ;" —phrases like these have no more of novelty than there might be, for instance, in the proposal of a Finance Minister to abolish the last of a long series of protective embargoes.   Free Trade and free inquiry have each of them advanced step by step, and by dint of the frequent repetition, under varying difficulties, of very similar, and very elementary, truths.   The special peculiarity of our topic is that it is an article (so to say) on which the Free Traders themselves have imposed an additional duty ; that it has been more sternly discountenanced by the men who appeal to experiment than by the men who appeal to authority ;—that its dispassionate discussion has since the rise of modern science been tabooed more jealously than when the whole province was claimed by theology alone.   There have been reasons, no doubt, for such an exclusion ; and I am not asserting that either Free Trade or free inquiry is always and under all circumstances to be desired.   But it is needful to point out yet once more how plausible the reasons for discouraging some novel research have often seemed to be, while yet the advance of knowledge has rapidly shown the futility and folly of such discouragement.

It was the Father of Science himself who was the first to circumscribe her activity.   Socrates, in whose mind the idea of the gulf between *knowledge* and mere *opinion* attained a dominant intensity which impressed itself on all ages after him,—Socrates expressly excluded from the range of exact inquiry all such matters as the movements and nature of the sun and moon.   He wished—and as he expressed his wish it seemed to have all the cogency of absolute wisdom—that men's minds should be turned to the ethical and political problems which truly concerned them,—not wasted in speculation on things unknowable—things useless even could they be known.

In a kindred spirit, though separated from Socrates by the whole result of that physical science which Socrates had deprecated, we find a great modern systematiser of human thought again endeavouring to direct the scientific impulse towards things serviceable to man; to divert it from things remote, unknowable, and useless if known. What then, in Comte's view, are in fact the limits of man's actual home and business? the bounds within which he may set himself to learn all he can, assured that all will serve to inform his conscience and guide his life? It is the *solar system* which has become for the French philosopher what the street and market-place of Athens were for the Greek. And this enlargement (it need hardly be said) is not due to any wider grasp of mind in Comte than in Socrates, but simply to the march of science; which has shown us that the whole solar system does, in fact, minister to our practical needs, and that the Nautical Almanack demands for its construction a mapping of the paths of those ordered luminaries which in the time of Socrates seemed the very wanderers of Heaven.

I need not say that Comte's prohibition has been altogether neglected. No frontier of scientific demarcation has been established between Neptune and Sirius, between Uranus and Aldebaran. Our knowledge of the fixed stars increases yearly; and it would be rash to maintain that human conduct is not already influenced by the conception thus gained of the unity and immensity of the heavens.

To many of the comments that have been made on our work, even by men who are not formal Comtists, the above reflections furnish a fitting reply. But it is not only, nor perhaps mainly, on account of the remoteness of our subject, or its unimportance to human progress, that objection is taken to our inquiry. The criticisms which have met us, from the side sometimes of scientific, sometimes of religious orthodoxy, have embodied, in modernised phraseology, nearly every well-worn form of timid protest, or obscurantist demurrer, with which the historians of science have been accustomed to give piquancy to their long tale of discovery and achievement. It would have been convenient had these objections been presented to us in a connected and formal manner. But this has not been the case; and, in fact, they are in their very nature too incoherent, too self-contradictory, for continuous statement. Sometimes we are told that we are inviting the old theological spirit to encroach once more on the domain of science; sometimes that we are endeavouring to lay the impious hands of Science upon the mysteries of Religion. Sometimes we are informed that competent *savants* have already fully explored the field which we propose for our investigation ; sometimes that no respectable man of science would condescend to meddle with such a reeking mass of fraud and hysteria. Sometimes we are pitied as laborious triflers who prove some infinitely small matter with mighty trouble and pains; sometimes we are derided as attempting the solution of gigantic problems by slight and superficial means.

§ 4. The best way of meeting objections thus confused and contradictory will be to show as clearly as we can at what points our inquiries touch the recent results of science ; what signs there are which indicate the need of vigorous advance along the lines which we have chosen. We shall show, perhaps, that there is a kind of convergence towards this especial need—that in several directions of research there is felt that kind of pause and hesitancy which is wont to precede the dawn of illuminating conceptions. We shall not, of course, thus prove that our own attempt has been *successful*, but we shall prove that it was *justified ;* that if the problems which we set ourselves to solve are found to be insoluble, the gaps thus left in the system of thought on which man's normal life is based will be such as can neither be ignored nor supplied, but will become increasingly palpable and increasingly dangerous.

Let us consider how far this remark can be justified with regard to some of the leading branches of human knowledge in turn. And let us take first Biology, the science which on the whole approaches the closest to our own inquiries. Biology has, during the last half-century, made an advance which, measured by the hold exercised on the mass of cultivated minds, has perhaps had no parallel since the forward stride of astronomy and physics in the days of Newton. A glance at the text-books of the last generation, in physical or mental science—Whewell's *History of the Inductive Sciences*, or Mill's *Logic,*—as compared, for instance, with the works of their immediate successor, Mr. Herbert Spencer, shows something which is not so much progress as revolution—the transformation of Biology from a mere special department of knowledge into the key to man's remotest history, the only valid answer to the profoundest questions as to his present being.

For, in truth, it is Biology above all other sciences which has profited by the doctrine of evolution. In evolution,—in the doctrine

that the whole cosmical order is the outcome of a gradual
development,—mankind have gained for the first time a working
hypothesis which covers enough of the known facts of the universe
to make its, possible extension to *all* facts a matter of hopeful
interest. And Biology, which even at the date of Whewell's
book could barely make good its claim to be regarded as a
coherent science at all, has now acquired a co-ordinating and
continuous principle of unity which renders it in some respects
the best type of a true science which we possess. It traces
life from the protozoon to the animal, from the brute to the man;
it offers to explain the complex fabric of human thought and
emotion, viewed from the physical side, as the development
of the molecular movements of scarcely-differentiated fragments
of protaplasm.

And along with this increased knowledge of the processes by
which man has been upbuilt has come also an increased knowledge
of the processes which are now going on within him. The same
inquiries which have brought our organic life into intelligible relation
with the whole range of animal and vegetable existence have
enabled us also to conceive more definitely the neural side of our
mental processes, and the relation of cerebral phenomena to their
accompanying emotion or thought. And hence, in the view of
some ardent physiologists, it is becoming more and more probable
that we are in fact physiological automata; that our consciousness
is a mere superadded phenomenon—a mere concomitant of some
special intensity of cerebral action, with no basis beyond or apart from
the molecular commotion of the brain.

But this view, as it would seem, depends in a great part upon
something which corresponds in the mental field to a familiar optical
illusion. When we see half of some body strongly illuminated, and
half of it feebly illuminated, it is hard to believe that the brilliant
moiety is not the larger of the two. And, similarly, it is the increased
definiteness of our conception of the physical side of our mental
operations which seems to increase its relative importance,—to give it
a kind of priority over the psychical aspect of the same processes.
Yet, of course, to the philosophic eye the central problem of the
relation of the objective and subjective sides of these psycho-neural
phenomena can be in no way altered by any increase of definiteness
in our knowledge of the objective processes which correspond to the
subjective states.

And, on the other hand, there is one singular logical corollary which seems thus far to have escaped the notice of physiologist and psychologist alike.   It is this : that our increased vividness of conception of the physical side of mental life, while it cannot possibly *disprove* the independence of the psychical side, may quite conceivably *prove* it.   I will again resort to the (very imperfect) analogy of a partially-illuminated body.   Suppose that one hemisphere of a globe is strongly lit up, and that the other is lit up by faint and scattered rays.[1]   I am trying to discern whether the two hemispheres are symmetrically marked throughout.   Now no clearness of marks on the bright hemisphere can disprove the existence of corresponding marks on the dim one.   But, on the other hand, it is conceivable that one of the few rays which fall on the dim hemisphere may reveal some singular mark which I can see that the bright hemisphere does not possess.   And the brighter the bright hemisphere is made, the more certain do I become that this particular mark is not to be found on it.

§ 5. I will give two concrete examples of what I mean—one of them drawn from the conclusions of a great physiologist, the other from the obvious condition of a new branch of experimental inquiry. I shall not discuss either instance in detail, since I am here only endeavouring to show that with increased precision in psycho-physical researches the old problems of free-will, soul and body, &c., are presenting more definite issues, and offering a far more hopeful field to the exact philosopher than their former vagueness allowed.

My first illustration, then, is from the form which the old free-will controversy has assumed in the hands of Wundt. Wundt stands, of course, among the foremost of those who have treated human thought and ·sensation as definite and measurable things, who have computed their rate of transit, and analysed their elements, and enounced the laws of their association.   It is not from him that we need look for any lofty metaphysical view as to the infinite resources of spiritual power,—the transcendental character of psychical phenomena.   But, nevertheless, Wundt believes himself able to assert that there is within us a residue—an all-important residue—of psychical action which is incommensurable with physio-

---

[1] The analogy will be closer if we suppose that the second half is lit, not *dimly* but *from within,*—since in one sense consciousness gives us *more* information as to the psychical than as to the physical side of life, though it is information of a different *quality.*

logical law. So far, he holds, is the principle of conservation of energy from covering the psychical realm, that the facts of mental evolution proclaim that the very contrary is the case ;—and that what really obtains is rather "an unlimited new creation of psychical energy."[1] Nay, so convinced is he of the inadequacy of any system of physiological determinism to explain psychical facts, that he holds that we must directly reverse the materialistic view of the relation of the corporeal to the psychical life. " It is not the psychical life," he says, " which is a product of the physical organisation ; rather it is the physical organism which, in all those purposive adjustments which distinguish it from inorganic compounds, is itself a psychical creation." [2]

I am not here expressing either agreement or disagreement with this general view. I am merely pointing out that here is an opinion which, whether right or wrong, is formed as a result not of *vagueness* but of *distinctness* of physiological conceptions. And my illustration shows at any rate that the development of physiology is tending not always to make the old psychical problems seem meaningless or sterile, but rather to give them actuality and urgency, and even to suggest new possibilities of their solution.

§ 6. But, to come to my second instance, it is perhaps from the present position of *hypnotism* that the strongest argument may be drawn for the need of such researches as ours, to supplement and co-ordinate the somewhat narrower explorations of technical physiology. For the actual interest of the mesmeric or hypnotic trance—I am not now dealing with the rival theories which these words connote—the central interest, let us say, of induced somnambulism, or the sleep-waking state—has hardly as yet revealed itself to any section of inquirers.

That interest lies neither in mesmerism as a curative agency, as Elliotson would have told us, nor in hypnotism as an illustration of inhibitory cerebral action, as Heidenhain would tell us now. It lies in the fact that here is a psychical experiment on a larger scale than was ever possible before ; that we have at length got hold of a handle which turns the mechanism of our being ; that we have found

---

[1] "Hier gilt vielmehr ein Gesetz unbegrenzter Neuschöpfung geistiger Energie, welches nur durch die sinnliche Bestimmtheit des geistigen Lebens gewisse Hemmungen erleidet."—Wundt, *Logik,* II., p. 507.

[2] "Nicht das geistige Leben ist ein Erzeugniss der physischen Organisation, sondern diese ist in allem, was sie an zweckvollen Einrichtungen der Selbstregulirung und der Energie-verwerthung vor den Substanzcomplexen der unorganischen Natur voraushat, eine geistige Schöpfung."—Wundt, *Logik,* II., p. 471.

a mode of shifting the threshold of consciousness which is a dislocation as violent as madness, a submergence as pervasive as sleep, and yet is waking sanity ; that we have induced a change of personality which is not *per se* either evolutive or dissolutive, but seems a mere allotropic modification of the very elements of man. The prime value of the hypnotic trance lies not in what it inhibits, but in what it reveals ; not in the occlusion of the avenues of peripheral stimulus, but in the emergence of unnoted sensibilities, nay, perhaps even in the manifestation of new and centrally-initiated powers.

The hypnotic trance is an eclipse of the normal consciousness which can be repeated at will. Now the first observers of eclipses of the sun ascribe them to supernatural causes, and attribute to them an occult influence for good or evil. Then comes the stage at which men note their effects on the animal organism, the roosting of birds, the restlessness of cattle. Then come observations on the intensity of the darkness, the aspect of the lurid shade. But to the modern astronomer all this is trifling as compared with the knowledge which those brief moments give him of the orb itself in its obscuration. He learns from that transient darkness more than the noon of day can tell ; he sees the luminary no longer as a defined and solid ball, but as the centre of the outrush of flaming energies, the focus of an effluence which coruscates untraceably through immeasurable fields of heaven.

There is more in this parallel than a mere empty metaphor. It suggests one of the primary objects which psychical experiment must seek to attain. Physical experiment aims at correcting the deliverances of man's consciousness with regard to the external world by instruments which extend the range, and concentrate the power, and compensate the fallacies of his senses. And similarly, *our* object must be to correct the deliverances of man's consciousness concerning the processes which are taking place *within* him by means of artificial displacements of the psycho-physical threshold ; by inhibiting normal perception, obliterating normal memory, so that in this temporary freedom from preoccupation by accustomed stimuli his mind may reveal those latent and delicate capacities of which his ordinary conscious self is unaware.

§ 7. It was thus, in fact, that thought-transference, or telepathy, was first discovered. In the form of community of sensation between operator and subject, it was noted nearly a century ago as a phenomenon incident to the mesmeric trance. Its full importance was not perceived, and priceless opportunities of experiment were almost wholly neglected. In order to bring out the value and extent of the phenomenon it was necessary, we venture to think, that it should be investigated by men whose interest in the matter lay not in the direction of practical therapeutics but of psychical theory, and who were willing to seek and "test for it" under a wide range of conditions, not in sleep-waking life only, but in normal waking, and normal sleep, and, as this book will indicate, up to the very hour of death.

The difficulties of this pursuit are not physiological only. But, nevertheless, in our endeavours to establish and to elucidate telepathy, we look primarily for aid to the most recent group of physiological inquirers, to the psycho-physicists whose special work—as yet in its infancy—has only in our own day been rendered possible by the increased accuracy and grasp of experimental methods in the sciences which deal with Life.

The list of Corresponding Members of our Society will serve to show that this confidence on our part is not wholly unfounded, and to indicate that we are not alone in maintaining that whatever may be the view of these perplexing problems which ultimately prevails, the recent advances of physiology constitute in themselves a strong reason—not, as some hold, for the abandonment of all discussion of the old enigmas, but rather for their fresh discussion with scientific orderliness, and in the illumination of our modern day.[1]

§ 8. From Biology we may pass, by an easy transition, to what is commonly known as Anthropology,—the comparative study of the different races of men in respect either of their physical characteristics, or of the early rudiments of what afterwards develops into civilisation.

The connection of anthropology with psychical research will be evident to any reader who has acquainted himself with recent expositions of Primitive Man. He may think, indeed, that the connection is *too* evident, and that we can hardly bring it into notice without proving a good deal more than we desire. For as the creeds and customs of savage races become better known, the part played by sorcery, divination, apparitions becomes increasingly predominant.

---

[1] The French Société de Psychologie Physiologique, whose President is M. Charcot, has already published several observations with an important bearing on our subject, some of which will be found in Vol. ii. of this work.

Mr. Tylor and Sir John Lubbock have made this abundantly
clear, and Mr. Spencer has gone so far as to trace all early religion
to a fear of the ghosts of the dead. In the works of these and similar
authors, I need hardly say, we are led to regard all these beliefs and
tendencies as due solely to the childishness of savage man—as
absurdities which real progress in civilisation must render increasingly
alien to the developed common-sense, the rational experience of
humanity. Yet it appears to me that as we trace the process of
evolution from savage to civilised man, we come to a point at which
the inadequacy of this explanation is strongly forced on our attention.
Certainly this was my own case when I undertook some years ago to
give a sketch of the Greek oracles. It soon became evident to me
that the mass of phenomena included under this title had, at any rate,
a psycho-physical importance which the existing works on the subject
for the most part ignored. I scarcely ventured myself to do more
than indicate where the real *nodi* of the inquiry lay. But when a
massive treatise on Ancient Divination appeared from the learned pen
of M. Bouché-Leclercq, I looked eagerly to see whether his erudition
had enabled him to place these problems in a new light. I found,
however, that he explicitly renounced all attempt to deal with the
phenomena in more than a merely external way. He would *record*,
but he would make no endeavour to *explain ;*—taking for granted,
as it appeared, that the explanation depended on fraud alone, and on
fraud whose details it would now be impossible to discover.

I cannot think that such a view can any longer satisfy persons
adequately acquainted with the facts of hypnotism. Whatever else,
whether of fraud or reality, there may have been on the banks of
Cassotis or Castaly,—*unde superstitiosa primum sacra evasit vox
fera,*—there were at least the hypnotic trance and hystero-epilepsy.
And until these and similar elements can be sifted out of the records
left to us, with something of insight gained by familiarity with their
modern forms, our knowledge of Pythia or of Sibyl will be shallow
indeed.

Still more markedly is such insight and experience needed in
anthropology proper—in the actual observation of the savage peoples
who still exist. It is to be hoped that shamans and medicine-men
will not vanish before the missionary until they have yielded some
fuller lessons to the psycho-physicist—until the annals of the
Salpêtrière and the experiments of Dean's Yard have been invoked in
explanation of the weird terrors of the Yenisei and the Congo.

§ 9. Passing on from Anthropology to history in its wider accepta-
tion, we find these psycho-physical problems perpetually recurring, and
forming a disturbing element in any theory of social or religious
evolution. The contagious enthusiasms of the Middle Ages—the
strange endemic maladies of witchcraft, vampirism, lycanthropy—
even the individual inspiration of a Mahomet or a Joan of Arc—
these are phenomena which the professed historian feels obliged to
leave to the physician and the alienist, and for which the physician
and the alienist, in their turn, have seldom a satisfactory explanation.
Nor do phenomena of this kind cease to appear with the advance
of civilisation. In detailed modern histories, in the biographies of
eminent men, we still come upon incidents which are, at any rate at
first sight, of a *supernormal*[1] kind, and over which the narrator is
forced to pass with vague or inadequate comment.

But it is, of course, in dealing with the history of *religions* that
our lack of any complete grasp of psychical phenomena is most
profoundly felt. And here, also, it is as a result of recent progress,—
of the growth of the comparative study of religions,—that we are able
to disengage, in a generalised form, the chief problems with which our
"psychical" science, if such could be established, would be impera-
tively called on to deal.

For we find throughout the world's history a series of great events
which, though differing widely in detail, have a certain general
resemblance both to each other and to some of those incidents both of
savage and of ordinary civilised life to which reference has already
been made.

The elements which are common to the great majority of religions
seem to be mainly two—namely, the promulgation of some doctrine
which the religious reformer claims to have received, or actually
to communicate, in some supernormal manner ; and the report of a

---

[1] "I have ventured to coin the word 'supernormal' to be applied to phenomena
which are *beyond what usually happens—beyond*, that is, in the sense of suggesting unknown
psychical laws. It is thus formed on the analogy of *abnormal.* When we speak of an
abnormal phenomenon we do not mean one which *contravenes* natural laws, but one which
exhibits them in an unusual or inexplicable form. Similarly by a supernormal phenomenon,
I mean, not one which *overrides* natural laws, for I believe no such phenomenon to exist,
but one which exhibits the action of laws higher, in a psychical aspect, than are discerned
in action in every-day life. By *higher* (either in a psychical or in a physiological sense), I
mean 'apparently belonging to a more advanced stage of evolution.'"—*Proceedings* of
the S.P.R., Vol. iii., p. 30. Throughout this treatise we naturally need a designation for
phenomena which are inexplicable by recognised physiological laws, and belong to
the general group into the nature of which we are inquiring. The term *psychical*
(which is liable to misapprehension even in the title of our Society) can hardly be used
without apology in this specialised sense. The occasional introduction of the word
supernormal may perhaps be excused.

concurrent manifestation of phenomena apparently inexplicable by ordinary laws.

Now, with the rise of one religion our Society has already had practically to deal. Acting through Mr. Hodgson, whose experiences in the matter have been elsewhere detailed,[1] a committee of the Society for Psychical Research has investigated the claim of the so-called "Theosophy," of which Madame Blavatsky was the prophetess, to be an incipient world-religion, corroborated by miraculous, or at least supernormal, phenomena,—and has arrived at the conclusion that it is merely a *réchauffé* of ancient philosophies, decked in novel language, and supported by ingenious fraud. Had this fraud not been detected and exposed, and had the system of belief supported thereon thriven and spread, we should have witnessed what the sceptic might have cited as a typical case of the origin of religions. A Gibbon of our own day, reviewing the different motives and tendencies which prompt, or spread, revelations, might have pointed to Theosophy and Mormonism as covering between them the whole ground ;—from the adroit advantage taken of mystical aspiration in the one religion, to the commonplace action of greed and lust upon helplessness and stupidity which forms the basis of the other.

But if it should be argued from these analogies that in no case of the foundation of a religion would any scientific method of psychical inquiry prove necessary or fruitful, if we knew all the facts ; but that such developments might be sufficiently dealt with by ordinary common-sense, or, like Mormonism, by the criminal law, the generalisation would be hasty and premature. We need not go far back to discover two religions whose central fact is not a fact of fraud at all, but an unexplained psychical phenomenon. I allude to the vision-life of Swedenborg, and the speaking with tongues which occurred in the church of Irving,—each of which constitutes a central point of faith for a certain number of intelligent and educated persons at the present day. Of neither of these facts can Science at present offer a satisfactory explanation. The speaking with tongues seems plainly to have been for the most part (though not entirely) a genuine automatic phenomenon. But as to the *origin* of such automatic utterances (conveyed in speech or writing), as to the range from which their contents are drawn, or the kind of attention which they can claim, there is little or nothing to be learnt from accepted textbooks. We are groping among the first experiments, the simplest instances, on which any valid theory can be based.[1]

The case of Swedenborg carries us still further beyond the limits of our assured knowledge. Of madness and its delusions, indeed, we know much ; but it would be a mere abuse of language to call Swedenborg mad. His position must be decided by a much more difficult analogy. For before we can even begin to criticise his celestial visions we must be able in some degree to judge of his visions of things terrestrial ; we must face, that is to say, the whole problem of so-called *clairvoyance*, of a faculty which claims to be not merely receptive but active,—a projection of super-sensory percipience among scenes distant and things unknown.

And the existence of such a faculty as this will assuredly never be proved by a mere study of the transcendental dicta of any single seer. This problem, too, must be approached, partly through the hypnotic trance, in which the best-attested instances of clairvoyance are alleged to have occurred, and partly through the collection of such supernormal narratives as some of those which find place in the present book.

Even a sketch like this may indicate how complex and various may be the problems which underlie that " History of Sects" in which a Bossuet might see only the heaven-sent penalty for apostasy against the Church,—a Gibbon, the mere diverting panorama of the ever-varying follies of men.

§ 10. But reflections like these lie on the outskirts of a still larger and graver question. What (it is naturally asked) is the relation of our study—not to eccentric or outlying forms of religious creed—but to central and vital conceptions ; and especially to that main system of belief to which in English-speaking countries the name of *religion* is by popular usage almost confined ?

Up till this time those who have written on behalf of the Society for Psychical Research have studiously refrained from entering on this important question. Our reason for this reticence is obvious enough when stated, but it has not been universally discerned. We wished to avoid even the semblance of attracting the public to our researches by any allurement which lay outside the scientific field. We could not take for granted that our inquiries would make for the spiritual view of things, that they would tend to establish even the independent existence, still less the immortality, of the soul. We

---

[1] See papers on " Automatic Writing " in *Proceedings* of the S.P.R., Vols. ii. and iii.

shrank from taking advantage of men's hopes or fears, from representing ourselves as bent on rescuing them from the materialism which forms so large a factor in modern thought, or from the pessimism which dogs its steps with unceasing persistency. We held it to be incumbent on us, in an especial degree, to maintain a neutral and expectant attitude, and to conduct our inquiries in the "dry light" of a dispassionate search for truth.

And this position we still maintain. This book, as will be seen, does not attempt to deal with the most exciting and popular topics which are included in our Society's general scheme. And we shall be careful in the pages that follow to keep within our self-assigned limits, and to say little as to any light which our collected evidence may throw on the possibility of an existence continued after our physical death.

That master-problem of human life must be assailed by more deliberate approaches, nor must we gild our solid arguments with the radiance of an unproved surmise. But it would, nevertheless, be impossible, in a discussion of this general kind, to pass over the relation of psychical research to religion altogether in silence. And, indeed, since our inquiries began, the situation has thus far changed that we have now not anticipation merely, but a certain amount of actual achievement, to which to appeal. We hold that we have proved by direct experiment, and corroborated by the narratives contained in this book, the possibility of communications between two minds, inexplicable by any recognised physical laws, but capable (under certain rare spontaneous conditions) of taking place when the persons concerned are at an indefinite distance from each other. And we claim further that by investigations of the higher phenomena of mesmerism, and of the automatic action of the mind, we have confirmed and expanded this view in various directions, and attained a standing-point from which certain even stranger alleged phenomena begin to assume an intelligible aspect, and to suggest further discoveries to come.

Thus far the authors of this book, and also the main group of their fellow-workers, are substantially agreed. But their agreement as to the facts actually proved does not extend,—it is not even to be desired that it *should* extend,—to the speculations which in one direction or another such facts must inevitably suggest. They are facts which go too deep to find in any two minds a precisely similar lodgment, or to adjust themselves in the same way to the complex of

d

pre-existent conceptions. The following paragraphs, therefore, must be taken merely as reflecting the opinions provisionally held by a single inquirer.

I may say, then, at once that I consider it improbable that tele-pathy will ever receive a purely physical explanation,—an explanation, that is to say, wholly referable to the properties of matter, as molecular matter is at present known to us. I admit, of course, that such an explanation is logically conceivable; that we can imagine that undulations should be propagated, or particles emitted, from one living organism to another, which should excite the percipient organism in a great variety of ways. But it seems to me,—and I imagine that in this view at any rate the majority of Materialists will concur,—that if the narratives in this book are to be taken as, on the whole, trustworthy, the physical analogies are too faint, and the physical difficulties too serious, to allow of our intruding among the forces of material Nature a force which—unlike any other—would seem (in some cases at least) neither to be diminished by any distance nor to be impeded by any obstacle whatsoever.

I lay aside, for the purposes of the present argument, the possibi-lity of a *monistic* scheme of the universe,—of a *consentiens conspirans continuata cognatio rerum* which may present in an unbroken sequence both what we know as Matter and what we know as Mind. Such a view,—though to higher intelligences it may perhaps be an intuitive certainty,—can for us be nothing more than a philosophic opinion. Our scientific arguments must needs be based on the *dualism* which our intellects, as at present constituted, are in fact unable to transcend.

I maintain, therefore, that if the general fact of telepathic communication between mind and mind be admitted, it must also be admitted that an element is thus introduced into our conception of the aggregate of empirically known facts which constitutes a serious obstacle to the materialistic synthesis of human experience. The psychical element in man, I repeat, must henceforth almost inevitably be conceived as having relations which cannot be expressed in terms of matter.

Now this dogma, though wholly new to experimental science, is, of course, familiar and central in all the higher forms of religions. Relations inexpressible in terms of matter, and subsisting between spirit and Spirit,—the human and the Divine,—are implied in the very notion of the interchange of sacred love and love, of grace and worship. I need hardly add that the reality of any such communion is rigidly excluded by the materialistic view. The Materialist, indeed, may regard prayer and aspiration with indulgence, or even with approval, but he must necessarily conceive them as forming merely the psychical side of certain molecular movements of the particles of human organisms, and he must necessarily regard the notion of Divine response to prayer as an illusion generated by subsequent molecular movements of the same organisms,—the mere recoil and reflux of the wave which the worshipper himself has created.

It would, of course, be mere offensive presumption to draw a parallel between our telepathic experiments and such a relation between a human and Divine spirit as the devout soul believes itself to realise in prayer. One side of that communion must *ex hypothesi* transcend the measurement or analysis of finite minds. But, confining our view wholly to the part played by the human organism, it seems to me incontestable that our experiments suggest possibilities of influence, modes of operation, which throw an entirely fresh light on this ancient controversy between Science and Faith. I claim at least that any presumption which science had established against the possibility of spiritual communion is now rebutted ; and that inasmuch as it can no longer be affirmed that our minds are closed to all influences save such as reach them through sensory avenues, the Materialist must admit that it is no longer an un-supported dream but a serious scientific possibility, that if any intelligences do in fact exist other than those of living men, influences from those intelligences may be conveyed to our own mind, and may either remain below the threshold of consciousness, or rise into definite consciousness, according as the presence or absence of competing stimuli, or other causes as yet unknown to us, may determine.

§ 11. I shall leave this proposition expressed thus in its most abstract and general form. And I may add—it is a reflection which I must ask the reader to keep steadily in mind,—that any support or illumination which religious creeds may gain from psychical inquiry is likely to affect not their *clauses* but their *preamble;* is likely to come, not as a sudden discovery bearing directly on some specific dogma, but as the gradual discernment of laws which may funda-mentally modify the attitude of thoughtful minds.

Now, in what I have called the *preamble* of all revelations two

d 2

theses are generally involved, quite apart from the subject-matter, or the Divine sanction, of the revelation itself. We have to assume, first, that human testimony to supernormal facts may be trustworthy ; and secondly, that there is something in the nature of man which is capable of responding to—I may say of participating in—these supernormal occurrences.

That is to say, revelations are not proved merely by large external facts, perceptible to every one who possesses the ordinary senses, nor again are they proved solely by what are avowedly mere subjective impressions, but they are largely supported by a class of phenomena which comes between these two extremes ; by powers inherent in certain individuals of beholding spiritual visions or personages unseen by common eyes, of receiving information or guidance by interior channels, of uttering truths not consciously acquired, of healing sick persons by the imposition of hands, with other faculties of a similarly supernormal kind.

And I hope that I shall not be thought presumptuous or irreverent if (while carefully abstaining from direct comment on any Revelation) I indicate what, in my view, would be the inevitable effect on the attitude of purely scientific minds towards these preliminary theses,—this *preamble,* as I have said, of definite religions,—were the continued prosecution of our inquiry to lead us after all to entirely negative conclusions, were all our evidence to prove untrustworthy, and all our experiments unsound.

For in the first place it is plain that this new science of which we are endeavouring to lay the foundations stands towards religion in a very different position from that occupied by the rising sciences, such as geology or biology, whose conflict or agreement with natural or revealed religion has furnished matter for so much debate. The discoveries of those sciences can scarcely in themselves add support to a doctrine of man's soul and immortality, though they may conceivably come into collision with particular forms which that doctrine has assumed. Religion, in short, may be able to assimilate them, but it would in no way have suffered had they proved altogether abortive.

But with our study the case is very different. For, to take the first of the two preliminary theses of religion already referred to, the question whether human evidence as to supernormal occurrences can *ever* be trusted has been raised by our inquiries in a much more crucial form than when Hume and Paley debated it with reference to *historical* incidents only. We discuss it with reference to alleged *contemporary* incidents; we endeavour to evaluate by actual inspection and cross-examination the part which is played in supernormal narratives by the mere love of wonder, "the mythopœic faculty," the habitual negligence and ignorance of mankind. And if all the evidence offered to us should crumble away on exact investigation—as, for instance, the loudly-vaunted evidence for the marvels connected with Theosophy has crumbled—it will no doubt be questioned whether the narratives on which the historic religions depend for their acceptance could have stood the test of a contemporaneous inquiry of a similarly searching kind.

And more than this, it will not only be maintained that the collapse of our modern evidence to supernormal phenomena discredits all earlier records of the same kind by showing the ease with which such marvels are feigned or imagined, but also that it further discredits those records by making them even more *antecedently* improbable than they were before. Not only will it be said that the proved fallibility of the modern witnesses illustrates the probable fallibility of the ancient ones, but the failure of the inquiry to elicit any indication that supernormal faculties do now exist in man will *pro tanto* throw a retrospective improbability on the second of the preliminary theses of religion, which assumes that some such supernormal faculty did at any rate exist in man at a given epoch. It may indeed be urged that such faculties were given for a time, and for a purpose, and were then withdrawn. But the instinct of scientific continuity, which even in the shaping of the solid continents is fain to substitute for deluge and cataclysm the tideway and the ripple and the rain, will rebel against the hypothesis of a bygone age of inward miracles,—a catastrophic interference with the intimate nature of man.

I will illustrate my meaning by a concrete example, which does not involve any actual article of Protestant faith. The ecstacy and the stigmata of St. Francis are an important element in Roman Catholic tradition. They are to some extent paralleled in the present day by the ecstacy and the stigmata of Louise Lateau. And Catholic instinct has discerned that if this modern case be decided to be merely *morbid*, and in no true sense *supernormal*, a retrospective discredit will be cast on the earlier legend. The old reluctance of the Catholic Church to submit her phenomena to scientific assessors has therefore to some extent been overcome; and Catholic physicians, under ecclesiastical authority, have discussed Louise Lateau's case in the forms of an ordinary medical report.

Enough will have been said to indicate the reality of the connection between our inquiries and the preliminary theses of religion. And so far as our positive results go in this direction, they will perhaps carry the more weight in that they are independently obtained, and intended to subserve scientific rather than religious ends ;—coming, indeed, from men who have no developed theory of their own to offer, and are merely following the observed facts wherever they may seem to lead. I see no probability, I may add, that our results can ever supply a convincing proof to any specialised form of religion. The utmost that I anticipate is, that they may afford a solid basis of general evidence to the independence of man's spiritual nature, and its persistence after death, on which basis, at any rate, religions in their specialised forms may be at one with science, and on which the structure of definite *revelation* (which must be up-built by historical or moral arguments) may conceivably be planted with a firmness which is at present necessarily lacking.

§ 12. I have been speaking thus far of religion in its full sense, as a body of doctrine containing some kind of definite assurance as to an unseen world. But the form of religious thought which specially characterises our own day is somewhat different from this. We are accustomed rather to varying attempts to retain the spirit, the aroma of religion, even if its solid substratum of facts previously supposed provable should have to be abandoned. The discoursers on things spiritual who have been most listened to in our own day—as Carlyle, Emerson, Mazzini, Renan, Tennyson, Matthew Arnold, Ruskin, &c.,— have been to a very small extent dogmatic on the old lines. They have expressed vague, though lofty, beliefs and aspirations, in which the eye of science may perhaps see little substance or validity, but which nevertheless have been in a certain sense more independent, more spontaneous, than of old, since they are less often prompted by any faith instilled from without, and resemble rather the awakening into fuller consciousness of some inherited and instinctive need.

And this brings us by an easy transition to the next topic, on which I wish to dwell. For I wish to point out that the *emotional* creed of educated men is becoming divorced from their *scientific* creed ; that just as the old orthodoxy of religion was too narrow to contain men's knowledge, so now the new orthodoxy of materialistic science is too narrow to contain their feelings and aspirations; and consequently that just as the fabric of religious orthodoxy used to be strained in order to admit the discoveries of geology or astronomy, so now also the obvious deductions of materialistic science are strained or overpassed in order to give sanction to feelings and aspirations which it is found impossible to ignore. My inference will, of course, be that in this vaguer realm of thought, as well as in the more distinctly-defined branches of knowledge which we have already discussed, the time is ripe for some such extension of scientific knowledge as we claim that we are offering here—an extension which, in my view, lifts us above the materialistic standpoint altogether, and which gives at least a possible reality to those subtle intercommunications between spirit and spirit, and even between visible and invisible things, of which Art and Literature are still as full as in any "Age of Faith " which preceded us.

I point, then, to the obvious fact that the spread of Materialism has not called into being Materialists *only* of those simple types which were commonly anticipated a century since as likely to fill a world of complete secularity.

Materialists, indeed, of that old unflinching temper do exist, and form a powerful and influential body. It would have been strange, indeed, if recent advances in physiology had not evoked new theories of human life, and a new ideal. For the accepted commonplaces of the old-fashioned moralist are being scattered with a ruthless hand. Our free will, over great portions at least of its once supposed extent, is declared to be an illusion. Our highest and most complex emotions are traced to their rudimentary beginnings in the instincts of self-preservation and reproduction. Our vaunted personality itself is seen to depend on a shifting and unstable synergy of a number of nervous centres, the defect of a portion of which centres may alter our character altogether. And meantime Death, on the other hand, has lost none of its invincible terrors. The easy way in which our forefathers would speak of " our mortal and immortal parts " is hard to imitate in face of the accumulating testimony to the existence of the one element in us, and the evanescence of the other. And since the decay and dissolution of man seem now to many minds to be so much more capable of being truly known than his survival or his further evolution, it is natural that much of the weight which once belonged to the prophets of what man *hoped* should pass to those who can speak with authority on what man needs must *fear.* Thus " mad-doctors " tend to supplant theologians, and the lives of lunatics are found to have more lessons for us than the lives of saints. For these thinkers know well that man can fall *below* himself; but that he can rise *above* himself they can believe no more. A corresponding ideal is gradually created; an ideal of mere sanity and normality, which gets to look on any excessive emotion or fixed idea, any departure from a balanced practicality, with distrust or disfavour, and sometimes rising to a kind of fervour of Philistinism, classes genius itself as a *neurosis.*

The alienists who have taken this extreme view have usually, perhaps, been of opinion that in thus discrediting the higher flights of imagination or sentiment we are not losing much ; that these things are in any case a mere surplusage, and that the ends which life is really capable of attaining can be compassed as well without them. But if the materialistic theory be the true one, these limitations of ideal might well be adopted even by men who would deeply regret what they were thus renouncing. It might well seem that, in abandoning the belief in any spiritual or permanent element in man, it were wise to abandon also that intensity of the affections which is ill-adapted to bonds so perishable and insecure, that reach of imagination which befitted only the illusory dignity which was once attached to human fates.

But in fact, as I have already implied, the characteristic movement of our own country, at any rate, at the present day, is hardly in this direction. Our prevalent temper is not so much *materialistic* as *agnostic ;* and although this renouncement of all knowledge of invisible things does in a sense leave visible things in sole possession of the field, yet the Agnostic is as far as anyone from being " a hog from Epicurus' sty." Rather, instead of sinking into the materialistic ideal of plain sense and physical well-being, the rising schools of thought are transcending that ideal more and more. Altruism in morals, idealism in art, nay, even the sentiment of piety itself, as a decorative grace of life,—all these, it is urged, are consistent with a complete and contented ignorance as to aught beyond the material world.

I need not here embark on the controversy as to how far this aspiration towards " the things of the spirit " is logically consistent with a creed that stops short with the things of sense. It is quite enough for my present purpose to point out that here also, as in the case of more definite religions, we have a system of beliefs and emotions which may indeed be able to *accommodate* themselves to modern science, but which are in no sense *supported* thereby ; rather which science must regard as, at best, a kind of phosphorescence which plays harmlessly about minds that Nature has developed by other processes and for other ends than these.

For my argument is that here again, as in the case of religion, telepathy, as we affirm it in this book, would be the first indication of a possible scientific basis for much that now lacks not only experimental confirmation, but even plausible analogy. We have seen how much support the preliminary theses of religion may acquire from an assured conviction that the human mind is at least *capable* of receiving supernormal influences,—is not closed, by its very structure, as the Materialists would tell us, to any " inbreathings of the spirit " which do not appeal to outward eye or ear. And somewhat similar is the added reality which the discovery of telepathy gives to the higher flights, the subtler shades, of mere earthly emotion.

> " Star to star vibrates light ; may soul to soul
> Strike thro' some finer element of her own ?"

The lover, the poet, the enthusiast in any generous cause, has in every age unconsciously answered Lord Tennyson's question for himself. To some men, as to Goethe, the assurance of this subtle intercommunication has come with vivid distinctness in some passion-shaken hour. Others, as Bacon, have seemed to gather it from the imperceptible indicia of a lifelong contemplation of man. But the step which actual experimentation, the actual collection and collation of evidence, has now, as we believe, effected, is a greater one than could have been achieved by any individual intuition of bard or sage. For we have for the first time a firm foothold in this impalpable realm ; we know that these unuttered messages do truly travel, that these emotions mix and spread ; and though we refrain as yet from further dwelling on the corollaries of this far-reaching law, it is not because such speculations need any longer be *baseless*, but because we desire to set forth the proof of our theorem in full detail before we do more than hint at the new fields which it opens to human thought.

§ 13. Pausing, therefore, on the threshold of these vaguer promises, I may indicate another direction, in which few will deny that a systematic investigation like ours ought to produce results eminently salutary. It ought to be as much our business to check the growth of error as to promote the discovery of truth. And there is plenty of evidence to show that so long as we omit to subject all alleged supernormal phenomena to a thorough comparative scrutiny, we are not merely postponing a possible gain, but permitting an unquestioned evil.

It should surely be needless in the present day to point out that no attempt to discourage inquiry into any given subject which strongly interests mankind, will in reality divert attention from the topic thus tabooed. The *savant* or the preacher may influence the readers of scientific hand-books, or the members of church congregations, but outside that circle the subject will be pursued with the more excited eagerness because regulating knowledge and experienced guidance are withdrawn.

And thus it has been with our supernormal phenomena. The men who claim to have experienced them have not been content to dismiss them as unseasonable or unimportant. They have not relegated them into the background of their lives as readily as the physiologist has relegated them into a few paragraphs at the end of a chapter. On the contrary, they have brooded over them, distorted them, misinterpreted them. Where *savants* have minimised, *they* have magnified, and the perplexing modes of marvel which the text-books ignore, have become, as it were, the ganglia from which all kinds of strange opinions ramify and spread.

The number of persons whose minds have been actually upset either by genuine psychical phenomena, or by their fraudulent imitation, is perhaps not large. But the mischief done is by no means confined to these extreme cases. It is mischievous, surely— it clashes roughly with our respect for human reason, and our belief in human progress—that religions should spring up, forms of worship be established, which in effect do but perpetuate a mistake and consecrate a misapprehension, which carry men not forward, but backward in their conception of unseen things.

The time has not yet come for an attempt to trace in detail the perversion which each branch of these supernormal phenomena has undergone in ardent minds;—the claims to sanctity, revelation, prophecy, which a series of enthusiasts, and of charlatans, have based on each class of marvels in turn. But two forms of creed already mentioned may again be cited as convenient examples—the Irvingite faith of the misinterpretation of *automatism*, the Swedenborgian of the misinterpretation of (so-called) *clairvoyance*. Still more singular have been the resultant beliefs when to the assemblage of purely *psychical* marvels a *physical* ingredient has been added, of a more disputable kind. For linked in various ways with records of automatic cerebration, of apparitions, of vision and revelation, come accounts of objective sounds, of measurable movements, which may well seem an unwarrantable intrusion into the steady order of the ponderable world. And in the year 1848 certain events, whose precise nature is still in dispute, occurred in America, in consequence of which many persons were led to believe that under appropriate circumstances these sounds, these movements, these tangible apparitions, could be evoked or reproduced at will. On this basis the creed of " Modern Spiritualism " has been upbuilt. And here arises the pressing question—notoriously still undecided, difficult and complex beyond any anticipation—as to whether supernormal phenomena of this *physical* kind do in fact occur at all ; or whether they are in *all* cases—as they undoubtedly have been in *many* cases —the product of mere fraud or delusion. This question, as it seems to us, is one to which we are bound to give our most careful attention ; and if we have as yet failed to attain a decisive view, it is not for want of laborious observation, continued by several of us throughout many years. But we are unwilling to pronounce until we have had ample opportunities—opportunities which so far we have for the most part sought in vain—of investigating phenomena obtained through private sources, and free, at any rate, from the specific suspicion to which the presence of a " paid medium " inevitably gives rise.

I need not add further illustrations of the cautionary, the critical attitude which befits such a Society as ours at the present juncture. This attitude is in one way unavoidably ungracious ; for it has sometimes precluded us from availing ourselves of the labours of predecessors whose zeal and industry we should have been glad to praise. The time, we hope, will come when enough of daylight shall shine upon our path to make possible a discriminating survey of the tracks which scattered seekers have struck out for themselves in the confusion and dimness of dawn. At present we have mainly to take heed that our own groping course shall at least avoid the pitfalls into which others have fallen. Anything like a distribution of awards of merit would be obviously premature on the part of men whose best hope must be that they may conduct the inquiry into a road firm enough to enable others rapidly to outstrip them.

II.

§ 14. Enough, however, has now been said to indicate the general tenor of the task which the Society for Psychical Research has undertaken. It remains to indicate the place which the present work occupies in the allotted field, and the reasons for offering it to public consideration at this early stage of our inquiry. We could not, of course, predict or pre-arrange the order in which opportunities of successful investigation might occur to the searchers in this labyrinth of the unknown. Among the groping experiments which seemed to have only too often led to mere mistake and confusion,—the " thousand pathways "

" qua signa sequendi
Falleret indeprensus et inremeabilis error,"—

it was not easy to choose with confidence our adit of exploration. The approach which proved most quickly productive was one from which it might have seemed that there was little indeed to hope. A kind of drawing-room game sprang up—it is hard to say whence—a method of directing a subject to perform a desired act by a contact so slight that no *conscious* impulsion was either received or given. Careful observers soon ranked the "willing-game" as an illustration of involuntary muscular action on the willer's part, affording a guidance to which the subject yielded sometimes without being aware of it. But while the *modus operandi* of public exhibitions of this misnamed " thought-reading " was not difficult to detect, Professor Barrett was one of the first who—while recognising all these sources of error— urged the duty of persistent watching for any residuum of true thought-transference which might from time to time appear. As will be seen from Chap. II. of this book it was not till after some six years of inquiry and experiment (1876-82) that definite proof of thought-transference in the normal state could be placed before the world. This was done in an article in the *Nineteenth Century* for June, 1882, signed by Professor Barrett, Mr. Gurney, and myself. The phenomenon of transmission of thought or sensation without the agency of the recognised organs of sense had been previously recorded in connection with the mesmeric state, but, so far as we know, its occasional occurrence in the normal state was now for the first time maintained on the strength of definite experiment. And the four years 1882-1886 have witnessed a great extension of those experiments, which no longer rest on the integrity and capacity of the earliest group of observers alone.

§ 15. The foundation of the Society for Psychical Research in 1882 gave an opportunity to Mr. Gurney and myself, as Hon. Secs. of a Literary Committee, to invite from the general public records of apparitions at or after death, and other abnormal occurrences. On reviewing the evidence thus obtained we were struck with the great predominance of alleged apparitions *at or near the moment of death*. And a new light seemed to be thrown on these phenomena by the unexpected frequency of accounts of apparitions of living persons, coincident with moments of danger or crisis. We were led to infer a strong analogy between our experimental cases of thought-transference and some of these spontaneous cases of what we call telepathy, or transference of a shock or impulse from one living person to another person at such a distance or under such conditions as to negative the possibility of any ordinary mode of transmission. An article, signed by Mr. Gurney and myself, in the *Fortnightly Review* for March, 1883, gave a first expression to the analogy thus suggested. The task of collection and scrutiny grew on our hands; Mr. Podmore undertook to share our labours; and the Council of the Society for Psychical Research requested us to embody the evidence received in a substantive work.

It will be seen, then, that the theory of Telepathy, experimental and spontaneous, which forms the main topic of this book, was not chosen as our theme by any arbitrary process of selection, but was irresistibly suggested by the abundance and the convergence of evidence tending to prove that special thesis. We were, and are, equally anxious to inquire into many other alleged marvels—clairvoyance, haunted houses, Spiritualistic phenomena, &c.—but telepathy is the subject which has first shown itself capable of investigation appearing to lead to a positive result; and it seemed well to arrange its evidence with sufficient fulness to afford at least a solid groundwork for further inquiry.

And having been led to this choice by the nature of the actual evidence before us, we may recognise that there is some propriety in dealing first with an issue which, complex though it is, is yet simple as compared to other articles of our programme. For the fact, if it be one, of the direct action of mind upon mind has at least a generality which makes it possible that, like the law of atomic combination in chemistry, it may be a generalisation which, though grasped at first in a very simplified and imperfect fashion, may prove to have been the essential pre-requisite of future progress.

§ 16. In a certain sense it may be said that this hidden action of one mind on another comes next in order of psychical discovery to the hidden action of the mind within itself. It will be remembered that the earliest scientific attempts to explain the phenomena of so-called Spiritualism referred them mainly to "unconscious cerebration," (Carpenter,) or to what was virtually the same thing, "unconscious muscular action" (Faraday).

Now these theories, in my view, were, so far as they went, not only legitimate, but the most logical which could have been suggested to explain the scanty evidence with which alone Faraday and Carpenter attempted to deal. This unconscious action of the mind was in reality the first thing which it was needful to take into account in approaching supernormal phenomena. I believe, indeed, that our knowledge of those hidden processes of mentation is still in its infancy, and I have elsewhere endeavoured to assign a wider range than orthodox science has yet admitted to the mind's unconscious operation.[1] But the result of this further analysis has been (as I hold) *not* to show that ordinary physiological considerations will suffice (as Dr. Carpenter seems to suppose) to explain all the psychical problems involved, but rather to reveal the fact that these unconscious operations of the mind do not follow the familiar channels alone, but are themselves the facilitation or the starting-point of operations which to science are wholly new.

To state the matter broadly, so as to include in a common formula the unremembered utterances of the hypnotic subject, and the involuntary writings of the waking automatist, I would maintain that when the horizon of consciousness is altered, the opening field of view is not always or wholly filled by a mere mirage or refraction of objects already familiar, but does, on rare occasions, include new objects, as real as the old. And amongst the novel energies thus liberated, the power of entering into direct communication with other intelligences seems to stand plainly forth. Among the objects in the new prospect are fragments of the thoughts and feelings of distant minds. It seems, at any rate, that some element of *telepathy* is perpetually meeting us throughout the whole range of these inquiries. In the first place, thought-transference is the only supernormal phenomenon which we have as yet acquired the power of inducing, even occasionally, in the *normal* state. It meets us also in the

---

[1] See *Proceedings* of the S.P.R., Vols. ii. and iii.

hypnotic trance, under the various forms of "community of sensation," "silent willing," and the like. Among the alleged cases of "mesmeric clairvoyance" the communication of pictures of places from operator to subject seems the least uncertain ground. And again, among phenomena commonly attributed to "spirits," (but many of which may perhaps be more safely ascribed to the automatic agency of the sensitive himself,) communication of thought still furnishes our best clue to "trance-speaking," "clairvoyant vision," answers to mental questions and the like. It need not, therefore, surprise us if, even in a field so apparently remote from all ordinary analogies as that of apparitions and death-wraiths, we still find that telepathy affords our most satisfactory clue.

§ 17. And here would seem to be the fitting place to explain why we have given the title of "Phantasms of the *Living*" to a group of records most of which will present themselves to the ordinary reader as narratives of apparitions of the *dead*.

When we began, in a manner to be presently described, to collect accounts of experiences which our informants regarded as inexplicable by ordinary laws, we were of course ignorant as to what forms these experiences would mainly take. But after printing and considering over two thousand depositions which seemed *primâ facie* to deserve attention, we find that more than half of them are narratives of appearances or other impressions coincident either with the death of the person seen or with some critical moment in his life-history.

The value of the accounts of apparitions *after* death is lessened, moreover, by a consideration which is obvious enough as soon as these narratives come to be critically considered. The difficulty in dealing with all these hallucinations—with all appearances to which no persistent three-dimensional reality corresponds—is to determine whether they are *veridical*, or *truth-telling*—whether, that is, they do in fact correspond to some action which is going on in some other place or on some other plane of being ;—or whether, on the other hand, they are merely morbid or casual—the random and meaningless fictions of an over-stimulated eye or brain. Now, in the case of apparitions at the moment of death or crisis, we have at any rate an objective fact to look to. If we can prove that a great number of apparitions coincide with the death of the person seen, we may fairly say, as we do say, that chance alone cannot explain this coincidence, and that there is a causal connection between the two events. But if I have a vision of a friend recently dead, and on whom my thoughts have been dwelling, we cannot be sure that this may not be a merely delusive hallucination—the mere offspring of my own brooding sorrow. In order to get at all nearly the same degree of evidence for a *dead* person's appearance that we can get for a *dying* person's appearance, it seems necessary that the apparition should either communicate some fact known only to the deceased, or should be noted independently by more than one person at once or successively. And our evidence of this kind is at present scarcely sufficient to support any assured conclusion.[1]

When, therefore, we are considering whether the phantasms of *dying* persons may most fitly be considered as phantasms of the dead or of the living, we find little support from analogy on the side of *posthumous* apparitions. And on the other hand, as already hinted, we have many cases where the apparition has coincided with violent shocks,—carriage accidents, fainting fits, epileptic fits, &c., which nevertheless left the *agent*,—as we call the person whose semblance is seen,—as much alive as before. In some cases the accident is *almost* a fatal one; as when a man's phantom is seen at the moment when he is half-drowned and insensible. In such a case it would seem illogical to allow the mere fact of his restoration or non-restoration to life to rank his phantom as that of a *living* person in the one case, of a *dead* person in the other. It seems simpler to suppose that if two men fall overboard to-day and their respective phantoms are seen by their friends at the moment,—then, though one man should be restored to life and the other not,—yet if the first phantom was that of a living man, so also was the second.

Nay more, even if the apparition be seen some hours later than the moment of apparent death, there are still reasons which prevent us from decisively classing it as the apparition of a dead man. In the first place, the moment of actual death is a very uncertain thing. When the heart's action stops the organism continues for some time in a state very different from that of ordinary inanimate matter. In such an inquiry as ours it is safer to speak, not of death, but of "the process of dissolution," and to allow for the possible prolongation of some form of psychical energy even when, for instance, the attempt to restore respiration to a drowned man has definitely failed. And in

[1] See Mrs. Sidgwick's paper on "The Evidence, collected by the Society, for Phantasms of the Dead," in *Proceedings* of the S.P.R., Vol. iii.

the second place, we find in the case of phantasms corresponding to some accident or crisis which befalls a living friend, that there seems often to be a latent period before the phantasm becomes definite or externalised to the percipient's eye or ear.   Sometimes a vague *malaise* seems first to be generated, and then when other stimuli are deadened,—as at night or in some period of repose,—the indefinite grief or uneasiness takes shape in the voice or figure of the friend who in fact passed through his moment of peril some hours before. It is quite possible that a deferment of this kind may sometimes intervene between the moment of death and the phantasmal announcement thereof to a distant friend.

These, then, are reasons, suggested by actual experience, for ascribing our phantasms at death to living rather than to dead men. And there is another consideration, of a more general order, which points in the same direction. We must not rashly multiply the problems involved in this difficult inquiry. Now Science, it is needless to say, offers no assurance that man survives the tomb ; and although in Christian countries our survival is an established doctrine, this does not carry with it any dogma as to the possibility that communications should reach us from departed spirits. The hypothesis, then, that apparitions are ever directly caused by dead persons is one which ordinary scientific caution bids us to be very slow in introducing. Should it afterwards be established that departed spirits can communicate with us, the interpretation placed upon various cases contained in these volumes may need revision. But for the present it is certainly safer to inquire how far they can be explained by the influences or impressions which, as we know by actual experiment, living persons can under certain circumstances exert or effect on one another, in those obscure supersensory modes which we have provisionally massed together under the title of Telepathy.

§ 18.   The main theses of this book, then, are now capable of being stated in a very simple form.

I. Experiment proves that telepathy—the supersensory [1] transference of thoughts and feelings from one mind to another,—is a fact in Nature.

---

[1] By "supersensory" I mean "independent of the recognised channels of sense." I do not mean to assert that telepathic perception either is or is not analogous to sensory perception of the recognised kinds.

II. Testimony proves that phantasms (impressions, voices, or figures) of persons undergoing some crisis,—especially death,—are perceived by their friends and relatives with a frequency which mere chance cannot explain.

III. These phantasms then, whatever else they may be, are instances of the supersensory action of one mind on another. The second thesis therefore confirms, and is confirmed by, the first. For if telepathy exists, we should anticipate that it would exhibit some *spontaneous* manifestations, on a scale more striking than our *experimental* ones. And, on the other hand, apparitions are rendered more credible and comprehensible by an analogy which for the first time links them with the results of actual experiment.

Such are the central theses of this work,—theses on which its authors, and the friends whom they have mainly consulted, are in entire agreement. The first thesis may, of course, be impugned by urging that our experiments are fallacious. The second thesis may be impugned by urging that our testimony is insufficient. The third thesis, as I have here worded it, is hardly open to separate attack ; being a corollary which readily follows if the first two theses are taken as proved.

This, however, is only the case so long as the third thesis, which asserts the analogy between thought-transference and apparitions—between experimental and spontaneous telepathy—is stated in a vague and general form. So soon as we attempt to give more precision to this analogy—to discuss how far the unknown agency at work can be supposed to be the same in both cases—or how far the apparitions may be referable to quite other, though cognate, laws,—we enter on a field where even those who have accepted the analogy in general terms are likely to find the evidence leading them to somewhat divergent conclusions. Of two men independently studying our records of apparitions, the one will almost inevitably press their analogy to simple telepathy further than the other. And each will be able to plead that he has been guided as far as possible by an instinct of scientific caution in thus judging of matters strange and new. The *first* will say that " causes are not to be multiplied without necessity," and that we have now in telepathy a *vera causa* whose furthest possibilities we ought to exhaust before invoking still stranger, still remoter agencies, whose very existence we are not in a position to prove. He will feel bound therefore to dwell on the points on which our knowledge either of telepathy, or of the mechanism of hallucinations in general, throws some light; and he will set aside as at present inexplicable such peculiarities of our evidence as cannot well be brought within this scheme.

The second inquirer, on the other hand, will perhaps feel strongly that telepathy, as we now know it, is probably little more than a mere preliminary conception, a simplified mode of representing to ourselves a group of phenomena which, as involving relations between *minds*, may probably be more complex than those which involve even the highest known forms of *matter*. He will feel that, while we hold one clue alone, we must be careful not to overrate its efficacy; we must be on the watch for other approaches, for hints of inter-relation between disparate and scattered phenomena.

It is to the first of these two attitudes of mind,—the attitude which deprecates extraneous theorising,—that Mr. Gurney and Mr. Podmore have inclined; and the committal of the bulk of this work to Mr. Gurney's execution indicates not only that he has been able to devote the greatest amount of time and energy to the task, but also that his view is on the whole the most nearly central among the opinions which we have felt it incumbent on us to consult. We have no wish, however, to affect a closer agreement than actually exists; and in a "Note on a Suggested Mode of Psychical Interaction," which will be found in Vol. II., I shall submit a view which differs from Mr. Gurney's on some theoretical points.

§ 19. The theories contained in this book, however, bear a small proportion to the mass of collected facts. A few words as to our method of collection may here precede Mr. Gurney's full discussion (Chapter IV.) of the peculiar difficulties to which our evidence is exposed.

It soon became evident that if our collection was to be satisfactory it must consist mainly of cases collected by ourselves, and of a great number of such cases. The apparitions at death, &c., recorded by previous writers, are enough, indeed, to show that scattered incidents of the kind have obtained credence in many ages and countries. But they have never been collected and sifted with any systematic care; and few of them reach an evidential standard which could justify us in laying them before our readers. And even had the existing stock of testimony been large and well-assured, it would still have been needful for us to collect our own specimens *in situ*,—to see, talk with, and correspond with the persons to whose strange experiences so much weight was to be given. This task of personal inquiry,—whose traces will, we hope, be sufficiently apparent throughout the present work,—has stretched itself out beyond expectation, but has also enabled us to speak with a confidence which could not have been otherwise acquired. One of its advantages is the security thus gained as to the *bona fides* of the witnesses concerned. They have practically placed themselves upon their honour; nor need we doubt that the experiences have been, as a rule, recounted in all sincerity. As to unintentional errors of observation and memory, Mr. Gurney's discussion will at least show that we have had abundant opportunities of learning how wide a margin must be left for human carelessness, forgetfulness, credulity. " God forbid," said the flute-player to Philip of Macedon, " that your Majesty should know these things as well as I !"

It must not, however, be inferred from what has been said that our informants as a body have shown themselves less shrewd or less accurate than the generality of mankind. On the contrary, we have observed with pleasure that our somewhat persistent and probing method of inquiry has usually repelled the sentimental or crazy wonder-mongers who hang about the outskirts of such a subject as this ; while it has met with cordial response from an unexpected number of persons who feel with reason that the very mystery which surrounds these incidents makes it additionally important that they should be recounted with sobriety and care. The straightforward style in which most of our informants have couched their narratives, as well as the honoured names which some of them bear, may enable the reader to share something of the confidence which a closer contact with the facts has inspired in our own minds.

Again, it seemed necessary that the collection offered to the public should be a very large one, even at the cost of including in a Supplement some remote or second-hand cases besides the first-hand cases which alone are admitted into the chapters of this book. If, indeed, our object had been simply to make out a case for the connection of deaths with apparitions, we might have offered a less assailable front, and should certainly have spared ourselves much trouble, had we confined ourselves to giving in detail a few of the best-attested instances. But what we desired was not precisely this. We hope, no doubt, that most of our readers may ultimately be led to conclusions resembling our own. But before our conclusions can expect to gain general acceptance, many other hypotheses will doubtless be advanced, and coincidence, superstition, fraud, hysteria, will be invoked in various combinations to explain the evidence given here. We think, therefore, that it is our duty in so new a subject to afford full material for hypotheses discordant with our own; to set forth cases drawn from so wide a range of society, and embracing such a variety of circumstances, as to afford scope for every mode of origination or development of these narratives which the critic may suggest.

Furthermore, the whole subject of hallucinations of the sane— which hitherto has received very scanty treatment—seems fairly to belong to our subject, and has been treated by Mr. Gurney in Chap. XI. We have throughout contended that a knowledge of abnormal or merely morbid phenomena is an indispensable pre-requisite for the treating of any supernormal operations which may be found to exist under somewhat similar forms of manifestation.

Once more, it was plainly desirable to inquire whether hypotheses, now admitted to be erroneous, had ever been based in past times on evidence in any way comparable to that which we have adduced. The belief in witchcraft, from its wide extent and its nearness to our own times, is the most plausible instance of such a parallelism. And Mr. Gurney, in his Note on Chapter IV., has given the results of an analysis of witch-literature more laborious than previous authors had thought it worth while to undertake. The result is remarkable; for it appears that the only marvels for which respectable testimony was adduced consist obviously of ignorant descriptions of hypnotic and epileptiform phenomena now becoming familiar to science; while as to the monstrous stories—copied from one uncritical writer into another—which have given to this confused record of hypnotic and hysterical illusions the special aromas (so to say) of witchcraft or lycanthropy,—these prodigies have scarcely ever the slightest claim to be founded on any first-hand evidence at all.

§ 20. But while the material here offered for forming an opinion on all these points is, no doubt, much larger than previous writers have been at the pains to amass, we are anxious, neverthe-less, to state explicitly that we regard this present collection of facts as merely preliminary; this present work as merely opening out a novel subject; these researches of a few persons during a few years as the mere first instalment of inquiries which will need repetition and reinforcement to an extent which none of us can as yet foresee.

A change in the scientific outlook so considerable as that to which these volumes point must needs take time to accomplish. Time is needed not only to spread the knowledge of new facts, but also to acclimatise new conceptions in the individual mind. Such, at least, has been our own experience; and since the evidence which has come to us slowly and piecemeal is here presented to other minds suddenly and in a mass, we must needs expect that its acceptance by them will be a partial and gradual thing. What we hope for first is an increase in the number of those who are willing to aid us in our labours; we trust that the fellow-workers in many lands to whom we already owe so much may be encouraged to further collection of testimony, renewed experiment, when they see these experiments confirming one another in London, Paris, Berlin,—this testimony vouching for cognate incidents from New York to New Zealand, and from Manchester to Calcutta.

With each year of experiment and registration we may hope that our results will assume a more definite shape—that there will be less of the vagueness and confusion inevitable at the beginning of a novel line of research, but naturally distasteful to the *savant* accustomed to proceed by measurable increments of knowledge from experimental bases already assured. Such an one, if he reads this book, may feel as though he had been called away from an ordnance survey, conducted with a competent staff and familiar instruments, to plough slowly with inexperienced mariners through some strange ocean where beds of entangling seaweed cumber the trackless way. We accept the analogy; but we would remind him that even floating weeds of novel genera may foreshow a land unknown; and that it was not without ultimate gain to men that the straining keels of Columbus first pressed through the Sargasso Sea.

§ 21. Yet one word more. This book is not addressed to *savants* alone, and it may repel many readers on quite other than scientific grounds. Attempting as we do to carry the reign of Law into a sanctuary of belief and emotion which has never thus been invaded in detail,—lying in wait, as it were, to catch the last impulse of the dying, and to question the serenity of the dead,—we may seem to be incurring the poet's curse on the man "who would peep and botanize upon his mother's grave,"—to be touching the Ark of sacred mysteries with hands stained with labour in the profane and common field.

How often have men thus feared that Nature's wonders would be degraded by being closelier looked into! How often, again, have they learnt that the truth was higher than their imagination; and that it is man's work, but never Nature's, which to be magnificent must remain unknown! How would a disciple of Aristotle,—fresh from his master's conception of the fixed stars as types of godhead, —of an inhabitance by pure existences of a supernal world of their own,—how would he have scorned the proposal to learn more of those stars by dint of the generation of fetid gases and the sedulous minuteness of spectroscopic analysis! Yet how poor, how frag- mentary were Aristotle's fancies compared with our conception, thus gained, of cosmic unity! our vibrant message from Sirius and Orion by the heraldry of the kindred flame! Those imagined gods are gone ; but the spectacle of the starry heavens has become for us so moving in its immensity that philosophers, at a loss for terms of wonder, have ranked it with the Moral Law.

If man, then, shall attempt to sound and fathom the depths that lie not without him, but within, analogy may surely warn him that the first attempts of his rude *psychoscopes* to give precision and actuality to thought will grope among " beggarly elements,"—will be concerned with things grotesque, or trivial, or obscure. Yet here also one handsbreadth of reality gives better footing than all the castles of our dream ; here also by beginning with the least things we shall best learn how great things may remain to do.

The insentient has awoke, we know not how, into sentiency ; the sentient into the fuller consciousness of human minds. Yet even human self-consciousness remains a recent, a perfunctory, a superficial thing ; and we must first reconstitute our conception of the microcosm, as of the macrocosm, before we can enter on those " high capacious powers " which, I believe, " lie folded up in man."

F. W. H. M.

ADDITIONS AND CORRECTIONS.

VOLUME I.

Page 33, line 20.   For 999,999, 98, read 999, 999, 999, 1.

Page 34, line 6.   For 1000 to 1, read "about 500 to 1."

Page 88.   Since the note on this page was written, some additional evidence has been obtained as to the effect of concentration of the operator's will in the process of hypnotising.   See the cases quoted in the Additional Chapter, (Vol. II., pp. 680, 684, 685,) from the records of the Société de Psychologie Physiologique.

Page 110, first note.   Two further examples of this interesting type will be found on pp. lxxxi-iv, below.

Page 118, second note.   After this note had been printed off, I came across a passage from *Die Christliche Mystik*, by J. J. von Goerres, in which a learned bishop, Prudencio de Sandoval, is made to describe a witch's journey through the air as though he had himself been a judicial spectator of it.   A reference to Sandoval's own account, however, in his *Historia de la vida y hechos del Emperador Carlos V.* (Pamplona, 1618), Vol. I., p. 830, shows that the trial of the witch in question took place in 1527.   Now Sandoval died in 1621; clearly, therefore, he could not have been a first-hand witness, as represented.   Nor does he even name his authority; and discredit is thrown on his sources of information by Llorente, in his *Anales de la Inquisicion de España* (Madrid, 1812), p. 319. As the passage from Goerres was quoted in a first-class scientific review, and, if accurate, would have told against my statements as to the absence of first-hand evidence for alleged magical occurrences, I have thought it worth while to forestall a possible objection.

The only instance that I can find, during the witch-epoch, of definite first-hand evidence for a marvel of a type which our present knowledge of abnormal bodily and mental states will not explain, is, as it happens, not part of the history of so-called magic, but is connected with the extraordinary epidemic of religious excitement which took place in the Cevennes at the beginning of the last century.   As the instance seems to be a solitary one, it may be worth while to give the facts.   *The Théâtre Sacré des Cevennes* (London, 1707) contains the depositions of two witnesses to the fact that they saw a man named Clary stand for many minutes, totally uninjured, in the midst of a huge fire of blazing wood; and that they immediately afterwards ascertained by their own senses that there was not a sign of burning on him or his clothes.   This is the sort of case which, if multiplied by scores or hundreds, and if nothing were known against the character of the witnesses, would support the view that an apparently strong evidential case can be made out for phenomena— being matters of direct observation—which nevertheless for the scientific mind are impossible; and that therefore the evidential case for telepathy presented in this book may be safely neglected (see p. 115). But the character of the two deponents mentioned is seriously impugned by a ·third witness, the celebrated Colonel Cavallier, who had no interest in decrying his own followers and partisans, and whose probity seems never to have been doubted even by those who most questioned his good sense.[1] *(Nouveaux Memoires pour Servir à l'Histoire des Trois Camisars*, London, 1708, pp. 6-9.) He describes them as worthless impostors, as to whom it was easy to see "qu' il n'y a pas beaucoup à compter sur ce qu' ils disent, et encore moins sur ce qu' ils sont." See also the account given of them by Dr. Hutchinson, a by no means over-sceptical writer, who seems to have had the means of ascertaining Cavallier's opinions when the latter was in England. (*A Short View of the Pretended Spirit of Prophecy*, London, 1708, pp. 9, 16. See also *A Preservative against the False Prophets of the Times*, by Mark Vernons, London, 1708, p. 72; and *Clavis Prophetica*, London, 1707, pp. 8, 9.) As regards Colonel Cavallier himself, we have to note (1) that in the history of the Cevennes disturbances, attributed to him and probably drawn up from recollections of his conversations, not a word on the subject occurs; and that the only direct testimony to the occurrence that we have from him, as far as I can discover, is the phrase, "Cela est vrai," applied to the fire of Clary, "et d'autres choses de cette nature" (*Memoires pour Servir*, &c, p. 10);[2] (2) that even supposing he was an eye-witness, it nowhere appears that he examined Clary after the ordeal, and ascertained that his clothes and hair were unsinged; and, as Hutchinson remarks, the fire may have been "a fire of straw, that is no sooner kindled but it is out again." And in fact, in the *Histoire des Troubles des Cevennes*, by A. Court (Villefranche, 1760), p. 442, the author professes to have found, from information gathered at the spot, that "(1) Clary ne séjourna pas dans le feu; (2) il y entra deux fois; (3) il se brûla au col du bras, et fut obligé de s'arrêter au lieu de Pierredon, pour se fair panser."

I confine myself to this single case, which bears directly on my discussion of evidence in Chapter IV.; but since no topic has been a greater favourite in the modern literature of the "supernatural" than the phenomena of the Cevennes, it may be useful to add that probably no chapter of history offers equal facilities for studying the natural genesis of modern miracles.

Page 127, line 16.   For wonder-mongerer read wonder-monger.

Page 140, last sentence of note.   Since this was written, a few other instances have been included where it is possible, but not certain, that the

---

[1] See, for instance, the *Histoire des Camisards* (London, 1754), p. 333, note. The view of Cavallier there cited from De Brueys' *Histoire du Fanatisme* (Utrecht, 1737), need not be discounted because in the same work he is called a *scélérat*; that being De Brueys' generic term for a Camisard leader.

[2] No further testimony of Cavallier's on the subject seems to have been known to the author of the *Examen du Théâtre Sacré des Cevennes* (London, 1708, p. 34). He is not even stated to have been present, except in the depositions of the discredited witnesses; but on this point they may probably be trusted, as falsehood would have been at once exposed.

12 hours' limit was exceeded. It was exceeded in case 138, and possibly in case 165.

Page 145, last sentence. Since this was printed, some further cases have been received of considerable exaggeration of the closeness of a coincidence, which should be added to the examples mentioned in the note.

(1) An informant sent us a sworn affidavit to the effect that, in January, 1852, when returning from China on board the "Pilot," and near the Cape, he had a vision of his sister, and learnt on his arrival in England that she had died "about the time" of the vision. We find, from an examination of various newspapers, that the "Pilot" was in the East Indies up to December, 1851, and was at Devonport in March, 1852; so that she may well have been near the Cape in January, 1852. But we find from the Register of Deaths that the sister died on June 29, 1851, at which date, as we learn from the Admiralty, the "Pilot" was at Whampoa. It is not likely that our informant was mistaken as to his own experience having taken place on the return voyage, and shortly before his arrival in England. What happened, we may surmise, is that he was told, when he arrived after a long absence, that his sister had *lately* died; and that on the strength of his vision, he assumed or gradually came to imagine, that the death had happened only several weeks before, instead of several months.

(2) A gentleman gave us a striking account of a phantasm of a friend, then in the Transvaal war, who appeared in his room early one morning, and announced that he had been shot through the right lung. Such a hallucination being absolutely unique in our informant's experience, he noted the time—4.10 a.m.—by a clock on the mantelpiece, and waited feverishly during the hours that elapsed before he could see a newspaper at his club. He found no news of the war. In the course of the day he mentioned his vision and his disquietude to an acquaintance at the club. The next morning he saw, in the first paper that he took up, the announcement that his friend had been killed—shot through the right lung, as it afterwards proved—at an hour (as he calculated) closely coincident with that of his vision. We found, however, from the *London Gazette*, that the battle in which this officer was killed did not begin till 9.30 a.m.; and the death took place at least two hours later, which would be between 9 and 10 a.m. in England. Clearly, therefore, the vision must have preceded the death by some hours, *if they occurred on the same day.* But an examination of the newspapers makes it seem very likely that the vision fell on the day *after* the death. The battle took place on Friday, and was announced in the Saturday papers; but the death was not announced in the morning papers till Monday, and the vision which is represented as having occurred on the day next before the announcement of the death may more easily be supposed to have occurred on the *second* day than on the *third* day before—*i.e.*, on the Saturday, not the Friday morning. As to the statement that the papers contained no war-news on the morning of the vision, that is a point on which our informant's memory might easily get wrong, as they did not contain what he searched them for.

(3) An account signed by three witnesses of unimpeachable character, and purporting to be a statement made to them on Sept. 7, 1859, by T. Crowley, of Dinish Island, records a hallucination which he experienced

on Saturday, Aug. 13, and afterwards connected with the unexpected death of his daughter, Ellen, which took place at a distance a few hours earlier. This daughter had been an inmate of a Deaf and Dumb Asylum. From the secretary of this institution we learnt that the day of her death was Sunday, July 24, 1859; and we procured a certificate of her burial on the following day. It is probable that those who took down the statement got an idea that the coincidence was a close one, and unconsciously forced the wrong date on an uneducated witness.

(4) Two letters have been handed to us, written by a husband to his wife on Nov. 7 and Dec. 28, 1874. The first letter describes an over-powering impression of calamity at home which the writer experienced, during a voyage, on Friday, Nov. 6, and which he immediately mentioned to a friend, who has given us full written confirmation of the fact. In that week the writer of the letters lost a child, who died, as we find from the Register of Deaths, on Tuesday, Nov. 3. Yet the second letter, written after the news of the death had reached the father, says, " It is very strange, but the very time—day and hour—of our boy's death, I could not sleep," and then follows another account of the very experience which was before described (and undoubtedly correctly) as having happened on the night of Nov. 6, three days after the death.

(5) A lady, who did not remember ever to have dreamt of death on any other occasion, told us that one night, in January, 1881, she had a remarkably vivid dream of the death of a relative whom she did not know to be ill or likely to die ; and that on coming down in the morning she found the death announced in the *Times* as having occurred on the previous day. She did not (for family reasons) communicate the name of the person who died. But it is not very common for deaths to appear in the *Times* on the day after that on which they occurred. A list was accordingly made out of all the persons, corresponding with her description in sex and age, whose deaths were so immediately announced during that month ; and the list, being submitted to her, her relative's name proved not to be in it. The death must therefore have preceded the dream by more than 24 hours.

(6) Another informant gives an account of an interesting experience said to have occurred on the night of Sunday, May 6, 1866, and remark-ably coinciding with the death of the narrator's brother, lost with the "General Grant." The fate of this ship was not known till January, 1868, when the *Melbourne Argus* published a "narrative of the survivors." From this account we find that the wreck occurred on the night of Sunday the 13th, and that the death in question probably occurred on the morning of the 14th ; which, allowing for longitude, would closely correspond with the time of the experience in England, supposing that our informant's date was wrong by a week. This may very likely have been the case, as he explains that all he is clear about is that the day was a Sunday in May which he spent at a particular place. But unfortunately he had said in a former letter that the date May 6 was impressed on his mind by its being his own birthday ; and that statement cannot, of course, be ignored ; although he makes it tolerably clear that he really only *inferred* long afterwards that that was the day, because he knew for certain that on his birthday he was at the place where the experience occurred.

Pages 149–51. The following instructive instance of the difference between first-hand and second-hand evidence shows how easily a spurious telepathic narrative may grow up. We received a second-hand account to the effect that a friend of our informant, as she was returning from a walk, saw her sister on the doorstep just entering the house, entered herself a few moments after, was told by the servant that her sister had not been out, went upstairs, and found her dying from a sudden fit. The first-hand account, which had been given to us some years before, contains every one of these facts, (modifying one of them by the statement that the sister died " *within 12 hours* " after,) but adds just two more. " I, *being very blind, thought* [1] I saw her before me." " I probably mistook the door, *there being two* on the same doorstep as mine." How completely the aspect of the case is altered by these few additional words, appears in the most natural way from the sentences that follow. The second-hand account says, " *She looked upon this as an apparition*, sent to her to break the sudden shock," &c. The first-hand account says, " *I never imagined I had really seen an apparition ;* but it certainly was a merciful mistake, as it in a certain sense broke the shock to me," &c.

Page 154, second paragraph. The particular form of exaggeration in second-hand evidence, which represents what was really only a dream as that far rarer and more striking phenomenon—a waking hallucination— is exemplified in connection with one of the narratives quoted later, No. 429. The first-hand account, it will be seen, describes the experience simply as a *dream ;* Aubrey (*Miscellanies*, London, 1696, p. 60) recounts it as a case of *apparition.*

Page 156, last part of note. The publication of this book has led to the verication of the incident here described. The gentleman concerned —Mr. G. H. Dickson, of 17, Winckley Street, Preston—has sent me (Dec. 22, 1886) an account which differs from the second-hand report in two points only :—the woman was not actually crushed to death, though Mr. Dickson "was told, before leaving the station, that her injuries would be fatal " ; and his wife did not describe her experience to him immediately on his arrival, but later in the day—whether before or after his mention of the scene they do not now remember.

Page 158, line 1. "No cases are given which are not first-hand." Cases 256 and 257 are exceptions ; but see Vol. II., p. 83.

Page 167, line 1 of note. "The suppressed names have in all cases been given to us in confidence." In the Supplement there are seven exceptions to this rule. Five of them are cases which have been previously published on apparently reliable authority, but which the death of the person responsible for them has prevented us from tracing to their source ; the sixth is a MS. case of the same description ; and in the seventh, our informant, though perfectly remembering the circumstances of his connection with the original witness, cannot recall his name. In a very few other cases the name of the *agent* has not been learnt.

Page 206, note. Some independent evidence has been received as to the manner of Captain Collyer's death. An advertisement was inserted for us in the *Daily Picayune*, the leading New Orleans newspaper, offering a small

---

[1] *Thought* is italicised in the original : all the other italics are mine.

reward for definite information as to the fatal accident on the "Alice." For some months no information was given; but on Jan. 6, 1886, the editor wrote to us as follows :—"To-day a party called at the *Picayune* office, and made the following statement : ' My name is J. L. Hall. I was a striker on the steamer "Red River" at the time she ran into the "Alice," John Collyer, master, at a point about 20 miles above New Orleans. The accident occurred at 10 o'clock at night, in January, 1856. The day of the month I do not remember. The "Red River" was bound up stream, and the "Alice" bound down. The collision broke the starboard engine of the "Alice" and stove in her upper guards and boiler deck. As soon as possible the "Red River" ·went to the assistance of the "Alice," when one of the crew of the disabled boat remarked that the captain had been killed. On investigation, Captain Collyer was found lying on his back on the starboard side of the boiler deck of his boat, with a severe wound in the head and life extinct. The crew of the "Alice," all of whom were negroes, stated that Captain Collyer had been killed by the collision, but the officers of the "Red River" thought otherwise, as the wound in his (Captain Collyer's) head appeared to have been made before the two boats met, and the blood on the deck was coagulated. Probably not more than 10 minutes elapsed from the time the collision took place until the body of Captain Collyer was viewed by the officers of the "Red River." After helping the "Alice" to make repairs, the "Red River" proceeded on her voyage. I cannot say positively, but I do not think the killing of Captain Collyer was ever investigated.' " [1]

It will be seen that there is a suggestion here that the death preceded the collision ; and if this was so, it is an additional reason for supposing the coincidence with Mrs. Collyer's experience to have been extremely close ; for the witness had no idea why the evidence was wanted, and cannot have adjusted his account to a narrative of which he knew nothing. If his idea is correct, then there is no reason to suppose (as I have too hastily done in p. 206, note) that he has made a mistake as to the hour of the collision.

Page 248, case 49. The following is a corroborative account from Mrs. Arundel, who wrote from Maniton, Colorado, on April 1, 1886 :—

"Not being very well, I was lying on the sofa (not asleep, for I had my baby sitting on the floor beside me, playing). Mr. Arundel was away on a sailing excursion with some friends, and I did not expect his return for some days. It seemed to me that I distinctly heard him call me by name, ' Maggie,' a slight pause and again ' Maggie.' The voice seemed far off and yet clear, but the tone such as he would use if needing me. The impression was so distinct that I rose and went out on to the porch with the thought, 'Can they possibly have returned sooner for some reason ?' and I so fully expected to see him there that I went back into the house with a feeling of disappointment and some anxiety, too, feeling so *sure* I had heard *his voice*. No one was in the house, my servant being out. When my husband came home, he was much startled to find how exactly

---

[1] The man who gave this account doubtless received the reward of a few dollars which had been placed in the editor's hands. In only one other instance has any payment been made to a witness : in that case the evidence had been spontaneously given, partly in writing and partly *vivâ voce*, and the payment was simply for the time occupied in drawing up a more complete written statement.

his experience on that Sunday afternoon corresponded with my vivid impressions. It could not have been mere coincidence. I must add that I mentioned *my* experience to Mr. Arundel before he had spoken to me of *his.* " I have had impressions more than once, but never a *false* one. When Mr. Arundel first crossed to America he met with a severe storm. The night that the ship was in great danger (though it is impossible to define how), I knew and felt that it was so. I mentioned it to my friends, who ridiculed the fancy ; nevertheless, the time corresponded precisely.[1]

" MARGUERITE ARUNDEL."

Page 249, case 52. Dr. and Mme. Ollivier are both now deceased.

Page 261, note. On *vivâ voce* examination of the witnesses, it seems probable that *Portugal* did enter into the impression ; but Mrs. Wilson, differing from her husband, thinks he knew that his brothers were going there—which certainly commends itself as the probable explanation of that detail. We had the door, which has been repainted, brought up to London, in order that the paint might be carefully removed. The expert whom we employed to do this told us that it was very improbable that the pencil marks would have resisted the action of turpentine and the friction of the repainting ; and nothing relating to the incident was discovered.

Page 304, bottom. Some further returns, received since this page was printed, leave unaltered the proportion stated.

Page 306, line 18. After " death " insert " dreamt by any previously specified individual." Lines 23 and 26. For $\frac{1}{27}$ read $\frac{1}{26}$. Line 28. After " will " insert " on an average, if chance alone rules."

Page 367, note. Visions of spectral funerals are mentioned by W. Howells, *Cambrian Superstitions*, pp. 54-6, 64 ; and by Wirt Sikes, *British Goblins*, pp. 231-2. An apparently telepathic instance, recorded in a collection of Border legends made by a Mr. Wilkie, may be found in W. Henderson's *Folk-lore of the Northern Counties of England and the Borders*, p. 29.

Page 394, note. It is true that Isaak Walton's account represents Dr. Donne as declaring that he was certainly awake ; but Walton is a third-hand witness. See p. 154, second paragraph, and the above remarks thereon.

Page 408, case 154. Asked by her daughter to say " whether she remembered anything particular taking place at home " on the night of the death, Mrs. Thompson wrote as follows, on June 30, 1886 :—

" 82, Talbot Street, Moss-side, Manchester.

" I remember distinctly my daughter coming to my room several times asking me if I had called her, or if I knew who had called her, the night during which my nephew, Harry Suddaby, died. " MARY THOMPSON."

Page 479. Since this page was printed, I have received another instance of hallucinations voluntarily originated. A lady who has had a scientific training tells me that one bright June day, two years ago—when lying ill in bed, but with her mind especially active—she saw the gradual formation, on the background of the blind, of a statuesque head, which then changed

---

[1] An impression of this sort, occurring at what may naturally have been a time of anxiety, has no evidential weight. The distinctly *auditory* character of the more recent experience places it in quite a different category.

into another. "I tired myself calling the pictures up again during the afternoon. They seemed as clear as if real, but after the first flash I was conscious of a mental effort with regard to them. Banishment was very easy ; it only needed a relaxed tension."

To the cases mentioned in the note should be added Dr. Abercrombie's description of a gentleman (not personally known to him) who " had the power of calling up spectral figures at his will, by directing his attention steadily to the conception of his own mind ; and this may either consist of a figure or a scene which he has seen, or it may be a composition created by his imagination. But though he has the faculty of producing the illusion, he has no power of banishing it ; and when he has called up any particular spectral figure or scene, he never can say how long it may continue. The gentleman is in the prime of life, of sound mind, in good health, and engaged in business. Another of his family has been affected in the same manner, though in a slighter degree." (*Inquiries concerning the Intellectual Powers*, 1838, p. 363.)

Pages 497–8. Chap. XI., § 2. The compatibility of sensory hallucinations, even of a very pronounced sort, with sound bodily and mental health is illustrated in the passage just quoted from Abercrombie.

Page 503, lines 17, 18. The statement that hallucinations of the sane and healthy, representing non-human objects, seem to be " rarely if ever " grotesque or horrible, is rather too sweeping. An exception should at any rate be made for certain endemic hallucinations. (See Vol. II., p. 189, note.)

Page 514, first paragraph. Some further examples of auditory hallucinations probably due to expectancy may be found in Howells' *Cambrian Superstitions* (Tipton, 1831), p. 65. See also Sikes's *British Goblins*, p. 229.

Page 534, case 199. The account, confirmed by Mr. B. in 1883, was written in or before 1876. Mrs. B. writes, on Dec. 31, 1886 :—"I perfectly recollect the occasion of Mrs. ——'s death, and that my husband for a whole week was considerably concerned about her. My husband mentioned the vision the same morning, at the time it occurred, and we did not hear of the death till seven or eight days afterwards." The death could not be traced in the register at Somerset House ; but on inquiring of the coroner of the district where it occurred, we find that it took place exactly as described, on April 9, 1873, which, however, was a Wednesday, not a Saturday. The mistake as to the day of the week seems neither to increase nor to decrease the probability that Mr. and Mrs. B. were able, after the short interval which elapsed before they heard the news, correctly to identify the day of the vision with that of the death.

Page 546, lines 14–16. Mr. Keulemans' statement that his little boy's fringe *could not* have grown to its usual length in a month might be questioned. But on my pointing this out to him, he explained that (being struck by the fact that the hair, as he saw it in his vision, was just as he had been accustomed to see it) he had expressly asked his mother-in-law what was the state of the child's hair at the time of his death ; and she had said that he " had very little hair—that it grew straight upright, and that he had no fringe when he died." Mr. Keulemans has no difficulty in accepting this description, as he has recently made experiments with two of his children, aged 4 and 6, with a result that entirely accords with it. The rate at which hair grows seems to differ greatly in different people.

Page 548, note. To the case mentioned add Mr. Wilkie's narrative, referred to above in connection with p. 367. Other possible examples of the bizarre investiture of a telepathic impression may be found in Kelly's *Curiosities of Indo-European Traditions and Folk-Lore*, p. 104 ; and in G. Waldron's *Description of the Isle of Man*, pp. 69-70,—a case to which we have a close parallel on good, but not first-hand, authority. See also Paul Sébillot's *Traditions de la Haute Bretagne*, Vol. I., pp 265-9.

Page 558, line 23. Major (now Colonel) Borthwick writes on Dec. 22, 1886, from the Chief Constable's Office, County Buildings, Edinburgh, that he is under the impression that Captain Russell Colt mentioned his experience to the party at breakfast on the morning after it occurred.

Page 559, case 211. In conversation, the narrator mentioned that the boots of the figure appeared clean, though it was pouring with rain ; and that the stick which she afterwards recognised had a silver *pomme*, not a curved handle. She was noticing the passage of time, as her father had to catch a train that afternoon. She added some details which increase the probability that the dying man's thoughts were running on her father at the last. As to the fact that it was she who was the percipient, and not her father, see Vol. II., pp. 268, 301 ; and compare cases 192, 225, 242, 307, 660.

The following "transitional" case is a fresh specimen of the rare and most important class to which Nos. 13, 14, 15, 16, 685, and 686 belong ; and is further of interest as being directly due to the publication of this book. The receipt of it justifies us in hoping that we may encounter more like it. On November 16th, 1886, the Rev. C. Godfrey, of 5, The Goffs, Eastbourne, wrote to Mr. Podmore as follows :—

"I was so impressed by the account on p. 105, that I determined to put the matter to an experiment.

"Retiring at 10.45, I determined to appear, if possible, to [a friend], and accordingly I set myself to work, with all the volitional and determinative energy which I possess, to stand at the foot of her bed. I need not say that I never dropped the slightest hint beforehand as to my intention, such as would mar the experiment, nor had I mentioned the subject to her. As the 'agent,' I may describe my own experiences.

"Undoubtedly the *imaginative* faculty was brought extensively into play, as well as the volitional ; for I endeavoured to *translate myself*, spiritually, into the room, and to attract her attention, as it were, while standing there. My effort was sustained for perhaps 8 minutes; after which I felt tired, and was soon asleep.

"The next thing I was conscious of was meeting the lady next morning, (*i.e.*, in a dream, I suppose?) and asking her at once if she had seen me last night. The reply came 'Yes.' 'How?' I inquired. Then in words strangely clear and low, like a well-audible whisper, came the answer, 'I was sitting beside you.' These words, so clear, awoke me instantly, and I felt I must have been dreaming; but on reflection, I remembered what I had been 'willing' before I fell asleep ; and it struck me, 'This must be a *reflex* action from the percipient.'

f

"My watch showed 3.40 a.m. The following is what I wrote immediately in pencil, standing in my night-dress :—'As I reflected upon those clear words, they struck me as being quite *intuitive*—I mean *subjective*, and to have proceeded *from within*, as *my own* conviction, rather than a communication from anyone else.[1] And yet I can't remember her face at all, as one can after a vivid dream!'

"But the words were uttered in a clear, quick tone, which was most remarkable, and awoke me at once.

"My friend, in the note with which she sent me the enclosed account of *her own* experience, says : 'I remember the man put all the lamps out soon after I came upstairs, and that is only done about a quarter to 4.'"

Mr. Godfrey went next morning to see someone who resided in the same house as Mrs. ——, and was leaving, when "she called out to me from the window that she had something special to tell me ; but being very busy, I could not return again into the house, and replied to the effect that it would keep. I am not quite certain now [2] whether it was on the afternoon of the same day, or later in the morning, that she called. I asked her, *as usual* [for she suffered from neuralgia], if she had had a good night, and she at once commenced to narrate as I have told you. When she had told me all, I begged her at once to go home and write it down. The account which I sent to you was the result ; and it compared accurately with a few scribbled notes in pencil which I had hastily jotted down as she was relating it to me originally."

The following is the percipient's account :—

"Yesterday, viz., the morning of Nov. 16, 1886, about half-past 3 o'clock, I woke up with a start, and an idea that someone had come into the room. I also heard a curious sound, but fancied it might be the birds in the ivy outside. Next I experienced a strange, restless longing to leave the room and go downstairs. This feeling became so overpowering that at last I rose, and lit a candle, and went down, thinking if I could get some soda-water it might have a quieting effect. On returning to my room, I saw Mr. Godfrey standing under the large window on the staircase. He was dressed in his usual style, and with an expression on his face that I have noticed when he has been looking very earnestly at anything. He stood there, and I held up the candle and gazed at him for 3 or 4 seconds in utter amazement ; and then, as I passed up the staircase, he disappeared. The impression left on my mind was so vivid that I fully intended waking a friend who occupied the same room as myself ; but remembering I should only be laughed at as romantic and imaginative, refrained from doing so.

[1] At first sight, this seems inconsistent with the idea of the "reflex" or reciprocal action in the preceding paragraph. But Mr. Godfrey explains what he means as follows :—" I was dreaming : reflection convinced me that the particular words were not uttered in course of *natural* dream, but by reflex [reciprocal] action : also that they proceeded from *myself*, and not from any one standing over my bed in the room. It was 'from any one else' that confused my meaning. I meant any one *in the room*, not any one in another house : from *her* they clearly *did* proceed." There does not seem, however, to be any such proof of reciprocal action as Mr. Godfrey supposes ; no reason appears why his dream should not have been purely subjective.

[2] The letter here quoted was written to me on Jan. 13, 1887. Mr. Podmore says that it entirely accords with Mr. Godfrey's and Mrs. ——'s independent *vivâ voce* accounts given on the previous Nov. 22. The reason why these details were not included in Mr. Podmore's notes was that at the moment he was under the impression that they had been mentioned in Mr. Godfrey's first letter, which was in my possession.

" I was not frightened at the appearance of Mr. Godfrey, but felt much excited and could not sleep afterwards."

In conversation with Mrs. —— (Nov. 22, 1886), Mr. Podmore learnt that she is a good sleeper, and not given to waking at nights. She does not remember ever before having experienced anything like the feeling which she had on first waking up. She was at the bottom of the stairs when she saw Mr. Godfrey's figure, which appeared on the landing, about 11 steps up. It was quite distinct and life-like at first,—though she does not remember noticing more than the upper part of the body ; as she looked, it grew more and more shadowy, and finally faded away. It must be added that she has seen in her life two other phantasmal appearances, which represented a parent whom she had recently lost. But a couple of experiences of this sort, coming at a time of emotional strain, cannot be regarded as a sign of any abnormal liability to subjective hallucinations (see p. 510) ; and even if she was destined anyhow to experience one other, the chances against its representing one particular member of her acquaintance, at the very time when he happened for the first time in his life to be making the effort above described, would be at least many hundreds of thousands to 1.

We requested Mr. Godfrey to make another trial, without of course giving Mrs. —— any reason to expect that he would do so. He made a trial at once, thinking that we wanted the result immediately, though he himself thought the time unsuitable ; and this was a failure. But on Dec. 8, 1886, he wrote as follows :—

" My friend Mrs. —— has just been in, and given me an account of what she experienced last night; she is gone home to write it out for you, and it will be enclosed with mine. I can state that I have not attempted one experiment since I last communicated with you ; therefore there are no failures to record. I was at Mrs. ——'s house last evening, and she testifies this morning that she had not the faintest suspicion that I intended attempting another experiment. The *first* words she used on seeing me this morning were (laughingly) ' Well, I saw you last night, anyway.'

" All the interest, as on the former occasion, of course lies with the percipient. I may simply explain that I acted as on the former occasion—viz., concentrated my attention on the percipient, while I was undressing ; then devoted some 10 minutes, when in bed, to intense effort to transport myself to her presence, and make my presence felt both by *voice* and *touch*,—viz., placing my hand upon the percipient's head. Then 1 fell asleep, slept well, and was conscious of nothing sufficiently vivid to *awake* me.

" Directly I awoke at my usual time, about 6.40 a.m., I guessed that I had succeeded, because I instantly remembered that I had dreamt (as last time) of meeting the lady next day, and asking her the same question—viz., whether she had seen me, and the answer was, ' Yes, I saw you indistinctly.' This reflex action is very important, and I would undertake to tell, on any occasion, whether I had failed or succeeded. The words of reply (above) were written down by me on paper[1] before hearing the percipient's account.

---

[1] As to this note, and the one made on the former occasion, Mr. Godfrey writes, " I am very sorry that I never kept the scraps of newspaper edge upon which I jotted down my reflections, and the words which reached me, in the middle of the night. I jotted them down to exclude any invalidation of the inferences on score of defective memory ; not thinking it needful to retain them as a check, when I had copied from them into my letters, they were committed to the flames."

"This case is, I think, very instructive, because of the *sound* of voice, as well as of *sight*."

Mr. Godfrey adds that Mrs. ——, though she appeared in good spirits, had been "frightened and a little unnerved"; and that he should not feel justified in repeating the experiment.

The percipient's account, written on Dec. 8, 1886, is as follows :—

"Last night, Tuesday, Dec. 7th, I went upstairs at half-past 10. I remember distinctly locking the bed-room door, which this morning, to my astonishment, was unlocked. I was soon asleep, and had a strange dream of taking flowers to a grave. Suddenly I heard a voice say 'Wake,' and felt a hand rest on the left side of my head. (I was lying on the right side.) I was wide awake in a second, and heard a curious sound in the room, something like a Jew's harp. I felt a cold breath streaming over me, and violent palpitation of the heart came on; and I also distinctly saw a figure leaning over me. The only light in the room was from the lamp outside, which makes a long line on the wall over the wash-stand. This line was partly obscured by the figure. I turned round at once, and the hand seemed to slip from my nead to the pillow beside me. The figure was stooping over me, and I felt it leaning up against the side of the bed. I saw the arm resting on the pillow the whole time it remained. I saw an outline of the face, but it seemed as if a mist were before it. I think the time when it came must have been about half-past 12. It had drawn the curtain of the bed slightly back, but this morning I noticed it was hanging straight as usual. The figure was undoubtedly that of Mr. Godfrey. I knew it by the appearance of the shoulders and the shape of the face. The whole time it remained, there was a draught of cold air streaming through the room, as if both door and window were open. I heard the dining-room clock strike half-past something; and as I could not sleep again, but heard the clock strike hours and half-hours consecutively up to 5 o'clock, I think I am right in saying the time was half-past 12."

I have drawn attention (pp. 165-6, and Vol. II., p. 170) to the fact that the first-hand evidence for telepathic experiences includes no reports of physical changes produced in the material world—which, if they occurred, would be impossible to account for by the hypothesis of a temporary psychical transference from one mind to another. A percipient may have the hallucination of seeing the door opening (p. 102, note); but the door not having really been moved, it of course is not afterwards found open. So, in the above account, the curtain, which seemed to the percipient to be shifted at the time of her experience, was found in its place in the morning. On the other hand, the door, which she says that she had locked, was found unlocked. On being questioned as to this, she replies that the door is habitually locked at night, and that she does not walk in her sleep; but she thinks it probable that, after locking the door, she left the room to get some matches, and that she omitted to lock it again on her return. If anyone, after this, should be inclined to connect the unlocking with the apparition, I would suggest to him that a "ghost" which has shown its capacity to walk through a closed hall-door would, on finding a bed-room door locked *on the inside*, be more likely to walk through it than to unlock it.

CHAPTER I.

§ 1. WHATEVER the advances of science may do for the universe, there is one thing that they have never yet done and show no prospect of doing—namely, to make it less marvellous. Face to face with the facts of Nature, the wonderment of the modern chemist, physicist, zoologist, is far wider and deeper than that of the savage or the child ; far wider and deeper even than that of the early workers in the scientific field. True it is that science *explains ;* if it did not it would be worthless. But scientific explanation means only the reference of more and more facts to immutable laws ; and, as discovery advances in every department, the orderly marvel of the comprehensive laws merely takes the place of the disorderly marvel of arbitrary occurrences. The mystery is pushed back, so to speak, from facts in isolation to facts in the aggregate ; but at every stage of the process the mystery itself gathers new force and impressiveness.

What, then, is the specific relation of the man of science to the phenomena which he observes ? His explanation of them does not lead him to marvel at them less than the uneducated person : what does it lead him to do for them that the uneducated person cannot do ? "To *predict* them with certainty," it will no doubt be replied ; "which further implies, in cases where the conditions are within his control, to produce them at will." But it is important to observe that this power of prediction, though constantly proclaimed as the authoritative test of scientific achievement, is very far indeed from being an accurate one. For it is a test which is only fulfilled with anything like completeness by a small group of sciences—those which deal with *inorganic* nature. The physicist can proclaim with confidence that gravitation, and heat, and electricity (as long as they act at all) will continue to act as they do now ; every discovery that the chemist makes about a substance is a

B

prophecy as to the behaviour of that class of substance for ever. But as soon as vital organisms appear on the scene, there is a change. Not only do the complexities of structure and process, and the mutual reactions of the parts and the whole, exclude all exact quantitative formulæ; not only is there an irreducible element of uncertainty in the behaviour from moment to moment of the simplest living unit; but there appear also developments, and varieties and " sports," which present themselves to us as arbitrary—which have just to be registered, and cannot be explained. Not, of course, that they are really arbitrary; no scientifically trained mind entertains the least doubt that they are in every case the inevitable results of prior conditions. But the knowledge of the expert has not approximately penetrated to the secret of those conditions; here, therefore, his power of prediction largely fails him.

This applies to a great extent even to events of a uniform and familiar order. Biological science may predict that an animal will be of the same species as its parents; but cannot predict its sex. It may predict the general characteristics of the next generation of men; but not the special attributes of a single individual. But its power of forecast is limited in a far more striking way—by the perpetual modification of the very material with which it has to deal. It is able to predict that, *given* such and such variations, natural selection will foster and increase them; that *given* such and such organic taints, heredity will transmit them: but it is powerless to say what the next spontaneous variation, or the next development of heredity will be. It is at work, not on steadfast substances with immutable qualities, like those of the inorganic world; but on substances whose very nature is to change. The evolution of animal existence, from protoplasm upwards, involves ever fresh elaborations in the composition of the vital tissues. Science traces the issue of these changes, and learns even to some extent to foresee and so to guide their course; it can thus lay down laws of scientific breeding, laws of medicine and hygiene. But the unconquerable spontaneity of the organic world is for ever setting previous generalisations at defiance; in great things and small, from the production of a new type of national physique to the production of a new variety of tulip, it is ever presenting fresh developments, whose necessity no one could divine, and of which no one could say aught until they were actually there. And so, though science follows closely after, and keeps up the game with spirit, its position in its Wonderland is always rather like that of Alice in hers, when the croquet-hoops consisted of soldiers who moved as often as they chose. The game is one on which it will never be safe to bet for very far ahead; and it is one which will certainly never end.

And if this is true of life in its *physical* manifestations, it is certainly not less true of its *mental* manifestations. It is to the latter, indeed, that we naturally turn for the highest examples of mobility, and the most marked exhibitions of the unexpected. An Athenian of Solon's time, speculating on "the coming race," might well have predicted for his countrymen the physical prowess that won Marathon, but not the peculiar intellectual vitality that culminated in the theatre of Dionysus. At the present moment, it is safer to prophesy that the next generation in Germany will include a good many hundreds of thousands of short-sighted persons than that it will include a Beethoven. Nor will it surprise us to find the "sports" and uncertainties of vital development most conspicuous on the psychical side, if we remember the nature of their physical basis. For mental facts are indissolubly linked with the very class of material facts that science can least penetrate—with the most complex sort of changes occurring in the most subtly-woven sort of matter—the molecular activities of brain-tissue.

§ 2. There exists, then, a large department of natural events where the test of prediction can be applied only in a restricted way. Whether the events be near or distant—whether the question be of intellectual developments a thousand years hence, or of the movements of an amœba or the success of a "thought-transference" experiment in the next five minutes—there is here no voice that can speak with absolute authority. The expert gets his cosmic prophecies accepted by pointing to the perpetual fulfilment of his minor predictions in the laboratory; or he refutes adverse theories by showing that they conflict with facts that he can at any moment render patent. But as to the implications and possibilities of *life*—the constitution and faculties of *man*—he will do well to predict and refute with caution; for here he may fail even to guess the relation of what will be to what is. If his function as a prophet is not wholly abrogated, he is a prophet ever liable to correction. He is obliged to deal largely in likelihoods and tendencies; and (if I may venture on a prophecy which is perhaps as fallible as the rest) the interest in the laws that he is able to lay down will never supersede the interest in the exceptions to those laws. Indeed it is in emphasising exceptions that his own *rôle* will largely consist. And above all must he beware of setting up any arbitrary " scientific frontier " between the part of Nature that he knows and the part that he does not know. He can trace the great flood of evolution to the point at which he stands; but a little beyond him it loses itself in the darkness; and though he may realise its general force and direction, and roughly surmise the mode in which its bed will be shaped, he can but dimly picture the scenes through which it will flow.

But if the science of life cannot be final, there is no reason why it should not be accurate and coherent. And if the scope of definite scientific comprehension is here specially restricted, and the unexpected is specially certain to occur, that is no reason for abating one jot of care in the actual work that it remains possible to do—the work of sifting and marshalling evidence, of estimating sources of error, and of strictly adjusting theories to facts. On the contrary, the necessity for such care is only increased. If incaution may be sometimes shown in too peremptorily shutting the door on alleged phenomena which are not in clear continuity with established knowledge, it is far more often and flagrantly shown in the claim for their admission. And it is undeniable that the conditions which have been briefly described expose speculation on the possible developments of vital phenomena to peculiar dangers and difficulties. In proportion as the expert moderates his tone, and makes his forecasts in a tentative and hypothetical manner, it is certain that those who are not experts will wax bold in assertion and theory. The part of the map that science leaves blank, as *terra incognita*, is the very one which amateur geographers will fill in according to their fancy, or on the reports of uncritical and untrustworthy explorers. The confidence of ignorance is always pretty accurately adjusted to the confidence of knowledge. Wherever the expert can put his foot down, and assert or deny with assurance, the uninstructed instinctively bow to him. He fearlessly asserts, for instance, that the law of the conservation of energy cannot be broken ; the world believes him, and the inventors of perpetual-motion-machines gradually die off. But suppose the question is of possible relations of human beings to inanimate things or to one another, new modes of influence, new forms of sensitiveness. Here responsible science can give no confident denial ; here, therefore, irresponsible speculation finds its chance.

It has, no doubt, modified its language under the influence of half a century of brilliant physical discovery.   It takes care to shelter its hypotheses under the name of law: the loosest of philosophers now-a-days would hesitate to appeal, as the elder Humboldt appealed sixty years ago, to a "sense of yearning in the human soul," as a proof that the course of nature may suffer exceptions.[1]   But the change is often rather in name than in fact; the "natural" lends itself to free guessing quite as easily as the "supernatural"; and nowhere in Nature is this freedom so unchartered as in the domain of psychic life.   Speculation here is not only easy; it is, unfortunately, also attractive.   The more obscure phenomena and the more doubtful assumptions are just those on which the popular mind most readily fastens; and the popular tongue rejoices in terms of the biggest and vaguest connotation. Something also must be set down to a natural reaction.   Even persons whose interest has been earnest and intelligent have found scientific *moral* hard to preserve, in departments surrendered by a long-standing convention to unscientific treatment.   Thus, in their practice, they have come to acquiesce in that surrender, and have dispensed with habits of caution for which no one was likely to give them credit; while in their polemic they have as much resented the stringent demands for evidence, in which their opponents have been right, as the refusal to look at it when it is there, in which their opponents have been wrong.

§ 3.   The above facts, and the peculiar obligations which they involve, should never be lost sight of by the serious student of "psychical"[2] phenomena.   His path is one that eminently craves wary walking.   On the one hand, he finds new dim vistas of study opening out, in an age whose ideal of scientific studies is formed from the most highly developed specimens of them; and the twilight which has in every class of knowledge preceded the illuminating dawn of law is made doubly dark and dubious for him by the advanced daylight of scientific conceptions from which he peers into it.   He finds, moreover, that the

[1] *Briefe an eine Freundin*, p. 61.

[2] The specific sense which we have given to this word needs apology.   But we could find no other convenient term, under which to embrace a group of subjects that lie on or outside the boundaries of recognised science, while seeming to present certain points of connection among themselves.   For instance, this book will contain evidences of the relation of *telepathy*—its main theme—both to *mesmerism* and to certain phenomena which are often, without adequate evidence, attributed to minds apart from material organisms.

marvellous recent extension of the area of the known through additions to its recognised departments and multiplication of their connections, has inevitably and reasonably produced a certain rigidity of scientific attitude—an increased difficulty in breaking loose from association, and admitting a new department on its own independent evidence.

And on the other hand, he finds himself more or less in contact with advocates of new departments who ignore the weight of the presumption against them—who fail to see that it is from the recognised departments that the standard of evidence must be drawn, and that if speculation is to make good its right to outrun science, it will certainly not be by impatience of scientific canons.   On this side the position of the psychical student is one in which the student of the recognised sciences is never placed.   The physicist never finds his observations confronted or confounded with those of persons who claim familiarity with his subject while ignoring his methods : he never sees his statements and his theories classed or compared with theirs.   He is marked out from his neighbours by the very fact of dealing with subject-matter which they do not know how even to begin to talk about.   The " psychicist " is not so marked out.   *His* subject-matter is in large measure common property, of which the whole world can talk as glibly as he ; and the ground which must be broken for science, if at all, by the application of precise treatment, has already been made trite in connection with quite other treatment.

§ 4.   The moral is one which the authors of the present undertaking have every reason to lay to heart.   For the endeavour of this book, almost throughout, is to deal with themes that are in a sense familiar, by the aid, partly, of improved evidential methods, but partly also of conceptions which have as yet no place in the recognised psychology. Not, indeed, that the reader is about to be treated to any large amount of speculation ; facts will be very much more prominent than theories.   Still, the facts to be adduced carry us at least one step beyond the accepted boundaries.   What they prove (if we interpret them rightly) is *the ability of one mind to impress or to be impressed by another mind otherwise than through the recognised channels of sense.*   We call the owner of the impressing mind the *agent,* and the owner of the impressed mind the *percipient ;* and we describe the fact of impression shortly by the term *telepathy.*   We began by restricting that term to cases where the distance through which the transference of impressions took place far exceeded the scope of the recognised senses ; but it may be fairly extended to *all* cases of impressions conveyed without any affection of the percipient's recognised senses, whatever may be his actual distance from the agent.   I of course do not mean by this merely that the channel of communication is unrecognised by the person impressed—as in the drawing-room pastime where hidden pins are found through indications which the finder receives and acts on without any consciousness of guidance. By the words "otherwise than through the recognised channels of sense," I mean that the cause or condition of the transferred impression is specifically unknown.   It may sometimes be necessary or convenient to conceive it as some special supernormal or supersensuous [1] *faculty ;* and in that case we are undoubtedly assuming a faculty which is new—or at any rate is new to science.   But we can at least claim that we take this step under compulsion ; not in the light-hearted fashion which formerly improvised occult forces and fluids to account for the vagaries of hysteria ; or which in our own day has discovered the dawn of a new sense, or the relic of some primeval instinct, in the ordinary exhibitions of the " willing-game."   Our inference of an unrecognised mode of affection has nothing in common with such inferences as these ; for it has been made only after recognised modes have been carefully excluded.

§ 5. It is not, however, with the ultimate conditions of the phenomena that the study of them can begin : our first business is with the reality, rather than with the rationale, of their occurrence.   Telepathy as a system of facts is what we have to examine. Discussion of the nature of the novel faculty in itself, and apart from particular results, will be as far as possible avoided.   That, if it exists, it has important relations to various very fundamental problems—metaphysical, psychological, possibly even physical—can scarcely be doubted.   So far from the scientific study of man being a region whose boundaries are pretty well mapped out, and which only requires to be filled in with further detail by physiologists and psychologists, we may come to perceive that we are standing only on the threshold of a vast *terra incognita,* which must be humbly explored before we can even guess at its true extent, or appreciate its relation to the more familiar

---

[1] It seems impossible to avoid these terms ; yet each needs to be guarded from a probable misunderstanding. *Supernormal* is very liable to be confounded with *supernatural ;* while *supersensuous* suggests a dogmatic denial of a physical side to the effect.

realms of knowledge. But such distant visions had better not be lingered over. Before the philosophical aspects of the subject can be profitably discussed, its position as a real department of knowledge must be amply vindicated. This can only be done by a wide survey of evidence ; the character of the present treatise will therefore be mainly evidential.

In demonstrating the reality of impressions communicated otherwise than through the known sensory channels, we rely on two distinct branches of evidence, each of which demands a special sort of caution. The larger portion of this work will deal with cases of *spontaneous* occurrence. Here the evidence will consist of records of experiences which we have received from a variety of sources—for the most part from living persons more or less known to us. Narratives of the same kind have from time to time appeared in other collections. These, however, have not been treated with any reference to a theory of telepathy such as is here set forth ; nor have their editors fulfilled conditions which, for reasons to be subsequently explained (Chap. IV.), we have felt bound to observe ; and we have found them of almost no assistance. In scarcely a single instance has a case been brought up to the standard which really commands attention.[1] The prime essentials of testimony in such matters—authorities, names, dates, corroboration, the *ipsissima verba* of the witnesses—have one or all been lacking ; and there seems to have been no appreciation of the strength of the *à priori* objections which the evidence has to overmaster, nor of the possible sources of error in the evidence itself. It is in analysing and estimating these sources of error, and in fixing the evidential standard which may fairly be applied, that the most difficult part of the present task will be seen to consist.

But though the records here presented will be more numerous, and on the whole better attested, than those of previous collections, the majority of them will be of a tolerably well-known type. The peculiarity of the present treatment will come out rather in the connection of this branch of our evidence with the other branch. For our conviction that the supposed faculty of supersensuous impression is a genuine one is greatly fortified by a body of evidence of an *experi-*

---

[1] An exception should perhaps be made in favour of a few of the late Mr. R. Dale Owen's narratives. The Rev. B. Wrey-Savile's book on *Apparitions* contains some careful work, but it deals chiefly with remote cases. Dr. Mayo, in his *Truths contained in Popular Superstitions*, adduces very inadequate evidence ; but he has given (p. 67) what is perhaps the first suggestion of a psychical explanation.

mental kind—where the conditions could be arranged in such a way as to exclude the chances of error that beset the spontaneous cases. In considering this experimental branch of our subject, I shall of course, after what has been said, be specially bound to make clear the distinction between what we hold to be genuine cases and the spurious "thought-reading" exhibitions which are so much better known. This will be easy enough, and will be done in the next chapter.

CHAPTER II.

THE EXPERIMENTAL BASIS : THOUGHT-TRANSFERENCE.

§ 1. IT is difficult to get a quite satisfactory name for the experimental branch of our subject. " Thought-reading " was the name that we first adopted ; but this had several inconveniences. Oddly enough, the term has got identified with what is not *thought*-reading at all, but *muscle*-reading—of which more anon. But a more serious objection to it is that it suggests a power to *read* anything that may be going on in the mind of another person—to probe characters and discover secrets—which raises a needless prejudice against the whole subject. The idea of such a power has, in fact, been converted into an *ad absurdum* argument against the existence of the faculty for which we contend. To suppose that people's minds can be thus open to one another, it was justly enough said, would be to contradict the assumption on which all human intercourse has been carried on. Our answer, of course, is that we have never supposed people's minds to be thus open to one another ; that such a supposition would be as remote as possible from the facts on which we rely ; and that the most accomplished " thought-reader's " power is never likely to be a matter of social inconvenience. The mode of experimentation may reassure those who look on the genuine faculty as dangerous or uncanny ; for the results, as a rule, have to be tried for by a distinct, and often a very irksome, process of concentration on the part of the person whose " thought " is to be " read." And this being so, it is clearly important to avoid such an expression as " thought-reading," which conveys no hint that his thought is anything else than an open page, or that his mental attitude has anything to do with the phenomenon.

The experiments involve, in fact, the will of *two* persons ; and of the two minds, it is rather the one which reads that is *passive* and the one which is *read* that is active. It is for the sake of recognising this that we distinguish the two parties as " agent " and "percipient," and that we have substituted for thought-reading the term *thought-transference.* *Thought* must here be taken as including more than it does in ordinary usage ; it must include sensations and volitions as well as mere representations or ideas. This being understood, the name serves its purpose fairly well, as long as we are on experimental ground. It will not be forgotten, however, that our aim is to connect an experimental with a spontaneous class of cases ; and according to that view it will often be convenient to describe the former no less than the latter as *telepathic.* We thus get what we need, a single generic term which embraces the whole range of phenomena and brings out their continuity—the simpler experimental forms being the first step in a graduated series.

§ 2. The history of experimental thought-transference has been a singular one. It was not by direct trial, nor in what we should now account their normal form, that the phenomena first attracted the attention of competent witnesses. Their appearance was connected with the discovery that the *somnambulic* state could be artificially induced. It was after the introduction of "mesmerism" or "magnetism" into France, and in the course of the investigation of that wider subject, that this special feature unexpectedly presented itself. The observations remained, it is true, extremely few and scattered. The greater part of them were made in this country, during the second quarter of the present century ; and took the form of *community of sensation* between the operator and the patient. The transference of impressions here depended on a specific *rapport* previously induced by mesmeric or hypnotic operations—passes, fixation, and the like. To us, now, this mesmeric *rapport* (in some, at any rate, of its manifestations) seems nothing more than the faculty of thought-transference *confined* to a single agent and percipient, and *intensified* in degree by the very conditions which limit its scope. But the course of discovery inverted the logical order of the phenomena. The recognition of the particular case, where the exercise of the faculty was narrowed down to a single channel, preceded by a long interval the recognition of the more general phenomena, as exhibited by persons in a normal state. The transference of impressions was naturally regarded as belonging essentially to mesmerism. As such, it was only one more wonder in a veritable wonderland ; and while obtaining on that account the readier acceptance among those who witnessed it, it to some extent shut out the idea of the possibility of similar manifestations where no specific *rapport* had been artificially established.

But there was a further result. The early connection of thought-transference with mesmerism distinctly damaged its chance of scientific recognition. Those who believed in cognate marvels might easily believe in this marvel: but cautious minds rejected the whole posse of marvels together. And one can hardly wonder at this, when one remembers the wild and ignorant manner in which the claims of Mesmer and his followers were thrust upon the world. A man who professed to have magnetised the sun could hardly expect a serious hearing; and even the operators who eschewed such extravagant pretensions still too often advocated their cause in a language that could only cover it with contempt. Theories of " odylic " force, and of imponderable fluids pervading the body—as dogmatically set forth as if they ranked in certainty with the doctrine of the circulation of the blood—were not likely to attract scientific inquiry to the facts. And in the later developments of hypnotism—in which many of the old " mesmeric " phenomena have been re-studied from a truer point of view, and *rapport* of a certain sort between the hypnotist and the " subject " has been admitted—there has been so much to absorb observation in the extraordinary range of mental and physical effects which the operator can command by verbal or visible *suggestion*, that the far rarer telepathic phenomena have, so to speak, been crowded out.[1] The consequence is that after nearly a century of controversy, the most interesting facts of mesmeric history are quite as little recognised as the less specialised kinds of thought-transference, which have only within the last few years been seriously looked for or definitely obtained.

Some of the older cases referred to will be found quoted *in extenso* in the first chapter of the Supplement. Though recorded for the most part in a fragmentary and unsatisfactory way, it will be seen that they do not lack good, or even high, scientific authority. The testimony of Mr. Esdaile, for many years Presidency Surgeon in Calcutta, cannot be despised by any instructed

---

[1] I refer specially to the eminent group of hypnotists at Nancy—Dr. Liébeault, and Professors Beaunis, Bernheim, and Liégeois. Dr. Liébeault has, however, personally described to us several instances of apparently telepathic transference which he has encountered in the course of his professional experience; and some observations recorded by Professor Beaunis (in his admirable article on hypnotism in the *Revue Philosophique* for August, 1885, p. 126), at any rate point, as he admits, to a new mode of sensibility. And since the above remarks were written, both these gentlemen have made definite experiments in telepathy, some of the results of which will be found in Vol. ii., pp. 333-4 and 657-60.

physiologist in our day; inasmuch as his work is now recognised as one of the most important contributions ever made to the rapidly-growing science of hypnotism. No one has denied the ability and integrity of Dr. Elliotson, nor (in spite of his speculative extravagances) of Reichenbach—who both witnessed instances of hypnotic telepathy. And though Professor Gregory, Dr. Mayo, the Rev. C. H. Townsend, and others, may not have been men of acute scientific intelligence, they were probably competent to conduct, and to record with accuracy, experiments the conditions of which involved no more than common care and honesty. We cannot but account it strange that such items of testimony as these men supplied should have been neglected, even by those who were most repelled by the ignorance and fanaticism which infected a large amount of the mesmeric literature. But since such was the fact, the observations will hardly now make their weight felt, except in connection with the fuller testimony of a more recent date. It is characteristic of every subject which depends on questions of fact, and which has yet failed to win a secure place in intelligent opinion, that any further advance must for the most part depend on *contemporary* evidence. I may, therefore, pass at once to the wholly new departure in thought-transference which the last few years have witnessed.

§ 3. The novelty of this departure— as has been already intimated —consists in the fact that successful results have been obtained when the percipient was apparently in a perfectly normal state, and had been subjected to no mesmerising or hypnotising process. The dawn of the discovery must be referred to the years 1875 and 1876. It was in the autumn of the latter year that our colleague, Professor W. F. Barrett, brought under the notice of the British Association, at Glasgow, a cautious statement of some remarkable facts which he had encountered, and a suggestion of the expediency of ascertaining how far recognised physiological laws would account for them. The facts themselves were connected with mesmerism;[1] but the discussion in the Press to which the paper gave rise led to a considerable correspondence, in which Professor Barrett found his first hints of a faculty of thought-transference existing independently of the specific mesmeric *rapport*.

That these hints happened to be forthcoming, just at the right moment, was a piece of great good fortune, and was due

---

[1] *Proceedings* of the Society for Psychical Research, Vol. i., pp. 241-2.

primarily to a circumstance quite unconnected with science, and from which serious results would scarcely have been anticipated—the invention of the " willing-game." In some form or other this pastime is probably familiar to most of my readers, either through personal trials or through the exhibitions of platform performers. The ordinary process is this. A member of the party, who is to act as " thought-reader," or percipient, leaves the room ; the rest determine on some simple action which he, or she, is to perform, or hide some object which he is to find. The would-be percipient is then recalled, and his hand is taken or his shoulders are lightly touched by one or more of the willers. Under these conditions the action is often quickly performed or the object found. Nothing could at first sight look less like a promising starting-point for a new branch of inquiry. The " willer " usually asserts, with perfect good faith, and often perhaps quite correctly, that he did not *push ;* but so little is it necessary for the guiding impression to be a push that it may be the very reverse—a slight *release* of tension when the " willed " performer, after various minute indications of a tendency to move in this, that, or the other wrong direction, at last hits on the right one. Even when the utmost care is used to main-tain the light contact with absolute neutrality, it is impossible to lay down the limits of any given subject's sensibility to such slight tactile and muscular hints. The experiments of Drs. Carpenter and Beard, and especially those of a member of our own Society, the Rev. E. H. Sugden, of Bradford,[1] and other unpublished ones on which we can rely, have shown us that the difference between one person and another in this respect is very great, and that with some organisations a variation of pressure so slight that the supposed " willer " may be quite unaware of exercising it, but which he applies according as the movements of the other person are on the right track or not, may afford a kind of *yes* or *no* indication quite sufficient for a clue. This, indeed, is the one direct piece of instruction which the game has supplied. We might perhaps have been to some extent prepared for the result by observing the infinitesimal touches to which a horse will respond, or the extremely slight indications on which we ourselves often act in ordinary life. But till this game was played, probably no one fully realised that muscular hints, so slight as to be quite unconsciously given, could be equally unconsciously

---

[1] *Proceedings* of the S.P.R., Vol. i , p. 291; Vol. ii., p. 11.

taken ; and that thus a definite course of action might be produced without the faintest idea of guidance on either side.   In some cases it appeared that even contact could be dispensed with, and the guidance was presumably of an auditory kind—the "subject" extracting from the mere footsteps of the "willer," who was following him about, hints of satisfaction or dissatisfaction at the course he was taking.[1]   But though this remarkable susceptibility to a particular order of impressions was an interesting discovery, the results which could be thus explained clearly involved nothing new in kind. That recognised faculties may exhibit unsuspected degrees of refinement is a common enough conception. The more important point was that there were certain results which, apparently, could *not* be thus explained, at any rate, in any off-hand way.   Occasionally the actions required of the "willed" performer were of so complicated a sort, and so rapidly carried out, as to cast considerable doubt on the adequacy of any muscular hints to evoke and guide them.   Here, then, was the first indication of something new—of a hitherto unrecognised faculty ; and by good fortune, as I have said, Professor Barrett's appeal for further evidence as to transferred impressions came just at the time when the game had obtained a certain amount of popularity, and when its more delicate and unaccountable phenomena had attracted attention.

Meanwhile similar observations were being made in America. America, indeed, was the original home of the "willing" entertainment ; and it is to an American, Dr. McGraw, that the credit belongs of having been the first (as far as I am aware) to detect in it the possible germ of something new to science.   In the *Detroit Review of Medicine* for August, 1875, Dr. McGraw gave a clear account of the ordinary physiological process—"the perception by a trained operator of involuntary and unconscious muscular movements" ; and then proceeded as follows:—

"It seemed to me that there were features in these exhibitions which could not be satisfactorily explained on the hypothesis of involuntary muscular action, for . . . . we are required to believe a man could unwillingly, and in spite of himself, give information by unconscious and involuntary signs that he could not give under the same circumstances by voluntary and conscious action. . . . . It seems to me there is a hint towards the possibility of the nervous system of one individual being used by the active will of another to accomplish certain simple motions."

[1] See the record of Mr. A. E. Outerbridge's experiments, published by Dr. Beard in the *American Popular Science Monthly* for July, 1877.

But though there might be enough in the phenomena to justify cautious suggestions of this sort, the ground is at best very uncertain. Even where some nicety of selection is involved, as, for instance, when a particular note is to be struck on the piano, or a particular book to be taken out of a shelf, still, unless the subject's hand moves with extreme rapidity, it will be perfectly possible for an involuntary and unconscious indication to be given by the " willer " at the instant that the right note or book is reached. In reports of such cases it is sometimes stated that there was no tentative process, and that the " subject's " hand seemed to obey the other person's will with almost the same directness as that person's own hand would have done. But this is a question of degree as to which the confidence of an eye-witness cannot easily be imparted to others. It may be worth while, however, to give an instance of a less common type by which the theory of muscular guidance does undoubtedly seem to be somewhat strained.

The case was observed by Mr. Myers on October 31st, 1877. The performers were two sisters.

"I wrote the letters of the alphabet on scraps of paper. I then thought of the word CLARA and showed it to M. behind R.'s back, R. sitting at the table. M. put her hands on R.'s shoulders, and R. with shut eyes picked out the letters C L A R V—taking the V apparently for a second A, which was not in the pack—and laid them in a heap. She did not know, she said, what letters she had selected. No impulse had consciously passed through her mind, only she had felt her hands impelled to pick up certain bits of paper.

"This was a good case as *apparently* excluding *pushing*. The scraps were in a confused heap in front of R., who kept still further confusing them, picking them up and letting them drop with great rapidity. M.'s hands remained apparently motionless on R.'s shoulders, and one can hardly conceive that indications could be given by *pressure*, from the rapid and snatching manner in which R. collected the right letters, touching several letters in the course of a second. M., however, told me that it was always necessary that she, M., should *see* the letters which R. was to pick up."

Such a case may not suggest thought-transference, but it at any rate tempts one to look deeper than crude sensory signs for the springs of action, and to conceive the governance of one organism by another through some sort of nervous induction. It at any rate differs greatly in its conditions from the famous bank-note trick, where a number is written on a board, so slowly, and in figures of so large a size, that at every point the " willer " may mark his opinion of the direction the lines are taking by involuntary muscular hints.

It would be useless to accumulate further instances. The best of them could never be wholly conclusive, and mere multiplication adds nothing to their weight. By some of them, as I have said, the theory of muscular guidance is undoubtedly strained. But then the theory of muscular guidance *ought* to be strained, and strained to the very utmost, before being declared inadequate ; and it would always be a matter of opinion whether the point of "utmost" strain had been overpassed. Dr. McGraw and Professor Barrett surmised that it had; Dr. Beard, of New York, was confident that it had not. The contention between "mind-reading" and "muscle-reading" could never reach a definite issue on this ground. But meanwhile the confident and exclusive adherents of the muscular hypothesis had a position of decided advantage over the doubters, for they could fairly enough represent themselves as the champions of science in its war with popular superstitions. The popular imagination *more suo* had fastened on the phenomena *en bloc*, and had decided that they were what they seemed to be—"thought-reading." To the average sight-seer a mysterious word is far more congenial than a physiological explanation ; and it was, of course, the interest of the professional exhibitor to adopt and advertise a description which seemed to invest him with novel and magical powers. What more natural, therefore, than that those who saw the absurdity of these pretensions should regard further inquiry or suspension of judgment as a concession to ignorant credulity ? "Irving Bishop," it seemed fair to argue, "is a professed 'thought-reader'; Irving Bishop's tricks are, at best, mere feats of muscular and tactile sensibility ; *ergo* whoever believes that there is such a thing as 'thought-reading' is on a par with the crowd who are mystified by Irving Bishop."

§ 4. If, then, the ground of experiment had remained unchanged— if the old "willing-game" had merely continued to appear in various forms—no definite advance could have been made. But on the path of the old experiments, a quite new phenomenon now presented itself, which no one could have confidently anticipated, but for which the suggestions drawn from the most advanced phenomena of the "willing-game" had to some extent prepared the way. It was discovered that not only transferences of impression could take place *without contact*, but that there was no necessity for the result aimed

c

at to involve movements ; the fact of the transference might be shown, not—as in the "willing-game "—by the subject's ability to *do* something, but by his ability to discern and describe an object thought of by the "willer." Both parties could thus remain perfectly still ; which was really a more important condition than even the absence of contact. In this form of experiment, muscle-reading and all the subtler forms of unconscious guidance are completely excluded; and the dangers which remain are such as can, with sufficient care, be clearly defined and safely guarded against. Indications of a visual kind —for instance, by the involuntary direction of glances—have no scope if the object which the percipient is to name is not present or visible in the room. There is, of course, an obvious danger in low whispering, or even soundless movements of the lips ; while the faintest accent of approval or disapproval in question or comment may give a hint as to whether the effort is tending in the right direction, and thus guide to the mark by successive approximations. Any exhibition of the kind before a promiscuous company is nearly sure to be vitiated by the latter source of error. But when the experiments are carried on in a limited circle of persons known to each other, and amenable to scientific control, it is not hard for those engaged to set a watch on their own and on each other's lips ; and questions and comments can be entirely forbidden.

I have been speaking of the danger of *involuntary* guidance. There is, of course, another danger to be considered—that of *voluntary* guidance—of actual *collusion* between the agent and percipient. Contact being excluded, such guidance would have to be by signals ; and it is impossible to lay down any precise limit to the degree of perfection that a plan of signalling may reach. The long and short signs of the Morse code admit of many varieties of application ; and though the channels of sight and touch may be cut off, it is difficult entirely to cut off that of hearing. Shufflings of the feet, coughs, irregularities of breathing, all offer available material. But though the precise line of possibilities in this direction cannot be drawn, we are at any rate able to suggest cases where the line would be clearly overpassed. For instance, if the idea to be transferred from the agent to the percipient is inexpressible in less than twenty words ; and if hearing is the only sensory channel left open ; and if it is carefully observed that there are no coughs or shufflings, and that the agent's breathing appears regular, then one seems justified in saying that the necessary information could not be conveyed by a code without a very considerable expenditure of time, and a very abnormally acute sense of hearing on the percipient's part. There is no relation whatever between a private experiment performed under such conditions as these, and the feats of a conjurer, like Mr. Maskelyne, who commands secret apparatus, and whose every word and gesture may be observed and interpreted by a concealed confederate.

It would be rash, however, to represent as crucial any apparent transferences of thought between persons not absolutely separated, where the good faith of at least one of the two is not accepted as beyond question, and where the genuineness of the result is left to depend on the perfection with which third parties have arranged conditions and guarded against signs. The conditions of a crucial result, for one's own mind, are either (1) that the agent or the percipient shall be oneself; or (2) that the agent or percipient shall be someone whose experience, as recorded by himself, is indistinguishable in certainty from one's own ; or (3) that there shall be several agents or percipients, in the case of each of whom the improbability of deceit, or of such imbecility as would take the place of deceit, is so great that the combination of improbabilities amounts to a moral impossibility. The third mode of attaining conviction is the most practically important. For it is not to be expected of most people that, within a short time, they will either themselves be, or have intimate friends who are, successful agents or percipients ; and they are justified, therefore, in demanding that the evidence to which they might fairly refuse credence if it depended on the veracity and intelligence of one or two persons, of however unblemished a reputation, shall be multiplied for their benefit. Whatever be the experimenter's assurance as to the perfection of his conditions, it is in the nature of things impossible that strangers, who only read and have not seen, should be infected by it. They cannot be absolutely certain that this, that, or the other stick might not break ; then enough sticks must be collected and tied together to make a faggot of a strength which shall defy suspicion.[1] As regards the experiments

---

[1] In reference to the objection that the demand for *quantity* of evidence shows that we know the *quality* of each item to be bad, I may quote the following passage from a presidential address of Professor Sidgwick's : " The quality of much of our evidence—when considered apart from the strangeness of the matters to which it refers—is not bad, but very good : it is such that one or two items of it would be held to establish the occurrence, at any particular time and place, of any phenomenon whose existence was generally accepted. Since, however, on this subject the best single testimony only yields an improbability of the *testimony being false* that is outweighed by the improbability of the *fact being true*, the only way to make the scale fall on the side of the testimony is to increase the quantity. If the testimony were not good, this increase of quantity would

of which I am about to present a sketch, it is not necessary to my argument that any individual's honesty shall be completely assumed, in the sense of being used as a certain basis for conclusions. The proof must depend on the *number* of persons, reputed honest and intelligent, to whom dishonesty or imbecility must be attributed if the conclusions are wrong, *i.e.*, it must be a cumulative proof. Not that my colleagues and I have any doubt as to the *bona fides* of every case here recorded. But even where our grounds of certainty are most obvious, they cannot be made entirely obvious to those to whom we and our more intimate associates are personally unknown; while outside this inner circle our confidence depends on points that can scarcely even be suggested to others—on views of character gradually built up out of a number of small and often indefinable items of conversation and demeanour. We may venture to say that a candid critic, present during the whole course of the experiments, would have carried away a far more vivid impression of their genuineness than any printed record can convey. But it must be distinctly understood that we discriminate our cases ; and that even where the results are to our own minds crucial—in that they can only be impugned by impugning the honesty or sanity of members of our own investigating Committee —we do not demand their acceptance on this ground alone, or attempt accurately to define the number of reputations which should be staked before a fair mind *ought* to admit the proof as over-whelming. As observations are accumulated, different "fair minds" will give in at different points; and until the most exacting are satisfied, our task will be incomplete.

§ 5. I mentioned above the correspondence which followed Professor Barrett's appeal for evidence. In this correspondence, among many instances of the higher aspects of the " willing-game," there was a small residue which pointed to a genuine transference of impression without contact or movement. Of this residue the most important item was that supplied by our friend, the Rev. A. M. Creery, then

be of little value ; but if it is such that the hypothesis of its falsity requires us to suppose abnormal motiveless deceit, or abnormal stupidity or carelessness, in a person hitherto reputed honest and intelligent, then an increase in the number of cases in which such a supposition is required adds importantly to the improbability of the general hypothesis. It is sometimes said by loose thinkers that the 'moral factor' ought not to come in at all. But the least reflection shows that the moral factor must come in in all the reasonings of experimental science, except for those who have personally repeated all the experiments on which their conclusions are based. Any one who accepts the report of the experiments of another must rely, not only on his intelligence, but on his honesty : only ordinarily his honesty is so completely assumed that the assumption is not noticed."

resident at Buxton, and now working in the diocese of Manchester.
He had his attention called to the subject in October, 1880 ; and was
early struck by the impossibility of deciding, in cases where contact
was employed, how far the powers of unconscious muscular guidance
might extend. He, therefore, instituted experiments with his
daughters and with a young maid-servant, in which contact was
altogether eschewed. He thus describes the early trials :—

" Each went out of the room in turn, while I and the others fixed on
some object which the absent one was to name on returning to the room.
After a few trials the successes preponderated so much over the failures
that we were all convinced there was something very wonderful coming
under our notice. Night after night, for several months, we spent an
hour or two each evening in varying the conditions of the experiments,
and choosing new subjects for thought-transference. We began by
selecting the simplest objects in the room ; then chose names of towns,
names of people, dates, cards out of a pack, lines from different poems,
&c., in fact any things or series of ideas that those present could keep
steadily before their minds ; and when the children were in good humour,
and excited by the wonderful nature of their successful guessing, they very
seldom made a mistake. I have seen seventeen cards, chosen by myself,
named right in succession, without any mistake. We soon found that a
great deal depended on the steadiness with which the ideas were kept
before the minds of ' the thinkers,' and upon the energy with which they
willed the ideas to pass. Our worst experiments before strangers have
invariably been when the company was dull and undemonstrative :
and we are all convinced that when mistakes are made, the fault rests, for
the most part, with the thinkers, rather than with the thought-readers."

In the course of the years 1881 and 1882, a large number of
experiments were made with the Creery family, first by Professor
Barrett, then by Mr. and Mrs. Sidgwick, by Professor Balfour Stewart,
F.R.S., and Professor Alfred Hopkinson, of Owens College, Manchester,
and, after the formation of the Society for Psychical Research, by the
Thought-transference Committee of that body, of which Mr. Myers
and myself were members. The children in turn acted as " percipients,"
the other persons present being " agents," *i.e.*, concentrating their
minds on the idea of some selected word or thing, with the intention
that this idea should be transferred to the percipient's mind. The
thing selected was either a card, taken at random from a full pack ; or
a name chosen also at random ; or a number, usually of two figures ;
or occasionally some domestic implement or other object in the house.
The percipient was, of course, absent when the selection was made,
and when recalled had no means of discovering through the exercise
of the senses what it was, unless by signals, consciously or uncon-

sciously given by one or other of the agents. Strict silence was maintained throughout each experiment, and when the group of agents included any members of the Creery family, the closest watch was kept in order to detect any passage of signals; but in hundreds of trials nothing was observed which suggested any attempt of the sort. Still, such simple objects would not demand an elaborate code for their description; nor were any effective means taken to block the percipient's channels of sense—it being thought expedient in these early trials not to disturb their minds by obtrusive precautions. We could not, therefore, regard the testimony of the investigators present as adding much weight to the experiments in which any members of the family were among the group of agents, unless the percipient was completely isolated from that group. Such a case was the following :—

"Easter, 1881. Present: Mr. and Mrs. Creery and family, and W. F. Barrett, the narrator. One of the children was sent into an adjoining room, the door of which I saw was closed. On returning to the sittingroom and closing its door also, I thought of some object in the house, fixed upon at random ; writing the name down, I showed it to the family present, the strictest silence being preserved throughout. We then all silently thought of the name of the thing selected. In a few seconds the door of the adjoining room was heard to open, and after a very short interval the child would enter the sitting-room, generally with the object selected. No one was allowed to leave the sitting-room after the object had been fixed upon ; no communication with the child was conceivable, as her place was often changed. Further, the only instructions given to the child were to fetch some object in the house that I would fix upon, and, together with the family, silently keep in mind, to the exclusion, as far as possible, of all other ideas. In this way I wrote down, among other things, a *hair-brush ;* it was brought : an *orange ;* it was brought : a *wine glass ;* it was brought : an *apple ;* it was brought : a *toasting-fork ;* failed on the first attempt, a pair of tongs being brought, but on a second trial it was brought. With another child (among other trials not here mentioned) a *cup* was written down by me ; it was brought : a *saucer ;* this was a failure, a plate being brought ; no second trial allowed. The child being told it was a saucer, replied, 'That came into my head, but I hesitated as I thought it unlikely you would name saucer after cup, as being too easy.'"

But, of course, the most satisfactory condition was that only the members of the investigating Committee should act as agents, so that signals could not possibly be given unless by one of *them.* This condition clearly makes it idle to represent the means by which the transferences took place as simply a trick which the members of the investigating Committee *failed to detect.* The trick, if trick there was, must have been one in which they, or one of them, *actively shared*; the only alternative to collusion on their part being some piece of carelessness amounting almost to idiocy—such as uttering the required word aloud, or leaving the selected card exposed on the table. The following series of experiments was made on April 13th, 1882. The agents were Mr. Myers and the present writer, and two ladies of their acquaintance, the Misses Mason, of Morton Hall, Retford, who had become interested in the subject by the remarkable successes which one of them had obtained in experimenting among friends.[1] As neither of these ladies had ever seen any member of the Creery family till just before the experiments began, they had no opportunities for arranging a code of signals with the children; so that any hypothesis of *collusion* must in this case be confined to Mr. Myers or the present writer. As regards the hypothesis of *want of intelligence*, the degree of intelligent behaviour required of each of the four agents was simply this: (1) To keep silence on a particular subject; and (2) to avoid unconsciously displaying a particular card or piece of paper to a person situated at some yards', distance. The first condition was realised by keeping silence altogether; the second by remaining quite still. The four observers were perfectly satisfied that the children had no means at any moment of seeing, either directly or by reflection, the selected card or the name of the selected object. The following is the list of trials:—

Objects to be named. (These objects had been brought, and still remained, in the pocket of one of the visitors. The name of the object selected for trial was secretly written down, not spoken.)

A White Penknife.—Correctly named, with the colour, the first trial.
Box of Almonds.—Correctly named.
Threepenny piece.—Failed.
Box of Chocolate.—Button-box said; no second trial given.
(A penknife was then hidden; but the place was not discovered.)

Numbers to be named.

Five.—Rightly given on the first trial.
Fourteen.—Failed.
Thirty-three.—54 (No). 34 (No). 33 (Right).
Sixty-eight.—58 (No). 57 (No). 78 (No).

Fictitious names to be guessed.

Martha Billings.—"Biggis" was said.

---

[1] See Miss Mason's interesting paper on the subject in *Macmillan's Magazine* for October, 1882.

Catherine Smith.—" Catherine Shaw " was said.
Henry Cowper.—Failed.

Cards to be named.

> *Two of clubs.*—Right first time.
> *Queen of diamonds.*—Right first time.
> *Four of spades.*—Failed.
> *Four of hearts.*—Right first time.
> *King of hearts.*—Right first time.
> *Two of diamonds.*—Right first time.
> *Ace of hearts.*—Right first time.
> *Nine of spades.*—Right first time.
> *Five of diamonds.*—Four of diamonds (No).   Four of hearts (No).
>   Five of diamonds (Right).
> *Two of spades.*—Right first time.
> *Eight of diamonds.*—Ace of diamonds said ; no second trial given.
> *Three of hearts.*—Right first time.
> *Five of clubs.*—Failed.
> *Ace of spades.*—Failed.

The chances against *accidental* success in the case of any one card are, of course, 51 to 1 ; yet out of *fourteen* successive trials *nine* were successful at the first guess, and only three trials can be said to have been complete failures. The odds against the occurrence of the five successes running, in the card series, are considerably over 1,000,000 to 1. On none of these occasions was it even remotely possible for the child to obtain by any ordinary means a knowledge of the object selected. Our own facial expression was the only index open to her; and even if we had not purposely looked as neutral as possible, it is difficult to imagine how we could have unconsciously carried, say, the two of diamonds written on our foreheads.

During the ensuing year, the Committee, consisting of Professor Barrett, Mr. Myers, and the present writer, made a number of experiments under similar conditions, which excluded contact and movement, and which confined the knowledge of the selected object—and, therefore, the chance of collusion with the percipient—to their own group. In some of these trials, conducted at Cambridge, Mrs. F. W. H. Myers and Miss Mason also took part. In a long series conducted at Dublin, Professor Barrett was alone with the percipient. Altogether these scrupulously guarded trials amounted to 497 ; and of this number 95 were completely successful at the first guess, and 45 at the second. The results may be clearer if arranged in a tabular form.

TABLE SHOWING THE SUCCESS OBTAINED WHEN THE SELECTED OBJECT WAS KNOWN TO ONE OR MORE OF THE INVESTIGATING COMMITTEE ONLY.

Place of Trial.	Object Chosen.	No. of Trials.	Probability of success by mere chance at each 1st guess.	Most probable number of successes at the 1st guess if chance alone acted.	Number of successes obtained		Number of successes reckoning both 1st and 2nd guesses.	Probability of attaining by mere chance the amount of success which the first guesses gave.
					At the 1st guess.	At the 2nd guess after the 1st had failed.		
Buxton	Playing Cards*	14	$\frac{1}{52}$	0	9	0	9	·000,000,000,000,7
,,	Numbers, &c.	15	$\frac{1}{90}$	0	4	0	4	·000,02
Cambridge	Playing Cards*	216	$\frac{1}{52}$	4	17	18	35	·000,000,1
,,	Numbers	64	$\frac{1}{90}$	1	5	6	11	·007
Dublin	Playing Cards*	30	$\frac{1}{52}$	1	3	0	3	·02
,,	Numbers, &c.	108	$\frac{1}{12}$	9	32	11	43	·000,000,000,2
,,	Words	50	$\frac{1}{4}$	13	25	10	35	·000,1
Totals		497		27†	95	45	140	·000,000,000,000,000,000,000,000,01‡

* A full pack was used, from which a card was in each case drawn at random.

† This number is obtained by multiplying each figure of the third column by the corresponding figure in the fourth column (e.g., 216 × $\frac{1}{52}$), and adding the products.

‡ This entry is calculated from the first three totals in the last horizontal row, in the same way that each other entry in the last column is calculated from the first three totals in the corresponding horizontal row.

Mr. F. Y. Edgeworth, to whom these results were submitted, and who calculated the final column of the Table, has kindly appended the following remarks:—

"These observations constitute a chain or rather coil of evidence, which at first sight and upon a general view is seen to be very strong; but of which the full strength cannot be appreciated until the concatenation of the parts is considered.

"Viewed as a whole the Table presents the following data. There are in all 497 trials. Out of these there are 95 successes at the first guess. The number of successes most probable on the hypothesis of mere chance is 27. The problem is one of the class which I have discussed in the *Proceedings* of the S. P. R., Vol. III., p. 190, &c. The approximative formula there given is not well suited to the present case,[1] in which the number of successes is very great, the probability of their being due to mere chance very small, in relation to the total number of trials. It is better to proceed directly according to the method employed in the paper referred to (p. 198) for the appreciation of M. Richet's result E P J Y E I O D [see below, p. 75]. By this method,[2] with the aid of appropriate tables,[3] I find for the probability that the observed total of successes have resulted from some other agency than pure chance

·999, 999, 999, 999, 999, 999, 999, 999, 98

"Stupendous as is this probability it falls short of that which the complete solution of our problem yields. For, measuring and joining all the links of evidence according to the methods described in the paper referred to, I obtain a row of *thirty-four nines* following a decimal point. *A fortiori,* if we take account of the second guesses.

"These figures more impressively than any words proclaim the certainty that the recorded observations must have resulted either from *collusion* on the part of those concerned (the hypothesis of illusion being excluded by the simplicity of the experiments), or from *thought-transference* of the sort which the investigators vindicate."

A large number of trials were also made in which the group of agents included one or more of the Creery family; and as bearing on the hypothesis of an ingenious family trick, it is worth noting that—except where Mr. Creery himself was thus included—the percentage of successes was, as a rule, not appreciably higher under these conditions than when the Committee alone were in the secret.[4] When

---

[1] The formula is adequate to prove that an inferior limit of the sought probability is ·9999.

[2] Owing to the rapid convergency of the series which we have to sum, it will be found sufficient to evaluate two or three terms.

[3] Tables of Logarithms, and of the values of log Γ $(x + 1)$.

[4] Here, for instance, is Professor Barrett's record of a casual trial made on August 4th, 1882—only he and Mrs. Myers knowing the card selected. Eight cards were successively drawn from a pack; of these, three were guessed completely right—two of them at the first attempt and the third at the second attempt; in this last case the first guess was the nine of clubs, and the second the nine of spades, that being the card chosen. In addition to these the suit was given rightly three out of the remaining five times, the pips or court card twice out of the five. Immediately after this experiment the two younger sisters of

Mr. Creery was among the agents, the average of success was far
higher ;[1] but his position in the affair was precisely the same as our
own ; and the most remarkable results were obtained while he was
himself still in a state of doubt as to the genuineness of the
phenomena which he was investigating.

One further evidential point should be noted. Supposing such
a thing as a genuine faculty of thought-transference to exist, and to
be capable, for example, of evoking in one mind the idea of a card on
which other minds are concentrated, we might naturally expect that
the card-pictures conveyed to the percipient would present various
degrees of distinctness, and that there would be a considerable number
of *approximate* guesses, as they might be given by a person who was
allowed one fleeting glimpse at a card in an imperfect light. Such
a person might often fail to name the card correctly, but his failures
would be apt to be far more nearly right than those of another
person who was simply guessing without any sort of guidance. This
expectation was abundantly confirmed in our experiments. Thus, in
a series of 32 trials, where only 5 first guesses were completely
right, the *suit* was 14 times running named correctly on the first
trial, and reiterated on the second. *Knave* was very frequently
guessed as *King*, and *vice versâ*, the suit being given correctly.

the guesser were called in and allowed to know the card chosen by Mrs. Myers and
Professor Barrett. The results, compared with the preceding, were as follows :—

In the absence of the sisters. Eight experiments. Two complete successes on the
first attempt and one on the second.

With the assistance of the sisters as agents. Seven experiments. Two complete
successes on the first attempt and one on the second.

And to make the coincidence more curious, the partial successes were identical in
number in the two series.

[1] Even the successes obtained when Mr. Creery was helping us were less remarkable than those which, according to his records, had been obtained in the earlier trials,
when the whole affair was regarded as an evening's amusement, and the children were
without any sort of *gêne* or anxiety. Still, with his assistance, we have had such
successes as the following. Out of 31 trials with cards (the chances against success by accident being in each case 51 to 1) 17 rightly guessed at the first attempt,
9 at the second, 4 at the third ; 8 *consecutive* successes in naming cards drawn
at random from a full pack ; and the following series, where the names on the left hand,
written down at random by one of ourselves, are what the agents silently concentrated
their minds on, and the names on the right hand are what the percipient said, usually
in two or three seconds after the experiment began :—

William Stubbs.—William Stubbs.
Eliza Holmes.—Eliza H——
Isaac Harding.—Isaac Harding.
Sophia Shaw.—Sophia Shaw.
Hester Willis.—Cassandra, then *Hester* Wilson.
John Jones.—John Jones.
Timothy Taylor.—Tom, then *Timothy* Taylor.
Esther Ogle.—Esther Ogle.
Arthur Higgins.—Arthur Higgins.
Alfred Henderson.—Alfred Henderson.
Amy Frogmore.—Amy Freemore. Amy Frogmore.
Albert Snelgrove.—Albert Singrove. Albert Grover.

The number of pips named was in many cases only one off the right number, this sort of failure being specially frequent when the number was over six. Again, the correct answer was often given, as it were, piecemeal—in two partially incorrect guesses—the pips or picture being rightly given at the first attempt, and the suit at the second ; and in the same way with numbers of two figures, one of them would appear in the first guess and the other in the second.[1]

Before we leave these early experiments, one interesting question presents itself, which has an important bearing on the wider subject of this book. In what form was the impression flashed on the percipient's mind? What were the respective parts in the phenomena played by the mental *eye* and the mental *ear*? The points just noticed in connection with the partial guessing of cards seem distinctly in favour of the mental eye. A king *looks* like a knave, but the *names* have no similarity. So with numbers. 35 is guessed piecemeal, the answers being 45 and 43 ; so 57 is attempted as 47 and 45. Now the similarity in *sound* between three and thirty in 43 and 35, or between five and fifty in 45 and 57, is not extremely strong ; while the *picture* of the 3 or the 5 is identical in either pair. On the other hand, names of approximate sound were often given instead of the true ones ; as "Chester" for Leicester, "Biggis" for

---

[1] To illustrate these various points, I will give one series where the success was below the average.

Cambridge, August 3rd, 1882.

Miss Mary Creery was outside the closed and locked door,—a thick and well-fitting one— and a yard or two from it, under the close observation of a member of the Committee, who observed her attentively. A card was chosen by one of the Committee cutting a pack ; the fact that the card had been selected was indicated to the guesser by a single tap on the door. The selected card was placed in view of all the agents, who regarded it intently. After the guesser had named a card loudly enough to be heard through the door, the word "No" or "Right," as the case might be, was said by one of the Committee ; otherwise complete silence preserved.

The cards chosen are printed on the left, the guesses on the right. Two guesses only were allowed.

1. *Three of hearts.*—Ten of spades (No). King of clubs (No).
2. *Seven of clubs.*—Nine of diamonds (No). *Seven* of hearts (No).
3. *Ten of diamonds.*—Queen of spades (No). Ten of diamonds (Right).
4. *Eight of spades.*—King of clubs (No). Ten of *spades* (No).
5. *Nine of hearts.*—*Nine* of clubs (No). Ace of *hearts* (No).
6. *Three of diamonds.*—Six of *diamonds* (No). Ten of *diamonds* (No).
7. *Knave of spades.*—*King* of spades (No). Queen of clubs (No).
8. *Six of spades.*—Six of spades (Right).
9. *Queen of clubs.*—*Queen* of diamonds (No). Ten of *clubs* (No).
10. *Two of clubs.*—Ten of diamonds (No). Ace of diamonds (No).

Here there were only two complete successes ; and in tabulating results and computing averages we should of course count all the trials except the third and eighth as complete failures. But the result numbered 7 was on the verge of complete success ; in 5 and 9 the correct description was given piecemeal ; and in 2 the number of pips was correctly given.

Billings, "Freemore" for Frogmore. Snelgrove was reproduced as "Singrore"; the last part of the name was soon given as "Grover," and the attempt was then abandoned—the child remarking afterwards that she thought of "Snail" as the first syllable, but it had seemed to her too ridiculous. Professor Barrett, moreover, successfully obtained a German word of which the percipient could have formed no visual image.[1] The children's own account was usually to the effect that they "seemed to see" the thing; but this, perhaps, does not come to much; as a known object, however suggested, is likely to be instantly visualised. On the whole, then, the conclusion seems to be that, with these "subjects," both modes of transference were possible; and that they prevailed in turn, according as this or that was better adapted to the particular case.

§ 6. I have dwelt at some length on our series of trials with the members of the Creery family, as it is to those trials that we owe our own conviction of the possibility of genuine thought-transference between persons in a normal state. I have sufficiently explained that we do not expect the results to be as crucial for persons who were not present, and to whom we are ourselves unknown, as they were for us; and that it cannot be "in the mouth of two or three witnesses" only that such a stupendous fact as the transmission of ideas otherwise than through the recognised sensory channels will be established. The testimony must be multiplied; the responsibility must be spread; and I shall immediately proceed to describe further results obtained with other agents and other percipients. But first it may perhaps be asked of us why we did not *exploiter* this remarkable family further. It was certainly our intention to do what we could in this direction, and by degrees to procure for our friends an opportunity of judging for themselves. This point, however, was one which could only be cautiously pressed. Mr. Creery was certainly justified in regarding his daughters as something more than mere subjects of experiments, and in hesitating to make a show of them to persons who might, or rather who reasonably must, begin by entertaining grave doubts as to their good faith. It must be remembered that we were dealing, not with chemical substances, but with youthful minds, liable to be reduced to confusion by anything in the demeanour of visitors which inspired distaste or alarm; and even with the best intentions, "a childly way

___

[1] In an account of some experiments with words, which we have received from a correspondent, it is stated that success was decidedly more marked in cases where there was a broad vowel sound.

with children " is not easy to adopt where the children concerned are objects of suspicious curiosity.   More especially might these considerations have weight, when failure was anticipated for the first attempts made under new conditions. And this suggests another difficulty, which has more than once recurred in the experimental branches of our work. The would-be spectators themselves may be unable or unwilling to fulfil the necessary conditions. Before introducing them, it is indispensable to obtain some guarantee that they on their part will exercise patience, make repeated trials, and give the " subjects " a fair opportunity of getting used to their presence. Questions of mood, of goodwill, of familiarity, may hold the same place in psychical investigation as questions of temperature in a physical laboratory ; and till this is fully realised, it will not be easy to multiply testimony to the extent that we should desire.

In the case of the Creery family, however, we met with a difficulty of another kind. Had the faculty of whose existence we assured ourselves continued in full force, it would doubtless have been possible in time to bring the phenomena under the notice of a sufficient number of painstaking and impartial observers. But the faculty did not continue in full force ; on the contrary, the average of successes gradually declined, and the children regretfully acknowledged that their capacity and confidence were deserting them. The decline was equally observed even in the trials which they held amongst themselves ; and it had nothing whatever ,to do with any increased stringency in the precautions adopted. No precautions, indeed, could be stricter than that confinement to our own investigating group of the knowledge of the idea to be transferred, which was, from the very first, a condition of the experiments on which we absolutely relied. The fact has just to be accepted, as an illustration of the fleeting character which seems to attach to this and other forms of abnormal sensitiveness. It seems probable that the telepathic faculty, if I may so name it, is not an inborn, or lifelong possession ; or, at any rate, that very slight disturbances may suffice to paralyse it. The Creerys had their most startling successes at first, when the affair was a surprise and an amusement, or later, at short and seemingly casual trials ; the decline set in with their sense that the experiments had become matters of weighty importance to us, and of somewhat prolonged strain and tediousness to them. So, on a minor scale, in trials among our own friends, we have seen a fortunate evening, when the spectators were interested and the percipient excited and confident, succeeded by a series of failures when the results were more anxiously awaited. It is almost inevitable that a percipient who has aroused interest by a marked success on several occasions, should feel in a way *responsible* for further results ; and yet any real pre-occupation with such an idea seems likely to be fatal. The conditions are clearly unstable. But of course the first question for science is not whether the phenomena can be produced to order, but whether in a sufficient number of series the proportion of success to failure is markedly above the probable result of chance.

§ 7. Before leaving this class of experiments, I may mention an interesting development which it has lately received. In the *Revue Philosophique* for December, 1884, M. Ch. Richet, the well-known *savant* and editor of the *Revue Scientifique,* published a paper, entitled " La Suggestion Mentale et le Calcul des Probabilités," in the first part of which an account is given of some experiments with cards precisely similar in plan to those above described. A card being drawn at random out of a pack, the " agent" fixed his attention on it, and the " percipient" endeavoured to name it. But M. Richet's method contained this important novelty—that though the success, as judged by the results of any particular series of trials, seemed slight (showing that he was not experimenting with what we should consider " good subjects "), he made the trials on a sufficiently extended scale to bring out the fact that the right guesses were *on the whole,* though not *strikingly,* above the number that pure accident would account for, and that their total was considerably above that number.

This observation involves a new and striking application of the calculus of probabilities. Advantage is taken of the fact that the larger the number of trials made under conditions where success is purely accidental, the more nearly will the total number of successes attained conform to the figure which the formula of probabilities gives. For instance, if some one draws a card at random out of a full pack, and before it has been looked at by anyone present I make a guess at its suit, my chance of being right is, of course, 1 in 4. Similarly, if the process is repeated 52 times, the most probable number of successes, according to the strict calculus of probabilities, is 13 ; in 520 trials the most probable number of successes is 130. Now, if we consider only a short series of 52 guesses, I may be accidentally right many more times than 13 or many less times. But if the series be prolonged—if 520 guesses be allowed instead of 52—the actual number of successes will vary from the probable number within much smaller limits; and if we suppose an indefinite prolongation, the proportional divergence between the actual and the probable number will become infinitely small. This being so, it is clear that if, in a very short series of trials, we find a considerable difference between the actual number of successes and the probable number, there is no reason for regarding this difference as anything but purely accidental; but if we find a similar difference in a very long series, we are justified in surmising that some condition beyond mere accident has been at work. If cards be drawn in succession from a pack, and I guess the suit rightly in 3 out of 4 trials, I shall be foolish to be surprised; but if I guess the suit rightly in 3,000 out of 4,000 trials, I shall be equally foolish *not* to be surprised.

Now M. Richet continued his trials until he had obtained a considerable total; and the results were such as at any rate to suggest that accident had not ruled undisturbed—that a guiding condition had been introduced, which affected in the right direction a certain small percentage of the guesses made. That condition, if it existed, could be nothing else than the fact that, prior to the guess being made, a person in the neighbourhood of the guesser had concentrated his attention on the card drawn. Hence the results, so far as they go, make for the reality of the faculty of " mental suggestion." The faculty, if present, was clearly only slightly developed; whence the necessity of experimenting on a very large scale before its genuine influence on the numbers could be even surmised.

Out of 2,927 trials at guessing the suit of a card, drawn at random, and steadily looked at by another person, the actual number of successes was 789; the most probable number, had pure accident ruled, was 732. The total was made up of thirty-nine series of different lengths, in which eleven persons took part, M. Richet himself being in some cases the guesser, and in others the person who looked at the card. He observed that when a large number of trials were made at one sitting, the aptitude of both persons concerned seemed to be affected; it became harder for the " agent " to visualise, and the proportion of successes on the guesser's part decreased. If we agree to reject from the above total all the series in which over 100 trials were consecutively made, the numbers become more striking.[1] Out of

---

It should be remarked, however, that the introduction of any principle of selection, *after* one experiment, is always objectionable. For some more or less plausible reason could probably always be found for setting aside the less favourable results.

1,833 trials, he then got 510 successes, the most probable number being only 458 ; that is to say, the actual number exceeds the most probable number by about $\frac{1}{10}$. Clearly no definite conclusion could be based on such figures as the above. They at most contained a hint for more extended trials, but a hint, fortunately, which can be easily followed up. We are often asked by acquaintances what they can do to aid the progress of psychical research. These experiments suggest a most convenient answer ; for they can be repeated, and a valuable contribution made to the great aggregate, by any two persons who have a pack of cards and a little perseverance.[1]

Up to the time that I write, we have received, in all, the results of 17 batches of trials in the guessing of suits. In 11 of the batches one person acted as agent and another as percipient throughout : the other 6 batches are the collective results of trials made by as many groups of friends. The total number of trials was 17,653, and the total number of successes was 4,760 ; which exceeds by 347 the number which was the most probable if chance alone acted. The probability afforded by this result for the action of a cause other than chance is ·999,999,98—or practical certainty.[2] I need hardly say that there has been here no selection of results ; all who undertook the trials were specially requested to send in their report, whatever the degree of success or unsuccess ; and we have no reason to suppose that this direction has been ignored. It is thus an additional point of interest that in *only one* of the batches did the result fall *below* the number which was the most probable one for mere chance to give. And if we take only those batches, 10 in number, in which a couple of experimenters made as many as 1,000 trials and over, the probability of a cause other than chance which the group of results yields is estimated by one method to be ·999,999,999,96, and by another to be ·999,999,999,999,2.

To this record must be added another, not less striking, of experiments which, (though part of the same effort to obtain large collective results,) differed in form from the above, and could not,

---

[1] The rules to observe are these : (1) The number of trials contemplated (1,000, 2,000, or whatever it may be) should be specified beforehand. (2) Not more than 50 trials should be made on any one occasion. (3) The agent should draw the card at random, and cut the pack between each draw. (4) The success or failure of each guess should be silently recorded, and the percipient should be kept in ignorance of the results until the whole series is completed. The results should be sent to me at 14, Dean's Yard, S.W.

[2] For these calculations we have again to thank Mr. F. Y. Edgeworth. For an explanation of the methods employed, see his article in Vol. iii. of the *Proceedings* of the S.P.R., already referred to, and also his paper on "Methods of Statistics" (*sub. fin.*) in the *Journal of the Statistical Society* for 1885.

therefore, figure in the aggregate. Thus, in a set of 976 trials, carried out by Miss B. Lindsay (late of Girton College), and a group of friends, where the choice was between 6 *uncoloured forms*— 9 specimens of each being combined in a pack from which the agent drew at random—the total of right guesses was 198, the odds against obtaining that degree of success by chance being 1,000 to 1. In another case, the choice lay between 4 things, but these were not suits, but simple *colours*—red, blue, green, and yellow. The percipient throughout was Mr. A. J. Shilton, of 40, Paradise Street, Birmingham; the agent (except in one small group, when Professor Poynting, of Mason College, acted) was Mr. G. T Cashmore, of Albert Road, Handsworth. Out of 505 trials, 261 were successes. The probability here afforded of a cause other than chance is considerably more than a trillion trillions to 1. And still more remarkable is the result obtained by the Misses Wingfield, of The Redings, Totteridge, in some trials where the object to be guessed was a number of two digits—*i.e.*, one of the 90 numbers included in the series from 10 to 99—chosen at random by the agent. Out of 2,624 trials, where the most probable number of successes was 29, the actual number obtained was no less than 275—to say nothing of 78 other cases in which the right digits were guessed in the reverse order. In the last 506 trials the agent (who sat some 6 feet behind the percipient) drew the numbers at random out of a bowl; the odds against the accidental occurrence of the degree of success—21 right guesses—obtained in this batch are over 2,000,000 to 1. The argument for thought-transference afforded by the total of 275 cannot be expressed here in figures, as it requires 167 nines—that is, the probability is far more than the ninth power of a trillion to 1.

Card-experiments of the above type offer special conveniences for the very extended trials which we wish to see carried out : they are easily made and rapidly recorded. At the same time it must not be assumed that the limitation of the field of choice to a very small number of known objects is a favourable condition ; it is probably the reverse. For from the descriptions which intelligent percipients have given it would seem that the best condition is a sort of inward blankness, on which the image of the object, sometimes suddenly but often only gradually, takes shape. And this inward blankness is hard to ensure when the objects for choice are both few and known. For their images are then apt to importune the mind, and to lead to guessing; the little procession of them marches so readily across the mental stage that it is difficult to drive it off, and wait for a single image to present itself independently. Moreover idiosyncrasies on the guesser's part have the opportunity of obtruding themselves—as an inclination, or a disinclination, to repeat the same guess several times in succession. These objections of course reach their maximum if the field of choice be narrowed down to *two* things— as where not the suit but the *colour* of the cards is to be guessed. And in fact some French trials of this type, and an aggregate of 5,500 carried out by the American Society for Psychical Research,[1] give a result only very slightly in excess of the most probable number.

§ 8. I may now pass to another class of experiments, in which the impression transferred was almost certainly of the visual sort, inasmuch as any verbal description of the object would require a group of words too numerous to present any clear and compact auditory character. An object of this kind is supplied by any irregular figure or arrangement of lines which suggests nothing in particular. We have had two remarkably successful series of experiments, extending over many days, in which the idea of such a figure has been telepathically transferred from one mind to another. A rough diagram being first drawn by one of the investigating Committee, the agent proceeded to concentrate his attention on it, or on the memory which he retained of it ; and in a period varying from a few seconds to a few minutes the percipient was able to reproduce the diagram, or a close approximation to it, on paper. No contact was permitted, except on a few occasions, which, on that very account, we should not present as crucial ; and in order to preclude the agent from giving unconscious hints—*e.g.*, by drawing with his finger on the table or making movements suggestive of the figure in the air—he was kept out of the percipient's sight.

Of the two series mentioned, the second is evidentially to be preferred. For in the first series the agent, as well as the percipient, was always the same person ; and we recognise this as *pro tanto* an objection. Not indeed that the simple hypothesis of collusion would

---

[1] Report by Professors J. M. Peirce and E. C. Pickering, in the *Proceedings of the American Society for Psychical Research*, Vol. i., p. 19. This Society has also carried out 12,130 trials with the 10 digits—which similarly gave a result only slightly in excess of theoretic probability. But here the digits to be thought of by the agent were not taken throughout in a purely accidental order, but in regularly recurring decads, in each of which each digit occurred once ; and consequently the later guesses (both within the same decad and in successive decads) might easily be biassed by the earlier ones. This system may lead to interesting statistics in other ways ; but to give thought-transference fair play in experiments with a limited number of objects, it seems essential that the order of selection shall be entirely haphazard, and that the guesser's mind shall be quite unembarrassed by the notion of a scheme.

at all meet the difficulties of the case. Faith in the power of a
secret code must be carried to the verge of superstition, before it
will be easy to believe that auditory signals, the material for which
(as I pointed out above) is limited to the faintest variations in the
signaller's method of breathing, can fully and faithfully describe a
complicated diagram ; especially when the variations, imperceptible to
the closest observation of the bystanders, would have to penetrate to
the intelligence of a percipient whose head was enveloped in bandage,
bolster-case, and blanket. But in spite of all, suspicion will,
reasonably or unreasonably, attach to results which are, so to speak,
a monopoly of two particular performers. In our second series of
experiments this objection was obviated. There were two percipients,
and a considerable group of agents, each of whom, when alone with one
or other of the percipients, was successful in transferring his impression. It is this series, therefore, that I select for fuller description.

We owe these remarkable experiments to the sagacity and energy
of Mr. Malcolm Guthrie, J.P., of Liverpool. At the beginning of 1883,
Mr. Guthrie happened to read an article on thought-transference in a
magazine, and though completely sceptical, he determined to make
some trials on his own account. He was then at the head of an
establishment which gives employment to many hundreds of persons ;
and he was informed by a relative who occupied a position of responsibility in this establishment that she had witnessed remarkable results
in some casual trials made by a group of his *employées* after business hours. He at once took the matter into his own hands, and
went steadily, but cautiously, to work. He restricted the practice of
the novel accomplishment to weekly meetings ; and he arranged
with his friend, Mr. James Birchall, the hon. secretary of the Liverpool Literary and Philosophical Society, that the latter should make
a full and complete record of every experiment made. Mr. Guthrie
thus describes the proceedings :—

" I have had the advantage of studying a series of experiments *ab ovo*.
I have witnessed the genuine surprise which the operators and the
' subjects ' have alike exhibited at their increasing successes, and at the
results of our excursions into novel lines of experiment. The affair has
not been the discovery of the possession of special powers, first made and
then worked up by the parties themselves for gain or glory. The experimenters in this case were disposed to pass the matter over altogether
as one of no moment, and only put themselves at my disposal in regard to
experiments in order to oblige me. The experiments have all been devised
and conducted by myself and Mr. Birchall, without any previous intimation
of their nature, and could not possibly have been foreseen. In fact they

have been to the young ladies a succession of surprises. No set of experiments of a similar nature has ever been more completely known from its origin, or more completely under the control of the scientific observer."

I must pass over the record of the earlier experiments, where the ideas transferred were of colours, geometrical figures, cards, and visible objects of all sorts, which the percipient was to name—these being similar in kind, though on the whole superior in the proportion of successes, to those already described.[1] The reproduction of diagrams was introduced in October, 1883, and in that and the following month about 150 trials were made. The whole series has been carefully mounted and preserved by Mr. Guthrie. No one could look through them without perceiving that the hypothesis of chance or guess-work is out of the question ; that in most instances some idea, and in many a complete idea, of the original must, by whatever means, have been present in the mind of the person who made the reproduction. In Mr. Guthrie's words,—

"It is difficult to classify them. A great number of them are decided successes ; another large number give part of the drawing ; others exhibit the general idea, and others again manifest a kind of composition of form. Others, such as the drawings of flowers, have been described and named, but have been too difficult to draw. A good many are perfect failures. The drawings generally run in lots. A number of successful copies will be produced very quickly, and again a number of failures— indicating, I think, faultiness on the part of the agent, or growing fatigue on the part of the 'subject.' Every experiment, whether successful or a failure, is given in the order of trial, with the conditions, name of 'subject' and agent, and any remarks made by the 'subject' specified at the bottom. Some of the reproductions exhibit the curious phenomenon of inversion. These drawings must speak for themselves. The principal facts to be borne in mind regarding them are that they have been executed through the instrumentality, as agents, of persons of unquestioned probity, and that the responsibility for them is spread over a considerable group of such persons ; while the conditions to be observed were so simple—for they amounted really to nothing more than taking care that the original should not be seen by the 'subject'—that it is extremely difficult to suppose them to have been eluded."

[1] The full record of the experiments will be found in the *Proceedings* of the S.P.R., Vol. i., p. 264, &c., and Vol. ii., p. 24, &c. There is one point of novelty which is thus described by Mr. Guthrie : "We tried also the perception of *motion*, and found that the movements of objects exhibited could be discerned. The idea was suggested by an experiment tried with a card, which in order that all present should see, I moved about, and was informed by the percipient that it was a card, but she could not tell which one because it seemed to be moving about. On a subsequent occasion, in order to test this perception of motion, I bought a toy monkey, which worked up and down on a stick by means of a string drawing the arms and legs together. The answer was : 'I see red and yellow, and it is darker at one end than the other. It is like a flag moving about—it is moving. . . . Now it is opening and shutting like a pair of scissors.'"

I give a few specimens—not unduly favourable ones, but illustrating the "spreading of responsibility" to which Mr. Guthrie refers. The agents concerned were Mr. Guthrie ; Mr. Steel, the President of the Liverpool Literary and Philosophical Society ; Mr. Birchall, mentioned above ; Mr. Hughes, B.A., of St. John's College, Cambridge ; and myself. The names of the percipients were Miss Relph and Miss Edwards. The conditions which I shall describe were those of the experiments in which I myself took part ; and I have Mr. Guthrie's authority for stating that they were uniformly observed in the other cases. The originals were for the most part drawn in another room from that in which the percipient was placed. The few executed in the same room were drawn while the percipient was blindfolded, at a distance from her, and in such a way that the process would have been wholly invisible to her or anyone else, even had an attempt been made to observe it. During the process of transference, the agent looked steadily and in perfect silence at the original drawing, which was placed upon an intervening wooden stand ; the percipient sitting opposite to him, and behind the stand, blindfolded and quite still. The agent ceased looking at the drawing, and the blindfolding was removed, only when the percipient professed herself ready to make the reproduction, which happened usually in times varying from half-a-minute to two or three minutes. Her position rendered it absolutely impossible that she should obtain a glimpse of the original. Apart from the blindfolding, she could not have done so without rising from her seat and advancing her head several feet ; and as she was very nearly in the same line of sight as the drawing, and so very nearly in the centre of the agent's field of vision, the slightest approach to such a movement must have been instantly detected. The reproductions were made in perfect silence, the agent forbearing to follow the actual process of the drawing with his eyes, though he was, of course, able to keep the percipient under the closest observation.

In the case of all the diagrams, except those numbered 7 and 8, the agent and the percipient were the only two persons in the room during the experiment. In the case of numbers 7 and 8, the agent and Miss Relph were sitting quite apart in a corner of the room, while Mr. Guthrie and Miss Edwards were talking in another part of it. Numbers 1-6 are specially interesting as being the complete and consecutive series of a single sitting.

No. 1. ORIGINAL DRAWING.　　　　No. 1. REPRODUCTION.

Mr. Guthrie and Miss Edwards. No contact.

No. 2. ORIGINAL DRAWING.　　　　No. 2. REPRODUCTION.

Mr. Guthrie and Miss Edwards. No contact

No. 3. ORIGINAL DRAWING.   No. 3. REPRODUCTION.

Mr. Guthrie and Miss Edwards
No contact.

No. 4. ORIGINAL DRAWING.   No. 4. REPRODUCTION.

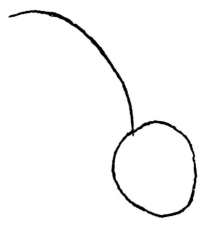

Mr. Guthrie and Miss Edwards.
No contact.

No. 5. ORIGINAL DRAWING.   No. 5. REPRODUCTION.

Mr. Guthrie and Miss Edwards.
No contact.

No. 6. ORIGINAL DRAWING.

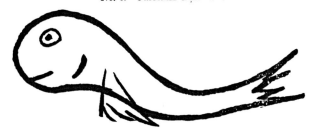

Mr. Guthrie and Miss Edwards. No contact

No. 6. REPRODUCTION.

Miss Edwards almost directly said, " Are you thinking of the bottom of the sea, with shells and fishes?" and then, " Is it a snail or a fish?"—then drew as above.

No. 7.   Original Drawing.

Mr. Gurney and Miss Relph.   Contact for half-a-minute before the reproduction was drawn.

No. 7.   Reproduction.

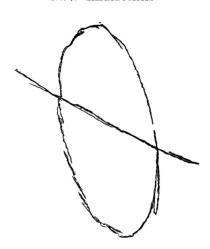

No. 8. ORIGINAL DRAWING.   No. 8. REPRODUCTION.

Mr Gurney and Miss Relph.   No contact.

No. 9. ORIGINAL DRAWING.

Mr. Birchall and Miss Relph.   No contact.

No. 9. REPRODUCTION.

Miss Relph said she seemed to see a lot of rings, as if they were moving, and she could not get them steadily before her eyes.

No. 10. ORIGINAL DRAWING.   No. 10. REPRODUCTION.

Mr. Birchall and Miss Relph.   No contact.

No. 11. ORIGINAL DRAWING.

No. 11. REPRODUCTION.

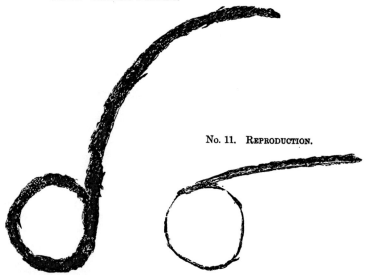

Mr. Birchall and Miss Edwards.   No contact.

No. 12. ORIGINAL DRAWING.

Mr. Steel and Miss Relph.   No contact.

No. 12.   REPRODUCTION.

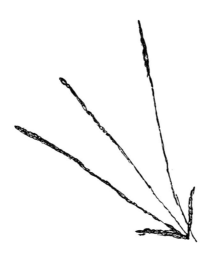

No. 13.   ORIGINAL DRAWING.   No. 13.   REPRODUCTION.

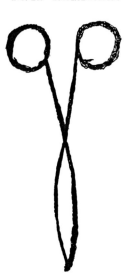

Mr. Steel and Miss Edwards. Contact before the
reproduction was made.

No. 14.   ORIGINAL DRAWING.   No. 14.   REPRODUCTION.

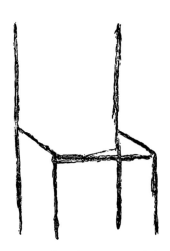

Mr. Hughes and Miss Edwards. Contact
before the reproduction was made.

Miss Edwards said, " A box or chair
badly shaped "—then drew as above.

No. 15. ORIGINAL DRAWING.

Mr. Hughes and Miss Edwards. No contact.

No. 15. REPRODUCTION.

Miss Edwards said, "It is like a mask at a pantomime," and immediately drew as above.

No. 16.   ORIGINAL DRAWING.

Mr. Hughes and Miss Edwards   No contact.

No. 16.   REPRODUCTION.

§ 9. Soon after the publication of these results, Mr. Guthrie was fortunate enough to obtain the active co-operation of Dr. Oliver J. Lodge, Professor of Physics in University College, Liverpool, who carried out a long and independent series of experiments with the same two percipients, and completely convinced himself of the genuineness of the phenomena. In his report[1] he says :—

" As regards collusion and trickery, no one who has witnessed the absolutely genuine and artless manner in which the impressions are described, but has been perfectly convinced of the transparent honesty of purpose of all concerned. This, however, is not evidence to persons who have not been present, and to them I can only say that to the best of my scientific belief no collusion or trickery was possible under the varied circumstances of the experiments. . . . . . When one has the control of the circumstances, can change them at will and arrange one's own experiments, one gradually acquires a belief in the phenomena observed quite comparable to that induced by the repetition of ordinary physical experiments. . . . . . We have many times succeeded with agents quite disconnected from the percipient in ordinary life, and sometimes complete strangers to them. Mr. Birchall, the headmaster of the Birkdale Industrial School, frequently acted ; and the house physician at the Eye and Ear Hospital, Dr. Shears, had a successful experiment, acting alone, on his first and only visit. All suspicion of a pre-arranged code is thus rendered impossible even to outsiders who are unable to witness the obvious fairness of all the experiments."

The objects of which the idea was transferred were sometimes things with names (cards, key, teapot, flag, locket, picture of donkey, and so on), sometimes irregular drawings with no name. Professor Lodge satisfied himself that auditory as well as visual impressions played a part—that in some cases the idea transferred was that of the object itself, and in others, that of its name ; thus confirming the conclusion which we had come to in the experiments with the Creery family. Of the two percipients one seemed more susceptible to the visual, and the other to the auditory impressions. A case where the auditory element seems clearly to have come in is the following. The object was a tetrahedron rudely drawn in projection, thus—

The percipient said : " Is it another triangle ? " No answer was given, but Professor Lodge silently passed round to the agents a scribbled message, " Think of a pyramid." The percipient then said, " I only see a triangle "—then hastily, "Pyramids of Egypt. No, I shan't do this." Asked to draw, she only drew a triangle.·

I will give only one other case from this series, which is important as showing that the percipient may be simultaneously influenced by two minds, which are concentrated on two different things. The two agents being seated opposite to one another, Professor Lodge placed between them a piece of paper, on one side of which was drawn a square, and on the other a cross. They thus had different objects to

ORIGINALS.   REPRODUCTION.

contemplate, and neither knew what the other was looking at ; nor did the percipient know that anything unusual was being tried. There was no contact. Very soon the percipient said, " I see things moving about . . . I seem to see two things . . . I see first one up there and then one down there . . . I don't know which to draw . . . I can't see either distinctly." Professor Lodge said : " Well, anyhow, draw what you have seen." She took off the bandage and drew first a square, and then said, " Then there was the other thing as well . . . afterwards they seemed to go into one,"— and she drew a cross inside the square from corner to corner, adding afterwards, " I don't know what made me put it inside." The significance of this experimental proof of *joint agency* will be more fully realised in connection with some of the spontaneous cases.

The following passage from the close of Professor Lodge's report has a special interest for us, confirming, as it does, the accounts which we had received from our own former " subjects," and the views above expressed as to the conditions of success and failure :—

"With regard to the feelings of the percipients when receiving an impression, they seem to have some sort of consciousness of the action of other minds on them ; and once or twice, when not so conscious, have complained that there seemed to be ' no power ' or anything acting, and that they not only received no impression, but did not feel as if they were going to.

"I asked one of them what she felt when impressions were coming freely, and she said she felt a sort of influence or thrill. They both say that several objects appear to them sometimes, but that one among them persistently recurs and they have a feeling when they fix upon one that it is the right one.

"One serious failure rather depresses them, and after a success others often follow. It is because of these rather delicate psychological conditions that one cannot press the variations of an experiment as far as one would do if dealing with inert and more dependable matter. Usually the presence of a stranger spoils the phenomena, though in some cases a stranger has proved a good agent straight off. "The percipients complain of no fatigue as induced by the experiments, and I have no reason to suppose that any harm is done them."

It is the "delicate psychological conditions" of which Professor Lodge here speaks that are in danger of being ignored, just because they cannot be measured and handled. The man who first hears of thought-transference very naturally imagines that, if it is a reality, it ought to be demonstrated to him at a moment's notice. He forgets that the experiment being essentially a mental one, his own presence—so far as he has a mind—may be a factor in it; that he is demanding that a delicate weighing operation shall be carried out, while he himself, a person of unknown weight, sits judicially in one of the scales. After a time he will learn to allow for the conditions of his instruments, and will not expect in the operations of an obscure vital influence the rigorous certainty of a chemical reaction.

I cannot conclude this division of the subject without a reference to a remarkable set of diagrams which appeared in *Science* for July, 1885—the first-fruits of the investigation of thought-transference set on foot by the American Society for Psychical Research. Most of the trials were carried out by Mr. W. H. Pickering (brother of the eminent astronomer at Harvard), and his sister-in-law. Though the success is far less striking to the eye than in the several English series, the evidence for some agency beyond chance seems, on examination, irresistible.

§ 10. So far the present sketch has included transference of impressions of the visual and auditory sorts only—impressions, moreover, which for the most part represented formed objects or definite *groups* of sensations, not sensations pure and simple. These are not only by far the most important forms of the phenomenon, in relation to the wider spontaneous operations of telepathy which we shall consider in the sequel; but are also the most convenient forms for experiment. Moreover, I have been tracing the development of the subject historically; and it was in connection with ideas belonging to the higher forms of sense that the transferences to percipients who were in a normal state were first obtained. But the existence of such cases would prepare us for transferences of a more elementary type,—transferences of a simple formless sensation and nothing more, which should impress the percipient not as an idea, but in its direct sensational character; and if the phenomena be arranged in a logical scale from the less to the more complex, such cases would have the priority. For their exhibition, it is naturally to the lower senses that we should look—taste, smell, and touch—which last (since a certain *intensity* of experience seems necessary) we should hardly expect to prove effective till it reached the degree of pain. These lower forms are, in fact, those which preponderate in the earlier observations of mesmeric *rapport* in this country; and our own experiments in mesmerism have included several instances of this sort.[1] Thus the discovery that a similar "community of sensation" might exist between persons in a normal state, and without any resort to mesmeric or hypnotic processes, not only filled up an obvious *lacuna*, but gave a fresh proof of the fundamental unity of our many-sided subject.

In the case of *taste*, we owe the discovery to Mr. Guthrie—the phenomenon having been, we believe, first observed by him on August 30th, 1883, and first fully examined in the course of a visit which Mr. Myers and the present writer paid to him in the following week. Failing to obtain very marked success in other lines of experiment, it occurred to us to introduce this novel form; but the superiority of the results was probably due simply to the fact that they were obtained on the later days of our visit, when the "subjects" had become accustomed to our presence.

I will quote the report made at the time :—

"The taste to be discerned was known only to one or more of the three actual experimenters ; and the sensations experienced were verbally described by the 'subjects' (not written down), so that all danger of involuntary muscular guidance was eliminated.

"A selection of about twenty strongly-tasting substances was made. These substances were enclosed in small bottles and small parcels, precisely similar to one another, and kept carefully out of the range of vision of the 'subjects,' who were, moreover, blindfolded, so that no grimaces made by the tasters could be seen. The 'subjects,' in fact, had no means whatever of knowing, through the sense of sight, what was the substance tasted.

---

[1] It is impossible here to give more than a selection of cases. I must refer the reader to Chap. i. of the Supplement, and to the *Proceedings* of the Society for Psychical Research, Vol. i., p. 225, &c., Vol. ii., p. 17, &c., and p. 205, &c. ; and Mr. Guthrie's "Further Report" in Vol. iii.

"*Smell* had to be guarded against with still greater care. When the substance was odoriferous the packet or bottle was opened outside the room, or at such a distance, and so cautiously as to prevent any sensible smell from escaping. The experiments, moreover, were conducted in the close vicinity of a very large kitchen, from whence a strong odour of beefsteak and onions proceeded during almost all the time occupied. The tasters took pains to keep their heads high above the 'subjects,' and to avoid breathing with open mouth. One substance (coffee) tried was found to give off a slight smell, in spite of all precautions, and an experiment made with this has been omitted.

"The tasters were Mr. Guthrie (M.G.), Mr. Gurney (E.G.), and Mr. Myers (M.). The percipients may be called R. and E. The tasters lightly placed a hand on one of the shoulders or hands of the percipients—there not being the same objection to contact in trials of this type as where lines and figures are concerned, and the 'subjects' themselves seeming to have some faith in it. During the first experiments (September 3rd and 4th) there were one or two other persons in the room, who, however, were kept entirely ignorant of the substance tasted. During the experiments silence was preserved. The last fifteen of them (September 5th) were made when only M. G., E. G., and M., with the two percipients, were present. On this evening E. was, unfortunately, suffering from sore throat, which seemed to blunt her susceptibility. On this occasion none of the substances were allowed even to enter the room where the percipients were. They were kept in a dark lobby outside, and taken by the investigators at random, so that often one investigator did not even know what the other took. Still less could any spy have discerned what was chosen, had such spy been there, which he certainly was *not*.

"A very small portion of each substance used was found to be enough. The difficulty lies in keeping the mean between the *massive* impression of a large quantity of a salt, spice, bitter, or acid, which confounds the specific differences under each general head, and the *fading* impression which is apt to give merely a residual pungency, from which the characteristic flavour has escaped. It is necessary to allow some minutes to elapse between each experiment, as the imaginary taste seems to be fully as persistent as the real one.

September 3rd, 1883.

TASTER.	PERCIPIENT.	SUBSTANCE.	ANSWERS GIVEN.
1.—M.	E.	Vinegar	"A sharp and nasty taste."
2.—M.	E.	Mustard	"Mustard."
3.—M.	R.	Do.	"Ammonia."
4.—M.	E.	Sugar	"I still taste the hot taste of the mustard."

September 4th.

5.—E. G. & M.	E.	Worcestershire sauce.	"Worcestershire sauce."
6.—M. G.	E.	Do.	"Vinegar."
7.—E. G. & M.	E.	Port wine	"Between eau de Cologne and beer."
8.—M. G.	R.	Do.	"Raspberry vinegar."
9.—E. G. & M.	E.	Bitter aloes	"Horrible and bitter."
10.—M. G.	R.	Alum	"A taste of ink—of iron—of vinegar. I feel it on my lips—it is as if I had been eating alum."

TASTER.	PERCIPIENT.	SUBSTANCE.	ANSWERS GIVEN.
11.—M. G.	E.	Alum	(E. perceived that M. G. was *not* tasting bitter aloes, as E. G. and M. supposed, but something different. No distinct perception on account of the persistence of the bitter taste.)
12.—E. G. & M.	E.	Nutmeg	"Peppermint—no—what you put in puddings—nutmeg."
13.—M. G.	R.	Do.	"Nutmeg."[1]
14.—E. G. & M.	E.	Sugar	Nothing perceived.
15.—M. G.	R.	Do.	Nothing perceived. (Sugar should be tried at an earlier stage in the series, as, after the aloes, we could scarcely taste it ourselves.)
16.—E. G. & M.	E.	Cayenne pepper	"Mustard."
17.—M. G.	R.	Do.	"Cayenne pepper." (After the cayenne we were unable to taste anything further that evening.

September 5th.

18.—E. G. & M.	E.	Carbonate of soda	Nothing perceived.
19.—M. G.	R.	Carraway seeds	"It feels like meal—like a seed loaf—carraway seeds." (The *substance* of the seeds seemed to be perceived before their *taste*.)
20.—E. G. & M.	E.	Cloves	"Cloves."
21.—E. G. & M.	E.	Citric acid	Nothing perceived.
22.—M. G.	R.	Do.	"Salt."
23.—E. G. & M.	E.	Liquorice	"Cloves."
24.—M. G.	R.	Cloves	"Cinnamon."
25.—E. G. & M.	E.	Acid jujube	"Pear drop."
26.—M. G.	R.	Do.	"Something hard, which is giving way—acid jujube."
27.—E. G. & M.	E.	Candied ginger	"Something sweet and hot."
28.—M. G.	R.	Do.	"Almond toffy." (M. G. took his ginger in the dark, and was some time before he realised that it was ginger.)
29.—E. G. & M.	E.	Home-made Noyau	"Salt."
30.—M. G.	R.	Do.	"Port wine." (This was by far the most strongly smelling of the substances tried, the scent of kernels being hard to conceal. Yet it was named by E. as salt.)
31.—E. G. & M.	E.	Bitter aloes	"Bitter."
32.—M. G.	R.	Do.	Nothing perceived.

[1] In some cases *two* experiments were carried on simultaneously with the same substance ; and when this was done, the first percipient was of course not told whether her answer was right or wrong. But it will perhaps be suggested that, when her answer was right, the agent who was touching her unconsciously gave her an intimation of the fact by the pressure of his hand ; and that she then coughed or made some audible signal to her companion, who followed suit. Whatever the theory may be worth, it will, we think, be seen that the success of the second percipient with the nutmeg was the only occasion, throughout the series, to which it can be applied.

" We should have preferred in these experiments to use only substances which were wholly inodorous. But in order to get any description of tastes from the percipients, it was necessary that the tastes should be either very decided or very familiar. It would be desirable, before entering on a series of experiments of this kind, to educate the palates of the percipients by accustoming them to a variety of chemical substances, and also by training them to distinguish, with shut eyes, between the more ordinary flavours. It is well known how much taste is helped by sight and determined by expectation ; and when it is considered that the percipients in these cases were judging blindfold of the mere shadow of a savour, it will perhaps be thought that even some of their mistakes are not much wider of the mark than they might have been had a trace of the substance been actually placed upon their tongues."

In later experiments, Mr. Guthrie endeavoured to meet the difficulty caused by odorous substances, and even succeeded in obtaining what appeared to be transferences of smell-impressions. The " subjects " and the agents were placed in different rooms. An opening, 10½ inches square, had been made in the wooden partition between the two rooms; and this had been filled in with a frame, covered with india-rubber and fitting tightly. Through a slit in this frame the agent (Mr. Guthrie or his relative, Miss Redmond) passed a hand, which both the " subjects " could then touch. Under these conditions, as far as could be judged, it was impossible for any scent to pass ; and, certainly, if any did pass, it would have needed extreme hyper-æsthesia to detect it. The following results were obtained on December 5th, 1883 :—

1.—Miss Redmond tasted powdered nutmeg.
   E. said " Ginger."
 · R. said " Nutmeg."
2.—Mr. G. tasted powder of dry celery.
   E. : " A bitter herb."
   R. : " Something like camomile."
3.—Miss Redmond tasted coffee.
   At the same time, without any previous intimation, Mr. G., with two pins, pricked the front of the right wrist of Miss Redmond.
   E. said : " Is it a taste at all ? "   Mr. G. : " Why do you ask ? "
   " Because I feel a sort of pricking in the left wrist." She was told it was the right wrist, but said she felt it in the left.
   R. : " Is it cocoa or chocolate ? " Answer given in the negative.
   E. : " Is it coffee ? "
4.—Mr. G. tasted Worcestershire sauce.
   R. : " Something sweet . . also acid . . a curious taste."
   E. : " Is it vinegar ? "
5.—Miss Redmond smelt eau de Cologne.
   R. : " Is it eau de Cologne ? "

6.—Miss Redmond smelt camphor.
    E. : " Don't taste anything."
    R. : Nothing perceived.
7.—Mr. G. smelt carbolic acid.
    R. : " What you use for toothache . . . creosote."
    E. afterwards said she thought of pitch.
8.—Mr. G. Right instep pricked with pins.
    E. guessed first the face, then the left shoulder ; then R. localised the
    pain on the right foot.
    The pain was then silently transferred to the left foot. E. localised it
    on the left foot. Both maintained their opinions.

I will quote one more taste-series, for the sake of illustrating a special point—namely, the *deferment* of the percipient's consciousness of the sensation until a time when the agent had himself ceased to feel it. This fact is of great interest, on account of the marked analogy to it which we shall encounter in many of the *spontaneous* telepathic cases. The instances below are too few to be conclusive ; but we used to notice the same thing in our experiments with the Creery family—the object on which the attention of the agents had been concentrated being sometimes correctly named after the experiment had been completely abandoned as a failure. (*Cf.*, Vol. II., p. 327.)

June 11th, 1885.

Dr. Hyla Greves was in contact with Miss Relph, having tasted salad oil.

Miss Relph said : " I feel a cool sensation in my mouth, something like that produced by sal prunelle."

Mr. R. C. Johnson in contact, having tasted Worcestershire sauce in another room.

" I taste something oily ; it is very like salad oil." Then, a few minutes after contact with Mr. Johnson had ceased, " My mouth seems getting hot after the oil." (N.B.—Nothing at all had been said about the substances tasted either by Dr. Greves or Mr. Johnson.)

Dr. Greves in contact, having tasted bitter aloes.

" I taste something frightfully hot . . . something like vinegar and pepper . . . Is it Worcestershire sauce ? "

Mr. Guthrie in contact, also having tasted bitter aloes.

" I taste something extremely bitter, but don't know what it is, and do not remember tasting it before . . . It is a very horrid taste."

The possibility of the transference of *pain*, to a percipient in the normal state, is also a recent discovery. In December, 1882, we obtained some results which—with our well-tried knowledge of the percipient's character—we regard as completely satisfactory ; but our more striking successes in this line happen to have been with hypnotic subjects.[1] The form of experiment has difficulties of its own. For, in mercy to the agent, the pain which it is hoped to transfer cannot be very severely inflicted; and, moreover, in such circumstances of investigation as Mr. Guthrie's, it is only a very limited amount of the area of the body that can practically be used—a fact which of course increases the percipient's chances of accidental success. Still, the amount of success obtained with Mr. Guthrie's "subjects," in a normal state, is such as certainly excludes the hypothesis of accident. In some of the most remarkable series, contact has been permitted, it being difficult to suppose that unconscious pressure of the hand could convey information as to the exact locality of a pain.[2] But complete isolation of the percipient is, no doubt, a more satisfactory condition; and at seven of the Liverpool meetings, which took place at intervals from November, 1884, to July, 1885, the experiment was arranged in the following way. The percipient being seated blindfolded, and with her back to the rest of the party, all the other persons present inflicted on themselves the same pain on the same part of the body. Those who took part in this collective agency were three or more of the following: Mr. Guthrie, Professor Herdman, Dr. Hicks, Dr. Hyla Greves, Mr. R. C. Johnson, F.R.A.S., Mr. Birchall, Miss Redmond, and on one occasion another lady. The percipient throughout was Miss Relph.

In all, 20 trials were made. The parts pained were—

1.—Back of left hand pricked. Rightly localised.
2.—Lobe of left ear pricked. Rightly localised.
3.—Left wrist pricked. "Is it in the left hand?"—pointing to the back near the little finger.
4.—Third finger of left hand tightly bound round with wire. A lower joint of that finger was guessed.
5.—Left wrist scratched with pins. "It is in the left wrist, like being scratched."
6.—Left ankle pricked. Rightly localised.
7.—Spot behind left ear pricked. No result.
8.—Right knee pricked. Rightly localised.
9.—Right shoulder pricked. Rightly localised.
10.—Hands burned over gas. "Like a pulling pain . . then tingling, like cold and hot alternately"—localised by gesture only.
11.—End of tongue bitten. "It is in the lip or the tongue."
12.—Palm of left hand pricked. "Is it a tingling pain in the hand, here?"—placing her finger on the palm of the left hand.
13.—Back of neck pricked. "Is it a pricking of the neck?"

[1] See *Proceedings* of the S.P.R., Vol. i., pp. 225-6; Vol. ii., p. 250.
[2] See, for instance, the record of Mr. Hughes's series in Mr. Guthrie's "Further Report," above referred to.

14.—Front of left arm above elbow pricked. Rightly localised.
15.—Spot just above left ankle pricked. Rightly localised.
16.—Spot just above right wrist pricked. " I am not quite sure, but I feel a pain in the right arm, from the thumb upwards, to above the wrist."
17.—Inside of left ankle pricked. Outside of left ankle guessed.
18.—Spot beneath right collarbone pricked. The exactly corresponding spot on the left side was guessed.
19.—Back hair pulled. No result.
20.—Inside of right wrist pricked. Right foot guessed.

Thus in 10 out of the 20 cases, the percipient localised the pain with great precision; in 6 the localisation was nearly exact, and with these we may include No. 10, where the pain was probably not confined to a single well-defined area in the hands of all the agents; in 2 no local impression was produced; and in 1, the last, the answer was wholly wrong.

§ 11. We may pass now to a totally new division of experimental cases. So far the effect of thought-transference on the receiving mind has been an effect *in consciousness*—the actual emergence of an image or sensation which the percipient has recognised and described. But it is not necessary that the effect should be thus recognised by the percipient; his witness to it may be unconscious, instead of conscious, and yet may be quite unmistakeable. The simplest example of this is when some effect is produced on his *motor* system—when the impression received causes him to perform some action which proves to have distinct reference to the thought in the agent's mind.[1]

The cases fall into two classes. In one class the actions are purely automatic : in the other some conscious idea of what was to be done has preceded and accompanied the muscular effect ; so that that effect would be at most semi-automatic. To begin with this semi-automatic class; it might be thought that examples would be found in those rarer cases of the " willing-game " where contact, and

---

[1] Even an effect on the *sensory* system may bear witness to an unconscious impression, if it is an *indirect* effect, led up to by certain hidden processes. In the *Proceedings* of the S.P.R., Vol. i., pp. 257-60, Vol. ii., pp. 203-4, and Vol. iii., pp. 453-9, a case in point is given. A young man's fingers having been concealed from him by a paper screen, anæsthesia and rigidity were repeatedly produced in one or another of them, by a process in which the concentrated attention of the " agent " on the particular finger proved to be an indispensable element. A psychical account of this result seems possible, if thought-transference can work, so to speak, underground. Such a case, however, may possibly indicate something beyond simple thought-transference—some sort of specific physical influence ; and it should be noted that the " subject," though at the time he was wide awake and in a perfectly normal state, had frequently on former occasions been hypnotised by the agent.

It is only in connection with hypnotism, again, that we find authentic cases of the direct effect of volition in producing the identical movement willed—such as raising the hand, dropping a book, &c. Some of these will be given in the next chapter.

movement on the agent's part, are avoided. But we have received no records of such cases where it is certain that the precautions necessary to exclude the barest possibility of slight unconscious physical signs were rigidly enforced ; and it will be preferable to describe some experiments made by members of our own group, where this point was kept steadily in view. We have had several interesting series in which the " subject's " power of utterance has been *inhibited* by the silent determination of the operator. Our first experiments of this sort were made in January, 1883. The "subject" was our friend, Mr. Sidney Beard, who had been thrown into a light hypnotic trance by Mr. G. A. Smith. A list of twelve *Yeses* and *Noes* in arbitrary order was written by one of ourselves and put into Mr. Smith's hand, with directions that he should successively "will" the " subject " to respond or not to respond, in accordance with the order of the list. Mr. Beard was lying back with closed eyes ; and a tuning-fork was struck and held at his ear, with the question, " Do you hear ? " asked by one of ourselves. This was done twelve times with a completely successful result, the answer or the failure to answer corresponding in each case with the " yes " or " no " of the written list—that is to say, with the silently concentrated will of the agent.[1]

A much more prolonged series of trials was made in November, 1883, by Professor Barrett, at his house in Dublin. The hypnotist was again Mr. G. A. Smith.

"The 'subject' was an entire stranger to Mr. Smith, a youth named Fearnley, to whom nothing whatever was said as to the nature of the experiment about to be tried, until he was thrown into the hypnotic state in my study. He was then in a light sleep-waking condition—his eyes were closed and the pupils upturned—apparently sound asleep ; but he readily answered in response to any questions addressed to him by Mr. Smith or by myself.

" I first told him to open the fingers of his closed hand, or not to open them, just as he felt disposed, in response to the question addressed to him. That question, which I always asked in a uniform tone of voice, was in

----

[1] Similar trials on other occasions were equally successful ; as also were trials where the tuning-fork was dispensed with, and the only sound was the question, "Do you hear ? " asked by one of the observers. On these latter occasions, however, Mr. Smith was holding Mr. Beard's hand ; and it might be maintained that "yes" and "no" indications were given by unconscious variations of pressure. How completely unconscious the supposed " reader " was of any sensible guidance will be evident from Mr. Beard's own account. " During the experiments of January 1st, when Mr. Smith mesmerised me, I did not entirely lose consciousness at any time, but only experienced a sensation of total numbness in my limbs. When the trial as to whether I could hear sounds was made, I heard the sounds distinctly each time, but in a large number of instances I felt totally unable to acknowledge that I heard them. I seemed to know each time whether Mr. Smith wished me to say that I heard them ; and as I had surrendered my will to his at the commencement of the experiment, I was unable to reassert my power of volition whilst under his influence."

each case, ' Now, will you open your hand ?' and at the same moment I pointed to the word ' Yes ' or ' No,' written on a card, which was held in sight of Mr. Smith, but entirely out of the range of vision of the ' subject,' even had his eyes been open, which they were not. Without the slightest change of expression or other observable muscular movement, and quite out of contact with the ' subject,' Mr. Smith then silently willed the subject to open or not to open his hand, in accordance with the ' Yes ' or ' No.' Twenty successive experiments were made in this way ; seventeen of these were quite successful, and three were failures. But these three failures were possibly due to inadvertence on Mr. Smith's part, as he subsequently stated that on those occasions he had not been prompt enough to direct his will in the right direction before the question was asked.

"The experiment was now varied as follows : The word ' Yes ' was written on one, and the word ' No ' on the other, of two precisely similar pieces of card. One or other of these cards was handed to Mr. Smith at my arbitrary pleasure, care, of course, being taken that the ' subject ' had no opportunity of seeing the card, even had he been awake. When ' Yes ' was handed, Mr. Smith was silently to will the ' subject' to answer aloud in response to the question asked by me, ' Did you hear me ?' When ' No ' was handed, Mr. Smith was to will that no response should be made in reply to the same question. The object of this series of experiments was to note the effect of increasing the distance between the willer and the willed,—the agent and the percipient. In the first instance Mr. Smith was placed *three feet* from the ' subject,' who remained throughout apparently asleep in an arm-chair in one corner of my study.

" At three feet apart, fifteen trials were successively made, and *in every case* the ' subject ' responded or did not respond in exact accordance with the silent will of Mr. Smith, as directed by me.

" At six feet apart, six similar trials were made without a single failure.

" At twelve feet apart, six more trials were made without a single failure.

"At seventeen feet apart, six more trials were made without a single failure.

" In this last case Mr. Smith had to be placed outside the study door, which was then closed with the exception of a narrow chink just wide enough to admit of passing a card in or out, whilst I remained in the study observing the ' subject.' To avoid any possible indication from the tone in which I asked the question, in all cases except the first dozen experiments, I shuffled the cards face downwards, and then handed the unknown ' Yes ' or ' No ' to Mr. Smith, who looked at the card and willed accordingly. I noted down the result, and then, and not till then, looked at the card.

" A final experiment was made when Mr. Smith was taken across the hall and placed in the dining-room, at a distance of about thirty feet from the ' subject,' two doors, both quite closed, intervening. Under these conditions, three trials were made with success, the ' Yes ' response being, however, very faint and hardly audible to me, who returned to the study to ask the usual question after handing the card to the distant operator. At this point, the ' subject ' fell into a deep sleep, and made no further replies to the questions addressed to him.

"Omitting these final experiments, the total number of successive trials at different distances was forty-three. If the result had been due to accident, there would have been an even chance of failures and of successes,—whereas in fact *there was not a single failure in the entire series.*

"I subsequently made a series of a dozen successive trials in an absolutely dark room, conveying my intention to Mr. Smith by silently squeezing his hand, once for 'No,' twice for 'Yes.' Every trial was successful. When Mr. Smith was placed outside the darkened room, I handed him the card through a small aperture, which could be closed. Eight trials gave six results quite right, one wrong, and one doubtful. Afterwards twenty trials, made when Mr. Smith was recalled, and the room lighted, were all entirely successful. There was, I need hardly say, no contact between operator and 'subject' in any of these experiments.

"The difference in the power of the will of the hypnotist and that of any other person was strikingly manifest, and the proof of the existence of a peculiar '*rapport*' between operator and subject was simply over-whelming. I several times exerted my will in opposition to that of Mr. Smith—that is to say, willed that the 'subject' should or should not respond, when Mr. Smith willed the opposite, both of us being equally distant from the 'subject.' In every case his will triumphed. As in the case of Mr. Beard, the 'subject,' on being aroused, stated that he had heard the question each time, but that when he gave no answer he felt unaccountably unable to control his muscles so as to frame the word.

"It was noticeable that neither in the normal nor in the hypnotic state was this subject able to tell any word or number or describe any diagram thought of or viewed by the operator. Only his ability to act in a particular way could be controlled, and he was not susceptible to even the most rudimentary form of thought-transference proper."

The following shorter series with another operator, Mr. Kershaw, of Southport, and with Mrs. Firth, a sick-nurse, as "subject," though the precautions were less elaborate than in the case just recorded, was to an eye-witness almost equally satisfactory. For the trial was quite suddenly suggested to Mr. Kershaw by the present writer; and not only was it planned out of Mrs. Firth's hearing, but Mr. Kershaw himself had some difficulty in understanding what was wanted. A variety of small circumstances combined to show that the form of experiment was entirely new both to operator and "subject."

The trial took place at Southport, on September 7th, 1883. Mrs. Firth, who had been previously thrown into a light stage of trance, was placed in a chair in the middle of a bare room. Mr. Kershaw and I stood about three yards behind her; and sight of us, or of any part of us, on her part was out of the question. The window was in the wall in front of her, but altogether on one side; and there were no other reflecting surfaces in the room. I drew up the subjoined list of *yeses* and *noes*, and held it for Mr. Kershaw to see. He made a quiet connecting motion of the hand (not touching me, and being many feet from Mrs. Firth), when there was to be an answer, and an equally quiet transverse or separating pass when there was to be none. I attribute no virtue to the passes, except so far as they were a means of vivifying Mr. Kershaw's silent intention to himself. The passes were almost absolutely noiseless, and the extremely faint sound which they made, from the very nature of the gentle motion, can scarcely have varied. Complete silence was preserved but for my question, " Do you hear ? " repeated time after time, in a perfectly neutral tone ; and there did not appear to be the very faintest chance of signalling, even had there been an opportunity for arranging a scheme.

1.—Yes............Right (*i.e.*, Mrs. Firth responded).
2.—No ....Right (*i.e.*, Mrs. Firth did not respond).
3.—Yes............Right.
4.—Yes............Right.
5.—No ....Right.
6.—Yes............Right.
7.—No ....At first no answer, which was right : then
                    I gave a very loud stamp, which pro-
                    voked a "Yes."
8.—No ....Right.
9.—Yes............Right.

I will add one more short series, which took place at my lodgings at Brighton, on September 10th, 1883. The operator was Mr. Smith ; the " subject " an intelligent young cabinet-maker, named Conway. Mr. Smith and I stood behind him, without any contact with him. I held the list, and pointed to .the desired answer each time. The silence was absolute. I repeated the question, "What is your name ?" in a perfectly neutral and monotonous manner.

1.—Yes.........Right (*i.e.*, the " subject " said " Conway ").
2.—Yes.........Right.
3.—No ....This time the answer " Conway " was given; but when
                 the *next* question was asked, the " subject " seemed
                 unable to answer for some seconds, as though Mr.
                 Smith's intention had taken effect a little too late.

4.—Yes.........Right.	7.—Yes.........Right.	10.—Yes.........Right.
5.—No ....Right.	8.—No ....Right.	11.—No ....Right.
6.—No ....Right.	9.—Yes.........Right.	12. Yes.........Right.

§ 12. But in experiments of this class it is clearly difficult to be sure that the *conscious idea* of the evoked or the inhibited action does not precede or accompany the muscular effects. Indeed, as we have seen, the percipient's own account has sometimes shown that it did so. I proceed, then, to our second class of cases. There is, fortunately, one sort of act where the verdict of the performer that it was automatically performed may be taken as conclusive ; the act of *writing*. If words are written down which the writer is obliged to read over, and even to puzzle over, just as anyone else might do, in order to learn what they are, his unconsciousness of them in the act of writing may be taken as established. Now written words are of course as good as spoken ones, as evidence that a particular idea has been in some way communicated. If, then, one person's automatic writing corresponds unmistakeably to the idea on which another person's mind was concentrated at the time, and if the possibility of sensory indications has been excluded, we have a clear example of some novel influence acting, not only without the participation of the recognised organs of sense, but without the participation of the percipient's conscious intelligence. Here again we find the advantage of the generic word " telepathy "—for it would clearly be inaccurate to call a phenomenon " thought-transference " where what is transferred does not make its appearance, on the percipient's side, as thought or any other form of conscious perception.

We have in our collection several examples of this *motor* form of experimental telepathy ; where a mental question on the part of some one present has been answered in writing, with a planchette[1] or a simple pencil, without any consciousness of either the question or the answer on the part of the person whose hand was automatically acting. But the following group of cases is decidedly the most remarkable that has come under our notice.

The Rev. P. H. Newnham, Vicar of Maker, Devonport, has had many indications of spontaneous transference of thought from himself to his wife ;[2] and at one period of his life, in 1871, he carried out a long and systematic series of experiments, which were of the motor type that we are now considering—he writing down a question, and the planchette under his wife's hands replying to it. He recorded the results, day by day, in a private diary, which he has kindly placed at our disposal. From this diary I quote the following extracts : —

My wife always sat at a small low table, in a low chair, leaning backwards. I sat about eight feet distant, at a rather high table, and with my back towards her while writing down the questions. It was absolutely impossible that any gesture or play of features, on my part, could have been visible or intelligible to her. As a rule she kept her eyes shut ; but never became in the slightest degree hypnotic, or even naturally drowsy.

---

[1] A planchette has two advantages over a simple pencil. It is very much more easily moved to write ; and it is very much easier to make with it the movements necessary for the formation of letters without realising what the letters are.
[2] See, *e.g.*, the cases quoted in Chap. v., §§ 2 and 8.

Under these conditions we carried on experiments for about eight months, and I have 309 questions and answers recorded in my note-book, spread over this time. But the experiments were found very exhaustive of nerve power, and as my wife's health was delicate, and the fact of thought-transmission had been abundantly proved, we thought it best to abandon the pursuit.

I may mention that the planchette began to move instantly, with my wife. The answer was often half written before I had completed the question.

On first finding that it would write easily, I asked three simple questions which were known to the operator ;[1] then three others, unknown to her, relating to my own private concerns. All six having been instantly answered in a manner to show complete intelligence, I proceeded to ask :—

7.[2] Write down the lowest temperature here this winter.

A. 8.

Now, this reply at once arrested my interest. The actual lowest temperature had been 7·6° so that 8 was the nearest whole degree ; but my wife said at once that, if she had been asked the question, she would have written 7 and not 8 ; as she had forgotten the decimal, but remembered my having said that the temperature had been down to 7 *something*.

I simply quote this, as a good instance, at the very outset, of perfect transmission of thought, coupled with a perfectly independent reply ; the answer being correct in itself, but different from the impression on the *conscious intelligence* of *both* parties.[3]

Naturally our first desire was to see if we could obtain any information concerning the nature of the intelligence which was operating through the planchette, and of the method by which it produced the written results. We repeated questions on this subject again and again, and I will copy down the principal questions and answers in the connection.

January 29th.

13. Is it the operator's brain, or some external force, that moves the planchette ? Answer " brain " or " force."
    A. Will.

14. Is it the will of a living person, or of an immaterial spirit, distinct from that person ? Answer " person " or " spirit."
    A. Wife.

15. Give first the wife's Christian name ; then, my favourite name for her.
    (This was accurately done.)

27. What is your own name ?
    A. Only you.

28. We are not quite sure of the meaning of the answer. Explain.
    A. Wife.

Failing to get more than this, at the outset, we turned to the same thought after question 114 ; when, having been closely pressed on another subject, we received the curt reply—" Told all I know."

---

[1] Mr. Newnham uses this word where we should use " subject " or " percipient."

[2] The numbers prefixed to the questions are those in the note-book.

[3] It will be borne in mind throughout that Mrs. Newnham had, at the time when the answer was produced, no conscious knowledge of the question which her husband had written down.

February 18*th.*

117. Who are you that writes, and has told all you know ?
    A. Wife.
118. But does no one tell wife what to write ?   If so, who ?
    A. Spirit.
119. Whose spirit ?
    A. Wife's brain.
120. But how does wife's brain know (certain) secrets ?
    A. Wife's spirit unconsciously guides.
121. But how does wife's spirit know things it has never been told ?
    A. No external influence.
122. But by what *internal* influence does it know (these) secrets ?
    A. You cannot know.

March 15*th.*

132. Who, then, makes the impressions upon her ?
    A. Many strange things.
133. What sort of strange things ?
    A. Things beyond your knowledge.
134. Do, then, things beyond our knowledge make impressions upon wife ?
    A. Influences which no man understands or knows.
136. Are these influences which we cannot understand external to wife ?
    A. External—invisible.
137. Does a spirit, or do spirits, exercise those influences ?
    A. No, never (written very large and emphatically).
138. Then from whom, or from whence, do the external influences come ?
    A. Yes ; you will never know.
139. What do you mean by writing " yes " in the last answer ?
    A. That I really meant never.

April 10*th.*

192. But by what means are my thoughts conveyed to her brain ?
    A. Electro-biology.
193. What is electro-biology ?
    A. No one knows.
194. But do not you know ?
    A. No.   Wife does not know.

My object in quoting this large number of questions and replies [N.B.
those here given are mere samples] has not been merely to show the
instantaneous and unfailing transmission of thought from questioner to
operator ; but, more especially, to call attention to a remarkable characteristic of the answers given.   These answers, consistent and invariable in
their tenor from first to last, *did not correspond with the opinions or
expectations of either myself or my wife.*   Neither myself nor my wife had
ever taken part in any form of (so-called) " spiritual " manifestations
before this time ; nor had we any decided opinion as to the agency by
which phenomena of this kind were brought about.   But for such
answers as those numbered 14, 27, 137, 192, and 194, we were both of us
totally unprepared ; and I may add that, so far as we were prepossessed
by any opinions whatever, these replies were distinctly opposed to such
opinions.   In a word, it is simply impossible that these replies should

F

have been either suggested or composed by the *conscious* intelligence of either of us.

I had a young man reading with me as a private pupil at this time. On February 12th he returned from his vacation ; and, on being told of our experiments, expressed his incredulity very strongly. I offered any proof that he liked to insist upon, only stipulating that I should see the question asked. Accordingly, Mrs. Newnham took her accustomed chair in my study, while we went out into the hall, *and shut the door behind us.* He then wrote down on a piece of paper :—

87. What is the Christian name of my eldest sister ?

We at once returned to the study, and found the answer already waiting for us :—

A. Mina.

(This name was the family abbreviation of Wilhelmina ; and I should add that it was unknown to myself.)

I must now go on to speak of a series of other experiments, of a very remarkable kind.

We soon found that my wife was perfectly unable to follow the motions of the planchette. Often she only touched it with a single finger ; but even with all her fingers resting on the board, she never had the slightest idea of what words were being traced out. It struck me that it would be a good thing to take advantage of this peculiarity on her part, to ask questions upon subjects that it was impossible for her to know anything about. I had taken a deep interest in Masonic archæology, and I now questioned planchette on some subjects connected therewith.

February 14th.

92. What is the English of the great word of the R.A. ?
   After an interruption, of which I shall speak hereafter, one great word of the degree, but not the one I meant, was written, very slowly and clearly.

February 18th.

112. What is the translation of the Great Triple Word ?
   A. (The first syllable of the word in question was written correctly, and then it proceeded.) The end unknown. Three languages. Greece. Egypt. Syriac.
115. Who are you that know ?
   (Answer scrawled and illegible.)
116. Please repeat same answer legibly.
   A. Manifestation triune person.

March 26th.

166. Of what language is the first syllable of the Great Triple R.A. Word ?
   A. Don't know.
167. Yes, you do. What are the three languages of which the word is composed ?
   A. Greek, Egypt, Syriac first syllable (*correctly given*), rest unknown.

168. Write the syllable which is Syriac.
    A. (First syllable correctly written.)
169. Write the syllable which is Egyptian.
    A. Second.
170. Can you not write the syllable itself ?
    A. Third Greek.
174. Write down the word itself.
    A. First three and last two letters were written correctly, but four incorrect letters, *partly borrowed from another word of the same degree,* came in the middle.
176. Why do you write a word of which I know nothing ?
    A. Wife tried hard to tell the word, but could not quite catch it.
177. Catch it from whom ?
    A. Not quite sure.
178. Not quite sure of what ?
    A. I know nothing. Wife doesn't quite know.

In the above series of answers we have, it seems to me, a very remarkable combination of knowledge and ignorance. There is a perfect appreciation of my thoughts, in the queries; but a strange, persistent, almost dogged, incapability of seeing my thoughts, in the replies. Especially in the answer to 116, and in some other answers [not here quoted], there is a reference to an opinion which was published by Dr. Oliver, whose works I had been carefully reading about four months before, but with whose theory, in this case, I most strongly disagreed. So that here was an opinion intimated which it was impossible that the operator could have been aware of, and which the questioner had absolutely rejected as untenable !

182. Write out the prayer used at the advancement of a Mark Master Mason.

    A. Almighty Ruler of the Universe and Architect of all worlds, we beseech Thee to accept this, our brother, whom we have this day received into our most honourable Company of Mark Master Masons. Grant him to be a worthy member of our brotherhood; and may he be in his own person a perfect mirror of all Masonic virtues. Grant that all our doings may be to Thy honour and glory, and to the welfare of all mankind.

This prayer was written off instantaneously and very rapidly. It is a very remarkable production indeed. For the benefit of those who are not members of the craft, I may say that no prayer in the slightest degree resembling it is made use of in the Ritual of any Masonic degree ; and yet it contains more than one strictly accurate technicality connected with the degree of Mark Mason. My wife has never seen any Masonic prayers, whether in "Carlile," or any other real or spurious Ritual of the Masonic Order.

Here, then, assuredly was a formula composed by some intelligence totally distinct from the conscious intelligence of either of the persons engaged in the experiment.

I proceeded to inquire as follows :—

183. I do not know this prayer.   Where is it to be found ?
   A. Old American Ritual.
184. Where can I get one ?
   A. Most likely none in England.
185. Can you not write the prayer that I made use of in my own Lodge ?
   A. No, I don't know it.

In these last answers we see a new moral element introduced.   There is evasion, or subterfuge, of a more or less ingenious kind ; and totally foreign to the whole character and natural disposition of the operator.   A similar attempt at deliberate invention, rather than plead guilty to total ignorance, is contained in the following answers :—

May 7th.

255. In what Masonic degree was the Triple Word first used ?
   A. Wife does not know.
256. Cannot you tell her ?
   A. How can wife know what no one else does ?
257. Does *no* one, then, know the answer to this ?
   A. No one knows now.
258. What do you mean by " now"?   Did anyone once know?
   A. The last one who knew died at least twenty years ago.
259. What was his name?
   A. In America ; don't know name.

[Many more instances of these evasive replies occur.]

May 10th.

Planchette again gave us an example of its sense of the humorous.

I had been obliged to engage a clergyman who was not a favourable specimen of his profession, as I could procure no one else in time to get the Sunday's work done.   He was much amused with planchette, and desired to ask :—

277. How should a bachelor live in this neighbourhood ?
   (The answer was illegible.)
278. Please repeat answer.
   A. Three months.

(Planchette evidently did not catch the exact query.)

279. I did not ask *how long* but *how* ?
   A. Eating and drinking and sleeping and smoking.

That clergyman never consulted planchette again.

I will conclude with a very pretty instance of a mistake instantly corrected.   It was on the same evening, May 10th ; I had to preach on the following Whit-Monday, on the occasion of laying a foundation-stone with Masonic ceremonial, so I asked :—

275. Give me a text for Whit-Monday's sermon.
   A. If I go not away, the Comforter will not come to you.

The selection of a subject suitable for *Whitsuntide* is plainly the first idea caught by the intelligence ; so I proceeded :—

276. That will not do for my subject.   I want a text for the *Monday's* sermon.

A. Let brotherly love continue.

I will add one example where, contrary to the usual rule, the idea of the answer, though not that of the question, reached the level of consciousness in Mrs. Newnham's mind.

59. What name shall we give to our new dog ?
    A. Nipen.

The name of Nipen, from *Feats on the Fiord*, shot into the operator's brain just as the question was asked.

The above quotations form a fair sample of Mr. Newnham's 309 experiments of the same type; and no one who admits the *bona fides* of the record, and believes that Mrs. Newnham, sitting with closed eyes eight feet behind her husband, did not obtain through her senses an unconscious knowledge of what he wrote, will deny that some sort of telepathic influence was at work, acting below the level of the percipient's consciousness. The experiments are further interesting as suggesting, in the character of many of the replies, an unconscious intelligence—a second self quite other than Mrs. Newnham's conscious self. " Unconscious intelligence " is no doubt a somewhat equivocal phrase, and it is necessary to know in every case exactly what is meant by it. It may be used in a purely *physical* sense—to describe the unconscious cerebral processes whereby actions are produced which as a rule are held to imply conscious intelligence ; as, for instance, when complicated movements, once performed with thought and effort, gradually become mechanical. But it may be used also to describe *psychical* processes which are severed from the main conscious current of an individual's life. Unconsciousness in any further sense it would be rash to assert ; for intelligent psychic process without consciousness of *some* sort, if not a contradiction in terms, is at any rate something as impossible to imagine as a fourth dimension in space. The events in question are outside the individual's consciousness, as the events in another person's consciousness are ; but they differ from these last in not revealing themselves as part of *any* continuous stream of conscious life ; and no one, therefore, can give an account of them as belonging to a self. What their range and conditions of emergence may be we cannot tell ; since, in general, their very existence can only be inferred from certain sensible effects to which they lead.[1] I may recall the undoubted phenomena of what

---

[1] It may be asked what right I have to make any such inference ; since *à la rigueur*, the effects, being sensible and physical, do not require us to suppose that they had any other than *physical* antecedents. It is true that it is impossible to *demonstrate* that the physical antecedents, which undoubtedly exist, have any psychical correlative. But the

has been termed "double consciousness," where a *double* psychical life is found connected with a *single* organism. In those cases the two selves, one of which knows nothing of the other, appear as *successive ;* but if we can regard such segregated existences as united or unified by bonds of reference and association which, for the partial view of one of them at least, remain permanently out of sight, then I do not see what new or fundamental difficulty is introduced by conceiving them as *simultaneous ;* and simultaneity of the sort is what seems to be shown, in a fragmentary way, by cases like the present. I shall have to recur to this conception in connection with some of the facts of spontaneous telepathy (see pp. 230-1).

A further noteworthy point is that so often the questions and not the answers in the agent's mind should have been telepathically discerned ; but we may perhaps conceive that the impulse first conveyed set the percipient's independent activity to work, and so put an end for the moment to the receptive condition. The power to reproduce the actual word thought of is sufficiently shown in the cases where names were given (15 and 87), and in some of the Masonic answers ; and the following examples belong to the same class.

48. What name shall we give to our new dog ?
    A. Yesterday was not a fair trial.
49. Why was not yesterday a fair trial ?
    A. Dog.

And again :—

108. What do I mean by chaffing C. about a lilac tree ?
    A. Temper and imagination.
109. You are thinking of somebody else. Please reply to my question.
    A. Lilacs.

Here a single image or word seems to have made its mark on the percipient's mind, without calling any originative activity into play ; and we thus get the naked reproduction. In these last examples we again notice the feature of *deferred* impression. The influence

results in question have often no analogy to the automatic actions which we are accustomed to attribute to "unconscious cerebration." They are not the effects of habit and practice ; they are *new* results, of a sort which has in all our experience been preceded by intention and reflection, and referable to a self. But perhaps the simplest illustration of what is here meant by "unconscious intelligence" is to be found in occasional facts of *dreaming.* Thus, it has occurred to me at least once, in a dream, to be asked a riddle, to give it up, and then to be told the answer—which, on waking, I found quite sufficiently pertinent to show that the question could not have been framed without distinct reference to it. Yet for the consciousness which I call *mine*, that reference had remained wholly concealed : so little had I known myself as the composer of the riddle that the answer came to me as a complete surprise. The philosophical problem of *partial selves* cannot be here enlarged on. For a discussion of the subject from the point of view of cerebral localisation, as well as for further quotations from Mr. Newnham's record, I may refer the reader to Mr. Myers' paper on "Automatic Writing," in Vol. iii. of the *Proceedings* of the S.P.R.

only gradually became effective, the immediate answer being irrelevant to the question. We may suppose, therefore, that the first effect took place below the threshold of consciousness.[1]

§ 13. I may now proceed to some further results which were obtained with percipients of less abnormal sensibility, and which demand, therefore, a careful application of the theory of probabilities.

[1] The following case, though not strictly experimental, is sufficiently in point to be worth quoting. Though unfortunately not recorded in writing at the time, it was described within a few days of its occurrence to Mr. Podmore, who is acquainted with all the persons concerned. The narrator is Miss Robertson, of 229, Marylebone Road, W.

"About three years ago I was speaking of planchette-writing to some of my friends, when a young lady, a daughter of the house where I was spending the evening, mentioned that she had played with planchette at school, and that it had always written for her. Thereupon I asked her to spend the evening with me, and try it again, which she agreed to do. On the morning of the day on which she had arranged to come to me, her brother, on leaving the house, said, laughing, 'Well, Edith, it is all humbug, but if planchette tells you the name and sum of money which are on a cheque which I have in my pocket, and which I am going to cash for mother, I will believe there is something in it.' Edith, on her arrival at my house in the evening, told me of this, and I said, 'We must not expect that; planchette never does what one wants,' or words to that effect. A couple of hours after, we tried the planchette, Edith's hand alone touching it. It almost immediately wrote, quite clearly :—

'I. SPALDING. £6 : 13 : 4.'

I had forgotten about the cheque, and I said, 'What can that mean?' Upon which Edith replied, 'It is H.'s cheque, perhaps.' I was incredulous, having a long acquaintance with planchette. I said, 'If it is right, send me word directly you get home ; I am sure it will not be.' But the next day I received a letter from Edith, telling me that she had astonished her brother greatly by telling him the name and the amount on the cheque, which was perfectly correct. I have read this account to the young lady and her brother, who sign it as well as myself.

"NORA ROBERTSON.
"E. C.
"D. C. H. C."

In answer to an inquiry, Miss Robertson adds, on Feb. 12, 1885 :—

"Miss E. C. says, in answer to your question, that she is quite certain she could not have known, or surmised, the name and amount of the cheque.

"I can confirm her on the first point, for I remember questioning everybody all round at the time. She had just returned from school, and knew nothing at all about her mother's business or money matters."

Here, it will be observed, the impression seems not only to have been unconscious, but to have remained latent for several hours before taking effect ; for it is at any rate the most natural supposition that the transference actually occurred at the time when the conversation on the subject took place between the brother and sister.

This *latency* of an impression which finally takes effect in distinct automatic or semi-automatic movements, may be seen in cases which have no connection with telepathy. It occurs, for instance, in the following "muscle-reading" experiment, described to us by Mr. George B. Trent, of 65, Sandgate Road, Folkestone :—

"March 24th, 1883.

"Some two months back, I was asked by a gentleman, who had read of my experiments in the paper, to oblige him with a séance. I called upon him one afternoon, and he told me that he had hidden some object, in the early morning, and he thought he had given me a puzzle. I first experimented with pins ; I led him to their hiding-places at once, without the least hesitation. I then asked him to concentrate the whole of his thoughts on what he had done in the morning. I immediately led him to a davenport, unlocked it, and from amongst, I may say, perhaps a hundred papers and other articles, I selected three photographs, and from the three I fixed upon one—that of his wife. He then said he was perfectly astonished, as I had positively gone through an experiment he had set himself to do, but abandoned in favour of another he *had* done."

It seems probable that, at any rate in the earlier stages of this performance, the idea of what was to be done was not consciously present in the "willer's" mind, which was apparently concentrated on something else. And if so, his muscular indications must have been the result of unconscious cerebration—an effect of nervous activity, continuing to act in accordance with a previous impulse which had lapsed from consciousness.

For the development of the motor form of experiment in this direction, we have again to thank M. Richet; who here, as in the case of the card-guessing, has brought the calculus to bear effectively on various sets of results many of which, if looked at in separation, would have had no significance.[1] The fact that the "subjects" of his trials were persons who had betrayed no special aptitude for "mental suggestion," made it clearly desirable that the bodily action required should be of the very simplest sort. The formation of words by a planchette-writer requires, of course, a very complex set of muscular co-ordinations: all that M. Richet sought to obtain was a single movement or twitch. In the earlier trials an object was hidden, and the percipient endeavoured to discover it by means of a sort of divining-rod—the idea being that he involuntarily twitched the rod at the right moment under the influence of "mental suggestion" from the agent, who was watching his movements. But where the subject of communication is of such an extremely simple kind, very elaborate precautions would be needed to guard against unconscious hints. Indications from the expression or attitude of the "agent" may be prevented by blindfolding the "percipient," and in other ways; but if the two are in close proximity, it is harder to exclude such signs as may be given by involuntary movements, or by changes of breathing. M. Richet's later experiments were ingeniously contrived so as to obviate this objection.

The place of a planchette was taken by a table, and M. Richet prefaces his account by a succinct statement of the orthodox view as to "table-turning." Rejecting altogether the three theories which attribute the phenomena to wholesale fraud, to spirits, and to an unknown force, he regards the gyrations and oscillations of séance-tables as due wholly to the unconscious muscular contractions of the sitters. It thus occurred to him to employ a table as an indicator of the movements that might be produced, by "mental suggestion." The plan of the experiments was as follows. Three persons (C, D, and E,) took their seats in a semi-circle, at a little table on which their hands rested. One of these three was always a "medium"—a term used by M. Richet to denote a person liable to exhibit intelligent movements in which consciousness and will apparently take no part. Attached to the table was a simple electrical apparatus, the effect of which was to ring a bell whenever the current was broken by the tilting of the table.

---

[1] I have given a fuller description and criticism of M. Richet's investigations in Vol. ii. of the *Proceedings* of the S.P.R.

Behind the backs of the sitters at the table was another table, on which was a large alphabet, completely screened from the view of C, D, and E, even had they turned round and endeavoured to see it. In front of this alphabet sat A, whose duty was to follow the letters slowly and steadily with a pen, returning at once to the beginning as soon as he arrived at the end. At A's side sat B, with a note-book ; his duty was to write down the letter at which A's pen happened to be pointing whenever the bell rang. This happened whenever one of the sitters at the table made the simple movement necessary to tilt it. Under these conditions, A and B are apparently mere automata. C, D, and E are little more, being unconscious of tilting the table, which appears to them to tilt itself; but even if they tilted it˙ consciously, and with a conscious desire to dictate words, they have no means of ascertaining at what letter A's pen is pointing at any particular moment ; and they might tilt for ever without producing more than an endless series of incoherent letters. Things being arranged thus, a sixth operator, F, stationed himself apart both from the tilting table and from the alphabet, and concentrated his thought on some word of his own choosing, which he had not communicated to the others. The three sitters at the first table engaged in conversation, sang, or told stories ; but at intervals the table tilted, the bell rang, and B wrote down the letter which A's pen was opposite to at that moment. Now, to the astonishment of all concerned, these letters, when arranged in a series, turned out to produce a more or less close approximation to the word of which F was thinking.

For the sake of comparing the results with those which pure accident would give, M. Richet first considers some cases of the latter sort. He writes the word NAPOLEON ; he then takes a box containing a number of letters, and makes eight draws ; the eight letters, in the order of drawing, turn out to be U P M T D E Y V He then places this set below the other, thus :—

N A P O L E O N

U P M T D E Y V

Taking the number of letters in the French alphabet to be 24, the probability of the correspondence of any letter in the lower line with the letter immediately above it is, of course $\frac{1}{24}$; and in the series of 8 letters it is more probable than not that there will not be a single correspondence. If we reckon as a success any case where the letter in the lower line corresponds not only with the letter above it, but with either of the neighbours of that letter in the alphabet[1] (*e.g.*, where L has above it either K, L, or M), then a single correspondence represents the most probable amount of success. In the actual result, it will be seen, there is just one correspondence, which happens to be a complete one—the letter E in the sixth place. It will not be necessary to quote other instances. Suffice it to say that the total result, of trials involving the use of 64 letters, gives 3 exact correspondences, while the expression indicating the most probable number was 2·7 ; and 7 correspondences of the other type, while the most probable number was 8. Thus even in this short set of trials, the accidental result very nearly coincided with the strict theoretic number.

We are now in a position to appreciate the results obtained when the factor of "mental suggestion" was introduced. In the first experiment made, M. Richet, standing apart both from the table and from the alphabet, selected from Littré's dictionary a line of poetry which was unknown to his friends, and asked the name of the author. The letters obtained by the process above described were J F A R D ; and there the tilting stopped. After M. Richet's friends had puzzled in vain over this answer, he informed them that the author of the line was Racine ; and juxtaposition of the letters thus—

J F A R D
J E A N R

shows that the number of complete successes was 2, which is about 10 times the fraction representing the most probable number; and that the number of successes of the type where neighbouring letters are reckoned was 3, which is about 5 times the fraction representing the most probable number. M. Richet tells us, however, that he was not actually concentrating his thought on the author's Christian name. Even so, it probably had a sub-conscious place in his mind, which might sufficiently account for its appearance. At the same time accident has of course a wider scope when there is more than one result that would be allowed as successful; and the amount of success was here not nearly striking enough to have any independent weight.

It is clearly desirable—with the view of making sure that F's mind, if any, is the operative one—not to ask a question of which the

---

[1] This procedure of counting neighbouring letters seems to require some justification. It might be justified by the difficulty, on the theory of mental suggestion, of obtaining an *exact* coincidence of time between the tilting and the pointing. But I think that M. Richet does justify it (*Rev. Phil.*, p. 654), by reference to some other experiments—not yet published, but of which he has shown us the record—where intelligible words were produced of which no one in the room was, or had been, thinking. For here also neighbouring letters appeared, but in such a way as left no room for doubt, in the reader's mind, as to what the letter should have been.

answer might possibly at some time have been within the knowledge of the sitters at the table; and in the subsequent experiments the name was silently fixed on by F. The most striking success was this:—

Name thought of: C H E V A L O N
Letters produced: C H E V A L

Here the most probable number of exact successes was 0, and the actual number was 6.

Taking the sum of eight trials, we find that the most probable number of exact successes was 2, and the actual number 14; and that the most probable number of successes of the other type was 7, and the actual number 24. It was observed, moreover, that the correspondences were much more numerous in the *earlier* letters of each set than in the later ones. The first three letters of each set were as follows—

J F A—N E F—F O Q—H E N—C H E—E P J—C H E—A L L
J E A—L E G—E S T—H I G—D I E—D O R—C H E—Z K O

Here, out of 24 trials, the most probable number of exact successes being 1, the actual number is 8; the most probable number of successes of the other type being 3, the actual number is 17. The figures become still more striking if we regard certain consecutive series in the results. Thus the probability of obtaining by chance the three consecutive correspondences in the first experiment here quoted was $\frac{1}{512}$; and that of obtaining the 6 consecutive correspondences in the C H E V A L O N experiment was about $\frac{1}{100,000,000}$.

The experiment was repeated four times in another form. A line of poetry was secretly and silently written down by the agent, with the omission of a single letter. He then asked what the omitted letter was; it was correctly produced in every one of the four trials. The probability of such a result was less than $\frac{1}{300,000}$.

And now follows a very interesting observation. In some cases, after the result was obtained, subsequent trials were made *with the same word*, which of course the agent did not reveal in the meantime; and the amount of success was sometimes markedly increased on these subsequent trials. Thus, when the name thought of was D'O R M O N T, the first three letters produced on the first trial were E P J

			second	„	E P F
„	„	„	third	„	E P S
„	„	„	fourth	„	D O R

Summing up these four trials, the most probable number of exact successes was 0, and the actual number was 3; the most probable number of successes of the other type was 1 or at most 2 ; and the actual number was 10. The probability of the 3 consecutive successes in the last trial was about $\frac{3}{10,000}$.

In respect of this name d'Ormont, there was a further very peculiar result. On the fourth trial, the letters produced in the manner described stood thus—   D O R E M I O D. Thus, if the name thought of were spelt D O R E M O N D, the approximation would be extraordinarily close, the probability of the accidental occurrence of the 5 consecutive successes being something infinitesimal.[1] Now, as long as we are merely aiming at an unassailable mathematical estimate of probabilities for each particular case, it does not seem justifiable to take *ifs* of any sort into consideration. M. Richet, who was the agent, expressly tells us that he *was* imagining the name spelt as d'Ormont ; and on the strict account, therefore, the success reached a point against which the odds, though still enormous, were decidedly less enormous than if he had been imagining the other spelling. But when we are endeavouring to form a correct view of what really takes place, it would be unintelligent not to take a somewhat wider view of the phenomena. And such a view seems to show that in those underground mental regions where M. Richet's results (if more than accidental) must have had their preparation, a mistake or a piece of independence in spelling is by no means an unusual occurrence. The records of automatism, quite apart from telepathy, afford many instances of such independence. Thus a gentleman, writing automatically, was puzzled by the mention of a friend at *Frontunac*—a place he had never heard of; weeks afterwards his own writing gave him the correct name—*Fond du Lac.* Mr. Myers' paper, above referred to, contains one case where a planchette wrote, "My name is *Norman*," presumably meaning *Norval ;* and another, witnessed by Professor Sidgwick, where the Greek letter χ was automatically written as K H, with the result that for a time the word completely puzzled the writer. And while engaged on this very point I have received a letter from Mr. Julian Hawthorne, in which he tells me that the spelling of the planchette-writing obtained through the automatism of a young child of his own was "much better than in her own letters and journals."

I will insert here an incident to which, since it occurred in connection with a person who has been detected in the production of spurious

---

[1] Moreover the E in the 4th place had appeared in two of the preceding trials and the final O D in one of them.

phenomena, I wish to attribute no evidential importance. Throughout this book care has been taken to rest our case exclusively on
phenomena and records of phenomena derived from (as we believe)
quite untainted sources; but there are two reasons which seem to me
to make the following experience worth describing. First, those who
already believe in thought-transference will feel little doubt that we
have here an instance of it, which is in itself independent of the
character and pretensions of the percipient; and this being so, they
will find, in the close parallelism that the case presents in some
points to M. Richet's experiments, an interesting confirmation of these.
And secondly, it may be useful to suggest that thought-transference
is probably the true explanation of certain results professedly
produced by "spiritualistic mediumship"; for till telepathic percipience is allowed for, as a natural human faculty, the occasional
manifestations of it in dubious circumstances are certain to be a
source of confusion and error.

On September 2, 1885, Mr. F. W. H. Myers, Dr. A. T. Myers, and
the present writer paid an impromptu visit to a professional "medium"
in a foreign town, who had no clue whatever to our names and
identity. We had decided beforehand on a name on which to concentrate our thoughts, with a view to getting it reproduced. There
was no opportunity for employing M. Richet's precautions and checks.
The "medium," her daughter, and the three visitors sat round a table
on which their hands were placed, and the present writer pointed to
the successive letters of a printed alphabet; at intervals the sound of
a rap was heard, and the letter thus indicated was written down.
Now these conditions could not have been considered adequate, had
the result been that the name in our minds was correctly given; for
though our two companions were not apparently looking at us and
not in contact with us, it might have been supposed that some
involuntary and unconscious movement on our part revealed to one of
them at what points to make the raps. But as the result turned out,
it will be seen, I think, that this objection does not apply. The name
that had been selected was John Henry Pratt. The result obtained
in the way described was ·   J O N H N Y E S R O S A T.
From the N in the fifth place to the end, Dr. Myers and myself
regarded the letters that were being given as purely fortuitous, and as
forming gibberish; and though Mr. F. W. H. Myers detected a
method in them, he was as far as we were from expecting the
successive letters before they appeared. On inspection, the method

becomes apparent. If in three places an approximation (of the sort so often met with by M. Richet) be allowed, and a contiguous letter be substituted, the complete name will be found to be given, thus :—

R   P T
J O N   H N Y E S   R O S A T

the first word being phonetically spelt, and the other two being correct anagrams. It is highly improbable that such an amount of resemblance was accidental; and it is difficult to suppose that it was due to muscular indications unconsciously given by us in accordance with an *unconscious* arrangement of the letters in our minds in phonetic and anagrammatic order. If these suppositions be excluded, the only alternative will be thought-transference—the letters whose image or sound was transferred being modified by the percipient herself, in a way which seems, from some experiments unconnected with thought-transference, to be quite within the scope of the mind's unconscious operations. [1] But in whatever way the knowledge of the letters or syllables reached the "medium's" mind, I see no reason to think that the expression of it by raps was other than a conscious act. The sounds were such as would be made by gently tapping the foot against the wooden frame of the table ; and at a subsequent trial with one of these so-called "mediums"— the daughter—I managed by very gradually advancing my own foot to receive on it first a part and ultimately the whole of the impact. The movement required to make the raps may have become semi-automatic from long habit, but can hardly have been unconscious. I may add that, out of a good many words and sentences which were spelt out in the same way at several different sittings, the case recorded was (with a single doubtful exception) the only one that contained the slightest indication of any abnormal faculty.

To return to M. Richet's experiments—a result of a different kind was the following, which is especially noteworthy as due to the agency of an idea that was itself on the verge of the unconscious. M. Richet chose a quotation at random from Littré's dictionary, and asked for the name of the author, which was Legouvé. The letters produced were J O S E P H C H D, which looked like a complete failure. But the quotation in the dictionary was adjacent to another from the works of Joseph Chénier ; and M. Richet's eye, in running over the page, had certainly encountered the latter name, which had probably retained a certain low place in his consciousness. Another

[1] For a curious case of the automatic production of anagrams, see *Proceedings* of the S.P.R., Vol. ii., pp. 226-31.

very interesting case of a result unintended by the agent, though probably due to something in his mind, was this.   The name thought of was Victor; the letters produced on three trials were

D A L E N
D A M E S
D A N D S

—seemingly complete failures. But it appeared that while the agent had been concentrating his thoughts on " Victor," the name of a friend, Danet, had spontaneously recurred to his memory.   We should, of course, be greatly extending the chances of *accidental* success, if we reckoned collocations of letters as successful on the ground of their resemblance, to any one of the names or words which may have momentarily found their way into the agent's mind while the experiment was in progress.   Here, however, the name seems to have suggested itself with considerable persistence, and the resemblance is very close.   And if the result may fairly be attributed to "mental suggestion," then, of the two names which had a certain lodgment in the agent's mind, the one intended to be effective was ineffective, and *vice versâ.*

It is a remarkable fact that in the few hitherto recorded cases of experimental telepathy, where words have been indicated by writing or by other movements on the percipient's part, the idea or word transferred seems as often as not to have been one which was not at the moment occupying the agent's consciousness ; that is to say, the influence has proceeded from some part of the agent's mind which is below the threshold of conscious attention.   (See p. 84 below, and Vol. II., pp. 670-1.)   This conception of *unconscious agency*—of an "unconscious intelligence" in the agent as well as in the percipient— will present itself again very prominently when we come to consider the cases of spontaneous telepathy.   But the experimental instances have a theoretic importance of another sort.   They seem to exhibit telepathic production of movements by what is at most an idea, and not a volition, on the agent's part.   This, indeed, is a hypothesis which seems justified even by M. Richet's less exceptional results.   For we must remember that in a sense A is throughout more immediately the agent than F ; it is what A's mind contributes, not what F's mind contributes, that produces the tilts at the right moments.[1]   But this

---

[1] When A, in pointing, began at the beginning of the alphabet, the sense of time might conceivably have led to an unconscious judgment as to the point arrived at.   This idea had occurred to M. Richet.   It seems, however, an unnecessary multiplication of hypotheses ; for we learn from him that in some trials A began at uncertain places, and

is of course through no *will* of A's ; he is ignorant of the required word, and has absolutely no opportunity of bringing his volition into play. His " agency " is of a wholly passive sort ; and his mind, as it follows the course of his pen, is a mere conduit-pipe, whereby knowledge of a certain kind obtains access to the " unconscious intelligence " which evokes the tilts. If, then, the knowledge manifests itself as impulse, can we avoid the conclusion that in this particular mode of access—in " mental suggestion " or telepathy as such—a certain *impulsive* quality is involved ? We shall encounter further signs of such an impulsive quality among the spontaneous cases.[1] (See pp. 294, 537-8.)

But of course the relation between F and the " medium " plays also a necessary part in the result ; the impulse to tilt when a particular letter is reached only takes effect when it falls (so to speak) on ground prepared by " mental suggestion " from F—on a mind in which the word imagined by him has obtained an unconscious lodgment. The unconscious part of the percipient's mind would thus be the scene of confluence of two separate telepathic streams, which proceed to combine there in an intelligent way—one proceeding from F's mind, which produces unconscious knowledge of the word, and the other proceeding from A's mind, which produces an unconscious image

that under these conditions coherent words were obtained. The fact that so often the approximate letter was given, instead of the exact one, might seem at first sight to favour the hypothesis of unconscious reckoning ; but it will be observed that exactly the same approximations took place in our own experiment (pp.77-8), where the alphabet was in the " medium's " sight.

[1] The impulse might no doubt be otherwise accounted for if we supposed that a close connection was established in F's mind between the idea of the *object*—*i.e.*, the successive letters—and the idea of the *movement*, and that this complex idea was what was transferred and what ultimately took effect. But it is hard to apply this hypothesis to cases where a word is produced which, though latent in F's mind, has no resemblance to the word whose production he is willing. The transference of the idea of the latent word, even to the exclusion of the right word, can be quite conceived ; but can we suppose that, subconsciously or unconsciously, an idea of *movement* was combined with the idea of its letters in the agent's mind, at the very moment when that on which his attention was fixed, and with which *ex hypothesi* the conscious idea of movement *was* connected, was a quite different set of letters ? Can we suppose that the idea of movement overflowed into the unconscious region of his mind, and there on its own account formed an alliance with alien elements, the effect of which on the percipient would prevent the effect intended ? It must be remembered that where a word which is not the one intended gets transferred from F to the " medium," there is no knowledge, conscious or unconscious, on F's part, as to what that word will be. A number of words are latent in his mind ; one of these finds an echo in another mind. But how should the idea of movement find out which particular one, out of all the words, is destined thus to find an echo, so as to associate itself with *its* letters and no others ? And if we suppose the association to be between the unconscious idea of movement and the unconscious idea of *letters in general*, this is no less dissimilar and opposed to anything that the conscious part of F's mind has conceived. For it is not in letters as such, but in the exclusive constituents of a particular word, that he is interested ; if indeed he is interested in anything beyond the word as a whole. The difficulty here seems to justify the suggestion—with which I imagine that M. Richet would agree—that the physiological impulse does not depend on any idea of *movement*, or any special direction of the agent's will to *that* result. This might be tested, if F were a person ignorant of the form of the experiment, and out of sight of the table.

of the successive letters.[1] Another possible supposition would be that F's thought affects, not the "medium," but A; or conversely, that A's thought affects not the "medium," but F;—that A obtains unconscious knowledge of the word, or that F obtains unconscious knowledge of the letter, and so is enabled to communicate an impulse to the "medium" at the right moment. And we should then have to suppose a secret understanding between two parts of A's or F's mind the part which takes account of the letters of the alphabet, and the part which takes account of the letters of the word—the former being conscious and the latter unconscious, or *vice versâ*, according as A or F is the party affected.

One hesitates to launch oneself on the conceptions which these experiments open up; but the only alternative would be to question the facts from an evidential point of view. So regarded, they are of an extremely simple kind; and if their genuineness be granted, we are reft once and for all from our old psychological moorings. The whole question of the psychical constitution of man is opened to its furthest depths; and our central conception—telepathy—the interest of which, even in its simpler phases, seemed almost unsurpassable, takes on an interest of a wholly unlooked-for kind. For it now appears as an all-important method or instrument for testing the mind in its hidden parts, and for measuring its unconscious operations.

§ 14. The above sketch (for it is little more) may give an idea of the chief experimental results so far obtained in the course of serious and systematic research.[2] But though the investigation may be laboriously and consecutively pursued by those who make a special study of the subject, it is one which admits also of being prosecuted in a more haphazard and sporadic manner. A group of friends may take it up for a few evenings, and then get tired of it; and it is quite possible for valuable results to be obtained without any recognition of their value. One or two specimens of these casual successes that we so

---

[1] It will be seen that the results of such "unconscious intelligence" go considerably beyond the received results of mere "unconscious cerebration." Unconscious cerebration is amply competent to produce such seemingly intelligent actions as ordinary writing; but what is now done more resembles the formation of a word by picking letters from a heap, or type-writing by a person who is unused to his instrument. The process is not one in which every item is connected by long-standing association with the one before and after it; every item is independent, and implies the recognition, at an uncertain moment, of a particular relation—that between the next letter required for the word and the same letter in its place in a quite distinct series.

[2] Some further experimental cases will be found in Chap. i. of the Supplement, and in the Additional Chapter at the end of Vol. ii.

G

frequently hear of may be worth citing, if only because the knowledge that such results are obtainable may stimulate further trials. Our own satisfaction in such fragments of evidence is often more than counterbalanced by the impossibility of getting our friends to devote time and trouble to the work.

The following case, received in September, 1885, from Mrs. Wilson, of Westal, Cheltenham, is interesting as an apparent victory of "thought-reading" over "muscle-reading." A group of five "willers" one of whom was in contact with the would-be percipient, were to concentrate their minds on the desire that the latter should sit down to the piano and strike the middle C. Had she done so, the result would have been worth little ; but this was what happened :—

"When A. I. entered blindfolded—her hand in the hand of B, held over the forehead—M. A. W. was possessed with the desire to will her, without bodily contact, to come to her and give her a kiss on the forehead, and she at once exerted (unknown to the others) all her will to achieve this object. A. I. came slowly up to M. A. W., till she stood quite close, touching her, and commenced bending down towards her, when M. A. W., thinking it was hardly fair to succeed against the other 'willers,' tried to reverse her will, and with intense effort willed A. I. to turn away and not give the intended kiss. Slowly A. I raised her head, stood a moment still, then turned in another direction towards the piano, but not near it, and sat down in an armchair. A few seconds after she said : 'I can't feel any impression now, nor any wish to do anything.' She was released from her bandage and questioned as to her feelings. 'Did you get any impression of what you had to do ? What did you feel ?' She replied : 'I had a distinct feeling that I had to go and kiss M. A. W. on the forehead ; but when I came up to someone and bent down to do it, I was sensible of a strong feeling that I was *not* to do it—and could not do it ; and after that I could get no impression whatever.'   "Mary A. Wilson.
"Alice M. W. Ingram."

The percipient in both the following cases was our friend, the Hon. Alexander Yorke. In the summer of 1884 he mentioned to two nieces, as a joke, that some one had suggested to him the possibility of discerning the contents of letters pressed to the forehead ; and this quack suggestion led by accident to an apparently genuine experiment in thought-transference.

The account is from the Misses Adeane, of 19, Ennismore Gardens, S.W.   "June, 1884.

"Taking a letter from a heap on my mother's table, I glanced at the contents, and then placed it on my uncle's head, where he held it. A minute had hardly elapsed before he said, quite quietly, 'This letter is not addressed to your mother.' He then paused, as if waiting for another impression. 'It is written to Charlie' (my brother), and another pause, 'by an uncle—not a real uncle—a sort of uncle.' Another pause, 'It must be about business.' At this point I was so much astonished that I could not help telling him how true and correct all his impressions had been, which practically put an end to the experiment by giving a clue as to what the business was, &c. My younger sister was the only other person in the room at the time. The letter was addressed to my brother at Oxford by his trustee, and uncle by marriage, and related to business ; he had forwarded it to my mother to read, and I selected it partly by chance, and partly because I thought, if there was only guessing in the case, it would have been a puzzler. My uncle, Mr. Yorke, does not know the writer of the letter or his handwriting.   "MARIE C. ADEANE.

"MAUDE ADEANE."

Again, the mother of these informants, Lady Elizabeth Biddulph, writes to us, on June 12, 1884 :—

" My girls came down to the drawing-room with my brother, Mr. Alexander Yorke, about 3.30 on Sunday afternoon, May 18th. I was sitting with one of Mr. Biddulph's brothers, and his sister, Mrs. L. They had just brought me a letter sent by mistake to 31, Eaton Place. Presently Captain and Lady Edith Adeane came in, and then my two girls began telling us of what had happened upstairs. I immediately rushed at the letter I had just received, and laughing, held it to Mr. Yorke's forehead : he objected, saying, ' I shall probably fail, and then you will only laugh at the whole thing.' He thrust my hand away, and I left the matter alone and went on talking to my relations. Presently my brother rose to go, and hesitating rather, said, ' Well, my dear, the impression about that letter is so strong that I must tell you the Duchess of St. Albans wrote it.' It *was* so. She does not correspond with me ; the letter, too, having been addressed by mistake to 31, Eaton Place, made it more unlikely there should be any clue, and its contents were purely of a business-like character.   " ELIZABETH P. BIDDULPH."

On another similar occasion, the present writer saw a letter taken up casually from a writing-table, and held to Mr. Yorke's forehead, in such a way that he could not possibly catch a glimpse of the writing. He correctly described the writer as an elderly man, formerly connected with himself, but could not name him. The writer had, in fact, been his tutor at one time. It need hardly be said that no importance is to be attributed to the holding of the letters to the forehead. In every case the writer and the contents of the letter were known to some person in the percipient's immediate vicinity, and that being so, any other hypothesis than that of thought-transference is gratuitous.

The following incident is an excellent casual illustration of the motor form of experiment to which the cases described on pp. 78-9 belonged. It presents, indeed, a point which would lead some to place it in a separate category: the names unexpectedly produced were those of *dead* persons. But where the "communication" contains nothing

G 2

beyond the content, or the possible manufacture, of the minds of the living persons present, it seems reasonable to refer it to those minds— at any rate until the power of the dead to communicate with the living be established by accumulated and irrefragable evidence.

One evening in August, 1885, some friends were assembled in a house at Rustington; and the younger members of the party suggested "table-turning" as an amusement. Three ladies—Mrs. W. B. Richmond, Mrs. Perceval Clark, and another—were seated apart from the larger group ; and a small table on which they laid their hands, and which was light enough to be easily moved by unconscious pressure, soon became lively. The alphabet being repeated, the sentence "Harriet knew me years ago," was tilted out. The name of *me* was asked for. "Kate Gardiner" was the answer. These names conveyed nothing to the three ladies at the table, but they caught the attention of a member of the other group, Mr. R. L. Morant. This gentleman was acting as holiday-tutor to Mrs. Richmond's boys, and had not before that been acquainted with any of the party; nor had Mrs. Richmond herself the slightest knowledge of his family-history. On hearing the names, he asked that "Harriet's" surname should be given. The name "Morant" was tilted out. In reply to further questions, put of course in such a way as not to suggest the answers, and while Mr. Morant remained at the further end of the room, the tilts produced the information that Harriet and Kate met at Kingstown, and that Harriet was Mr. Morant's great-aunt, his father "Robin" Morant being her nephew.

We have received in writing three independent and concordant accounts of this occurrence—from Mrs. Richmond, from the third lady at the table (who is hostile to the subject, but who was probably the unconscious percipient), and from Mr. Morant, who adds :—

"I felt distinctly and always rightly, when it would answer, and *what* it would answer. I found that it always answered the questions of which *I knew* the answer ; and was silent when I did not : *e.g.*, it would not say how many years ago [the meeting was]. I was quite ignorant of where they met ; that was the only answer beyond my knowledge. [It is not known if this answer was correct.] All the names given are correct : my father's name was Robert, but he was always called *Robin*. Kate Gardiner was a friend of my father ; I believe she helped to arrange his marriage. Harriet Morant was his aunt. I am ignorant of much about this aunt ; and from reading some old correspondence in June, I was particularly anxious to learn more about these names. No one at the table can possibly have known *anything whatever* about any one of the names given."[1]

It is, of course, a matter of interest to know what indications of genuine telepathy may be afforded by these less systematic trials. For experiments with a comparatively small number of " subjects " (like those before described), however conclusive we may consider them as to the existence of a special faculty, afford no means of judging how common that faculty may be. If it exists,

----

[1] See another very similar case in Vol. ii., pp. 670-1.

we have no reason to expect it to be extremely uncommon; on the contrary, we should rather expect to find an appreciable degree of it tolerably widely diffused. But (putting aside the results of § 7, above,) our only means, at present, for judging how far this is the case is by considering the evidence of persons who were, so to speak, amateur observers, and who in some cases were not even aware that the matter had any scientific importance. Such evidence must, of course, be received with due allowances, and, if it stood alone, might be wholly inadequate to establish the case for telepathic phenomena; but if these be otherwise established, it would be illogical to shut our eyes to alleged results which fall readily into the same class, provided the trials appear to have been conducted with intelligence and care.

It is unnecessary to say that this last proviso at once excludes the vast majority of the cases which one reads about in the newspapers, or hears discussed in private circles. We have already seen that the subject of "thought-reading" has obtained its vogue by dint of exhibitions which, however clever and interesting, have no sort of claim to the name. The prime requisite is that the conditions shall preclude the possibility of unconscious guidance; that contact between the agent and the percipient shall be avoided; or that the form of experiment shall not require movements, but the percipient shall give his notion of the transferred impression—card, number, taste, or whatever it may be—by word of mouth. That these conditions have been observed is itself an indication that experiments have been intelligently conducted; and the cases of this sort of which we have received records are at any rate numerous enough to dispel the disquieting sense that the possibility of accumulating evidence for our hypothesis depends on the transient endowment of a few most exceptional individuals. I have spoken above of the urgent importance of spreading the responsibility for the evidence as widely as possible—in other words, of largely increasing the number of persons, reputed honest and intelligent, who must be either knaves or idiots if the alleged transference of thought took place through any hitherto recognised channels. And our hopes in this direction are, of course, the better founded, in so far as the necessary material for experimentation is not of extreme rarity. If what has been here said induces a wider and more systematic search for this material, and increased perseverance in following up all indications of its existence, a very distinct step will have been taken towards the general acceptance of the facts.

CHAPTER III.

THE TRANSITION FROM EXPERIMENTAL TO SPONTANEOUS
TELEPATHY.

§ 1. IN all the cases of the action of one mind on another that were considered in the last chapter, both the parties concerned—percipient as well as agent—were consciously and voluntarily taking part in the experiment with a definite idea of certain results in view. Spontaneous telepathy, as its name implies, differs from experimental in precisely this particular—that neither agent nor percipient has consciously or voluntarily formed an idea of any result whatever. Something happens for which both alike are completely unprepared. But between these two great classes of cases there is a sort of transitional class, which is akin to each of the others in one marked feature. In this class the *agent* acts consciously and voluntarily ; he exercises a concentration of mind with a certain object, as in experimental thought-transference ; he is in this way truly experimenting.[1] But the *percipient* is not consciously or voluntarily a party to the experiment ; as in spontaneous telepathy, his mind has not been in any way adjusted to the result ; he finds himself affected in a certain manner, he knows not by what means.

In another way, also, this class of cases serves as a connecting link between the other two. For it introduces us to results produced at a much greater *distance* than any of those that have been so far described. Not that greater distance between the agent and percipient is in any way a distinguishing mark of the spontaneous, as opposed to the experimental, effects ; the former no less than the latter—as we shall see reason to think—may take place between persons in the same room. But in the large majority of the spontaneous cases that we shall have to notice, the distance was considerable. And in the transitional class we meet

---

[1] It should be observed, however, that unless he records his experiment at the time, the case will stand on a different footing from those of the last chapter.

with specimens of both kinds—effects produced in the same room, and effects produced at a distance of many miles.

§ 2. In these transitional cases—as in those of the last chapter—the effect may show itself either in ideas and sensations which the percipient describes, or in actions of a more or less automatic sort. The *motor* cases have been by far the most heard of, and are, indeed, popularly supposed to be tolerably common ; but this idea has no real foundation. The allegations of certain persons that, *e.g.*, they can make strangers in church or in a theatre turn their heads, by "willing" that they should do so, cannot be accepted as establishing even a *primâ facie* case. Till accurate records are kept, such cases must clearly be reckoned as mere illusions of *post hoc propter hoc*—of successes noted and failures forgotten. Authentic instances of the kind seem, as it happens, always to be more or less closely connected with mesmerism. And even as regards mesmeric cases where a definite action or course of action is produced by silent or distant control, the first thing to remark is that many phenomena are popularly referred to this category which have not the slightest claim to a place in it. The common platform exhibition, where a profession is made of "willing" a particular person to attend, and he rushes into the room at the appointed moment, is not to be attributed to any influence then and there exercised, but is the effect of the command or the threat impressed on his mind when in its wax-like condition of trance on a previous evening. Nor, as a rule, do the cases where "subjects" are said to be drawn by their controller from house to house, or even to a distant town, prove any specific power of his will, or anything beyond the *general* influence and attraction which he has established, and which is liable every now and then to recrudesce in his absence, and to manifest itself in this startling form.[1]

---

[1] Signs of this general mesmeric influence occur occasionally in the records of witchcraft. (See, *e.g.*, *The Discovery of Sorcery and Witchcraft practised by Jane Wenham*, London, 1712.) It would scarcely be safe to interpret in any other way such an isolated case as the following of the late Mr. H. S. Thompson's :—

"Mr. John Dundas, who was very much interested in mesmerism, was staying with me at Fairfield, about eight miles from Sutton. He one evening suggested that I should try and influence Mrs. Thornton at a distance ; this was about 9 o'clock. I tried, but only for a few minutes, never thinking I should succeed. We went over to Sutton next day, when Mr. Harland said, 'You must take care what experiments you try on Mrs. Thornton, as she has become so sensitive to you, that she not only goes to sleep when you are present, but last night after dinner she went to sleep, and rushed to the hall door, saying she must go to Fairfield, as Mr. Thompson wanted her. And we had great difficulty in waking her.' "

The incident is a striking one ; but we need to know whether Mrs. Thornton ever behaved in the manner described at times when Mr. Thompson was *not* trying to influence her.

Very much rarer are the really crucial cases where the intended effect—the origination or inhibition of a motor-impulse—is brought about at the moment by a deliberate exercise of volition. In some of the more striking instances, the inhibition has been of that specific sort which temporarily alters the whole condition of the "subject," and induces the mesmeric trance. In the *Zoist* for April, 1849, Mr. Adams, a surgeon of Lymington, writing four months after the event, describes how a guest of his own twice succeeded in mesmerising the man-servant of a common friend at a distance of nearly fifty miles, the time when the attempt was to be made having in each case been privately arranged with the man's master. On the first occasion, the unwitting "subject" fell at the time named, 7.30 p.m., into a state of profound coma not at all resembling natural sleep, from which he was with difficulty aroused. He said that "before he fell asleep he had lost the use of his legs; he had endeavoured to kick the cat away, and could not do so." On the second occasion a similar fit was induced at 9.30 a.m., when the man was in the act of walking across a meadow to feed the pigs. But the following case is more striking, as resting on the testimony of a man whose name must perforce be treated with respect. Dr. Esdaile says:—[1]

(1) "I had been looking for a blind man on whom to test the imagination theory, and one at last presented himself. This man became so susceptible that, by making him the object of my attention, I could entrance him in whatever occupation he was engaged, and at any distance within the hospital enclosure. . . . My *first attempt* to influence the blind man was made by gazing at him silently over a wall, while he was engaged in the act of eating his solitary dinner, at the distance of twenty yards. He gradually ceased to eat, and in a quarter of an hour was profoundly entranced and cataleptic. This was repeated at the most untimely hours, when he could not possibly know of my being in his neighbourhood, and always with like results."

[1] *Natural and Mesmeric Clairvoyance*, pp. 227-8. See also Mr. Cattell's case in the *Zoist*, Vol. viii., p. 143 ; where the special circumstances seem sufficiently to exclude the hypothesis of expectancy.

These examples of distant influence have a bearing on the question as to the efficacy of concentrated attention in more ordinary mesmeric processes. Elliotson asserts that his own manipulations were often successful, however mechanically and inattentively carried out ; and Bertrand (*Du Magnétisme Animal*, p. 341) makes a similar remark. Other operators have said that their passes were ineffectual, unless accompanied by distinct intention. The Rev. C. H. Townshend made this observation in an experiment with the celebrated naturalist, Agassiz, whom he was mesmerising while himself distracted by the non-arrival of some expected letters. "Although I was at the time engaged in the mesmeric processes to all appearance as actively as usual, my patient called out to me constantly and coincidently with the remission of my thought, 'You influence me no longer ; you are not exerting yourself.'" And the above cases certainly favour the view that the exercise of any specific influence will normally have a well-marked psychical side. (See also Nos. 688, 689, 690.) It is interesting to find Esdaile making the same observation as Townshend in respect even of the very definite manipulations of his Hindoo assistants, where, if anywhere, we might have assumed a purely physical and mechanical agency.

Cases of *waking* a hypnotic "subject" by the silent exercise of the will have been recorded by Reichenbach,[1] and by the Committee appointed by the French Royal Academy of Medicine to investigate "animal magnetism." In their Report, published in 1831, this Committee say that they "could entertain no doubt as to the very decided effects which magnetism produced upon the 'subject,' even without his knowledge, and at a certain distance." A more recent case will be found in Vol. II., p. 685.

§ 3. But, besides such examples of the induction of trance, the records of mesmerism contain a good many cases of the induction or inhibition of particular actions ; and where persons who appeared to be in a perfectly normal state have had their will similarly dominated, or their actions dominated against their will, it has almost always, I think, been through the agency of some person who has given indications of considerable mesmeric power. The Rev. J. Lawson Sisson, Rector of Edingthorpe, North Walsham, (whose interest in mesmerism, like that of so many others, began with the discovery of his own power to alleviate pain,) describes the following experiment as having been performed on an incredulous lady, whose first experience of his influence had been a few moments' subjection to the slightest possible hypnotic process in the course of the evening.[2]

(2) " Conversation went on on other topics, and then followed a light supper. Several of the gentlemen, myself among the number, were obliged to stand. I stood talking to a friend, against the wall, and at the back of Miss Cooke, some three or four feet off her. Her wine-glass was filled, and I made up my mind that she should not drink without my ' willing.' I kept on talking and watching her many futile attempts to get the glass to her mouth. Sometimes she got it a few inches from the level of the table, sometimes she got it a little higher, but she evidently felt that it was not for some reason to be done. At last I said, ' Miss Cooke, why don't you drink your wine ? ' and her answer was at once, ' I will when you let me.' "

The *Zoist* contains several cases of apparently the same kind ; though, unfortunately, the narrators have seldom recognised the need of making it clear that the possibility of physical indications was completely excluded. Thus Mr. Barth records of a patient of his own (Vol. VII., p. 280) :—

---

[1] *Der Sensitive Mensch* (Stuttgart, 1855), Vol. ii., pp. 665-6.

[2] For results of a still simpler type, see the record of the experiments made on M. Petit, in the Report of the French Committee above mentioned. Mr. Sisson says of one of his subjects that, when she was walking many yards in front of him, and engaged in conversation, "I could, by raising my hand and *willing* it, draw her head quite back. It fell back, neither to right nor left, as though it had been pulled by a cord."

(3) " When she wished to leave the room, I could at any time prevent her, by willing that she should stay, and this silently. I could not arrest her progress whilst she was in motion, but if she stood for a moment and I mentally said ' Stand,' she stood unable to move from the spot. If she placed her hand on the table I could affix it by my will alone, and unfix it by will. If she held a ruler or paper-knife in her closed hand, I could compel her by will alone to unclose her hand and drop the article. Frequently when she has been at the tea-table, and I quite behind and out of sight, have I locked her jaws or arrested her hand with her bread-and-butter in it, when half way betwixt her plate and her mouth."

And Mr. N. Dunscombe, J.P. (*Zoist*, Vol. IX., p. 438), narrates of himself that, having attended some mesmeric performances, he was for some time at the mercy of the operator's silent will.

(4) " He has caused me, by way of experiment, to leave my seat in one part of my house, and follow him all through it and out of it until I found him. He was not in the room with me, neither had I the slightest idea of his attempting the experiment. I felt an unaccountable desire to go in a certain direction."

Most remarkable of all are the cases of acts performed under the silent control of the late Mr. H. S. Thompson, of Moorfields, York, though here again we have to regret that the signed corroboration of the persons affected was not obtained at the time. Mr. Thompson's interest in mesmerism lay almost entirely in the opportunities which his power gave him of alleviating suffering ; and having succeeded in giving relief to a patient, it is to him a comparatively small matter to be able to say (*Zoist*, Vol. V., p. 257):—

" I have often, by the will, made her perform a series of trifling acts, though, when asked why she did them, she has answered that she did them without observing them, and had no distinct wish to do them as far as she was aware."

Some of his descriptions, however, are more explicit. He gave us permission to publish, for the first time on his authority, an account of an after-dinner incident which made much sensation in Yorkshire society when it occurred, and which even twenty years afterwards was still alluded to with bated breath, as a manifest proof of the alliance of mesmerists with the devil. The account was sent to us in November, 1883.

(5) " In 1837, I first became acquainted with mesmerism through Baron Dupotet. The first experiment I tried was upon a Mrs. Thornton, who was staying with some friends of mine, Mr. and Mrs. Charles Harland, of

Sutton. She told me that no one had ever succeeded in mesmerising her, though she soon submitted to being mesmerised by me. She went to sleep at once, and was very strongly influenced by my will. One night when I was dining with Mr. Harland, after the ladies had left the room, some gentleman proposed that I should will her to come back again, which I did. She came directly, and after this I could not go to the house without her going to sleep, even if she did not know that I was there."

In the same letter, Mr. Thompson continues :—

"I have met with many cases of thought-reading, but none so distinct as in a little girl named Crowther. She had had brain fever, which had caused a protrusion of the eyes. Of this ill effect I soon relieved her, and found that she was naturally a thought-reader. I practised on her a good deal, and at length there was no need for me to utter what I wished to say, as she always knew my thoughts. I was showing some experiments to a Dr. Simpson, and he asked me to will her to go and pick a piece of white heather out of a large vase full of flowers there was in the room, and bring it to me. She did this as quickly as if I had spoken to her. All these experiments were performed when the girl was awake, and not in a mesmeric sleep."

The next account (received in 1883) is none the less interesting that it is of a partial *failure* ; and in this case we have the advantage of the percipient's own testimony. The lady who sent it to us is a cousin of Mr. Thompson's and has had other similar experiences; but at this distance of time can only recollect the following, whose absurdity vividly impressed her mind.

(6) " I was sitting one day in the library. No one else was in the room except my cousin, Henry Thompson, who was reading at the other end of the room. Gradually I felt an unaccountable impulse stealing over me, an impulse to go up to him and kiss him. I had been in the habit of kissing him from childhood upwards at intervals, when I left the sitting-room before going to bed, or when he came to say good-bye at the termination of a visit, &c., as a matter of course, not of pleasure. In this instance the inclination to kiss him struck me as being so extraordinary and ridiculous as to make it an impossibility. I have no recollection of leaving the room, though I *may* have done so, but in the evening when he said to me at dinner, ' I tried to will you to-day and failed,' I answered at once, ' I know perfectly *when* you were willing me, and what you wanted me to do, though I did not suspect it at the time. But you were willing me to kiss you in the library, and I had the greatest inclination to do so!' 'And why would you not?' he asked, and laughed immoderately at my answering that I was so astonished at myself for feeling an inclination to kiss him that I resisted it at once. I had never been mesmerised by him, and my will was not subservient to his.

"L. F. C."

And here a word may be in place as to the relation of the *will* to telepathic experiments in general. That the will of the agent or operator is usually in active play, admits, of course, of no doubt ; but the nature and extent of its operation are sometimes misconceived. In ordinary thought-transference, it is probably effective only so far as it implies strong concentration of the agent's own attention on the sensation or image which he seeks to convey. As a rule he will naturally desire that the experiment should succeed ; but, provided only that the necessary concentration be given, there is nothing to show, or even to suggest that, if for some special reason he desired failure, his desire would ensure that result. It is somewhat different with cases like the above, where a distinct set of visible actions—as that the performer shall walk to a particular spot or select a particular object —is the thing aimed at ; in so far as there the desire is likely to be keener and more persistent. When we are picturing a series of move-ments to be performed by a person in our sight, we easily come to regard that person's physique under a half-illusion that we can direct it from moment to moment, as though it were our own ; and we are more on edge, so to speak, than when we are merely imagining (say) a word or a number, and waiting for the " subject " to name it, or write it down. But even here there is little founda-tion for the idea that the operator's will in any way *dominates* the other will, or that he succeeds by superior " strength of will " in any ordinary sense. It is still primarily an *image*, not any form of force, that is conveyed—but an image of *movement*, *i.e.*, an image whose nervous correlate in the brain is in intimate connection with motor-centres ; and the muscular effect is thus evoked while the " subject " remains a sort of spectator of his own conduct. The last example of Mr. Thompson's powers goes as near as any I know to the actual production of an effect on the *self-determining* faculty of a person in a normal state ; but even here, it will be observed, the action suggested was of a simple sort, and one which the " subject " had often voluntarily performed. And in mesmeric cases —as in the experiments on inhibition of utterance in the last chapter —where, no doubt, the self-determining faculty is often to a great extent abrogated, we must still beware of concluding that the " subject's " will is dominated and directed this way or that by a series of special jets of energy. It is rather that his instinct of choice, his free-will as a whole, has lapsed, as one of the general features of the trance-condition. It is worth noting, moreover, that in none of the cases quoted have the "willer" or the "willed" been further removed from one another than two neighbouring rooms. The liability to have definite acts compelled from a distance, which figures in romance and in popular imagination as the natural and terrible result of mesmeric influence, is precisely the result for which we can find least evidence.

We have, however, in our own collection, two first-hand instances where the distance between the agent and the percipient was greater, and where the action to be performed was of a rather more complicated sort.[1] We received the following case in 1883 from the agent, Mr. S. H. B., a friend of our own. The first part of the account was copied by us from a MS. book, in which Mr. B. has recorded this and other experiments.

(7) "On Wednesday, 26th July, 1882, at 10.30 p.m., I willed very strongly that Miss V., who was living at Clarence Road, Kew, should leave any part of that house in which she might happen to be at the time, and that she should go into her bedroom, and remove a portrait from her dressing-table.

"When I next saw her she told me that at this particular time and on this day, she felt strongly impelled to go up to her room and remove something from her dressing-table, but she was not sure which article to misplace. She did so and removed an article, but not the framed portrait which I had thought of.

"Between the time of the occurrence of this fact and that of our next meeting, I received one or two letters, in which the matter is alluded to and my questions concerning it answered.

"S. H. B."[2]

Mr. B. was himself at Southall on the evening in question. He has shown the letters of which he speaks to the present writer, and has allowed him to copy extracts.

On Thursday, July 27th, without having seen or had any communication with Mr. B., Miss Verity (now residing in Castellain Road, W., who allows the publication of her name) wrote to him as follows :—

"What were you doing between ten and eleven o'clock on Wednesday evening? If you make me so restless, I shall begin to be afraid of you. I positively *could not* stay in the dining-room, and I believe you meant me to be upstairs, and to move something on my dressing-table. I want to see if you know what it was. At any rate, I am *sure* you were thinking about me."

Mr. B. then wrote and told Miss Verity that the object he had thought of was Mr. G.'s photograph. She answered :—

"I must tell you it was not G.'s photo, but something on my table

---

[1] See Vol. ii., pp. 680-1. In case 687 the distance was about 100 yards.
[2] This entry is undated ; but Mr. B. assures us that it was written very soon after the event.

which perhaps you would never think of. However, it was really wonderful how impossible I found it to *think* or do anything until I came upstairs, and I *knew* for certain that your thoughts were *here ;* in fact, it seemed as if you were very near."

[More than a year after these letters were written, an absolutely concordant account was given *vivâ voce* to the present writer by Miss Verity, whom he believes to be a thoroughly careful and conscientious witness.]

We have a parallel instance to this on equally trustworthy authority; but the person impressed has a dread of the subject, and will not give his testimony for publication.[1]

§ 4. I now turn to the second class of transitional cases ; that where *ideas* and *sensations* unconnected with movement are excited, in a person who is not a conscious party to the experiment, by the concentrated but unexpressed will of another. And here, even more than before, I have to admit how scanty in every sense are the accounts which former observers have published.[2] Of *ideational* cases, one of the most striking, if correctly reported, is that given by the Rev. L. Lewis in the *Zoist*, Vol. V., p. 324.

"Gateacre, October, 1847.

(8) " One evening, at a friend's house, and in the presence of several spectators, E. C. was put into the sleep, when I suggested to the magnetiser [Mr. Lewis's son] that he should attempt inducing *personation*, that is, making the magnetised person assume different characters by means of the will and passes alone.

"The first individual agreed upon was myself, with whom E. C. was well acquainted, and my name was given to the magnetiser on paper. After a

---

[1] The following case, though sufficiently like the above to be worth quoting, cannot be pressed as evidence ; for there is an appreciable chance that the impulse felt was accidental. Its interest partly depends on the fact that the ladies concerned report that they have occasionally had very striking successes in the ordinary experimental thought-transference. The account was received in 1884, from the Misses Barr, of Apsley Town, East Grinstead.

"I and my sister E. had been in the habit, for some years, of trying our power of 'will' over my youngest sister H., and had succeeded so well that in the winter of 1874-5, E., being then in London, determined to test her will-power over H., who was then living in the North of Scotland. E. was very anxious to have a certain pair of shoes sent to her in time for a ball to which she was going, and there was not time enough for a letter to go to Scotland, and for the shoes to be sent by post. She therefore determined to ' will H.' to go into her room in the house in Scotland, fetch the shoes, and start them off by post.

"On the afternoon of that day H. brought the shoes into the drawing-room, where we were sitting, saying, 'I've a fixed idea that E. wants these shoes, so I am just going to send them off to her.'

"E. was delighted, yet half-surprised, to receive them on the following day.
"Lizzie M. Barr."

" I perfectly remember the above incident, and also the vague but impressed feelings which prompted my actions. My sister E. had been absent in England for some weeks, and I did not know she was going to a ball. It was a most unusual thing for me to enter her room while she was away, and I wondered at myself for doing so, and especially for opening one of her drawers.   "Harriet A. S. Barr."

[2] See however Vol. ii., pp. 334-6 and 676-8.

few passes having been made by him over E. C., she assumed rather a dictatorial tone, complaining of interruption when spoken to, as it was Saturday night, when she was busy writing. I shall draw a curtain over my other frailties, and proceed to the mention of characters well known in the world, but whom E. C. had never seen.

"The first of these was Queen Victoria. With regard to this name the company observed the same silence as before, only writing it on paper, and the magnetiser pursued the same method also with E. C. But the dignity which she very soon assumed, the lofty tone with which she asked questions, so contrary to her usual disposition, the orders she issued to the various persons of the household, and especially her conversation with Prince Albert (whose person the magnetiser had assumed),[1] her remonstrances at his staying so long from the castle contrary to her express commands, and her threats that he should not be permitted to leave again, excited instantly peals of laughter, and on reflection, the most intense astonishment.

"The name of Sir Robert Peel was then written by one of the company, and given to the magnetiser. He then magnetised her, and she soon gave unequivocal proofs of her personating the noble baronet by conversations with the Queen on the state of the country, and answering several political questions in accordance with his well-known sentiments.

"From Conservatism it was thought the best step next to take was Liberalism, and the name of Daniel O'Connell was handed to the magnetiser. Now E. C.'s replies were of a different nature, whether political or religious ; but there was one question which she answered in a peculiar manner, yet whether in unison with the views of the late celebrated ' Liberator' I know not. When the magnetiser asked her what she thought of the English Church Establishment, she replied that the ' Establishment was already on crutches, and would soon be down.'

"The last personation was that of a young lady whom E. C. had never seen or heard of, and who was then more than one hundred miles distant, but her mother and sisters were present. The same mode of secrecy was adopted in this as well as in all other instances, so that it was impossible E. C. should have been able to guess the name. The absent person was the daughter of a lady at whose house these experiments were made. When E. C. was willed to personate the proposed character, the first thing she uttered was an exclamation of surprise at finding herself suddenly at home. Being asked her name, she ridiculed the idea of such a question being put in the presence of her family, but being pressed by her magnetiser to pronounce it, and promised not to be troubled with any further questions, she ingeniously said, and with somewhat of an arch look, that it began with the third letter in the alphabet. On being told that she had not given a direct reply, she rather pettishly answered, ' Well, then, it is Clara.' *This was the fact.*

"Except in the precise order in which these cases occurred, I can vouch for their correctness, having been present when they happened.

"L. LEWIS."

---

[1] It is probably to be understood that the magnetiser assumed this part *after* his "subject" had assumed the other.

The following instance, however, has more weight with us, who know the observer, and have had ample proof of his accuracy. Mr. G. A. Smith, of 2, Elms Road, Dulwich, (who has assisted us in most of our mesmeric work,) narrated the incident to us within two months of its occurrence ; and has now supplied a written account.

(9) "One evening in September, 1882, at Brighton, I was trying some experiments with a Mrs. W., a 'subject' whom I had frequently hypnotised. I found that she could give surprisingly minute descriptions of spots which she knew—with details which her normal recollection could never have furnished.   I did not for a moment regard these descriptions as implying anything more than intensified memory, but resolved to see what would happen when she was requested to examine a place where she had *never been to*.   I therefore requested her to look into the manager's room at the Aquarium, and to tell me all about it.   Much to my surprise, she immediately began to describe the apartment with great exactness, and in perfect conformity with my own knowledge of it.   I was fairly astonished ; but it occurred to me that although my subject's memory could not be at work, my own mind might be acting on hers.   To test this, I imagined strongly that I saw a large open umbrella on the table, and in a minute or so the lady said, in great wonder : ' Well ! how odd, there's a large open umbrella on the table,' and then began to laugh.   It, therefore, seemed clear that her apparent knowledge of the room had been derived somehow from my own mental picture of it ; but I may add I was never able to produce the same effect again."

This may be fairly reckoned among transitional cases, inasmuch as the lady was quite unaware at the time that any person's influence was being brought to bear upon her.

§ 5. It will be seen that in both these last examples the agent and percipient were close together, and the latter was in the hypnotic state. And among transitional cases, we have absolutely no specimens of the deliberate transference of a perfectly unexciting idea—as of a card or a name—to a *distant* and *normal* percipient.   This may appear an unfortunate *lacuna* in the transition that I am attempting to make ; but the fact itself can hardly surprise us.   It must be remembered that in most of our experimental cases there was a true analogy to the passivity of hypnotism, in the adjustment of the percipient's mind, the sort of inward blankness and receptivity which he or she established by a deliberate effort ; that even where this was absent, the *rapport* involved in the mere sense of personal proximity to the agent probably went for something in the results ; and also that (with few exceptions) the *sort* of image to be expected was known—that the percipient realised whether it was a card, a

name, or a taste. That an impression should flash across a mind in
this state of preparation is clearly no guarantee that anything similar
will occur when the percipient is occupied with wholly different
things, while the agent is secretly concentrating his thoughts on a
card or a taste in another place. And indeed the supposed conditions
—a purely unemotional idea on the part of the would-be agent, and
a state of complete unpreparedness on the part of the person whom
it is attempted to influence—seem the most unfavourable possible :
where the percipient mind is unprepared—that is, where the condition
on one side is unfavourable—we should naturally expect that a
stronger impulsive force must be supplied from the other side. But
we have further to note that, even if the trial succeeded, the success
would be hard to establish. For to the percipient the impression
would only be a fleeting and uninteresting item in the swarm of faint
ideas that pass every minute through the mind; and as he is *ex
hypothesi* ignorant that the trial is being made, there would be
nothing to fix this particular faint item in his memory. It would
come and go unmarked, like a thousand others. And this same
possibility must be equally borne in mind in respect of *spontaneous*
telepathy. For though in most of the cases to be quoted in the
sequel, a special impulsive force will be inferred from the fact that
the agent was at the time in a state psychically or physically
abnormal, we must not be too positive that the telepathic action is
confined to the well-marked or ostensive instances on which the
proof of it has to depend. The abnormality of the agent's state,
though needed to make the coincidence striking enough to be
included in this book, may not for all that be an indispensable condition ; genuine transferences of idea, of which we can take no
account, may occur in the more ordinary conditions of life ; and the
continuity of the experimental and the spontaneous cases may thus
conceivably be complete. Meanwhile, however, a certain gap in the
evidence has to be admitted ; and there is nothing for it but to pass
on to the more extreme cases where the *senses* begin to be affected—
the percipients having been for the most part in a normal state, and
at various distances from the agents.

§ 6. The sensory cases to be found in the *Zoist* are a trifle less
fragmentary than some that I have quoted, but depend again on the
uncorroborated statement of a single observer. Mr. H. S. Thompson
(Vol. IV., p. 263) says :—

(10) "I have tried an amusing experiment two or three times very successfully. I have taken a party (without informing them of my intentions) to witness some galvanic experiments, and whilst submitting myself to continued slight galvanic shocks, have fixed my attention on some one of the party. The first time I tried this I was much amused by the person soon exclaiming, 'Well, it is very strange, but I could fancy that I feel a sensation in my hands and arms as though I were subject to the action of the battery.' I found that out of seven persons, *four* experienced similar sensations more or less. None of them showed any symptom of being affected before I directed my attention towards them. After that [*sic*] they were made acquainted with the experiment, I found their imagination sometimes supplied the place of my will, and they fancied I was experimenting upon them when I was not so. This we so often see in other cases."

Muscular and tactile hallucinations are, of course, eminently of a sort which may be produced by expectancy; and all that can be said is that Mr. Thompson seems to have been alive to this danger. I may perhaps be allowed to state of this gentleman that, as far as we are aware, (and we have questioned both a near relative of his and a bitter detractor,) it was never alleged that he was an untrustworthy witness, or prone to exaggerate his powers.

The impression in the next example seems to have been on the borderland between sensation and idea. It is given by the Rev. L. Lewis in the same paper as the account above quoted. His son had resolved to test the statement that in a mesmeric state a "subject" might, by the operator's unexpressed will, be impressed with delusions such as are usually only produced by direct suggestion.

(11) "The girl [one whom he had often hypnotised] being gone into the sleep, the first thing that occurred to him was that she should imagine herself a camphine lamp, which was then burning on the table. He wrote down the words, which were not uttered by anyone, and were handed to the company. Then, without speaking, he strongly willed that she should be a lamp, making over her head the usual magnetic passes. E. C. was in a few minutes perfectly immovable, and not a word could be elicited from her. When she had continued in this strange state for some time, he dissipated the illusion by his *will*, without awaking her, when she immediately found her tongue again, and on being asked how she had felt when she would not speak, she replied, 'Very hot, and full of naphtha.'"

The next case (contained in a letter from Mr. H. S. Thompson, to Dr. Elliotson, *Zoist*, Vol. V., p. 257,) takes us a little further, for the agent and percipient were at a considerable distance from one another; and though the experience was of a vague sort, very much more was produced than a mere idea—namely, a physical impression of the agent's presence, strong enough to be described as *felt*.

(12) " I have tried several experiments on persons not in the mesmeric state, and some who had never been mesmerised. I have repeatedly found that I have been able, by will, to suggest a series of ideas to some persons, which ideas have induced corresponding actions ; and again, by fixing my attention upon others, and thinking on some particular subject, I have often found them able most accurately to penetrate my thoughts. Neither have I observed that it was always necessary to be near them, or to be in the same room with them, to produce these effects. . . . Some months ago I was staying at a friend's house, and this subject came under discussion. Two friends had left the house the day before.[1] Neither of them, that I am aware of, had ever been in the mesmeric state ; but I knew that to some extent they had this faculty. I proposed to make trial whether I could will them to think I was coming to see them at that moment. I accordingly fixed my attention upon them for some little time. Six weeks elapsed before I saw either of them again ; and when we met I had forgotten the circumstance, but one of them soon reminded me of it by saying, 'I have something curious to tell you, and want also to know whether you have ever tried to practise your power of volition upon either of us ; for on the evening of the day I left the house where you were staying, I was sitting reading a book in the same room with Mr. ——. My attention was withdrawn from my book, and for some moments I felt as though a third person was in the room, and that feeling shortly after became connected with an idea that you were coming or even then present. This seemed so very absurd that I tried to banish the idea from my mind. I then observed that Mr. ——'s attention was also drawn from the book which he was reading, and he exclaimed, ' It is positively very ridiculous, but I could have sworn some third person was in the room, and that impression is connected with an idea of Henry Thompson.' "

§ 7. But the most pronounced cases are of course those where an actual affection of *vision* is produced. Here previous observations of an authentic sort almost wholly fail us.[2] I have no wish to extenuate the negative importance of this fact. At the same time, it must be remembered how very exceptional, probably, are the occasions on which

---

[1] It seems practically certain, from what follows, that by "the day before " Mr. Thompson meant " earlier in the day." Otherwise the case would have had no relation to what he is speaking of.

[2] It is hardly necessary to say that we cannot reckon in this class hallucinations, even though dependent on the special influence of another person, where no definite exercise of will has been exerted by that person at the time. For instance, the following case of Mr. H. S. Thompson's may (in default of more precise detail) be ascribed to faith and imagination on the part of the " subject."

"Mr. Harland's wife had been ill for three years, said to be heart-disease, with spasms of the heart, and neuralgic pains in head and spine. A few passes removed the pains, and in the course of a few days she gained so much strength that she walked round the garden, which she had not done for three years. In a few days she was able to walk to a friend's house two miles off ; she became very sensitive and slept well. I frequently put her to sleep at night, but when I did not go to her house I always used to *will* her to go to sleep, and when I asked if she had had a good night, she used to say, ' I always have a good night when you mesmerise me,' and when I said, ' I was not here last night,' she answered, ' Oh, yes, but you were, I heard you come up stairs after I had gone to bed, and knock at my door. I said, " Come in," but you would not speak to me, and walked up to me, and held your hand over my head, saying, " Sleep," and I did sleep, and had a very good night ; you surely were in the house, for I saw you as plainly as I do now.' "

the experiment has been attempted. When the two persons concerned in a " willing " experiment have been together, the object, as a rule, has been to produce the effect which shall present the most obvious test for spectators or for the agent himself—namely, *motor* effects. And when some one of the few persons who possess an appreciable degree of the abnormal power has attempted to exercise it at a distance, it is still the production of *actions* that he would most naturally aim at ; for it is in this direction that such a power has been popularly expected to show itself. Thus it is reasonable to conclude that deliberate attempts to produce a visual hallucination in another person, by the exercise of the will, have been very few and far between. Still this is, of course, no complete explanation of the rarity of the phenomenon ; for no definable line separates these rare attempts from the ordinary experiments in thought-transference, when the agent concentrates his attention on a visible object. In those experiments there is, so to speak, an opportunity for a visual hallucination, if the agent is able to produce one. But the percipient has never (as far as I know) received more than a vivid idea, or at most a picture of the object in the mind's eye. And this fact sufficiently indicates that the more pronounced sensory result is one requiring most special conditions—one which would remain extremely rare however much it were sought for, and the proof of which will rightly be regarded with all the more jealous scrutiny.

The previous records of the phenomenon to which I can point are really only four in number;[1] and these are so far from conclusive, that they would hardly even be worth mentioning, if stronger examples could not be added from our own collection. The first case is thus meagrely described by Dr. Elliotson (*Zoist,* Vol. VIII., p. 69) :—

" I have a friend, who can, by his will, make certain patients think of any others he chooses, and fancy he sees those persons : he silently thinking of certain persons, the brain of the patient sympathises with his brain. Nay, by silently willing that these persons shall say and do certain

---

[1] We cannot, of course, recognise as even on the threshold of evidence the following remote and third-hand case from *A Treatise on the Second-Sight,* &c., by "Theophilus Insulanus " (Edinburgh, 1763), p. 40. But it is curious enough to be worth quoting, the imperfection of the alleged transference being very parallel to what has been already observed in some of our own experiments.

" The said ensign [viz., Ensign Donald Macleod], a person of candour, who lived then at Laoran, informed me that, having gone with his wife to visit his father-in-law in the Isle of Skye, night coming on, they were obliged to put up with a cave on the side of Lough Urn, to pass the night ; and as they were at supper, his wife took a cabbock of cheese in her hand, and, having covered it with three or four apples, wished it in a seer's hand, who lived with her father, and who, that night, by her second-sight, saw the gentlewoman offering her a cabbock of cheese, but was at a loss to know what the round things were that covered it, as, perhaps, she had seen none of the kind in her lifetime, until her master's daughter, upon her arrival, told her the whole."

things which he chooses, he makes the patients believe they see these imaginary appearances doing and uttering those very things."

That a man of indisputable ability should have thought such a statement of such a fact adequate is truly extraordinary. The same may be said of the following sentence of Dr. Charpignon's *Physiologie du Magnétisme,* (Paris, 1848,) p. 325:—

"Nous avons maintes fois formé dans notre pensée des images fictives, et les somnambules que nous questionnions voyaient ces images comme des réalités."

Even if these descriptions be accurate in the main, we are unable to judge how far the vision was really *externalised* by the patients. In the next case this point is clear; but the distinct assurance is still lacking that the agent was on his guard against the slightest approach to a suggestive movement. The incident is cited in the *Annales Médico-Psychologiques,* 6th series, Vol. V., p. 379, by Dr. Dagonet, doctor at the Saint Anne Asylum.

"Un interne [house-physician] lui dit: 'Regardez donc, Didier, voilà une jolie femme.' Il n'y avait personne. Didier reprit: 'Mais non, elle est laide,' et il ajoute: 'Qu'a-t-elle dans les bras?' Ces questions se rapportaient exactement à ce que pensait son interlocuteur. A un certain moment Didier se précipita même pour empêcher de tomber l'enfant qu'il croyait voir dans les bras de la femme imaginaire dont on lui parlait."

This is a specimen of the stray indications of thought-transference that may be found even in strictly scientific literature; but the significance of the phenomenon seems to have been altogether missed. It is described among a number of observations of an ordinary kind, made on an habitual somnambulist, and as though it were quite on a par with the rest.

The next account, though, like Dr. Charpignon's, first-hand from the agent, is more remote, and equally uncorroborated. It is to be found in an article by Councillor H. M. Wesermann, in the *Archiv für den Thierischen Magnetismus,* Vol. VI., pp. 136-9; and is dated Düsseldorf, June 15th, 1819. The first four items in the list are impressions alleged to have been made on a sleeping percipient but the fifth is a waking and completely externalised hallucination.

"*First Experiment at a Distance of Five Miles.*—I endeavoured to acquaint my friend, the Hofkammerrath G. (whom I had not seen, with whom I had not spoken, and to whom I had not written, for thirteen years), with the fact of my intended visit, by presenting my form to him in his sleep, through the force of my will. When I unexpectedly went to him on the following evening, he evinced his astonishment at having seen me in a dream on the preceding night.

"*Second Experiment at a Distance of Three Miles.*—Madame W., in her sleep, was to hear a conversation between me and two other persons, relating to a certain secret ; and when I visited her on the third day she told me all that had been said, and showed her astonishment at this remarkable dream.

"*Third Experiment at a Distance of One Mile.*—An aged person in G. was to see in a dream the funeral procession of my deceased friend S., and when I visited her on the next day her first words were that she had in her sleep seen a funeral procession, and on inquiry had learned that I was the corpse. Here then was a slight error.

"*Fourth Experiment at a Distance of One-Eighth of a Mile.*—Herr Doctor B. desired a trial to convince him, whereupon I represented to him a nocturnal street-brawl. He saw it in a dream, to his great astonishment. [This means, presumably, that he was astonished when he found that the actual subject of his dream was what Wesermann had been endeavouring to impress on him.]

"*Fifth Experiment at a Distance of Nine Miles.*—The intention was that Lieutenant N. should see in a dream, at 11 o'clock p.m., a lady who had been five years dead, who was to incite him to a good action. Herr N., however, contrary to expectation, had not gone to sleep by 11 o'clock, but was conversing with his friend S. on the French campaign. Suddenly the door of the chamber opens ; the lady, dressed in white, with black kerchief and bare head, walks in, salutes S. thrice with her hand in a friendly way, turns to N., nods to him, and then returns through the door. Both follow quickly, and call the sentinel at the entrance ; but all had vanished, and nothing was to be found. Some months afterwards, Herr S. informed me by letter that the chamber door used to creak when opened, but did not do so when the lady opened it—whence it is to be inferred that the opening of the door was only a dream-picture, like all the rest of the apparition." [1]

To such a record, if it stood alone, we should attach very little importance, in default of any evidence as to the intellectual and moral trustworthiness of Wesermann. There is, fortunately, no necessity for dwelling on these cases, as the possibility of the alleged phenomenon will certainly not be admitted except on the strength of *contemporary* and *corroborated* instances.

§ 8. In the examples that I am about to quote, one grave defect must at once be admitted. Though in all of them testimony is given by both agent and percipient, the agent in every case, and the percipient in one, withhold their names from publication. We, of course, regret this restriction exceedingly ; but it can hardly be deemed unnatural or unreasonable. It must be remembered that

---

[1] Other cases of the hallucination of a door opening or shutting are Nos. 15, 30, 190, 198, 495, 530, 537, 591, 659, 670, 676, 696, 698. In Nasse's *Zeitschrift für Psychische Aertze* (Leipzig) for 1820, Part IV., pp. 757-67, Wesermann again describes the first and fifth of these experiments, and states that the trials were made in the autumn of 1808.

these cases of apparitions intentionally produced stand in a most peculiar position, as compared even with the other remarkable incidents with which we are concerned in the present work. In the case of the more normal telepathic phantasm, neither party is in the least responsible for what occurs. A dies or breaks his leg; B thinks that he sees A's form or hears his voice : neither can help it; if their experiences coincide, that is not their business ; perhaps it is a chance. But in the present class of cases, the agent *determines* to do something that to most of his educated fellow-creatures will appear a miracle ; and however little he himself may share that view, he may still have good grounds for shrinking from the reputation either of a miracle-worker or of a miracle-monger. The percipient's position is somewhat different ; but modern miracles are by no means tempting things to get publicly mixed up with, even for a person whose share in them has been passive. And the extreme rarity of the phenomenon is another daunting fact. For a single specimen of this deliberate type of phantasm, we have a hundred specimens of the wholly spontaneous type : and the witness who is willing to give his name for publication, where he is assured that he will find himself in numerous and respectable company, may fairly hesitate when aware that the incident he records is almost unexampled.

However, it may be hoped that this difficulty, like others, will gradually be removed by a modification of public opinion on the whole subject. Meanwhile, I can but give the evidence under the conditions imposed. In the first case, the agent is slightly known to us. The percipient is our friend, the Rev. W. Stainton Moses, who believes that he has kept a written memorandum of the incident, but has been prevented by a long illness, and by pressure of work, from hunting for it among a large mass of stored-away papers. The agent's account was written in February, 1879, and includes a few purely verbal alterations made in 1883, when Mr. Moses pronounced it correct.

(13) "One evening early last year, I resolved to try to appear to Z, at some miles distance. I did not inform him beforehand of the intended experiment; but retired to rest shortly before midnight with thoughts intently fixed on Z, with whose room and surroundings, however, I was quite unacquainted. I soon fell asleep, and awoke next morning unconscious of anything having taken place. On seeing Z a few days afterwards, I inquired, 'Did anything happen at your rooms on Saturday night?' 'Yes,' replied he, 'a great deal happened. I had been sitting over the fire with M, smoking and chatting. About 12.30 he rose to leave, and I let him out myself. I returned to the fire to finish

my pipe, when I saw you sitting in the chair just vacated by him. I looked intently at you, and then took up a newspaper to assure myself I was not dreaming, but on laying it down I saw you still there. While I gazed without speaking, you faded away. Though I imagined you must be fast asleep in bed at that hour, yet you appeared dressed in your ordinary garments, such as you usually wear every day.' 'Then my experiment seems to have succeeded,' said I. 'The next time I come, ask me what I want, as I had fixed on my mind certain questions I intended to ask you, but I was probably waiting for an invitation to speak.'

"A few weeks later the experiment was repeated with equal success, I, as before, not informing Z when it was made. On this occasion he not only questioned me on the subject which was at that time under very warm discussion between us, but detained me by the exercise of his will some time after I had intimated a desire to leave.[1] This fact, when it came to be communicated to me, seemed to account for the violent and somewhat peculiar headache which marked the morning following the experiment; at least I remarked at the time that there was no apparent cause for the unusual headache; and, as on the former occasion, no recollection remained of the event, or seeming event, of the preceding night."

Mr. Moses writes :—   "21, Birchington Road, N.W.
                                "September 27th, 1885.

"This account is, as far as my memory serves, exact; and, without notes before me, I cannot supplement it.   "W. STAINTON MOSES."

Mr. Moses tells us that he has never on any other occasion seen the figure of a living person in a place where it was not.

The next case, otherwise similar, was more remarkable in that there were two percipients. The narrative has been copied by the present writer from a MS. book of Mr. S. H. B.'s, to which he transferred it from an almanack diary, since lost.

(14) "On a certain Sunday evening in November, 1881, having been reading of the great power which the human will is capable of exercising, I determined with the whole force of my being that I would be present in spirit in the front bedroom on the second floor of a house situated at 22, Hogarth Road, Kensington, in which room slept two ladies of my acquaintance, viz., Miss L. S. V. and Miss E. C. V., aged respectively 25 and 11 years. I was living at this time at 23, Kildare Gardens, a distance of about 3 miles from Hogarth Road, and I had not mentioned in any way my intention of trying this experiment to either of the above ladies, for the simple reason that it was only on retiring to rest upon this Sunday night that I made up my mind to do so. The time at which I determined I would be there was 1 o'clock in the morning, and I also had a strong intention of making my presence perceptible.

---

[1] As regards the interchange of remarks with a hallucinatory figure, see below, p. 476, and Vol. ii., p. 460. But it is possible, of course, that this detail as to the prolonging of the interview has become magnified in memory; or that the second vision partook more of the nature of a dream than the first.

" On the following Thursday I went to see the ladies in question, and, in the course of conversation (without any allusion to the subject on my part), the elder one told me, that, on the previous Sunday night, she had been much terrified by perceiving me standing by her bedside, and that she screamed when the apparition advanced towards her, and awoke her little sister, who saw me also.

" I asked her if she was awake at the time, and she replied most decidedly in the affirmative, and upon my inquiring the time of the occurrence, she replied, about 1 o'clock in the morning.

" This lady, at my request, wrote down a statement of the event and signed it.

" This was the first occasion upon which I tried an experiment of this kind, and its complete success startled me very much.

" Besides exercising my power of volition very strongly, I put forth an effort which I cannot find words to describe. I was conscious of a mysterious influence of some sort permeating in my body, and had a distinct impression that I was exercising some force with which I had been hitherto unacquainted, but which I can now at certain times set in motion at will.   " S. H. B."

[Of the original entry in the almanack diary, Mr. B. says : " I recollect having made it within a week or so of the occurrence of the experiment, and whilst it was perfectly fresh in my memory."]

Miss Verity's account is as follows :—

                                        "January 18th, 1883.

" On a certain Sunday evening, about twelve months since, at our house in Hogarth Road, Kensington, I distinctly saw Mr. B. in my room, about 1 o'clock. I was perfectly awake and was much terrified. I awoke my sister by screaming, and she saw the apparition herself. Three days after, when I saw Mr. B., I told him what had happened ; but it was some time before I could recover from the shock I had received, and the remembrance is too vivid to be ever erased from my memory.

                                        " L. S. VERITY."

In answer to inquiries, Miss Verity adds :—

" I had never had any hallucination of the senses of any sort whatever."

Miss E. C. Verity says :—

" I remember the occurrence of the event described by my sister in the annexed paragraph, and her description is quite correct. I saw the apparition which she saw, at the same time and under the same circumstances.

                                        " E. C. VERITY."

Miss A. S. Verity says :—

" I remember quite clearly the evening my eldest sister awoke me by calling to me from an adjoining room ; and upon my going to her bedside, where she slept with my youngest sister, they both told me they had seen S. H. B. standing in the room. The time was about 1 o'clock. S. H. B. was in evening dress, they told me.[1]   " A. S. VERITY."

---

[1] Mr. B. does not remember how he was dressed on the night of the occurrence.

[Miss E. C. Verity was asleep when her sister caught sight of the figure, and was awoke by her sister's exclaiming, " There is S." The name had therefore met her ear before she herself saw the figure ; and the hallucination on her part might thus be attributed to suggestion. But it is against this view that she has never had any other hallucination, and cannot therefore be considered as predisposed to such experiences. The sisters are both equally certain that the figure was in evening dress, and that it stood in one particular spot in the room. The gas was burning low, and the phantasmal figure was seen with far more clearness than a real figure would have been.

The witnesses have been very carefully cross-examined by the present writer. There is not the slightest doubt that their mention of the occurrence to S. H. B. was spontaneous. They had not at first intended to mention it ; but when they saw him, their sense of its oddness overcame their resolution. I have already said that I regard Miss Verity as a careful and conscientious witness ; I may add that she has no love of marvels, and has a considerable dread and dislike of this particular form of marvel.]

The next case of Mr. S. H. B.'s is different in this respect, that the percipient was not consciously present to the agent's mind on the night that he made his attempt. The account is copied from the MS. book mentioned above.

(15) " On Friday, December 1st, 1882, at 9.30 p.m., I went into a room alone and sat by the fireside, and endeavoured so strongly to fix my mind upon the interior of a house at Kew (viz., Clarence Road), in which resided Miss V. and her two sisters, that I seemed to be actually in the house. During this experiment I must have fallen into a mesmeric sleep, for although I was conscious I could not move my limbs. I did not seem to have lost the power of moving them, but I could not make the effort to do so, and my hands, which lay loosely on my knees, about 6 inches apart, felt involuntarily drawn together and seemed to meet, although I was conscious that they did not move.

" At 10 p.m. I regained my normal state by an effort of the will, and then took a pencil and wrote down on a sheet of note-paper the foregoing statements.

" When I went to bed on this same night, I determined that I would be in the front bedroom of the above-mentioned house at 12 p.m., and remain there until I had made my spiritual presence perceptible to the inmates of that room.

" On the next day, Saturday, I went to Kew to spend the evening, and met there a married sister of Miss V. (viz., Mrs. L.) This lady I had only met once before, and then it was at a ball two years previous to the above date. We were both in fancy dress at the time, and as we did not exchange more than half-a-dozen words, this lady would naturally have lost any vivid recollection of my appearance, even if she had remarked it.

" In the course of conversation (although I did not think for a moment of asking her any questions on such a subject), she told me that on the previous night she had seen me distinctly upon two occasions. She had spent the night at Clarence Road, and had slept in the front bedroom. At about half-past 9 she had seen me in the passage, going from one room to another, and at 12 p.m., when she was wide awake, she had seen me enter the bedroom and walk round to where she was sleeping, and take her hair (which is very long) into my hand. She also told me that the apparition took hold of her hand and gazed intently into it, whereupon she spoke, saying, ' You need not look at the lines, for I have never had any trouble.' She then awoke her sister, Miss V., who was sleeping with her, and told her about it. After hearing this account, I took the statement which I had written down on the previous evening, from my pocket, and showed it to some of the persons present, who were much astonished although incredulous.

" I asked Mrs. L. if she was not dreaming at the time of the latter experience, but this she stoutly denied, and stated that she had forgotten what I was like, but seeing me so distinctly she recognised me at once.

" Mrs. L. is a lady of highly imaginative temperament, and told me that she had been subject, since childhood, to psychological fancies,[1] &c., but the wonderful coincidence of the time (which was exact) convinced me that what she told me was more than a flight of the imagination. At my request she wrote a brief account of her impressions and signed it.

"S. H. B."

[Mr. B. was at Southall when he made this trial. He tells me that the above account was written down about ten days after the experiment, and that it embodies the entry made in his rough diary on the night of the trial.]

The following is the lady's statement, which was forwarded to Mr. B., he tells us, " within a few weeks of the occurrence."

" 8, Wordsworth Road, Harrow.

"On Friday, December 1st, 1882, I was on a visit to my sister, 21, Clarence Road, Kew, and about 9.30 p.m. I was going from my bedroom to get some water from the bathroom, when I distinctly saw Mr. S. B., whom I had only seen once before, about two years ago, walk before me past the bathroom, towards the bedroom at the end of the landing. About 11 o'clock we retired for the night, and about 12 o'clock I was still awake, and the door opened[2] and Mr. S. B. came into the room and walked round to the bedside, and there stood with one foot on the ground and the other knee resting on a chair. He then took my hair into his hand, after which he took my hand in his, and looked very intently into the palm. ' Ah,' I said (speaking to him), ' you need not look at the lines, for I never had any trouble.' I then awoke my sister ; I was not nervous, but excited, and began to fear some serious illness would befall her, she being delicate at the time, but she is progressing more favourably now.

" H. L." [Full name signed.]

---

[1] Asked to explain this phrase, Mr. B. says : " I have never heard of Mrs. L. having had any *hallucinations.* The fancies I alluded to were simply a few phenomena accounted for on the ground of ' telepathic ' *rapport* between herself and Mr. L., such as having a distinct impression that he was coming home unexpectedly (whilst absent in the North of England), and finding on several occasions that the impressions were quite correct."

[2] See p. 102, note.

Miss Verity corroborates as follows :—

" I can remember quite well Mrs. L.'s mentioning her two visions—one at 9.30 and one at 12—at the time, and before S. H. B. came. *When he came*, my sister told him, and immediately he took a card (or paper, I forget which) out of his pocket, containing an account of the previous evening. I consider this testimony quite as good as if Mrs. L. were giving it, because I can recall *so well* these two days.

" My sister has told me that she never experienced any hallucination of the senses except on this occasion.   " L. S. VERITY."

The present writer requested Mr. B. to send him a note on the night that he intended to make his next experiment of the kind, and received the following note by the first post on Monday, March 24th, 1884.

                                                            " March 22nd, 1884.

(16) " DEAR MR. GURNEY,—I am going to try the experiment to-night of making my presence perceptible at 44, Norland Square, at 12 p.m.   I will let you know the result in a few days.—Yours very sincerely,

                                                                   " S. H. B."

The next letter was received in the course of the following week :—

                                                            " April 3rd, 1884.

" DEAR MR. GURNEY,—I have a strange statement to show you, re-specting my experiment, which was tried at your suggestion, and under the test conditions which you imposed.

" Having quite forgotten which night it was on which I attempted the projection, I cannot say whether the result is a brilliant success, or only a slight one, until I see the letter which I posted you on the evening of the experiment.

" Having sent you that letter, I did not deem it necessary to make a note in my diary, and consequently have let the exact date slip my memory.

" If the dates correspond, the success is complete in every detail, and I have an account signed and witnessed to show you.

" I saw the lady (who was the subject) for the first time last night, since the experiment, and she made a voluntary statement to me, which I wrote down at her dictation, and to which she has attached her sig-nature. The date and time of the apparition are specified in this statement, and it will be for you to decide whether they are identical with those given in my letter to you. I have completely forgotten, but yet I fancy that they are the same.   " S. H. B."

This is the statement :—

                                                      " 44, Norland Square, W.

" On Saturday night, March 22nd, 1884, at about midnight, I had a distinct impression that Mr. S. H. B. was present in my room, and I distinctly saw him whilst I was quite widely awake. He came towards me, and stroked my hair.   I *voluntarily* gave him this information, when he called to see me on Wednesday, April 2nd, telling him the time and the circumstances of the apparition, without any suggestion on his part. The appearance in my room was most vivid, and quite unmistakeable.

"L. S. VERITY."

Miss A. S. Verity corroborates as follows :—

"I remember my sister telling me that she had seen S. H. B., and that he had touched her hair, *before* he came to see us on April 2nd.

"A. S. V."

Mr. B.'s own account is as follows :—

"On Saturday, March 22nd, I determined to make my presence perceptible to Miss V., at 44, Norland Square, Notting Hill, at 12 midnight, and as I had previously arranged with Mr. Gurney that I should post him a letter on the evening on which I tried my next experiment (stating the time and other particulars), I sent a note to acquaint him with the above facts.

"About ten days afterwards I called upon Miss V., and she voluntarily told me, that on March 22nd, at 12 o'clock midnight, she had seen me so vividly in her room (whilst widely awake) that her nerves had been much shaken, and she had been obliged to send for a doctor in the morning.

"S. H. B."

[Unfortunately Mr. B.'s intention to produce the impression of touching the percipient's hair is not included in his written account. On August 21st, 1885, he wrote to me, "I remember that I had this intention;" and I myself remember that, very soon after the occurrence, he mentioned this as one of the points which made the success "complete in every detail"; and that I recommended him in any future trial to endeavour instead to produce the impression of some spoken phrase.]

It will be observed that in all these instances the conditions were the same—the agent concentrating his thoughts on the object in view before going to sleep. Mr. B. has never succeeded in producing a similar effect when he has been awake. And this restriction as to time has made it difficult to devise a plan by which the phenomenon could be tested by independent observers, one of whom might arrange to be in the company of the agent at a given time, and the other in that of the percipient. Nor is it easy to press for repetitions of the experiment, which is not an agreeable one to the percipient, and is followed by a considerable amount of nervous prostration. Moreover, if trials were frequently made with the same percipient, the value of success would diminish ; for any latent expectation on the percipient's part might be argued to be itself productive of the delusion, and the coincidence with the agent's resolve might be explained as accidental. We have, of course, requested Mr. B. to try to produce the effect on ourselves ; but though he has more than once made the attempt, it has not succeeded. We can therefore only wait, in the hope that time will bring fresh opportunities, and that other persons may be

induced to make the trial.[1] I am strongly sensible of the natural
repulsion which descriptions of such isolated marvels are likely to
produce in most educated minds, and the more so when the details are
of a slightly ludicrous kind. But the evidence to the facts is of such
a quality that it could not have been suppressed without doing grave
injustice to the case for telepathy.[2]

§ 9. But even a reader who can sufficiently rely on our knowledge
of the witnesses to feel that the evidence is important, may find an
objection of another kind. He may question our right to make
any *theoretic connection* between the experimental results before
discussed and these last-described cases. I have called the phenomena of the present chapter *transitional,* and have pointed out
the way in which they form a bridge from the experimental thought-
transference of the last chapter to the spontaneous telepathy that
will occupy us for the future. But it may seem that the line of
connection is after all only an external one ; and that there is a deep
essential difference—a gulf which cannot be thus lightly crossed—
between the more ordinary facts of thought-transference and these
apparitions of the agent. It is not only that in the latter the
percipient's impression has been of an external object—of something
not merely flashed on the mind, but independently located in space :

[1] Since this was written two further cases have been received—Nos. 685 and 686 in
the Additional Chapter at the end of Vol. ii.

[2] It is, of course, of prime importance in cases of this sort to obtain the direct testimony
of *both* the parties concerned. Partly for the lack of this, and partly because the percipient
had received an intimation (though a considerable time before) that the experiment was
some day to be tried, I do not lay stress on the following example. At the same time it
is worth quoting, as I believe the narrator (who is personally known to me) to be a careful,
as he is certainly an honest, witness. Mr. John Moule, of Codicote, Welwyn, Herts,
after describing how, as a young man, he had considerable success as a mesmerist, adds :—
"In the year 1855, I felt very anxious to try and affect the most sensitive of my
mesmeric subjects away from my house, and unknown to them. I chose for this purpose
a young lady, a Miss Drasey, and stated that some day I intended to visit her wherever
she might be, although the place might be unknown to me; and told her, if anything
particular should occur, to note the time, and when she called at my house again, to state
if anything had occurred. One day about two months after (I not having seen her in the
interval) I was by myself in my chemical factory, Redman's Row, Mile End, London, all
alone, and I determined to try the experiment, the lady being in Dalston, about three
miles off. I stood up, raised my hands, and willed to act upon the lady. I soon felt that
I had expended energy. I immediately sat down in a chair, and went to sleep. I then saw
in a dream, my friend coming down the kitchen stairs, where I dreamt I was. She saw
me, and suddenly exclaimed, 'Oh ! Mr. Moule,' and fainted away. This I dreamt, and
then awoke. I thought very little about it, supposing I had had an ordinary dream ; but
about three weeks after she came to my house, and related to my wife the singular occurrence of her seeing me sitting in the kitchen, where she then was, and that she fainted
away, and nearly dropped some dishes she had in her hands. All this I saw exactly in
my dream, so that I described the kitchen furniture, and where I sat, as perfectly as if I
had been there, though I had never been in the house. I gave many details, and she said,
'It is just as if you had been there.' After this, she made me promise that I would never
do it again, as she would never feel happy with the idea of me appearing to her. Some
time after this, she left this country for Australia, and died a few years afterwards."
    If this record is accurate, the case differs from those given in the text, inasmuch as
the effect was *reciprocal,* the agent himself being telepathically impressed. *Cf.* case 685.

that might be a mere question of degree. The more radical difference is this—that what the one party perceived was not that on which the mind of the other party had been concentrated. In a " thought-transference " experiment of the normal type, the percipient's image or idea of a card or diagram is due (as we hold) to the fact that the agent has been directing his attention to that very image or idea. But in the case of these will-produced phantasms, the agent has not been picturing his own visible aspect. So far as he has been thinking of himself at all, it has been not of his aspect particularly, but of his personality, and of his personality in relation to the percipient. It is thus probable that the *percipient's* aspect has formed a larger part of the agent's whole idea than his own ; yet it is *his* aspect, and nothing else, that is telepathically perceived. And a similar departure from the normal experimental type will meet us again in the large majority of the *spontaneous* telepathic cases. In some of these, the content of the agent's mind, at the time when the percipient received some sensory impression of him, has been a forcible idea of the percipient, and of himself in relation to the percipient ; in others, we shall find that even this bond was lacking, and that the percipient's impression cannot be even loosely identified with any part of the conscious contents of the agent's mind.

These facts have, no doubt, a very real theoretic importance : they reveal a certain incompleteness in the transition which I have been endeavouring to make. As long as the impression in the percipient's mind is merely a reproduction of that in the agent's mind, it is possible to conceive some sort of *physical* basis for the fact of the transference. The familiar phenomena of the transmission and reception of vibratory energy are ready to hand as analogies—the effect, for instance, of a swinging pendulum on another of equal length attached to the same solid support; or of one tuning-fork or string on another of the same pitch ; or of glowing particles of a gas on cool molecules of the same substance. Still more tempting are the analogies of magnetic and electrical induction. A permanent magnet brought into a room will throw any surrounding iron into a similar condition ; an electric current in one coil of wire will induce a current in a neighbouring coil; though here even the medium of communication is unknown. So it is possible to conceive that vibration-waves, or nervous induction, are a means whereby activity in one brain may evoke a kindred activity in another—with, of course, a similar correspondence of psychical impressions. Even here, perhaps, the conception should rather be regarded as a metaphor than an analogy. We have only to remember that the effect of all the known physical forces diminishes with distance—whereas we shall find reason to think that, under appropriate conditions, an idea may be telepathically reproduced on the other side of the world as easily as on the other side of a room. The employment, therefore, of words like *force*, *impulse*, *impact*, in speaking of telepathic influences, must not be held to imply the faintest suspicion of what the force is, or any hypothesis whatever which would co-ordinate it with the recognised forces of the material world. Not only, as with other delicate phenomena of life and thought, is the *subjective* side of the problem the only one that we can yet attempt to analyse : we do not even know where to look for the *objective* side. If there really is a physical counterpart to the *fact* of transmission— over and above the movements in the two brains which are the *termini* of the transmission—that counterpart remains wholly unknown to us.

But a much more serious difficulty in the way of any physical conception of telepathy presents itself as soon as we pass to the cases where the image actually present in the agent's mind is no longer reproduced in the percipient's. A is dying at a distance ; B sees his form. We may perhaps trace a relation between the processes in their two minds ; but it certainly does not amount to anything like identity or distinct parallelism. That being so, there can be no such simple and immediate concordance as we have supposed, between the nervous vibrations of their two brains ; and that being so, there is no obvious means of translating into physical terms the causal connection between their experiences. This difficulty will take a somewhat different aspect when we come later to consider the part which the mind's *unconscious* operations may bear in telepathic phenomena. We may see grounds for thinking that a considerable community of experience (especially in emotional relations) between two persons may involve nervous records sufficiently similar to retain for one another some sort of revivable affinity, even when the experience has long lost its vividness for conscious memory. Meanwhile it is best to admit the difficulty without reserve, and to state in the most explicit way that in the *rapprochement* between experimental thought-transference and spontaneous telepathic impressions we are confining ourselves to the *psychical* aspect ; we connect the phenomena as being in all cases affections of one mind by another, occurring otherwise than through the recognised channels of sense. The objector may urge that if we have not, we ought to have, a *physical* theory which will embrace all the phenomena—that we ought not to talk about a *rapport* between A's mind and B's unless we can establish a *bridge* between their two brains. This seems rather to assume that the standing puzzle of the relation between cerebral and psychical events *in the individual*, B, can only be stated in one crude form—viz., that the former are prior and *produce* the latter; and though for ordinary purposes such an expression is convenient, the convenience has its dangers. Still, as the converse proposition—that the psychical events are ' the prior—would be equally dangerous, a *crux* remains which we cannot evade. Since we cannot doubt that B's unwonted experience has its appropriate cerebral correlate, we have to admit that the energy of B's brain is directed in a way in which it would not be directed but for something that has happened to A. In this physical effect it is impossible to assume that an external physical antecedent is not involved; and the relation of the antecedent to the effect is, as I have pointed out, hard to conceive, when the neural tremors in A's brain are so unlike the neural tremors in B's brain as they must presumably be when A's mind is occupied with his immediate surroundings, or with the idea of death, and B's mind is occupied with a sudden and unaccountable impression or vision of A.

But however things may be on the physical plane, the facts recorded in this book are purely *psychical* facts; and on the psychical plane it is possible to give to a heterogeneous array of them a certain orderly coherence, and to present them as a graduated series of natural phenomena. Can it be asserted that this treatment is illegitimate unless a concurrent physical theory can also be put forward? It is surely allowable to do one thing at a time. There is an unsolved mystery in the background; that we grant and remember; but it need not perpetually oppress us. After all, is there not that standing mystery of the cerebral and mental correlation in the individual—a mystery equally unsolved and perhaps more definitely and radically insoluble—at the background of every fact and doctrine of the recognised psychology? The psychologists work on as if it did not exist, or rather as if it were the most natural and intelligible thing in the world, and no one complains of them. All that we claim is a similar freedom.

I

CHAPTER IV.

GENERAL CRITICISM OF THE EVIDENCE FOR SPONTANEOUS TELEPATHY.

§ 1. WE have now to quit the experimental branch of our subject. We have been engaged, so far, with cases of thought-transference deliberately sought for and observed within the four walls of a room, both the agent and the percipient being aware of the object in view ; and with the further cases where—though the distance between the agent and the percipient was often greater, and the latter had no intimation of what was intended—there was still a deliberate desire on the agent's part to exert a telepathic influence, and a concentration of his mind on that object. For the remainder of our course we shall be entirely occupied with cases where no such desire or idea existed —where the effect produced on the percipient, though we may connect it with the state of the agent, was certainly not an effect which he was aiming at producing. And this change in the character of the facts is accompanied by a marked change in the character of the evidence —a change for which some of the transitional cases in the last chapter have already prepared us. Our conclusions will now have to be drawn from the records of persons who, at the time when the phenomena which they describe took place, were quite unaware that these would ever be used as evidence for telepathy or anything else. Nor have my colleagues and I any observations of our own to compare with what our witnesses tell us ; the facts are known to us only through the medium of their report, and we shall have to decide how far the medium may be a distorting one. Our method of inquiry will thus be the historical method ; and success will depend upon the exercise of a wider and less specialised form of common-sense than was required in the experimental work. A great many more points have to be taken into account in weighing human testimony than in arranging the conditions of a crucial trial of thought-transference. There, one precise and simple form of danger had to be guarded against—the possibility of conscious or unconscious physical signs : here, dangers multiform and indeterminate will have to be allowed for. We shall be brought face to face with questions of character, of the general behaviour of human beings in various circumstances, and of the unconscious workings of the human mind ; and a quite different sort of logic must come into play, involving often a very complex estimate of probabilities.

So all-important is it for our purpose to form a correct judgment as to the possible sources of error in this new department of evidence, that I have thought it best to devote the present chapter entirely to that subject.

§ 2. First, then, to face the most general objection of all. This may perhaps be stated as follows. All manner of false beliefs have in their day been able to muster a considerable amount of evidence in their support, much of which was certainly not consciously fraudulent. The form of superstition varies with the religious and educational conditions of the time ; but within certain limits a diligent collector will be able to obtain evidence for pretty well anything that he chooses.   There is, of course, a line—and every age will have its own line—beyond which it would be impossible for anyone who wished to be thought sane and educated to go; for instance, it would be impossible in the present day to obtain anything like respectable contemporary testimony for the transformation of old women into hares and cats. But short of this line there is always a range of ideas and beliefs as to which opinion is divided—which it is perfectly allowable to repudiate, and which science may treat with scorn, but which it is not a sign of abnormal ignorance or stupidity to entertain.   And within this range evidence, and even educated evidence, for the beliefs will pretty certainly be forthcoming.   For however much advancing knowledge may have limited the field of superstition, the fund of possibilities in the way of mal-observation, misinterpretation, and exaggeration of facts is still practically inexhaustible ; and with such a fund to draw on, the belief, or the mere desire or tendency to believe, in any particular order of phenomena is sure, now and again, to light on facts which can be made to yield the semblance of a proof.

Now, though it is difficult to deny the force of this argument when stated in general terms, I think that it can be shown not seriously to invalidate the evidence which is here relied on as proof of the reality of spontaneous telepathy.   For the sake of comparison, it will be worth while to glance at the most striking example that modern times supply of the support of false beliefs by a large array of contemporary evidence—the case of witchcraft.

We may begin by excluding the enormous amount of the witch-evidence which consisted in confessions extracted by torture, terror, or false promises—" the casting evidence in most tryals," as Hutchinson says; and also the large class of cases where the actual facts attested would not be disputed ;—as where a woman was condemned because a child who had been with her hung its head on its return home, and rolled over in its cradle in the evening; or because a good many people or cattle had fallen sick in her village ; or because she kept a tame frog, presumed to be her "imp"; or because on the very day that she had scolded a carter whose cart knocked up against her house, the self-same cart stuck in a gate, and the men who should have emptied it at night felt too tired to do so.[1] Putting these cases aside as irrelevant, anyone who looks carefully into the remaining records will find (1) that the actual testimony on which the alleged facts were believed came exclusively from the uneducated classes ; and (2) that the easy acceptance of this evidence by better educated persons was due to the ignorance which was at that time all but universal respecting several great departments of natural phenomena —those of hallucination, trance, hysteria, and mesmerism. This ignorance took effect in the following way—that every piece of evidence to marvellous facts was perforce regarded as presenting one simple alternative :—either the facts happened as alleged ; or the witnesses must be practising deliberate fraud. The latter hypothesis was, of course, an easy one enough to make in respect of this or that individual case, and was supported by indisputable examples ; but it could not long be applied in any wholesale manner. The previous character of many of the persons involved, the aimlessness of such a fraud, the vast scale of the conspiracy which would have had to be organised in order to impose it on the world, and above all the fact that many of the witnesses brought on themselves nothing but oppro-brium and persecution by their statements, made it practically impos-sible to doubt that the testimony was on the whole honestly given. Fraud, then, being excluded, there remained nothing but to believe

---

[1] Lilienthal, *Die Hexenprocesse der beiden Städte Braunsberg* (Königsberg,1861),p. 152; *A Detection of Chelmsford Witches* (London, 1579) ; *Malleus Maleficarum* (Lyons, 1620), Vol. i., p. 242; Müller, *Beiträge zur Geschichte des Hexenglaubens* (Brunswick, 1854), p. 35, &c.; Ady, *Candle in the Dark* (London, 1656), p. 135 ; Hutchinson, *Historical Essay Concerning Witchcraft* (London, 1720), p. 147.

the facts genuine. Sane men and women spoke with obvious sincerity of what they had seen with their own eyes ; how could such a proof be gainsaid ? This is a point which Glanvil and other writers of the witch-epoch are for ever urging ; if we reject these facts, they argue, we must reject all beliefs that have their basis in human testimony. Happily we have now a totally different means of escaping from the dilemma. We know now that subjective hallucinations may possess the very fullest sensory character, and may be as real to the percipient as any object he ever beheld. I have myself heard an epileptic subject, who was perfectly sane and rational in his general conduct, describe a series of interviews that he had had with the devil, with a precision, and an absolute belief in the evidence of his senses, equal to anything that I ever read in the records of the witches' compacts. And further, we know now that there is a condition, capable often of being induced in uneducated and simple persons with extreme ease, in which any idea that is suggested may at once take sensory form, and be projected as an actual hallucination. To those who have seen robust young men, in an early stage of hypnotic trance, staring with horror at a figure which appears to them to be walking on the ceiling, or giving way to strange convulsions under the impression that they have been changed into birds or snakes, there will be nothing very surprising in the belief of hysterical girls that they were possessed by some alien influence, or that their distant persecutor was actually present to their senses. It is true that in hypnotic experiments there is commonly some preliminary process by which the peculiar condition is induced, and that the idea which originates the delusion has then to be suggested *ab extra.* But with sensitive " subjects " who have been much under any particular influence, a mere word will produce the effect ; nor is there any feature in the evidence for witchcraft that more constantly recurs than the *touching* of the victim by the witch.[1] Moreover, no hard and fast line exists between the delusions of induced hypnotism and those of spontaneous trance, or of the grave hystero-epileptic crises which mere terror is now known to develop. And association between persons who were possessed with certain exciting ideas would readily account for the generation of a mutually contagious influence ; as in cases where magic rites were performed by several persons in company ; or

---

[1] Thus, in a case mentioned by De l'Ancre, in the *Tableau de l'Inconstance des mauvais Anges et Démons* (Paris, 1612), p. 115, all the children who believed themselves to have been taken to a " Sabbath," stated that the witch had passed her hand over their faces, or placed it on their heads.

where a whole household or community was affected with some particular delusion.[1]

The above seems a sufficient explanation of the testimony which to the eyes of contemporaries appeared the strongest—the testimony of "possessed" persons, and of the professed participators in the incantation scenes and nocturnal orgies. As regards the alleged statements of independent persons who testified to having witnessed the aërial rides, transformations into animal forms, and such-like marvels, I would remark in the first place that the literature of witchcraft may be searched far and wide without encountering half-a-dozen *first-hand* statements of the sort;[2] and in the second place, that there is a characteristic of uneducated minds which is only exceptionally observed in educated adults—the tendency to confound mental images, pure and simple, with matters of fact. This tendency naturally allies itself with any set of images which is prominent in the beliefs of the time; and it is certain now and then to give to what are merely vivid ideas the character of *bonâ fide* memories. The imagination which may be unable to produce, even in feeble-minded persons, the belief that they *see* things that are not there, may be quite able to produce the belief that they *have seen* them—which is all, of course, that their testimony implies.[3]

There is, however, one small class of phenomena connected with witchcraft which stands on different ground, as regards the quality of

---

[1] *A True and Just Record of the Information taken at St. Osey, in Essex* (London, 1582); Potts, *Wonderfull Discoverie of Witches in the Countie of Lancaster, &c.* (London, 1613); the case of the Flowers in *A Collection of Rare and Curious Tracts relating to Witchcraft between the Years 1618 and 1664*, pp. 19, 21; Glanvil, *Sadducismus Triumphatus*, p. 581: Hutchinson, *Op. cit.*, p. 53; Durbin, *A Narrative of Some Extraordinary Things* (Bristol, 1800), p. 47; Horst, *Zauber-Bibliothek*, p. 219; Madden, *Phantasmata*, Vol. i., pp. 346-7; T. Hutchinson, *History of Massachusetts Bay* (Boston, 1692), Vol. ii., p. 18; Richet, *L'Homme et l'Intelligence* (Paris, 1884), p. 392.

[2] If "first-hand" be restricted (as it is throughout this book) to statements in the witness's own words, I cannot point to a single such statement; but in the above phrase I mean merely the author's statement of what was told directly to herself. The *circumstantial* evidence (also very meagre) for these miracles stands on different ground; as there the *facts* recorded are quite credible, and only the *inference* need be rejected. For example, the external evidence relied on for the supposed transformations was usually that the accused proved to have some bodily hurt on the same day as a wolf or some other animal had been wounded.

[3] Another explanation might be attempted, if (on the analogy of certain Indian juggling tricks) we could suppose the spectator to have been unawares subjected to a "mesmeric glamour," whereby the suggestion of the magical occurrence was enabled to develop in his mind into an actual vision of it. One story in the *Malleus Maleficarum*, where a girl appeared to herself and to her friends to be a mare, while a priest (over whom the evil influence had no power) saw her as a girl, strongly recalls some of the Indian stories. See also the curious account of imps which appears in *Witches of Huntingdon, Renfrew, and Essex* (London, 1646). Such a result would, however, enormously transcend the range of mesmeric influence as so far recognised in the West; and we certainly need not strain hypotheses to save the credit of writers like Sprenger.

the evidence adduced for it.   A few cases are recorded, on really
respectable authority, of a remarkable susceptibility, shown by
persons whom we might now recognise as hypnotic " subjects," to the
conscious or unconscious influence of some absent person supposed
to be a witch ; and perhaps also of abnormal powers of discernment
on the part of the supposed witches themselves.   These alleged
telepathic cases naturally fell into discredit along with all the other
phenomena of occult agency.   For the belief in witchcraft faded
and ultimately died as a whole ; not because each sort of phenomenon
was in turn exposed or explained, or because any critical account
of hallucinations and popular delusions was forthcoming, or even
because a certain amount of distinct fraud was proved, but because
the general tide of uncritical opinion took a turn towards scepticism
as to matters supernatural.   Now we are certainly not concerned
to maintain that this or that instance of alleged telepathic influence
ought to have been allowed to stand as genuine, when belief in
the more phantastic phenomena was undermined.   Is is probable
that in the former, as in the latter, the influence of imagination
was not allowed for, and that the different items of evidence
were never tested and compared in the manner that true
scientific scepticism would dictate.   We, at any rate, have difficulty
enough in testing the accuracy of contemporary evidence, and
certainly are not going to rest any part of our case on the records
of a by-gone age.   But if anyone who has studied the evidence for
witchcraft urges these cases as a proof that the more recent telepathic
evidence is unworthy of attention, it is reasonable to remark that if
telepathy is in operation now, it was probably in operation then ;
and that the only cases of supposed magic with which persons of sense
and education seem, at the time, to have come to close quarters were
similar in character to cases for which persons of sense and education
are still found to offer their personal testimony.[1]

---

[1] Of the early records the best known is the evidence of the Père Surin and others in
respect of the hysterical epidemic in the Ursuline convent at Loudun, in 1633.   But
perhaps the most carefully observed case is the older one given in the *Most Strange and
Admirable Discovery of the Three Witches of Warboys* (London, 1593), of which Sir W.
Scott's account (*Demonology and Witchcraft*, p. 238) gives a very imperfect idea.   Another
example of much the same kind is given in G. More's *True Discourse against S.
Harsnet* (London, 1600).   The cases where the victim showed uneasiness when the
absent witch was at large, and relief when she was bolted, though quite inconclusive,
seem occasionally to have been rationally tested.   (*Witchcraft further Displayed*,
London, 1712, p. 21 ; *History of the Witches of Renfrewshire*, Paisley, 1809, p. 134 ;
Sadducismus Debellatus, London, 1698, p. 47.)   The assertions that " possessed persons "
were able to read secrets present sometimes this sign of sobriety, that the revelations are
said to have concerned only past and present, not future, things (see, *e.g.*, Lercheimer,
Ein Christlich Bedenken und Erinnerung von Zauberei, Heidelberg, 1585 ; and Majolus, *Dies*

But in whatever light these residual cases be regarded, the general conclusion remains the same—that the phenomena which were characteristic of witchcraft, and which are an accepted type of exploded superstitions, never rested on the first-hand testimony of educated and intelligent persons; and the sweeping assertion which is often made that such persons were, in their day, witnesses to the truth of these absurdities needs, therefore, to be carefully guarded. What the educated and intelligent believers did was to accept from others, as evidence of *objective* facts, statements which were really only evidence of *subjective* facts. And they did this naturally and excusably, because they lived at a time when the science of psychology was in its infancy, and the necessary means of correction were not within their reach.[1]

One further criticism may be made as to the mental condition of those who were in any direct sense witnesses to the facts. They were invariably persons inclined to such beliefs to begin with—who had been brought up in them and had accepted them as a matter of course. We have no record of anyone who had all his life declined to admit the reality of the alleged phenomena, and who was suddenly convinced of his mistake by coming into personal contact with them.

§ 3. We are now in a position to perceive, by comparison, how the case stands with the evidence for telepathy which awaits examination. It would almost be sufficient to say that the comparison is an absolute contrast in respect of every point which has been mentioned. A very large number of our first-hand witnesses are

---

Caniculares, Mainz, 1614, p. 593); but as such a power finds no parallel in the telepathy of our day, it is satisfactory rather than otherwise to find that it is supported by hardly anything that can be called evidence. The strongest item is perhaps the testimony of Poncet to the powers of some of the *convulsionnaires* of St. Médard (see Bertrand, *Du Magnétisme Animal*, Paris, 1826, p. 435). Nor do the "thought-reading" stories about Somers (*e.g.*, in Darrell's *Brief Apologie and Detection*, London, 1599 and 1600), and about Escot de Parme (De l'Ancre, *L'Incredulité et Mescréance du Sortilège*, Paris, 1622) reach even the lowest evidential grade. It would be useless to multiply indecisive instances. If the *least* wretchedly-attested cases, even in the most wretched collections of witch-anecdotes, turn out to be those which admit of a telepathic explanation, yet much stronger cases might well be damned by such company. And though some of the less credulous authors, who have a real notion of natural causes and of what constitutes proof, seem to have felt the evidence for supersensuous communications to be too strong to resist (*e.g.*, Cotta in *The Infallible, True and Assured Witch*, London, 1625) their general position is too wavering for their authority to have any weight. One rises from their works feeling that this was the side of the subject which had produced on them the strongest impression of reality; and that is all that can be said.

[1] I am speaking—it must be remembered—of the attitude of educated and intelligent persons towards assertions which might (however loosely) be described as *evidence*. That such persons often showed themselves credulous and uninquiring in attaching value to mere legends and local gossip is of course true enough, but does not concern the present argument. For a justification of the above remarks, see the Note on Witchcraft at the end of this chapter.

educated and intelligent persons, whose sobriety of judgment has never been called in question. For the most part, moreover, they have been in no way inclined to admit the reality of the phenomena, prior to themselves encountering them. By many of them even what they themselves narrate has not been regarded with special interest ; while others, who have been unable to get behind their own experience, have expressed scepticism as to the existence of the phenomena as a class.[1] The facts themselves have no special affinity with any particular form of faith ; they are not facts in a belief of which any one is specially brought up. And here we may contrast telepathy, not only with the comparatively modern superstition of witchcraft, but with phenomena of much older and wider acceptance—the alleged apparitions of the dead. The continued existence of departed friends and relatives has been one of the most constant elements of religious belief ; and that myths should grow up respecting their appearances to survivors is what might have naturally been looked for. But even in respect of the most striking sort of phenomena with which we shall here be concerned—apparitions at the time of death— we do not find in men's prevalent habits of thought, at any stage of culture, elements which would be particularly likely to produce a myth on the subject. And as a matter of fact, if we go to the classes of persons whose beliefs have no special relation to evidence, we do actually find the one myth prevalent, and not the other. The idea of apparitions after death has a wide and strong hold on the popular mind ; the idea of apparitions at the time either of death, or of serious crises in life, has no established vogue. Instances are, no doubt, to be met with in books of history, biography, and travel ; and the range which such notices cover is itself important, as showing that the idea, though so far from universally prevalent, is for all that not in any sense a speciality of particular times or localities. But though numerous, the instances are sporadic ; they appear as isolated marvels, which even those who experienced them regarded as such, and not as evidences to any widely-believed reality. So much is this the case that to many persons with

---

[1] It is amusing sometimes to encounter arbitrary fragments of scepticism, combined with a belief in the " supernatural " character of many of the coincidences which we are endeavouring to account for as natural. Thus a gentleman contributes a case to *Knowledge* (May 16th, 1884) and concludes his letter thus : " Personally, I do not believe in apparitions, nor in anything akin thereto ; but coincidences such as you record from week to week must have happened to most of us, and obtuse indeed must the individual be who does not think that there is something supernatural sometimes even in coincidences."

whom we have conversed on the subject we find that the very idea of such phenomena is practically new; and that "apparitions," whether delusions or realities, have always been considered by them as apparitions of the *dead*.[1] And if this is true of the more striking telepathic cases, *à fortiori* is it true of the less striking. The class of apparitions and impressions which have corresponded with the death of the "agent" has only been vaguely recognised; the class which have corresponded with a state of passing excitement or danger can hardly be said to have been recognised at all. Even persons with whose general way of thinking they might seem compatible are apt to be repelled by their apparent uselessness, and certainly are not wont to exhibit any *à priori* belief in their reality ; while to others who have encountered them, they have appeared in the objectionable light of a puzzle, without analogies and without a place in the recognised order of Nature.

But though I think that it is not hard to distinguish the evidence on which we rely from the evidence for various forms of popular superstition, and to show that, as a matter of fact, telepathy is *not* a popular superstition, I am far from denying a certain degree of force to the line of objection above suggested. Ignorance, credulity, and a predisposition to believe in a particular order of marvels, are not the only sources of unconscious falsification in human testimony; and it by no means follows, because these particular elements of error are absent, that a *bonâ fide* first-hand narrative of contemporary facts is trustworthy. And having briefly considered certain dangers and objections from which we think that our telepathic evidence is free, I proceed now to consider certain others to which it is to a certain extent exposed, and to explain the means by which we have endeavoured to obviate or reduce them.

---

[1] Next to these, the best-recognised class are undoubtedly the *premonitory* apparitions of "second-sight."

Since the above remarks were written, I am glad to find them implicitly confirmed by a very high authority on myth and folk-lore, Mr. Andrew Lang. In the *Nineteenth Century* for April, 1885, he showed very clearly and amusingly how the same types of "ghost-story" are found in the most distant places, and in the most diverse stages of culture—whether owing to some common basis of fact, or to the same pervading love of the mysterious, or (as is sometimes undoubtedly the case) to the survival of remnants of primitive superstitions in the midst of an advancing civilisation. But though most of his instances are drawn from barbarous countries, he "has not encountered, among savages, more than one example" pointing to a belief in what we call telepathic impressions ; and even that one is a very doubtful example. There is, as I have said, a certain amount of sporadic evidence that the phenomena have been noticed at many different times and places ; but of any pervading belief, such as would cause people to be on the *qui vive* for them and would ensure a perpetual supply of spurious evidence, neither we nor apparently Mr. Lang can find any indication whatever.

§ 4. It will be best to enumerate, one by one, the general sources of error which may affect the testimony of honest and fairly-educated persons, to events that are both unusual and of a sort unrecognised by contemporary science. We shall thus be able to observe in detail how far each is likely to have affected the evidence here brought forward.

The most obvious danger may seem to lie in errors of observation and inference. And first as to errors of *observation*. The phenomena with which these have to do are naturally *objective* phenomena. It is only in reference to the objective world that observation can be proved to be accurate or faulty; the faulty observation is that which interprets real things in a way that does not correspond with reality. Now misinterpretation of this sort may undoubtedly produce spurious telepathic cases; and wherever we can suppose it to have been possible, we are bound to exclude the case from our evidence. Thus we have a group of narratives of the following type, suggesting a mistake of identity.

Mrs. Campbell, of Dunstaffnage, Oban, wrote, in June, 1884 :—

" Two years ago one of our tenant farmers was very ill, and my brother asked me to inquire how he was, on my way back from a walk I was going to take with a cousin of mine. We went, but on passing the old man's house I forgot to go in, and soon we arrived at our avenue, when my cousin reminded me of not having asked for the sick man. I thought of returning, when I distinctly saw the old man, followed by his favourite dog, cross a field in front of us, and go into his house, and I remarked to my cousin, who also had seen the old man and his dog, that as he was so well that he was able to walk about, there was not much use in going to inquire for him, so we went on home. But on arriving there, my brother came to tell us that the old man's son had just been to say that his father had just died."

Here it is possible, and therefore for evidential purposes necessary, to suppose that the figure seen was a neighbour, or perhaps the old man's son.[1] The next incident, given in the words of Mrs. Saxby, of Mount Elton, Clevedon, was narrated to her and other friends by the late Rev. G. Ridout, Vicar of Newland, Gloucestershire, on whom it had made a very serious impression.

" My sister and I were left orphans when we were extremely young. We were very fond of each other. When I was nearly grown up, I was sent to Magdalen College, Oxford. While there, one day when I was

---

[1] I may say here, once for all, that our gratitude to an informant is none the less because his or her experience may not have appeared relevant to the direct argument of this book. Such cases have often been very useful and instructive in other ways.

walking in the cloisters, I saw my sister walking before me, dressed in white. I knew that she was not staying in Oxford, and I was much surprised at seeing her there—but I had no doubt whatever that it was my sister. She passed along the cloister before me, I following close behind her till she turned the first angle. To my surprise, when I reached the same place, instead of seeing her before me, she was gone. Immediately the conviction that she was dead seized me, and I felt myself strengthened to receive the tidings of her death, which reached me next day."

The disappearance here seems to have been strangely sudden; but we have not been able to cross-examine the witness ; and one knows that people of flesh and blood do sometimes get out of sight round corners in odd ways. Again, the Rev. C. Woodcock, Rector of All Saints', Axminster, writes :—

"January 8th, 1884.

" The following fact was often narrated in my presence by my father, who has been dead upwards of thirty years. He was once invited, when a young man, to breakfast on the ground floor at St. James's Palace, to meet a particular friend. He was punctual to the appointed hour ; but not so the expected guest. The hour had struck, but neither party present was willing to sit down without the mutual friend. They had not long to wait for seeming satisfaction, for as each stood at a window opposite the thoroughfare to the park, both exclaimed at the same moment, ' Oh ! there he is,' and the host, so fully satisfied in his ocular assurance, went to the door on the other side of the house, to welcome his friend, instead of waiting for his announcement. He stood there in vain ; the friend never appeared, to the great astonishment of all present ; for two persons standing at different windows agreed that they saw him pass at the identical moment. Within an hour, a man-servant appeared to announce that his master, the expected guest, was found dead in his bed that morning. My father was a member of the Madras C. S.; the name of his host I forget."

Here the eyes of two persons were concerned ; but they were in an expectant state of mind, which is eminently favourable to such mistakes. In another case, two gentlemen crossed Piccadilly under the impression that they saw a friend, who, as it turned out, died in India on that day. But it is needless to multiply instances ; in all of them the figure seen has been out of doors, and at some yards' distance; and these being the very circumstances in which we know that spurious recognitions often take place, there is nothing surprising in an occasional coincidence of the sort described. Similarly, a person may hear a call, perhaps of his own Christian name, outside his house, and may mistake the voice for that of a friend ; and, " in due course," as our informants sometimes say, the news of that friend's death may arrive.[1] But it is only to an inconsiderable fraction of the evidence here presented that such explanations could by any possibility be applied. The large majority of the alleged experiences are, on the face of them, *subjective* phenomena, in the sense that they are independent of any real objects in the environment, and of any mistakes possible in connection with such objects, and are due to a peculiar affection of the percipient's own mind. This mode of regarding them (and the reservations with which the word "subjective" must be used) will be fully explained in the sequel. It is enough for the present to note that the witness who would be an unsafe authority if he said "Sea-serpents exist," may be a safe authority if he says, "I saw what appeared to be a sea-serpent"; and this amount of assertion is all that the telepathic evidence involves. All the accuracy of observation required of the witness has to do with what he *seemed to himself* to see, or to hear, or to feel.

Nor in our cases is the danger of errors of *inference* so serious as might be imagined. A man may, no doubt, see something odd or indefinite, at the time that his mother dies at a distance, and may infer that it bodes calamity ; and if, after he hears of the death, he infers and reports that he saw his mother's form, the error will be a very grave one. But it will be more convenient to treat retrospective mistakes of this sort under the head of errors of *memory*. And with a percipient's interpretation of his impression *at the moment* we have really very little concern. He may see the apparition of a relative in his room, and infer first that it is the relative's real figure in flesh and blood, and next that it is the relative's spirit. Neither inference has any relation to our argument.

---

[1] The following example has a comic as well as a tragic side. A gentleman, with whom the present writer is well acquainted, had attained some skill in "ventriloquism," and used occasionally to amuse himself by mystifying his friends. He was one day idly swinging on a trapeze in the Ramsgate Gymnasium, and was chatting with the wife and daughter of Mr. R., the manager of the place, who were at a window above him.

"It occurred to me to put my powers into practice for the benefit of everybody, so I delivered myself of a long, low wail, carefully muffled and made distant, so as to resemble a cry from the rocks on the seashore below. Without really thinking much of what I was doing, I amused myself for about a minute by producing 'Oh's!' Suddenly there was a disturbance above, Mr. R. rushed upstairs, and I saw his wife hurried off by her family in a state of collapse. I supposed she had been taken ill, and thought no more of the matter.

"I did not attend the gymnasium for the next few days ; but a friend who *did* learnt what the mystery was. It appears that Mrs. R., who had several sons abroad, had received, at one time or another, what you call 'telepathic' indications of any illness or death happening to any of them. My imitation of a distant person in distress had been heard and regarded by her as one of these telepathic messages, and implanted in her mind the belief that a son, who was abroad, and from whom they had not heard for some time, had *at that moment died*. So convinced was she that the voice she heard was that of her dying son, that she refused to listen to any comfortings, and gave herself up to despair. She did not recover from the shock for upwards of three weeks, and never quite forgave me."

The only fact that concerns us is the fact that he had the subjective impression of seeing his relative. I may refer once more, by way of contrast, to the case of witchcraft, where the very basis of the superstition was error of inference,—error shown (and by the more intelligent class exclusively shown) not in the giving but in the interpreting of testimony.

§ 5. The tendencies to error which more vitally concern us fall broadly into two classes—tendencies to error in *narration*, and tendencies to error of *memory*. Let us ask, then, what are the various conscious or unconscious motives which may cause persons who belong to the educated class, and who have a general character for truthfulness, to *narrate* experiences of telepathic impressions in a manner which is not strictly accurate ?

One motive which has undoubtedly to be allowed for in some cases is the desire to make the account *edifying*. This danger naturally attaches to the evidence for any class of facts which can be regarded, however erroneously, as transcending natural law. Enthusiastic persons will value an unusual occurrence, not for its intrinsic interest, but for its tendency, if accepted, to convert others to their own way of belief; and they will be apt to shape and colour their account of it with a view to the desired effect. Intent on pointing the moral, they will unconsciously adorn the tale. This source of error is one which it is specially necessary to bear in mind where some particular type of story is connected with a particular religious sect. The literature of the Society of Friends, for instance, is remarkably rich in accounts of providential monitions and premonitions ; and it supplies also a considerable number of telepathic cases. But we have already seen that telepathy does not specially lend itself to the support of definite articles of faith. Nor is any one who takes the trouble to study our evidence likely to maintain that errors of narration have largely entered into it under the influence of a propagandist zeal. It is rather for the sake of completeness than on account of its practical importance that such a possibility has been mentioned.[1]

---

[1] Curiously enough, the only specially "edifying" incident which has reached us on what seemed good authority, turns out to be quite inadmissible as evidence. The account was received from the Rev. G. B. Simeon, of St. John's Vicarage, Gainsborough, of whose accuracy as a narrator we feel no doubt. He says :—   "January 10th, 1884.

"When I was in Oxford, a story was going about to the effect that Dr. Pusey had seen an apparition *in High Street*, and I undertook to ask him whether it was true. He said No, but that the report was probably founded on the following truth :—

"Two clergymen, A and B, well known to himself and very great friends, were together in the neighbourhood of Oxford. One of them, B, went away on a visit. The

A far more frequent and effective source of error in narration is the tendency to make the account *graphic and picturesque*. Among human beings, the motives which prompt narration of matters unconnected with business or the mere machinery of life are mainly two, —a desire to interest one's auditor; and a desire to put oneself *en evidence*, to feed one's own self-esteem by attracting and retaining the attention of others. The influence of each of these motives is towards making the story as good a one as possible. And though, as I have already said, a good deal of our evidence comes from persons who profess to have had no bias in favour of the reality of such events as they describe, and wish rather that they had not occurred, still the instinct to make what one says seem worth saying is too general for it ever to be safe to assume its absence. In such a subject as ours, this instinct will find its chief opportunity in making things appear *marvellous*. The reader must decide for himself how far the evidence to be here presented bears the stamp of the wonder-mongerer or *raconteur*. The desire to make people open their eyes is no doubt perfectly compatible with a habit of truthfulness in the ordinary affairs of life. Still, the desire, as a rule, is actually to see the eyes opening; and the danger is therefore greater in the case of a story which is told off-hand and *vivâ voce* for the sake of immediate effect, than in the case of evidence which is first written down at leisure, and has then to undergo the ordeal of a careful and detailed scrutiny. Nor must we forget that there is another instinct which tends directly

other, A, was in the garden, and saw his friend B come in at the gate and approach him. On expressing his surprise at seeing him return sooner than was expected, his friend B replied, in an agitated manner, '*I have been in hell for half an hour because I loved the praise of men more than the praise of God,*' and turning, immediately left the garden. In the course of the next day, A, going out into the parish, met a third person, who stopped him and said, '*Do you know, sir, that devoted servant of God, B, is dead suddenly?*' On further inquiry he found he had died the previous day shortly before his appearance in the garden.

"The underlined words were exactly those used by Dr. Pusey, and the whole manner of his telling made me feel sure that A was himself, although I did not like to ask him point blank. But he assured me he knew it to be true, and that, doubtless, it had given rise to the story going about Oxford. I fear you will think that, like most of these things, it lacks the full details, which probably none but Dr. Pusey could give, and which I felt it would be presumptuous to ask for."

The same story—with some differences of detail—is reported to have been told by Dr. Pusey, as a personal experience, to the Sisters in Osnaburgh Street (see p. 25 of *Sisterhoods of the Church of England*, by Margaret Goodman). Nevertheless, we are forced to conclude that those to whom Dr. Pusey narrated the incident were mistaken in supposing him to refer to himself. For it is scarcely possible to doubt that a story published as long ago as 1819, in the *Imperial Magazine* (Liverpool), p. 963, and given also in the *Life of Mr. W. Bramwell*, 1839, is the original of what he told. The vision appears there as a dream, not a waking percept. Otherwise the central incident is the same, and the very words used by the phantom are almost identical. But the names of the parties are not given, and all our guarantee for the correctness of the account vanishes. This case is of interest, as showing the importance of probing a witness as thoroughly as possible whiles one is in the way with him.

to discourage wonder-mongering, at any rate in the narration of unusual personal experiences—the instinct to *win belief*. Where the risk of being disbelieved is appreciable, a sense of accuracy becomes also a sense of security; a thing being credible to oneself just because it is fact, the consciousness of not exaggerating the fact begets a sort of trust that others may somehow find it credible. And with the class from whom our evidence is chiefly drawn, this influence seems not less likely to be operative than the desire to say something startling. The latter tendency is more prone on the whole to affect *second-hand* witnesses, who do not feel bound to exercise any economy of the miraculous, who can always fall back on the plea that they are only telling what was told to them, and who may easily be led into inaccuracies by the analogy of other marvellous stories.

And indeed it is a matter of ordinary observation, by no means confined to " psychical research," that where the subject of narration has nothing to do with merit, and what is alleged to have been done or suffered is not of a sort to attract admiration to the doer or sufferer, the more extravagant sort of stories are given, not as personal experiences, but on the authority of someone else. If there is exaggeration, it is " a friend " who is to blame ; and this term is used on such occasions with considerable latitude. I have already noted how, in the case of witchcraft, the more bizarre incidents do not rest on anything like traceable first-hand testimony. This remark is applicable in a general way to the whole field of evidence for marvellous events, as recorded in modern literature ; and the same fact has been very noticeable with respect to the evidence, of very various sorts and qualities, which has come under the attention of my colleagues and myself during the last few years. We have often taken the trouble to trace and test the matter of those sensational newspaper-paragraphs which get so freely copied from one journal into another ; but in scarcely one per cent. of the cases has the evidence held water. And in the ordinary talk of society, where there is often a show or assertion of authority for the statements made, one gradually learns to diagnose with confidence the accounts which profess to be second or third hand from the original, but of which no original will ever be forthcoming. An example is the well-known tale of the dripping letter, handed to a lady by the phantasmal figure of a midshipman who had been drowned before he could execute his commission. If the newspaper-anecdotes were like bubbles that break in the pursuer's hand, a society-marvel of this stamp may be more fitly compared to a will-o'-the-wisp : one never gets any nearer to it. Then there is the young lady who was preserved from a railway accident by seeing the apparition of her *fiancé* on the platform of three consecutive stations—which induced her to alight. Here I was actually promised an introduction to the heroine : what I finally received was a reference to "a friend of the lady who told the story." Or, again, there is the tale of second-sight, so widely told during the last three years, where the visitor saw a daughter of the house stabbed by a stranger, whom he has since identified as her husband, and has remorselessly dogged in hansom cabs. Three or four times have we been, so to speak, "one off" this story; but the various clues have shown no sign of converging; and we still occasionally hear of the happy couple as on their honeymoon.

§ 6. Turning now to the sources of error in *memory*, we find the danger here is of a more insidious kind, in that comparatively few persons realise the extent to which it exists in their own case. For one who is innocent of any desire to impress his auditor in any particular way, and who simply desires to tell the truth, it is not easy to realise that he may be an untrustworthy witness about matters concerning himself. The weaknesses of human memory, and the precautions which they necessitate, will be so frequent a topic in the sequel that a brief classification will here suffice.

We must allow, in the first place, for a common result of the belief in supernatural influences and providential interpositions. Persons who are interested in such ideas will be keenly alive to any phenomena which seem to transcend a purely materialistic view of life. They will be apt to see facts of this class where they do not exist, and to interpret in this sense small or vague occurrences which if accurately examined at the time might have been otherwise explained. And where this tendency exists, it is almost inevitable that, as time goes on, the occurrence should represent itself to memory more and more in the desired light, that inconvenient details should drop out, and that the remainder should stand out in a deceptively significant and harmonious form. Of the cases to be here presented, however, only a very small proportion betray any idea on the part of the witness that what he recounts has any special religious or philosophical significance. Our informants have had no motive to conceal from us their real view of the facts ; and if they narrate an incident as simply strange or

K

unaccountable, we have no right to assume their evidence to have been coloured by an emotional sense that materialism had been refuted in their person, or that supernatural communications had been permitted to them. Indeed, as regards religious and emotional pre-possessions, we are certainly justified in thinking that they have rather been hindrances than helps to the presentation of an abundant array of evidence. For it has happened in many instances that persons whose testimony would have been a valuable addition to the case for telepathy, have felt their experiences to be too intimate or too sacred for publication.[1]

But apart from any bias of an emotional or speculative sort, we must certainly admit a general tendency in the human mind to make any picture of facts definite. To many people vagueness of emotion or of speculation is a delight; but no one enjoys vagueness of memory. In thinking of an event which was in any way shadowy or uncertain, there is always a certain irksomeness in realising clearly how little clear it was. The same applies, of course, to events at which we look back through any considerable interval of time. The very effort to recall them implies an effort to represent them to the mind as precisely and completely as possible, and it is often not observed that the precision thus attained is not that of reality.

Lastly, there is a general tendency to lighten the burden of memory by *simplifying* its contents—by bringing any group of connected events into as round and portable a form as possible. This may, of course, only result in the loss of excrescences and subordinate features, while the essential incident is left intact. But we shall find instances further on where simplification really alters the character of the evidence. Details may not simply drop out; they may undergo a change, and group themselves conveniently round some central idea. It might reasonably be expected, and we ourselves certainly began by expecting, that error from this source would always tell in the direction of actual distortion and exaggeration; if the aspect of the case was to some extent striking and significant to begin with, it would seem likely that this aspect of it should become

---

[1] To take a single instance—a lady sends us an unsensational narrative of the ordinary type, as to how one day in 1882, when just about to sit down to the piano, she saw close to her the figure of an old school-friend, who, as it turned out, died on that day at a distance. " I am confident," she says, " of having seen the vision, though my common-sense makes me wish to put it down to imagination. I never saw any vision of any kind before or since." But we are withheld from quoting the account in a form which could have any evidential value, by her feeling that such publication would be wrong.

more pronounced as it assumed a more isolated place in the mind, and lost its connection with the normal stream of experience in the course of which it appeared. As a matter of fact, however, this is by no means always what happens. For instance, we have met with several cases of the following sort. An impression of a remarkable kind, and which, if telepathy exists, may fairly be regarded as telepathic, has been produced on a percipient while in a state which he recognised at the time as one of complete wakefulness, and which was practically proved to be so by the fact that he did not wake from it—that it formed a connected part of his waking life. But in the natural gravitation towards *easy* accounts of things, he gradually gets to look back on this experience as a *dream;* that is, he allows the verdict of subsequent memory to supplant the verdict of immediate consciousness. We must not then say in our haste, all men—or all memories—are exaggerators. Even where evidence has been modified in passing through several mouths, a comparison between later and earlier versions of the same occurrence has sometimes shown that its more striking and significant characteristics have lost rather than gained by the transmission. But this is no doubt the exception.

§ 7. Such, in brief outline, are the principal sources of error which may in a general way be supposed to affect the sort of evidence with which we are concerned ; and our next step must be to fix with precision what the actual opportunities for perversion are. The evidence for telepathy has a certain type and structure of its own, and we must realise what this is, in order to know where to look for the weak points. What, then, are the essential elements of a typical telepathic phenomenon ? They consist in two events or two states, of a more or less remarkable kind, and connected, as a rule, by certain common characteristics ; and of a certain time-relation between the two. For example, if a flawless case is to be presented, it would be of the following type and composition: It would comprise (1) indisputable evidence that A (whom we call the agent) has had an unusual experience—say, has died; (2) indisputable evidence that B (whom we call the percipient) has had an unusual experience which includes a certain impression of A—say, has, while wide awake, had a vision of A in the room ; (3) indisputable evidence that the two events coincided in time—which, of course, implies that their respective dates can be accurately fixed. When I call such evidence as this *flawless,* I do not, of course, mean that it is *conclusive :* the fact that the two

K 2

events occurred, and the fact that they occurred simultaneously, might be placed beyond dispute, and the coincidence might, for all that, be due not to telepathy, but to chance alone. But though no single case can prove telepathy, no case where the above conditions are not to some extent realised can even help to prove it. Briefly, then, if the account of some alleged instance of telepathy is evidentially faulty, there must be misrepresentation as to one or more of the following items: (1) the state of the agent; (2) the experience of the percipient; (3) the time of (1); (4) the time of (2).

Now the evidence where the chances of misrepresentation have primarily to be considered is clearly that of the *percipient*. It is the percipient's mention of his own experience which makes, so to speak, the ground-work of the case; unless the percipient gives his own account of this experience, the case is in no sense a first-hand one; whereas if such an account is given we should consider the evidence first-hand, even though the account of the *agent's* state is not obtained from himself. Of course when the agent is in a position to give an account, it is important that his evidence should be procured; but this is impossible in the numerous cases where his share in the matter consists simply in dying. In these cases, then, we are dependent on others for evidence as to the agent's side of the occurrence; and primarily often on the percipient, who is our first and indispensable witness for the whole matter. This being premised, we shall have no difficulty in discovering where the risks of misrepresentation really lie.

§ 8. Taking the above four items in order, the first of them—the state of the agent—is the one where the risk is smallest. To take the commonest case, the very fact, death, which makes it impossible to obtain the agent's personal testimony, is an event as to which, of all others in his history, it is least likely that a person who knew him should be in error. It is one also as to which corroboration of the percipient's statement is often most easily obtained; either from the verbal testimony of surviving relatives and friends, or from contemporary letters, notices, and obituaries. And where the event which has befallen the agent falls short of this degree of gravity, it is probably still sufficiently out of the common for the ascertainment of it by the percipient and others to have been natural and easy; and *à fortiori* sufficiently out of the common to have stamped itself on

the memory of the agent himself, who may now be available as a
witness.[1]

When we come to the next item—the experience of the percipient
—the risk of misrepresentation seems decidedly to increase. For the
witness is now recounting something purely personal, for the occurrence
of which he can produce no objective proofs. He says that he saw
something, or heard something, or felt something, which struck him as
remarkable (in many cases, indeed, as *unique* in his experience), and
this has to be taken on his word; no external observation of him (even
were anyone present with him at the time) could reveal whether he
was actually experiencing these sensations which he afterwards
described. Now to a careless glance it may seem that there is a
loophole here, through which enough error may enter to invalidate
the whole case. It may be said that the percipient was perhaps
nervous, or unwell, or imaginative ; and that a report of impressions
which are received under such conditions cannot be relied on as
evidence. But in what was said above as to errors of observation,
this objection has been practically answered. It would be in place if
the question were whether what he thought he perceived was really
there ; but it is not in place when the question is simply what he
thought he perceived. We are discussing the experience of the
percipient as the second of the four heads under which misrepresentation may enter. Now, *misrepresentation* of this experience would
consist simply in the statement that he had had certain sensations or
impressions which he had not had : *misinterpretation* of the
experience—*e.g.*, if he imagined that his friend was actually physically
present where his form had been seen or his voice heard—has nothing
to do with the evidential point. Grant that the percipient's senses
played him false—that his impression was a hallucination ; that, as I
have implied, is the very light in which we ourselves regard it ; it may
even be the light in which he regarded it himself. That does not
prevent its being an unusual experience ; and it is simply as an

---

[1] The less exceptional the event, the less of course is the evidential force of the case,
and the more important it is to obtain the direct testimony of the agent. A lady of my
acquaintance informed me that on the 21st of October, 1883, she had a startling
and distressing vision of a kind unique in her experience—in which she seemed to pay a
visit to a former school-fellow, whom she had not heard of for more than ten years, to
console her in a recent bereavement. The extent of my informant's agitation and distress
was testified to by a near relative, to whom she had at once narrated her experience.
A few days afterwards a notice in the *Times* obituary showed that her friend's husband
had died on October 20th. Had the widow's thoughts, then, in her fresh sorrow, turned
to her early associate and sympathetically impressed her ? The *widow*, perhaps, might
have told us ; but on inquiry we find that the *wife* had died some years before her
husband.

unusual experience, which included an impression of his friend, that it has a place in the evidence.

Now the probability that this unusual experience has been misrepresented will be very different, according as the mention of it by the percipient precedes or follows his knowledge of what has befallen the agent. If he gives his account in ignorance of that event, and independently of any ideas which it might be calculated to awake in his mind, there seems no ground at all for supposing that he has coloured his statement, at any rate in any way which would affect its evidential value. If A, a person with a general character for truthfulness, and with no motive to deceive, mentions having had an unusual experience—a hallucination of the senses, an unaccountable impression, or whatever he likes to call it—which was strongly suggestive of B, no one will tell him that he is romancing or exaggerating, and that he had no such impression as he reports. He will simply be told that his nerves are overstrung, or that he has had a waking dream, or something of that sort. And this assumption of the truth of the statement could of course not be impugned merely because it subsequently turned out that B died at the time.

Hence, one of the points to which we have, throughout our inquiry, attached the highest value, is the proof that evidence of the percipient's experience was in existence prior to the receipt of the news of the agent's condition. This prior evidence may be of various sorts. The percipient may at once make a written record in a diary, or in a letter which may have been preserved. Where this has been the case, we have always endeavoured to obtain the document for inspection.[1] Or he may have mentioned his hallucination or

---

[1] There are cases where a sort of exactitude is required which makes documentary evidence almost indispensable. An instance may be found in the following account, sent to us by Miss Weale, who wrote from Nepaul, Croft Road, Torquay.

"January 26th, 1884.

"I had been—not on the day when the following was heard, but for some days previously—wondering why Dr. Pusey had not replied to a letter which I had written to him; when, sitting in our London drawing-room one day at about half-past 2 in the day, I suddenly heard Dr. Pusey speaking as if in a low voice close beside me. I was not cogitating about him, but suddenly and distinctly heard his voice speaking. The words were an answer to my letter written many days previously, and I so felt it to be *the* reply that I went to my writing-table and wrote it all down, and the day and hour; and moreover (how I know not) it was borne in on me, 'Why he is at Pusey Hall, and that is why he has not sooner replied,' and so it turned out to be. A few days after came a letter from him, written from Pusey Hall. The beginning of the letter bore the date of the day in question when I had heard his voice, but the end was dated the day previous, and in the letter *were the precise sentences I had heard.*

"C. J. DORATEA WEALE."

In answer to inquiries, Miss Weale adds :—

"It was not one sentence or two, but one side full of a small sheet of note-paper, such as he usually wrote on, but I don't carry long letters about with me, and could not tell you the wording now. I scribbled down my waking dream as to Dr. Pusey's words, being

impression to some one who made a note of it, or who distinctly remembers that it was so mentioned; and whenever this has been done, we have endeavoured to get written corroboration from this second person. Evidence of this class affords comparatively little opportunity for the various sorts of error which have been passed in review. No amount of carelessness of narration, or of love of the marvellous, would enable a witness to time his evidence in correspondence with an event of which he was ignorant, nor to fix on the right person with whom to connect his alleged experience. Errors of *memory* are equally unlikely to take a form which makes the impression correspond with an *unknown* event ; and danger from that source is, moreover, at a minimum, in cases which are distinguished by the very fact that the impression has been itself recorded immediately, or very shortly, after its occurrence.

But apart from the actual records of the experience in writing or in someone else's memory, it may have produced *action* of a sufficiently distinct sort on the percipient's part ; for instance, it may have so disturbed him as to make him take a journey, or write at once for tidings of the agent's condition. Such immediate action, which can often be substantiated by others, affords a strong independent proof that the impression had occurred, and had been of an unusual kind. And even if he has done none of these things, yet if

amazed at the vivid sense of his presence and voice, and all I wrote down was in the note."

Now everything here depends on the exact accuracy of the words. They were admittedly an answer to a letter, and their general tenor might easily have been surmised; unless, therefore, the words were *identical,* the case could be explained as a hallucination of hearing of a sufficiently ordinary type. We have obtained no complete assurance as to the verbal identity : and we have not been able to compare the letter with the note made at the time, which has probably been destroyed.

A similar criticism will apply to the following well-known case, written down in the first instance by the Rev. Joseph Wilkins, a Dissenting minister at Weymouth (who died in 1800), and endorsed by the late Dr. Abercrombie, of Edinburgh, a man, I need hardly say, of great scientific acumen :—

"Joseph Wilkins, while a young man, absent from home, dreamt, without any apparent reason, that he returned home, reached the house at night, found the front door locked, entered by the back door, visited his mother's room, found her awake, and said to her, 'Mother, I am going on a long journey, and am come to bid you good-bye.' A day or two afterwards this young man received a letter from his father, asking how he was, and alleging his mother's anxiety on account of a vision which had visited her on a night which was, in fact, that of the son's dream. The mother, lying awake in bed, had heard some one try the front door and enter by the back door, and had then seen the son enter her room, heard him say to her, 'Mother, I am going on a long journey, and am come to bid you good-bye,' and had answered, 'O dear son, thou art dead !' words which the son also had heard her say in his dream."

From an evidential point of view, everything again depends on the identity of the words dreamt and the words heard. And as we do not hear that Dr. Abercrombie compared a note of the dream made at the time with the father's letter, we have no assurance that Mr. Wilkins (by a lapse of memory, or through failure to perceive where the critical point lay) did not afterwards convert into absolute identity what was really a mere general resemblance. This would at once reduce the case to a mere "odd coincidence."

he describes a state of discomfort or anxiety, following on his experience and preceding his receipt of the news, this must, at any rate,
be accounted a fresh item of testimony, confirmatory of the mere
statement that such-and-such an unusual experience had befallen
him; and it is sometimes possible to obtain the corroboration of
others who have noticed or been made aware of this anxiety, even
though the source of it was not mentioned. If, however, he has kept
his feelings as well as their cause, to himself, there is, of course,
nothing but his subsequent memory to depend on. Here, therefore,
we shall have a transitional step to the next evidential class, where
the percipient's own perception of the importance of the experience,
and any possibilities of confirmation, date from a time when the condition of the agent has become known.

§ 9. Cases of this type are of course, as a class, less satisfactory.
It is here that some of the recognised tendencies to error—the impulse
to make vague things definite, and the impulse to make a group of facts
compact and harmonious—may find their opportunity. The error will,
of course, not arise without a certain foundation in fact: the news
that a friend has died is not in itself calculated to create a wholly
fictitious idea that one has had an unusual experience shortly before
the news arrived. But an experience which has been somewhat out
of the common may look quite different when recalled in the light of
the subsequent knowledge. It may not only gain in significance ; its
very content may alter. A person perhaps heard his name called
when no one was near, and, not being subject to hallucinations of
hearing, he was momentarily struck by the fact, but dismissed it from
his mind. A day or two afterwards he hears of a friend's death. It
then occurs to him that the events may have been connected. He
endeavours to recall the sound that he heard, and seems to hear in it
the tones of the familiar voice. Gradually the connection that he has
at first only dimly surmised, becomes a certainty for him ; and in
describing the occurrence, without any idea of deceiving, he will
mention his friend's voice as though he had actually recognised it at
the time. In the same way something dimly seen in an imperfect
light may take for subsequent memory the aspect of a recognisable
form ; or a momentary hallucination of touch may recur to the mind
as a clasp of farewell.

Now such possibilities cannot be too steadily kept in view, during
the process of collecting and sifting evidence. At the same time, the

interrogation of witnesses, and the comparison of earlier and later accounts, have not revealed any definite instance of this sort of inaccuracy. Now the number of alleged telepathic cases which we have examined (a number of which the narratives given in this book form less than a third) seems sufficiently large for the various types of error that really exist to have come to light ; and, as a matter of fact, certain types *have* come to light, and have helped us to a view of what may be called the laws of error in such matters. If, then, a particular form of inaccuracy is conspicuous by its absence from our considerable list of proved inaccuracies, it may be concluded, we think, not to have been widely operative. It would be a different matter if the cases of the lower evidential class stood alone—if we were unable to present any cases where the percipient's identification of his impression with the particular personality of the agent had been established beyond dispute. But in face of the large number of those stronger instances, it would be unwarrantably violent to suppose that in all, or nearly all, the other cases where the percipient declares that the identification was clear and unmistakeable, he is giving fictitious shape and colour to a purely undistinctive experience.

But there is yet another reason for allowing this inferior evidence to stand for what it is worth. For even if we make very large allowance for inaccuracy, and suppose that in a certain number of these cases the visible or audible phantasm, afterwards described as recognised, was really unrecognised at the moment, the evidence for a telepathic production of it does not thereby vanish. If, indeed, a witness's mental or moral status were such that he might be supposed capable of giving retrospective and objective distinctness to what was an utterly indefinite impression, with no external or sensory character at all, his testimony would, of course, be valueless ; simply because we could not assure ourselves that he had not had experiences of that sort daily, so that the coincidence with the real event would lose all significance. But in the case of a witness of fair intelligence, the point remains that the presence of a human being was suggested to his senses in a manner which was in his experience markedly unusual or unique, at the time that a human being at a distance with whom he was more or less closely connected, was in a markedly unusual or unique condition. By itself such evidence might fairly, perhaps, be regarded as too uncertain to support any hypothesis. But if a case for telepathy can be founded on the stronger cases, where the immediate reference of the impression to the agent is as much

established as the fact of the impression itself, then we have no right
to lay down as an immutable law of telepathic experience that
such a reference is indispensable. Recognition is beyond doubt the
best of tests ; and in a vast majority of our cases we have the
percipient's testimony, and in a very large number corroborative
testimony as well, to the fact of recognition. But distinctness and
unusualness in the experience are also evidential points. We have,
indeed, a whole class of cases where the percipient has expressly
stated that a phantasm which coincided with the supposed agent's
death was unrecognised, and where, therefore, the distinctness and
unusualness of the impression were the only grounds for paying any
attention to the coincidence. Such cases may be far from proving
telepathy ; yet if telepathy be a *vera causa*, it would be unscientific
to leave them out of account.

§ 10. So much for the evidence of the state of the agent, and of
the experience of the percipient, regarded simply as events, of which
we want to know (1) to what extent we can rely on the description that
we receive of them ; (2) to what extent the presumption of a
telepathic connection between them is affected by the sort of inaccuracies that may be revealed or surmised. The sketch that has
been given is, of course, a mere outline. It must wait for further
amplifications of detail till we come to examine the evidence itself.
Meanwhile it may serve to prepare the reader's mind, and to indicate
what special points to be on the look-out for. But of those four
essential items of a case, as to which the opportunities and the effect
of misrepresentation were to be specially considered, two still remain,
namely, the precise *times* of the two items already discussed—of the
agent's and the percipient's respective shares in the incident. It is
clearly essential to a telepathic case that these times should approximately coincide ; and error in the assertion of this coincidence is a
possibility requiring fully as much attention as error in the description
of the two events.

But here the reader may fairly ask where the line of error is to be
drawn. Must the coincidence be exact to the moment ? And, if not,
what degree of inexactness may be permitted before we cease to regard
a case as supporting the telepathic hypothesis ? It is unfortunately not
easy for the moment to give any satisfactory answer to this question.
Two distinct questions are in fact involved. The first is a question
of natural fact : What are the furthest limits of time within which it

appears, on a review of the whole subject, that a single telepathic phenomenon may really be included ? At what distance of time, from the death of an absent person, may a friend receive telepathic intimation of the fact ? The second question is one of interpretation and argument. It will be a most important part of our task hereafter to estimate the probability that it was *by chance*, and not as cause and effect, that the two events occurred at no very great distance of time from one another. The wider the interval, the greater, of course, does this probability become ; in other words, the larger the scope that we give to " coincidences " which we are willing to regard as *primâ facie* telepathic in origin, the greater is the chance that we shall be wrong in so regarding them. Now, unless some provisional limit were assigned to the interval which may separate the two events, it would be impossible to obtain numerical data for calculating what the force of the argument for chance really is, and how far the hypothesis of some cause beyond chance is justified. This point will be made clear in the first chapter of the second volume, which deals with " the theory of chance-coincidence " ; meanwhile it will be convenient to defer both these questions, and to make the following brief statement without discussion or explanation.

There is one class of cases which are not available for a numerical estimate at all—those, namely, where the agent's condition is not strictly limited in time ; for instance, where he is merely very ill, and no particular crisis takes place at or near the time when the percipient's impression occurs. This indefiniteness is, of course, a serious evidential weakness. But in a vast majority of the cases to be brought forward, the event that befalls the agent is short and definite. If, then, the experience of the percipient does not exactly coincide with that event, it must either follow or precede it. And, first, if it *follows* it ; then it will be convenient to limit the interval within which this must happen to 12 hours. I may mention at once that in most of our cases the coincidence seems to have been very considerably closer than this. But in a few cases the 12 hours' limit has been reached ; and if we found that, though some error in evidence had made the coincidence appear to have been closer than it really was, yet after correction the 12 hours seemed not to have been over-passed, we should still treat the case as having a *primâ facie* claim to be considered telepathic. Next as to the cases where the percipient's impression *precedes* some marked event or crisis in the existence of the other person concerned ; the question will then be, What was that other person's condition at the actual time that the impression occurred ? If it was *normal,* we should not argue here for any connection between the experiences of the two parties. For instance, we should not treat as evidence for telepathy an impression, however striking, which preceded by an appreciable interval an *accident* or *sudden* catastrophe of any sort.[1] But it may happen that the percipient's impression falls within a season in which the condition of the other party is distinctly *abnormal*—say a season of serious illness ; and that it likewise precedes by less than 12 hours the crisis—usually death—with which that season closes. And these cases will not only have a *primâ facie* claim to be considered telepathic, but will also admit of being used in a strict numerical estimate.

§ 11. To return now to the evidential question, it is really in the matter of dates, rather than facts, that the risk of an important mistake is greatest. In the first place, dates are hard things to remember : many persons who have a fairly accurate memory for facts which interest them have a poor memory for dates. This is a natural failing, and it is also one that may easily escape notice ; for in the vast majority of instances where a personal experience is afterwards recounted, the whole interest centres in the fact, and none at all in the date. But in examining the evidence for· an

---

[1] For instance, a trustworthy informant has given us the following account :—

"December, 1883.

"On November 5th, 1855, I was staying at a country house with several friends. It being a wet day, we amused ourselves by reading aloud, of which I did a large share ; but I was so overcome by the impression that a very dear brother was drowning, that ice had broken, and that he was drawn under it by the current, that I could not at all follow the purport of the book, and when alone, dressing for dinner, could only control my distress by arguing that there could be no fear of ice accidents, as the weather was exceptionally mild at that time. We afterwards learned my brother had been in very actual peril, having jumped into a canal dock to rescue a companion, who, being short-sighted, had fallen in in the dusk of the evening. He was then an undergraduate at Cambridge, and I was in Wales. He received a medal from the 'Humane Society,' and a watch, &c., from members of his college, in recognition of the act. I have never had any similar impression of death or danger to any one." [The friends with whom our informant was staying perfectly remember her mentioning to them what she had experienced.]

The brother—the Rev. J. C. Williams Ellis, of Gayton Rectory, Blisworth— confirms the facts as far as he was concerned ; but from his account, and that of Mr. A. Tibbits, of 44, Oakfield Road, Clifton, who was also present, we can fix the time of the accident at about 6.30 p.m. Now further inquiry has elicited the fact that the sister's depression began early in the afternoon, and reached its climax soon after 5. Her experience was certainly, therefore, not telepathic in origin.

The history of the Wheatcroft case, quoted in Chap. ix., affords another illustration of this point : had the death not been eventually proved to have preceded, and not followed, the vision, the case could not have been used. I may add that in this instance, the 12 hours' limit was possibly, but not certainly, exceeded.

alleged telepathic case, much more than ordinary human frailty in the matter of dates has to be considered. It is just here that the action of the various positive tendencies to error, above enumerated, is really most to be apprehended. Two unusual events—say the death of a friend at a distance, and the hearing of a voice which certainly sounded like his—have happened at no very great distance of time. The latter event recalls the former to the mind of the person who experienced it; and on reflection he feels that the character of the one connects it in a certain way with the other. True, he has kept no record of the day and hour when he heard the voice ; or his friend may have died in South America, and no accurate report of the date of the occurrence may ever have reached England ; but the connection which has been surmised cannot but raise a presumption that the two events corresponded in time as well as in character. " Why, otherwise, should I have heard the voice at all ? " the person who heard it will argue : " I am not given to hearing phantasmal voices. I did not know how to account for it before ; but now I see my way to doing so." This train of thought being pursued, it will seem in a very short time that the two events *must* have been simultaneous ; and what can that mean but that they *were* simultaneous ? And the fact thus arrived at will remain the point of the story, as long as it continues to be told. In allowing his mind to act thus, it will be seen that the percipient has merely followed the easy and convenient course. There was something baffling and aimless in the occurrence of the phantasmal voice, without rhyme or reason, at a time when the hearer was in good health and not even thinking of his friend. Rhyme and reason—significance and coherence—are supplied by the hypothesis that his friend, finding death imminent, was thinking of him. It does not occur to him that this account of the matter is in itself harder to accept than the fact of a subjective auditory hallucination. To realise this would require a certain amount of definite psychological know-ledge. Things are sufficiently explained to him if they seem to cohere in an evident way. Or if he is sensible that his version of the matter introduces or suggests a decided element of the marvellous, still the marvel is of a sort which is a legitimate subject of human speculation, and with which it is interesting to have been in personal contact. And not only has his reason thus followed the line of least resistance ; his memory has also been relieved by the unity which he has given to its contents. It has now got a single and well-compacted story to carry, instead of two disconnected items. It has, so to speak, exchanged two silver pieces, of different coinages and doubtful ratio, for a single familiar florin.

The above is no mere fancy sketch ; it represents what is really not unlikely to occur. When we were just now considering how far an honest and intelligent witness is likely to imagine afterwards that a passing impression which at the time was vague and unrecognised had really been distinct and recognised, it will be remembered that such a perversion seemed decidedly unlikely—that we saw no ground for assuming that an error of that type had entered into anything like a majority of the cases where we have no conclusive evidence that it has not entered. But with the dates it is otherwise. We have received several illustrations of the liability of even first-hand witnesses to make times exactly coalesce without due proof of their having done so, or even in spite of proof that they did not do so. Having by a reasoning process of a vague kind come to the conclusion that the two events were simultaneous, they will be apt to note any items of facts or inference which tell in this direction, and not such as may tell in the other. An informant sometimes by his very accuracy reveals the attitude of mind which might easily produce inaccuracy in other cases. He will tell us that all that was proved was that the death fell in the same month as the impression ; but that it is " borne in on him " that it was at the same hour. A good many people upon whom such a conviction is " borne in " will treat that as if it were itself the evidence required. One sort of case in which the tendency in question has been specially evident is that where the death has taken place at a great distance from the percipient. The instinct of artistic perfection overshoots the mark, when a ship's log in the Indian Ocean shows that death took place at a quarter-past 3, and a clock on an English mantelpiece reveals that that is the very minute of the apparition. Telepathy, like electricity, may " annihilate space "; but it will never make the time of day at two different longitudes the same. This particular error would not, it is true, completely vitiate the case from our point of view, since the 12 hours' interval would not have been exceeded ; but *pro tanto* it, of course, diminishes the credit of the witness.

§ 12. Let us now examine the two dates separately, and see where the danger more particularly lies, and what tests and safeguards can be adopted. And first as to the date of the event that has befallen the agent. As we have seen, it is almost always first from the percipient's side that we hear of this event; and to him the knowledge of it came as a piece of news, sometimes by word of mouth, sometimes in a letter or telegram, occasionally in some printed form. In very many cases the date would, of course, be part of the news. Now, if his own experience was impressive enough to have caused him real anxiety or curiosity, and if his recollection is clear that the news came almost immediately afterwards—say within a couple of days—and that the time of the two events was there and then compared, and found to coincide, the coincidence will then rest on something better, at any rate, than the mere memory of a date. It will depend on the memory that a certain unusual and probably painful state of mind received remarkable justification, and that this justification in turn produced another state of mind which was also of an unusual type. If there was really no such synchronism as is represented, then not only the abstract fact of correspondence, but a distinct and interesting piece of mental experience must have been fictitiously imagined.[1] Now, it may be said, I think, as a rule, that a fictitious imagination of this sort needs some little time to grow up ; that it is decidedly improbable that any case which is definitely recorded very soon after the event will have suffered this degree of misrepresentation. But a few years will give the imagination time to play very strange tricks. We have had one very notable proof of this, in a case where a curiously detailed vision of a dead man, which (so far as we can ascertain) must have followed the actual death by at least three months, was represented to us, after an interval of ten years, by the person who had seen it—a witness of undoubted integrity—as having occurred on the very night of the death. We may be right in regarding so complete a lapse of memory on the part of an intelligent witness as exceptional ; but we should certainly not be justified in *assuming* that it is exceptional; and no case of anything like that degree of remoteness can be relied on, without some

---

[1] The Rev. W. G. Payne, of Toppesfield, Essex, sends us a case of a parishioner, Mrs. Ellen Dowsett—"a quiet, sensible person," of whose good faith he was certain—who narrated to him the fact of her having been startled by the appearance of her husband, who was absent at Alexandria, and who died suddenly at that very time. "Feeling sure that this foreboded evil tidings, she became very anxious ; so much so that the clergyman of the parish came several times to try to console her. All his efforts to dismiss the thought from her mind availed nothing, and a settled conviction laid hold of her that her husband was dead." The case is not one that we should lay any stress on, as it comes to us second-hand (the percipient being dead), and we do not know who the clergyman was who was told of the apparition before the news arrived. But it illustrates the point in the text. Where an apparition causes such distress and apprehension as this, its date has at least a good chance of getting fixed in the mind ; and the greater, therefore, is the likelihood for the coincidence to be noted correctly.

evidence beyond the percipient's mere present recollection that the event which befell the agent took place at the time mentioned. The evidence may be of various sorts. If the exact date of the percipient's experience can be proved, then it is often possible to fix the other date as the same, by letters, diaries, or obituaries, or by the verbal testimony of some independent witness. If no such evidence is accessible, or even if the exact date of the percipient's experience is forgotten, it may still be possible to obtain corroboration of the coincidence from someone who was immediately cognisant of the percipient's experience, and who had independent means of ascertaining the further fact and of noting the connection at the time. But the absence of a written record of either event is, of course, a decidedly weak point.

§ 13. But on the whole, the danger that the closeness of the coincidence may be exaggerated depends rather on mis-statement of the date of the *percipient's* than of the *agent's* share in the alleged occurrence. Clearly the fact that some one has died or has had a serious accident, or has been placed in circumstances of some unusual sort, is likely to be known to more persons, and to be more frequently recorded in some permanent form, than the fact that some one has had, or says he has had, an odd hallucination. And clearly also, if one of the points is fixed, and the other, by hasty assumption or defective memory, is moved up to it, the moveable date is likely to be that of the event which has no ascertainable place in the world of objective fact. As a rule, it is at any rate possible at the time to obtain certainty as to the date of what has befallen the agent; and therefore if the percipient has been struck by his experience and retains evidence of its date, either in writing or in the memory of others to whom he mentioned it, he will very likely be prompted, when he hears of the other event, to assure himself as to what the degree of coincidence really was. But the converse case is very different. If the percipient does not record his experience at the time of its occurrence, even a week's interval may destroy the possibility of making sure what its exact date was ; and therefore, however certain the date of the other event may be, assurance as to the degree of coincidence will here be unattainable. It is often expressly recognised as such by the percipient himself ; and then one can only regret that the importance of the class of facts—if facts indeed they are—has been so little realised that the simple measures which would have ensured accurate evidence have not been taken. But where the account given is one of accurate coincidence, we cannot be satisfied without good evidence that the point was critically examined into at the time. It may, of course, happen that the percipient has a clear recollection that the coincidence was adequately made out at the time, although he can produce no documentary evidence which would establish it; and if others confirm his memory in this respect, that is so far satisfactory. Such unwritten confirmation, however, will have little independent force, unless the person who gives it was made aware of the percipient's experience within a very short time of its occurrence.

But though the danger here must be explicitly recognised, it is important not to exaggerate its practical scope. The coincidence may have been reported as closer than it was; but it may still, in a majority of cases, be fairly concluded to have fallen within the 12 hours' limit. As a rule, the news of what has befallen the agent arrives soon enough for not more than a space of two days to intervene between the percipient's knowledge of this event and the time when, to make the coincidence complete, his own experience must have taken place. We are not, therefore, making a large demand on his memory ; we are only requiring that he shall remember that an experience, which he represents as remarkable, befell him, or did not befall him, on the day before yesterday. No doubt, after a lapse of years, the evidential value of what a person reports ceases to have a close relation to the knowledge of the facts which it seems pretty certain he must have had at the time. But the demands made at the time on the intelligence either of the percipient, or of anyone else who had the opportunity of asking questions and forming conclusions, are so slight that we may fairly take contemporary written records of the matter, or even later verbal corroboration, as having a considerable claim to attention, even when the best evidence of all—evidence whose existence preceded the arrival of the news—is wanting. And it is important to notice that, while we have had several coincidences reported to us as having been close to the hour, which turned out, on further inquiry or examination of documents, to have been only close to the day, we have had very few cases where a similar correction has proved that the 12 hours' limit was really overpassed.[1] A good many coincidences,

---

[1] We have, however, a case where a death was reported to us as having taken place at 3 a.m., and where, on reference to the letter in which it was announced, it was found to have taken place at 6 p.m. The evidence on the percipient's side seemed satisfactory, as we received confirmation of the fact that she mentioned her impression at the time as a unique and very distressing one, without any knowledge that her brother, who died in Jamaica, was even ill ; and there can be no doubt that the impression did actually fall

no doubt, have been represented as extremely close, where no independent evidence on this point has been accessible, and closer inquiry has occasionally revealed that the assertion rested only on a guess. But wholly to neglect cases where the exactitude of the coincidence is not brought within the 12 hours' limit would clearly be unreasonable, provided that—on the evidence—it is not likely that this limit was much exceeded,[1] and not certain that it was exceeded at all. Such cases must, of course, be excluded from any numerical estimate based on precise data ; but they may fairly be allowed their own weight on the mind.

§ 14. We see, then, that cases where the alleged correspondence of facts and coincidence of dates are sufficiently close to afford a *primâ facie* presumption of telepathic action, may present very various degrees of strength and weakness; and it may be convenient to summarise the evidential conditions according to their value, in the following tabular form. (The words " the news " mean always the news of what has befallen the supposed agent.)

A. Where the event which befell the agent, with its date, is recorded in printed notices, or contemporary documents which we

---

within the period of serious illness. But the impression was a dream ; and a dream of death, however remarkable in its character, which is separated from the actual event by 18 hours, cannot be included in our evidence. In another very similar case, the percipient's impression was stated, and apparently correctly, to have occurred in the Crimea on January 11th, 1878, and the death (of a sister) in England to have taken place on the same day. But on examining the letter in which the news was announced, we find that the death actually took place on a Wednesday ; and Wednesday fell not on the 11th but on the 9th. The assumed coincidence, therefore, altogether breaks down. For some further instances see the " Additions and Corrections " which precede Chap. i.

1 This question of likelihood must be carefully weighed, according to the circumstances. The following case, from the Rev. Canon Sherlock, of Sherlockstown, Naas, which was published in our first report on the subject as possibly telepathic, is a specimen of what we certainly should not now feel justified in regarding as evidence.

"During the Indian Mutiny, my brother was serving (as ensign) in the 72nd Highlanders. At that time I was an undergraduate of Trinity College, Dublin, and living at Sandycove, near Kingstown. One night about 2 o'clock I was reading by the fire, when I heard myself distinctly called by my brother, the tone of his voice being somewhat raised and urgent; looking round I saw his head and the upper part of his body quite plainly. He appeared to be looking at me, and was about 7 or 8 feet distant. I looked steadily at him for about half a minute, when he seemed gradually to fade into a mist and disappear. The date of this occurrence I, unfortunately, lost note of, but upon my brother's return from India and my casually mentioning that I had so seen him, we talked the matter over, and both came to the conclusion that the apparition coincided with a dangerous attack of illness, in which my brother suddenly awoke with the impression that he was suffocating, at which moment he thought of me. The attack was brought on by sleeping during a forced march through a country great part of which was under water. This is the only apparition that I have ever experienced, and there was no anxiety on my mind which could have given rise to it, as we had quite recently had a letter from my brother, written in good health and spirits.
" W. SHERLOCK."

If one dismisses all *à priori* leanings to a telepathic explanation, there is nothing in this account which renders it unlikely that the two events were separated by (say) 10 days, or that the event in England preceded the one in India.

have examined; or is reported to us by the agent himself independently, or by some independent witness or witnesses ; and where

(1) The percipient (a) made a written record of his
experience, with its date, at the time of its occurrence,
which record we have either seen or otherwise ascertained
to be still in existence; or (β) before the arrival of the
news, mentioned his experience to one or more persons, by
whom the fact that he so mentioned it is corroborated ;
or (γ) immediately adopted a special course of action on
the strength of his experience, as is proved by external
evidence, documentary or personal.

(2) The documentary evidence mentioned in (1a) and
(1γ) is alleged to have existed, but has not been accessible
to our inspection ; or the experience is alleged to have been
mentioned as in (1β), or the action taken on the strength
of it to have been remarked as in (1γ), but owing to death
or other causes, the person or persons to whom the
experience was mentioned, or by whom the action was
remarked, can no longer corroborate the fact.

This second class of cases is placed here for convenience,
but should probably rank below the next class. At the same
time the fact that the percipient's experience was noted in
writing by him, or was communicated to another person,
or was acted on, before the arrival of the news, is not one
which is at all specially likely to be unconsciously invented
by him afterwards.

(3) The percipient did not (a) make any written record,
nor (β) make any verbal mention of his experience until
after the arrival of the news, but then did one or both ; of
which fact we have confirmation.

This class is of course, as a rule, decidedly inferior to the
first class. At the same time, cases occur under it in which
the news was so immediate that the fact of the coincidence could only be impugned by representing the whole story
as an invention.[1]

(4) The immediate record or mention on the arrival
of the news is alleged to have been made, but owing to
loss of papers, death of friends, or other causes, cannot be
confirmed.

[1] See, for instance, case 17, pp. 188-9.

L 2

(5) The percipient alleges that he remarked the coincidence when he heard the news; but no record or mention of the circumstance was made until some time afterwards.

Such cases, of course, rapidly lose any value they may have as the time increases which separates the account from the incident. Still, sometimes we have been able to obtain the independent evidence of some one who heard an account previous to the present report to us; or we have ourselves obtained two reports separated by a considerable interval. And where a comparison of accounts given at different times shows that they do not vary, this is to some extent an indication of accuracy.

B. Where the percipient is our sole authority for the nature and date of the event which he alleges to have befallen the agent.

In many of these cases, the percipient is also our sole authority for his own experience; and the evidence under this head will then be weaker than in any of the above classes. But where we have independent testimony of the percipient's mention of the two events, and of their coincidence, soon after their occurrence—he having been at the time in such circumstances that he would naturally know the nature and date of what had befallen the agent—the case may rank as higher in value than some of those of Class A (5).

§ 15. The evidence which I have so far analysed is *first-hand* evidence—in the sense that the main account comes to us direct from the percipient. The present collection, however, includes (in the Supplement) a certain number of second-hand narratives; and it will be well, therefore, to consider briefly what are the best sorts of second-hand evidence, and what kinds of inaccuracy are most to be apprehended in the transmission of telepathic history from mouth to mouth.

There is one, and only one, sort of second-hand evidence which can on the whole be placed on a par with first-hand; namely, the evidence of a person who has been informed of the experience of the percipient while the latter was still unaware of the corresponding event; and who has had equal opportunities with the percipient for learning the truth of that event, and confirming the coincidence. The second-hand witness's testimony in such a case is quite as likely to be accurate as the percipient's for though his impression of the actual details will no doubt be less vivid, yet on the other hand he will not be under the same temptation to exaggerate the force or strangeness of the impression in subsequent retrospection. Specimens of this class have therefore been admitted to the body of the work, as well as to the Supplement. Putting this exceptional class aside, the value of second-hand evidence chiefly depends on the relation of the first narrator to the second. A second-hand account from a person only slightly acquainted with the original narrator is of very little value ; not only because it is probably the report of a story which has been only once heard, and that, perhaps, in a hurried or casual way ; but also because the less the reporter's sense of responsibility to his informant, the less also will be his sense of responsibility to the facts, and the greater the temptation to improve on the original.¹ But we cannot so lightly dismiss the testimony of near relatives and close friends to a matter which they have heard the first-hand witness narrate more than once, or narrate in such a manner as convinced them that the alleged facts were to him realities, and had made a lasting impression on his mind. Here we at any rate' have a chance of forming a judgment as to the character of the original authority ; we can make tolerably certain that what we hear was never the mere anecdote of a *raconteur ;* and we have grounds for assuming in our own informants a certain instinct of fidelity which may at any rate preserve their report from the errors of wilful carelessness and exaggeration. It not infrequently happens, too, that we can obtain several independent versions from several second-hand witnesses, which may mutually confirm one another ; and contemporary documentary evidence may give further support to the case.

The risks of error in *transmitted* evidence are, of course, in many respects the same, in an intensified form, as those of original evidence. To a person who is told something which sounds surprising by some one else who has experienced it, the central marvel is apt to stand out in memory with undue relief ; and the various details and considerations which might modify the marvellous element will drop out of sight. One is, of course, familiar with the same process in the case of almost any anecdote or witticism that gets at all *répandu :* the

---

¹ A lady has described to us a hallucination which presented to her the form of her father-in-law, who had been dead 14 years. An acquaintance, to whom she once mentioned this experience, had reported it to us as the apparition of her brother, with the addition that "a short time afterwards she received news of her brother's death, which had taken place at the very time of the apparition." There is a touch of nature in the fact that the author of this amended version considers the original witness "not at all an imaginative person."

point is retained, the details and surroundings vary. For purposes of amusement such variations may be wholly unimportant; for purposes of evidence they may be all-important. Facts, moreover, are very much easier to improve than *bon mots* and the like, and with the second-hand narrator the tendency to make things picturesque and complete, by the addition, omission, or transformation of details, is naturally stronger in that there is no deeply-graven sense of the reality to act as a check on it. A gentleman, who signs himself " Rector," writes to the *Daily Telegraph*, and describes a number of clergymen sitting round a table, on the evening when the late Bishop of Winchester met with his fatal accident. " One of them said, ' There is the Bishop looking in at that window.' Another immediately said, ' No, he is at this window.' " What really happened—as we learn from Mr. G. W. Paxon, who was present at the scene referred to—was that a strange figure passed the three windows of the dining-room at Wotton, but that " it was not possible for the gentlemen present " (who, by the way, were three only, and all laymen) to identify it. Mr. Evelyn went out to see who it could be, but it had disappeared with mysterious rapidity. And that is the whole story. Again, a young man, we are told, was dying in London, his friends being unaware of his whereabouts. A sister of his in Edinburgh, who was also dying, " said that she was present at the death-bed of her brother; she gave an outline of his room, and *told the name and number* of the street." A friend of our informant's, Mr. David Lewis, of 21, St. Andrew Square, Edinburgh, was then asked to inquire, went to the address, and found (as he informs us) that the young man had just died there. But on more careful inquiry from the lady's husband, we learn that though his wife described the room, she did not see the name of the street; and that he himself knew his brother-in-law's address at the time, and had actually received a letter saying that he was very ill and not expected to live. The description of the room—even if proved to be correct—could have no evidential force unless extremely minute. All that remains to be accounted for, therefore, is the lady's impression as to her brother's condition; and though her husband is sure that she could not have known it in any ordinary way, it is impossible for outsiders—remembering that the knowledge did exist in the house at the time—to share his confidence. Again, a gentleman tells us how his grandfather, when taking a walk at Honfleur, on November 24th, 1859, saw the apparition of his (our informant's) sister, who expired at that time in England. He followed the figure, and it disappeared on reaching his garden. "In conversation afterwards the very wrapper worn by the deceased was described." We obtain a copy of the original letter in which the grandfather described the occurrence, and find that he was walking "in the dark and a drizzling rain" when he observed something very white. "It appeared to be a lady in white, without a bonnet, but a large white veil over her head. It disappeared at the door of a house. This took place as near the time of dear Sarah's departure as possible." Here, therefore, the second-hand account *introduced* the recognition, *omitted* the uncertain light, and *altered* the place of disappearance. Once more, a lady has had a strong impression of her husband's being in danger, at a time when he actually had a narrow escape in a railway accident. In this accident a number of cattle were killed, and the line was red with their blood. The story comes round to us that the wife had not only an impression of danger, but a vivid picture of blood.

It is amusing sometimes to find that evidence breaks down on the exact point which has been held to be its most convincing feature. The following narrative, though a third-hand one, seemed to have some claim to attention, as it reached us from two independent quarters; and the two accounts so completely agree that we may assume that we have the correct version of the second-hand witness. Mr. W. C. Morland, of Lamberhurst Court Lodge, Kent, (who vouches for no more than that he repeats exactly what he was told,) writes to us as follows:—

"August 11th, 1883.

"My wife's great-uncle was private secretary to Warren Hastings in India, and one day, when sitting in Council, they all saw a figure pass through the Council-room into an inner room, from which there was no other exit. One of the Council exclaimed, 'Good God! that is my father.' Search was made in the inner room, but nothing could be found, and Warren Hastings, turning to his secretary, said, 'Cator, make a note of this, and put it with the minutes of to-day's Council.' As a small incident in the story, it was noticed that the figure had one of our modern pot hats. Some months after, a ship arrived bringing the news of the old gentleman's death and the first pot hats that had been seen in India.

"I simply tell it you as I heard it from a Mr. Sparkes, who is now dead, and who, as well as my wife, was a great-nephew to—and probably heard it from—the old Mr. Cator who was present at the Council. I never heard him say whether he heard it direct from Mr. Cator, but I think it likely, as he was rather nearly related, and from his age must have known him."

Precisely similar details were given by Mr. Sparkes to the Rev. B. Wrey Savile, who has published the case in his book on *Apparitions;* in this account the Member of Council who recognised his father figures as Mr. Shakespeare. Now the official minutes of the Supreme Council have been searched for us; but it does not appear either that Mr. Shakespeare was a Member of Council at the time, or that Mr. Cator was Hastings' private secretary, though he was certainly in the Company's service. We learn, however, from the Superintendent of Records at the India Office that "it is believed that the registers of the Company's servants in India at that early date were not always quite accurate "; so that these discoveries would not alone have thrown serious suspicion on the report. And the chimney-pot hat seemed, at any rate, something respectable to stand by. The phantom, in fact, owed his character to his hat ; for it is hard to imagine how Mr. Cator or Mr. Sparkes could have gratuitously introduced such a feature into the story. But the curious perfection of the detail as to the simultaneous arrival of the news and of the real hats at once suggests scrutiny of the dates. All the accounts of chimney-pot hats that we have been able to find agree that they came into use between 1790 and 1795, though they seem to have been worn in France as early as 1787. They cannot, therefore, have reached India before the termination of Hastings' governorship in 1785. Thus the case at once assumes a mythical air ; and the most we can assume is that probably some odd coincidence occurred.[1]

I will add a case where the instinct that we have noticed, to make evidence *picturesque,* has so far overleapt itself as to supply the very means of confutation. The late Mrs. Howitt Watts gave us the narrative as from her mother, who had "many times heard it related " by *her* mother, the percipient, and so far it is third-hand. But Mrs. Watts had also heard it from her grandmother's own lips. The occurrence took place at Heanor, in Derbyshire.

"My mother's family name, Tantum, is an uncommon one, which I do not recollect to have met with, except in a story of Miss Leslie's. My mother had two brothers, Francis and Richard. The younger, Richard, I

---

[1] Very comparable is an account which we have received, written by the late Lieut.-Colonel Balneavis—describing how, when a child, he was woke by his mother, who had had a terrifying vision of her husband "putting a corpse in full uniform on a sofa, and afterwards covering it over with a white sheet "; and how his father was "at the very time" performing these offices for Sir T. Maitland, Governor of Malta, with whom he had been dining, and who "dropped down dead at table." We find from the *Annual Register* that Sir T. Maitland was taken ill in the middle of the day, at the house of a friend, and died there in the evening, in bed, after being speechless for 8 hours.

knew well, for he lived to an old age.   The elder, Francis, was at the time of the occurrence I am about to report, a gay young man, about twenty, unmarried, handsome, frank, affectionate, and extremely beloved by all classes throughout that part of the country.   He is described, in that age of powder and pigtails, as wearing his auburn hair flowing in ringlets on his shoulders, like another Absalom, and was much admired, as well for his personal grace as for the life and gaiety of his manners.

" One fine calm afternoon, my mother, shortly after a confinement, but perfectly convalescent, was lying in bed, enjoying, from her window, the sense of summer beauty and repose : a bright sky above, and the quiet village before her.   In this state she was gladdened by hearing footsteps which she took to be those of her brother Frank, as he was familiarly called, approaching the chamber-door.   The visitor knocked and entered. The foot of the bed was towards the door, and the curtains at the foot, notwithstanding the season, were drawn, to prevent any draught.   Her brother parted them, and looked in upon her.   His gaze was earnest, and destitute of its usual cheerfulness, and he spoke not a word.   ' My dear Frank,' said my mother, ' how glad I am to see you.   Come round to the bedside ; I wish to have some talk with you.'

"He closed the curtains, as complying ; but instead of doing so, my mother, to her astonishment, heard him leave the room, close the door behind him, and begin to descend the stairs.   Greatly amazed, she hastily rang, and when her maid appeared she bade her call her brother back.   The girl replied that she had not seen him enter the house.   But my mother insisted, saying, ' He was here but this instant. Run ! quick ! call him back ! I must see him.'

"The girl hurried away, but, after a time, returned, saying that she could learn nothing of him anywhere ; nor had anyone in or about the house seen him either enter or depart.

" Now, my father's house stood at the bottom of the village, and close to the high-road, which was quite straight ; so that anyone passing along it must have been seen for a much longer period than had elapsed.   The girl said she had looked up and down the road, then searched the garden— a large, old-fashioned one, with shady walks.   But neither in the garden nor on the road was he to be seen.   She had inquired at the nearest cottages in the village ; but no one had noticed him pass.

"My mother, though a very pious woman, was far from superstitious ; yet the strangeness of this circumstance struck her forcibly.   While she lay pondering upon it, there was heard a sudden running and excited talking in the village street."

Briefly, the cause of the disturbance was that Mr. Francis Tantum had just been killed.   He had been dining at Shipley Hall, about a mile off, and was riding home after the early country dinner of that day— somewhat elated, it may be, with wine.   He stopped at the door of an ale-house at Heanor, where he offended the young man who served him, by striking him with his whip.   The youth ran into the house, seized a carving-knife, darted back, and stabbed him.

This story obtained a certain currency, having been published by Mr. Dale Owen in his *Footfalls.*   Yet the simple precaution of getting independent evidence as to the time of the death goes far to ruin its character. A certificate sent to us by the rector of the parish shows that Mr. F. Tantum was buried on the *4th of February*, and that his age was 36. And this does more than merely disturb our picture of the quiet summer scene, and of the Absalom of twenty. The time of year shows that the percipient's vision probably took place *after dark;* so that "any one passing along the high-road" might very well *not* have been seen a minute after his departure; and the inquiries at the cottages would have been worth little or nothing. But these researches, as they are described, must have taken time ; and as the news of the murder would be likely to spread fast, we should conclude that that event took place decidedly *after* the vision. Thus there appears no adequate reason why the apparition should not have been the *real man*—his conduct, though undoubtedly odd, being explicable by the state of slight intoxication which the narrative suggests.

But apart from sensational additions, details are apt to creep in which seem sober and innocent enough, but which make the whole difference from an evidential point of view. A very striking narrative reaches us from a second-hand source, as to how an officer in India one day saw his father, long deceased, issue from a wood leading his mother by the hand ; how the latter addressed some words to her son, and the pair then vanished ; and how he afterwards learnt that his mother had died in England on that very day. We happened already to have a first-hand account of the incident, in which the visitation that coincided with the death was described not as a *waking percept*, but as a *dream*. The enormous difference, for the purpose of our argument, which this point involves will abundantly appear in the sequel. Again, in transmitted cases it is quite remarkable how often the percipient "made a note" of his experience at the time of its occurrence—an act of foresight in which percipients, to judge from their own first-hand accounts, seem only too apt to fail.

In transmitted evidence, which is more remote than second-hand, another frequent point is that the chain of transmission is shortened —that a narrative which has really passed through two or through three mouths will be represented as having passed only through one or through two. For instance, a gentleman tells us of a striking telepathic phantasm which appeared to a friend of his, a sea-captain, on board ship. Nautical phantasms are not a favourite class of ours; the evidence is too apt to "suffer a sea-change"; and even the guarantee offered to us in respect of another specimen, that "the crew had no difficulty in believing it," is not completely reassuring. But the present example, at any rate, proved quite too superlatively nautical; for it turned out that the sea-captain was not the original witness, but had heard the story from another sea-captain; and that *this* sea-captain had heard it from the "man at the wheel"; whom we have not troubled for it. Again, a story which has been more than once printed by Spiritualistic writers begins as follows:—"Mrs. Crawford, in the *Metropolitan Magazine* in 1836, tells us that the *then* Lord Chedworth was a man who suffered deeply from doubts"— and then describes how the apparition of a sceptical friend of Lord Chedworth's presented itself one night, told him that there was a judgment to come, and disappeared—the news of the friend's death arriving "in due course" next morning. On referring to Mrs. Crawford's own account, we find the hero of the story described as "Lord Chedworth, the *father* of the *late* lord": and even this description is incorrect, as the fourth baron—with whose death in 1804 the title became extinct—succeeded, not his father, but his uncle.[1] This possible shortening of the chain of evidence is a point that must never be lost sight of when the account was given orally to the last witness, and was not made the subject of minute inquiry.[2] But perhaps no feature of the transmitted narratives is on the whole so suggestive as the wonderful exactness of the all-important time-coincidence; which in these cases we must be doubly careful of

---

[1] The story which "drags at each remove a lengthening chain," even though the removes be in the direction of its source, is a type that has become very familiar to us. The following is a sample of many a correspondence which is more amusing in retrospect than in reality,

Miss A. described to me a remarkable incident, as related to her by the Rev. B., who had heard of it from the lady to whom it occurred.

The Rev. B., on being applied to, said that he had heard of it, not from the lady to whom it occurred, but from the Rev. C.

The Rev. C. was applied to, but had only heard the story from the Rev. D.; with whose appearance on the scene hope revived.

The Rev. D. reported that he had not heard the story from the heroine of it, but from a friend of hers, Mrs. E., who would procure it from the heroine.

Mrs. E., in turn, reported that her authority, Miss F., was not herself the heroine, but had been informed by Miss G., who was.

Miss F., on being applied to, had only heard Miss G.'s story *third-hand*, but referred me to Miss H., a nearer friend of Miss G.'s.

Miss H. kindly applied to Miss G., but reported, as the result, that Miss G.'s own information was only *third* or *fourth* hand.

Such is the last state (as far as I am concerned at any rate) of a story which began by being third-hand, and has been traced back through seven mouths.

[2] For instance, a friend of the present writer reports as follows:—

"About ten years ago Admiral Johnson, of Little Baddow, Essex, told me as follows: One day he was walking with companions in a wood, when he suddenly saw his brother Arthur, in uniform, and said, 'There's my brother!' It was discovered afterwards that the brother died at that time."

We have failed to trace this occurrence; and it may be surmised as possible that the hero of the story, which was told in casual conversation, was not Admiral Johnson

assuming to have been founded on a genuine coincidence of a less exact kind (p. 139). Thus, a gentleman strikingly describes to us how a friend of his, while walking in Barnsley, and when no one was within 30 yards of her, felt herself seized by two hands round the waist ; her only " enlightenment on the matter " being that " on the very same afternoon her brother went down with the ill-fated training ship, the ' Eurydice.' " On applying direct to the lady, we find that the hallucination took place " two days before the dreadful accident." The more remote the incident, and the less the authority for the story, the more clinching the correspondence becomes, till its perfection is really quite wearisome. " On the day of his vision, and *at that very moment,*

himself, but some one else. That is, the story may be third-hand, and is of no evidential value.

The following narrative from Mrs. Lonsdale, of Lichfield, is another instance in point :—

" I was sitting next my dear old friend, Dr. (since Sir Thomas) Watson, at a London dinner-party. I think some one on the opposite side of the table said to him, ' A physician in your extensive practice must hear and see strange things sometimes.' He said, ' Indeed we do.' He then turned to me and said, ' *You* know that I am a matter-of-fact person, and I will now tell you the strangest of all the strange things that ever happened to me.

" ' I was called in, some years ago, to see a man, a stranger to me, who had been taken dangerously ill at his chambers in the Temple. Directly I saw him I knew that he had not more than 24 hours to live, and I told him that he must lose no time in settling any worldly affairs, and in sending for any relations whom he might wish to see. He told me he had only one near relation, a brother, who was in one of the Midland counties. By my patient's desire, I sat down and wrote to the brother, telling him that if he would find the sick man still alive he must come off at once, on receipt of my letter. The next morning, while I was visiting my patient, who was then sinking fast, the brother arrived. As he came in at the door, the dying man fixed his eyes on his face and said, " Ah ! brother, how d'ye do—I saw you last night, you know." To my infinite surprise, the brother, instead of appearing to take these words as I did, for the dreamy wanderings of extreme weakness, replied quietly, " Ah ! yes—so you did—so you did." All was over in a very short time, and when we left the bedroom together, I could not help asking the brother what those strange words meant. He said, " You may well ask, but as sure as I see you now, I saw my brother in the middle of last night ; he came out of a cupboard at the foot of my bed, and after gazing at me for a minute or two, without speaking, he disappeared." ' "

An account of what appears to be the same incident is given, as authentic, but without names, by Dr. Elliotson, in the *Zoist*, Vol. viii., p. 70. But on the other hand, Sir T. Watson's family, to whom we applied, seem never to have heard of the story ; which we may therefore not unreasonably suppose to have been narrated as a friend's experience.

I give one more instance—worth nothing of course as it stands—in the hope of inducing some readers to take down at the time the names and addresses of casual acquaintances who seem to have *bonâ fide* evidence to produce. The account was sent to us by Mrs. Pritchard, of The Cottage, Bangor, North Wales, on February 7th, 1884.

" I much regret that I am not able to give you the name and address of the lady [*i.e.,* Mrs. Pritchard's informant], for I do not know it myself. I met her at the Barmouth Hotel last summer. She told me that upon one occasion, when her husband had left home for a couple of days, she had a most painful impression that he was being crushed. When he returned she ran up to him, saying, ' Oh, I'm so glad you have come back safely, for I've had a dreadful feeling that you were crushed.' Her husband then told her that he had seen a woman crushed to death by the train close by where he stood, and it affected him greatly—he couldn't get it out of his mind, and it prevented him sleeping.

" I have written to Barmouth to try and find out the name of these people, but as no visitors' book is kept at the hotel, they were unable to give me any information. I think the name was Dickenson, and I know that the husband is a solicitor in one of the English towns—a young man."

Here, if we could have discovered the address, the account might possibly have been made first-hand ; at present we should not be safe in giving it even as second-hand.

his friend was passing away," is quite the accepted sort of formula. We may hunt far in such accounts before we find any guarding clauses, as that " the hour of death was never exactly ascertained," or " the vision was in the morning, but the death did not take place till the afternoon "—clauses which are common enough, be it observed, in first-hand records.

It would, however, not be fair to leave this list of causes which diminish the amount of presentable second-hand evidence, without adding that of the more reliable sort of second-hand (no less than of first-hand) cases, a considerable number are withheld from publication from motives with which it is hard altogether to sympathise. Persons who have a really accurate knowledge of some incident in which a deceased relative has been concerned, and who—seeing that the incident did no dishonour to any one's head or heart—have no scruple in publishing it at casual dinner-parties, become sometimes almost morbidly scrupulous when there is a question of making it available, even in an anonymous form, for a scientific purpose.

Here I may close this preliminary survey of the possibilities of error which must be constantly kept in view in the investigation of alleged telepathic cases, and which must be either excluded by evidence or carefully allowed for. Both the dangers and the safe-guards will, of course, be better realised when we come to the details of particular cases. It does not seem necessary to give a similar synopsis of the evidential flaws and weaknesses which are not in any sense *errors*. Some of these may be apparent on the very face of the evidence ; as when the percipient expressly states that his impression was of an undefined sort, or was of a sort which he had experienced on other occasions without the correspondence of any real event, or that the coincidence of dates, though close, was not exactly ascertained. Others may appear when we take all the circumstances into considera-tion, although the percipient may fail to admit them ; for instance, a person who is in decided anxiety about an absent relative or friend may be regarded as to some extent predisposed to subjective impres-sions which suggest his presence, so that the accidental coincidence of such an impression with some actual crisis that is apprehended may be regarded as not violently improbable. All such topics, however, will find a more convenient place in the sequel.

§ 16.   And now with regard to the cases that have been included in the evidential part of the present work.   A certain separation has been attempted. In the main body of the book, no cases are given which are not first-hand, or of the particular second-hand sort which (as explained on p. 148) is on a par with first-hand; or in which the *primâ facie* probability that the facts stated are substantially correct is not tolerably strong. But the Supplement includes a good many second-hand accounts;[1] as well as first-hand accounts where the evidence, from lack of corroboration or other causes, falls short of the standard previously attained.[2] Our principle in selecting cases for the Supplement has been to take only those which—supposing telepathy to be established as a fact in Nature—would reasonably be regarded as examples of it. Their existence adds force to the proof of telepathy; but we should not have put them forward as an adequate proof by themselves. This separation, however, does not apportion the evidential weight of the two divisions with rigid precision. For, given a certain amount of assurance that the facts are correctly reported, the value of the facts *in the argument for telepathy* will vary according to the class to which they belong. There are strong classes and weak classes. Now the body of the work includes specimens of purely emotional impressions, and of dreams— classes which we shall find by their very nature to be weak; and more weight might reasonably be attached to some case in the Supplement, even though less completely attested, if it belonged to the strongest class, which we shall find to be the class of waking visual phantasms. And even within the limits of a single class, it is impossible to evaluate the cases with exactness. A phantasm of sight or sound which does not at the moment suggest the appearance or voice of an absent friend, may still—if unique in the percipient's experience, and if the coincidence of time with the friend's death is exact—have about an equal claim to be considered telepathic with a distinctly recognised phantasm, the coincidence of which with the death (though it may have been exact) cannot with certainty be brought closer than three or four days.

Then as regards the mere accuracy of the records—though it has been possible to draw up a sort of table of degrees, such a table, of course, affords no final criterion. It is a guide in the dissection of

---

[1] We have seen that there is one sort of second-hand evidence which must rank as on a par with first-hand. On the same principle there is one sort of third-hand evidence which must rank as on a par with second-hand. A few third-hand accounts of this type have been admitted to the Supplement; and one or two others by special exception.

[2] There are, however, a few first-hand cases in the Supplement which would have found a place in the main body of the work (in substitution probably for some which now appear there), had they been received earlier.

testimony; it directs attention to important structural points; but it takes no account of the living qualities, the character, training, and habits of thought of witnesses. We have included no cases where the witnesses were not, to the best of our belief, honest in intention, and possessed of sufficient intelligence to be competent reporters of definite facts with which they had been closely connected. But the report, say, of a sceptical [1] lawyer or a man of science, who had totally disbelieved in the whole class of phenomena until convinced by his own experience, is naturally stronger evidence than the report of a lady who, whether owing to natural proclivities or to want of scientific training, has no sense of any *à priori* objections to the telepathic hypothesis. The report of a person who has seen the phantasm of a friend at the time of his death, but considers that the coincidence may have been accidental, is stronger evidence than the report of a person who would regard such a supposition as irreverent. Each case must be judged on its merits, by reference to a considerable number of points; [2] and as far as

---

[1] It occasionally happens, however, that scepticism, no less than superstition, may mar the evidence. We have received a case where two sisters in England, sleeping apparently in different rooms, saw the form of another sister who was just dying in Germany; but, "having a horror of encouraging superstitious fancies," they purposely abstained from making an exact note of the day and hour, and neither of them mentioned what she had seen to the other. And thus the triumph of robust common-sense has been to prevent the verification of a date!

[2] Among the variety of considerations involved, it is impossible to hope for more than a general approval of our principles of admission. The cases on the line often present a very puzzling array of *pros* and *cons.* Take, for instance, the following first-hand instance.

On February 10th, 1884, Mrs. Longley, of 4, Liverpool Lawn, Ramsgate, a respectable married woman, who has never had any other hallucination of the senses, heard a voice call "Mother" three times. She knew that she had been awake, as she had been restless, and was amusing herself by seeing how long the moon would take to cross a certain pane of glass. She thought that her son, who was sleeping in a room above her own, must be ill; but on going up, she found him fast asleep. She tells us that she looked at the clock on the stairs, and noticed that it was 3.15 a.m. Nine days afterwards she received the news that her eldest and much-loved son, who was at sea, had been drowned, at about that hour, on a moonlight night, and that his first cry was, "Mother, mother, mother! Save me for my mother's sake." Her husband, she says, went to Grimsby, and learnt these details from the captain of the vessel, and also made out that the night was the same as that of her own experience.

Now the incidents here are recent; and we need feel no doubt as to the fact either of the unusual auditory impression (which Mrs. Longley mentioned to several people besides her own family before the news arrived), or of the death. These are the *pros.* The *cons.* are as follows. (1) The voice was unrecognised. This, however, would not alone be fatal to the evidence; and in one way it even tells in favour of the telepathic explanation, as, had the voice suggested the son at sea, it would have been easier to ascribe the impression to latent anxiety on his account. (2) The narrator is quite uneducated; and times and intervals are matters in which the memory of uneducated persons is specially apt to get hazy. (3) She is certain that her husband, and the son who was at home, would not corroborate her statement in writing—her husband in particular having an aversion to signing documents. (4) No note having been taken, nothing that the husband could say now would convince us that he was justified in his conclusion as to the coincidence of the day; and though the date of the *death* might still be ascertained by independent inquiry, this would not help us, as the exact date of the *voice* is irrecoverable.

The inclusion of such a case would perhaps not have injured our argument; but we have felt it safer to reject it.

written testimony goes, the reader will have the same opportunities as we have had for forming an opinion. We have done our best to obtain corroborative evidence of all sorts, whether from private sources, from public notices, or from official records. We have often failed ; and these failures, and other evidential flaws, have been brought into (I fear) wearisome prominence. In quotations, care has, of course, been taken to give the exact words of witnesses. The only exceptions are that (1) we have occasionally omitted reflections and 'other matter which formed no part of the evidence ; and (2) we have corrected a few obvious slips of writing, and introduced an occasional word for the sake of grammatical coherence, where the narrative has come to us piecemeal, or where the above-named omissions have been made. But in no case have we made the slightest alteration of meaning, or omitted anything that could by any possibility be held to modify the account given. A few cases have been summarised, in whole or in part ; but here the form of the sentences will show that they are not quotations. Any word or phrase interpolated for other than grammatical reasons is clearly distinguished by being placed within square brackets.

One advantage, however, which we ourselves have had, cannot be communicated to our readers—namely, the increased power of judgment which a personal interview with the narrator gives. The effect of these interviews on our own minds has been on the whole distinctly favourable. They have greatly added to our confidence that what we are here presenting is the testimony of trustworthy and intelligent witnesses. And if the collection be taken as a whole, this seems to be a sufficient guarantee. It follows from the very nature of telepathic cases (as distinguished, say, from the alleged phenomena of "ghost-seeing" or of "Spiritualism") that the evidence often in great measure, so to speak, *makes itself*—the agent's side in the matter being beyond dispute. Thus a valid case, as has been shown above, might perfectly well rest on the testimony of a person whose own interpretation of it was totally erroneous, and whose intelligence and memory were only adequate to reporting truthfully that he thought he saw so-and-so in his room yesterday or the day before. But we have naturally preferred to be on the safe side. We have, therefore, excluded all narratives where, on personal acquaintance with the witnesses, we felt that we should be uneasy in confronting them with a critical cross-examiner ; and we have frequently thought it right to exclude

FOR SPONTANEOUS TELEPATHY.

cases, otherwise satisfactory, that depended on the reports of uneducated persons.[1] Nor, I think, will the reader find much to suggest perversion of facts through superstitious à priori fancies. The greater part of our witnesses, as already stated, have had no special belief in the phenomena, except so far as they have themselves come in contact with them; and even where their interest has been awakened, it has seldom been of a more intense kind than might naturally be excited by a remarkable passage of personal or family experience. They have not, for instance, been at all in the attitude towards the subject which is now ours, and which it is hoped that the reader may come to share. Thus even on this score, their common-sense, in the ordinary straightforward meaning of the term, could hardly be impugned. Perhaps even so general a testimony to character as this is somewhat of an impertinence; to give it precision in particular cases would, as a rule, be out of the question. But however little weight such an expression of opinion may have, the mere statement that we are, in the large majority of cases, personally acquainted with our witnesses, has a distinct bearing on the evidence; for it practically implies that they gave us their account in such a way that their good faith is pledged to it.

§ 17. But there is quantity as well as quality to consider: the basis of our demonstration needs to be broad as well as strong. We might have a few correspondences perfect in every detail, a few

---

[1] First-hand evidence, where the witness cannot be cross-questioned, is at once invalidated by any doubt as to the case that may have been felt by persons who were more immediately cognisant of it. The well-known Norway story is an instance. In *Early Years and Late Reflections*, by Clement Carlyon, M.D., there is a signed account by Mr. Edmund Norway of a vision of his brother's murder that he had while in command of the Orient, on a voyage from Manilla to Cadiz. Mr. Arthur S. Norway, son of the murdered man and nephew of Mr. Edmund Norway, tells us that the account was taken down by Dr. Carlyon from his uncle, at the latter's house; he himself also has heard it from his uncle's own lips. It describes with some detail how in a vision, on the night of February 8th, 1840, Mr. Edmund Norway saw his brother set upon and killed by two assailants at a particular spot on the road between St. Columb and Wadebridge : and how he immediately mentioned the vision to the second officer, Mr. Henry Wren. The brother was actually murdered by two men at that spot, on that night, and the details—as given in the confession of one of the murderers, William Lightfoot—agree with those of the vision. But Mr. Arthur Norway further tells us that another of his uncles and the late Sir William Molesworth "investigated the dream at the time. Both were clever men, and they were at that time searching deeply and experimenting in mesmerism—so that they were well fitted to form an opinion. They arrived at the conclusion that the dream was imagined." Mr. Arthur Norway has also heard Mr. Wren speak of the voyage, but without any allusion to the dream. This is just a case, therefore, where we may justly suspect that detail and precision have been *retrospectively* introduced into the percipient's experience.

It almost goes without saying, in a case like this, that sooner or later we shall be told that the vision was inscribed in the ship's log ; and Mr. Dale Owen duly tells us so. Mr. Arthur Norway expressly contradicts the fact.

M

coincidences precise to the moment, established by evidence which was irresistible; and pure accident might still be the true explanation of them. Later, however, it will be proved, as I think, beyond the shadow of a doubt, that that line cannot be taken in respect of the several hundreds of coincidences included in these volumes. And the majority of persons who regard the book from an evidential point of view, and who start with the legitimate à priori prejudice against the whole class of phenomena, will certainly take other ground. They will take exception to the evidence as it stands. They will not be concerned to deny that there would be an enormously strong case for the reality of telepathy, supposing the correspondences and coincidences to have occurred exactly as stated; but they will take the ground that they did not so occur; and will frame various hypotheses, according to which it should be possible that the evidence should be thus, and the facts otherwise.

Now not only is the endeavour to frame such hypotheses legitimate : it has been throughout an indispensable part of our own work. Even improbable hypotheses ought to be carefully considered; for we have no desire to underrate the à priori improbability of our own hypotheses of telepathy. It is extremely difficult to compare the improbability of any particular combination of known conditions with the improbability of the existence of a hitherto unknown condition. But the point on which we desire to lay stress is the *number* of improbable hypotheses that will have to be propounded if the telepathic explanation is rejected. Of course, this point may be evaded by including all the hypotheses needed in a single sweeping assumption, as to the general untrustworthiness of human testimony. This mode of argument would be perfectly legitimate if we were presenting a collection of unsifted second and third-hand stories; but it will scarcely seem equally so in application to what we do present. The evidence (or at any rate a very large amount of it) is of a sort which merits attention, even from those who most fully share the views that I have endeavoured to express as to the chances of error in the records of unusual occurrences. It cannot be summarily dismissed; if it is to be got rid of, it must be explained away in detail. And it is the continued process of attempts to explain away which may, we think, produce on others the same cumulative effect as it has produced on ourselves. The attempts have been made on the lines already sketched; and so far as any reader agrees that the risks and vulnerable points have been carefully considered in the abstract, he may be willing provisionally to accept an assurance that a similar careful and rationally sceptical mode of examination has been applied to the concrete instances. The work is, no doubt, wearisome; but there is no avoiding it, for anyone who wishes to form a fair independent opinion as to what the strength of the case for telepathy really is. The narratives are very various, and their force is derived from very various characteristics; the endeavour to account for them without resorting to telepathy must, therefore, be carried through a considerable number of groups, before it produces its legitimate effect on the mind. That effect arises from the number and variety of the improbable suppositions, now violent, now vague—contradictory of our experience of all sorts of human acts and human relations—that have to be made at every turn. Not only have we to assume such an extent of forgetfulness and inaccuracy, about simple and striking facts of the immediate past, as is totally unexampled in any other range of experience. Not only have we to assume that distressing or exciting news about another person produces a havoc in the memory which has never been noted in connection with distress or excitement in any other form. We must leave this merely general ground, and make suppositions as detailed as the evidence itself. We must suppose that some people have a way of dating their letters in indifference to the calendar, or making entries in their diaries on the wrong page and never discovering the error; and that whole families have been struck by the collective hallucination that one of their members had made a particular remark, the substance of which had never even entered that member's head; and that it is a recognised custom to write mournful letters about bereavements which have never occurred; and that when A describes to a friend how he has distinctly heard the voice of B, it is not infrequently by a slip of the tongue for C; and that when D says he is not subject to hallucinations of vision, it is through momentary forgetfulness of the fact that he has a spectral illusion once a week; and that when a wife interrupts her husband's slumbers with words of distress or alarm, it is only her fun, or a sudden morbid craving for undeserved sympathy; and that when people assert that they were in sound health, in good spirits, and wide awake, at a particular time which they had occasion to note, it is a safe conclusion rhat they were having a nightmare, or were the prostrate victims of nervous hypochondria. Every one of these improbabilities is, perhaps, in itself a possibility; but as the

M 2

narratives drive us from one desperate expedient to another, when time after time we are compelled to own that deliberate falsification is less unlikely than the assumptions we are making, and then again when we submit the theory of deliberate falsification to the cumulative test, and see what is involved in the supposition that hundreds of persons of established character, known to us for the most part and unknown to one another, have simultaneously formed a plot to deceive us—there comes a point where the reason rebels. Common-sense persists in recognising that when phenomena, which are united by a fundamental characteristic and have every appearance of forming a single natural group, are presented to be explained, an explanation which multiplies causes is improbable, and an explanation which multiplies improbable causes becomes, at a certain point, incredible.

§ 18. I am aware that in its abstract form, and apart from actual study of the cases, this reasoning must be wholly unconvincing. But meanwhile the argument for the *general* trustworthiness of our evidence may be put in another, and, perhaps, clearer light. Amid all their differences, the cases present one general characteristic—an unusual affection of one person, having no apparent relation to anything outside him except the unusual condition, otherwise unknown to him, of another person. It is this characteristic that gives them the appearance, as I have just said, of a *true natural group*. Now the full significance of these words may easily escape notice. They have an *evidential* as well as a *theoretic* bearing. They involve, of course, the hypothesis that the facts, if truly stated, are probably due to a single cause; but they involve, further, a very strong argument that the facts *are* truly stated. Let us suppose, for the moment, that any amount of laxity of memory and of statement may be expected even from first-hand witnesses, belonging to the educated class. And let us ignore all the heterogeneous improbabilities which we were just now considering; and assume that the mistakes mentioned, and others like them, may occur at any moment. What, then, is the likelihood that all these various causes—all these errors of inference, lapses of memory, and exaggerations and perversions of narration—will issue in a consistent body of evidence, presenting one well-defined type of phenomenon, free in every case from excrescences or inconsistent features and explicable, and completely explicable, by one equally well-defined hypothesis ? What is the likelihood that a number of narratives, which are assumed to have diverged in various ways from the actual facts, should thus converge to a single result ?   Several hundreds of independent and first-hand reporters have, wittingly or unwittingly, got loose from the truth, and are well started down the inclined plane of the marvellous. Yet all of them stop short at or within a given line—the line being the exact one up to which a particular explanation, not of theirs but of ours, can be extended, and beyond which it could not be extended. Tempting marvels lie further on—marvels which in the popular view are quite as likely to be true as the facts actually reported, and which the general traditions of the subject would connect with those facts. But our reporters one and all eschew them.   To take, for instance, the group of cases which the reader will probably find to be the most interesting, as it is also the largest, in our collection—apparitions at the time of death.   Why should not such apparitions hold prolonged converse with the waking friend ?   Why should they not produce *physical* effects—shed tears on the pillow and make it wet, open the door and leave it open, or leave some tangible token of their presence ? It is surely noteworthy that we have not had to reject, on grounds like these, a single narrative which on other grounds would have been admitted.   Have all our informants drawn an arbitrary line, and all drawn precisely the same arbitrary line, between the mistakes and exaggerations of which they *will* be guilty, and the mistakes and exaggerations of which they will *not ?*   We might imagine them as travellers, ignorant of zoology, each of whom reports that he has landed on a strange shore, and has encountered a strange animal.   Some of the travellers have been nearer the animal, and have had a better view of him than others, and their accounts vary in clearness ; but these accounts, though independently drawn up, all point to the same source ; they all present a consistent picture of the self-same animal, and what is more, the picture is one which zoology can find no positive cause to distrust.   We find in it none of the familiar features of myth or of untrained fancy ; the reports have not given wings to a quadruped, or horns and hoofs to a carnivor; they contradict nothing that is known.   Can we fairly suppose that this complete agreement, alike in what they contain and in what they do not contain, is the accidental result of a hundred disconnected mistakes ?

It is most instructive, in this connection, to compare first-hand (and the better sort of second-hand) narratives with others.   I have already spoken of the greater general sobriety of the first-hand evidence. I may now add that the suspiciously startling details which often characterise the more remote narratives are precisely of the sort which the telepathic hypothesis could by no possibility be made to cover. To wet the pillow or leave the door open would be quite an ordinary breach of manners in the popular "ghost," or the second-hand apparition of doubtful authority. I have mentioned the real dripping letter conveyed by the phantasmal midshipman. I may further recall the scar reported to have been left on the lady's wrist by the touch of the well-known " Beresford " apparition; and the wounds alleged to have been produced on the bodies of absent witches, by blows and sword thrusts directed to their " astral " appearances. No marvels in the least resembling these find any place in our first-hand records; yet why should they not, if those records are fundamentally untrustworthy? The existence of such features in other narratives sufficiently shows how wide is the possible range of incidents, in stories where the ordinary limitations of communication between human beings are alleged to have been transcended. Of this wide field, the hypothesis of the action of mind on mind, which we are endeavouring to develop, covers only a single well-defined portion. By what fatality, if error is widely at work in the case of our first-hand evidence, do its results always fall inside and not outside this very limited area? If our witnesses are assumed to sit loose to the facts which they *have* known, why should they bring their accounts into rigid (though purely accidental) conformity with a theory which they have *not* known?

§ 19. What I have here indicated is the general impression produced by the evidence in our own minds. In our view, the reality of telepathy (even apart from a consideration of the experimental evidence) may be not unreasonably taken as proved. Having formed this view, we are bound to state it; but we expressly refrain from putting it forward dogmatically, and from saying that to reject it would argue want of candour or intelligence. We hold that, in such a matter, it is idle to attempt to define the line of complete proof; and the proof given—if it be one—is far from being of an *éclatant* or overwhelming sort. To those who do not realise the strength of the *à priori* presumption against it, it may easily look more overwhelming than it is. To others, again, it may appear that, on the hypothesis that the faculty has acted as widely as we have supposed, the highest evidential standard ought to have been reached in a larger number of cases. To us it rather seems that the evidence that we find is just about what might have been expected. We see nothing in the mere existence of telepathy that would tend to make reserved people mention strange experiences, or to make careless or busy people keep conscientious diaries—or generally that would lead the persons immediately connected with a telepathic case, in which their emotions may be deeply involved, to act with a single eye to producing a clinching piece of evidence for the future benefit of critical psychological inquirers. It would, of course, be useless for us to urge that evidence which falls short of the best is still as good as can be expected, unless we were able to present a certain nucleus of fairly conclusive cases, and this we think we can do. But if the proof is held to demand more cases of the highest evidential quality, we must trust to time for them. The ideal collection would, of course, be one where every independent instance should be so evidentially complete that it must be either (1) telepathic, or (2) a purely accidental coincidence of a most striking kind, or (3) the result of a fraudulent conspiracy to deceive, in which several persons of good character and reputation have taken part. In our view, this point has been reached in a sufficient number of the examples here given to exclude the second and third of these alternatives; but these examples constitute only a very small minority compared with the mass of cases which are merely confirmatory—strongly confirmatory, as we think, but still confirmatory only and not crucial. And the collection so far falls short of the ideal.

In saying, then, that telepathy may not unreasonably be taken as proved, I do not wish for a moment to imply that the proof which we give is the one which we should eventually desire to see given. To no reader, we think, will the various imperfections and weak spots of our case be more patent than they have been to ourselves. Some of these are beyond remedy—as the absence of contemporary documents. Others may possibly be remedied at a later stage—for instance, the suppression of names.[1] It has been impossible to bring home to all

---

[1] The suppressed names have in all cases been given to us in confidence; and in some instances with permission to mention them to any persons who have any *bonâ fide* interest in the subject. Purely anonymous cases can of course have no weight at all. I subjoin a couple of cases which are of a normal type, and have quite the air of being *bonâ fide*, as samples of a numerous class which have to be treated as waste paper. The following account appeared in the *Times* for December 26th, 1868, in a review of Scott's *Demonology and Witchcraft*. The writer, who is here perforce anonymous, says that it "has quite recently fallen under our own observation."

"A young English lady had been betrothed to an officer before his departure to the East. During her lover's absence she was taken abroad by her mother, and on their

our informants that where a person refuses to a phenomenon, belonging to a certain class, the direct testimony which he would give, if needful, to any other sort of personal experience, the world is sure to take the view that he lacks that complete assurance of the reality of the experience which alone can make his evidence worthy of serious

arrival late one evening at a French inn, they found it necessary to occupy rooms on different floors. As Miss C. was in the act of getting into bed late at night, she suddenly beheld the form of her lover standing in a remote corner of her chamber. His countenance was extremely sad, and she observed that round his right arm he wore a band of crape. Indignant at the conduct of her betrothed in entering her sleeping apartment, she called on him loudly to depart ; the form of her lover remained speechless, but as she lifted up her voice, his brow grew yet sadder, and as he glided silently out of the room he seemed a prey to the gloomiest feelings. After a time Miss C. summoned up sufficient courage to descend to her mother and recite her adventure. They caused diligent search to be made for the returned officer, but without success. Nor could the smallest trace of him be afterwards discovered. Several weeks later the young lady received the news of her lover's death in a general action in India."

If such an account as this appeared in a leading newspaper now, we should hope of course to obtain the means of sifting it. But cases like the following could not be pursued without great expense in local advertising.

"Birmingham, December 15th, 1882.

"Dear Sir,—I have much pleasure in forwarding the following perfectly authentic account. It has never before been made known beyond our own immediate circle, and I relate it to you in the hope that it may be instrumental, with others of greater importance, in establishing the fact that there is indeed, and in truth, a future existence.

"A long time ago when my mother—who is now dead—was a girl, she was staying with her cousin, who was in delicate health ; they were reading or chatting when, suddenly, the latter's attention was drawn to the door, and she exclaimed, with delight, 'Why, there's grandma ! Why did you not say she was here ? ' The two—especially the latter—were great favourites of the old lady. Mother, hearing this, at once turned round, but saw nothing, but at once left the room, fully expecting to find her among the other members of the family. But being told that the old lady was not there she returned with the information to her cousin, who loudly protested that they were deceiving her, as she had been again, during mother's absence, and she had a ribbon in her cap which she had sent her a short time before, on her birthday anniversary. Mother again went to the other members of the family with this news. They, of course, thought it strange, and told the girl that it was only imagination. On the following day, however, news arrived that at that very time the old lady had passed away.

"This is perfectly true, and can, if neccessary, be corroborated by my brother, who is a clergyman.

"You may make any use you like of this communication, but I do not wish my name and address to be published, and so subscribe myself, yours, &c.,

"WELL-WISHER."

The signature probably expresses the truth ; but for all that it effectually prevents the narrative from being "instrumental in establishing" any fact whatever. But even more tantalising than anonymity is an insufficient or undecipherable address. The following is a case which this cause has rendered abortive. Inquiries for the locality have been made all over the British Isles without success.

"Gurnet Bay.

"January 1st, 1884.

"I do not believe in supernatural visitations, and the following experiences of my mother may be outside the range of your inquiries.

"My mother, while an infant, lost her father by an accident, and was brought up by a maternal uncle, who was greatly attached to her, and for whom she had the most unbounded affection. Learning that he was about to be married, and not being able to endure a divided affection, she left him, came up to Hampshire, married, and settled there, occasionally hearing from him. The night on which her uncle died, she was sleeping with a middle-aged lady named Day. At the moment of her uncle's death, as it afterwards appeared, she awoke in great agitation, exclaiming, 'My God ! my uncle's dead,' and frightened her companion, who awoke at the same time. So vivid was the impression that she made immediate preparation to go to Box, near Bath, where her uncle's residence was. On her arrival she found that he had died at the time and under exactly the circumstances she had seen in her dream, having strongly desired to see her at the last. "E. J. A'COURT SMITH."

attention. This is not always just; since the reason why he suppresses his name may be, not that he doubts the truth of his evidence, but that he regards the truth in this particular department of Nature as something disgraceful or uncanny ; or it may be mere fear of ridicule, or a shrinking from any form of publicity. But meanwhile the defect must not be extenuated. Even minor points may detract from the businesslike look of the work. Informants whose evidence is otherwise satisfactory sometimes feel it a sort of mysterious duty to throw a veil over something—if it is only to put C—— for Clapham. A dash is the last refuge of the occult. We must not be held to be blind to these blots because we have printed the evidence in which they occur. But the case, as it stands, seemed worth presenting, and the time for presenting it seemed to have arrived. Even if it be weaker than we think it, there is the future as well as the past to think of. By far the greater part of the telepathic evidence, even of the last twenty years, has undoubtedly perished, for all scientific purposes ; we want the account for the next twenty years to be different. But it is only by a decided change in the attitude of the public mind towards the subject that the passing phenomena can be caught and fixed ; and it is only by a wider knowledge of what there already is to know that this change can come about. Thus our best chance of a more satisfactory harvest hereafter is to exhibit our sheaf of gleanings now. If telepathy is a reality, examples of it may be trusted to go on occurring; and with the increase of intelligent interest in psychical research we may hope that the collection and verification of good first-hand evidence will gradually become easier, and that the necessity of careful contemporary records, and of complete attestation, will be more widely perceived.

§ 20. Meanwhile it may be just worth while to forestall an objection—which, as it has been made before, may be made again—to the argument from numbers. It has been urged that no accumulation of instances can make up a solid case, if no individual instance can be absolutely certified as free from flaw. But the different items of inductive proof are, of course, not like the links of a deductive chain. The true metaphor is the sticks and the faggot ; and our right to treat any particular case as a stick depends, not on its being so flawlessly strong, as evidence for our hypothesis, that no other hypothesis can possibly be entertained with regard to it, but on the much humbler fact that any other hypothesis involves the assumption of *something in itself improbable.* Third-hand ghost-stories, and the ordinary examples of popular superstitions, have no claim to be regarded as sticks at all, since the rejection of the popular explanation of them involves no improbable assumptions of any kind ; at best they are dry reeds, and no multiplication of their number could ever make a respectable faggot. But in every one of the examples on which we rest the telepathic hypothesis, the rejection of that hypothesis does, as I have pointed out, involve the assumption of something in itself improbable ; and every such example adds to the cumulative force of the argument for telepathy. The multiplication of such examples, therefore, makes a faggot of ever-increasing solidity.

When made explicit, this seems too plain to be denied ; but an extreme case may perhaps make the point even clearer. If, since the world began, nobody had ever died without a phantasm of him appearing to one or more of his friends, the joint occurrence of the two events would have been a piece of universally recognised knowledge ; of the cause of which we should to this day possibly not know more, and could not possibly know less, than we know of the cause of gravitation. Nor, if the attestation had been forthcoming in the case of only *half* the deaths, would its significance have been much more likely to be disputed ; nor if it had been forthcoming in the case of a quarter, or a tenth, or even a hundredth of the number. But those who admit this, practically admit that there is a conceivable number of well attested cases which they would regard as conclusive evidence of telepathy. We may ask them, then, to name their number ; and if they do so, we may not unreasonably proceed to inquire the grounds of their selection. A writer on the subject lately named 5000 as the mark ; but can he make his reasons explicit for considering 5000 as conclusive, and 4000, or even 1000, as inconclusive ? In course of time we hope that his minimum may be reached ; but any limit must be to a great extent arbitrary. We shall be content if impartial readers, who do not feel convinced that an adequate inductive proof has been attained, are yet brought to see that our object and method are scientifically defensible ; while we, on our side, fully admit that the adequacy of the present collection does not admit of demonstration, and are perfectly willing that it should be regarded as only a first imperfect instalment of what is needed.

§ 21. Perhaps, after all, the difference of instinct as to what really
is needed may be considerably less than at first sight appears. For we
have not been able to regard the alleged phenomena in the completely
detached fashion which most of those who consider them naturally
adopt. We are unable to determine how far the impression on our
own minds of the evidence for *spontaneous* telepathy has been
dependent on our conviction of the genuineness of cognate
experimental cases. These latter being for the most part trivial,
recent, and little known, it is not surprising that comparatively
few persons should have considered them, and that still fewer should
have grasped their bearing on the spontaneous cases. But to anyone
who accepts the experimental results, the *à priori* presumption
against other forms of supersensuous communication can hardly
retain its former aspect. The presumption is diminished—the
hospitality of the mind to such phenomena is increased—in a
degree which is none the less important that it does not admit of
calculation. A further step of about equal importance is made
when we advance to the better-evidenced of the *transitional* cases ;
though here again the effect on our own minds, due to our knowledge of the persons concerned, cannot be imparted to others.
Attention has been duly drawn to the difficulty of embracing these
several classes in a common *physical* conception ; but on *psychological* ground we cannot doubt that we are justified (provisionally
at any rate) in regarding them as continuous. Remembering the
existence of the transitional class, we may regard the extremes as
not more remote from one another than the electrical phenomena
of the cat's coat from those of the firmament. Electricity, indeed,
affords in this way a singularly close parallel to telepathy. " The
spontaneous apparitions of the dying " (I quote Mr. Myers' words)
" may stand for the lightning ; while the ancient observations on
the attraction of amber for straw may fairly be paralleled by our
modest experiments with cards and diagrams. The spontaneous
phenomena, on the one hand, have been observed in every age,
but observed with mere terror and bewilderment. And, on the
other hand, candid friends have expressed surprise at our taking
a serious interest in getting a rude picture from one person's
mind into another, or proving that ginger may be hot in the
mouth by the effect of unconscious sympathy alone. Yet we
hold that these trivial cases of community of sensation are the
germinal indications of a far-reaching force, whose higher manifes-

tations may outshine these as the lightning outshines the sparks on Puss's back. We hold that the lowest telepathic manifestations may be used to explain and corroborate the highest." Their con- ditions differ widely; so widely, indeed, as to supply indirectly an argument for the genuineness of the facts, since totally distinct and independent hypotheses—that of collusion in the one case, and of forgetfulness or exaggeration in the other—would be needed to refute them. Yet, with all this difference of conditions, when we compare the facts of either class with any facts which the accepted psychology includes, we cannot help recognising the great common characteristic—a supersensuous influence of mind on mind —as a true generic bond. Where that characteristic is found, there we have a natural group of phenomena which differ far more fundamentally from all other known phenomena than they can possibly differ among themselves. Their unity is found in contrast. Till more is known of their causes, it may be impossible for science to establish their inner relationships, just as it is impossible to establish the degrees of affinity between casually selected members of a single human community. But they draw together, so to speak, on the field of science, even as men of one race draw together when cast among an alien population.

NOTE ON WITCHCRAFT.

In saying that there is a total absence of respectable evidence, and an almost total absence of any first-hand evidence at all, for those alleged phenomena of magic and witchcraft which cannot be accounted for as the results of diseased imagination, hysteria, hypnotism, and occasionally, perhaps, of telepathy, I have made a sweeping statement which it may perhaps seem that nothing short of a knowledge of the whole witch-literature of the world could justify. I have, of course, no claim to this complete knowledge. My statement depends on a careful search through about 260 books on the subject (including, I think, most of the principal ones of the 16th, 17th, and 18th centuries), and a large number of contemporary records of trials.[1] Such a list is certainly very far from exhaustive. But as, on the one hand, the 450 works which Le

---

[1] The greater part of this irksome task has been carried out for me with rare zeal and intelligence by my friend, Miss Porter, to whom I must here once again express my obligations.

Loyer professed to have studied, before writing his *Livre des Spectres*, did not fortify him with the trustworthy record of a single case, so, on the other hand, a much smaller assortment may suffice to support very wide negative conclusions. To those who have travelled over the same ground, the reason will be obvious. Every student of records of abnormal or "supernatural" events must have been struck by the way in which the same cases keep on reappearing in one work after another. Even the most credulous partisans exercise a sort of economy of the marvellous, in so far as they find that copying out old marvels is a great saving of time and responsibility. And this is very specially the case with the literature now in question. Bodin's *Démonomanie* and the *Malleus Maleficarum* supplied generations of theorists with their pittance of facts ; and not even the Beresford ghost has done such hard and continuous duty in the cause of superstition as some few of the witch-cases.

Considering the enormous place that lycanthropy, for instance, plays in the interminable discussions as to what the devil could do, and how he did it, it is strange to realise what the evidence (outside confessions[1]) actually was. Putting Nebuchadnezzar and Lot's wife out of the question, the main burden of the proof seems really to rest on about four cases. Either it is the 11th century legend, quoted from William of Malmesbury, of the two old women who kept an inn, and transformed their guests into asses : or it is the equally mythical tale of the wood-cutter who wounded three cats, and declared that three women afterwards accused him of having wounded *them ;* or it is Peter Stubbe, against whom the evidence was that the villagers lit on him unexpectedly, while they were hunting a wolf ; or it is the man who, having cut off a wolf's paw, drew from his pocket the hand of his host's wife, whom he found sitting composedly without it—a story told to Boguet (as a joke for aught we can tell) by a person who professed to have picked it up in travelling through the locality. Even the credulous De l'Ancre [2] admits that, with wide opportunities, he has not come on the track of any transformations —a fact which seems to have a good deal impressed him. But in the eyes of other writers, perpetual citation seems to have imparted to the classical legends just mentioned the virtue of good first-hand testimony. Glanvil gives

---

[1] When we remember the ways in which confessions were obtained, the regard in which they were held appears the most amazing fact in the whole history of witchcraft. The common view is quaintly illustrated in an account of Peter Stubbe (translated from the Dutch, London, 1590) ; where it is said that Peter "after being put to the rack, and fearing the torture, *volluntarilye* confessed his whole life." Even where no violent means were used, the mind of the accused would be unhinged by starvation, enforced sleeplessness, or mere despair. And as if this was not enough, we have the dismal record of cheats and quibbles—*e.g.*, the promising his life to the accused if he would confess, meaning *eternal* life. We have also, no doubt, to allow for the morbid vanity and shame-lessness which is a symptom of advanced hysteria. (See Richet, *Op. cit.*, p. 364.)

[2] *Tableau de l'Inconstance des Mauvais Anges et Démons* (Paris, 1612), p. 312.

another case where a panting old woman was suddenly seen in the place of a hunted hare, on the authority of a huntsman;[1] but there are features in the account which strongly suggest, as Glanvil admits, that the huntsman was a wag. I find another less known English example of the kind; and the manner of its appearance is significant. The record of the trial of the Essex witches in 1645 [2] contains, first, all manner of *first-hand* evidence to witches' "familiars"—evidence which must have been easy enough to get, considering that a man who had looked through a cottage window, and seen a woman holding a lock of wool that cast a shadow, was believed when he described these objects as her white and black imps;[3] and then at last we have a case of transformation into an animal, at which point, sure enough, the evidence becomes *second-hand*, and the witness has heard the tale from a man who he knew "would not speak an untruth." A transformation case which Webster mentions as given on first-hand testimony was afterwards confessed to have been an imposture.[4] I have found but a single item of independent evidence to the phenomenon which is first-hand, in the sense of having been given direct to the writer who records it. This is in Spina's *Quæstio de Strigibus* (Rome, 1576, p. 53), and is to this effect :—a cobbler, being annoyed by a cat, dealt blows at it, after which an old woman turned out to have some hurts which she was not known to have received.[5] To be quite fair, I should add that Bodin says that one Pierre Mamor wrote a little treatise, in which he professed to have actually seen a transformation—this being the only case that I have come across where a man of sufficient education to write something that was printed is even cited as bearing personal testimony to such marvels.

It is the same with the witches' compacts, and with the nocturnal rides and orgies. Putting aside confessions, the evidence is of the flimsiest sort, and is copied and re-copied with untiring pertinacity; while many of the miraculous tales are mere country gossip, which do not even pretend to

---

[1] *Sadducismus Triumphatus* (London, 1689), p. 387. Glanvil's own theory is that the hare was a demon, and that the witch was invisibly hurried along with it, to put her out of breath.

[2] *A Collection of Curious Tracts relating to Witchcraft,* &c. (London, 1838).

[3] Hutchinson, *Historical Essay Concerning Witchcraft* (London, 1720), p. 60. It is an interesting instance of the intimate relation between persecution and the vitality of the persecuted doctrines, that *imps* are little mentioned except in this country, where, as Hutchinson says, "the law makes the feeding, suckling, or rewarding of them to be felony."

[4] *The Displaying of Supposed Witchcraft* (London, 1677), p. 278.

[5] This story also appears as a treasure in the *Compendium Maleficarum* (Milan, 1620). In the only other case given by Spina (who, be it observed, is one of the very chief authorities) the evidence was that a witch told two people that certain deceased cats had been witches. In the treatment of the old dateless legends, the taste of the narrator counted for something. Thus, Olaus Magnus (*Historia de Gentibus Septentrionalibus,* Rome, 1555, p. 644) reports that once upon a time an accused person was closely confined and watched, till he duly transformed himself. Majolus, telling the story half a century later, says that the watchers watched in vain.

rest on any authority. Holland says, " I cannot hear that any wise man or honest man tell us any thing, which hath been himself either a party or a witness of such horrible bargains."[1] " What credible witness is there brought at any time," says Reginald Scot, " of this their corporal, visible, and incredible bargain ; saving the confession of some person diseased both in body and mind, wilfully made or injuriously constrained?"[2] As regards transportations, the most superstitious writers have never themselves come into anything like close contact with the marvels that they record. Habbakuk, and the Sabine peasant who inadvertently dispersed an assembly by a pious ejaculation, figure in the records with almost unbroken regularity. I am aware of only two cases in which it is even rumoured that a person has been actually observed travelling through the air ;[3] and whenever a " Sabbath " has been seen, or persons have been found far from their homes in the morning—presumably because the devil, who was carrying them back from the revels, dropped them at the sound of the Angelus—the witnesses are shepherds or peasants (in one case a butler), who have not been cross-examined or even interviewed. Grillandus[4] says that he had been at first inclined to disbelieve in bodily transportations, but that longer experience had changed his view. He then gives a couple of hearsay stories about people found in the fields, and a few confessions. Binsfeld[5] considers transportation certain, on the strength of some village gossip (copied in part from Grillandus). A story quoted by Horst from the *De Hirco Nocturno* of Scherertz, of a young man found on the roof towards morning, is apparently a typical case of natural somnambulism. The *Malleus* (Vol. I., p. 171) tells how some young men saw a comrade carried off by invisible means ; but the prominent fact in the story is that they were having a drinking bout.[6]

---

[1] *A Treatise against Witchcraft* (Cambridge, 1590), p. 31.

[2] *The Discovery of Witchcraft* (London, 1584), p. 48. See also his criticism on Bodin, p. 23 ; and cf. Christian Thomas, *Kurtze Lehrsätze von dem Laster der Zauberey* (1706), p. 31.

[3] *Malleus*, Vol. i., p. 175 ; Scot, *Op. cit.*, p. 67. On the general omission of any sort of investigation of stories, see Dell' Osa, *Die Nichtigkeit der Hexerey* (Frankfort, 1766), p. 508.

[4] *Tractatus de Sortilegiis* (Lyons, 1536), cap. 7.

[5] *Tractatus de Confessionibus Maleficarum et Sagarum* (Trèves, 1591), pp. 223-30 and 343-5.

[6] See also Spina, *Op. cit.*, p. 108; Remy, *Dæmonolatria* (Lyons, 1595), pp. 112,115; Glanvil, *Op. cit.*, p. 143. The testimony to the effect that the persons reputed to have been at the nocturnal orgies had never really left their beds, must have been well known—see, *e.g.*, J. Baptista Porta, *Magia Naturalis* (Naples, 1558), p. 102 ; Wier, *De Præstigiis Dæmonum*, &c. (Basle, 1568), p. 275 ; Godelmann, *Tractatus de Magis, Veneficis, et Lamiis* (Frankfort, 1591), Lib. ii., p. 39 ; Remy, *Op. cit.*, p. 110 ; *Compendium Maleficarum*, p. 81 ; Menghi, *Compendio dell' Arte Essorcista* (Bologna, 1590), p. 439 ; Elich, *Dæmonomagia* (Frankfort, 1607), p. 131 ; Hutchinson, *Op. cit.*, pp. 100, 125 ; but the figure that remained at home might, of course, be accounted for as an optical delusion caused by the devil, or as due to his direct personation (see Gayot de Pitaval, *Causes Célèbres*, Amsterdam, 1775, p. 153). But if the superstition could thus defy direct counter-evidence, we get a fresh idea of the feebleness of its own evidential support from the fact that both sceptics and believers seem sometimes to have forgotten that the question was one of evidence at all. Thus, G. Tartarotti (*Del Congresso Notturno delle Lamie*, Venice, 1749) bases his elaborate argument

In all these matters we may be sure that, had there been better evidence to record, it would have been recorded.

Similarly in the trials of witches, where (if we exclude the confessions) nearly all the alleged facts can now be accepted and explained on physiological and psychological principles, the sameness is so great that, after our research has been carried to a certain point, we feel sure that no new types will be forthcoming.[1] Even the questions and suggestions used for entrapping the accused seem to have become stereotyped forms, and the very indictments came to be hurried over, as almost taken for granted.[2] Spee says that it never even entered into his head to doubt the existence of witches, till he studied the judicial evidence.[3]

On the whole, then, the sweeping statement considered at the beginning of the foregoing chapter—that in modern societies a more or less imposing array of so-called evidence can be obtained for the support of any belief or crotchet that is less than an outrage on the popular common-sense of the time—is very far from receiving support from the history of witchcraft. The stock example which was to prove the view goes, in fact, somewhat surprisingly far to disprove it. For at no period would the conditions seem to be more favourable for a really impressive record of marvellous phenomena than during the 15th and 16th centuries. The art and literature of the epoch show high imaginative development, and a keen appetite for variety and detail; while, at the same time, the majority of able and educated minds were not fore-armed, in at all the same way as now, by a sense of à priori impossibilities and of a uniform Nature, and the belief in the incalculable power and malignity of the devil was nearly universal.[4] One would have

entirely on collateral difficulties—as that, if the witches really feasted at their meetings, they ought to come back surfeited and happy, instead of hungry and tired; and that if they could escape from their bedrooms they ought to be able to escape from prison. And, similarly, the author of the *Critiche* on this book, (Venice, 1751) refutes Tartarotti by a long chain of theoretic reasoning supported by many orthodox authorities, but not by a single fact.

[1] Compare, for instance, the cases in Pitcairn's *Criminal Trials of Scotland* (Edinburgh, 1833); Cannaert's *Olim Procès des Sorcières en Belgique* (Ghent, 1845); Rueling's *Auszüge einiger merkwürdigen Hexenprozessen* (Göttingen, 1786); Müller, *Op. cit.* See also Reuss, *La Sorcellerie au 16me et au 17me Siècle, particulièrement en Alsace* (Paris, 1871), p. 107; Haas, *Die Hexenprozesse* (Tübingen, 1865), p. 80; and Soldan, *Geschichte der Hexenprozessen* (Stuttgart, 1880), pp. 385-9. A similar repetition of stock stories, and a similar monotony of detail, are observable in the New England records.

[2] See Haas, *Op. cit.*, p. 79; Lilienthal, *Op. cit.*, p. 93; Rapp, *Die Hexenprozesse* (Innsbruck, 1874), pp. 21-27. Rapp (p. 143) specially remarks on the sameness of the confessions as due to the sameness of the judge's questions.

[3] *Cautio Criminalis* (Frankfort, 1632), p. 398.

[4] This belief was held alike by the credulous majority and the sensible minority; and it is interesting to see how the latter contrived to make controversial use of it. For instance, G. Gifford, an author who is almost modern in his view of the influence of the mind on the body, in his *Dialogue concerning Witches* (London, 1603), p. L, argues for the worthlessness of confessions on the ground that "the testimonie of a witch in many things at her death is not any other than the testimonie of the divell, because the divell hath deceived her, and made her beleeve things which were nothing so." And Hutchinson, *Op. cit.*, p. 99, ridicules the test of torture on similar grounds, "since the devil will pretend torture when he feels none, and fall down when he needs not." Cf. D'Autun, *L'Incrédulité Scavante et la Crédulité Ignorante* (Lyons, 1671), p. 791.

expected, then, that every village would swell the direct testimony to transformations and witches' "Sabbaths"; and that even philosophers who regarded the Evil One as an abiding source of sensory delusion might occasionally have had their own senses deluded. But we can only take the record that we find, and it is as monotonous as it is meagre. Not only do the philosophers and their friends seem to have enjoyed complete immunity from Satanic visitations, but even in the lower social strata the magical incidents (other than those which modern science can accept and explain) are extremely few and far between; and the evidence for them—if the word be used with any degree of strictness—is practically non-existent.[1]

I must specially insist on this point; as my view seems completely opposed to that given in the account from which most English readers have probably formed their idea of the subject—the brilliant first chapter of Mr. Lecky's *History of Rationalism.* Mr. Lecky's treatment appears to me to suffer from the want of two important distinctions. In the first place, he does not separate the fact of the wide belief in the magical phenomena, and the array of authorities that could be cited on the side of that belief, from the evidence for particular events—the statements of *bonâ fide* witnesses. For every grain of *testimony* there is no difficulty in finding a ton of *authority.*[2] And in the second place, he does not explicitly discriminate between the wholly bizarre

---

[1] Writers of the most opposite views confirm what the records of trials would sufficiently prove—that the natural stronghold of witchcraft was among the most ignorant and backward sections of the population. Bodin (*Op. cit.,* p. 168) says that witches were commonest in villages. Bernard (*Guide to Grand Jurymen in Cases of Witchcraft,* London, 1627, p. 22) says that "fear and imagination make many witches among country-people," and asserts that only those who think much about witches are ever troubled with them. Glanvil (*Op. cit.,* p. 498) thinks it an important fact that "all people in the country about were fully persuaded" of the reality of one of his cases. D'Autun (*Op. cit.,* p. 507) traces the rumour of witchcraft to the imagination of villagers. Tartarotti (*Op. cit.,* p. 105) describes the supposed attendants at the "Sabbath" as poor, weak, ill-fed creatures. Hutchinson (*Op. cit.,* p. 153) remarks that "country-people are wonderfully bent to make the most of all stories of witchcraft." Sir G. Mackenzie (*The Laws and Customs of Scotland in Matters Criminal,* Edinburgh, 1699) says: "Those poor people who are ordinarily accused of the crime, are poor ignorant creatures, and ofttimes women who understand not the nature of what they are accused of"; and Pitcairn speaks of convictions "on the slenderest evidence, afforded by the testimony of ignorant and superstitious country-people." These extracts might be multiplied to any extent.

[2] Thus Bodin's chapter on lycanthropy contains, as Mr. Lecky truly observes, "immense numbers of authorities." But it is surely important to notice that among the chief of them are Homer, Ovid, and Apuleius; that Virgil is quoted as a frequent eye-witness of the phenomenon on the strength of the 8th Eclogue; and that the only instances for which a shadow of evidence is adduced are the following:—Three confessions unsupported by any external evidence, one of which (to be just) is said *not* to have been extorted; one confession with the additional piece of evidence reported at third-hand, that the accused man had a wound which the witness recognised as one that he had inflicted on a wolf; a report of a prosecution which was abandoned, against some men who had wounded some cats; the eternal story above mentioned of the wood-cutter and the three cats; and Pierre Mamor's testimony, also mentioned above. The list is surely not an imposing one; and becomes even less so when we find Bodin quite equally impressed with the fact that the author of another book, dedicated to an emperor, had seen a man, not committing the crime, but condemned for it; or that someone who had been in Livonia reported that the people there were all believers.

N

and incredible side of the subject, and its scientific or pathological side.
Of course "belief in witchcraft" may be taken to mean simply a group or
system of wrong inferences, drawn under a strong instinct of demonic
agency ; and in that light the belief can doubtless be treated as a whole—
as a single though complex superstition. But "witchcraft" may also be
used, and is frequently used in Mr. Lecky's own pages, to denote the facts
alleged—for instance, that old women were carried through the air—and
not the inference drawn, that it was the devil who carried them. And
this is the meaning that naturally becomes prominent when the question is
of the *evidence* for witchcraft—the actual testimony that men's senses bore
to it. For instance, Mr. Lecky says (pp. 14-16) that "the historical
evidence establishing the reality of witchcraft is so vast and varied that it
is impossible to disbelieve it without what, on other subjects, we should
deem the most extraordinary rashness. . . . In our own day, it may
be said with confidence that it would be altogether impossible for such an
amount of evidence to accumulate round a conception which had no
substantial basis in fact. . . . If it were a natural but a very
improbable fact, our reluctance to believe it would have been completely
stifled by the multiplicity of the proofs." Here the "evidence" and
"proofs" clearly refer rather to facts than to inferences ; and it is implied
in the whole tone of the passage that the facts referred to belong to the
miraculous class which is now universally discredited. I can, therefore,
only express my entire dissent from the statements made, at any rate
until they receive better support than Mr. Lecky supplies. He tells us,
for instance, that Boguet "is said to have burnt 600 persons, chiefly for
lycanthropy." If this be true, it still gives us no hint as to what the
evidence was ; judging by analogy, we should suppose that it consisted in
confessions, probably made under torture.[1] Did 600 persons, or 100, or
even 10 persons ever bear testimony before Boguet that they had seen a
man or woman converted into a wolf? If so, it is surely remarkable that
his own book *(Discours des Sorciers,* Lyons, 1608) contains (besides a few
confessions and a few of the stock fables) *only two* lycanthropy cases—the
evidence for one being that a child who had been injured by a wolf
declared, in the fever which followed, that the animal's paws were like
hands ; and for the other that a peasant woman who had been desperately
frightened by a wolf, said afterwards that its hind feet had had human
toes. So again, Mr. Lecky (p. 127) seems completely to sympathise with
Glanvil's statement that the evidence for "the belief of things done by
persons of despicable power and knowledge, beyond the reach of art and

---

[1] See Kanoldt, *Supplementum iii curieuser und nutzbarer Anmerkungen,* &c. (Bautzen,
1728), p. 63. For a proof that even a writer who was rather inclined to ridicule
the subject could still regard confession under torture as conclusive of this crime see
Peucer, *Commentarius de præcipuis Divinationum Generibus* (Hanover, 1607) p. 280.

ordinary nature," was overwhelming.[1] And truly Glanvil does speak of "the attestation of thousands of eye and ear witnesses, and those not of the easily deceivable vulgar only, but of wise and grave discerners." But this is a typical example of the very confusion which I am trying to clear up. If thousands of wise and grave discerners *saw* the incredible marvels with their own eyes, how is it that in not a single case has the record been preserved? If on the other hand they *saw* only the credible marvels—fits and the like—and *believed* the incredible ones, on extraordinarily feeble testimony but under an extraordinarily strong prepossession, in what sense can it be asserted that there was then "overwhelming evidence" for what would now be denied?

In brief, when it is a question of evidence, we should naturally expect to find a strongly-marked division between that part of the superstition where the wrong inference was drawn from *spurious* facts, such as lycanthropy and the nocturnal orgies, and that part where the wrong inference was drawn from *genuine* facts, such as the phenomena of somnambulism or epilepsy. And my contention is that this strongly marked division actually exists, and that for the former class of marvels there was practically no evidence—no professedly first-hand observation. For the latter class, on the other hand, the evidence was naturally abundant, however wrongly interpreted.

To pass now to this latter class—that is to say, to the physiological and psychological aspects of the subject. I have said that many phenomena, which in their way were sufficiently genuine, were misinterpreted, because the sciences which should have explained them were still unborn. But though anything like a complete and critical explanation of these phenomena was impossible, it is to be remarked that the witch-literature presents a constant succession of sensible writers (chiefly English and German), who wholly rejected the common view of them. As early as the 15th century, and often during the 16th, works appeared in which the objective nature of the more bizarre incidents is denied, and they are treated as hallucinations; almost invariably, however, as hallucinations of a supernatural kind, caused directly by the devil.[2] This comparatively rational view of the transportations, transformations,

---

[1] *Sadducismus Triumphatus*, p. 3.

[2] Molitor, *De Lamiis* (Cologne, 1489), cap. vi. ; Wier, *Op. cit.*, pp. 216, 236, 352, 371 ; Daneau, *Les Sorciers* (Geneva, 1574), p. 104 ; Remy, *Op. cit.*, Lib. ii. cap. v. ; Saur, *Ein kurtze Warnung*, &c. (Frankfort, 1582) ; Del Rio, *Disquisitiones Magicæ* (Louvain, 1599), Vol. i., pp. 207-8 ; Gifford, *Op. cit.*, p. K 3, (but cf. his *Discourse of Subtill Practices*, London, 1587, p. E, where he attributes to certain of the devil's "counterfeite shewes of a bodie" a kind of objectivity); *Flagellum Hereticorum Fascinariorum* (Frankfort, 1581), p. 5 ; Holland, *Op. cit.*, p. 31. Neuwaldt (*Exegesis Purgationis*, Helmstedt, 1585, p. D 6) gives an elaborate description of the process. The view could claim the authority of St. Augustine (*De Civitate Dei*, Lib. xviii.). Godelmann (*Tractatus de Magis, Veneficis, et Lamiis*, Frankfort, 1591) is perhaps the only one of the German 16th century writers—and in this respect may be bracketed with Scot and Montaigne—who gets distinctly beyond this notion ; but see

&c., was gradually adopted in the course of the 17th century even by the credulous writers ;[1] while the rational writers come to recognise more distinctly the influence of terror and excitement on weak minds, and hallucination begins to be regarded as a natural phenomenon.[2] Ady even recognises a case (*Candle in the Dark*, p. 65) where mere *entraînement*, apart from terror, was sufficient to produce a hallucination in an excitable " subject "—a boy who was employed to assist in calling up imps, by imitating the quacking of ducks, having so imposed on a minister that, even when shown the cheat, "he would not be persuaded but that he saw real ducks squirming about the room." And throughout we meet with cases of sensory delusion which may with great probability be referred to hypnotic suggestion ; being very similar to the effects which are produced in our day on the platform of professional "mesmerists." I have mentioned De l'Ancre's instance of the children supposed to have been taken to a "Sabbath." Bodin (*Op. cit.*, p. 138) describes how Trois-Eschelles made a circle of spectators mistake a breviary for a pack of cards ; Boguet (*Op. cit.*, p. 360) mentions the celebrated Escot de Parme as having been able to make persons see cards differently to what they really were, and mentions another case (*Six Advis*, p. 89) where a witch made a woman see rubbish as money ; Remy and Del Rio describe similar feats performed by one Jean de Vaux. It is of course impossible to be sure that these were not mere conjuring feats; but Del Rio seems to have been awake to that hypothesis, and to have thought it quite untenable.

As specimens of other effects which may fairly be accounted for as hypnotic, I may mention the following. Occasionally witches are said to have shown insensibility to torture ; of which a self-induced trance

---

also Valrick *Von den Zaüberern, Hexen*, &c. (translated from the Dutch, Cologne, 1576) ; Erastus, *Deux Dialogues* (translated from the Latin, 1579), p. 776 ; and Scribonius, *De Sagarun Naturâ* (Marburg, 1588), p. 76. It was naturally in connection with the human organism that the idea of Satanic control survived longest. The devil's power over the external world—shown, *e.g.*, in raising tempests—was as completely believed in as his power over men, by the ablest writer of the Middle Ages ; but on this question Professor Huxley does not stand further from St. Thomas Aquinas than did Wier (*Op. cit.*, p. 264).

[1] *E.g.*, King James I., *Dæmonologie* (London,1603), p. 40 ; Nynauld, *De la Lycanthropie* (Paris, 1615), p. 20 ; Glanvil, *Op. cit.*, p. 507. As to transportations, it remained a very favourite compromise that they were *occasionally* genuine, but *as a rule* illusory ; see, for instance, the *Corollaria* to the *Disputatio de Fascinatione*, held at Coburg in 1764. For a proof that the possibility of a purely subjective hallucination had as little dawned on Glanvil in the 17th century as on Michael Psellus in the 11th, see *Sadd. Triumph.*, p. 405 ; where the only alternative to supposing an apparition to have been "Edward Avon's ghost " is to suppose it a "ludicrous dæmon." D'Autun (*L'Incrédulité Scavante*, &c.), an author whose desire to be just to both sides gives him a sort of half-way position, still believes, in 1671, that the witch or the devil, and not the brain of the percipient, is responsible for hallucinations (pp. 65, 876). It is more remarkable that Hutchinson, an eminently sensible writer, who belonged to a later date, still seems to believe (*Op. cit.*, p. 106) that the devil assumed the form of the delusive image.

[2] Bekker, *De Betoverde Wereld* (Leewarden, 1691), p. 247, in the German translation of 1781.

affords the readiest explanation.[1] There are occasional cases of inhibition, of a sort to which we have abundant modern parallels in connection with hypnotism, but none, as far as I am aware, except in that connection.[2] Remy (*Op. cit.*, p. 221) gives an apparent example of the inability of the " subject " to drop an object which his controller insists on his holding. In *Dr. Lamb Revived, or Witchcraft Condemned*, (London, 1653), p. 20, a case of the production of hypnotic sleep is described by an eye-witness. The description in Glanvil (*Op. cit.*, p. 342) of a " subject " who showed the well-known symptoms of muscular rigidity, and of *rapport* with a single person, is again strongly suggestive of hypnotic trance.   The *rapport*, shown in exclusive sensitiveness to the witch's touch or approach, reappears in Saint André's *Lettres au Sujet de la Magie* (Paris, 1725), p. 213 ; and in *The Tryal of Bridget Bishop* at Salem in 1692 ;[3] where also the " subjects " are described as having displayed the phenomenon of *imitation* of the witch's postures and gestures.   The " subject's " craving to get to the witch is another significant feature.   (See above, p. 87, note.)   We should probably have had a much larger amount of definite hypnotic evidence had such a thing as hypnotism been recognised at the time—observations made under the influence of wrong theories being naturally one-sided and defective.

With respect to demoniacal possession, we find a progress of opinion to some extent parallel with that observed in the treatment of hallucinations ; but the belief in the Satanic agency was here naturally more tenacious ; and where the actual possession was doubted, the investigators often fell into the opposite error of concluding that the victims could have nothing the matter with them, and must be consciously shamming.[4]

---

[1] Wier, *Op. cit.*, 482; Scot, *Op. cit.*, p. 22, quoting Grillandus ; Del Rio, *Op. cit.*, Vol. ii., p. 66 ; Le Loyer, *Livre des Spectres*, chap. 12 ; *Hexen-processe aus dem 17en Jahrhundert* (Hanover, 1862), p. 78.   The phenomenon was much discussed as the "maleficium taciturnitatis."   The same has, of course, been recorded of religious martyrs, and has been ascribed to ecstasy ; but we have no reason to suppose the mental and spiritual condition of the supposed witches to have been such as would make that term applicable ; and it is difficult to see why merely hysterical anæsthesia should supervene at the critical moment.   It is, however, probably to hysteria that we should attribute whatever of truth there may have been in the idea of the devil's mark—the alleged insensibility of restricted areas of the body.   (See Richet, *Op. cit.*, p. 364.)

[2] A case in the *Pathologia Dæmoniaca* of J. Caspar Westphal (Leipzig, 1707), p. 48, which the author seems to have personally observed, closely resembles some of the cases given above in Chap. iii.   The mere inhibition of utterance, either produced in the victim by the supposed persecutor's presence (*A Philosophical Endeavour in the Defence of the Being of Witches and Apparitions*, London, 1668, p. 129), or by the idea of it (G. More, *A True Discourse*, &c., London, 1600, p. 20 ; *Witchcraft further Displayed*, London, 1712, p. 7) ; or in the witch herself when attempting to repeat the Lord's Prayer (Glanvil, *Op. cit.*, p. 377), may, of course, be sufficiently accounted for by hysteria or imagination.

[3] Mather, *Wonders of the Invisible World* (Boston, 1693), p. 106.

[4] See, for instance, Dr. Harsnet's *Discovery of the Fraudulent Practices of John Darrell, B.A.* (London, 1599), and the controversy to which it gave rise.   But of course, a certain number of cases were undoubtedly fraudulent ; see *The Disclosing of a Late Counterfeyted Possession*, &c. (London, 1574.)   It seems to have depended very much on accidental circumstances whether hysterical girls were pitied as victims or denounced as cheats.

Webster (*Op. cit.*, p. 248) is, perhaps, the earliest English writer who insists on purely natural causes as sufficient to explain possession. As regards the whole question of the influence of the reputed witches on health, it is here probably that we should have had the most distinct indications of hypnotic agency had the idea of hypnotism been there to colligate the facts.[1] And much must, no doubt, be set down to the morbid craving for notoriety which is now one of the best known symptoms of hysteria. But as regards the larger number of the alleged phenomena, the rational inference—that the effects were due to imagination or fright—might, as we now see, have been drawn from the evidence of even the most credulous writers. Bodin, for instance, insists on the necessity of *faith* on the part of the sufferer,[2] and reports not a single case of curing where the witch was not actually present.[3] His records, and those of · many others, are precisely parallel to what our newspapers describe of the "mind-cures" in Boston and Bethshan, and might be accepted to-day without difficulty by orthodox medical opinion.[4] Cases where there was rapid improvement in the victim's health on the condemnation of the supposed witch come into the same category.[5] Similarly in cases of injurious effects— we constantly hear that the sufferer had been touched, or at the very least fixedly looked at, by the supposed witch.[6] Great stress was laid on the confession of the celebrated Gaufridi that he had breathed on his numerous victims.[7] And if we bear in mind the prevalent belief that the witch commanded the full powers of the devil, we need not refuse to connect the threats and angry words of unpopular old women with a certain proportion, at any rate, of the

---

[1] On the beneficial effects of the supposed witch's touch and strokings, see, for instance, the sensible Cotta, *The Infallible, True and Assured Witch,* (London, 1625), p. 138; Deodat Lawson, *Further Account of the Trials of the New England Witches* (London, 1693), p. 8 ; Lamberg, *Criminal Verfahren* (Nuremberg, 1835), p. 27 ; *Miscellany of the Spalding Club* (Aberdeen, 1841), Vol. i., pp. 92, 119. Even in the present century mesmeric cures have been attributed to the devil. (See Lecky, *Op. cit.*, p. 109.)

[2] Cf. *A Pleasant Treatise of Witches* (London, 1673), p. 109 ; Remy, *Op. cit.*, p. 348.

[3] Bodin has a firm belief that a witch could cause death by a word ; but characteristically adduces no evidence. He is also persuaded that the disease which is removed from one person must be transferred to another—a view which he supports by a single supposed instance.

[4] See, for example, Prof. G. Buchanan's paper on "Healing by Faith" in the *Lancet,* for 1885, Vol. i., p. 1117. Cf. Dell' *Osa, Op. cit.*, pp. 29, 30.

[5] See, for instance, Mackenzie, *Op. cit.*, p. 50 ; and the account of Dorothy Durant's restoration when the verdict was given against Amy Duny, in the *Tryal of Witches at the Assizes held at Bury St. Edmunds, before Sir Matthew Hale* (London, 1682).

[6] Remy, *Op. cit.*, p. 312 ; Del Rio, *Op. cit.*, Vol. i., p. 34 ; De l'Ancre, *L'Incrédulité et Méscréance du Sortilège* (Paris, 1622), p. 108 ; Goldschmidt, *Verworffener Hexen-und Zauber-Advocat* (Hamburg, 1705), p. 454 ; Pitcairn, *Op. cit.*, *passim.*

[7] Michaelis, *Histoire Admirable* (Paris, 1613), Part II., p. 118 ; Calmet, *Traité sur les Apparitions* (Senones, 1759), Vol. i., pp. 37, 138. See also Westphal, *Op. cit.*, p. 48 ; and the history of Hartley, the kissing witch, in G. More's *True Discourse.*

illnesses which are so freely testified to as having soon after supervened.[1]
It must also be borne in mind that the reputed witches possibly included
in their ranks a fair sprinkling of the amateur medical practitioners of
the time.[2]   This is a feature of the witch-history which is more prominent
in foreign than in English records.   In Cannaert. (*Op. cit.*) and Reuss
(*Op. cit.*) constant mention is made of bewitched powders ; and in the
foreign trials generally, more stress is laid on poisoning than on
anything else.   Reuss is of opinion that the hallucinations were in many
cases the result of drugs.   At the same time we find that, among the
credulous writers of the witch-epoch, a witch and a poisoner were often
regarded as synonymous ; and the stories of the powders may have
rested on much the same evidence as those of the imps.   As far as I
know, no one ever deposed to having seen the drug administered.[3]

The above slight sketch may serve to suggest that *learned* opinion on
the question of witchcraft has a history of its own of a rather complex
kind ; and some recognition of this seems necessary to supplement the
view of the decline of the belief so forcibly set forth by Mr. Lecky.   As
regards the place of witchcraft in the *popular* regard, the effect of the
advancing spirit of rationalism was no doubt more unconscious and
indiscriminate—undermining the superstition without exactly attacking
it in detail ; putting the whole subject, so to speak, out of court, not
through a reasonable refutation of its claims, but through a general
change of instinct and mood in respect of miraculous events.   But
professed students still felt it their business to analyse the phenomena, and
exercised their minds on the various points in turn.   And the consequence
is that the works of the abler writers present us with a curious and
gradually-shifting medley of *à priori* convictions and scientific reasonings
and of beliefs and disbeliefs, often oddly inconsistent and oddly
harmonised in the same mind.   Binsfield, who firmly believes in the
" Sabbaths," draws the line at the dancing with Diana and Herodias ;
because as for Diana, there is no such person, and Herodias, though
existing in hell, is a soul only and not a woman.[4]   Boguet thinks that
witches pursue and eat children, but that they are not really wolves.
Majolus and Nynauld believe in transportations, but not in transformations.   Wier pours scorn alike on lycanthropy and on the night-rides; but he
has not the slightest doubt that the devil *can* transport people, and that he

[1] Mackenzie, *Op. cit.*, p. 48; D'Autun, *Op. cit.*, p. 480; *Miscellany of the Spalding Club*, Vol. i., pp. 84, 131, 144; Pitcairn, *Op. cit.*, *passim.*   Wagstaffe (*The Question of Witchcraft Debated*, London, 1671) seems to be the first author who expressly recognises that, in questions of coincidence, allowance must be made for the operation of chance.
[2] See P. Christian, *Histoire de la Magie* (Paris, 1870), p. 400 ; he gives quite an elaborate witches' *pharmacopœia.*   Cf. Sir A. C. Lyall, *Asiatic Studies*, p. 85.
[3] See Saint André, *Op. cit.*, p. 285.
[4] *Op. cit.*, p. 349.

does prevent his votaries from feeling torture.[1] Neither he nor Cotta has grasped the idea that hysterical girls can play tricks, and produce from their mouths objects which they have previously placed there.[2] Perkins considers that such effects as transformation, and injury by the mere power of the eye, quite transcend the devil's range;[3] but this view in no way shakes his faith in the reality of magical powers. Méric Casaubon, though so far emancipated as to surmise that "supernatural" things may in time be explained, yet writes expressly to confute "the Sadducism of these times," disapproves of Scot, and can say nothing harsher of Bodin and Remy than that they were "in some things perchance more credulous than I should be."[4] His impartiality is quite tantalising. Thus, as regards certain alleged cures, he presents us with four alternatives, quoted from Franciscus à Victoria, from which we may suit ourselves :—either the healers cheat ; or they heal by the power of the devil ; or by the grace of God ; or by some specific natural gift. D'Autun, a writer who wholly repudiates the extremer marvels, and who is remarkable for his humanity, yet cannot resist the evidence of confession, which a modern writer regards with mingled scorn and indignation.[5] Even in the 18th century, Acxtelmeir, who does not lack sense, and who attributes the midnight revels to dream, yet cannot shake off the effect on his mind of the feeble stories about the persons found in the fields in the morning ;[6] and a little earlier Wagstaffe, one of the most open-minded of all the writers on the subject—who expressly attributes much of the deception to "want of knowledge in the art of physic "—is yet convinced that there were genuine cases of wounding the witch at a distance by striking at her apparition.[7] Bayle and La Bruyère, as Mr. Lecky has observed, held a similar uncertain position.

For any wide historical analysis of the grounds of opinion and of certainty in the human mind, no literature could better repay detailed study than that which these brief citations illustrate. But enough has perhaps been said for my present purpose—which is merely to show that, if the gradual tendency of the great body of public opinion on the subject of witchcraft was to put aside evidential questions, and simply to

---

[1] *Op. cit.*, pp. 236, 238, 242. Cf. Cooper, *Mystery of Witchcraft* (London, 1617), p. 258.

[2] A case where the fraud was exposed is given by Hutchinson, *Op. cit.*, p. 283.

[3] *A Discourse of the Damned Art of Witchcraft* (Cambridge, 1608), pp. 33, 140.

[4] *Of Credulity and Incredulity* (title of the first edition, London, 1668), pp. 28, 147, 169.

[5] *Op. cit.*, p. 164.

[6] *Misanthropus Audax* (Augsburg, 1710), pp. 32, 36.

[7] *Op. cit.*, pp. 118, 114. Of the more bizarre ideas, this was perhaps the one that lingered longest among rational writers. The author of *A Philosophical Endeavour*, &c., p. 128, Glanvil (*Op. cit.*, p. 34), and Mather (*Op. cit.*, p. 106), have, of course, no doubt on the subject. A case in which fraud was afterwards discovered is given by Thacker, *Essay on Demonology* (Boston, 1831), p. 107.

turn away from the phenomena as incredible and absurd, there was in the reflective and literary world a strong tendency to cling, wherever possible, to tradition and *à priori* conceptions, and for that purpose to press to the very utmost such items of evidence as were to be found. Had evidence and inference, necessarily and throughout, gone hand in hand, and had the abnormal occurrences all been of a piece—all of that bizarre and incredible kind which Mr. Lecky's treatment too much implies—then critical as well as uncritical minds might have drifted away from them in the silent and indifferent way which he depicts. But many of the abnormalities were far too real and tangible to be thus drifted away from ; and it often happened that these, through the wrong inferences to which they gave rise, lent a sort of unsound support to the more incredible and the worse-attested incidents. Thus, one author after another, in the gradual recession to the rational standpoint, draws and defends what, to us now, looks like an arbitrary line between fact and fable ; but the effect of this more critical treatment was, on the whole, to keep in view the large mass of phenomena which science can still accept as fact, and some of which, indeed—notably those of hysteria, hystero-epilepsy, and hypnotism—are only now beginning to make their full importance felt. And thus the position taken up in the foregoing chapter is maintained. The part of the case for witchcraft which is now an exploded superstition had never, even in its own day, any real evidential foundation ; while the part which had a real evidential foundation is now more firmly established than ever. It is with the former part that we would directly contrast, and with the latter that we might in some respects compare, our own evidential case for telepathy.

CHAPTER V.

SPECIMENS OF THE VARIOUS TYPES OF SPONTANEOUS
TELEPATHY.

§ 1. WE now come to the actual evidence for spontaneous telepathy.
As has been explained, the proof is cumulative, and its strength can
only be truly estimated by a patient study of a very large mass
of testimony. But to wade through a number of the cases is far
from an attractive task. They are very unexciting—monotonous
amid all their variety—as different from the *Mysteries of Udolpho*
as from the dignified reports of a learned society, and far more likely
to provoke slumber in the course of perusal than to banish it afterwards. And for the convenience of those who desire neither to toil
nor to sleep, it will be well to disregard logical arrangement, and to
present at once a few preliminary samples. This chapter, therefore,
will include a small batch of narratives which may serve as types of
the different classes of telepathic phenomena, while further illustrating various important evidential points. At the present stage it will,
no doubt, be open to anyone who accepts the facts in these cases as
essentially correct to regard every one of the coincidences as accidental. The reasoning that will prevent this conclusion must still
be taken on trust ; it could not be given now without delaying the
concrete illustrations till the reader would be weary of waiting for
them. Nor would it be profitable at this place to enter fully into the
principles of the classification, which can only be made clear in connection with the evidence. I will therefore sketch here the main
headings, without comment, trusting to the further development of
the work to justify the arrangement adopted.

We find our most distinct line of classification in the nature of
the percipient's impression. This at once divides the cases into two
great families—those (A) where the impression is *sensory and externalised*, and those (B) where it is *not sensory or externalised*. In
the first division the experience is a percept or quasi-percept—some-

thing which the person seems to see, hear, or feel, and which he instinctively refers to the outer world. In the second division, the impression is of an inward or ideal kind—either a mental image, or an emotion, or a mere blind impulse towards some sort of action. There is also a small group of cases (C) which it is not easy to assign to either division—those, namely, where the experience of the percipient is sensory, without being an external-seeming affection of sight, hearing, or touch—for instance, a physical feeling of illness or malaise. This small group will be most conveniently treated with the emotional division, into which it shades. Further, each of these divisions is represented in sleeping as well as in waking life, so that *dreams* form a comprehensive class (D) of their own ; and the *externalised* division is also strongly represented in a region of experience which is on the *borderland* (E) between complete sleep and complete normal wakefulness. Lastly, there are two peculiarities, attaching to certain cases in all or nearly all the above divisions, which are of sufficient importance to form the basis of two separate classes. The first of these is the *reciprocal* class (F), where each of the persons concerned seems to exercise a telepathic influence on the other; and the second is the *collective* class (G), where more percipients than one take part in a single telepathic incident.

§ 2. Now the logical starting-point for the following inquiry will naturally be found in the cases which present most analogy to the results of experimental thought-transference. All those results, it will be remembered, were of the *non-externalised* type. I shall therefore start with inward impressions, ideal and emotional, and shall advance, through dreams—where each of us has, so to speak, an outer as well as an inner world of his own—to the "borderland" and waking impressions which seem to fall on the senses in an objective way from the outer world that is common to us all.

But though the impressions received by the percipient in the experimental cases had no *external* quality, a good many of them were distinctly *sensory*—one important branch being transference of *pains*. And if the parallel between experimental and spontaneous effects be a just one, we might fairly expect to find cases where a localised pain has been similarly transferred from one person to another at a distance. I will open this preliminary batch of narratives with just such a case, the simplest possible specimen of group C, and as pure an instance of transference of sensation, unattended by any idea

or image, as can well be conceived. The parties concerned are Mr. Arthur Severn, the distinguished landscape-painter, and his wife; and the narrative was obtained through the kindness of Mr. Ruskin. Mrs. Severn says :—   " Brantwood, Coniston.
                                                            "October 27th, 1883.

(17) " I woke up with a start, feeling I had had a hard blow on my mouth, and with a distinct sense that I had been cut, and was bleeding under my upper lip, and seized my pocket-handkerchief, and held it (in a little pushed lump) to the part, as I sat up in bed, and after a few seconds, when I removed it, I was astonished not to see any blood, and only then realised it was impossible anything could have struck me there, as I lay fast asleep in bed, and so I thought it was only a dream !—but I looked at my watch, and saw it was seven, and finding Arthur (my husband) was not in ·the room, I concluded (rightly) that he must have gone out on the lake for an early sail, as it was so fine.

" I then fell asleep. At breakfast (half-past nine), Arthur came in rather late, and I noticed he rather purposely sat farther away from me than usual, and every now and then put his pocket-handkerchief furtively up to his lip, in the very way I had done. I said, 'Arthur, why are you doing that ? ' and added a little anxiously, ' I know you have hurt yourself ! but I'll tell you why afterwards.' He said, ' Well, when I was sailing, a sudden squall came, throwing the tiller suddenly round, and it struck me a bad blow in the mouth, under the upper lip, and it has been bleeding a good deal and won't stop.' I then said, ' Have you any idea what o'clock it was when it happened ? ' and he answered, ' It must have been about seven.'

" I then told what had happened to *me*, much to *his* surprise, and all who were with us at breakfast.

" It happened here about three years ago at Brantwood, to me.

                                                    " JOAN R. SEVERN."
In reply to inquiries Mrs. Severn writes :—

" There was no doubt about my starting up in bed wide awake, as I stuffed my pocket-handkerchief into my mouth, and held it pressed under my upper lip for some time before removing it to 'see the blood,'—and was much surprised that there was none. Some little time afterwards I fell asleep again. I believe that when I got up, an hour afterwards, the impression was still vividly in my mind, and that as I was dressing I did look under my lip to see if there was any mark."

Mr. Severn's account, dated Nov. 15, 1883, is as follows :—

" Early one summer morning, I got up intending to go and sail on the lake ; whether my wife heard me going out of the room I don't know ; she probably did, and in a half-dreamy state knew where I was going.

" When I got down to the water I found it calm, like a mirror, and remember thinking it quite a shame to disturb the wonderful reflections of the opposite shore. However, I soon got afloat, and as there was no wind, contented myself with pulling up my sails to dry, and putting my boat in order. Soon some slight air came, and I was able to sail about a mile below Brantwood, then the wind dropped, and I was left becalmed for half-an-hour or so, when, on looking up to the head of the lake, I saw a dark blue line on the water. At first I couldn't make it out, but soon saw that it must be small waves caused by a strong wind coming. I got my boat as ready as I could, in the short time, to receive this gust, but somehow or other she was taken aback, and seemed to spin round when the wind struck her, and in getting out of the way of the boom I got my head in the way of the tiller, which also swung round and gave me a nasty blow in the mouth, cutting my lip rather badly, and having become loose in the rudder it came out and went overboard. With my mouth bleeding, the mainsheet more or less round my neck, and the tiller gone, and the boat in confusion, I could not help smiling to think how suddenly I had been humbled almost to a wreck, just when I thought I was going to be so clever ! However, I soon managed to get my tiller, and, with plenty of wind, tacked back to Brantwood, and, making my boat snug in the harbour, walked up to the house, anxious of course to hide as much as possible what had happened to my mouth, and getting another handkerchief walked into the breakfast-room, and managed to say something about having been out early. In an instant my wife said, ' You don't mean to say you have hurt your mouth ? ' or words to that effect. I then explained what had happened, and was surprised to see some extra interest on her face, and still more surprised when she told me she had started out of her sleep thinking she had received a blow in the mouth ! and that it was a few minutes past seven o'clock, and wondered if my accident had happened at the same time ; but as I had no watch with me I couldn't tell, though, on comparing notes, it certainly looked as if it had been about the same time.   " ARTHUR SEVERN."

Considering what a vivid thing pain often is, it might seem likely that this form of telepathy, if it exists, would be comparatively common, in comparison with the more ideal or intellectual forms which are connected with the higher senses. This, however, is not so. It is conceivable, of course, that instances occur which go unnoticed. For, apart from injury, even a sharp pain is soon forgotten ; and unless the copy reproduced the original with excruciating fidelity, a sudden pang might be referred to some ordinary cause, and the coincidence would never be noted. We, however, can only go by what *is* noted. I mentioned that even in experimental trials the phenomenon has been little observed except with hypnotised " subjects " ; and on the evidence we must allow its spontaneous appearance to be even rarer. The stock instance is that of the brothers, Louis and Charles Blanc, the latter of whom professed to have experienced a strong physical shock at the time that his brother was felled in the streets of Paris by (as was supposed) some Bonapartist bully.[1] But this is a third-hand story at best ; and the above is our

[1] I received this version of the incident from Mrs. Crawford, of 60, Boulevard de Courcelles, Paris, to whom Louis Blanc narrated it in 1871, in a long and intimate *tête-à-tête*. Charles made his appearance in Paris, unexpectedly, some days after the event,

only first-hand instance where the pain was of an unusual kind, and was very exactly localised. It is specially for cases of this sort—most interesting to science, but with neither pathos nor dignity to keep them alive—that the chance of preservation will, we trust, be improved by the existence of a classified collection, where they may at once find their proper place.

What has been said of pains applies, *mutatis mutandis*, to all affections of the lower senses. In the first place, it is the exception and not the rule for the spontaneous transferences to reproduce in the percipient the exact sensation of the agent (p. 111); and, in the second place, such reproduction (or at any rate the evidence for it) seems almost wholly confined to the higher senses of sight and hearing. Thus, though we found that transference of *tastes* had been a very successful branch of the experimental work, we have no precisely analogous record in the spontaneous class. The nearest approach is a case which concerned the sense of smell, but where there was no direct transference of sensation as such. The case is, however, worth quoting here on another ground, as illustrating one of the evidential points of the last chapter—namely, that the strength of any evidence, in the sense of the assurance which it produces that the facts are correctly reported, is a very different thing from its strength as a contribution to the proof of telepathy. Thus, no one probably will care to dispute the facts in the following narrative ; but the coincidence recorded is little, if at all, more striking than most of us occasionally encounter ; and recourse to the telepathic explanation can only be justified by our knowledge that the two persons concerned have, on other occasions, given very much more conclusive signs of their power of super-sensuous communication.[1] The Rev. P. H. Newnham, of Maker Vicarage, Devonport, writes to us :—

alleging as the reason of his visit the anxiety which the shock had caused him; and his brother at any rate, who knew him thoroughly, accepted this as the true reason.   The case affords an interesting instance of the transformations which a story that becomes at all celebrated is almost sure to undergo.   See, *e.g.*, *A Memoir of C. Mayne Young* (1871), pp. 341-2, where the injury is localised as a stab in the arm, and the parts of the brothers are inverted.   The lady who gave the account to the subject of the memoir professed to have heard it from Louis Blanc, at Dr. Ashburner's dinner-table; and also to have been shown the scar on Charles Blanc's arm after dinner !   A parallel case—where the absent husband was struck by a ball in the forehead, and the wife felt the wound —is recorded by Borel, *Historiarum et Observationum Medicophysicarum Centuriæ iv.* (Paris, 1656), Cent. ii., obs. 47 ; but only on the authority of "persons worthy of credit."   This is the earliest record that I can recall of a non-externalised telepathic impression of at all a definite sort.

[1] See pp. 63-9. Mr. Newnham has further told us that coincidences of thought of a more or less striking kind occur to himself and his wife as matters of daily experience. But to differentiate these from the numerous domestic cases which pure accident will account for (Chap. vi., § 1), a written record would have to be accurately kept from day to day.

"January 26th, 1885.

(18) "In March, 1861, I was living at Houghton, Hants. My wife was at the time confined to the house, by delicacy of the lungs. One day, walking through a lane, I found the first wild violets of the spring, and took them home to her.

"Early in April I was attacked with a dangerous illness; and in June left the place. I never told my wife exactly where I found the violets, nor, for the reasons explained, did I ever walk with her past the place where they grew, for many years.

"In November, 1873, we were staying with friends at Houghton; and myself and wife took a walk up the lane in question. As we passed by the place, the recollection of those early violets of $12\frac{1}{2}$ years ago flashed upon my mind. At the usual interval of some 20 or 30 seconds my wife remarked, 'It's very curious, but if it were not impossible, I should declare that I could smell violets in the hedge.'

"I had not spoken, or made any gesture or movement of any kind, to imdicate what I was thinking of. Neither had my memory called up the perfume. All that I thought of was the exact locality on the hedge bank; my memory being exceedingly minute for locality."

Mr. Newnham's residence at Houghton lasted only a few months, and with the help of a diary he can account for nearly every day's walking and work. "My impression is," he says, "that this was the first and only time that I explored this particular 'drive'; and I feel certain that Mrs. Newnham never saw the spot at all until November, 1873. The hedges had then been grubbed, and no violets grew there."

The following is Mrs. Newnham's account:—

"May 28th, 1885.

"I perfectly remember our walking one day in November, 1873, at Houghton, and suddenly finding so strong a scent of violets in the air that I remarked to my husband, 'If it were not so utterly impossible, I should declare I smelt violets!' Mr. Newnham then reminded me of his bringing me the first violets in the spring of 1861, and told me that this was just about the spot where he had found them. I had quite forgotten the circumstance till thus reminded."

§ 3.   We may now pass to illustrations of Class B—the class of ideal and emotional impressions. The following is a well-attested case of the transference of an idea. It was sent to us, in 1884, by our friend, the Rev. J. A. Macdonald, who wrote:—

"19, Heywood Street, Cheetham, Manchester.

(19) "When I was in Liverpool, in 1872, I heard from my friend, the late Rev. W. W. Stamp, D.D., a remarkable story of the faculty of second sight possessed by the Rev. John Drake, of Arbroath, in Scotland. I visited Arbroath in 1874, and recounted to Mr. Drake the story of Dr. Stamp, which Mr. Drake assented to as correct, and he called his faculty 'clairvoyance.' Subsequently, in 1881, I had the facts particularly verified by Mrs. Hutcheon, who was herself the subject of this clairvoyance of Mr. Drake.

"When the Rev. John Drake was minister of the Wesleyan Church at Aberdeen, Miss Jessie Wilson, the daughter of one of the principal lay office bearers in that church, sailed for India, to join the Rev. John Hutcheon, M.A., then stationed as a missionary at Bangalore, to whom she was under engagement to be married. Mr. Drake, one morning, came down to Mr. Wilson's place of business and said, ' Mr. Wilson, I am happy to be able to inform you that Jessie has had a pleasant voyage, and is now safely arrived in India.' Mr. Wilson said, ' How do you know that, Mr. Drake ? ' to which Mr. Drake replied, ' I saw it.' ' But,' said Mr. Wilson, ' it cannot be, for it is a fortnight too soon. The vessel has never made the voyage within a fortnight of the time it is now since Jessie sailed.' To this Mr. Drake replied : ' Now you jot it down in your book that John Drake called this morning, and told you that Jessie has arrived in India this morning after a pleasant voyage.' Mr. Wilson accordingly made the entry, which Mrs. Hutcheon assures me she saw, when she returned home, and that it ran thus : ' Mr. Drake. Jessie arrived India morning of June 5th, 1860.' This turned out to have been literally the case. The ship had fair winds all the way, and made a quicker passage by a fortnight than ever she had made before."

The above account was sent by Mr. Macdonald to Mr. Drake for verification, and the following reply was received from the Rev. Crawshaw Hargreaves, of the Wesleyan Manse, Arbroath :—

"April 29th, 1885.

" MY DEAR SIR,—Mr. Drake is sorry your communication of the 2nd inst. has been so long unanswered ; but two days after receiving it he had a paralytic seizure, which has not only confined him to bed, but taken from him the use of one side.

"He now desires me to answer your inquiries, and to say that the account, which you enclosed and which he now returns to you, is correct, except that he has no recollection of ever calling it ' clairvoyance.' It was neither a ' dream,' nor a ' vision,' but an impression that he received between the hours of 8 and 10 in the morning, when his mind was as clear as ever it was, an impression which he believes was given him by God for the comfort of the family. Moreover this impression was so clear and satisfactory to himself that when Mr. Wilson said, ' It cannot be,' Mr. Drake replied, ' You jot it down,' as warmly as if his statement of any ordinary circumstances had been doubted by a friend.

"Mr. Drake hopes these particulars will be enough for your purpose.— Believe me, dear sir, yours very truly,   " C. HARGREAVES."

The following is Mrs. Hutcheon's account of the incident, given quite independently :—

" Weston-super-Mare.

" February 20th, 1885.

"The facts are simply these. I sailed for India on March 3rd, 1860, in the ' Earl of Hardwicke,' a good, but slow, sailing-vessel. About 16 weeks were usually allowed for the voyage, so that we were not due in Madras till about the middle of June. Our voyage, however, being an uncommonly rapid one, we cast anchor in the roads of Madras on the morning of June 5th, taking our friends there quite by surprise.

"On this same morning, my former pastor, an able and much esteemed Wesleyan minister, called on my father at an unusually early hour, when the following conversation passed :—

"'Why, Mr. D., what takes you abroad at this early hour?'

"'I have come to bring you good news, Mr. W. Your daughter Jessie has reached India this morning, safe and well.'

"'That would indeed be good news, if we could believe it; but you forget that the ship is not due at Madras before the middle of June. Besides, how could you get to know that?'

"'Such, however, is the fact,' replied Mr. D., and seeing my father's incredulous look, he added : 'You do not believe what I say, Mr. W., but just take a note of this date.'

"To satisfy him, my father wrote in his memo. book : 'Rev. J. D. and Jessie. Tuesday, 5th June, 1860.'

"In due time, tidings confirming Mr. D.'s statement arrived, greatly to the astonishment of my friends. He, however, manifested no surprise, but simply remarked, 'Had I not known it for a fact, I certainly should not have told you of it.'

"These particulars I received by letter at the time, and on our return home 7 years later, we heard it from my father's own lips. He is no longer with us, but the above are the plain facts as he gave them, and the little memo. in his handwriting, which he gave me as a curiosity, lies before me now.

"JESSIE HUTCHEON."

In answer to inquiries, Mrs. Hutcheon adds :—

"March 23rd.

"I felt inclined to smile at the idea that I could possibly be mistaken as to a date so memorable in my life's history, and immediately preceding my marriage. However, to render assurance doubly sure, I have referred to both my husband's diary and my own, in each of which my landing in India on the 5th of June has an important place.

"The entry made by my husband is as follows: 'N.B.—5th June, 1860 ; a memorable day ! The 'Hardwicke' has arrived. What a quick voyage! Miss Wilson and mission party well.'"

[Mr. Macdonald tells us that he believes Mr. Drake had many such experiences, but that he found him so reticent that he despaired of getting an account of them from him. And Mr. Drake's death has now made the attempt impossible.]

As regards the facts here, the narrative will probably be accepted as trustworthy. As regards the inference that may be drawn, the case is eminently of a sort where the character of the professing percipient (in other points than the mere desire to be truthful) ought to be taken into account. From a person "given to little surprises," or who posed as a diviner if one out of a hundred guesses hit the mark, the evidence would deserve no attention ; from a person of grave and reticent character, it is at any rate worthy of careful record.

In the last example, the idea apparently transferred was of a somewhat abstract kind—the impression of a mere event, without any

o

concrete imagery. But the ideal class includes many instances of a distinctly pictorial kind, where a scene is as clearly presented to the inward eye as the image of a card or diagram in some of our experimental cases. The following account of a vivid mental picture of this sort was received from Mrs. Bettany, of 2, Eckington Villas, Ashbourne Grove, Dulwich.

"November, 1884.

(20) "When I was a child I had many remarkable experiences of a psychical nature, which I remember to have looked upon as ordinary and natural at the time.

"On one occasion (I am unable to fix the date, but I must have been about 10 years old) I was walking in a country lane at A., the place where my parents then resided. I was reading geometry as I walked along, a subject little likely to produce fancies or morbid phenomena of any kind, when, in a moment, I saw a bedroom known as the White Room in my home, and upon the floor lay my mother, to all appearance dead. The vision must have remained some minutes, during which time my real surroundings appeared to pale and die out; but as the vision faded, actual surroundings came back, at first dimly, and then clearly.

"I could not doubt that what I had seen was real, so, instead of going home, I went at once to the house of our medical man and found him at home. He at once set out with me for my home, on the way putting questions I could not answer, as my mother was to all appearance well when I left home.

"I led the doctor straight to the White Room, where we found my mother actually lying as in my vision. This was true even to minute details. She had been seized suddenly by an attack at the heart, and would soon have breathed her last but for the doctor's timely advent. I shall get my father and mother to read this and sign it.

"JEANIE GWYNNE-BETTANY."

Mrs. Bettany's parents write :—

"We certify that the above is correct.   "S. G. GWYNNE.
                                                "J. W. GWYNNE."

In answer to inquiries, Mrs. Bettany says :—

(1) "I was in no anxiety about my mother at the time I saw the vision I described. She was in her usual health when I left her.

(2) "Something a little similar had once occurred to my mother. She had been out riding alone, and the horse brought her to our door hanging half off his back, in a faint. This was a long time before, and she never rode again. Heart-disease had set in. She was not in *the habit* of fainting unless an attack of the heart was upon her. Between the attacks she looked and acted as if in health.

(3) "The occasion I described was, I believe, the only one on which I saw a scene transported apparently into the actual field of vision, to the exclusion of objects and surroundings actually present.

"I have had other visions in which I have seen events happening as they *really were*, in another place, but I have been also conscious of *real* surroundings.

In answer to further inquiries, she adds :—

(1) " No one could tell whether my vision preceded the fact or not. My mother was supposed to be out. No one knew anything of my mother's being ill, till I took the doctor and my father, whom I had encountered at the door, to the room where we found my mother as I had seen her in my vision.

(2) " The doctor is dead. He has no living relation. No one in A. knew anything of these circumstances.

(3) " The White Room in which I saw my mother, and afterwards actually found her, was out of use. It was unlikely she should be there.

" She was found lying in the attitude in which I had seen her. I found a handkerchief with a lace border beside her on the floor. This I had distinctly noticed in my vision. There were other particulars of coincidence which I cannot put here."

Mrs. Bettany's father has given the following fuller account :—

" I distinctly remember being surprised by seeing my daughter, in company with the family doctor, outside the door of my residence ; and I asked ' Who is ill ? ' She replied, ' Mamma.' She led the way at once to the ' White Room,' where we found my wife lying in a swoon on the floor. It was when I asked when she had been taken ill, that I found it must have been after my daughter had left the house. None of the servants in the house knew anything of the sudden illness, which our doctor assured me would have been *fatal* had he not arrived when he did.

" My wife was quite well when I left her in the morning.

"S. G. GWYNNE."

If this vision suggests *clairvoyance*, owing to the amount of detail presented, we must still notice that it includes nothing which was not, or had not recently been, within the consciousness of the supposed agent. This point will claim further notice at a later stage. But the case is chiefly useful as illustrating an evidential point, which it will be very important to bear in mind in studying the mass of narratives in the sequel—namely, that possible inaccuracy as to details may leave the substantial fact which makes for telepathy quite untouched. It might, no doubt be fairly urged that the vision described may have assumed its distinctness of detail in the percipient's mind only after the details of the actual scene had met her eyes. A child's mind might easily be undiscriminating in this respect ; and moreover Mrs. Bettany is by nature a good visualiser ; which may perhaps be supposed to involve a slight tendency to *retrospective hallucination*—to mistaking vividly-conceived images for memories of actual experiences. But even if this hypothesis be pressed to the uttermost, the fact that she unexpectedly fetched the doctor remains ; and if her whole impression of her mother's critical condition was only a subsequent fancy, this very exceptional step must have been taken without a reason. That is to say, we can only reject what is the substantial part of the evidence by supposing a distinctly improbable thing to have happened. And that being so, the evidence is a true stick in the telepathic faggot (p. 169).

I will supplement these two last cases by a third, in which their respective points, the abstract idea of an event and the concrete picture of a scene, were both presented. This case will also illustrate an evidential point. It occasionally happens that a number of occurrences, perhaps trivial in character, and each of them likely enough to be dismissed as merely a very odd coincidence, fall to the experience of one person; and if he is observant of his impressions, he may gradually become conscious of a certain similarity between them, which leads him to regard them as telepathic, or at any rate as something more than accidental. Before it can be worth while to consider such evidence, we must have reason to believe that the witness is a good observer, and alive to the very general mistake of noting hits and not misses in these matters. Such an observer we believe that we have found in Mr. Keulemans, of 34, Matilda Street, Barnsbury, N., a well-known scientific draughtsman, of whose care and accuracy we have had several examples. He has experienced so many of these coincidences that, even before our inquiries quickened his interest in the matter, he had been accustomed to keep a record of his impressions—which, according to his own account, were invariably justified by fact. Some more of his cases will be given in the sequel. The one here quoted is trivial enough (except perhaps to the baby who fell out of bed), and of little force if it were a single experience. Yet it will be seen that the impression was precise in character, was at once written down, and proved to be completely correct. We may perhaps assume Mrs. Keulemans to have been the agent.

"October 16th, 1883.

(21) " My wife went to reside at the seaside on September 30th last, taking with her our youngest child, a little boy 13 months old.

" On Wednesday, October 3rd, I felt a strong impression that the little fellow was worse (he was in weak health on his departure). The idea then prevailed on my mind that he had met with a slight accident; and immediately the picture of the bedroom in which he sleeps appeared in my mind's eye. It was *not* the strong sensation of awe or sorrow, as I had often experienced before on such occasions ; but, anyhow, I fancied he had fallen *out of the bed*, upon chairs, and then rolled down upon the floor. This was about 11 a.m., and I at once wrote to my wife, asking her to let me know how the little fellow was getting on. I thought it rather bold to tell my wife that the baby had, to my conviction, really met with an accident, without being able to produce any confirmatory evidence. Also I considered that she would take it as an insinuation of carelessness on her part ; therefore I purposely wrote it as a *post scriptum.*

" I heard no more about it, and even fancied that this time my impression was merely the consequence of anxiety. But on Saturday last I went to see my wife and child, and asked whether she had taken notice of my advice to protect the baby against such an accident. She smiled at first, and then informed me that he had tumbled out of bed upon the chairs placed at the side, and then found his way upon the floor, without being hurt. She further remarked, ' You must have been thinking of that when it was just too late, because it happened the same day your letter came, some hours previously.' I asked her what time of the day it happened. Answer : ' About 11 a.m.' She told me that she heard the baby fall, and at once ran upstairs to pick him up.

" I am certain, without the shadow of a doubt, that I wrote immediately after the impression ; and that this was between 11 and 11.30 in the morning."

I have seen the letter which Mr. Keulemans wrote to his wife. The envelope bears the post-mark of Worthing, October 3rd ; and the postcript contained the following words :—

" Mind little Gaston does not fall out of bed. Put chairs in front of it. You know accidents soon happen. The fact is, I am almost certain he has met with such a mishap this very morning."

Mrs. Keulemans' aunt supplied the following testimony a day or two after Mr. Keulemans' letter of October 16th.

" 36, Teville Street, Worthing.

" Mrs. Keulemans (my niece) and her baby are staying at my house. The baby had fallen out of bed the morning of the day the letter [*i.e.,* Mr. Keulemans' letter] was received.   " C. GRAY."

The next account illustrates an emotional impression, with a certain amount of physical discomfort. The experience appears to have been of a very unusual sort, and the coincidence of time to have been exact ; the case is therefore a strong example of a weak class. The narrator is Miss Martyn, of Long Melford Rectory, Suffolk.

" September 4th, 1884.

(22) " On March 16th, 1884, I was sitting alone in the drawing-room, reading an interesting book, and feeling perfectly well, when suddenly I experienced an undefined feeling of dread and horror ; I looked at the clock and saw it was just 7 p.m. I was utterly unable to read, so I got up and walked about the room trying to throw off the feeling, but I could not : I became quite cold, and had a firm presentiment that I was dying.[1] The feeling lasted about half-an-hour, and then passed off, leaving me a good deal shaken all the evening ; I went to bed feeling very weak, as if I had been seriously ill.

" The next morning I received a telegram telling me of the death of a near and very dear cousin, Mrs. K., in Shropshire, with whom I had been

---

[1] Cf. cases 70 and 76.

most intimately associated all my life, but for the last two years had seen
very little of her.   I did not associate this feeling of death with her or
with anyone else, but I had a most distinct impression that something
terrible was happening.   This feeling came over me, I afterwards found.
just at the time when my cousin died (7 p.m.).   The connection with her
death may have been simply an accident.   I have never experienced anything of the sort before.   I was not aware that Mrs. K. was ill, and her
death was peculiarly sad and sudden.   " K. M."

Mr. White Cooper, through whose kindness we obtained this account,
writes as follows :—

                                    " 19, Berkeley Square, W.
                                        " April 7th, 1885.
" I have asked Miss Martyn whether she had told anyone about her
feeling of horror on March 16th, *before* she heard of the death of her
cousin.   She told me she had.   She was quite convinced, and perfectly
remembered telling Miss Mason the same evening, after Miss Mason had
come from church, that she had had a peculiar feeling of horror and dread
for which she could give no account.   I then questioned Miss Mason, and
enclose what she dictated."

Miss Mason says :—
                            " The Rectory, Long Melford, Suffolk.
                                        " April 5th, 1885.
" I well remember Miss Martyn telling me that a feeling of horror and
an indescribable dread came over her on Sunday evening, March 16th,
1884, while we were in church, and she was alone in the drawing-room ;
that she was unable to shake it off, and felt very restless, and got up and
walked about the room.   She did not refer to anyone, and could give no
cause for this peculiar feeling.   I am under the impression that she told
me the same evening (Sunday), and before she heard of the death of her
cousin, bnt I am not certain whether it was Sunday or Monday that she
told me about it.   " ANNA M. MASON."

We have verified the date of the death in two local newspapers.   The
day was a Sunday, which is in accordance with the evidence.

§ 4.   The next case illustrates the class of *dreams* (D).   I am
aware that the very mention of this class is apt to raise a prejudice
against our whole inquiry.   I shall explain later why it is extremely
difficult to draw conclusive evidence of telepathy from dreams, and
why we mark off the whole class of dreams, which are simply remembered as such, from the cases on which we rest our argument ; but I
shall also hope to show that dreams, though needing to be treated
with the greatest caution, have a necessary and instructive place in
the conspectus of telepathic phenomena.   As to the evidential force
of the present case, it will be enough to point out that the percipient
states the experience to have been unique in his life; and that
the violence of the effect produced, leading to the very unusual entry
in the diary, puts the vision outside the common run of dreams which

may justly be held to afford almost limitless scope for accidental coincidences. The narrative is from Mr. Frederick Wingfield, of Belle Isle en Terre, Côtes du Nord, France.

"20th December, 1883.

(23) "I give you my most solemn assurance that what I am about to relate is the exact account of what occurred. I may remark that I am so little liable to the imputation of being easily impressed with a sense of the supernatural [1] that I have been accused, and with reason, of being unduly sceptical upon matters which lay beyond my powers of explanation.

"On the night of Thursday, the 25th of March, 1880, I retired to bed after reading till late, as is my habit. I dreamed that I was lying on my sofa reading, when, on looking up, I saw distinctly the figure of my brother, Richard Wingfield-Baker, sitting on the chair before me. I dreamed that I spoke to him, but that he simply bent his head in reply, rose and left the room. When I awoke, I found myself standing with one foot on the ground by my bedside, and the other on the bed, trying to speak and to pronounce my brother's name. So strong was the impression as to the reality of his presence and so vivid the whole scene as dreamt, that I left my bedroom to search for my brother in the sitting-room. I examined the chair where I had seen him seated, I returned to bed, tried to fall asleep in the hope of a repetition of the appearance, but my mind was too excited, too painfully disturbed, as I recalled what I had dreamed. I must have, however, fallen asleep towards the morning, but when I awoke, the impression of my dream was as vivid as ever—and I may add is to this very hour equally strong and clear. My sense of impending evil was so strong that I at once made a note in my memorandum book of this 'appearance,' and added the words, 'God forbid.'

"Three days afterwards I received the news that my brother, Richard Wingfield-Baker, had died on Thursday evening, the 25th of March, 1880, at 8.30 p.m., from the effects of the terrible injuries received in a fall while hunting with the Blackmore Vale hounds.

"I will only add that I had been living in this town some 12 months; that I had not had any recent communication with my brother; that I knew him to be in good health, and that he was a perfect horseman. I did not at once communicate this dream to any intimate friend—there was unluckily none here at that very moment—but I did relate the story after the receipt of the news of my brother's death, and showed the entry in my memorandum book. As evidence, of course, this is worthless; but I give you my word of honour that the circumstances I have related are the positive truth.

"FRED. WINGFIELD."

"February 4th, 1884.

"I must explain my silence by the excuse that I could not procure till to-day a letter from my friend the Prince de Lucinge-Faucigny, in which he mentions the fact of my having related to him the particulars of my dream on the 25th of March, 1880. He came from Paris to stay a few

---

[1] This expression cannot be excluded, when the words of our informants are quoted. We, ourselves, of course, regard all these occurrences as strictly *natural*.

days with me early in April, and saw the entry in my note-book, which I
now enclose for your inspection. You will observe the initials R. B. W. B.,
and a curious story is attached to these letters. During that sleepless
night I naturally dwelt upon the incident, and recalled the circumstances
connected with the apparition. Though I distinctly recognised my brother's
features, the idea flashed upon me that the figure bore some slight
resemblance to my most intin ae and valued friend, Colonel Bigge, and in
my dread of impending evil to one to whom I am so much attached, I wrote
the four initials, R. B. for Richard Baker, and W. B. for William Bigge.
When the tidings of my brother's death reached me I again looked at the
entry, and saw with astonishment that the four letters stood for my
brother's full name, Richard Baker Wingfield-Baker, though I had always
spoken of him as Richard Baker in common with the rest of my family.
The figure I saw was that of my brother ; and in my anxious state of mind
I worried myself into the belief that possibly it might be that of my old
friend, as a resemblance did exist in the fashion of their beards. I can
give you no further explanations, nor can I produce further testimony in
support of my assertions.

"FRED. WINGFIELD."

With this letter, Mr. Wingfield sent me the note-book, in which,
among a number of business memoranda, notes of books, &c., I find the
entry—" Appearance—Thursday night, 25th of March, 1880. R. B. W. B.
God forbid ! "

The following letter was enclosed :—

"Coat-an-nos, 2 février, 1884.

" Mon cher ami,—Je n'ai aucun effort de mémoire à faire pour me
rappeler le fait dont vous me parlez, car j'en ai conservé un souvenir très
net et très précis.

"Je me souviens parfaitement que le dimanche, 4 avril, 1880, étant
arrivé de Paris le matin même pour passer ici quelques jours, j'ai été
déjeûner avec vous. Je me souviens aussi parfaitement que je vous ai
trouvé fort ému de la douloureuse nouvelle qui vous était parvenue
quelques jours [1] auparavant, de la mort de l'un des messieurs vos
frères. Je me rappelle aussi comme si le fait s'était passé hier, tant j'en
ai été frappé, que quelques jours avant d'apprendre la triste nouvelle,
vous aviez un soir, étant déjà couché, vu, ou cru voir, mais en tous cas
très distinctement, votre frère, celui dont vous veniez d'apprendre la
mort subite, tout près de votre lit, et que, dans la conviction où vous
étiez que c'était bien lui que vous perceviez, vous vous étiez levé et lui
aviez addressé la parole, et qu'à ce moment vous aviez cessé de le voir
comme s'il s'était évanoui ainsi qu'un spectre. Je me souviens encore
que, sous l'impression de l'émotion bien naturelle qui avait été la suite
de cet évènement, vous l'aviez inscrit dans un petit carnet où vous
avez l'habitude d'écrire les faits saillants de votre très paisible existence,
et que vous m'avez fait voir ce carnet. Cette apparition, cette vision,
ou ce songe, comme vous voudrez l'appeler, est inscrit, si j'ai bon
souvenir, à la date du 24 ou du 25 février,[1] et ce n'est que deux ou trois

[1] The words "*quelques jours* auparavant," coupled with the fact that the *number of
the day* is right, suggest that *février* is a mere slip of the pen for *mars*.

jours après que vous avez reçu la nouvelle officielle de la mort de votre frère.

" J'ai été d'autant moins surpris de ce que vous me disiez alors, et j'en ai aussi conservé un souvenir d'autant plus net et précis, comme je vous le disais en commençant, que j'ai dans ma famille des faits similaires auxquels je crois absolument.

" Des faits semblables arrivent, croyez-le bien, bien plus souvent qu'on ne le croit généralement ; seulement on ne veut pas toujours les dire, parceque l'on se méfie de soi ou des autres.

" Au revoir, cher ami, à bientôt, je l'espère, et croyez bien à l'expression des plus sincères sentiments de votre tout devoué

"FAUCIGNY, PRINCE LUCINGE."

In answer to inquiries, Mr. Wingfield adds :—

" I have never had any other startling dream of the same nature, nor any dream from which I woke with the same sense of reality and distress, and of which the effect continued long after I was well awake. Nor have I upon any other occasion had a hallucination of the senses."

The *Times* obituary for March 30th, 1880, records the death of Mr. R. B. Wingfield-Baker, of Orsett Hall, Essex, as having taken place on the 25th. The *Essex Independent* gives the same date, adding that Mr. Baker breathed his last about 9 o'clock.

It will be seen here that the impression followed the death by a few hours—a feature which will frequently recur. The fact, of course, slightly detracts from the evidential force of a case, as compared with the completely simultaneous coincidences ; inasmuch as the odds against the *accidental* occurrence of a unique impression of someone's presence within a few hours of his death, enormous as they are, are less enormous than the odds against a similar accidental occurrence within five minutes of the death. But the deferment of the impression, though to this slight extent affecting a case as an item of telepathic *evidence,* is not in itself any obstacle to the telepathic *explanation.* We may recall that in some of the experimental cases the impression was never a piece of conscious experience at all ; while in others the latency and gradual emergence of the idea was a very noticeable feature (pp. 56, 63-71, 84). This justifies us in presuming that an impression which ultimately takes a sensory form may fail in the first instance to reach the threshold of attention. It may be unable to compete, at the moment, with the vivid sensory impressions, and the crowd of ideas and images, that belong to normal seasons of waking life ; and it may thus remain latent till darkness and quiet give a chance for its development. This view seems at any rate supported by the fact that it is usually *at night* that the delayed impression —if such it be—emerges into the percipient's consciousness. It is supported also by analogies which recognised psychology supplies. I may refer to the extraordinary exaltation of memory sometimes observed in hypnotic and hystero-epileptic "subjects"; or even to the vivid revival, in ordinary dreaming, of impressions which have hardly affected the waking consciousness.

Mr. Wingfield's vision had another unusual feature besides the violence of its effect on him. It represented a single figure, without detail or incident. It was, so to speak, the *dream of an apparition;* and in this respect bears a closer affinity to "borderland" and waking cases than to dreams in general. It will be worth while to quote here one dream-case of a more ordinary type so far as its content is concerned, but resembling the last in its unusual and distressing vividness. The supposed agent in this instance experienced nothing more than a brief sense of danger and excitement, which, however, may have been sufficiently intense during the moments that it lasted. The account is from Mrs. West, of Hildegarde, Furness Road, Eastbourne.

"1883.

(24) "My father and brother were on a journey during the winter. I was expecting them home, without knowing the exact day of their return. The date, to the best of my recollection, was the winter of 1871-2. I had gone to bed at my usual time, about 11 p.m. Some time in the night I had a vivid dream, which made a great impression on me. I dreamt I was looking out of a window, when I saw father driving in a Spids sledge, followed in another by my brother. They had to pass a cross-road, on which another traveller was driving very fast, also in a sledge with one horse. Father seemed to drive on without observing the other fellow, who would without fail have driven over father if he had not made his horse rear, so that I saw my father drive under the hoofs of the horse. Every moment I expected the horse would fall down and crush him. I called out 'Father! father!' and woke in a great fright. The next morning my father and brother returned. I said to him, 'I am so glad to see you arrive quite safely, as I had such a dreadful dream about you last night.' My brother said, 'You could not have been in greater fright about him than I was,' and then he related to me what had happened, which tallied exactly with my dream. My brother in his fright, when he saw the feet of the horse over father's head, called out, 'Oh! father, father!'

"I have never had any other dream of this kind, nor do I remember ever to have had another dream of an accident happening to anyone in whom I was interested. I often dream of people, and when this happens I generally expect to receive a letter from them, or to hear of them in the course of the next day. I dreamt of Mrs. G. Bidder the night before I received her letter asking me for an account of this dream; and I told Mr. West, before we went down to breakfast, that I should have a letter that day from her. I had no other reason to expect a letter from her, nor had I received one for some time, I should think some years, previously.

"HILDA WEST."

Mrs. West's father, Sir John Crowe, late Consul-General for Norway, is since dead ; but her brother, Mr. Septimus Crowe, of Librola, Mary's Hill Road, Shortlands, sends us the following confirmation :—

"I remember vividly, on my return once with my father from a trip to the north of Norway in the winter time, my sister meeting us at the hall-door as we entered, and exclaiming how pleased she was to see us, and that we were safe, as she said at once to me that she had had such an unpleasant dream the evening before. I said, 'What was it?' She then minutely explained to me the dream, as she related it to you, and which is in accordance with the facts. It naturally astonished my father and myself a good deal, that she so vividly in her sleep saw exactly what happened, and I should say, too, she dreamt it at the very time it happened, about 11.30 p.m. "SEPTIMUS CROWE."[1]

This, again, is a good example of a weak class. But in the present instance we at any rate possess Mrs. West's testimony that her experience was unique ; and we have, further, Mr. Crowe's testimony that the dream was accurately described before the facts were known. It was described, no doubt, in a conversation with *him*—a person whose mind was full of the facts, and he probably did not keep silence during the whole course of his sister's narration : I have already noted that the unprepared actors in these cases are not likely to conduct themselves at the moment with a deliberate eye to the flawlessness of their evidence for our purposes some years afterwards. But it would be straining a sceptical hypothesis too far to assume that his interposed comments formed the real basis of the scene in Mrs. West's memory, while he himself remained completely unconscious that he was supplying the information which he appeared to be receiving.

§ 5. We now come to an example of the "borderland" class (E)— the class where the percipient, though not asleep, was not, or cannot be

---

[1] Our friend Mrs. Bidder, the wife of Mr. G. Bidder, Q.C., sends us the following recollection of the narrative as told at her table by Mr. S. Crowe, who is her husband's brother-in-law.

"Ravensbury Park, Mitcham, Surrey.

"10th January, 1883.

"The following was related at our table by my husband's brother-in-law, Mr. Septimus Crowe. His father, since dead, was Sir John Crowe, Consul-General for Norway.

"'My father and I were travelling one winter in Norway. We had our carrioles as sledges, and my father drove first, I following. One day we were driving very quickly down a steep hill, at the bottom of which ran a road, at right angles with the one we were on. As we neared the bottom of the hill we saw a carriole, going as quickly as ourselves, just ready to cross our path. My father reined in suddenly, his horse reared and fell over, and I could not, at first, see whether he was hurt or not. He, luckily, had sustained no injury, and in due time we reached home. My sister, on our approach, rushed out, exclaiming : "Then you are not hurt? I saw the horse rear, but I could not see whether you were hurt or not."'"

It will be seen that if Mrs. Bidder's report is strictly accurate, there is a discrepancy as to which of the two horses it was that reared. But even eye-witnesses of a sudden and confusing accident might afterwards differ in such a point as this.

proved to have been, in a state of complete normal wakefulness. The case was first published in the *Spiritual Magazine* for 1861, by Dr. Collyer, who wrote from Beta House, 8, Alpha Road, St. John's Wood, N.W.

"April 15th, 1861.

(25) " On January 3rd, 1856, my brother Joseph being in command of the steamer ' Alice,' on the Mississippi, just above New Orleans, she came in collision with another steamer. The concussion caused the flagstaff or pole to fall with great violence, which, coming in contact with my brother's head, actually divided the skull, causing, of necessity, instant death. In October, 1857, I visited the United States. When, at my father's residence, Camden, New Jersey, the melancholy death of my brother became the subject of conversation, my mother narrated to me that at the very time of the accident, the apparition of my brother Joseph was presented to her. This fact was corroborated by my father and four sisters. Camden, New Jersey, is distant from the scene of the accident, in a direct line, over 1,000 miles, and nearly double that distance by the mail route. My mother mentioned the fact of the apparition on the morning of the 4th of January to my father and sisters ; nor was it until the 16th, or 13 days after, that a letter was received confirming in every particular the extraordinary visitation. It will be important to mention that my brother William and his wife lived near the locality of the dreadful accident, now being in Philadelphia ; they have also corroborated to me the details of the impression produced on my mother."

Dr. Collyer then quotes a letter from his mother, which contains the following sentences :—   " Camden, New Jersey, United States.

"March 27th, 1861.

" My beloved Son,—On the 3rd of January, 1856, I did not feel well, and retired to bed early. Some time after, I felt uneasy and sat up in bed ; I looked round the room, and to my utter amazement, saw Joseph standing at the door, looking at me with great earnestness, his head bandaged up, a dirty night-cap on, and a dirty white garment on, something like a surplice. He was much disfigured about the eyes and face. It made me quite uncomfortable the rest of the night. The next morning, Mary came into my room early. I told her that I was sure I was going to have bad news from Joseph. I told all the family at the breakfast table ; they replied, ' It was only a dream, and all nonsense,' but that did not change my opinion. It preyed on my mind, and on the 16th of January I received the news of his death ; and singular to say, both William and his wife, who were there, say that he was exactly attired as I saw him.   " Your ever affectionate Mother,

Dr. Collyer continues :—   "ANNE E. COLLYER."

" It will no doubt be said that my mother's imagination was in a morbid state, but this will not account for the fact of the apparition of my brother presenting himself at the exact moment of his death. My mother had never seen him attired as described, and the bandaging of the head did not take place until hours after the accident. My brother William told me that his head was nearly cut in two by the blow, and that his face was dreadfully disfigured, and the night-dress much soiled.

"I cannot wonder that others should be sceptical, as the evidences I have had could not have been received on the testimony of others ; we must, therefore, be charitable towards the incredulous.

"ROBERT H. COLLYER, M.D., F.C.S., &c."

On our applying to Dr. Collyer, he replied as follows :—

"25, Newington Causeway, Borough, S.E.
"March 15th, 1884.

"In replying to your communication, I must state that, strange as the circumstances narrated in the *Spiritual Magazine* of 1861 are, I can assure you that there is not a particle of exaggeration. As there stated, my mother received the mental impression of my brother on January 3rd, 1856. My father, who was a scientific man, calculated the difference of longitude between Camden, New Jersey, and New Orleans, and found that the mental impression was at the exact time of my brother's death. I may mention that I never was a believer in any *spiritual* intercourse, or that any of the phenomena present during exalted conditions of the brain are spiritual. I am, and have been for the last 40 years, a materialist, and think that all the so-called spiritual manifestations admit of a philosophical explanation, on physical laws and conditions. I do not desire to theorise, but to my mind the sympathetic chord of relationship existed between my mother and my brother (who was her favourite son), when that chord was broken by his sudden death, she being at the time favourably situated to receive the shock.

"In the account published in the *Spiritual Magazine*, I omitted to state that my brother Joseph, prior to his death, had retired for the night in his berth ; his vessel was moored alongside the levee, at the time of the collision by another steamer coming down the Mississippi. Of course, my brother was in his *nightgown*. He ran on deck on being called and informed that a steamer was in close proximity to his own. These circumstances were communicated to me by my brother William, who was on the spot at the time of the accident. I do not attempt to account for the apparition having a bandage, as that could not have been put for some time after death. The difference of time between Camden, New Jersey, and New Orleans is nearly 15°, or one hour.

"My mother retired for the night on 3rd January, 1856, at 8 p.m., which would mark the time at New Orleans 7 p.m. as the time of my brother's death."

Mr. Podmore says :—

"I called upon Dr. Collyer on 25th March, 1884. He told me that he received a full account of the story verbally from his father, mother, and brother in 1857. All are now dead ; but two sisters—to one of whom I have written—are still living. Dr. Collyer was quite certain of the precise coincidence of time."

The following is from one of the surviving sisters :—

"Mobile, Alabama, 12th May, 1884.

"I resided in Camden, New Jersey, at the time of my brother's death. He lived in Louisiana. His death was caused by the collision of two steamers on the Mississippi. Some part of the mast fell on him, splitting his head open, causing instantaneous death. The apparition appeared to my mother at the foot of her bed. It stood there for some time gazing at her, and disappeared. The apparition was clothed in a long white garment, with its head bound in a white cloth. My mother was not a superstitious person, nor did she believe in Spiritualism. She was wide awake at the time. It was not a dream. She remarked to me when I saw her in the morning, ' I shall hear bad news from Joseph,' and related to me what she had seen. Two or three days [1] from that time we heard of the sad accident. I had another brother who was there at the time, and when he returned home I inquired of him all particulars, and how he was laid out. His description answered to what my mother saw, much to our astonishment.

" A. E. COLLYER."

Here we have no direct proof of the exactness of the coincidence ; but Dr. Collyer is clear on the fact that the matter was carefully inquired into at the time. As to the alleged resemblances between the phantasm and the real figure, we shall find reason further on to think that the impression of the white garment may have been really transferred. But the criticism made above in respect of Mrs. Bettany's narrative again applies : we cannot account it certain that points were not read back into the vision, after Mrs. Collyer had learnt the actual aspect which the dead man presented. It will be observed, too, that the more striking details—especially that of the bandage—could not in any case help the telepathic argument. For if the son who was killed was the " agent " of his mother's impression, any correspondence of the phantasmal appearance with features of reality which did not come into existence till *after* death must plainly have been accidental. We shall afterwards encounter plenty of instances where the percipient supplements the impression that he receives with elements from his own mind, and especially, in death-cases, with elements symbolic of death; and it is not impossible that in the present instance the white garment and bandaged head were a dim representation of grave-clothes.

Mrs. Collyer would probably have affirmed that at the time of her vision she was completely awake. That the percipient in the next example was completely awake is, I think, nearly certain ; but as he was in bed, the account may serve as a transition to the cases where the matter admits of no doubt. Mr. Marchant, of Linkfield Street, Redhill, formerly a large farmer, wrote to us in the summer of 1883:—

---

[1] This is probably incorrect, as it differs from Dr. Collyer's and the mother's statement ; but the point does not seem important. For a piece of independent testimony respecting Captain Collyer's death, see the "Additions and Corrections" which precede Chap. I. The hour there mentioned is 10 p.m. ; but this can hardly weigh against Dr. Collyer's evidence. After 30 years' interval, a mistake of 3 hours might easily be made as to the time of an event which occurred after dark on a winter's night.

(26) "About 2 o'clock on the morning of October 21st, 1881, while I was perfectly wide awake, and looking at a lamp burning on my washhand-stand, a person, as I thought, came into my room by mistake, and stopped, looking into the looking-glass on the table. It soon occurred to me it represented Robinson Kelsey, by his dress and wearing his hair long behind. When I raised myself up in bed and called out, it instantly disappeared.[1] The next day [2] I mentioned to some of my friends how strange it was. So thoroughly convinced was I, that I searched the local papers that day (Saturday) and the following Tuesday, believing his death would be in one of them. On the following Wednesday, a man, who formerly was my drover, came and told me Robinson Kelsey was dead. Anxious to know at what time he died, I wrote to Mr. Wood, the family undertaker at Lingfield ; he learnt from the brother-in-law of the deceased that he died at 2 a.m. He was my first cousin, and was apprenticed formerly to me as a miller ; afterwards he lived with me as journeyman ; altogether, 8 years. I never saw anything approaching that before. I am 72 years old, and never feel nervous ; I am not afraid of the dead or their spirits. I hand you a rough plan of the bedroom, &c."

In answer to inquiries, Mr. Marchant replied :—

" Robinson Kelsey had met with an accident. His horse fell with him, and from that time he seemed at times unfit for business. He had a farm at Penshurst, in Kent. His friends persuaded hin to leave it. He did, and went to live on his own property, called Batnors Hall, in the parish of Lingfield, Surrey. I had not been thinking about him, neither had I spoken to him for 20 years. About 3 or 4 years before his death I saw him, but not to speak to him. I was on the up-side platform of Red-hill Station, and I saw him on the opposite down-side. In the morning after seeing the apparition, I spoke about it to a person in the house. In the evening, I again spoke about it to two persons, how strange it was. It was several days after our conversation about what I had seen that I heard of the death. These people will confirm my statement, for after I heard of his death I spoke of it to the same people, that my relation died the same night as I saw the apparition. When I spoke to these three persons I did not know of his death, but had my suspicions from what I had seen. As the apparition passed between my bed and the lamp I had a full view of it ; it was unmistakeable. When it stopped looking in the glass I spoke to it, then it gently sank away downwards.

"Probably it was 10 days before I found out, through Mr. Wood, the hour he died, so that these persons I spoke to knew nothing of his death at the time.   " GEORGE MARCHANT."

We have received the following confirmation of this incident :—

" July 18th, 1883.

" We are positive of hearing Mr. Marchant one day say that he saw the apparition of Robinson Kelsey during the previous night.

" ANN LANGERIDGE, Linkfield Street, Redhill.
" MATILDA FULLER, Station Road, Redhill.
" WILLIAM MILES, Station Road, Redhill."

[1] As to the disappearance on sudden speech or movement, see Vol. ii., p. 91, first note.
[2] This means the day following the night of the experience ; but, two lines lower, *that* day should no doubt be the *next* day, as Oct. 21, 1881, was a Friday.

Mr. Anthony Kelsey, of Lingfield, Surrey, brother-in-law and cousin of Robinson Kelsey, has confirmed October 21st, 1881, as the date of the death (which we have also verified in the Register of Deaths), but he has forgotten the hour ; and Mr. Robinson Kelsey's widow having since died, Mr. Marchant's recollection on this point cannot now be independently confirmed. As to the hour of the apparition, again, Mr. Marchant's statement is only a conclusion, drawn from his regular habit of waking once in the middle of the night at about 2. But there can be no reasonable doubt that the *day* of the death and of the vision was the same.

On February 12th, 1884, I had an interview with Mr. Marchant, who is a very vigorous and sensible old man, with a precise mind. He went through all the details of his narrative in a methodical manner, and his description corresponded in every particular with the written account, which was sent to me many months before. Mr. Marchant was positive that he never had any other hallucination of the senses, and laughed at the very idea of such things. He quite realised the ordinary criticisms which might be made about a nocturnal vision, *e.g.*, that he had had a glass too much, and also realised their absurdity as applied to his own case. I cannot doubt his statement that he has been a most temperate man. He showed me in his bedroom the precise line that the figure took ; appearing at his right hand, then passing along in front of a lamp which was on the washhand-stand, and finally standing between the foot of his bed and the dressing-table. He described Kelsey's long and bushy black hair as a very distinct peculiarity. In answer to inquiries on this point he says : " I have not any doubt whatever that Robinson Kelsey did have that peculiarity of the hair at the day of his death. My recollection of him is as clear as if I had his photo before me." The figure was visible, he thinks, for nearly a minute ; but the length of time in such cases is of course likely to be over-estimated.

I likewise saw Mrs. Langeridge, a sensible person, without any belief in " ghosts," who at once volunteered the remark that Mr. Marchant described his vision to her next morning.

This case is remarkable from the fact that there was no immediate interest between the two parties—though it is of course possible that the dying man's thoughts reverted to his kinsman and old employer. But comments on this point must be reserved.

§ 6. We now come to examples of the most important class of all, Class A—externalised impressions, occurring to persons who are up, and manifestly in the full possession of their waking senses. Of this class the most important examples are *visual* impressions, or apparitions. But I will first give a case which is on the line between Classes A and B, a vision not absolutely externalised in space, but where the mental image took on a sort of vividness and objectivity which the percipient believes to have been unexampled in his experience. The coincidence with the death of the agent was apparently quite exact; and we have the testimony of a third person to the fact that the percipient mentioned his impression immediately on its occurrence. The narrator is Mr. Rawlinson, of Lansdown Court West, Cheltenham.

"September 18th, 1883.

(27) "I was dressing one morning in December, 1881, when a certain conviction came upon me that someone was in my dressing-room. On looking round, I saw no one, but then, instantaneously (in my mind's eye, I suppose), every feature of the face and form of my old friend, X., arose. This, as you may imagine, made a great impression on me, and I went at once into my wife's room and told her what had occurred, at the same time stating that I feared Mr. X. must be dead. The subject was mentioned between us several times that day. Next morning, I received a letter from X.'s brother, then Consul-General at Odessa, but who I did not know was in England, saying that his brother had died at a quarter before 9 o'clock that morning. This was the very time the occurrence happened in my dressing-room. It is right to add that we had heard some two months previously that X. was suffering from cancer, but still we were in no immediate apprehension of his death. I never on any other occasion had any hallucination of the senses, and sincerely trust I never again shall.

"ROB. RAWLINSON."

The following is Mrs. Rawlinson's account :—

"June 18th, 1883.

"My husband was dressing, a few months ago, one morning about a quarter to 9 o'clock, when he came into my room, and said : 'I feel sure X.' (an old friend of his) 'is dead.' He said all at once he felt as if there was someone in the room with him, and X.'s face came vividly before his *mind's* eye ; and then he had this extraordinary conviction of X.'s death. He could not get the idea out of his mind all day. Strange to say, the next morning he had a letter saying X. had died the morning before, at a quarter to 9, just the very time my husband came into my room. About two months before, we had heard that X. had an incurable complaint, but we had heard nothing more, and his name had not been mentioned by anyone for weeks. I ought to tell you that my husband is the last person in the world to imagine anything, and he had always been particularly unbelieving as to anything supernatural." [1]

A reference to the Consul's letter, and to the *Times* obituary, has fixed the date of the *death* as December 17th ; but the date of the *vision* was not written down at the time: we therefore have to trust to Mr. and Mrs. Rawlinson's memory for the fact that it took place on the day before the letter was received. Not, however—be it observed—to their memory *now*, but to their memory at the time when the letter was received ; and considering the effect that the

---

[1] See p. 199, note. "X." in the above accounts is our own substitution for the real name.

occurrence had on their minds, we can scarcely suppose them to have agreed in referring it to the preceding day, if several days had really intervened.

In the next case the coincidence was certainly close to within a very few minutes, and may have been exact. The impression was again completely unique in the percipient's experience, and was at once communicated to a third person, whose testimony to that point we have obtained. " N. J. S.," who, though he uses the third person, is himself the narrator, is personally known to us. Occupying a position of considerable responsibility, he does not wish his name to be published ; but it can be given to inquirers, and he " will answer any questions personally to anyone having a wish to arrive at the truth." The account was received within a few weeks of the occurrence.

(28) " N. J. S. and F. L. were employed together in an office, were brought into intimate relations with one another, which lasted for about eight years, and held one another in very great regard and esteem. On Monday, March 19th, 1883, F. L., in coming to the office, complained of having suffered from indigestion ; he went to a chemist, who told him that his liver was a little out of order, and gave him some medicine. He did not seem much better on Thursday. On Saturday he was absent, and N. J. S. has since heard he was examined by a medical man, who thought he wanted a day or two of rest, but expressed no opinion that anything was serious.

" On Saturday evening, March 24th, N. J. S., who had a headache, was sitting at home. He said to his wife that he was what he had not been for months, rather too warm ; after making the remark he leaned back on the couch, and the next minute saw his friend, F. L., standing before him, dressed in his usual manner. N. J. S. noticed the details of his dress, that is, his hat with a black band, his overcoat unbuttoned, and a stick in his hand ; he looked with a fixed regard at N. J. S., and then passed away. N. J. S. quoted to himself from Job, ' And lo, a spirit passed before me, and the hair of my flesh stood up.' At that moment an icy chill passed through him, [1] and his hair bristled. He then turned to his wife and asked her the time ; she said, ' 12 minutes to 9.' He then said, ' The reason I ask you is that F. L. is dead. I have just seen him.' She tried to persuade him it was fancy, but he most positively assured her that no argument was of avail to alter his opinion.

" The next day, Sunday, about 3 p.m., A. L., brother of F. L., came to the house of N. J. S., who let him in. A. L. said, ' I suppose you know what I have come to tell you ? ' N. J. S. replied, ' Yes, your brother is dead.' A. L. said, ' I thought you would know it.' N. J. S. replied, ' Why ? ' A. L. said, ' Because you were in such sympathy with one another.' N. J. S. afterwards ascertained that A. L. called on Saturday to see his brother, and on leaving him noticed the clock on the stairs was 25 minutes to 9 p.m. F. L.'s sister, on going to him at 9 p.m., found him dead from rupture of the aorta.

[1] See Vol. ii., p. 37, first note, and the addition thereto in the " Additions and Corrections " at the beginning of Vol. ii.

"This is a plain statement of facts, and the only theory N. J. S. has on the subject is that at the supreme moment of death, F. L. must have felt a great wish to communicate with him, and in some way by force of will impressed his image on N. J. S.'s senses."

In reply to our inquiries Mr. S. says :—

"May 11th, 1883.

"(1) My wife was sitting at a table in the middle of the room under a gas chandelier, either reading or doing some wool work. I was sitting on a couch at the side of the room in the shade ; she was not looking in the direction I was. I studiously spoke in a quiet manner to avoid alarming her ; she noticed nothing particular in me.

"(2) I have never seen any appearance before, but have disbelieved in them, not seeing any motive.

"(3) Mr. A. L. told me that in coming to inform me of his brother's death, he wondered what would be the best way of breaking the matter to me, when, without any reason except the knowledge of our strong mutual regard, it seemed to flash upon his mind that I might know it.

"There had been no instances of thought-transmission between us.

"There are many slight details which it is nearly impossible to describe in writing, so I may say that I shall be most willing to give you a personal account and answer any questions at any time you should be in town.

"There is one thing which strikes me as singular—the instant certainty I felt that my friend was dead, as there was nothing to lead up to the idea ; and also that I seemed to accept all that passed without feeling surprise, and as if it were an ordinary matter of course.

"N. J. S."

Mrs. S. supplies the following corroboration :—

"September 18th, 1883.

"On the evening of the 24th March last, I was sitting at a table reading, my husband was sitting on a couch at the side of the room ; he asked me the time, and on my replying 12 minutes to 9, he said, 'The reason why I ask is that L. is dead, I have just seen him.' I answered, 'What nonsense, you don't even know that he is ill ; I daresay when you go to town on Tuesday you will see him all right.' However, he persisted in saying he had seen L., and was sure of his death. I noticed at the time that he looked very much agitated and was very pale					"MARIA S."

We find from the *Times* obituary that F. L.'s death took place on March 24th, 1883.

In a later communication Mr. S. says :—

"February 23rd, 1885.

"In compliance with your request, I have asked Mr. A. L. to send you the statement of what came to his knowledge with reference to the time of his brother's death.

"I have often thought the matter over since. I am unable to satisfy my own mind as to the *why* of the occurrence, but I still adhere to every particular, having nothing to add or withdraw."

Mr. L.'s brother corroborates as follows :—

"Bank of England.

"February 24th, 1885.

"Mr. S. having informed me that you have expressed a wish that I should corroborate some statements made by him relative to my brother Frederick's sudden death, I beg to send you the following particulars.

"On Saturday, March 24th, 1883, my brother having been absent from business, I called about 8 p.m. to see him, and found him sitting up in his bedroom. I left him, apparently much better, and came down to the dining-room about 8.40, where I remained with my sister for about half-an-hour, when I left, and she, going upstairs, immediately upon my departure, found her brother lying dead upon the bed, so that the exact time of his death will never be known. On my way over to Mr. S. the next day, to break the news to him, the thought occurred to me—knowing the strong sympathy between them—'I should not be surprised if he has had some presentiment of it'; and when he came to the door to meet me, I felt certain from his look that it was so, hence I said, 'You know what I have come for,' and he then told me that he had seen my brother Frederick in a vision a little before 9 on the previous evening. I must tell you I am no believer in visions, and have not always found presentiments correct ; yet I am perfectly certain of Mr. S.'s veracity, and having been asked to confirm him, willingly do so, though I strengthen a cause I am not a disciple of.

"A. C. L."

An attempt to form a numerical estimate of the probability (or improbability) that the coincidence in this case was accidental will be found in a subsequent chapter on "The Theory of Chance-Coincidence" (Vol. II., pp. 18-20).

The next case again exhibits the slight *deferment* of the percipient's experience which I have already mentioned (p. 201). But its chief interest is as illustrating what may be called a *local*, as distinct from a *personal, rapport* between the parties concerned.[1] The percipient, at the moment of his impression, was contemplating a spot with which the agent was specially connected, and which may even have had a very distinct place in her dying thoughts ; and it is natural to find in this fact a main condition why he, of all people, should have been the one impressed. The case was thus narrated to us by the Rev. C. T. Forster, Vicar of Hinxton, Saffron Walden :—

"August 6th, 1885.

(29) "My late parishioner, Mrs. de Fréville, was a somewhat eccentric lady, who was specially morbid on the subject of tombs, &c.

"About two days after her death, which took place in London, May 8th, in the afternoon, I heard that she had been seen that very night by Alfred Bard. I sent for him, and he gave me a very clear and circumstantial account of what he had seen.

---

[1] As to this point, see Vol. ii., pp. 268 and 301-2.

"He is a man of great observation, being a self-taught naturalist, and I am quite satisfied that he desires to speak the truth without any exaggeration.

"I must add that I am absolutely certain that the news of Mrs. de Fréville's death did not reach Hinxton till the next morning, May 9th. She was found dead at 7.30 p.m. She had been left alone in her room, being poorly, but not considered seriously or dangerously ill.

"C. T. FORSTER."

The following is the percipient's own account :—

"July 21st, 1885.

"I am a gardener in employment at Sawston. I always go through Hinxton churchyard on my return home from work. On Friday, May 8th, 1885, I was walking back as usual. On entering the churchyard, I looked rather carefully at the ground, in order to see a cow and donkey which used to lie just inside the gate. In so doing, I looked straight at the square stone vault in which the late Mr. de Fréville was at one time buried. I then saw Mrs. de Fréville leaning on the rails, dressed much as I had usually seen her, in a coal-scuttle bonnet, black jacket with deep crape, and black dress. She was looking full at me. Her face was very white, much whiter than usual. I knew her well, having at one time been in her employ. I at once supposed that she had come, as she sometimes did, to the mausoleum in her own park, in order to have it opened and go in. I supposed that Mr. Wiles, the mason from Cambridge, was in the tomb doing something. I walked round the tomb looking carefully at it, in order to see if the gate was open, keeping my eye on her and never more than five or six yards from her. Her face turned and followed me. I passed between the church and the tomb (there are about four yards between the two), and peered forward to see whether the tomb was open, as she hid the part of the tomb which opened. I slightly stumbled on a hassock of grass, and looked at my feet for a moment only. When I looked up she was gone. She could not possibly have got out of the churchyard, as in order to reach any of the exits she must have passed me.[1] So I took for granted that she had quickly gone into the tomb. I went up to the door, which I expected to find open, but to my surprise it was shut and had not been opened, as there was no key in the lock. I rather hoped to have a look into the tomb myself, so I went back again and shook the gate to make sure, but there was no sign of any one's having been there. I was then much startled and looked at the clock, which marked 9.20. When I got home I half thought it must have been my fancy, but I told my wife that I had seen Mrs. de Fréville.

"Next day, when my little boy told me that she was dead, I gave a start, which my companion noticed, I was so much taken aback.

"I have never had any other hallucination whatever.

"ALFRED BARD."

Mrs. Bard's testimony is as follows :—

"July 8th, 1885.

"When Mr. Bard came home he said, 'I have seen Mrs. de Fréville to-night, leaning with her elbow on the palisade, looking at me. I turned again to look at her and she was gone. She had cloak and bonnet on.'

---

[1] See the remark within brackets, which follows the case.

He got home as usual between 9 and 10; it was on the 8th of May, 1885
"SARAH BARD."

The *Times* obituary confirms the date of the death.

[Mr. Myers was conducted over Hinxton churchyard by Mr. Forster, and can attest the substantial accuracy of Mr. Bard's description of the relative position of the church, the tomb, and the exits. The words " must have passed me," however, give a slightly erroneous impression ; " must have come very near me " would be the more correct description.]

The next case is of a more abnormal type. We received the first account of it—the percipient's evidence—through the kindness of Mrs. Martin, of Ham Court, Upton-on-Severn, Worcester.

"Antony, Torpoint, December 14th, 1882.

(30) " Helen Alexander (maid to Lady Waldegrave) was lying here very ill with typhoid fever, and was attended by me. I was standing at the table by her bedside, pouring out her medicine, at about 4 o'clock in the morning of the 4th October, 1880. I heard the call-bell ring (this had been heard twice before during the night in that same week), and was attracted by the door of the room opening,[1] and by seeing a person entering the room whom I instantly felt to be the mother of the sick woman. She had a brass candlestick in her hand, a red shawl over her shoulders, and a flannel petticoat on which had a hole in the front. I looked at her as much as to say, ' I am glad you have come,' but the woman looked at me sternly, as much as to say, ' Why wasn't I sent for before ? ' I gave the medicine to Helen Alexander, and then turned round to speak to the vision, but no one was there. She had gone. She was a short, dark person, and very stout. At about 6 o'clock that morning Helen Alexander died. Two days after her parents and a sister came to Antony, and arrived between 1 and 2 o'clock in the morning ; I and another maid let them in, and it gave me a great turn when I saw the living likeness of the vision I had seen two nights before. I told the sister about the vision, and she said that the description of the dress exactly answered to her mother's, and that they had brass candlesticks at home exactly like the one described. There was not the slightest resemblance between the mother and daughter.

"FRANCES REDDELL."

This at first sight might be taken for a mere delusion of an excitable or over-tired servant, modified and exaggerated by the subsequent sight of the real mother. If such a case is to have evidential force, we must ascertain beyond doubt that the description of the experience was given in detail before any knowledge of the reality can have affected the percipient's memory or imagination. This necessary corroboration has been kindly supplied by Mrs. Pole-Carew, of Antony, Torpoint, Devonport.

" December 31st, 1883.

" In October, 1880, Lord and Lady Waldegrave came with their Scotch maid, Helen Alexander, to stay with us. [The account then describes how Helen was discovered to have caught typhoid fever.] She did not seem to be very ill in spite of it, and as there seemed no fear of danger, and Lord

[1] See p. 102, note.

and Lady Waldegrave had to go a long journey the following day (Thursday), they decided to leave her, as they were advised to do, under their friends' care.

"The illness ran its usual course, and she seemed to be going on perfectly well till the Sunday week following, when the doctor told me that the fever had left her, but the state of weakness which had supervened was such as to make him extremely anxious. I immediately engaged a regular nurse, greatly against the wish of Reddell, my maid, who had been her chief nurse all through the illness, and who was quite devoted to her. However, as the nurse could not conveniently come till the following day, I allowed Reddell to sit up with Helen again that night, to give her the medicine and food, which were to be taken constantly.

"At about 4.30 that night, or rather Monday morning, Reddell looked at her watch, poured out the medicine, and was bending over the bed to give it to Helen, when the call-bell in the passage rang. She said to herself, ' There's that tiresome bell with the wire caught again.' (It seems it did occasionally ring of itself in this manner.) At that moment, however, she heard the door open, and looking round, saw a very stout old woman walk in. She was dressed in a nightgown and red flannel petticoat, and carried an old-fashioned brass candlestick in her hand. The petticoat had a hole rubbed in it. She walked into the room, and appeared to be going towards the dressing-table to put her candle down. She was a perfect stranger to Reddell, who, however, merely thought, ' This is her mother come to see after her,' and she felt quite glad it was so, accepting the idea without reasoning upon it, as one would in a dream. She thought the mother looked annoyed, possibly at not having been sent for before. She then gave Helen the medicine, and turning round, found that the apparition had disappeared, and that the door was shut. A great change, meanwhile, had taken place in Helen, and Reddell fetched me, who sent off for the doctor, and meanwhile applied hot poultices, &c., but Helen died a little before the doctor came. She was quite conscious up to about half-an-hour before she died, when she seemed to be going to sleep.

"During the early days of her illness Helen had written to a sister, mentioning her being unwell, but making nothing of it, and as she never mentioned anyone but this sister, it was supposed by the household, to whom she was a perfect stranger, that she had no other relation alive. Reddell was always offering to write for her, but she always declined, saying there was no need, she would write herself in a day or two. No one at home, therefore, knew anything of her being so ill, and it is, therefore, remarkable that her mother, a far from nervous person, should have said that evening going up to bed, ' I am sure Helen is very ill.'

"Reddell told me and my daughter of the apparition, about an hour after Helen's death, prefacing with, ' I am not superstitious, or nervous, and I wasn't the least frightened, but her mother came last night,' and she then told the story, giving a careful description of the figure she had seen. The relations were asked to come to the funeral, and the father, mother, and sister came, and in the mother Reddell recognised the apparition, as I did also, for Reddell's description had been most accurate, even to the expression, which she had ascribed to annoyance, but which was due to deafness. It was judged best not to speak about it to the mother, but Reddell told the sister, who said the description of the figure corresponded exactly with the probable appearance of her mother if roused in the night ; that they had exactly such a candlestick at home, and that there was a hole in her mother's petticoat produced by the way she always wore it. It seems curious that neither Helen nor her mother appeared to be aware of the visit. Neither of them, at any rate, ever spoke of having seen the other, nor even of having dreamt of having done so.

" F. A. POLE-CAREW."

Frances Reddell states that she has never had any hallucination, or any odd experience of any kind, except on this one occasion. The Hon. Mrs. Lyttelton, of Selwyn College, Cambridge, who knows her, tells us that " she appears to be a most matter-of-fact person, and was apparently most impressed by the fact that she saw a hole in the mother's flannel petticoat, made by the busk of her stays, reproduced in the apparition."

Mrs. Pole-Carew's evidence goes far to stamp this occurrence as having been something more than a mere subjective hallucination. But it will be observed that there is some doubt as to who was the agent. Was it the mother? If so, we find nothing more definite on the agent's part, as a basis for the distant effect, than a certain amount of anxiety as to her daughter's condition ; while the fact that Reddell and she were totally unknown to one another, would show, even more conclusively than the two preceding narratives, that a special personal *rapport* between the parties is not a necessary condition for spontaneous telepathic transference. Thus regarded, the case would considerably resemble the instance of local *rapport* last quoted—the condition of the telepathic impression being presumably the common occupation of the mind of both agent and percipient with one subject, the dying girl. But it is also conceivable that Helen herself was the agent ; and that in her dying condition a flash of memory of her mother's aspect conveyed a direct impulse to the mind of her devoted nurse.

The last five cases have all been recent. I will now give an example which is 70 years old. It will show the value that even remote evidence may have, if proper care is exercised at the time ; and it points the moral which must be enforced *ad nauseam*, as to the importance of an immediate written record on the percipient's part. The account was received from Mrs. Browne, of 58, Porchester Terrace, W. On May 29th, 1884, Mr. Podmore wrote :—

"May 29th, 1884.

(31) " I called to-day on Mrs. Browne, and saw (1) a document in the handwriting of her mother, Mrs. Carslake (now dead), which purported to be a copy of a memorandum made by Mrs. Browne's father, the late Captain John Carslake, of Sidmouth. Appended to this was (2) a note,

also in Mrs. Carslake's handwriting, and signed by her; and (3) a copy also in Mrs. Carslake's handwriting, of a letter from the Rev. E. B——r, of Sidmouth.

" Mrs. Browne told me that, as far as she knows, the originals of (1) and (3) are no longer in existence.

" Document (4) is a note from Mrs. Browne herself.

" The Middleburg referred to is apparently the town of that name in the Netherlands."

(1)

" Thursday, July the 6th, 1815.—On returning to-day from Middleburg with Captain T., I was strongly impressed with the idea that between 2 and 3 I saw my uncle John cross the road, a few paces before me, and pass into a lane on the left leading to a mill, called Olly Moulin, and that when he arrived at the edge of the great road, he looked round and beckoned to me.

" Query.—As he has long been dangerously ill, may not this be considered as an omen of his having died about this time ?

" JOHN CARSLAKE."

(2)

" He had not been thinking of his uncle, but talking with Captain T. about a sale where they had been ; he was quite silent afterwards, and would not tell the reason. On going on board, he went to his cabin and wrote the time he saw his uncle, and wrote to Mr. B.

" T. CARSLAKE."

(3)

" Long, in all probability, before this can reach you, you will have been informed that, precisely *at the minute* in which his apparition crossed your path in the neighbourhood of Middleburg, your dear and venerable uncle expired. I think it proves, beyond all contradiction, that his last and affectionate thoughts were fixed on you. The fact you have stated is the strongest of the kind, in which I could place such full confidence in the parties, that *I* ever knew.—E. B."

[Judging from Mr. Carslake's own account, it seems unlikely that the writer of this can have *known* the coincidence to have been as close as he describes.]

(4)

" May 29th, 1884.

" I remember more than once hearing this story, exactly as it is told here, from my father's own lips. I remember that he added that the figure wore a peculiar hat, which he recognised as being like one worn by his uncle.   " T. L. BROWNE."

The next example repeats the peculiarity that the percipient's impression, though unique in his experience, did not at the moment suggest the agent; but it differs, as will be seen, from Frances Reddell's case. We received it from the Rev. Robert Bee, now residing at 12, Whitworth Road, Grangetown, near Southbank, Yorkshire.

"Colin Street, Wigan.
"December 30th, 1883.

(32) "On December 18th, 1873, I left my house in Lincolnshire to visit my wife's parents, then and now residing in Lord Street, Southport. Both my parents were, to all appearance, in good health when I started. The next day after my arrival was spent in leisurely observation of the manifold attractions of this fashionable seaside resort. I spent the evening in company with my wife in the bay-windowed drawing-room upstairs, which fronts the main street of the town. I proposed a game at chess, and we got out the board and began to play. Perhaps half-an-hour had been thus occupied by us, during which I had made several very foolish mistakes. A deep melancholy was oppressing me. At length I remarked : ' It is no use my trying to play, I cannot for the life think about what I am doing. Shall we shut it up and resume our talk ? I feel literally wretched.'

" 'Just as you like,' said my wife, and the board was at once put aside.

" This was about half-past 7 o'clock ; and after a few minutes' desultory conversation, my wife suddenly remarked : '*I* feel very dull to-night. I think I will go downstairs to mamma, for a few minutes.'

" Soon after my wife's departure, I rose from my chair, and walked in the direction of the drawing-room door. Here I paused for a moment, and then passed out to the landing of the stairs.

" It was then exactly 10 minutes to 8 o'clock. I stood for a moment upon the landing, and a lady, dressed as if she were going on a business errand, came out, apparently, from an adjoining bedroom, and passed close by me. I did not distinctly see her features, nor do I remember what it was that I said to her.

" The form passed down the narrow winding stairs, and at the same instant my wife came up again, so that she must have passed close to the stranger, in fact, to all appearance, brushed against her.

" I exclaimed, almost immediately, ' Who is the lady, Polly, that you passed just now, coming up ? '

" Never can I forget, or account for, my wife's answer. 'I passed nobody,' she said.

" ' Nonsense,' I replied ; ' You met a lady just now, dressed for a walk. She came out of the little bedroom. I spoke to her. She must be a visitor staying with your mother. She has gone out, no doubt, at the front door.'

" ' It is impossible,' said my wife. ' There is not any company in the house. They all left nearly a week ago. There is no one in fact at all indoors, but ourselves and mamma.'

" ' Strange,' I said ; ' I am certain that I saw and spoke to a lady, just before you came upstairs, and I saw her distinctly pass you ;[1] so that it seems incredible that you did not perceive her.'

" My wife positively asserted that the thing was impossible. We went downstairs together, and I related the story to my wife's mother, who was busy with her household duties. She confirmed her daughter's previous statement. There was no one in the house but ourselves.

[1] In conversation Mr. Bee reiterated to me his certainty as to having seen the two figures simultaneously.

" The next morning, early, a telegram reached me from Lincolnshire ; it was from my elder sister, Julia (Mrs T. W. Bowman, of Prospect House, Stechford, Birmingham), and announced the afflicting intelligence that our dear mother had passed suddenly away the night before ; and that we (*i.e.*, myself and wife) were to return home to Gainsborough by the next train. The doctor said it was heart-disease, which in a few minutes had caused her death."

After giving some details of his arrival at home, and of the kindness of friends, Mr. Bee continues :—

" When all was over and Christmas Day had arrived, I ventured to ask my brother the exact moment of our mother's death.

" ' Well, father was out,' he said, ' at the school-room, and I did not see her alive. Julia was just in time to see her breathe her last. It was, as nearly as I can recollect, 10 *minutes to* 8 *o'clock.*'

" I looked at my wife for a moment, and then said : ' Then I saw her in Southport, and can now account, unaccountably, for my impressions.'

" Before the said 19th of December I was utterly careless of these things ; I had given little or no attention to spiritual apparitions or impressions.   " ROBT. BEE."

In answer to inquiries, Mr. Bee adds :—

" My mother died in her dress and boots ; she was taken ill in the street, and had to be taken to a neighbour's house in Gainsborough a few paces from her own house. The figure resembled my mother exactly as to size, dress, and appearance, but it did not recall her to my mind at the time. The light was not so dim that, if my mother had actually passed me in flesh and blood, I should not have recognised her."

We learn from the obituary notice in the *Lincolnshire Chronicle* that Mr. Bee's mother died on December 19, 1873, in Mr. Smithson's shop, in Gainsborough, of heart-disease ; and that her usual health was pretty good.

In answer to the question whether this is the only case of hallucination that he has experienced, Mr. Bee answers " Yes."

He further adds :—

" The gas light over the head of the stairway shone within a frosted globe, and was probably not turned on *fully*.

" The fact is, there was ample light to see the figure in, but just as the face might have been turned to me, or was turned to me, I could not, or did not, clearly discern it. Many, many times, my regret and disappointment when I recall this fact have been deeply felt."

Mrs. Bee writes to us as follows :—

" January 9th, 1884.

" If anything I can say to you will be of any use, I will willingly give my testimony to all my husband has said. I remember perfectly ten years ago my visit to my mother's, and my husband's unaccountable restlessness on the particular evening mentioned, also Mr. Bee asking me, after I had been downstairs, if I had met a lady on the stairs. I said, ' No, I do not think there is any one in the house but us.' Mr. Bee then said, ' Well, a lady has passed me just now on the landing ; she came out of the small bedroom and went downstairs; she was dressed in a black bonnet and shawl.' I said, 'Nonsense, you must be mistaken.' He said, 'I am certain I am not, and I assure you I feel very queer.' I then went to ask mamma if there was anyone in the house, and she said no, only ourselves ; still Mr. Bee insisted someone had passed him on the landing, although we tried to reason him out of it.

"In the morning while we were in bed, we received a telegram stating that Mrs. Bee had died suddenly the night before. I said at once, ' Robert, that was your mother you saw last night.' He said it was. When we got to Gainsborough we asked what time she died; we were told about 10 minutes to 8, which was the exact time ; also that she was taken suddenly ill in the street (wearing at the time a black bonnet and shawl) and died in 10 minutes.

" MARY ANN BEE."

Mrs. Bourne, a sister of Mr. Bee's, writes to us :—

" Eastgate Lodge, Lincoln.
" October 2nd, 1885.

"My mother died on December 19th, 1873, about 10 minutes to 8 in the evening ; it might be a little later or a little earlier. Her attack resembled a fainting fit, and lasted from 30 to 40 minutes. At the commencement of it, she said a few words to my sister, when I was not present ; afterwards I believe she never opened her eyes or spoke again, though we tried our utmost to induce her to do so.

" MARIAN BOURNE."

If this case is accurately reported, the figure seen cannot be supposed to have been a real person; for—to say nothing of the unlikelihood that a strange lady would be on the upper floor on some unknown errand—Mrs. Bee, who seemed to her husband to come into actual contact with the figure, could hardly have failed to observe that some one passed her on the stairs. The fact that the form did not at the moment suggest Mr. Bee's mother tends, no doubt, to weaken the case as evidence for telepathy, to this extent,—that if a person has the one hallucination of his life at the moment that a near relative dies, this singular coincidence may with less violence be ascribed to accident if the hallucination is merely *an* appearance—an unrecognised figure—than if it is *the* appearance of that particular relative. The phantasm not being individualised, the conditions for the operation of chance are so far widened. Still, there are two strong evidential points. The coincidence of time seems to have been precise ; and the resemblance to the supposed agent " as to size, dress, and appearance " is described as exact. As for any theoretic difficulty that might be felt in the fact of non-recognition, I will make at this point only one remark.

If we are prepared (as experiment has prepared us) to admit that telepathic impressions need not even affect consciousness at all—if it is possible for some of them to remain completely unfelt—it does not seem specially surprising that others should issue on the mental stage with various degrees of distinctness and completeness.

§ 7. So much for visual examples. I will now give an illustration of externalised impressions of the *auditory* sort. The case differs in another respect from the foregoing visual examples ; for though, as in most of them, the agent died, the percipient's experience *preceded* the death by some hours ; and that being so, we must clearly connect this experience with the serious condition in which her friend actually was, not with that in which he was about to be. The narrative is from a lady who prefers that her name and address should not be published. She is a person of thorough good sense, and with no appetite for marvels.

"1884.

(33) "On the morning of October 27th, 1879, being in perfect health and having been awake for some considerable time, I heard myself called by my Christian name by an anxious and suffering voice, several times in succession. I recognised the voice as that of an old friend, almost play-fellow, but who had not been in my thoughts for many weeks, or even months. I knew he was with his regiment in India, but not that he had been ordered to the front, and nothing had recalled him to my recollection. Within a few days I heard of his death from cholera on the morning I seemed to hear his call. The impression was so strong I noted the date and fact in my diary before breakfast."

In answer to inquiries, the narrator says :—

"I was never conscious of any other auditory hallucination whatever. I do not think I mentioned the subject to any one, as I believe we had friends with us. I still have my diary preserved."

The present writer has seen the page of the diary, and the reference to the strange experience, under the date of Monday, October 27th, 1879.

We find from the *East India Service Register* for January, 1880, that the death of Captain John B., Native Infantry (Bombay Division), took place on October 27th, 1879, at Jhelum. (This is the gentleman referred to in the account.) The *Times* obituary of November 4th, 1879, mentions that the death was due to cholera.

Our informant was requested to find out the exact hour of the death, and learnt that it took place, not in the morning, as she had supposed, but at 10 p.m. (about 5 p.m. in England). She adds : "So that would not make the time agree with the hour of hearing his call. The cry may have come, however, when the illness began first."

In the last-quoted visual example, the figure seen was unrecognised. I will now give a parallel auditory case, where the sound heard by the percipient suggested at the moment no particular person. The account is from a gentleman of good position, whom I must term Mr. A. Z. He is as far removed as possible from superstition, and takes no general interest in the subject. He has given us the full names of all the persons concerned, but is unwilling that they should be published, on account of the painful character of the event recorded.

"May, 1885.

(34) " In 1876, I was living in a small agricultural parish in the East of England, one of my neighbours at the time being a young man, S. B.,[1] who had recently come into the occupation of a large farm in the place. Pending the alteration of his house, he lodged and boarded with his groom at the other end of the village, furthest removed from my own residence, which was half a mile distant and separated by many houses, gardens, a plantation, and farm buildings. He was fond of field sports, and spent much of his spare time during the season in hunting. He was not a personal friend of mine, only an acquaintance, and I felt no interest in him except as a tenant on the estate. I have asked him occasionally to my house, as a matter of civility, but to the best of my recollection was never inside his lodgings.

" One afternoon in March, 1876, when leaving, along with my wife, our railway station to walk home, I was accosted by S. B. ; he accompanied us as far as my front gate, where he kept us in conversation for some time, but on no special subject. I may now state that the distance from this gate, going along the carriage drive, to the dining and breakfast room windows is about 60 yards ; both the windows of these rooms face the north-east and are parallel with the carriage drive.[2] On S. B. taking leave of us my wife remarked, ' Young B. evidently wished to be asked in, but I thought you would not care to be troubled with him.' Subsequently— about half-an-hour later—I again met him, and, as I was then on my way to look at some work at a distant part of the estate, asked him to walk with me, which he did. His conversation was of the ordinary character ; if anything, he seemed somewhat depressed at the bad times and the low prices of farming produce. I remember he asked me to give him some wire rope to make a fence on his farm, which I consented to do. Returning from our walk, and on entering the village, I pulled up at the cross-roads to say good evening, the road to his lodgings taking him at right angles to mine. I was surprised to hear him say, ' Come and smoke a cigar with me to-night.' To which I replied, ' I cannot very well, I am engaged this evening.' ' Do come,' he said. ' No,' I replied, ' I will look in another evening.' And with this we parted. We had separated about 40 yards when he turned around and exclaimed, ' Then if you will not come, good-bye.' This was the last time I saw him alive.

" I spent the evening in my dining-room in writing, and for some hours I may say that probably no thought of young B. passed through my mind. The night was bright and clear, full or nearly full moon, still, and without

---

[1] These are not the right initials of the name.
[2] The position of the house, as I found on visiting it, is particularly retired and quiet.

wind. Since I had come in slight snow had fallen, just sufficient to make the ground show white.

"At about 5 minutes to 10 o'clock I got up and left the room, taking up a lamp from the hall table, and replacing it on a small table standing in a recess of the window in the breakfast-room. The curtains were not drawn across the window. I had just taken down from the nearest book-case a volume of ' Macgillivray's British Birds ' for reference, and was in the act of reading the passage, the book held close to the lamp, and my shoulder touching the window shutter, and in a position in which almost the slightest outside sound would be heard, when I distinctly heard the front gate opened and shut again with a clap, and footsteps advancing at a run up the drive; when opposite the window the steps changed from sharp and distinct on gravel to dull and less clear on the grass slip below the window, and at the same time I was conscious that someone or some-thing stood close to me outside, only the thin shutter and a sheet of glass dividing us. I could hear the quick panting laboured breathing of the messenger, or whatever it was, as if trying to recover breath before speaking. Had he been attracted by the light through the shutter? Suddenly, like a gunshot, inside, outside, and all around, there broke out the most appalling shriek—a prolonged wail of horror, which seemed to freeze the blood. It was not a single shriek, but more prolonged, com-mencing in a high key, and then less and less, wailing away towards the north, and becoming weaker and weaker as it receded in sobbing pulsations of intense agony. Of my fright and horror I can say nothing—increased tenfold when I walked into the dining-room and found my wife sitting quietly at her work close to the window, in the same line and distant only 10 or 12 feet from the corresponding window in the breakfast-room. *She had heard nothing.* I could see that at once ; and from the position in which she was sitting, l knew she could not have failed to hear any noise outside and any footstep on the gravel. Perceiving I was alarmed about some-thing, she asked, ' What is the matter?' ' Only someone outside,' I said. ' Then why do you not go out and see? You always do when you hear any unusual noise.' I said, ' There is something so queer and dreadful about the noise. I dare not face it. It must have been the Banshee shrieking.'

"Young S. B., on leaving me, went home to his lodgings. He spent most of the evening on the sofa, reading one of Whyte Melville's novels. He saw his groom at 9 o'clock and gave him orders for the following day. The groom and his wife, who were the only people in the house besides S. B., then went to bed.

"At the inquest the groom stated that when about falling asleep, he was suddenly aroused by a shriek, and on running into his master's room found him expiring on the floor. It appeared that young B. had undressed upstairs, and then came down to his sitting-room in trousers and night-shirt, had poured out half-a-glass of water, into which he emptied a small bottle of prussic acid (procured that morning under the plea of poisoning a dog, which he did not possess). He walked upstairs, and on entering his room drank off the glass, and with a scream fell dead on the floor. All this happened, as near as I can ascertain, at the *exact time* when I had been so much alarmed at my own house. It is utterly impossible that any sound short of a cannon shot could have reached me from B.'s lodgings, through closed windows and doors, and the many intervening obstacles of houses and gardens, farmsteads and plantations, &c.

"Having to leave home by the early train, I was out very soon on the following morning, and on going to examine the ground beneath the window found no *footsteps* on grass or drive, still covered with the slight sprinkling of snow which had fallen on the previous evening.

"The whole thing had been a dream of the moment—an imagination, call it what you will; I simply state these facts as they occurred, without attempting any explanation, which, indeed, I am totally unable to give. The entire incident is a mystery, and will ever remain a mystery to me. I did not hear the particulars of the tragedy till the following afternoon, having left home by an early train. The motive of suicide was said to be a love affair."

In a subsequent letter dated June 12th, 1885, Mr. A. Z. says :—

"The suicide took place in this parish on Thursday night, March 9th, 1876, at or about 10 p.m. The inquest was held on Saturday, 11th, by ——, the then coroner. He has been dead some years, or I might perhaps have been able to obtain a copy of his notes then taken. You will probably find some notice of the inquest in the —— of March 17th. I did not myself hear any particulars of the event till my return home on Friday afternoon, 17 hours afterwards. The slight snow fell about 8 o'clock —*not later*. After this the night was bright and fine, and very still. There was also a rather sharp frost. I have evidence of all this to satisfy any lawyer.

"I went early the next morning under the window to look for footsteps, just before leaving home for the day. Perhaps it is not quite correct to call it snow; it was small frozen sleet and hail, and the grass blades just peeped through, but there was quite enough to have shown any steps had there been any.

"I was not myself at the inquest, so in that case only speak from hearsay. In my narrative I say the groom was awoke by 'a shriek.' I have asked the man [name given], and cross-questioned him closely on this point ; and it is more correct to say by 'a series of noises ending in a crash' or 'heavy fall.' This is most probably correct, as the son of the tenant [name given], living in the next house, was aroused by the same *sort of sound* coming through the wall of the house into the adjoining bedroom in which he was sleeping.

"I do not, however, wish it to be understood that any *material* noises heard in that house or the next had any connection with the peculiar noises and scream which frightened me so much, as anyone knowing the locality must admit at once the *impossibility* of such sounds travelling under any conditions through intervening obstacles. I only say that the scene enacted in the one was coincident with my alarm and the phenomena attending it in the other.

"I find by reference to the book of ——, chemist, of ——, that the poison was purchased by young S. B., on March 8th. I enclose a note from Mrs. A. Z., according to your request."

The enclosed note, signed by Mrs. A. Z., also dated June 12th, 1885, is as follows : —

"I am able to testify that on the night of March 9th, 1876, about 10 o'clock, my husband, who had gone into the adjoining room to consult a book, was greatly alarmed by sounds which he heard, and described as the gate clapping, footsteps on the drive and grass, and heavy breathing close to the window—then a fearful screaming.

"I did not hear anything. He did not go to look round the house, as he would have done at any other time, and when I *afterwards* asked him why he did not go out, he replied, ' Because I felt I could not.' On going to bed he took his gun upstairs; and when I asked him why, said, ' Because there must be someone about.'

"He left home early in the morning, and did not hear of the suicide of Mr. S. B. until the afternoon of that day."

An article which we have seen in a local newspaper, describing the suicide and inquest, confirms the above account of them.

Asked if he had had any similar affections which had *not* corresponded with reality, Mr. A. Z. replied in the negative.

The criticism made on Mr. Bee's case will of course apply again here; the percipient's failure to connect his impression with the agent is, *pro tanto*, an evidential defect. But the fact remains that he received an impression of a vividly distressful and horrible kind— of a type, too, rarely met with as a purely subjective hallucination among sane and healthy persons [1]—at the very time that his companion of a few hours back was in the agony of a supreme crisis.

§ 8. Telepathic impressions of the sense of *touch* are naturally hard to establish, unless some other sense is also affected. In the cases in our collection, at all events, a mere impression of touch has rarely, if ever, been sufficiently remarkable or distinctive for purposes of evidence. The case, therefore, which I select to illustrate tactile impression is one where the sense of hearing was also concerned. And the example, as it happens, will serve a double purpose; for it will also illustrate the phenomenon of *reciprocality*, which, as I have said, we make the basis of a separate class (F). The narrator is again the Rev. P. H. Newnham, of whose telepathic *rapport* with his wife we have had such striking experimental proof, and who describes himself as " an utter sceptic, in the true sense of the word."

(35) " In March, 1854, I was up at Oxford, keeping my last term, in lodgings. I was subject to violent neuralgic headaches, which always culminated in sleep. One evening, about 8 p.m., I had an unusually violent one; when it became unendurable, about 9 p.m., I went into

---

[1] See Chapter xi., § 4.

my bedroom, and flung myself, without undressing, on the bed, and soon fell asleep.

"I then had a singularly clear and vivid dream, all the incidents of which are still as clear to my memory as ever. I dreamed that I was stopping with the family of the lady who subsequently became my wife. All the younger ones had gone to bed, and I stopped chatting to the father and mother, standing up by the fireplace. Presently I bade them goodnight, took my candle, and went off to bed. On arriving in the hall, I perceived that my *fiancée* had been detained downstairs, and was only then near the top of the staircase. I rushed upstairs, overtook her on the top step, and passed my two arms round her waist, under her arms, from behind. Although I was carrying my candle in my left hand, when I ran upstairs, this did not, in my dream, interfere with this gesture.

"On this I woke, and a clock in the house struck 10 almost immediately afterwards.

"So strong was the impression of the dream that I wrote a detailed account of it next morning to my *fiancée*.

"*Crossing my letter*, not in answer to it, I received a letter from the lady in question : 'Were you thinking about me, very specially, last night, just about 10 o'clock? For, as I was going upstairs to bed, I distinctly heard your footsteps on the stairs, and felt you put your arms round my waist.'

"The letters in question are now destroyed, but we verified the statement made therein some years later, when we read over our old letters, previous to their destruction, and we found that our personal recollections had not varied in the least degree therefrom. The above narratives may, therefore, be accepted as absolutely accurate.   "P. H. NEWNHAM."

Asked if his wife has ever had any other hallucinations, Mr. Newnham replied, 'No, Mrs. N. never had any fancy of either myself or any one else being present on any other occasion."

The following is Mrs. Newnham's account :—

"June 9th, 1884.

"I remember distinctly the circumstance which my husband has described as corresponding with his dream. I was on my way up to bed, as usual, about 10 o'clock, and on reaching the first landing I heard distinctly the footsteps of the gentleman to whom I was engaged, quickly mounting the stairs after me, and then I as plainly felt him put his arms round my waist. So strong an impression did this make upon me that I wrote the very next morning to the gentleman, asking if he had been particularly thinking of me at 10 o'clock the night before, and to my astonishment I received (at the same time that my letter would reach him) a letter from him describing his dream, in almost the same words that I had used in describing my impression of his presence.

"M. NEWNHAM."

[It is unfortunate that the actual letters cannot be put in evidence. But Mr. Newnham's distinct statement that the letters were examined, and the coincidence verified, some years after the occurrence, strongly confirms his own and his wife's recollections of the original incident.]

In this case it would, no doubt, be possible to suppose that Mr. Newnham was the sole agent, and that his normal dream was the source of his *fiancée's* abnormal hallucination. But it is at least equally natural to suppose a certain amount of *reciprocal* percipience—a mutual influence of the two parties on one another. We shall meet with more conclusive examples of the mutual effect further on ; and it need in no way disturb our conception of telepathy. For if once the startling fact that A's mind can affect B's at a distance be admitted, there seems no *à priori* reason for either affirming or denying that the conditions of this affection are favourable to a reverse telepathic communication from B's mind to A's. Indeed, if in our ignorance of the nature of these conditions any sort of surmise were legitimate, it might perhaps rather lean to the probability of the reciprocal influence ; and the natural question might seem to be, not why this feature is present, but why it is so generally absent. Meanwhile it is enough to note the type, and observe that the telepathic theory, as so far evolved, will sufficiently cover it.

§ 9. Finally, the class of *collective* percipience (G) may be illustrated by an instance which (since visual cases have preponderated in this chapter) I will again select from the auditory group. It was received in the summer of 1885, from Mr. John Done, of Stockley Cottage, Stretton, Warrington.

(36) " My sister-in-law, Sarah Eustance, of Stretton, was lying sick unto death, and my wife was gone over to there from Lowton Chapel (12 or 13 miles off), to see her and tend her in her last moments. And on the night before her death (some 12 or 14 hours before) I was sleeping at home alone, and awaking, heard a voice distinctly call me. Thinking it was my niece, Rosanna, the only other occupant of the house, who might be sick or in trouble, I went to her room and found her awake and nervous. I asked her whether she had called me. She answered, ' No ; but something awoke me, when I heard someone calling ! '

" On my wife returning home after her sister's death, she told me how anxious her sister had been to see me, ' craving for me to be sent for,' and saying, ' Oh, how I want to see Done once more ! ' and soon after became speechless. But the curious part was that about the same time she was ' craving,' I and my niece heard the call.   " JOHN DONE."

In a subsequent letter Mr. Done writes :—

" In answer to your queries respecting the voice or call that I heard on the night of July 2nd, 1866, I must explain that there was a strong sympathy and affection between myself and my sister-in-law, of pure brotherly and sisterly love ; and that she was in the habit of calling me by the title of ' Uncle Done,' in the manner of a husband calling his wife

'mother' when there are children, as in this case. Hence the call being
'Uncle, uncle, uncle!' leading me to think that it was my niece (the only
other occupant of the house that Sunday night) calling to me.

"Copy of funeral card : 'In remembrance of the late Sarah Eustance,
who died July 3rd, 1866, aged 45 years, and was this day interred at
Stretton Church, July 6th, 1866.'

"My wife, who went from Lowton that particular Sunday to see her
sister, will testify that as she attended upon her (after the departure of
the minister), during the night she was wishing and craving to see me,
repeatedly saying, 'Oh, I wish I could see Uncle Done and Rosie once
more before I go!' and soon after then she became unconscious, or at
least ceased speaking, and died the next day ; of which fact I was not aware
until my wife returned on the evening of the 4th of July.

"I hope my niece will answer for me ; however, I may state that she
reminds me that she thought I was calling her and was coming to me,
when she met me in the passage or landing, and I asked her if she called me.

"I do not remember ever hearing a voice or call besides the above case."

On August 7th, 1885, Mr. Done writes :—

"My wife being sick and weak of body, dictates the following statement to me :—

"I, Elizabeth Done, wife of John Done, and aunt to Rosanna Done
(now Sewill), testify that, on the 2nd of July, 1866, I was attending
upon my dying sister, Sarah Eustance, at Stretton, 12 miles from my home
at Lowton Chapel, Newton le Willows ; when during the night previous to
her death, she craved for me to send for my husband and niece, as she
wished to see them once more before she departed hence, saying often 'Oh,
I wish Done and Rosie were here. Oh, I do long to see Uncle Done.'
Soon after she became speechless and seemingly unconscious, and died
some time during the day following.   "ELIZABETH DONE."

Mr. Done adds :—

"Several incidents have come to my mind, one of which is that, feeling
unsettled in my mind during the day after having heard the voice calling
me, and feeling a presentiment that my dear sister-in-law was dead, I,
towards evening, set off to meet a train at Newton Bridge, which I believed
my wife would come by, returning home, *if her sister was dead as I
expected*. There was an understanding that she was to stay at Stretton
to attend upon Mrs. Eustance until her demise or convalescence.

"I met my wife some few hundred yards from the station, and could
see by her countenance that my surmises were correct. She then told me
the particulars of her sister's death, how she *longed* to see me and Rosanna.
I then told her of our being called by a voice resembling hers *some time*
in the night *previous*, when she (my wife) said she (Mrs. Eustance) often
repeated our names during the night before becoming unconscious."

The niece, Mrs. Sewill, writes as follows :—

"11, Smithdown Lane, Paddington, Liverpool.
"August 21st, 1885.

"At my uncle's and your request, I write to confirm the statement of
uncle respecting the voice I heard, as follows : I was awakened suddenly
without apparent cause, and heard a voice call me distinctly, thus : '*Rosy,*

Rosy, Rosy![1] Thinking it was my uncle calling, I rose and went out of my room, and met my uncle coming to see if I was calling him.[2] We were the only occupants of the house that night, aunt being away attending upon her sister. The night I was called was between 2nd and 3rd of July, 1866. I could not say the time I was called, but I know it was the break of day. I never was called before or since.   " ROSANNA SEWILL."

[The last words—an answer to the question whether the narrator had ever experienced any other hallucination—perhaps need correction, as I learnt in conversation that on another occasion she (and two other persons in the same house) had been woke by a voice resembling that of a deceased relative. But she is by no means a fanciful or superstitious witness.]

The percipients in this case may perhaps have been in a somewhat anxious and highly-wrought state. Now that is a condition which—as we shall see in the sequel—tends occasionally to produce purely subjective hallucinations of the senses. It is true that the impression of a call which was imagined to be that of a healthy person close at hand, and was in no way suggestive of the dying woman, does not seem a likely form for subjective hallucination due to anxiety about her to take ; still, the presence of the anxiety would have prevented us from including such a case in our evidence, had only a single person been impressed. But it must be admitted as a highly improbable accident that *two* startling impressions, so similar in character, and each unique in the life of the person who experienced it, should have so exactly coincided.

§ 10. The above may serve as examples of the several groups classified with reference to the nature of the *percipient's* impression. But it will be seen that the *agent* has also been exhibited in a great variety of conditions—in normal waking health, in apparently dreamless sleep (pp. 103-9), in dream, in physical pain, in a swoon, in the excitement of danger, in dangerous illness, and *in articulo mortis*, the death being in one case accidental and instantaneous, in another the result of a sudden seizure, and in others the conclusion of a prolonged illness. And amid this variety the reader will, no doubt, have been struck by the large proportion of *death* cases—a proportion which duly represents their general preponderance among alleged cases of spontaneous telepathy. They constitute about half of our whole collection. Now this fact raises a question with respect to the interpretation of the phenomena which may be conveniently noticed at once since it bears an equal relation to nearly all the

---

[1] Each of the percipients, it will be noted, heard his or her own name. This point receives its explanation in Chap. xii., § 5.

[2] Mrs. Sewill, (who was 14 or 15 at the time) is certain that she is correct on this point ; and in conversation with her uncle, I found that his memory agrees with hers.

chapters that follow, while such answer as I can give to it depends to some extent on what has preceded.

We are, of course, accustomed to regard death as a completely unique and incomparably important event; and it might thus seem, on a superficial glance, that if spontaneous telepathy is possible, and the conditions and occasions of its occurrence are in question, no more likely occasion than death could be suggested. But on closer consideration, we are reminded that the actual psychical condition that immediately precedes death often does not seem to be specially or at all remarkable, still less unique; and that it is this actual psychical condition—while it lasts, and not after it has ceased—that really concerns us here. Our subject is phantasms *of the living :* we seek the conditions of the telepathic impulse on the hither side of the dividing line, in the closing passage of life ; not in that huge negative fact—the apparent cessation or absence of life—on which the common idea of death and of its momentous importance is based. And the closing passage of life, in some of the cases above quoted and in many others that are to follow, was, to all appearance, one of more or less complete lethargy ; a state which (on its psychical side at any rate) seems in no way distinguishable from one through which the agent has passed on numerous previous occasions—that of deep sleep. Nor are the cases which issue in death the only ones to which this remark applies : in the more remarkable cases of Chap. III., the agent was actually in deep sleep ; Mrs. Bettany's mother was in a swoon (p. 194) ; and other similar instances will meet us. Here, then, there appears to be a real difficulty. For how can we attribute an extraordinary exercise of psychical energy to a state which on its psychical side is quite ordinary, and in which psychical and physical energies alike seem reduced to their lowest limits ?

It may, no doubt, be replied that we have no right to assume that the psychical condition is ordinary ; that the *nervous* condition in the lethargy of approaching death, and even in a fainting-fit, may differ greatly from that of normal sleep, and that this difference may be somehow represented on the psychical side, even though the *ostensible* psychical condition is approximately *nil.* But a completer answer may possibly be found in some further development of the idea of the "unconscious intelligence" which was mentioned above (pp. 69, 70). We there noted stray manifestations of psychical action that seemed unconnected with the more or less coherent stream of experience which we recognise as a *self ;* and a probable relation of these was pointed

out to those curious cases of "double consciousness," in which two more
or less coherent streams of experience replace one another by turns,
and the same person seems to have two selves. Many other cognate
facts might be mentioned, which enable us to generalise to some
extent the conceptions suggested by the more prominent instances.
But since for present purposes the topic only concerns us at the point
where it comes into contact with telepathy, I must ask the reader
to seek those further facts elsewhere ; and to accept here the
statement that the more these little-known paths of psychology
are explored, the more difficult will it appear to round off the idea of
personality, or to measure human existence by the limits of the
phenomenal self.[1] Now the very nature of this difficulty cannot but
suggest a deeper solution than the mere connection of various
streams of psychic life in a single organism. It suggests the
hypothesis that a single individuality may have its psychical being,
so to speak, on different planes ; that the stray fragments of
"unconscious intelligence," and the alternating selves of "double
consciousness," belong really to a more fundamental unity, which
finds in what we call life very imperfect conditions of manifestation ;
and that the self which ordinary men habitually regard as their
proper individuality may after all be only a partial emergence.
And this hypothesis would readily embrace and explain the special
telepathic fact in question ; while itself drawing from that fact a
fresh support. By its aid we can at once picture to ourselves how it
should be that the near approach of death is a condition exceptionally favourable to telepathic action, even though vital faculties
seem all but withdrawn, and the familiar self has lapsed to the very
threshold of consciousness. For to the hidden and completer self
the imminence of the great change may be apparent in its full and
unique impressiveness ; nay, death itself may be recognised, for
aught we can tell, not as a cessation but as a liberation of energy.
But this line of thought, though worth pointing out as that along
which the full account of certain phenomena of telepathy may in
time be sought, is not one that I can here pursue.

[1] In addition to Dr. Azam's well-known case of Félida, I may refer specially to
Professor Verriest's "Observation de trois existences cérébrales distinctes chez le
même sujet," in the *Bulletin de l'Académie Royale de Médecine de Belgique*, 3rd Series,
Vol. xvi.; the case of Louis V——, with his six different personalities, reported by
various French observers (Camuset, *Annales Médico-psychologiques*, 1882, p. 75 ; Jules
Voisin, *Archives de Neurologie*, September, 1885 ; Bourru and Burot, *Revue Philosophique*,
October, 1885, and *Archives de Neurologie*, November, 1885) ; and the hypnotic experiments
described by Mr. Myers, in his paper on "Human Personality," *Proceedings* of the S.P.R.
Part x. A theory of the transcendental self, in its relation to various abnormal states,
has been worked out at length in Du Prel's *Philosophie der Mystik* (Leipzig, 1885).

CHAPTER VI.

TRANSFERENCE OF IDEAS AND OF MENTAL PICTURES.

§ 1. THE advance-guard of cases in the last chapter has afforded a glance at the whole range of the phenomena. But I must now start on a methodical plan, and take the narratives in groups according to their subject-matter. The groups will follow the same order as the preceding specimens; but though theoretically the best, this order has the practical disadvantage that it puts the weakest classes first. Of the two great divisions, the *externalised* impressions are by far the most remarkable in themselves, and by far the most conclusive as evidence; but as they constitute the extreme examples of telepathic action, they are logically led up to through the *non-externalised* group, which presents more obvious analogies with the experimental basis of our inquiry. I must, therefore, beg the reader who may be disappointed by much of the evidence in this and the two following chapters, to note that it is no way presented as conclusive; and that though it is well worthy of attention if'the case for spontaneous telepathy is once made out, it is only when we come to the "borderland" examples of Chap. IX. that the strength of the case begins rapidly to accumulate.

The great point which connects many of the more inward impressions of spontaneous telepathy with the experimental cases is this—that what enters the percipient's mind is the exact reproduction of the agent's thought at the moment. It is to this class of direct transferences, especially between persons who are in close association with one another, that popular belief most readily inclines—as a rule, without any sufficient grounds. Nothing is commoner than to hear instances of sympathetic flashes between members of the same household—cases where one person suddenly makes the very remark that another was about to make—adduced as evidence of some sort of supersensuous communication. But it is tolerably evident that a number of such "odd coincidences" are sure to occur in a perfectly normal way. Minds which are in habitual contact with one another will constantly react in the same way, even to the most trifling influences of the moment; and the sudden word which proves them to have done so would have nothing startling in it, if the whole train of association that led up to it could be exposed to view. Moreover, physical signs which would be imperceptible to a stranger, may be easily and half-automatically interpreted by a familiar associate ; and thus what looks sometimes like divination may perfectly well be due to unconscious inference. It is very rarely that conditions of this sort can be with certainty excluded. Still, experimental thought-transference would certainly prepare us to encounter the phenomenon occasionally in ordinary social and domestic life ; and one or two examples may be given which have a strong *primâ facie* air of being genuine specimens.

One frequent form of the alleged transferences is that of *tunes.* It is matter of very common observation that one person begins humming the very tune that is running in some one else's head. This admits, as a rule, of a perfectly simple explanation. It is easy to suppose that some special tune has been a good deal " in the air " of a house, half unconsciously hummed or whistled, as tunes often are, and that thus the coincidence is an accident which may very readily occur. At the same time, if the telepathic faculty exists tunes should apparently be a form of " thought " well calculated for transference. With many people the imagining of a tune is the sort of idea which comes nearest to the vividness of actual sensation. And moreover, it contains not only the representation of sensory experience, but also a distinct *motor* element—an impulse to reproduction. A person with a musical ear can silently reproduce a tune, with such an inward force as almost produces the illusion of driving it into objective existence. Such an incident as the following therefore, where there is no question of a family knowledge of the tune, or of its having been in any way in the air, is of decided interest ; though, of course, the actual force of any single case of the sort is very small.[1] We received the account from Sir Lepel Griffin, K.C.S.I.

---

[1] The phenomenon is not without experimental support. Just a century ago, Puységur wrote, of one of his "magnetised" subjects : "Je le forçais à se donner beaucoup de mouvement sur sa chaise, comme pour danser sur un air, qu'en chantant *mentalement* je lui faisais répéter tout haut." *(Mémoires, &c., du Magnetisme Animal,* 3rd edition, p. 22. See also Dr. Macario, *Du Sommeil, des Rêves, et du Somnambulisme,*

" 53A, Pall Mall.

" February 14th, 1884.

(37) " Colonel Lyttleton Annesley, Commanding Officer of the 11th Hussars, was staying in my house some time ago, and one afternoon, having nothing to do, we wandered into a large unoccupied room, given up to lumber and packing cases. Colonel A. was at one end of this long room reading, to the best of my recollection, while I opened a box, long forgotten, to see what it contained. I took out a number of papers and old music, which I was turning over in my hand, when I came across a song in which I, years before, had been accustomed to take a part, 'Dal tuo stellato soglio,' out of ' Mosé in Egitto,' if I remember right. As I looked at this old song, Colonel A., who had been paying no attention whatever to my proceedings, began to hum, ' Dal tuo stellato soglio.' In much astonishment I asked him why he was singing that particular air. He did not know. He did not remember to have sung it before ; indeed I have not ever heard Colonel A. sing, though he is exceedingly fond of music. I told him that I was holding the very song in my hand. He was as much astonished as I had been, and had no knowledge that I had any music in my hand at all. I had not spoken to him, nor had I hummed the air, or given him any sign that I was looking over music. The incident is curious, for it is outside all explanation on the theory of coincidence."

Later, Sir L. Griffin wrote:—   " 28th April, 1884.

" I promised to write to you when I received a reply from General Lyttleton Annesley, to whom I had written, in the same words I had used to you, the little incident which struck you as noteworthy. I may mention that it had never formed the subject of conversation or correspondence between us from the day that it happened until now. He says: ' I perfectly recollect the incident you refer to about the song " Dal tuo stellato soglio." I had my back to you at the time you were taking out the music, and did not even know what you were doing. I was close to a window and you were at the bottom end of the room. In fact your account is exact to the minutest point.'   " LEPEL GRIFFIN."

We have other cases in which the transferred impression was not of a tune, but of a word or phrase, while still apparently of an auditory sort, conveying the *sound* of the word rather than its meaning. When the two persons concerned have been in close proximity, it is, of course, difficult to make sure that some incipient sound or movement of the lips, on the part of the supposed agent, did not

p. 184.) Mr. Guthrie has successfully repeated the experiment several times with a "subject " in a normal state *(Proceedings* of the S.P.R., Vol. iii.)—with contact, it is true, which prevents the results from being quite conclusive. Still, the only element in a tune which could be conveyed with any accuracy by minute movements is the *rhythm.* Now this could only be conveyed by *sudden* movements at definite moments—a very different matter from the continuous slightly-varied pressure of the willing-game ; while even supposing that these discrete and accurate indications could be unconsciously given, it is hard to believe that they could lead to the identification of the tune, unless their rhythmic character were consciously perceived.

supply an unconscious suggestion.[1] But the following case cannot be so explained. We received it from Mr. J. G. Keulemans, who was mentioned above (p. 196) as having had a number of similar experiences.

"November, 1882.

(38) "In the summer of the year 1875, about eight in the evening, I was returning to my home in the Holloway Road, on a tramcar, when it flashed into my mind that my assistant, Herr Schell, a Dutchman, who knew but little English (who was coming to see me that evening), would ask me what the English phrase, ' to wit,' meant in Dutch. So vivid was the impression that I mentioned it to my wife on arriving at my house, and I went so far as to scribble it down on the edge of a newspaper which I was reading. Ten minutes afterwards Schell arrived, and almost his first words were the inquiry, ' Wat is het Hollandsch voor " *to wit* "?' (The words scribbled on the newspaper were not in his sight, and he was a good many yards from it.) I instantly showed him the paper, with the memorandum on it, saying, ' You see I was ready for you.' He told me that he had resolved to ask me just before leaving his house in Kentish Town, as he was intending that evening to do a translation of an English passage in which the words occurred. He was in the habit of making such translations in order to improve his knowledge of English. The time of his resolution corresponded (as far as we could reckon) with that of my impression."

[Unfortunately no corroboration of this occurrence is now obtainable; but the incident of the newspaper does not seem a likely one to have been unconsciously invented.]

The next case, if correctly reported, is of a transitional sort ; for though it was a distinct idea, and not a mere sound-image, that seems to have been transferred, the transference was probably connected with the fact that the words were actually on the tip of the agent's tongue. This fact, of course, suggests again the chance of unconscious suggestion by actual sound or movement of the lips;

---

[1] For instance, we should not be justified in laying stress on such an occurrence as the following, described to us by Mr. Dismorr, of Thelcrest Lodge, Gravesend.
"November 19th, 1884.
" A somewhat curious little incident occurred this morning, which, though not of any value, might be of interest to you.
" Last evening a friend of mine, Mr. F. P., and I, unable to fix upon a suitable name for a new invention of ours, agreed to think it over and communicate the names selected this morning.   The only names I could think of at all suitable were three, ' Matchless,' ' Marvel,' and ' Express.'
" We met in the train, and I said to P., ' Have you thought of any name ? ' he replied ' Yes,' and leant across to mention it, but suddenly stopped short, and said, ' Tell me yours.' I at once commenced, as I thought, to give the three I had selected in the order named ; but quite as much to my surprise as that of Mr. P., the first name I mentioned was the word ' Superb,' a name that had never entered my mind, but strangely enough the actual name that P. had settled on and was about to mention.
" As there was not any reflection whatever, nor time for it, between P.'s question and my rejoinder, it struck me as rather curious.   "J. S. DISMORR."
[Mr. P. admits the fact, but would rather his name did not appear.]
This may have been a lucky chance, or it may have been that Mr. P., before checking himself, had given a hint of the coming word.

but such an explanation seems here practically excluded by the length of the sentence. The case was recorded in the *Spectator* of June 24th, 1882, and has been confirmed to us by the writer.

"Ferndene, Abbeydale, near Sheffield.

"June 22nd.

(39) "I had one day been spending the morning in shopping, and returned by train just in time to sit down with my children to our early family dinner. My youngest child—a sensitive, quick-witted little maiden of two years and six weeks old—was one of the circle. Dinner had just commenced, when I suddenly recollected an incident in my morning's experience which I had intended to tell her; and I looked at the child with the full intention of saying, 'Mother saw a big, black dog in a shop, with curly hair,' catching her eyes in mine, as I paused an instant before speaking. Just then something called off my attention, *and the sentence was not uttered.* What was my amazement, about two minutes afterwards, to hear my little lady announce, 'Mother saw a big dog in a shop.' I gasped. 'Yes, I did!' I answered; 'but how did you know?' 'With funny hair,' she added, quite calmly, and ignoring my question. 'What colour was it, Evelyn?' said one of her elder brothers; 'was it black?' She said, 'Yes.'

"Now, it was simply impossible that she could have received any hint of the incident verbally. I had had no friend with me when I had seen the dog. All the children had been at home, in our house in the country, four miles from the town; I had returned, as I said, just in time for the children's dinner, and I had not even remembered the circumstance until the moment when I fixed my eyes upon my little daughter's. We have had in our family circle numerous examples of spiritual or mental insight or foresight; but this, I think, is decidedly the most remarkable that has ever come under my notice.   "CAROLINE BARBER."

Mrs. Barber has shown to Mr. Podmore the note-book in which she noted the occurrence, and from which her letter to the *Spectator* was taken almost verbatim. The incident was recorded on Jan. 11, 1880, as having taken place on Jan. 6. She adds that the governess and the other children at table were positive that she had not said anything about the dog, and were as much astonished as she was.

§ 2. In the next case (which might fairly have been included under the head of experiments) we break away altogether from the auditory symbols of thought, and have a transference of an idea pure and simple. For even if the agent was formulating his thought to himself, he would naturally do so in English, while the percipient described *his* impression in Italian. The account is from Mr. Robert Browning, and was first cited by Mr. James Knowles, in a letter to the *Spectator* of January 30th, 1869.

(40) "Mr. Robert Browning tells me that when he was in Florence some years since, an Italian nobleman (a Count Giunasi, of Ravenna), visiting at Florence, was brought to his house without previous introduction, by an intimate friend. The Count professed to have great mesmeric or

clairvoyant faculties, and declared, in reply to Mr. Browning's avowed scepticism, that he would undertake to convince him, somehow or other, of his powers. He then asked Mr. Browning whether he had anything about him then and there, which he could hand to him, and which was in any way a relic or memento. This, Mr. Browning thought, was, perhaps, because he habitually wore no sort of trinket or ornament, not even a watch-guard, and might, therefore, turn out to be a safe challenge. But it so happened, that by a curious accident, he was then wearing under his coat-sleeves some gold wrist-studs to his shirt, which he had quite recently taken into wear, in the absence (by mistake of a sempstress) of his ordinary wrist-buttons. He had never before worn them in Florence or elsewhere, and had found them in some old drawer, where they had lain forgotten for years. One of these studs he took out and handed to the Count, who held it in his hand awhile, looking earnestly in Mr. Browning's face, and then he said, as if much impressed, 'C'é qualche cosa che mi grida nell' orecchio, " Uccisione, uccisione ! " ' [There is something here which cries out in my ear, ' Murder, murder ! ']

" ' And truly,' says Mr. Browning, ' those very studs were taken from the dead body of a great-uncle of mine, who was violently killed on his estate in St. Kitts, nearly 80 years ago. These, with a gold watch and other personal objects of value, were produced in a court of justice, as proof that robbery had not been the purpose of the slaughter, which was effected by his own slaves. They were then transmitted to my grandfather, who had his initials engraved on them, and wore them all his life. They were taken out of the night-gown in which he died, and given to me, not my father. I may add that I tried to get Count Giunasi to use his clairvoyance on this termination of ownership, also ; and that he nearly hit upon something like the fact, mentioning a bed in a room, but he failed in attempting to describe the room—situation of the bed with respect to windows and door. The occurrence of my great-uncle's murder was known only to myself, of all men in Florence, as certainly was also my possession of the studs.' "

Mr. Browning, in a letter to us, dated the 21st of July, 1883, affirms that the account "is correct in every particular"—adding, " My own explanation of the matter has been that the shrewd Italian felt his way by the involuntary help of my own eyes and face. The guess, however attained to, was a good one."

If a spurious diviner can thus feel his way as far as murder, and even Mr. Browning's expression is so inadequate to veil his thought, then indeed is our daily life compassed with dangers of which genuine telepathy has shown no trace.

With this account it is interesting to compare the following, from Miss Caroline B. Morse, of Northfield, Vermont.

" April, 1884.

(41) " I early became conscious of a peculiar sensitiveness to the undertones — the unuttered thoughts — of others. Later, this tendency developed into an occasional lightning-like reading of facts that apparently came to me through none of the ordinary sensory

channels, and which always, whatever their nature, gave me a shock of surprise. As an instance : About 13 years ago I went with an uncle to a jeweller's shop to see a wonderful clock. I had never met the proprietor of the shop ; he was known to my uncle, who introduced him as he came forward and stood with us before the clock. At that instant came a sensation as if every nerve in my body had been struck. The affable jeweller had extended his hand, but with a shudder, that only habitual self-control repressed, I said within myself : ' I cannot touch your hand— there is blood upon it—you are a murderer.' Outwardly, I merely bowed and looked at the clock, as if nothing could interest me so much, thus ignoring the proffered hand. Several weeks after, I learned that the jeweller and a companion, when young men, had been accused of and tried for the murder of a pedlar. They escaped conviction through the garbled testimony of the chief witness, who at the preliminary hearing had made a clear statement strongly against them.   " CAROLINE B. MORSE."

The following corroboration is from Mr. B. T. Merrill :—

" Montpelier, Vermont.
" May 31st, 1884.

" I think it was in the fall of 1871 that I asked my niece, Miss C. B. Morse, to go with me to see a musical clock. We went into the shop. I introduced the jeweller ; he reached out his hand to shake hands with her, but she refused to take his hand. After we left the shop, I asked her why she did not shake hands with him. She did not make much reply, and I did not know the real reason till long afterwards. I did not then know that the jeweller had been tried for murder, but some time after learned the facts from some of the residents of this place.

" BENJAMIN T. MERRILL."[1]

In contrast to this purely ideal sort of horror, I may quote the following two cases where the impression, though still extremely indefinite in character, was yet sufficiently concrete to suggest the very presence of the object.

The first account was given to us by Miss Charlotte E. Squire, then residing at Feltham Hill, Middlesex (now Mrs. Fuller Maitland).

---

[1] Compare case 379, where the impression seems to have been received when the agent's hand was actually touched. The following account of a parallel incident occurs in the *Zoist*, Vol. x., p. 409, in a letter from the Rev. C. H. Townshend to Dr. Elliotson.

" October 6th, 1852.
" There is a curious story that M. Woodley de Cerjat wanted you to know. I believe he wrote it to Dickens to tell you again. However, I may as well repeat it.
" A young lady, a friend of M. Cerjat's, who had been with her family at Lausanne, was taken ill at Berne with typhus fever. Her doctor found her one day in a lucid interval (she was generally delirious), but no sooner had he touched her hand than she seemed to pass into an extraordinary state, and cried out, 'Oh that poor child ! that poor little boy ! why did you cut his head open ? How is he now ?' The doctor, astonished, replied, ' I left him well ; I hope he will recover,' and tried to calm the patient. But when he got out of the room, he said, 'That was the most extraordinary thing I ever knew in my life. I am come from trepanning a boy whose head had been injured, but there was no human means by which Miss —— could have known it, as I am only this moment come direct from the boy here, and no one knew of the accident, nor had Miss ——'s nurse ever left the room.' The explanation seems to be that the *touch* of the doctor's hand threw the young lady into clairvoyance. She is since dead, and M. de Cerjat attended her funeral."

"January 17th, 1884.

(42) "My brother and I were travelling together from Cologne to Flushing. We were alone in the carriage when suddenly my brother, who had been half asleep, said to me that he had an odd idea that some one else was in the carriage sitting opposite to me. The very same idea had struck me just before he spoke.

"Though my feet were on the opposite seat, I was *certain* that some one was there, though I was wide awake and never saw the slightest appearance of anything. The impression only lasted for a moment, but it was strange that our thoughts should have been simultaneous. This happened three years ago."

Asked if this impression was a *unique* experience in her life, Miss Squire replied that it was.

The following corroboration is from Mr. W. Barclay Squire :—

"The incident took place in the second week of February, 1881. My sister and myself had been to Hanover, and were returning home *viâ* Flushing. We were alone in a first-class carriage, I sitting with my face to the engine, she with her back, at the diagonal corners of the carriage. In the evening, as we drew near to Flushing, I was dozing, or rather in that half-awake, half-asleep state when dreams become mixed up with reality, and actual objects become mingled with dream images. From this state I suddenly woke, under the vivid impression that a figure was seated in the corner of the carriage opposite my sister, *i.e.*, at the other end of the seat on which I was. The impression was quite transitory, but so vivid as to wake me thoroughly, though the figure was vague and dark, as if muffled up in a cloak, no features being visible. I immediately mentioned the hallucination to my sister, when she told me she had a similar one. I was careful to note that there were no bags or rugs on the seat on which I saw the figure, which could have given rise to its appearance by some fanciful combination.   "W. BARCLAY SQUIRE."

Asked whether he had ever had any other hallucinations of vision, Mr. Squire replied that when quite a child he had seen figures, which were to be accounted for by an "almost continual state of delicate health. I never saw figures from the time I was about 7 or 8 until this experience in the railway carriage."

It naturally occurred to us that the impression might have been unconsciously suggested to one of the two persons by the other, through some unconscious gesture or sudden change of feature. But the following communications seem decisive against this hypothesis :—

"39, Phillimore Gardens, W.
"March 15th, 1885.

"The idea of a third presence in the railway carriage occurred to both my brother and myself, without either of us ever having seen the other's face. I had my eyes closed at the time, and as we were sitting on the same side of the carriage we could not see each other's faces.
                    "C. E. FULLER MAITLAND."

"I am certain the impression on my part was entirely spontaneous, and not suggested by any action or look of my sister.
                    "W. BARCLAY SQUIRE."

[It will be seen, however, that there is a discrepancy as to the positions in the carriage.]

Supposing this incident to have been telepathic, it is natural to regard Mr. Squire as the agent, and his impression of the strange presence as the momentary survival of a dream. But in the next example, if we surmise that a sort of waking nightmare of one of the three sisters affected the other two, we cannot at all assign their respective shares in the occurrence. The writer of the narrative is well known as an authoress and practical philanthropist.

"1884.

(43) "It was on a Saturday night, the end of October, or early in November, 1848, that I was staying at St. M——'s Vicarage, Leicester. My two sisters were at home, at H., about 14 or 15 miles from Leicester. The room in which I slept was large and low, opening into a broad, low corridor; the nursery was on the same floor; the rest of the family slept on the one below. I had been asleep for some time, and was not consciously dreaming at all. I was awoke instantaneously, not by any sound, but intensely awake, starting up in a panic—not of fear, but of horror, knowing that something horrible was close by. The room was still dimly lighted by the dying-out fire. I suppose it was seeing the room empty made me at once know that whatever it was, it was still outside the door, for I rushed at once to lock it. The impression I had was so vivid that I can only describe it by speaking of 'It' as objective. 'It' was living, not human, not physically dangerous ; I think it was malevolent, but the overpowering consciousness I had was horrible ; I did not represent it to myself in any shape even, except as an indefinite blackness, like a cloudy pillar, I suppose. The presence seemed to stay outside the door five minutes (but probably it was a much shorter time), and then it simply was not there. Whilst it was there I knew that it was nearly 2 o'clock, and the church bells chimed 2, about ten minutes, as I suppose, after it ceased. Whilst it was there I was very angry with myself for being so absurd ; and I remember wondering whether a young German, who was living there as a pupil, a *protégé* of Chauncey Townsend's, could be mesmerising me. He had been telling us about mesmerism and clairvoyance the day before, but I had not the slightest faith in either, at any rate not in C. H. T.'s accuracy of observation.

"I went home on the following Tuesday, and that night, in talking over my visit with my two sisters, I told them what a strange delusion I had had.

"They were both astonished, and related a similar experience each had had on the same Saturday night, or rather Sunday morning, for both agreed their impression at the time had been it was about or near 2. They were sleeping in separate rooms, but next each other.

"R. was awoke in the same sudden manner, with the consciousness that something dreadful or harmful was near, not in her room, but a little way off. Her impression was the same in character, but less vivid than mine.

"E. was awoke suddenly, as I had been, with a sense of intense horror,

Some presence, fearful, evil and powerful, was standing close by her side ; she was unable to move or cry out ; it seemed to her also to be a spiritual presence. Her room was quite dark, so she could see nothing. Her impression was at the time so much more overpowering, and it was so much closer to her, that it seemed to me, on talking it over, to have been the cause of ours. Not one of us for a moment connected it with a ghost. That notion never occurred to us.

"R. and E. had told each other before my return, I believe on the next day. Afterwards we told the strange coincidence to my father and mother. She thought she had also been awoke by a cry, if I remember right, that night ; but her recollection was too vague to be relied upon.

"Nothing ever came of it, except that the known date of the commencement of E.'s fatal illness was the Saturday following. But neither she, so far as I know, nor we ever thought of it in this connection. She was very much interested in it afterwards, but not in the slightest degree uneasy or alarmed at it, only eager to find out how the coincidence could be accounted for. I was 28 at the time ; E. was just 25."

[R. remembers this incident vaguely, and can add nothing.]

§ 3. I now come to cases where the impression was of a more definite sort, representing actual people and actual events. We sometimes encounter persons who allege that they have repeatedly experienced some occult sort of perception of what was happening to friends or relatives at a distance. As a rule their statements have no force at all as evidence for telepathy ; partly because we have no means of judging how far the idea of the distant event may have been suggested in some normal way ; partly because the impressions have not been recorded at the time, and it is specially easy to suppose that failures may have been forgotten, while a lucky guess has been remembered. We have, however, one example of marked correspondence where two witnesses were concerned, each of whom professes to have had other similar experiences, and where the particular incident narrated is adequately confirmed. The witnesses are Mr. and Mrs. L. H. Saunders, of St. Helen's, near Ryde. As to former experiences, Mr. Saunders says :—

"I have mentally noted frequent 'vivid impressions' during many years past, and in the majority of instances, when such impressions have appeared to be spontaneous and intuitive, the facts have actually corresponded."

Mrs. Saunders says :—

"I have had other similar strong impressions at distant intervals, and as far as I can recollect they have corresponded with the reality. I cannot say if I have had any such impressions which have *not* corresponded with the reality, but my opinion is that I have had none such."

Mr. Saunders' account of the particular incident is as follows :—

R

" San Claudio, Sandown, Isle of Wight.

" March 12th, 1883.

(44) " On Thursday evening last (8th inst.) in the house of friends with
whom we were staying at Tavistock, Devon, I suddenly asked my wife
' What she was thinking of ?' She replied, 'I cannot get M. R. and A. F.
out of my head all day ; they *will* run through all my thoughts.' I
replied, ' What makes you think of them ?' She said, ' I don't know, but
it seems just as if they were married,' to which I asked, ' Have you any
reason to suppose they would be married to-day ?' She replied, ' Oh no !
I am *sure* Mary would not be married during Lent.' I then allowed my
mind to travel to the house where M. R. resided in London, when I became
immediately conscious of receiving the strongest possible conviction that
they were married that day, so that I quickly but firmly replied, '*They are
married to-day, and we shall see the wedding announced in the Times on
Saturday,*' at which there was a general titter. However, I was so
convinced of the accuracy of our joint thoughts that I foolishly offered to
wager the whole of my belongings on the truth of it, and until seeing the
confirmation, I was anxious to risk anything in support of my belief. I
may here mention that there were present, who could testify to the foregoing conversation, *three* independent witnesses, quite unknown to the
persons referred to as M. R. and A. F. Neither of the latter had been
seen nor communicated with by my wife for nearly six months, but I had
seen them once about three months before. We knew they were to be
married, but understood not until April or May. This knowledge and the
question of Lent made my wife doubtful as to the fulfilment of her
presentiment when I pressed her finally at noon on Saturday ; soon after
which, on reaching Exeter station, I procured a copy of the *Times*, and
before opening it again declared my conviction absolutely unshaken. As
you may have guessed, there was the notice of marriage, as having taken
place on the 8th inst., all right. [We have verified this fact independently.]
I may conclude by saying this notice is all we know of the wedding, no
communication having passed between us and any member of the bride's
or bridegroom's family, &c. Further, if you deem it of sufficient
importance I will supply correct names and addresses of all parties
interested, as I feel sure our Tavistock friends could not object to
contributing to scientific truth by testifying to the facts."

The ladies who were present when Mr. and Mrs. Saunders had this
impression corroborate as follows, in a letter written to Mr. Saunders from
Harleigh House, Tavistock :—

" After a lengthy discussion you both emphatically concluded that she
was married on that day. We were quite sceptical at the time, but on
receipt of the *Times* the proofs were quite convincing.

" LILY SAMPSON.
" KATHLEEN SAMPSON."

Here the state of the supposed agent or agents was presumably
excitement of a happy nature. This, however, is rarely the case—
which may perhaps be taken as indicating the superior vividness of
pains over pleasures. Impressions of death, illness, or accident are

the almost unbroken rule. I will first quote cases where a distinct idea of the particular event was produced, without any distinct representation of the actual scene.

The following account is from Mrs. Herbert Davy, of 1, Burdon Place, Newcastle-on-Tyne.

"December 20th, 1883.

(45) "A very old gentleman, living at Hurworth, a friend of my husband's and with whom I was but slightly acquainted, had been ill many months. My sister-in-law, who resides also at H., often mentioned him in her letters, saying he was better or worse as the case might be.

"Late last autumn, my husband and I were staying at the Tynedale Hydropathic Establishment. One evening I suddenly laid down the book I was reading, with this thought so strong upon me I could scarcely refrain from putting it into words : 'I believe that Mr. C. is at this moment dying.' So strangely was I imbued with this belief—there had been nothing whatever said to lead to it—that I asked my husband to note the time particularly, and to remember it for a reason I would rather not state just then. 'It₀ is exactly 7 o'clock,' he said, and that being our dinner hour, we went downstairs to dine. The entire evening, however, I was haunted by the same strange feeling, and looked for a letter from my sister-in-law next morning. None came. But the following day there was one for her brother. In it she said : 'Poor old Mr. C. died last night at 7 o'clock. It was past post time, so I could not let you know before.'"

Mr. Davy corroborates as follows :—

"December 27th, 1883.

"I have a perfect recollection of the night in question, the 20th October, 1882, when my wife asked me to tell her the time. I told her the time, as she 'had a reason for knowing it,' she said. She afterwards told me that reason. "HERBERT DAVY."

The following is a copy of an obituary card, referring to the Mr. C. of the narrative :—

"In loving memory of John Colling, of Hurworth-on-Tees, who died October the 20th, 1882, aged 84 years."

Mrs. Davy has had one other experience, to be quoted later (case 395), which also corresponded with a death. With this exception, she states that the present case was quite unique in her experience.

In an interview with Professor Sidgwick, on April 15th, 1884, Mrs. Davy described the impression as strong and sudden, not emotional, but merely the sudden conviction that Mr. Colling was at that moment dying, though a strange feeling of sadness followed and remained during the evening. "She called it strange," says Professor Sidgwick, "meaning (as I understand) that her interest in Mr. C. was too slight to account for it ; and she has no reason to suppose that he thought of her at the moment of death. In this case her recollection of the uniqueness and strength of her conviction is confirmed by her request to her husband to note the time ; she was certain that she had never on any other occasion made a similar request in consequence of a similar impression. Her belief at the time was not the result of any reasoning process leading her to have confidence in her impression." More than two years later, in conversation with the present writer, Mrs. Davy mentioned the surprise which she herself afterwards felt at having made the request to her husband.

The next case is from Miss A. S. Jarry, of Settle, Yorkshire.

"June 2nd, 1884.

(46) "I was making a hurried tour in the North of Italy, having left a sister at home, who for some time past had been subject to sudden attacks of illness. Owing to short halts, and some uncertainty as to these, I had not had any tidings from home for nearly a fortnight. Although much disappointed at this, I can confidently say that I had not dwelt upon the thought so as to induce any nervous anxiety. One evening, in Venice, at about half-past 10, the certain conviction was suddenly forced upon me that my sister was ill. The impression was so distinct that it would have been impossible, in any case, to doubt the reality of the fact, but having had two similar communications some years before in the case of my mother's illness, I knew quite well that my sister was ill. Under these circumstances, it would be difficult to measure time accurately; my impression was that I had been about two hours arranging in my own mind to leave Venice by the earliest morning train, when suddenly an assurance as strong as the first was conveyed that all cause for anxiety had passed away. On my return home I found that both impressions had been correct, as my sister's account subjoined will show. I also send the evidence of a friend to whom, on the following morning, I communicated the impressions of the night. "A. S. JARRY."

Miss Jarry's sister writes:—

"Having for some time been liable to sudden attacks in my head, the symptoms of which were great confusion of thought, an attack was never surprising. On the night of April 21st, 1882, as I was preparing for bed (being at the house of a friend), I all at once felt that I was not in my own room at home, and I could not account for that circumstance; for some moments, it might be minutes, I did not know where I was. At last I became clear on that point, but not as to the reason of my being there. I was so far clear as to know that at the time I was ill, and that I must hasten into bed as soon, but with as little movement, as possible. It was about 10.30 p.m. the attack came on; it continued to cause great and distressing confusion for about 2 hours. The time I was quite aware of, as a clock near, striking the quarters, marked the time accurately. After this, clearness of mind gradually returned, and I felt convinced I was recovering. I heard 2 a.m. strike before I fell asleep, but before that time I had felt convinced all danger was over. "M. L. JARRY."

In answer to inquiries, Miss A. S. Jarry says:—

"June 30th, 1884.

"My impression of my sister's illness occurred on the same night, and, as exactly as can be ascertained at that distance, at the same time as her illness occurred. By comparing notes as strictly as can be, the certainty of all danger being over coincided exactly with her consciousness that she was going to fall into a refreshing sleep. I told my impression to Miss Barnett on the following morning. The previous correct impression to which I alluded in the account I sent you, referred to two communications of precisely the same nature in the cases of two distinct illnesses of my mother's.[1] The impressions were equally clear and unmistakeable. I have never had any false impression."

Miss Julia Barnett confirms as follows :—

"81, Fitzwilliam Street, Huddersfield.

"Miss Barnett begs to say that she is able to bear testimony to the accuracy of the statements contained in Miss Jarry's letter, as she shared her room the night the strong impression of her sister's illness came over her, and, on awaking in the morning, received from her a vivid account of the distress she had endured whilst (as it appeared to her) her sister's attack lasted.

"Miss Barnett can also state that, on arriving at home, she learned from the elder Miss Jarry that the latter had really had an attack on the night, and at the hour, when the certainty of it was felt by her sister.   "JULIA BARNETT."

Here the noteworthy points are, of course, the sudden resolution to start homewards next morning, and the distinct and unaccountable cessation of the anxiety. But in both these last cases the percipient was aware that the supposed agent was in a state where the event surmised was not wholly improbable, which reduces the force of the evidence. There are many cases of sudden accident where this objection does not apply.

The following account is from Mrs. Muir, of 42, Holland Park, W.

"April 7th, 1885.

(47) "In the year 1849 I was staying in Edinburgh. One Sunday as I was dressing my second boy (aged 5 years) for church at about 10.30 a.m., he looked up at me and said, 'Mother, Cousin Janie is dead.' I asked him which Cousin Janie he meant, and he answered, 'Cousin Janie at the Cape, she's dead.' I then tried to make him explain why he thought so, but he only kept repeating the statement. This 'Cousin Janie' was a girl of about 16 who had been staying in Edinburgh, and had gone out to the Cape with her parents some months before. She had been very fond of my boys, and had often played with them. I was rather struck by the way the child kept repeating what he had said, and wrote down the day and the hour, and told my mother and sisters. Some time afterwards the Cape mail brought the news that the girl had died on that very Sunday. She had been badly burnt the night before, and had lingered on till a little after midday.   "ALICE MUIR."

In answer to questions, Mrs. Muir says :—

(1) "The child was not in the habit of saying odd things of this kind.

---

[1] We have received full accounts of these other cases; but as they occurred at a time when Miss Jarry was in distinct anxiety about her mother, they cannot be presented as evidence.

(2) " As to the kind of impression I could discover nothing.

(3) "I have no record in writing, but it is possible that my mother and sisters may remember the occurrence."

On November 25th, 1885, Miss M. A. Muir wrote :—

" All that we have gathered is that neither my grandmother nor my mother's two sisters have any distinct remembrance of the occurrence. The person who seemed to have been most impressed by it was a sister who died some years ago. I remember hearing her describe her feeling of wonder and awe, when the news came and they found the child's words were true."

Very similar is the following incident, of which the first account was sent to us by Mr. C. B. Curtis, of 9, East 54th Street, New York.

" November 20th, 1884.

(48) " The incident I have to relate occurred 18 years ago, the present month. My wife at the time was making a visit at the house of her sister, about 300 miles from this city, in the central part of the State of New York. Thirty miles distant a brother resided with his family, among them a son, David, about 12 years of age.

" One afternoon, my wife was sitting with her sister, while a child of the latter, a girl 3 years of age, was amusing itself with toys in another part of the room. Suddenly the child ceased its play and ran to my wife, exclaiming, ' Auntie, Davie's drowned.' Not being attended to at once, the child repeated the words ' Davie's drowned.' The aunt, thinking she had not heard correctly, asked the mother what the child said, when the words were again repeated. Nothing, however, was thought of the matter at the time, the mother simply saying the little one was probably only repeating what it had heard from some one.

" A few hours later a telegram was received, announcing that at just about the time these words were spoken, David, the child's cousin, with a brother, a year or two older, were drowned while skating 40 miles away.

" CHARLES B. CURTIS."

[The *Penn Yan Express* for January 9th, 1867, describes the accident as having occurred on the afternoon of January 2nd. Mr. Curtis is, therefore, not correct in saying that it occurred in November.]

On February 6th, 1885, Mr. Curtis sent us a copy of the following statement from his sister-in-law, Mrs. Ogden.

" Kings Ferry, New York.

"On the afternoon of January 2nd, 1867, my little daughter, Augusta, aged 3 years, was playing with her dolly, sitting near her aunt, who was spending the day at my house in Genoa, New York. Her little cousins, Darius and David Adams, aged 11 and 9 years, to the younger of whom she was tenderly attached, were living in Penn Yan, New York, 25 miles away. The cousins had not met since the preceding summer or early autumn.

" While busy with her play, the child suddenly spoke, and said, ' Auntie, Davie is drowned ! ' Her father who was present, and I, heard her distinctly. I answered, ' Gussie, what did you say?' She repeated the words, ' Davie is drowned!' Her aunt, who was not familiar with the childish accent, said, ' Gussie, I do not understand you '; when the child repeated for the third time, ' Auntie, Davie is drowned!' I chanced to look at the clock, and saw it was just 4.

" I immediately turned the conversation, as I did not wish such a painful thought fastened on the child's mind.

" I cannot recall that any allusion had been made to the boys that day; neither was I aware that my daughter even knew the meaning of the word *drowned*. She simply uttered the words without apparent knowledge of their import.

" That evening a telegram came from my brother, saying, ' My little boys, Darius and Davie, were drowned at 4 o'clock to-day while skating on Kenks Lake.'   " E. M. O."

The impression of a very young child, corresponding to such an accident as this, has far more force than that of an adult would generally have; for seasons when relatives are supposed to be skating or boating are likely times for nervous apprehensions, which will naturally now and then be fulfilled.[1] The following case ·is a strong one of its kind; since the coincidence appears to have been close to the hour, while the ground for nervousness, such as it was, extended over a good many days. The impression, moreover, seems to have been of a peculiarly definite and startling kind, being almost if not quite externalised as actual sound. The account is from the Rev. A. W. Arundel, who wrote from Colorado Springs, U.S.A., in 1884.

(49) " In the fall of 1875, I took a trip to Madison, Ohio, to Johnson's Island, Kelly's Island, and neighbouring points. There were nine of us in all, and our conveyance was a small sailing vessel. One Sunday morning we crossed from Cedar Point to Sandusky, in order to attend church. During the service a heavy storm came up, and when we went down to the landing, on our return, we found a pretty rough sea. We ventured, however, to try and get across, and in the end succeeded; but in the trial we

---

[1] To a person who is constitutionally free from nervousness, and who recognises the impression received as having been a unique one, such an incident will naturally seem more striking than it does to others. This description applies to Mrs. Rachel Tuckett, of Southwood Lawn, Highgate (a member of the Society of Friends), who tells us that on August 10th, 1878, she was impressed, in a way unknown in her previous experience, with a sense that some member of a party who had gone out on a steam yacht had fallen overboard. This accident had actually happened at that very time to her daughter (now Mrs. Green), who remembers her mother's mentioning the impression to her when she returned home, dripping wet.

We have a similar case from Mr. J. N. Maskelyne, the celebrated conjurer. When a boy he was nearly drowned. He says : " The last thing I could remember was a vivid picture of my home. I saw my mother, and could describe minutely where she sat, and what she was doing." This, however, would clearly not be evidence for telepathy, unless what the mother was doing was something very unusual, which does not seem to have been the case. But on Mr. Maskelyne's return home, though he concealed from her what had happened, " she questioned me closely, and said she felt strangely anxious about me, and thought some accident had befallen me." The percipient's first-hand testimony cannot, however be obtained. Nor have we any means of knowing the number of such maternal impressions about childish accidents that go unconfirmed.

had a very narrow escape. We had gone about halfway, when a very heavy gust of wind struck our little vessel, and turned her over on her side. The water rushed in, and it seemed almost impossible to keep her afloat. There we were clinging to the side that was still out of water, and expecting every moment to be swamped. By dint of almost superhuman effort, those who had sufficient presence of mind cut away all the sail we were carrying, and the boat righted just enough to allow the men to bale out some of the water. We managed, after one or two almost hopeless struggles, to get ashore. Now just at the moment of greatest danger, when escape seemed impossible, I thought of my wife and child a hundred miles away. I thought of them in a sort of agony, and felt that to leave them was impossible. If ever there was an unuttered cry for loved ones, it was at that moment. This was on the Sunday afternoon.

"I reached home on the following Saturday afternoon. Having to preach that Sunday, I held no conversation with my wife that morning, and it was not until Sunday after dinner that we had an opportunity for a chat. Just as I was about to commence an account of my trip, my wife said, 'By-the-way, I had a very peculiar experience last Sunday, just about this time. I was lying on the lounge, when all at once I had a startling impression that you wanted me, and even fancied I heard you call. I started up and listened, and went out on to the porch, and looked up and down the road, and acted altogether in a very agitated way.'

"This happened, as nearly as we could determine by comparing notes, at precisely the same hour that I was clinging to that side of the sinking boat, and facing what seemed to be the possibility of a watery grave. I do not believe it was coincidence. It must, I think, be explained in some other way.   "Alfred W. Arundel,
                                                        "Pastor 1st U.E. Church."

[For Mrs. Arundel's testimony, see the "Additions and Corrections."]

The next case is well-known, having been published in the *Life of Bishop Wilberforce*, Vol. I., p. 397.

(50) "The Bishop was in his library at Cuddesdon, with three or four of his clergy, writing with him at the same table. The Bishop suddenly raised his hand to his head, and exclaimed, 'I am certain that something has happened to one of my sons.' It afterwards transpired that just at that time his eldest son's foot (who was at sea) was badly crushed by an accident on board his ship. The Bishop himself records the circumstance in a letter to Miss Noel, dated March 4th, 1874; he writes: 'It is curious that at the time of his accident I was so possessed with the depressing consciousness of some evil having befallen my son Herbert, that at last on the third day after, the 13th, I wrote down that I was quite unable to shake off the impression that something had happened to him, and noted this down for remembrance.'"

[If the Bishop was correct in stating that he connected the impression at the time with the particular son who was hurt, the exclamation put into his mouth in the earlier part of the account is perhaps not exactly what he uttered. We have not been able to learn who were present at the scene. Here, as in other cases, I shall be most grateful for further testimony, should this book fall into the hands of anyone able to supply it.]

In the next case, though it seems certain that the percipient's experience was mentioned at the moment, we unfortunately cannot obtain her own account, or her friend's confirmation, as Mr. Smith has changed his residence, and we have failed to trace him. He was personally known to Professor Barrett, to whom the account was sent.

"Leslie Lodge, Ealing, W.

"October 10th, 1876.

(51) "I had left my house, 10 miles from London, in the morning as usual, and in the course of the day was on my way to Victoria Street, Westminster, having reached Buckingham Palace, when in attempting to cross the road, recently made muddy and slippery by the water cart, I fell, and was nearly run over by a carriage coming in the opposite direction. The fall and the fright shook me considerably, but beyond that I was uninjured. On reaching home I found my wife waiting anxiously, and this is what she related to me : She was occupied wiping a cup in the kitchen, which she suddenly dropped, exclaiming, 'My God ! he's hurt.' Mrs. S. who was near her heard the cry, and both agreed as to the details of time and so forth. I have often asked my wife why she cried out, but she is unable to explain the state of her feelings beyond saying, 'I don't know why ; I felt some great danger was near you.' These are simple facts, but other things more puzzling have happened in connection with the singular intuitions of my wife.   "T. W. SMITH."

As Mr. Smith was cognisant of his wife's distress, and probably heard her tale before informing her of what had befallen him, this evidence is practically first-hand (see p. 148); but it is incomplete, since, for aught we can tell, Mrs. Smith may have had similar alarms that did *not* correspond with reality—which would diminish the improbability of an accidental success.

There is a similar defect in the next piece of evidence—this time owing to the fact that M. Ollivier will not answer our letters. He probably thinks his own account sufficient, and does not see the importance, for our purposes, of fuller information.

"Janvier 20, 1883.

(52) "Le 10 octobre, 1881, je fus appelé pour service médical à la campagne à trois lieues de chez-moi. C'était au milieu de la nuit, une nuit très sombre. Je m'engageai dans un petit chemin creux, dominé par des arbres venant former une voute au dessus de la route. La nuit était si noire que je ne voyais pas à conduire mon cheval. Je laissai l'animal se diriger à son instinct. Il était environ 9 heures ; le sentier dans lequel je me trouvais en le moment était parsemé de grosses pierres rondes et présentait une pente très rapide. Le cheval allait au pas très lentement. Tout à coup, les pieds de devant de l'animal fléchissent et il tombe subitement, la bouche portant sur le sol. Je fus projeté naturellement par-dessus sa tête, mon épaule porta à terre, et je me fracturai une clavicule.

" En le moment même, ma femme, qui se déshabillait chez elle et se préparait à se mettre au lit, eut un pressentiment intime qu'il venait de m'arriver un accident ; un tremblement nerveux la saisit, elle se mit à pleurer et appelle la bonne. ' Venez vite, j'ai peur ; il est arrivé quelque malheur ; mon mari est mort ou blessé.' Jusqu'à mon arrivée elle retint la domestique près d'elle, et ne cessa de pleurer. Elle voulait envoyer un homme à ma recherche, mais elle ne savait pas dans quel village j'étais allé. Je rentrai chez moi vers 1 heure du matin. J'appela la domestique pour m'éclairer et desseller mon cheval. ' Je suis blessé,' dis-je, ' je ne puis bouger l'épaule.'

" Le pressentiment de ma femme était confirmé.

" Voilà, monsieur, les faits tels qu'ils se sont passés, et je suis très heureux de pouvoir vous les envoyer dans toute leur vérité.

" A. OLLIVIER,

" Médecin à Huelgoat, Finistère."

I have mentioned that occasionally, where the same percipient has had several such impressions, all of them are alleged to have corresponded with a real event—or (as we may say for brevity) to have been *veridical ;* and this special susceptibility, though often imagined or exaggerated, is more likely to have been correctly observed, if the impressions have been connected with marked incidents, befalling one or more members of the witness's immediate circle. We found such a percipient in Mrs. Gates, of 44, Montpelier Road, Brighton, who has given us several instances of the singular sympathy existing between herself and her children, and manifesting itself by marked disquiet at moments when they are in danger or pain, although she may have no means of knowing it.

To our inquiries whether she had ever noticed any failures, she said :—

" I cannot recall any occasion of my experiencing ominous sensations with regard to certain of my children that have been entirely groundless ; still, the results have been of less importance than my emotions presaged. For instance, on a certain evening, about three months ago, I was troubled about my son Ross. I received a letter, which he must have been writing while I was so nervous about him, and this is the postscript :—

" ' Excuse bad writing. I am feeling downright ill to-night, cold shivers, headache, and intense thirst. I think I'm in for a fever, &c., &c.'

" He had, however, no illness ; the feverish symptoms passed away.'

Now, this, of course, is quite unavailable as evidence ; but several such inconclusive incidents could hardly be held to *weaken* the force of more striking ones. Here, for instance, is a case where the coincident crisis was more sudden and serious.

" November 21st, 1882.

" My son Ross, a fine, tall young fellow, is musical attendant at an establishment for the mentally afflicted near Bath. Sitting with my

family, on Monday afternoon, I remarked to my son-in-law, Mr. Evelyn
Dering, 'I'm so unhappy this afternoon about Ross, I can think of
nothing but him. What a nuisance I am to people!' This morning I
received a letter from my son in which he says, 'I had a narrow escape on
Monday afternoon; one of our patients, named Rummell, attacked me with
a chair. After a close struggle, I managed to blow my whistle, and get
help from the next apartment. I was by myself with a large number of
men, the other attendants being out and on duty in other places; but
thank goodness I did not get hurt,' &c., &c. This, then, was happening
at the very time those singular feelings possessed me."

Mr. Evelyn Dering corroborates as follows :—

"5, Hova Villas, West Brighton.

"I write to confirm what Mrs. H. S. Gates gave you particulars of.
It was certainly previous to receiving the letter from her son Ross that
she expressed to me the painful anxiety she was suffering on his account."

The next instance is more definite still, and may be numbered as
an evidential case.

(53) "One August morning, in 1874 or 1875, at breakfast, the well-
known feeling stole over me. Waiting till all had left the table excepting
my second daughter, I remarked to her, 'I am feeling so restless about one
of my absent boys! It is ——; and I feel as if I was looking at blood!'"

The son in question, in a letter received a few days later, inquired of
Mrs. Gates as follows : "Write in your next if you had any presentiments
during last week. We were going to —— canal, fishing, and I got up at
the first sound of the bell, and taking my razor to shave, began to sharpen
it on my hand, and being, I suppose, only half awake, failed to turn the
razor, and cut a piece clean out of my left hand. An artery was cut in
two places, and bled dreadfully."

The fact of Mrs. Gates's alarm and vision of blood has been confirmed
to us independently by the daughter, Mrs. Darnley, to whom she described
it at the moment. The letter, which we have seen, was dated August 16th,
but without the year. The full description shows that the pain was
exceedingly severe, and that the writer had fainted.

§ 4. There is one interesting group of cases where the idea
apparently impressed on the percipient has been simply that of the
agent's approach. But here, again, great caution is necessary. Popular
opinion is extremely apt to invest presentiments of this sort with a
character to which they have no claim. Every day, probably, a large
number of people have a more or less strong impression, for which they
can assign no distinct reason, that some particular person is near them
or is coming to see them. That with some people such an impression
should prove correct often enough to be remarked on, is only what we
should naturally expect; and it is probable that the impression, when
apparently confirmed in this way, would look to memory more

definite and confident than it had really been. When it is always about the same person that the impression is felt, there is more *primâ facie* ground for supposing that it may be telepathic. But still the circumstances may make it quite unavailable as evidence. For instance, Mr. Rowland Rowlands, of Bryncethin, Bridgend, tells us that when he was manager of the Pen-y-graig Collieries, a man who was acting under him as foreman (since dead) had constantly to come to his house on business in the middle of the night.

"I was invariably aware of his coming, in dream, before he actually appeared, and would leave my bed and watch for him at the window. He himself noticed this, and told the other men that he never came but he found me at the window watching for him."

But those who are in the habit of being waked at night for a special purpose know the way in which the expectation will often haunt their dreams ; and in the absence of more definite assurance that the man was never expected when he did not come, and that he never came unexpected, accident is the reasonable explanation of the coincidences. Mrs. Wheeler, of 106, High Street, Oxford, tells us that in the summer of 1869, she had a similar impression " dozens of times " with respect to the coming of a friend from Iffley, and that it never played her false. But this friend was a constant visitor, and if she came thirty times in the course of a few months, and Mrs. Wheeler had the impression on six of these occasions (which is, perhaps, a fair scientific translation of " dozens "), accident again would easily account for the case. Mrs. Stella, of Chieri, Italy, tells us how, when she was ill years ago, a son, who was quartered six miles off, got away at night on five or six occasions, against rules and at considerable risk, to inquire about her at the lodge.

"Although unconscious and frequently delirious, I always knew when he came, and called him, showing signs of eagerness and restlessness. At first they treated it as pure raving on my part, but on inquiry they found that he had been there during the night."

This is a more plausible sample, since telepathic sensibility seems often heightened in illness; still, the necessary precision is wholly lacking. We have, however, stronger cases, of which a couple may be worth quoting here. The first is remarkable from the extreme improbability of the visit ; the second from the number of times in succession that the impression proved correct.

Miss M. E. Pritchard, of Tan-y-coed, Bangor, says :—

"January 30th, 1884.

(54) "One night, at 12 o'clock, I felt a conviction that a friend of ours, Mr. Jephson, was coming to see us very shortly.   I mentioned it to my sister, who merely said it was very improbable, as he must be on his way to Canada, as such was his intention when we had last seen him.

" It was greatly to her astonishment when he actually arrived next morning at 9 a.m.   When questioned as to the time of his arrival, we found it corresponded to the time of my remark, and, still more curious, he was then thinking of coming straight down to see us, but decided to wait till morning.   This was in March, 1880, as far as I can remember."

In reply to inquiries, Miss Pritchard adds :—

"February 7th, 1884.

" In reply to your question as to whether any other previous impressions had *not* turned out true, I think, as far as I can remember, any deep impression I have ever had as to anyone calling has invariably been true."

The following corroboration is from Miss Pritchard's sister :—

"Tan-y-coed, February 8th, 1884.

"I distinctly remember my sister telling me (at the time) of her impression that a friend was on his way to see us, which turned out to be the fact.—E. B. Pritchard."

Mr. Robert Castle, estate agent to many of the Oxford colleges, and well known to Mr. Podmore, writes as follows :—

"Oxford, 13th October, 1883.

(55) " In the years 1851 and 1852, when I was from 15 to 17 years of age, I was left in charge of a considerable extent of building and other estate work at Didcot, Berks, at which some 50 or 60 men were employed ; and for so young a person a good deal of responsibility was put upon me, as I was only visited occasionally, about once a fortnight on an average, by one of the seniors responsible for the work.

" Occasionally this senior was my brother Joseph, about eight years older than myself, and who had always taken, even for a brother, a very great deal of interest in my welfare, and between whom and myself a very strong sympathy existed.

" I was very rarely apprised by letter of these visits, but almost invariably before my brother came (sometimes the day before, at other times at some previous hour on the same day) it would suddenly come into my mind as a quite clear and certain thing, how, I cannot say, that my brother was coming to see me, and would arrive about a certain hour, sometimes in the morning and sometimes in the afternoon, and I cannot remember a single occasion on which I had received one of these vivid impressions, on which he did not arrive as expected.

" I had, without thinking particularly about it, got to act upon the faith of these impressions as much as if I had received a letter ; and the singularity of the occurrence was not brought very forcibly to my own mind until one day when the foreman asked me to give him instructions as to how a portion of the work should be carried out—when I answered him quite naturally, ' Oh, leave it to-day, Joe will be here about 4 o'clock this afternoon, and I would rather wait and ask his advice about it.'

" The foreman, who had access to my office, and usually knew what letters I received, said, ' Perhaps it would be as well, but I didn't know that you had received a letter from Oxford.'

" I had to explain to him that I had not received a letter, and that it was merely by an impression I knew my brother was coming, and upon this I got a hearty laugh only for my credulity.

" As my brother turned up all right at the time named, the foreman would not be convinced that I had not been playing a trick upon him, and that I had not received a letter and put it away so that he might not know of it.

" The strangeness of the matter then induced me to arrange with the foreman always to let him know, as soon as I might have the opportunity, of the occurrence of these impressions, so that he might check them as well as myself ; and he, although he gave up all attempts to explain the singularity of the thing, came afterwards to trust the certainty of their being right as much as I did myself.

" I told my brother of them, who was very much puzzled, and could not account for so strange an occurrence; but on comparing my statements as to the time when the impressions occurred to me, in a number of cases, he said that, so far as he could check the time, it would seem to have been always at or about the time when he first received his instructions, or knew of the arrangement having been made for him to come.

" As both the foreman and my brother have been dead for some years past, I have no means of comparing their recollections of these matters with my own.

" Perhaps I should add that my brother was living at Oxford at the time, 10 miles or so from Didcot; and that although I was visited from time to time by other gentlemen beside my brother, I cannot remember having had these previous impressions in any case except his.

" ROBERT CASTLE."

Here real pains seem to have been taken to test the phenomenon fairly ; but the case is rather remote, and it is very unfortunate that no notes were taken at the time. Some further specimens will be found in the Supplement; and parallel cases where there was an actual sensory impression of the person about to arrive will be found in Chap. XIV., § 7.

§ 5. So far, the impressions that corresponded with real events have all been ideas of a more or less abstract kind ; the *fact* was realised, but no image of the actual *scene* was called up in the percipient's mind. We now come to a series of more concrete impressions—still belonging, however, to the non-sensory family ; for though they have evoked sensory images with more or less distinctness, they have not suggested to the percipient any actual affection of the senses. And they continue to present this marked point of analogy to the results of experimental thought-transference, that the images or the scene evoked before the percipient's mind reflected (either wholly or in great part) the images or scene with which the agent's attention was actually occupied.

In alleged transferences of this distinct and detailed sort, it is, of course, essential to the evidence that the scene with which the percipient is inwardly impressed should not be one that might, in the ordinary course of things, have been pictured correctly, or with sufficient correctness for the description to seem applicable. The tendency to make the most of such correspondences must here be carefully borne in mind. For instance, a lady of our acquaintance communicated the following experience. An old friend of hers in Wales had been earnestly longing to receive the Communion on a particular Sunday, but was prevented by illness. On this Sunday, our informant, who was in London, and who was unaware of her friend's desire, and had never seen the church—

" Had a vision of her sitting quietly in her place in the little village church, waiting to receive the rite. The church was evidently much neglected, and the floor and the matting were thickly covered with dust. On inquiry, I was assured that such was the condition of the church. The phantasm appeared as really present at the spot to which my friend's desire had focussed her thoughts."

But here, it will be seen, the one detail that the narrator (who was much given to *visualising*) would not have been quite likely to imagine spontaneously, was the dusty condition of the church. Even that is a doubtful exception; and it is moreover a point which would be very likely to get unconsciously worked into the vision *after* the actual state of the case was learnt. The following cases seem to be free from these objections. The first shall be another specimen from the remarkable series of impressions which have been experienced by Mr. J. G. Keulemans (see pp. 126 and 235).

"November, 1882.

(56) " One morning, not long ago, while engaged with some very easy work, I saw in my mind's eye a little wicker basket, containing five eggs, two very clean, of a more than usually elongated oval and of a yellowish hue, one very round, plain white, but smudged all over with dirt ; the remaining two bore no peculiar marks. I asked myself what that insignificant but sudden image could mean. I never think of similar objects. But that basket remained fixed in my mind, and occupied it for some moments. About two hours later I went into another room for lunch. I was at once

struck with the remarkable similarity between the eggs standing in the egg-cups on the breakfast table, and those two very long ones I had in my imagination previously seen. 'Why do you keep looking at those eggs so carefully ?' asked my wife ; and it caused her great astonishment to learn from me how many eggs had been sent by her mother half an hour before. She then brought up the remaining three ; there was the one with the dirt on it, and the basket, the same I had seen. On further inquiry, I found that the eggs had been kept together by my mother-in-law, that she had placed them in the basket and thought of sending them to me ; and, to use her own words,' I did of course think of you at that moment.' She did this at 10 in the morning, which (as I know from my regular habits) must have been just the time of my impression.   " J. G. KEULEMANS."

Mrs. Keulemans tells us that she has almost forgotten the incident. " All I can say is that my husband looked at some eggs and made the remark that he had seen them before. I know he told me my mother had sent them."

Here the very triviality of this incident, as well as the smallness and definiteness of the object visualised, makes the resemblance to cases of experimental thought-transference specially close.[1]

In the examples which follow, the idea of something less circumscribed than a single object, and more of the nature of a complete scene, seems to have been transmitted. I will begin with a case where the visualisation, if there was any, was extremely vague. Miss M. E. Pritchard, Tan-y-coed, Bangor, (the contributor of case 54 above,) writes :—   "January 30th, 1884.

(57) " Two years ago I awoke, one night, with a curious sensation of being in a sick room, and of the presence of people who were anxiously watching the bedside of some person, who was dangerously ill. It was not till some time after that we heard that one of the sisters, then living in Florida, had been very ill of a fever, and was at the time of the incident in a most critical state.   " MAGGIE E. PRITCHARD."

In reply to inquiries, Miss Pritchard adds :—

" I have never had any other experience of an impression of sickness or death.

" The impression of sickness was not the continuation of a dream, and hardly a distinct waking impression. I woke from a heavy sleep with a

---

[1] Mr. Keulemans is a trained observer, and has made a careful study of his peculiar mental pictures, the subjects of which range from single objects, as in the above case, to complete scenes. He says: "They are always marked by a strange sensation. There is no attempt on my part to conjure them up—on the contrary, they come quite suddenly and unexpectedly, binding my thoughts so fixedly to the subject as to render all external influences imperceptible. Whenever I took the trouble to ascertain whether my impressions corresponded to real events, I found them invariably to do so, even in the most minute details." But his cases naturally differ in their evidential force. He tells us, for instance, that on New Year's Eve, 1881, he had a vivid picture of his family circle in Holland, but missed from the group his youngest sister, a child of 14, whose absence from home on such an occasion was most improbable. He wrote at once to ask if this sister was ill ; but the answer was that, contrary to all precedent, she had been away from home. This may plainly have been an accidental coincidence.

great sense of oppression, which gradually seemed to assume a distinct impression. It lasted about half an hour, that is the actual impression, but I had a great feeling of uneasiness for several days. I have never had any hallucinations or dreams of death."

The following corroboration is from Miss Pritchard's sister :—

"February 8th, 1884.

"I recollect my sister telling me of her feeling of being in a sick room with people watching round a bedside. She did not mention it to me till the morning (it occurred during the night). It did not make much impression on me at the time—not till afterwards, when we heard of our sister's dangerous illness. "E. B. PRITCHARD."

The next instance is somewhat more definite. It is from Mr. John Hopkins, of 23, King Street, Carmarthen.

"May 2nd, 1884.

(58) "One evening, in the early spring of last year (1883), as I was retiring to bed, and whilst I was in the full enjoyment of good health and active senses—I distinctly saw my mother and my younger sister crying. I was here in Carmarthen, and they were away in Monmouthshire, 80 miles distant. They distinctly appeared to me to be giving way to grief, and I was at once positive that some domestic bereavement had taken place. I said to myself, 'I shall hear something of this in the morning.' When the morning came, the first thing which was handed to me was a letter from my father in Monmouthshire, stating that they had, on the day of writing, had intelligence that my nephew had just died. The little boy was the son of my elder sister, living in North Devon. There was no doubt but that my mother and younger sister had both given way to grief on the day of my strange illusion, and it was in some mysterious manner communicated to my mind—together with a certain presentiment that I was on the eve of intelligence of a death in the family. I thought it most probable, though, that the imaginative faculty added—in a purely local manner—the idea of speedy intelligence to the communication which the mind received in some way from Monmouthshire.

"It was the only occurrence of the sort I have ever experienced.

"JOHN HOPKINS."

In answer to inquiries, Mr. Hopkins writes, on May 15, 1884 :—

"I, at Carmarthen, had news on the following morning, as I thoroughly expected to, of a death—that of a nephew. I had no opportunity of mentioning the circumstance to anyone before the letter came. I am sorry to say, too, that I have destroyed the letter.

"As to the reality of the scene in my mind—speaking as correctly as I can at this distance of time from the occurrence (about a year ago)— I don't think the affair did produce a picture on my mind *more* vivid than might have been summoned there by closing the eyes and putting some strain upon the imagination. It certainly did not make the outward eye fancy it saw something, as the Bishop of Carlisle has suggested may be the case in some instances. But there was this peculiarity. The scene was impressed upon my mind without closing of the eyes or any other

S

inducement to absent-mindedness, and without the *imagination* from myself, so far as I can say, going out in that direction. It was also more firmly rivetted upon my mind than any passing, or what one may term accidental, impression would be. It was *fixed* there. I could not get rid of it, and I felt certain it meant something, which it certainly did.

"Although the *locale* was familiar to me, I don't think there had been more wanderings of memory to it than to other places I knew, and the state of grief which my relatives were in may be said to have been the only exceptional feature."

In conversation with Mr. Hopkins, I learnt that his father, mother, and younger sister were the only three relatives at home ; and that his impression as to the grief of the two latter resulted in apprehension about his father—led him, that is, to a wrong guess. On the other hand I am sure, from his account, that the impression itself was of a very strong and peculiar kind.

The scene, however, sometimes makes a much more vivid impression than this. Here are a couple more cases from the rather considerable group where the event that befalls the agent is either death or a near approach to death by drowning. One example of this sort has already occurred (p. 246) ; and their number altogether is sufficient to suggest that this particular condition on the agent's part is, for some unknown reason, a specially favourable one for the generation of the telepathic impulse.

The following account is from Mrs. Paris (*née* Griffiths), of 33, High Street, Lowestoft.

"April 30th, 1884.

(59) "We were a family of eight. Twenty years ago we were all at home but one, H. This was by no arrangement, but by what seemed a series of coincidences. H. was to join us on Wednesday, August 3rd, to leave his situation, and spend a few days at home before entering on his new one. On the Sunday previous to his coming we had been to church—I for the first time after a protracted illness. My sister was too much occupied with her infant niece, and had not been with us. We met my sister's friend, Miss J., a Russian lady, highly accomplished, and very intelligent. She walked home with us, and we insisted on her staying to our early dinner. My sister was delighted to have her to recount the precocious charms of our infantile treasure. It was a very pleasant morning,

"I have given these details rather minutely to show that there was nothing in the surrounding circumstances to cause depression. My sister was in good health, even better than usual. Well, we had gone through the first course, the second was being placed on the table, when Miss J. asked 'Where is Marianne ?'—my sister. My mother remarked that she had left the room some minutes since, and did not seem well. I immediately went out, and after looking all through the house and not finding her, went into the garden. There I found her sitting with her head resting on her hands, looking into what was called the 'quarry'—an unused working, then and for years before flooded. From where she sat she could see the water looking so still and black. She was quite unaware of my presence. I put my hands on her shoulders, and asked, ' What is the matter ?' She evidently neither felt nor heard me. I then went to her side and shall never forget the expression of her face. She looked perfectly paralysed with fear and horror. Her eyes seemed rivetted to that water, as if she was witnessing an awful scene, and could give no help. ' *What* is the matter, my dear ?' She was still insensible to my presence and touch. In a few seconds she gave such a cry of suppressed agony and said,' ' Oh, he's gone.' She then seemed to become aware of my presence and turned a look of agonised entreaty on me, and yet there was a little relief. Presently she said, 'Oh, J., do go away and leave me.' I begged her to come in, and then as if she could bear it no longer she said, ' Oh, J., he's gone. Oh, God, he's gone, my poor dear H.' I begged her not to restrain herself so terribly, but to tell me what was wrong. Very slowly, as if it cost her unspeakable suffering, she said, 'There is something terrible taking place.' I lightly answered, ' Of course, that is true all the year round. When is the moment but that some soul is meeting its Author?' She shivered, and after a good deal of persuasion she returned with me into the room—*she* evidently not wishing to excite or trouble me. I thought no more of it. Miss J. had gone with her to her room and had insisted on her lying down, and induced her to relieve herself by telling her, Miss J., all about it. *She* was so much impressed with what she had heard that she left my sister, promising to return after afternoon service.

"At about 3 o'clock that afternoon, we received the news of the death of our dear H. by drowning. He was on his way to church with the other members of the choir. Tempted by the delightful weather, and the inviting look of the water, several of them proposed a ' dip,' 'just one for the last time, H.' He complied, was first in, and had only gone into water up to his knees, when he called out that he was drowning. His companions were panic-stricken, and declared afterwards that they could not move. One at last recovered presence of mind sufficient to shout, and then to run the short distance to the church, and called out, ' G., H. is drowning, come, quick.' G. rushed out, undressing as he went, and throwing his clothes along the road, jumped in, and would undoubtedly have saved him, but H. clutched hold of him, and they both sank to rise no more, just a few minutes before 2 o'clock, and at the moment my sister called out, ' He's gone.'

" We found her in a deep sleep, looking years older, but quite prepared for the news, for when my brother roused her, she said, ' Have they come? They have not brought him home yet, have they?' Miss J. came, seemingly quite prepared to hear of our sorrow. She told me afterwards that my sister had described the scene and the place, although she had certainly never been there. There was no precedent for his bathing on Sunday, nothing to suggest to her mind the possibility of his doing so.

" Had I been the recipient of this 'warning,' 'presentiment,' 'revelation,' or whatever it may be called, weakness and consequent nervousness might have been urged as a predisposing cause, but it could not be urged in my sister's case. She was twenty-seven at the time, and we have always been pronounced 'sensible women with no nonsense about them.' "

In answer to inquiries, Mrs. Paris writes, on May 10, 1884 :—
" My sister and Miss J. are both dead. . . . In answer to your
next inquiry I have written to my father to ask the questions as to the
distance, &c. He thinks ' Bo'ness,' where the accident took place, was
about 13 or 14 miles from Blackhall (where the family were then residing).
I think I said 3 o'clock the news reached us. He puts it a little later. As
to the character of the water, it was the Firth of Forth ; but I know
nothing of the place. My father says there was a steep place, caused by
water running in from an engine in connection with Mr. Wilson's works
there, and that H. got into that deep pool. The time of afternoon service
was from 2 till 3.30. Perhaps you know that in the Scotch churches
there is only a short interval between the services. My brother was nearly
19. As to there being any special reason why my sister should have had
the experience rather than myself, there are, to my mind, two. First, she
was of a much more contemplative cast of mind. She was dreamy, I very
active. But the second is, to my mind, the most powerful reason in
this instance. You will have observed in all large families the members
pair off, on the principle of like drawing to like, I suppose. She and H.
paired off.   "JANE PARIS."

The *Airdrie Advertiser* for Saturday, August 6th, 1864, confirms the
fact that the accident took place on the afternoon of the previous Sunday.

In conversation, Mrs. Paris told me of another apparently veridical
impression which her sister mentioned to her at the time of its occurrence,
relating to the death of a cousin who was drowned at sea.

The following case is given on the authority of the late Dr.
Goodall Jones, of 6, Prince Edwin Street, Liverpool; and as he
was not only made cognisant of the percipient's impression immediately after its occurrence, but also actually saw the percipient in the
state of excitement which the impression had produced, and many
hours before the coincident event had been heard of, his account may
be taken as on a level with first-hand evidence, and perhaps even
in this particular instance as preferable to first-hand evidence. Dr.
Jones wrote to us :—

"November 28th, 1883.
(60) " Mrs. Jones, wife of William Jones, a Liverpool pilot, living at
46, Virgil Street [since removed to 15, St. George's Street, Everton], was
confined on Saturday, February 27th, 1869. On my calling next day,
Sunday, February 28th, at 3 p.m., her husband met me, saying he was
just coming for me, his wife was delirious. He said that about half-an-
hour before, he was reading in her room, when she suddenly woke up from
a sound sleep, saying that her brother, William Roulands (also a Liverpool
pilot), was drowning in the river (Mersey). Her husband tried to soothe
her by telling her that Roulands was on his station outside, and could
not be in the river at the time. She, however, persisted that she had *seen*
him drowning. News arrived in the evening that about the time named,
2.30 p.m., Roulands was drowned. There was a heavy gale outside ; the
pilot boat was unable to put a pilot on board an inward-bound ship, and

had to lead the way in. When *in* the river, opposite the rock lighthouse, another attempt was made, but the small boat upset, and Roulands and another pilot were drowned. When Mrs. Jones was informed of his death she calmed down, and made a good recovery."

The following two cases differ from most of the preceding, in that the condition of the agent was only slightly abnormal, and the probability that the impressions of the percipients were telepathic rests entirely on the exactitude of detail in the correspondence. The first is from Mr. and Mrs. Wilson, of Wale House, Winding Road, Halifax.

"May, 1884.

(61) "About the year 1858, on a Sunday afternoon, as I sat with my wife by my fireside in Halifax (my brothers Tom and George having gone to Africa), in awaking from a nap, I saw my brothers in Portugal [1] in a row in the street over a dog which I saw Tom take by the tail, and, with a swing round, pitch over a bridge into the water. I told my wife what I had seen, and the impression was so strong that I wrote the particulars, together with the date, with a pencil on the cupboard door. In about a month after, I had a letter from my brothers stating that they had arrived safely in Africa, and mentioning that on their way they called at Lisbon, and there got into a row through Tom's throwing a dog over a bridge into the water, and that they had narrowly escaped getting locked up about it. The information contained in the letter showed also that the time of the incident corresponded exactly to the time of my vision.

"JOHN AMBLER WILSON."

"The foregoing statement is quite true.—SARAH ANN WILSON."

In answer to inquiries, Mr. Wilson says :—

"March 30th, 1885.

"I did not know that my brothers were likely to go near Lisbon. I do not remember either churches or ships. I was standing on a bridge over a river, and all along, so far as I saw, were woodyards with wooden workshops. With regard to the letter in which my brother spoke of the accident, I never keep letters."

The following is from a daughter of Mr. Wilson :—

"Heath Villas, Halifax.
"April 12th, 1885.

"I remember, when a child, seeing my father start up, open the cupboard door, and write there something which he had just related to my mother that he had seen in a vision. And I remember that a letter came from my uncles, which was said to confirm the truth of the vision. I have often heard the particulars referred to by my father since.

"ANNIE S. OAKES."

The next case is much fuller of detail. The name of the narrator, Mrs. L., is only withheld from publication because her friends would

---

[1] It is not meant that the idea of Portugal formed part of Mr. Wilson's impression.

object to its appearance. She has had other similar experiences, but the following is the only one that she can accurately recall.

"January, 1885.

(62) " Some years ago, the writer, when recovering from an illness, had a remarkable experience of 'second-sight.' It was thus :—

"A friend had been invited to dinner, whom the writer was most anxious to consult on a subject of grave anxiety. At 7 o'clock the servant came to ask, 'If dinner should be served or not, as the guest had not arrived.'

"The writer said at once, and without hesitation, 'No, put off the dinner till 8 o'clock. Mr. A. will arrive at —— Station by 7.45 train ; send the carriage there to meet him.'

"The writer's husband, surprised at this announcement, said, 'Why did you not tell us this before, and when did Mr. A. let you know of the delay in his arrival ?'

"The writer then explained that there had been no intimation from Mr. A., but that as she had been lying there, on the couch, and anxiously hoping to see her guest, she had had a distinct vision of him, at a certain place (mentioning the name of the town) ; that she had seen him going over a 'House to Let' ; that, having missed the train and also the ferry, he had crossed the river in a small boat and scrambled up the steep bank, tripping in doing so, and that he had run across a ploughed field, taking up the train at a side station, which would arrive at —— at a quarter to 8 p.m.

"The writer gave all these particulars without any sort of mental effort, and felt surprised herself at the time that they should arise to her mind and tongue.

" Presently Mr. A. arrived full of apologies, and surprised beyond measure to find his friend's carriage awaiting him at the station. He then went on to explain that he had had that morning quite suddenly taken it into his head to leave town for ——, and finding it so fresh and healthy a place, he had been tempted to look over some houses to let, hoping to be able to get one for a few weeks in the season ; that he had lost time in doing this, and missed both train and ferry ; that he had bribed a small boat to row him over ; that in getting up the side bank, he fell, which delayed him again, but that he had just contrived to catch the train at a siding, by running breathless over a field ; that he had intended to telegraph on arriving at the station, but, meeting the carriage there, he had felt bound to come on, to explain and apologise, in spite of delay, and 'morning dress,' &c., &c."

The following is a letter from Mr. A. to Mrs. L. :—

"February 16th, 1885.

" DEAR MRS. L.,—Anent that Indian incident, your seeing me, and what I was doing at Barrackpore one evening, you yourself being in Calcutta at the time.

" It is now so long ago, 13 years, I think, that I cannot recall all the circumstances, but I do remember generally.

" I left home one morning without the intention of going from Calcutta during the day, but I did go from Calcutta to Barrackpore and spent some time in looking through the bungalows to let.

"I remember I crossed in a small boat—not by the ferry, and my impression is that I did not land at the usual jetty, but, instead, at the bank opposite the houses which I wished to see.

"I missed the train by which I would ordinarily have travelled, and consequently arrived in Calcutta considerably later than your usual dinner-hour.

" I cannot remember distinctly that I found any gharry at the Barrackpore train, Calcutta Station, but you may probably remember whether you sent the gharry ; but I do remember my astonishment that you had put back dinner against my return from Barrackpore by that particular train, you having had no previous direct knowledge of my having gone to Barrackpore at all.

"I remember, too, your telling me generally what I had been doing at Barrackpore, and how I had missed the earlier train. And on my inquiry, 'How on earth do you know these things?' you said, 'I saw you.' Expecting me by that train, I can quite understand your having sent the carriage for me, although that particular item is not clearly on my memory.

"I can well remember that at the time of the incident you were in a very delicate state of health.

"Do you remember that other occasion in Calcutta, a holiday, when Mrs. —— called, I being out, and on her inquiring for me your informing her that I had gone to the bootmakers and the hatters, you having had no previous intimation from me of any such intention on my part? and our astonishment and amusement when I did a little later turn up, a new hat in my hand, and fresh from registering an order at the bootmakers ?

" These have always appeared to me very extraordinary incidents, and the first, especially, incapable of explanation in an ordinary way."

Mrs. L. recollects the other incident referred to, but she is not inclined to think it of much importance.

She adds :—

" The river crossed was the Hooghly from Serampore to Barrackpore, where the house was situated which Mr. A. looked over. The station he arrived at was in Calcutta, I think called the South Eastern, but of this I am not sure."

The next account is from a lady who is an active philanthropist, and as practical and unvisionary a person as could be found. She has no special interest in our work, and withholds her name on the ground that her friends would dislike or despise the subject. This is one of the ways in which the present state of thought and feeling often prevents the facts from having their legitimate force.

" May 9th, 1883.

(63) " It happened one Tuesday last January. I was going to start for one of my usual visits to Southampton. In the morning I received a letter from a friend saying he was going to hunt that day, and would write next day, so that I should get the letter on my return home. In the train, being tired, I put down my book and shut my eyes, and presently the

whole scene suddenly occurred before me—a hunting field and two men riding up to jump a low stone wall. My friend's horse rushed at it, could not clear it, and blundered on to his head, throwing off his rider, and the whole scene vanished. I was wide awake the whole time. My friend is a great rider, and there was no reason why such an accident should have befallen him. Directly I arrived at Southampton I wrote to him, simply saying I knew he had had a fall, and hoped he was not hurt. On my return late on Wednesday night, not finding the promised letter, I wrote a few lines, merely saying I should expect to hear all about his *spill* next day, and I mentioned to two people that evening on my return what I had seen ; also that Tuesday evening, dining with friends, I spoke of what had happened in the train, and they all promptly laughed at me. On Thursday morning I received a letter from my friend, telling me he had had a fall, riding at a low stone wall, that the horse had not been able to clear it, and had blundered on to his head, that he was not much hurt, and had later on remounted. He had not, when he wrote, received either of my letters, as my Tuesday one only arrived in Scotland on Thursday morning, and my Wednesday one on Friday. When he received my letters, he only declared I must have been asleep. Nothing of the sort ever happened to me before or since. It all seemed very natural and did not alarm me.   " H. G. B."

In answer to inquiries, Mrs. B. adds :—

" My friend, who is a hard-headed Scotchman, declined to say another word about it. All I know is that there were two horsemen riding up to the same spot."

In a personal interview, Mrs. B. told the present writer that her vision took place about 3 o'clock in the afternoon, and that she had heard from her friend that his accident took place "after lunch." She had no idea of *disaster*, and felt sure he was not much hurt. She cannot say whether her eyes were open or shut, but is certain that the experience was an altogether unique one.

Very similar to this incident is the following, which seems to take us up to the very furthest point where the experience can still be described as a mental picture. The percipient herself might have been puzzled to say afterwards whether the vision had or had not seemed to engage her bodily eye. (Compare the parallel quasi-auditory impression above, case 49.) The account is in Sir —— L.'s own words. His reason for withholding his name is Lady L.'s dislike of the subject.

(64) "Some time ago Mr. and Mrs. [now Sir — and Lady] L. were at his father's country house at S., where they generally spent the autumn. Mrs. L. was not feeling well, and lay on the sofa or bed all the day.

"About 11 o'clock Mr. L. told her he was going to drive *in the dog-cart* to the neighbouring town, about nine miles off. This was not an unusual thing, and he left her to go. Some four or five hours afterwards, on his return home, he went straight up to her room to see how she was, and found her greatly disturbed. She said, ' Oh, I am so glad to see you back ;

I have had such a horrid fright, a sort of dream, or rather vision, for I was not asleep.   I thought I saw you run away with ; but it was quite absurd, for I knew you were in the dog-cart, and *I fancied I saw two horses.*'   Mr. L. inquired when she saw it, and she said about an hour ago.

"Now the facts were these : On leaving Mrs. L. about 11 that morning, Mr. L.'s father said he would accompany him, and Mr. L. accordingly counter-ordered the dog-cart and ordered a phaeton and pair, but naturally he did not think of telling Mrs. L. of the change of plan. Coming out of the town, Mr. L. was driving, and they *were run away with*, one of the horses having bolted, and for about 200 yards or more it was found impossible to stop the horses, when an intervening hill gave them the opportunity.   The time when this happened, as nearly as possible, coincided with the time when Mrs. L. saw what she described as a *vision, not a dream*, and the detail as to the two horses is remarkable, because Mrs. L. was ignorant of the change of plan."

In answer to inquiries, Sir — L. adds :—

"September 15th, 1884.

" The narrative has often been told by me in my wife's presence, and there can be no discrepancy or doubt.   It is a true and circumstantial account of what happened, about 1866 or 1867, I think."

We received the next account through the kindness of Mr. J. Bradley Dyne, of 2, New Square, Lincoln's Inn.   The incident took place in his house at Highgate, and the narrator is his sister-in-law. The case brings us again to the very verge of actual sensory hallucination.   It seems also to be an extreme instance of a *deferred* or a *latent* telepathic impression—the death of the agent (allowing for longitude) having preceded the percipient's experience by about 10 hours.   This feature does not seem specially surprising, when we remember how actual impressions of sense may pass unnoted, and yet emerge into consciousness hours afterwards, either in dream or in some moment of silence or *recueillement.*   (See above, pp. 201-2.)

" 1883.

(65) " I had known Mr. —— as a medical man, under whose treatment I had been for some years, and at whose hands I had experienced great kindness.   He had ceased to attend me for considerably more than a year at the time of his death.   I was aware that he had given up practice, but beyond that I knew nothing of his proceedings, or of the state of his health.   At the time I last saw him, he appeared particularly well, and even made some remark himself as to the amount of vigour and work left in him.

" On Thursday, the 16th day of December, 1875, I had been for some little time on a visit at my brother-in-law's and sister's house near London. I was in good health, but from the morning and throughout the day I felt unaccountably depressed and out of spirits, which I attributed to the gloominess of the weather.   A short time after lunch, about 2 o'clock, I thought I would go up to the nursery to amuse myself with the children, and try to recover my spirits.   The attempt failed, and I returned to the dining-room, where I sat by myself, my sister being engaged elsewhere. The thought of Mr. —— came into my mind, and suddenly, with my eyes open, as I believe, for I was not feeling sleepy, I seemed to be in a room in which a man was lying dead in a small bed.   I recognised the face at once as that of Mr. ——, and felt no doubt that he was dead, and not asleep only.   The room appeared to be bare and without carpet or furniture.   I cannot say how long the appearance lasted.   I did not mention the appearance to my sister or brother-in-law at the time.   I tried to argue with myself that there could be nothing in what I had seen, chiefly on the ground that from what I knew of Mr. ——'s circumstances it was most improbable that, if dead, he would be in a room in so bare and unfurnished a state.   Two days afterwards, on December 18th, I left my sister's house for home.   About a week after my arrival, another of my sisters read out of the daily papers the announcement of Mr. ——'s death, which had taken place abroad, and on December 16th, the day on which I had seen the appearance.

"I have since been informed that Mr. —— had died in a small village hospital in a warm foreign climate, having been suddenly attacked with illness whilst on his travels."

In answer to an inquiry Mr. Dyne says :—

"My sister-in-law tells me that the occasion which I mentioned to you is absolutely the only one on which she has seen any vision of the kind."

We learn from Mr. ——'s widow that the room in which he died fairly corresponded with the above description, and that the hour of death was 3.30 a.m.

These latter narratives might suggest a sort of incipient *clairvoyance*.[1]   But in the present state of our knowledge, it would be rash to ascribe any phenomenon to independent clairvoyance, which could by any possibility be regarded as telepathic ; for the simple reason that the phenomena on record which (if correctly reported) must beyond doubt have been due to independent clairvoyance, are extremely rare in comparison with those which, if correctly reported, can be accounted for by thought-transference.   Thus in the last example—granting the possibility of deferred impressions—there is no difficulty in connecting the idea of the room, and even the idea of actual death, with the perceptions and thoughts of the dying man.   It would be inconvenient, however, to refuse the term *clairvoyance* to cases where telepathic action reaches such a pitch that the percipient seems actually to be using the senses of some person or persons at the distant scene.   And it will perhaps suffice to save confusion, if I note at once the difference between clairvoyance of this extreme telepathic type (which is still fairly

_____
[1] As regards the appearance of the agent's own figure in the scene, see the remarks on some parallel dream-cases, Chap. viii., Part ii., end of § 5.

within the scope of this book), and any supposed extension, for which no conditioning "agency" can be assigned, of the percipient's own senses.

Among the cases to be here quoted, none perhaps strains the hypothesis of a conditioning "agency" more than the following. It is from a Fellow of the College of Physicians, who fears professional injury if he were "supposed to defend opinions at variance with general scientific belief," and does not therefore allow his name to appear. He is candid enough to admit that if every one argued as he does, "progress would be impossible."

"May 20th, 1884.

(66) "Twenty years ago [abroad] I had a patient, wife of a parson. She had a peculiar kind of delirium which did not belong to her disease, and perplexed me. The house in which she lived was closed at midnight, that is, the outer door had no bell. One night I saw her at 9. When I came home I said to my wife, 'I don't understand that case; I wish I could get into the house late.' We went to bed rather early. At about 1 o'clock I got up. She said, 'What are you about; are you not well?' I said, 'Perfectly so.' 'Then why get up?'. 'Because I can get into that house.' 'How, if it is shut up?' 'I see the proprietor standing under the lamp-post this side of the bridge, with another man.' 'You have been dreaming.' 'No, I have been wide awake; but dreaming or waking, I mean to try.' I started with the firm conviction that I should find the individual in question. Sure enough there he was under the lamp-post, talking to a friend. I asked him if he was going home. (I knew him very well.) He said he was, so I told him I was going to see a patient, and would accompany him. I was positively ashamed to explain matters; it seemed so absurd that I knew he would not believe me. On arriving at the house I said, 'Now I am here, I will drop in and see my patient.' On entering the room I found the maid giving her a tumbler of strong grog. The case was clear; it was as I suspected—delirium from drink. The next day I delicately spoke to the husband about it. He denied it, and in the afternoon I received a note requesting me not to repeat the visits. Three weeks ago I was recounting the story and mentioned the name. A lady present said : 'That is the name of the clergyman in my parish, at B., and his wife is in a lunatic asylum from drink!'"

In conversation with the present writer, the narrator explained that the vision—though giving an impression of externality and seen, as he believes, with open eyes—was not definitely located in space. He had never encountered the proprietor on the spot where he saw him, and it was not a likely thing that he should be standing talking in the streets at so late an hour.

This is certainly a perplexing incident. But if we regard it as more than an accidental coincidence, we can hardly help supposing that the connection between the proprietor of the house and the desire with which the physician was preoccupied was at any rate one of the conditions which enabled the proximity of the former to affect the latter; so that we may still be within the limits of telepathic communication between mind and mind.

I had hoped to conclude this chapter with a case showing how a special condition of the percipient's mind may open the door (so to speak) to a telepathic impression, and also exemplifying the occurrence of a series of these vivid mental pictures to a single percipient. On the occasions referred to, a deliberate effort on the percipient's part seems to have been involved in receiving, or rather in obtaining, a true impression of the aspect and surroundings of absent persons; but unless we would assert (which we have no grounds for doing) that the continued existence of those persons, and their pre-established relation to the percipient, were not necessary conditions for the impression, we must still hold them to have been technically the *agents.* One of these agents, however—a medical man—while unable to resist the proofs which he has received of this sort of telepathic invasion, has so invincible a dread and dislike of the subject that for the present, in deference to his wishes, the account is withheld from publication. To "believe and tremble" is not a very scientific state of mind, and it is one for which we trust that there will be less and less excuse, as psychical research is gradually redeemed from supernatural and superstitious associations. Meanwhile, we must treat it with indulgence; merely noting how the very qualities which have so often operated to swell lists of spurious marvels may equally operate to hamper the record and recognition of facts.

CHAPTER VII.

EMOTIONAL AND MOTOR EFFECTS.

§ 1. WE come next to a class of cases which are characterised not so much by the distinctness of the idea as by the strength of the emotion produced in the percipient. In some of these the emotion has depended on a definite idea, and has been connected with a sense of calamity to a particular individual, or a particular household : in others it has not had reference to any definite idea, and has seemed at the time quite causeless and unreasonable. Sometimes, again, the analogy with experimental cases, in the direct reflection of experience from mind to mind, is distinctly retained,[1] the experience of the percipient seeming actually to reproduce that of a relative or friend who is in some physical or mental crisis at a distance ; while in other cases a peculiar distress on the one side is so strikingly contemporaneous with a unique condition on the other, that we cannot refuse to consider the hypothesis of a causal connection.

From the point of view of evidence, this class of emotional impressions clearly requires the most careful treatment. There is all the difference between a sensory impression, and even between the more distinct " mental pictures " of the last chapter, and a mere mood. We have no grounds for assuming that the news (for instance) of a

---

[1] The emotional class of impressions is, of course, a field peculiarly ill-adapted for deliberate experiment. Strong emotion cannot be summoned up at will by an experimenter even in his own mind ; while, if it exists, it probably betrays itself in ways beyond his control. Cases are, indeed, alleged where a secret grief or anxiety on a mesmeriser's part has been reflected in the demeanour of his "subject." But this would not necessarily prove more than that the "subject" was, so to speak, hyperæsthetic to slight physical signs of mental disturbance—which would be quite in accordance with the one-sided concentration of his mind that is shown in other ways, e.g., in his frequent deafness to any other voice than that of his operator. I may quote for what they are worth the following observations of Mr. H. S. Thompson (*Zoist*, v. 257): " One patient who was highly sensitive, and whom I mesmerised for a nervous disorder, could, when awake, point out immediate y whatever part of my head was touched by a third person. If I mesmerised her when I was in spirits, she was in spirits also ; if I was grave, she was grave ; and I never dared mesmerise her when I was suffering from any annoyance. I did not find that she often had *distinct thoughts* corresponding with my own, even when I tried to impress her by will with them. But she has experienced and shown a *feeling corresponding* with the thoughts I had."

friend's death will incite a man of sense and honesty to say that he saw, heard, felt, or strongly pictured, something unusual at or near the time of its occurrence, unless he really did so ; but it is easy to suppose that, having chanced to be slightly out of spirits at the time, he afterwards seems to remember that he was very much depressed indeed, and even filled with a boding of some impending calamity. Nay, since a person who is oppressed by gloom and apprehension will often embrace in mental glances the small group of persons with whom his emotional connection is strongest, he may recall, when one of these persons proves actually to have been passing through a crisis at the time, that this particular one was present to his mind, and may easily glide on into thinking that it was with him that the sense of apprehension was specially connected. In these cases, then, it is of prime importance that the percipient's impression shall be mentioned or otherwise noted by him in an unmistakeable way, before the receipt of news as to the supposed agent's condition. And even when we have clear proof that the emotion was really of a strongly-marked character, it is necessary further to obtain some assurance that such moods are not of common occurrence in the percipient's experience. Failing this, it is safest to regard any unusual character that may afterwards be attributed to the emotion as the result of its being afterwards dwelt on in connection with the coincident event.

It need hardly be added that all cases must be rejected where there has been any appreciable cause for anxiety, however unmistakeable and unique the impression may be shown to have been. Thus it cannot be regarded as usual for a lady who is at a friend's house, and intending to remain there for a week or two, to find herself suddenly and irrationally impelled, by the certainty of a domestic calamity, to pack her boxes and sit waiting for a telegram—which (to borrow the phrase of a business-like informant) was shortly delivered "as per presentiment." But the surmise which was thus confirmed related to a baby grandchild at home ; and though she had not heard that it was ailing, those who watch over the health of young children are often, of course, in a more or less chronic state of nervousness.

§ 2. I will first quote a case where the emotional impression had a certain definiteness of embodiment. The narrator unfortunately does not allow the publication of his complete name ; but he impressed Professor Sidgwick, who examined him personally, as a sensible and trustworthy witness.

"Edinburgh.
"December 27th, 1883.

(67) "In January, 1871, I was living in the West Indies. On the 7th of that month I got up with a strange feeling that there was something happening at my old home in Scotland. At 7 a.m. I mentioned to my sister-in-law my strange dread, and said that even at that hour what I dreaded was taking place.

"By the next mail I got word that at 11 a.m. on the 7th January my sister died. The island I lived in was St. Kitts, and the death took place in Edinburgh. Please note the hours and allow for difference in time, and you will notice at least a remarkable coincidence. I may add I never knew of her illness.

"ANDREW C——N."

The longitude of St. Kitts is about 62°—which makes 4 hours and a few minutes difference of time.

In answer to inquiries, Mr. C——n adds :—

"January 8th, 1884.

"I never at any other times had a feeling in any way resembling the particular time I wrote about.

"It would be very difficult to get the note from my sister-in-law, as she now lives in Cincinnati, Ohio, and I seldom hear of her.

"At the time I wrote about I was in perfect health, and in every way in comfortable circumstances."

[We have, of course, repeatedly urged our informant to apply, or to allow us to apply, for his sister-in-law's recollection of this incident ; but without success.]

The next case, from our friend the Hon. Mrs. Fox Powys, is still more indefinite, and would not be worth quoting but for our own well-grounded assurance that the account is free from exaggeration.

"Milford Lodge, Godalming.
"February 16th, 1884.

(68) "About 3 months ago as I was sitting, quietly thinking, between 5 and 7 p.m., I experienced a very curious sensation. I can only describe it as like a cloud of calamity gradually wrapping me round. It was *almost* a physical feeling, so strong was it ; and I seemed to be certain, in some inexplicable way, of disaster to some one of my relations or friends, though I could not in the least fix upon anybody in particular, and there was no one about whom I was anxious at the time. I do not remember ever experiencing such a thing before. I should say it lasted about half-an-hour. This happened on a Saturday, and on Monday I got a letter from my sister, written on the Saturday evening to go by the post which leaves at 7 p.m., in which she told me she had received a telegram, an hour or so ago, informing her of the dangerous illness of her brother-in-law, at which she was greatly upset. This appeared to be a very probable explanation of my extraordinary presentiment, and I wrote and told her all about it at once.

"A. C. POWYS."

[Mrs. Powys tells us that she mentioned her impression at the time to her husband ; but he cannot recall the fact.]

272 EMOTIONAL AND MOTOR EFFECTS. [CHAP.

A single impression of so vague a kind as this cannot, of course, go for much. And though it is so far against the hypothesis of accidental coincidence that the narrator states—and we believe, accurately—that the experience was unique, yet this very uniqueness involves a certain difficulty. For if she could be once telepathically impressed by an agent whose emotional excitement at the time, though considerable, was clearly not extreme, we cannot but wonder that so remarkable a sensibility should have found no other occasion to manifest itself. There is more evidential force in the occurrence of *several* such impressions to the same person—provided, of course, that they have all corresponded with facts. Such seems to have been the experience of Mr. J. D. Harry, whom we do not know personally, but who has been described to us by two common acquaintances as an acute man of the world. He wrote to us as follows, in 1882, from The Palms, St. Julian's, Malta :—

(69) "I lost my brother in Cornwall, and my uncle in Devonshire. Neither of them had been ill more than three days, and no communication whatever had taken place with me from the time they were first attacked until their deaths ; nevertheless I felt so depressed on each occasion, from the time they were taken ill, that I could scarcely perform the duties of my office, the peculiar feeling lasting until the announcements in each case were made. It was nearly the same feeling of depression previous to my mother's death, whose illness was likewise very sudden and unknown to me.

"JOHN D. HARRY."

In answer to the question whether he had ever had similar depressions which had *not* had any correspondence with reality, Mr. Harry replied :—

"You ask if I ever felt similarly depressed. You have my assurance that I never experienced a like feeling, except in the three instances named ; indeed, all those who know me well would tell you that in their belief I am the last person to become so affected. During the three or four serious illnesses I have undergone, when the hopes of my family and friends were despaired of, I was still cheery."

[Here we have to depend entirely on the narrator's memory ; and the case does not conform to the rule that the marked character of the experience shall be *en évidence* before the news is known.]

In the next example there can no doubt as to the striking nature of the percipient's experience ; which, indeed, was so distinctly physical in character as to suggest the actual sensory transference of which Mrs. Severn's case (p. 188) was our most precise example. The narrator is Mrs. Reay, of 99, Holland Road, Kensington.

"August 14th, 1884.

(70) " I will endeavour to write you an account of the incident, related for you by my friend, Mr. E. Moon. His sister was staying with me at the time. It was in February, but I don't remember what year. We were sitting chatting over our 5 o'clock tea; I was perfectly well at the time, and much amused with her conversation. As I had several notes to write before dinner, I asked her to leave me alone, or I feared I should not get them finished. She did so, and I went to the writing-table and began to write.

" All at once a dreadful feeling of illness and faintness came over me, and I felt that I was dying. I had no power to get up to ring the bell for assistance, but sat with my head in my hands utterly helpless.

" My maid came into the room for the tea things. I thought I would keep her with me, but felt better while she was there, so did not mention my illness to her, thinking it had passed away. However, as soon as I lost the sound of her footsteps, it all came back upon me worse than ever. In vain I tried to get up and ring the bell or call for help; I could not move, and thought I was certainly dying.

" When the dressing bell rang it roused me again, and I made a great effort to rise and go to my room, which I did ; but when my maid came in I was standing by the fire, leaning upon the mantelpiece, trembling all over. She at once came to me and asked what was the matter. I said I did not know, but that I felt very ill indeed.

" The dinner-hour had arrived, and my husband had not come home. Then, for the first time, it flashed upon my mind that something had happened to him when I was taken ill at the writing-table. This was the first time I had thought about him, so that it was no anxiety on my part about him that had caused my illness. The next half-hour was spent in great suspense ; then he arrived home with his messenger with him ; he was almost in an unconscious state, and remained so for about 24 hours. When he was well enough for me to ask him about his illness, he said he had been very well indeed all day, but just as he was preparing to leave his office he became suddenly very ill (just the same time that I was taken ill at the writing-table), and his messenger had to get a cab and come home with him ; he was quite unable to be left by himself.

"EMILY REAY."

Mr. Reay, Secretary of the London and North-Western Railway, confirms as follows :—

"September 18th, 1884.

" I perfectly well recollect, on the evening of my severe and sudden attack of illness, my wife asking me some questions about it, when, after hearing what I had to say, she told me that almost at the same instant of time (soon after 5 p.m.), when writing, she was seized with a fit of trembling and nervous depression, as if she were dying. She went to her room and remained there in the same state until the dinner hour, and as I did not arrive by that time she instinctively felt that something had happened to me, and was on the point of sending to the office to inquire when I left, when I was brought home in a cab. At the time of my seizure I was writing, and it was with much difficulty that I was enabled to finish the letter.   "S. REAY."

In answer to inquiries, Mrs. Reay adds :—

" I never at any other time in my life had the slightest approach to the sensations I experienced when the sudden illness came over me, under the circumstances mentioned to you. I never in my life fainted, nor have I any tendency that way. The feeling which came over me was a dreadful trembling, with prostration, and a feeling that I was going to die ; and I had no power to rise from the writing-table to ring for assistance. I have never had the same feeling since, and never before that time."

The uniqueness of the experience may be readily accepted as stated, in a case where its physical character was so distinct as this. But even in judging of more doubtful cases, an inference which the percipient's description might hardly warrant may sometimes be fairly drawn from the permanent effect made on his mind. The following account, for instance, is very likely to provoke a smile, and is in itself wholly inconclusive ; yet the impression was at any rate sufficiently marked to force the reality of sympathetic transferences on the mind of a scientific witness, who candidly records it in a book largely devoted to the exposure of spurious "psychical" marvels. Dr. E. L. Fischer, of Würzburg, in his *Der Sogenannte Lebens-Magnetismus oder Hypnotismus* (Mainz, 1883), says that as a student at the University he enjoyed extremely good spirits, but was one morning oppressed by an extraordinary gloom, which his companions noticed.

(71) " During the whole afternoon I remained in this state of dismal wretchedness. All at once a telegram arrived from home, informing me that my grandmother was taken very ill, and that she was earnestly longing for me. There I had the solution of the riddle. Nevertheless from that hour my melancholy gradually decreased, and in spite of the telegram it completely disappeared in the course of the afternoon. In the evening I received a second message, to the effect that the danger was over. In this way the second phenomenon, the rapid decrease of my wretchedness—a circumstance which in itself was surprising, inasmuch as the melancholy should naturally rather have *increased* after the receipt of the first news— received its explanation. For the afternoon was just the time when the change in the patient's condition for the better took place ; and the danger to her life once over, her yearning for my presence had decreased ; while simultaneously my anxiety was dispelled."

Dr. Fischer was, I think, wrong in accepting this incident, (and a very few more like it), as sufficient evidence for the fact of telepathy ; but right in placing it on record for what it is worth.

In the majority of the emotional cases, the natural bond between the two persons concerned has been of the closest. And, *ceteris paribus,* the nearer tie of blood increases the probability of the telepathic explanation, wherever the hypothesis of natural anxiety for a beloved relative is excluded by the fact that the emotion is connected with no special person. We received the following case from Mrs. Bull, of Mossley Vicarage, Congleton.

"January 3rd, 1885.

(72) "On the evening of January 28th, 1863, I had met several old friends at dinner at a friend's house near Manchester, in which neighbourhood I had been paying visits. My return home to my father's house was fixed for the next afternoon. I ought to say that between that father and me, his first-born child, a more than common bond of affection and sympathy existed, arising from circumstances I need not mention, and I was looking forward to my return with earnest longing. The evening had been bright and happy, surrounded by friends I valued. When I was about to leave, my hostess pressed me to play for her a very favourite old march. I declined, on account of the lateness of the hour, and keeping horses standing. She said, ' It is not yet 12, and I have sent the carriage away for a quarter of an hour.' I sat down laughing, and before I played many bars, such an indescribable feeling came over me, intense sadness heralded a complete break down, and I was led away from the piano in hysterics. By 10 o'clock the next morning I got a telegram, to say my father had gone to bed in his usual health, and at a quarter to 12 the night before had passed away in an epileptic fit, having previously said to my sister how glad he was to think of seeing me so soon, and when she bid him good-night, praying God to give them both a quiet night and sleep.

"A. M. BULL."

The *Chester Courant* for February 4th, 1863, says that the death of the Rev. J. Jackson took place on January 28th, very suddenly. He had preached on the Sunday, and had been out on the Tuesday preceding the Wednesday night when his fatal fit attacked him.

In reply to inquiries, Mrs. Bull says :—

"Since reading your letter last night, I have carefully gone over the guests of that dinner party, and find them all gone but one, Frank Ashton, Esq., The Laurels, Twickenham, and he is too ill to read or to answer a letter. At the time I speak of, I was the widow of the Rev. J. Lowthian, vicar of Wharton. My father was the Rev. John Jackson, vicar of Over. *I never experienced* a similar feeling. I am not at all naturally inclined to depression, and am *perfectly free* from what is commonly understood by superstition."

In conversation, Mrs. Bull told me that she has never in her life had a fit of hysterics, or of unaccountable weeping, except on this occasion.

The writer of the following narrative is the editor of a well-known northern newspaper, and was formerly special foreign correspondent of a London paper. A few weeks before the occurrence here described, he had a curious impression corresponding with the death of a friend, which is narrated in the following chapter (case 103).

T 2

"December 11th, 1884.

(73) "On the 3rd of May in the same spring [1882], my wife, while taking tea with my daughter, was suddenly seized with an epileptic fit, and fell heavily to the floor, striking her forehead on the fender ; she was never conscious again, but died the next day. This accident happened between 3 and 4 o'clock in the afternoon. For nearly 5 years my wife had intermittently suffered from epilepsy, but for some 3 months before her death seemed to have completely recovered, which apparent fact had caused much joy in our little family circle, as the poor dear had been a great sufferer. I set this down to show that her death or serious illness was not at all expected at the time it happened.

" On the morning of the 3rd of May I left for the City, and as my wife kissed her hand to me at the window, I thought how remarkably well and ' like her old self ' she appeared. I went to business in ' high spirits,' and left her in the same ; but *somewhere* about the time she fell—neither my daughter nor I have been able to fix the time within an hour—I suddenly fell into such a fit of gloom that I was powerless to go on with my work, and could only sit with my face between my hands, scarcely able to speak to my colleagues in the same office, who became alarmed as they had never seen me in any but a cheerful mood. I was at the time editing *England,* and as friend after friend dropped into my room, and wanted to know what ailed me, I could only explain my sensation in a phrase (which they and I well remember) which I kept repeating, namely, ' I have a horrible sense of some impending calamity.' So far as I am aware, my thoughts never once turned to my home. If they had, I think I should not have accepted, as I did, an invitation to dine with a friend at a restaurant in the Strand, pressed on me for the express purpose of ' cheering me up.'

"I was telegraphed for to our office in the Strand, but by an accident it was not forwarded to me to Whitefriars Street at my editorial room: so that I never saw my wife until after 12 at night, when my 8 or 9 hours of fearful depression of spirits (as it instantly struck me) were accounted for. I may add that I am naturally of a buoyant temperament, in fact I may say far above the average of people in that respect, and I was never to my knowledge ever so suddenly or similarly depressed before. My wife, in this case, you will observe, was not dead but simply unconscious when my fit of low spirits set in.

"There are several witnesses who can testify to these facts, for when it became known at the office that my wife was dead the strong coincidence of my suddenly ' turning so queer ' was a topic of conversation there. I have nothing to add but that we (my wife and I) had been married for 25 years, and were extremely fond of each other, and we were both, I should say, of a sympathetic temperament, perhaps more than ordinarily so."

Mr. Podmore writes on Sept. 1, 1885 :—

" I called to-day at Mr. ——'s house. He was out of town, but his son and daughter were at home.[1]

" As regards Mr. ——'s depression on the day of his wife's fatal attack,

---

[1] Our informant has since this date removed to the North of England, where a personal interview with him might easily have been obtained, but was lately missed through an accident.

they both assured me that he spoke of this immediately after his return home on the evening of that day, and has frequently mentioned it since The son has also heard one of his father's colleagues, Mr. Green, describe the circumstance as something quite remarkable. Mr. Green told him that both himself and others present in the office did all they could to rally Mr. —— but failed."

[A full *vivâ voce* account of the incident has been given by the narrator to our friend and helper, Mr. A. G. Leonard.]

Mr. Green writes:—
" Netherworton House, Steeple Aston, Oxon.
" September 16th, 1885.
" DEAR SIR,—My friend, Mr. ——, of *England*, has asked me to corroborate the fact that he suffered from a singular depression all the day of his wife's fatal seizure. I was in his company most of the day, and can fully corroborate his statement.—Yours truly,   " C. E. GREEN."

The next case is from a lady who is willing that her name should be given to any one genuinely interested in this case. She is known to the present writer as a sensible and clear-headed witness, as far from sentimentality or superstition as can well be conceived.

" October 27th, 1885.
(74) " On the Saturday before Easter, 1881, my husband left London for Paris. On the Saturday or Sunday evening he was taken ill, at the hotel, with congestion of the brain, and wandered about the place delirious. Subsequently he was put in a room, and although a man was in attendance, he was, in regard to medical advice, &c., quite neglected. He remained there some days, and by looking in his papers his name was discovered, and his family were communicated with.

" On the afternoon of Easter Monday, my sons and my daughter had gone out, leaving me at home. I fell into an altogether extraordinary state of depression and restlessness. I tried in vain to distract myself with work and books. I went upstairs and felt beside myself with distress, for what reason I could not tell; I argued with myself, but the feeling increased. I even had a violent fit of weeping—a thing absolutely alien to my character. I then put on my things, and, in the hope of ridding myself of the uncomfortable feeling, took a hansom cab, and drove about Hyde Park for about three hours—a thing which I should have considered myself stark mad for doing at any other time. I should have been the last person to spend eight shillings on cab fare for nothing. On receiving the news I went over to Paris, where I arrived on the Thursday, and my husband just knew me. The nurse engaged to nurse him told me that she was asked by the waiter if my Christian name was M. [Mrs. S.'s name, and a not very common one], as that was the name that my husband was constantly calling out during his delirium. He died some days afterwards.
" M. S."

I learn from both Mrs. S. and her son that she mentioned her remarkable experience to her family on the Monday evening. Her son writes as follows :—

"I beg to corroborate my mother's account of the circumstances mentioned. Her distress and the circumstances of the cab drive are entirely foreign to her character. My father was in delicate health, although seldom actually ill.

"E. S."

In answer to some questions addressed to Mrs. S., Mr. E. S., replies :—

"My mother had no particular anxiety about my father's health. He left on the Saturday for Paris, and was then in his usual health, and she did not particularly connect her feelings with him."

[I suggested a difficulty as to the driving *about* Hyde Park, since it is only in a restricted portion of that park that cabs are permitted to pass. But Mrs. S. adheres to the word.]

In the following case a very marked depression of spirits was followed by a vivid dream. The latter may of course be easily accounted for as following naturally on the former ; but the emotional depression, which coincided in time with the fatal turn in the illness of a near relative, seems to have been a unique experience in the life of a person of strong mental and physical health. The narrator, a physician, refuses permission to publish his name on the ground that he is a "confirmed unbeliever"; though in conversation with him I was unable to learn what exactly his unbelief was of, and in what exactly its confirmation had consisted.

"March 7th, 1885.

(75) "When a boy about 14 years of age, I was in school in Edinburgh, my home being in the West of Scotland. A thoughtless boy, free from all care or anxiety, in the 'Eleven' of my school, and popular with my companions, I had nothing to worry or annoy me. I boarded with two old ladies, now both dead.

"One afternoon—on the day previous to a most important cricket match in which I was to take part—I was overwhelmed with a most unusual sense of depression and melancholy. I shunned my friends and got 'chaffed' for my most unusual dulness and sulkiness. I felt utterly miserable, and even to this day I have a most vivid recollection of my misery that afternoon.

"I knew that my father suffered from a most dangerous disease in the stomach—a gastric ulcer—and that he was always more or less in danger, but I knew that he was in his usual bad health, and that nothing exceptional ailed him.

"That same night I had a dream. I was engaged in the cricket match. I saw a telegram being brought to me while batting, and it told me that my father was dying, and telling me to come home at once. I told the ladies with whom I boarded what my dream had been, and told them how real the impression was. I went to the ground, and was engaged in the game, batting, and making a score. I saw a telegram being brought out, read it, and fainted. I at once left for home, and found my father had just died when I reached the house. The ulcer in the stomach had suddenly burst about 4 o'clock on the previous day, and it was about that hour that I had experienced the most unusual depression I have described. The sensations I had on that afternoon have left a most clear and distinct impression on my mind, and now, after the lapse of 15 years, I well remember my miserable feelings.

" J. D., M.D."

In reply to inquiries, Dr. D. says :—

" I most certainly never had a similar experience of depression, or such a vivid dream as the one I tried in my letter to explain. Both the depression and the dream were quite exceptional, and have left a most clear impression on my memory.

" I fear I cannot name any individual schoolfellow who noticed my most unwonted silence and quietness on that afternoon, but I distinctly remember their chaffing me for not joining as usual in the afternoon's practice."

§ 3. On the supposition that a close natural bond between two persons is a favourable condition for telepathic influence, there is one group of persons among whom we might expect to find a disproportionate number of instances—namely, *twins*. As a matter of fact, we have a certain number of twin cases, which, though actually small, is indisputably disproportionate, if we remember what an infinitesimally small proportion of the population twins form. I will quote here the three examples which properly belong to this chapter. It may be of interest to compare them with the cases given by Mr. F. Galton (*Inquiries into Human Faculty*, pp. 226-31), of consentaneous thought and action on the part of twins. Mr. Galton attributes the coincidences to a specially close similarity of constitution. The pair may be roughly compared to two watches, which begin to go at the same hour, and keep parallel with one another in their advance through life. This theory seems fairly to account for the occurrence of special physiological or pathological crises at the same point of the two lives. The twins, though separated, have their croup or their whooping-cough simultaneously. The explanation, however, seems a little strained when applied to the simultaneous purchase in different towns of two sets of champagne-glasses of similar pattern, owing to a sudden impulse on the part of each of the twins to surprise the other with a present. If it were possible—which it can hardly be—to make sure that there had been no previous mention of the subject between the brothers, and that the idea was really and completely impromptu, one might hint that the coincidence here was telepathic. And, at any rate, the cases to be now quoted seem outside the range of a pre-established physiological harmony; with them, the alternative is between telepathy and accident.

The first account is from the Rev. J. M. Wilson, head-master of Clifton College, a Senior Wrangler and well-known mathematician.

"Clifton College.

"January 5th, 1884.

(76) "The facts were these, as nearly as I can remember.

"I was at Cambridge at the end of my second term, in full health, boating, football-playing and the like, and by no means subject to hallucinations or morbid fancies. One evening I felt extremely ill, trembling, with no apparent cause whatever; nor did it seem to me at the time to be a physical illness, a chill of any kind. I was frightened. I was totally unable to overcome it. I remember a sort of struggle with myself, resolving that I *would* go on with my mathematics, but it was in vain: I became convinced that I was dying.

"I went down to the rooms of my friend, W. E. Mullins, who was on the same staircase, and I remember that he exclaimed at me before I spoke. He put away his books, pulled out a whisky bottle and a backgammon board, but I could not face it. We sat over the fire for a bit, and then he fetched some one else (Mr. E. G. Peckover), to have a look at me. I was in a strange discomfort, but with no symptoms I can recall, except mental discomfort, and the conviction that I should die that night.

"Towards 11, after some 3 hours of this, I got better, and went upstairs and got to bed, and after a time to sleep, and next morning was quite well.

"In the afternoon came a letter to say that my twin brother had died the evening before in Lincolnshire. I am quite clear of the fact that I never once thought of him, nor was his presence with me even dimly imagined. He had been long ill of consumption; but I had not heard of him for some days, and there was nothing to make me think that his death was near. It took me altogether by surprise.

"JAMES M. WILSON."

We have applied to Mr. Mullins, but he cannot now recall the incident.

In answer to inquiries, Mr. Wilson says :—

"I never experienced any similar nervous depression. It was a sort of panic fear, the chill of approaching death that was on me. The hours did not exactly coincide; my brother died some 4 hours before I was so seized."

If we are right in regarding this incident as probably telepathic, it is one of the numerous cases where the impression has lain latent for a considerable time before affecting consciousness. Mr. Wilson's description of his experience strongly recalls case 22, where the percipient, it will be remembered, "became quite cold, and had a firm presentiment that she was dying"; and compare also case 70.

The next case is from Mr. James Carroll, who, when he wrote, was in attendance on an invalid, under the care of Dr. Wood, The Priory, Roehampton. I have had a long interview with him, as well as a good deal of correspondence ; and I have no doubt whatever that the facts are correctly recorded.

"July, 1884.

(77) " I beg to forward my experience of about six years ago, while living in the employment of Colonel Turbervill, near Bridgend, Glamorgan, and a twin brother in the same capacity with a lady at Chobham Place, Bagshot, Surrey.

"I may mention that my brother and I were devotedly attached from children, and our resemblance to each other so remarkable that only one or two of our family then living, and oldest friends, could distinguish any difference between us. Up to June 17th, 1878, I had not known my brother to have one day's illness, and in consequence of having about this time recovered heavy financial loss, there was this and other unusual cause for cheerfulness. But on the morning of the date given, about half-past 11, I experienced a *strange sadness* and depression. Unable to account for it, I turned to my desk, thinking of my brother. I looked at his last letter to see the date, and tried to detect if there was anything unusual in it but failed. I wrote off to my brother, closed my desk, and felt compelled to exclaim quite aloud, ' My brother or I will break down.' This I afterwards found was the first day of his fatal illness.

" I wrote again to him, but in consequence of his being ill I received no reply. We usually wrote twice a-week. I tried to persuade myself his silence was due to being busy. On the following Saturday, the 22nd, while speaking to Mr. Turbervill, a sudden depression, which I had never before realised, and which I feel impossible to describe, came over me. I felt strange and unwell. I retired as soon as possible, thankful my state of mind had not been noticed. I would have gone to my room, but felt it might be noticed, and felt frightened too, as if something might suddenly happen to me.

" I went, instead, into the footman's pantry, where they were cleaning the plate, and sat down, suppressed my feelings, but alluded to a dulness and concern for my brother. I was speaking, when a messenger entered with a telegram to announce my brother's dangerous state, and requesting my immediate presence. He died on the following Monday morning. It is clearly proved that at the time I felt the melancholy described he was speaking of me in great distress. We were never considered superstitious, and I was never apt to feelings of melancholy.

"My brother and I were well known to Dr. Young, of 30, West-bourne Square, Paddington ; and to Mr. Trollope, Solicitor, 31, Abingdon Street, Westminster.

"JAMES CARROLL."

In reply to inquiries Mr. Carroll says :—

"August 8th, 1884.

"I find it difficult now, after the lapse of time and many changes, to get the memory of friends to recall the subjects of our correspondence. I left South Wales on the death of my brother, and have been moving about among strangers ever since ; circumstances on this part of the matter are singularly against me.

" You asked in your previous letter, was the impression of distress and apprehension which I described, rare to me in my experience ? I never before felt anything like it, except in a milder form, before the death of my mother, about 14 years ago, while I was at Lord Robarts' seat in Arnhill, and my mother in London. The sensation then was about two or three days previous to her death. I have always been an opponent to ghost theory, and till my brother's death I never thought to entertain the idea that there could be any unseen power in the thought of apparitions.

" My brother's death was from a cold neglected, and inflammation rapidly setting in. We were twins, his age at time of death 39 about. From our extraordinary resemblance we were well known. I may mention my brother being the only near relation left.

" I sent to Ireland for signatures to a distant relative, who was with me as an adopted son shortly after my brother's death, for about two years. He is about 18 years of age ; his name, too, is James Carroll. His corroboration comes very close to the time.

" An old friend, of 25 years, 30 I think, holding a good position in one of our chief banking houses, also promised to corroborate, a day or two ago. I enclose now a note from him, just received. He remembers the subject. I often, just after my brother's death, spoke of it to him.

" J. C."

A nephew and namesake of Mr. Carroll's writes as follows :—

" Clonmel, Ireland.
" August 10th, 1884.

" I hereby certify that Mr. Carroll frequently, during the early part of my residence with him, about 5 years ago, spoke of the presentiment he describes in a letter written to you, a copy of which he has sent me.

" JAMES CARROLL."

The following is a letter to Mr. Carroll from Mr. James Martin, of 1, Oak Villa, Avenue Road, Acton.

" August 16th, 1884.

" DEAR JAMES,—From the time of your brother's death till the present, I have spent much time in your society. I remember well the account you gave me of the dreadful depression of mind you passed through just previous to his death. It was singular, but true.

" JAMES MARTIN."

Mr. Carroll showed me a letter written by Mrs. Benyan, his brother's employer, at the time when the brother was dangerously ill. The letter is to a solicitor, and expresses a desire that he, James Carroll, should be informed of the illness. It proves that the illness was sudden and that Mr. Carroll was unaware of it.

The following case is less striking, but is worth giving in connection with the others. We received it from Mr. (now the Rev.) A. J. Maclean, of Tewkesbury.

"Clergy School, Leeds.
"June 8th, 1884.

(78) " About three years ago my twin brother was yachting off Norway for six weeks.   One Sunday I (who was then at college) felt certain that there was something wrong with my brother and spoke of it freely (I cannot remember to whom).   When I saw my brother I mentioned this circumstance.   My brother had kept a diary, and on the day in question they had encountered a storm, in which the masts were injured and things washed away.   .They gave up all for lost."
In answer to inquiries, Mr. Maclean says :—
"June, 1884.

" I could not say whether my brother had any thoughts about me on the day he was in danger of being shipwrecked, but I certainly had a vivid impression that he was in danger the same day on which it happened.   He was yachting at the time, and was off the coast of Norway.   He is not the sort of man to experience anything in the way of hallucination, and if he did think of me at the time he would take no notice of it, or even forget it altogether the next minute.   I feel sure I should get very little information bearing on the subject from him.   I only know that he *was* in actual danger, and furthermore that I myself was convinced at the time that something was happening to him, and mentioned the fact to several friends at the time—being at Oxford—though I cannot possibly remember to whom I expressed my fears.   He is a twin brother.
"ARTHUR J. MACLEAN."

In answer to further inquiries, especially as to whether he had ever had similar impressions which had *not* corresponded with reality, Mr. Maclean says :—
"June 20th, 1884.
" My impression with regard to my brother's danger is the *only one* I ever remember having.
" I am afraid I cannot possibly remember to whom I mentioned my fears at the time, as I was at college, and there were so many I might have told."

§ 4.   We may now pass to a group of these cases in which the primary element of the emotional impression is a sense of *being wanted*—an impulse to go somewhere or do something.

The first example is from the Rev. E. D. Banister, of Whitechapel Vicarage, Preston.
"November 12th, 1885.
(79) " My father on the day of his death had gone out of the house about 2.30 p.m., to have his usual afternoon stroll in the garden and fields.   He had not been absent more than 7 or 8 minutes when, as I was talking to my wife and sister, I was seized with a very urgent desire to go to him.   (The conversation related to a visit which we proposed to pay that afternoon to a neighbour, and no allusion was made to my father.)   The feeling that I ought to go and see him came upon me with irresistible force.   I insisted upon all in the house going out to find my father.   I was remonstrated with—my very anxiety seeming so unreasonable.   My father's afternoon stroll was a regular habit of life in fine

weather, and I had no reason to give why on that particular occasion I must insist on his being found. Search was made, and it was my sad lot to find him dead in the field, in a place which, according to the route he ordinarily adopted, he would have reached about 7 or 8 minutes after leaving the house.

" My idea is that when he felt the stroke of death coming upon him he earnestly desired to see me, and that, by the operation of certain psychical laws, the desire was communicated to me.

" E. D. BANISTER."

In reply to inquiries Mr. Banister adds :—

" In reply to your letter I have to state :—

" 1. Vivid impressions of the kind I have related are utterly unknown to me ; the one related is unique in my experience.

" 2. There was not the least cause for anxiety owing to the absence of my father. It only seemed a short time since he had gone out of the room, and on this account my urgency was deemed unreasonable.

" 3. The date was January 9th, 1883."

We have confirmed this date by the obituary notice in the *Preston Chronicle.*

Mr. Banister's wife and sister supply the following corroboration :—

" We have seen the statement which Mr. Banister has forwarded to the Psychical Research Society, relating to the strong impression by which he was irresistibly urged in search of his father on the afternoon of January 9th, 1883, and we are able to confirm all details given in that statement.

" MARY BANISTER.
" AGNES BANISTER."

In conversation Mr. Banister informed me that his father was a remarkably hale old man, and there had never been the slightest anxiety about his being out alone. He further mentioned that the compulsion seemed to come to him " from outside."

The following instance is from Mrs. C., of 11, Upper Hamilton Terrace, N.W.

" December 17th, 1883.

(80) " On December 2nd, 1877, I was at church. My children wished to remain to a christening. I said, ' I cannot, somebody seems calling me ; something is the matter.' I returned home to find nothing ; but next morning two telegrams summoned me to the deathbed of my husband, from whom I had had a cheerful letter on the Saturday, and who left me in excellent spirits the Thursday before. I only arrived in time to see him die."

The following is the sons' corroboration :—

" We remember, perfectly, our mother leaving the church, saying she felt she was wanted, someone was calling her. The next day our father died, December 3rd, 1877.

" GEORGE C.
" JOHN A. C."

In answer to inquiries, Mrs. C. says :—

" February 19th, 1884.

(1) " I cannot say that the experience of some one calling me was

unique. I have often had strong impressions of things occurring, and such things have happened, but not having set down the dates, I could not be sufficiently certain to satisfy myself.[1]

(2) " My husband wrote me a cheerful letter on the Friday, November 30th, and on the Saturday, December 1st, only mentioning that he was a little bilious, but that he was going to Leicester that afternoon. He was, however, so much worse that afternoon that he went to bed. In the night he was found by a gentleman to be out of bed, and unable to get in, and he mistook the gentleman for me. All Sunday he was dying, and my friends could not telegraph, and there was no train. On Monday I received two telegrams, early in the morning. As soon as I read your letter my sons both said they remembered the circumstance quite well and signed the enclosed. George was 10 years old, John 12 years."

Asked whether she would have been certain to stay for the christening under ordinary circumstances, Mrs. C. replied in the affirmative ; and that the boys were disappointed. She is without any theory on these matters ; and simply reports an undoubted experience.

The following case is very similar. The narrator is Mr. A. Skirving, foreman at Winchester Cathedral.

"Cathedral Yard, Winchester.
"January 31st, 1884.

(81) " I respectfully beg to offer you a short statement of my experience on a subject which I do not understand. Let me premise that I am not a scholar, as I left school when 12 years of age in 1827, and I therefore hope you will forgive all sins against composition and grammar. I am a working foreman of masons at Winchester Cathedral, and have been for the last 9 years a resident in this city. I am a native of Edinburgh.

" It is now more than 30 years ago that I was living in London, very near where the Great Western Railway now stands, but which was not then built. I was working in the Regent's Park for Messrs. Mowlem, Burt, and Freeman, who at that time had the Government contract for 3 years for the masons' work of the capital, and who yet carry on a mighty business at Millbank, Westminster. I think it was Gloucester Gate, if I mistake not. At all events, it was that gate of Regent's Park to the eastward of the Zoological Gardens, at the north-east corner of the park. The distance from my home was too great for me to get home to meals, so I carried my food with me, and therefore had no call to leave the work all day. On a certain day, however, I suddenly felt an intense desire to go home, but as I had no business there I tried to suppress it,—but it was not possible to do so. Every minute the desire to go home increased. It was 10 in the morning, and I could not think of anything to call me away from the work at such a time. I got fidgety and uneasy, and felt as if I must go, even at the risk of being ridiculed by my wife, as I could give no reason vhy I should leave my work and lose 6d. an hour for nonsense. However, I could not stay, and I set off for home under an impulse which I could not resist.

---

[1] One of these cases, however, seems to have been quite precise, and will be found below (No. 204).

"When I reached my own door and knocked, the door was opened by my wife's sister, a married woman, who lived a few streets off. She looked surprised, and said, ' Why, Skirving, how did you know ? ' ' Know what ? ' I said. ' Why, about Mary Ann.' I said, ' I don't know anything about Mary Ann ' (my wife). ' Then what brought you home at present ? ' I said, ' I can hardly tell you. I seemed to want to come home. But what is wrong ? ' I asked. She told me that my wife had been run over by a cab, and been most seriously injured about an hour ago, and she had called for me ever since, but was now in fits, and had several in succession. I went upstairs, and though very ill she recognised me, and stretched forth her arms, and took me round the neck and pulled my head down into her bosom. The fits passed away directly, and my presence seemed to tranquillise her, so that she got into sleep, and did well. Her sister told me that she had uttered the most piteous cries for me to come to her, although there was not the least likelihood of my coming. This short narrative has only one merit ; it is strictly true.

"ALEXANDER SKIRVING."

In answer to the question whether the time of the accident corresponded with the time when he felt a desire to go home, Mr. Skirving says :—

"I asked my wife's sister what time the accident occurred, and she said, 'An hour and a-half ago '—that is from the time I came home. Now, that was exactly coincident with the time I wanted to leave work. It took me an hour to walk home ; and I was quite half-an-hour struggling in my mind to overcome the wish to leave work before I did so."

He adds : "You ask me if I ever had a similar impression on any other occasion. I never had. It was quite a single and unique experience."

Mr. Skirving's wife is dead. His sister-in-law, Mrs. Vye, is in New Zealand. Her husband, writing from Otago on July 1st, 1885, says that she cannot now give particulars of the occurrence, though she remembers the accident very well.

In the next case—from Mrs. Wirgman, of 121, Dawson Place, Westbourne Park, W.—the percipient's line of action was still more abnormal.

(82) "In 1845 I had moved from Germany to a small town in Belgium ; on my arrival an English lady called on me to offer her aid in finding a house. While talking to her I suddenly exclaimed, ' I must go to England.' I then and there started in order to catch the boat from Antwerp. On reaching London I remarked the numerous persons I saw in mourning.[1] I drove to my parents' lodgings at the West End, and on my cousin coming to the cab door, I inquired who it was, my father or my mother. I found my mother well, my father dying; his last conscious words had been, ' Fan will be here on Thursday,' and so I was, to the intense surprise of my relations, some of whom had written, not anticipating immediate danger, and had it not been for the inexplic-

---

[1] This is merely intended to mark the gradually increasing definiteness of the alarm.

able impulse, I certainly should not have reached London in time to see my father again."

In conversation Mrs. Wirgman described to Mr. Myers the extreme inconvenience, and apparent folly, of her return to England, which she undertook without any definite notion as to its object, and, as it were, in spite of herself.

In the next case—from Mr. Pae, of 30, Gordon Street, Gateshead-on-Tyne—there may have been a certain amount of latent anxiety on the narrator's part respecting his father's condition of health. On the other hand his impression seems to have reached the pitch of actual physical discomfort, and certainly affected his actions in an unexpected way.

(83) " I dreamt that my father died before I got his portrait painted. This dream I told so often when my father was in good health that it became a standing jest. Three months before he died he took a slight pain in his shoulder, and I said to myself, ' Is he going to die ? ' So I *did* begin to paint his portrait, but next day he was all right again, so the portrait did not make headway. Three months after, Isabella (my wife) and I had arranged to go to the theatre one night. It was arranged that I would get tea in Newcastle, and meet Isabella at the High Level Bridge end (she had to come in from the Low Fell, where we lived). All went well. I got to the High Level. As I was standing waiting for her, I felt all of a sudden that if I could wish myself anywhere in the world at that moment it would be in our kitchen at the Low Fell. I tried to shake the feeling off, but it got worse and worse. When Isabella came, I didn't make any movement in the direction of the theatre. She saw something was the matter. I explained the feeling. She said, ' Try and shake it off.' But no ! I couldn't. She said, ' Then let us go home.' When we got home to the kitchen we found my father in an apoplectic fit—quite powerless. He had remained to take care of the children. He died the next day. He never spoke ; and of course the portrait was never finished.

"WILLIAM PAE."

" I distinctly remember my husband's concern when I met him at the High Level, and confirm all he relates about his father's death.

"ISABELLA PAE."

[Our active helper, Mr. E. T. Nisbet, of 51, Eldon Street, Newcastle-on-Tyne, mentions that "Mr. Pae, when describing the feeling that came over him while waiting at the High Level, put his hands on his chest and pressed them against it at short intervals, saying, ' Just like that.' "]

The late Mr. Cromwell F. Varley, F.R.S., the well-known electrician, records an experience in which, as he believed, he made a deliberate and successful attempt to impress his wife's mind, not, however, by way of experiment, but in a crisis of great danger *(Report of*

a Committee of the Dialectical Society on Spiritualism, p. 162).
He had been in the habit of inhaling chloroform to relieve constriction of the throat, and one day fell back on his bed, powerless to move, with the sponge on his mouth. Mrs. Varley was in the room above, nursing a sick child.

(84) "I made, of my will, a distinct impression on her brain that I was in danger. Thus aroused, she came down, and immediately removed the sponge, and was greatly alarmed. I then used my body to speak to her, and I said, ' I shall forget all about it, and how this came to pass, unless you remind me in the morning, but be sure to tell me what made you come down, and I shall then be able to recall the circumstances.' The following morning she did so, but I could not remember anything about it ; I tried hard all the day, however, and at length I succeeded in remembering, first a part, and ultimately the whole."

With so much forcing of the memory, however, the evidence here cannot be ranked as much better than second-hand; and Mrs. Varley's account of the incident has not, I believe, been placed on record.[1]

The next case involves a less momentous experience, but perhaps a more improbable coincidence. Still, it is scarcely too much to say that cases of this character, in whatever number accumulated, could never decisively exclude the hypothesis of accident. The narrator is Bt. Major Kobbé, U.S. Army.

"Mt. Vernon Barracks, Ala.
"July 31st, 1884.

(85) "In 1858 or 1859, while at home in New York city, I one day felt a desire to visit Greenwood Cemetery some six or seven miles distant, on Long Island, where my family owned a vault, &c.

"When I arrived there I found my father standing uncovered at an open grave, in which he had just had placed the remains of an infant son, who had died before my birth; he had had the remains removed from the vault and placed in the grave for final interment, and the workmen were on the point of putting in the first spadeful of earth as I came up.

"When we left the cemetery together I remarked on the singular coincidence which had brought me there at the nick of time ; it quickly and naturally came out that my father had left a message at home for me to meet him there at the time I really did do so. *This message I never received,* for the simple reason that I had not gone home.

"The ' coincidence ' is remarkable because—

" 1. In those days the cemetery was not pleasant or convenient of access.

---

[1] I should mention that Mr. Varley's own view of this occurrence, and of another which will be quoted later (case 305), is different from that here adopted. But telepathy seems quite adequate to cover the facts. The sense of being "out of the body," which is what appears most powerfully to have impressed him, is a known form of pathologic experience, or—as I should regard it—of hallucination. (See p. 555, note.)

" 2. Neither my father, myself, nor other members of the family ever went there, or for that matter ever spoke of the place. With the exception of two infant children who had died many years before, none of our relatives were buried there, and, as far as I know, no one of the family had been there for many years. Most of them had never been there.

" 3. There was and had been no reason why I should ever think of the place, and I had never had any intention or desire to visit it.

" 4. Had I been a few minutes earlier or later (say half-an-hour at the most) I would not have met my father, and it is probable would never have heard of the matter. His messenger would have reported to him that I had not received his message, and he would probably not have mentioned it to me.

" To put the matter in a nutshell, a message was left for me to be at a certain undesirable and unfrequented place, inconvenient of access and taking some hours to reach by boat and other conveyance. I do not receive the message, but obey it implicitly to the minute.

"WILLIAM A. KOBBÉ."

In answer to inquiries, Major Kobbé says :—

" My father died about 4 years ago. Since my very remarkable meeting with him in the cemetery I have been at home at long intervals only, and for short periods of time, and for this reason, I suppose, never had occasion to mention the matter to him, or to any other member of the family. I have, since his death, spoken of it to others. I am now, and always have been, entirely free from superstition of any kind, and have, in common with all of my relatives and race, uncommonly strong nerves, unexcitable temperament, and an aversion to 'isms' of all kinds. Nothing of a similar nature ever happened to me before or since, and I never had any premonition or impression of any kind that I could not and did not care- fully and easily trace to its source."

We requested Major Kobbé to find out if his mother remembered the incident. He finds that she does not remember it, adding, " The part my mother played in the matter, while all-important as evidence, was a matter of slight moment to her at the time."

It is necessary, of course, to be sure that the line of action adopted by the percipient was really an unlikely one. It may look so, without really having been so. For instance, Miss Lindsay, of 58, Lloyd Street, Greenheys, Manchester, has given us an account of an unusually long walk which she suddenly undertook against advice, with the view of seeing an aunt who was almost a stranger to her.

" The day was very unsuitable for a walk of a number of miles. It threatened to rain, and began before I had got far on my way. I took a wrong turning, too, in a brown study, and returned in a loop to the same road, so that I found myself, late in the afternoon, again near the tram terminus, by which I might have gone home, instead of near my destination. By this time my thin print dress was soaked through by the rain, for I had

U

no cloak, yet I never thought of turning homewards. After walking some 14 miles, I arrived at the house, to find that my aunt had died suddenly of acute rheumatism that morning.

"Now, looking back on the matter, I see that native obstinacy might account for my starting in spite of counsel and weather, but it would *not* account for my visiting a relation I did not know well, and whom I did know to be particular about appearances, in a dripping dress. What I am particularly sure about is that it never once struck me that my proceeding was odd ; which, to my mind, proves conclusively that the initial impulse must have been stronger than an every-day freak."

Still, it may have been a freak, though not an " every-day " one. Miss Lindsay had just returned from the seaside " in excellent health, though in circumstances of considerable worry." Thus an excuse for a long walk may have been readily caught at, and the "native obstinacy" may have done the rest. The case, moreover, lacks the important evidential point which marked those that preceded it—the *desire* on the part of the supposed agent for the other person's presence. We have another case where a walk was suddenly taken, and pursued in torrents of rain, in spite of two attempts to return, under an idea that an acquaintance was on the point of death. She died the same evening. But she had been for some years an object of care to the person who visited her, and though the latter says, " I had not seen her for some weeks, possibly months before, and I did not know she was ill or likely to die," the case is one which we can hardly include.

The doubt as to what can be considered unlikely conduct on the percipient's part has relegated several alleged cases of this class to the Supplement. Among these are two of considerable interest. One of them is from Mr. Frederick Morgan, of Nugent Hill, Bristol, who records how he once made a sudden and unaccountable exit in the middle of a lecture, and walked home, unconscious of having done anything unusual, to find his house in imminent danger from fire, and his mother strongly desiring his presence. We have Mr. Morgan's assurance that he was thoroughly interested in the discourse, and had even noticed a friend with whom he had planned to walk home when it was over ; otherwise the impulse to leave a lecture-room might not seem the best possible specimen of an abnormal experience. The second case is from the Dr. Fischer quoted a few pages back ; who went to a jubilee dinner, and " had not been at table more than an hour," when he was forced to go out by an overpowering conviction that some one was in need of his assistance. This heroic step, taken on a comparatively empty stomach, was (as it turned out) fully justified. But we must remember that an impression of being wanted is a very deep and abiding element of a medical man's experience. The following case is better worth quotation, for the very reason that the percipient was not a doctor. We received it from Mr. Rowlands, of Bryncethin, near Bridgend, mentioned above (p. 252).

"July 2nd, 1884:

(86) "There was a Calvinistic Methodist minister, named Thomas Howell, Kinffig Hill, near Bridgend. He was preaching at Pen-y-graig, and resided not far from my house. 'I was disturbed in my mind about him about 12 or 1 o'clock in the morning. I rose from bed, and put my clothes on, went to his lodgings and knocked at his door, and told them that I was disturbed about the minister. I went in and up to his bedroom, and found him sitting down on the side of the bed, sweating, and as ill and as painful as could be. This happened about 6 years ago. You can write to Mr. Howell if you wish.

"ROWLAND ROWLANDS."

Mr. Howell writes to us as follows :—

"Longlands, Wyle.

"July 16th, 1884.

"I beg to inform you that the contents of the enclosed letter, which I received from you, sent to you from Mr. Rowland Rowlands, are quite true, and more than is stated in his letter. The night it took place, August 10th, 1879, I shall never forget, for, I believe, had it not been that some unknown agency sent me assistance, that I would have realised the mysteries of another world in a short time.

"The narrative is simply this. I was preaching at Pen-y-graig, the Sabbath referred to. I slept in a house near the chapel. After the service a few friends sat awhile with me conversing. After they left, about 10 o'clock, I took a little food, a cup of tea and a small bit of bread and butter, and retired to sleep about half-past 10, quite healthy, feeling no pain or uneasiness whatever. Somewhere between 12 and 1 o'clock I awoke with a severe attack of pain in the stomach,—remained a little in bed, but thinking death had struck me, I turned out on the bedside and attempted to call the landlady, but failed to do so. I could not move any further nor speak. In a few minutes I heard a voice at the door, outside, calling the landlady, who was in bed. He succeeded in awaking her and she replied from the landing—'Who is there?' To which Mr. Rowlands replied, 'Open the door at once; I have been disturbed in bed; there is something the matter with the preacher.' To which she replied, 'I don't think so; he has not called.' I heard Mr. Rowlands speak again : 'Make haste, Mrs. Phillips,' which time I believe, Mrs. Phillips, the landlady, was dressing herself, and ran downstairs and opened the door. Mr. Rowlands and herself came to my bedroom at once and knocked at my door. Receiving no answer, Mr. Rowlands opened the door, and found me in the position mentioned in his letter to you. He asked me, 'What is the matter with you, Mr. Howell?' to which I could not reply. I was by this time speechless. He told me again, 'I was disturbed in my bed about you ; shall we have a doctor?' to which I shook my head, meaning 'No.' I thought everything was almost over. A few moments again I was unconscious and for hours after knew nothing. When I came to myself, I saw Mr. Rowlands and Mrs. Phillips in the room. They remained with me till the morning. I gradually got better, and when Mr. Rowlands left me between 7 and 8 o'clock he remarked to me, 'I really thought you were going to die. How strange, was it not, that I was disturbed so! Can you account for it?' I replied 'No, if it was not that the Almighty had sent you to save me.'

"I have no more to say nor explain, but I know the facts are true.

"Thos. Howell."

Another letter of Mr. Howell's explains that the illness consisted in painful spasms, from which he had occasionally suffered, and that Mr. Rowlands "held him quiet." It is not clear that Mr. Rowlands' presence had anything to do with his recovery, though it was a great support to him. But as the illness and pain seem to have been extremely sudden, the coincidence is striking.

And here I may recall what was said above (p. 92) on the subject of *will* in relation to telepathy. The remarks which were made *à propos* of experimental cases derive strong confirmation from the more recent evidence. It is clear, I think, that in the cases last considered the telepathic influence should be interpreted as primarily *emotional*, rather than controlling or directive. In none of them should I regard the determination of the percipient's motor-impulse as at all directly due to the strong desire of the agent that he should act in that particular manner. I doubt if any amount of the most determined "willing," on the part of the strongest-minded friend or relative, would have brought Mr. Skirving from his work, Mr. Rowlands from his bed, or Dr. Fischer from his dinner. But we may quite conceive that Mrs. Skirving's distress and agitation might set up in her husband's mind a disturbance associated with the idea that he was needed ; and this might naturally affect his behaviour in the same way as an actual knowledge of the circumstances would have done, without the slightest abrogation of his normal power of choice. In Mr. Morgan's case the transferred impression (if it was one) did not reach the level of an idea at all, nor did the disturbance even take the form of distress, but only made itself felt in the complete distraction of his mind from its obvious and normal activities. But such distraction implies a genuine disturbance ; and since the idea of the locality— home—would naturally have a permanent place at the background of his mind, it is not hard to see how the disturbance might be attracted into this obvious channel, and might thus transform itself into a motor-impulse by a process which quite eluded consciousness.

I will illustrate this view by a final and extreme case, where the movements produced in the percipient were not such as the agent can have desired, or even thought of. The narrator is Dr. Liébeault, of 4, Rue Bellevue, Nancy.

"4 Septembre, 1885.

(87) "Je m'empresse de vous écrire au sujet du fait de communication de pensée dont je vous ai parlé, lorsque vous m' avez fait l'honneur d'assister à mes séances hypnotiques à Nancy. Ce fait se passa dans une famille française de la Nouvelle-Orléans, et qui était venue habiter quelque temps Nancy, pour y liquider une affaire d'intérêt. J'avais fait connaissance de cette famille parceque son chef, M. G., m'avait amené sa nièce, Mlle. B., pour que je la traitasse par les procédés hypnotiques. Elle était atteinte d'une anémie légère et d'une toux nerveuse contractées à Coblentz, dans une maison d'éducation où elle était professeur. Je parvins facilement à la mettre en somnambulisme, et elle fut guérie en deux séances. La production de cet état de sommeil ayant démontré à la famille G. et à Mlle. B. qu'elle pourrait facilement devenir médium (Mme. G. était médium spirite), cette demoiselle s'exerça à evoquer, à l'aide de la plume, les esprits, auxquels elle croyait sincèrement, et au bout de deux mois elle fut un remarquable médium écrivante. C'est elle que j'ai vue de mes yeux tracer rapidement des pages d'écriture qu'elle appelait des messages, et cela en des termes choisis et sans aucune rature, en même temps qu'elle tenait conversations avec les personnes qui l'entouraient. Chose curieuse, elle n'avait nullement conscience de ce qu'elle écrivait ; 'aussi,' disait-elle, 'ce ne peut être qu'un esprit qui dirige ma main, ce n'est pas moi.'[1]

"Un jour—c'était, je crois, le 7 Février, 1868—vers 8 heures du matin, au moment de se mettre à table pour déjeûner, elle sentit un besoin, un quelque chose qui la poussait à écrire (c'était ce qu'elle appelait une *trance*)—et elle courut immédiatement vers son grand cahier, où elle traça fébrilement, au crayon, des caractères indéchiffrables. Elle retraça les mêmes caractères sur les pages suivantes, et enfin l'excitation de son esprit se calmant, on put lire qu'une personne nommée Marguérite lui annonçait sa mort. On supposa aussitôt qu'une demoiselle de ce nom qui était son amie, et habitait, comme professeur, le même pensionnat de Coblentz où elle avait exercé les même fonctions, venait d'y mourir. Toute la famille G., compris Mlle. B., vinrent immédiatement chez moi, et nous decidâmes de vérifier, le jour même, si ce fait de mort avait réellement eu lieu. Mlle. B. écrivit à une demoiselle anglaise de ses amis, qui exerçait aussi les mêmes fonctions d'institutrice dans le pensionnat en question ; elle prétexta un motif, ayant bien soin de ne pas revéler le motif vrai. Poste pour poste, nous reçumes une réponse en anglais, dont on me copia la partie essentielle—réponse que j'ai retrouvée dans une portefeuille il y

---

[1] I need hardly point out the fallacy of this argument. See the discussion and examples of automatic writing in Chap. ii., § 12.

a à peine quinze jours, et égarée de nouveau. Elle exprimait l'etonnement de cette demoiselle anglaise au sujet de la lettre de Mlle. B., lettre qu'elle n'attendait pas sitôt, vu que le but ne lui en paraissait pas assez motivé. Mais en même temps, l'amie anglaise se hâtait d'annoncer à notre médium que leur amie commune, Marguérite, était morte le 7 Février vers les 8 heures du matin. En outre, un petit carré de papier imprimé était interré dans la lettre ; c'était un billet de mort et de faire part. Inutile de vous dire que je vérifiai l'enveloppe de la lettre, et que la lettre me parut venir réellement de Coblentz.

" Seulement j'ai eu depuis des regrets. C'est de n'avoir pas, dans l'intérêt de la science, demandé à la famille G. d' aller avec eux vérifier au bureau télégraphique si, réellement, ils n'auraient pas reçu une dépêche télégraphique dans la matinée du 7 Février. La science ne doit pas avoir de pudeur ; la verité ne craint pas d'être vue. Je n'ai comme preuve de la véracité du fait qu'une preuve morale : c'est l'honorabilité de la famille G., qui m' a paru toujours au dessus de tout soupçon.

"A. A. LIÉBEAULT."

[Apart from the improbability that the whole family would join in a conspiracy to deceive their friend, the nature of the answer received from Coblentz shows that the writer of it cannot have been aware that any telegraphic announcement had been sent. And it is in itself unlikely that the authorities of the school would have felt it necessary instantly to communicate the news to Mdlle. B.]

This example, it will be seen, differs from the preceding in the distinctness of the idea which—albeit latent in the percipient's mind—we must hold to have been transferred. Its chief interest, however, lies in the completeness and complexity of the automatism evolved. It exhibits a spontaneous telepathic impulse taking effect through the motor-system of the percipient in the very way that M. Richet's or our own deliberate efforts took effect on the "medium" (pp. 72-8). The parallel could not well be closer; and our view of the essential continuity of experimental and spontaneous telepathy [1] could hardly receive stronger support.

---

[1] See above, pp. 171-2.

CHAPTER VIII.

DREAMS.

PART I.—THE RELATION OF DREAMS TO THE ARGUMENT FOR TELEPATHY.

§ 1. THE inward impressions of distant events with which I have so far dealt have all been *waking* impressions. They have visited the percipient in the midst of his daily employments, and have often caused emotions that seemed quite incongruous with the normal current of life in which they mingled. But there is another department of experience which we are accustomed to consider as *par excellence* the domain of inward impressions, and from which the normal current of life is altogether shut off—the department of dreams. And this department, where inward ideas and images dominate unchecked, is also one which covers so large a period of human existence as to make it *à priori* probable that a considerable number of " transferred impressions " (supposing such things to exist) would fall within it. It would naturally, therefore, suggest itself as our next field of inquiry.

But dreams not only fall in naturally at this point; they are a means of advance. They comprise in themselves the whole range of transition from *ideal and emotional* to distinctly *sensory* affections; and they thus supply a most convenient link between the vaguer sort of transferred impressions and the more concrete and definitely embodied sort. The telepathic communications of the last two chapters, even where connected with recognisable images of persons and things, did not affect sight or hearing in such a way as to suggest the physical presence of the objects. Now many dreams are of just this impalpable kind. The material objects which figure in them are often the very vaguest of images, not localised in any particular spot. It is the general idea, the generalised form, of a person that presents itself, not a figure in a special attitude or clad in a special dress; events pass through the mind clothed in the faintly represented imagery in which a waking train of memory or of reverie will embody its contents. Such a dream only differs from a waking reverie in that it has not to compete, on the field of attention, with any objective facts; it is not contrasted with the immediate experience which the external world forces at every moment on the waking senses; and it is, therefore, itself accepted as immediate experience. With some persons it is rare for their dreams ever to emerge into more concrete actuality than this; and telepathy often seems to act in dreams of just such a veiled and abstract kind. From this lowest stage the transition is a gradual one up to the most vivid and detailed dream-imagery, the features of which are engraved on the memory as sharply as those of a striking scene in waking life;[1] and at every step of the transition we find evidence (how far conclusive will be seen later) to the action of telepathy.

It is only, however, when we come to the most distinctly sensory class of all, that the full theoretic importance of dreams can be realised. To make this clear, I must ask a moment's indulgence for a statement of some very obvious facts. Vivid dreams present themselves to us in *two* very different aspects. There is first the standpoint which we occupy when we are dreaming them. From that standpoint, the world with which they present us is often as external as the real one; and our perceptions in that world are perceptions of outward and abiding things, among which we live and move with as much sense of reality as if we had never known the disillusion of waking. To the dreamer, his more vivid and concrete images are actual *percepts*, calling his senses (in physiological language his sensory centres) into play just as external reality would. But there is of course a totally different standpoint from which to regard dreams, namely, the external and critical one that we habitually assume during waking life. We then think of them merely as that floating phantasmagoria whose transience and unreality have been the theme of philosophers and poets; which has very singular relations to time, and no real relations

---

[1] Those whose dreams are habitually of the more ideal and impalpable sort have sometimes a difficulty in realising the extreme sensory vividness of dreams at the other end of the scale, dreamt often by persons who have no exceptional power of visualising when awake. I myself lately dreamt that, meeting a stranger in Bond Street, I was arrested by a certain familiarity in the face, which I continued to scrutinise with puzzled eagerness, till I at last identified it with a portrait in the Grosvenor Gallery of the preceding year. Awake, I can scarcely recall the portrait at all.

I have also heard it asserted that (apart from actual external sounds) the sense of *hearing* is never distinctly exercised in dreams. I never had a more vivid dream than one of a few nights back, where some rifle-shooting, in the midst of which I found myself, caused me again and again precisely the same dread before the sound came, and the same intense irritation when it came, as I associate with the firing of a pistol on the stage. I could distinctly trace this dream to a similar (though less acute) irritation which I had suffered from the cracking of whips in a foreign city on the previous day.

at all to our familiar space—unless, indeed, we loosely identify it with its physical conditions, and localise it in the brain. Dreams, then, have this peculiarity : they are distinct affections of the senses, which yet, in reflecting on them, we rarely or never confound with objective facts ; waking hallucinations, on the other hand—spectral illusions or ghostly visitants—are often so confounded. The sleeping experiences are marked off from external reality in the minds of all of us by the very fact that we wake from them ; our change of condition makes their vanishing seem natural ; and thus looked back on, they will often seem to have been mere vague representations, *i.e.*, something *less* than affections of the senses. The waking experiences cannot be woke from ; their vanishing seems unconnected with the percipient and therefore *un*natural ; and thus looked back on, they will often seem to have been independent realities, *i.e.*, something *more* than affections of the senses.

Now it is as affections of the senses, and not as independent realities, that our Class A, the externalised sort of "phantasms of the living," are treated in this book. In the theory that the percipient is impressed *from a distance*, and in the very word *phantasm*, it is implied that what he sees or hears has no objective basis or existence in that part of the external world where his body is situated ; and whether he be asleep or awake, his relation to what he perceives, and of this to reality, is the same. But I shall be proceeding by the easiest route if (so far as the evidence will allow) I first trace the occurrence of the telepathic phantasms in the region of experience where sensory phantasms of some sort are normal and familiar, and are habitually judged of rightly as affections of the *inner* sense,[1] before passing to the region where phantasms of any sort are abnormal and unfamiliar, and are perpetually judged of wrongly as affections of the *outer* sense. The *rapprochement* which will thus be established between the sleeping and the waking cases will receive further and interesting illustration in certain interme- diate stages which we shall encounter on the way. We shall find that one set of phenomena merges into the other by gradual steps, and that this " borderland " is itself a region specially rich in the telepathic impressions.

---

[1] This term implies that sensation, from a physical point of view, is inverted ; that the initial stimulation takes place in the higher tracts of the brain, and that the stimulation of the special sensory apparatus is produced by a downward centrifugal current. The point will be further noticed in connection with waking hallucinations (see pp. 487-8).

§ 2. But though dreams thus present a logical point of departure, they also form in many ways the most assailable part of our case. They are placed almost in a separate category by their intimate connection with the lowest physical, as well as the highest psychical, operations. The grotesque medley which constantly throng through the gate of ivory thrust into discredit our rarer visitants through the gate of horn. And before proceeding further, it will be well to examine with some care the *general evidential value* of dreams, in relation to a theory of transferred impressions. The field may seem a fair one enough, as long as we keep to general expectations ; if telepathy is a reality, here is a probable scene of telepathic events. But what opportunities does it afford for confirming these expectations by accurate and convincing evidence ? This is a question which may rapidly convert our hopes into doubts.

The first objection to dreams, as evidence for transferred impressions of distant conditions or events, is this—that dreams being often somewhat dim and shapeless things, subsequent knowledge of the conditions or events may easily have the effect of giving body and definiteness to the recollection of a dream. When the actual facts are learnt, a faint amount of resemblance may often suggest a past dream, and set the mind on the track of trying accurately to recall it. This very act involves a search for details, for something tangible and distinct ; and the real features and definite incidents which are now present in the mind, in close association with some general scene or fact which actually figured in the dream, will be apt to be unconsciously *read back* into the dream. They make part of the original, of which the mind conceives the dream to have been a picture ; and the picture, when evoked in memory, will only too probably include details drawn from the original. After we have once realised the matter in its full distinctness, it becomes almost impossible to recall with due *in*distinctness the distant and shadowy suggestion of it.[1] Dreams in this way resemble objects seen in the dusk ; which begin by puzzling the eye, but which, when once we

---

[1] The possibilities referred to may be illustrated by the following cases.
Mr. R. O'Shaughnessy, M.P., writes to us :—
                          " House of Commons, April 20th, 1883.
" One night, when I was in my teens, I dreamt that I was passing by the house of Mr. J., who lived near us ; that I saw his nursery maid coming down the steps, carrying a baby in her arms, and preceded by a boy five or six years old ; that I asked her if this boy was Mr. J.'s eldest son ; that she said ' Yes,' and that I then said, ' Well, he's not a beauty, but he promises to be a fine fellow. He is very like his father.' Such was my dream. A few minutes after I awoke, *my* father, in whose room I slept, told me, without my having made any allusion to Mr. J., that he had on the previous day passed by Mr. J.'s house ; had seen the nurse and baby coming out, and the boy preceding

know or think we know what they are, seem quite unmistakeable and even full of familiar detail. For our purposes, therefore, it is of prime importance that the dream shall be told in detail to some one on whose memory we can rely; or, better still, written down, or in some way acted on, at the time, and before the confirmation arrives. Nearly all the evidence to be brought forward has, at any rate, this mark of accuracy.

But there is a more general and sweeping objection. Millions of people are dreaming every night; and in dreams, if anywhere, the range of possibilities seems infinite; can any positive conclusion be drawn from such a chaos of meaningless and fragmentary impressions? Must not we admit the force of the obvious *à priori* argument, that among the countless multitude of dreams, one here and there is likely to correspond in time with an actual occurrence resembling the one dreamed of; and that when a dream thus "comes true," unscientific minds are sure to note and store up the fact as something extraordinary, without taking the trouble to reflect whether such incidents occur oftener than pure chance would allow? Can the chances be at all estimated? Are any valid means at hand for distinguishing between a transferred impression and a lucky coincidence? What degree of exactitude of date and circumstance

them; had addressed to the nurse the very questions and remarks I had dreamt I addressed to her, and received the answer I had dreamt she made me."

In a case like this, one realises how a vague dream, excited, perhaps, by some remark heard over night, may have fallen into definite shape as the details of the real scene were one by one recounted.

Mrs. Nind, of Midleton House, Westcombe Park, Blackheath, tells us how, when about 20 years of age, she saw in a dream a brother, of whose whereabouts his family had long been ignorant, "lying on the deck of a ship, greatly exhausted. I saw in my dream the name of the ship, 'Zenobia.' A few days after, in the morning paper, I read the 'Zenobia' was picked up at sea waterlogged, near the south coast of Ireland, the crew and passengers suffering from great exhaustion, having been many hours working at the pumps, exactly as I had dreamt. I told it at once, and was impressed by the facts coming true in the course of a few days."

The brother was actually on that ship. But the whole pith of the statement is that the name of the ship was correctly seen; and this is just a point where unsupported memory cannot be relied on. The name might so easily *seem* to have been seen, when once it became associated with the reality; and a coincidence which is striking to begin with is all the more likely to become perfect in memory. (It is fair, however, to mention that the same lady has had at least two other dreams which strikingly corresponded with reality, and were mentioned by her before the reality was known; one of the bursting of a gun on board the "Viper," of which her brother was master; the other of her sister "lying faint in someone's arms," at a time when the sister had fallen and severely sprained her ankle.)

Again, Mrs. Liddell, of 18, Brae Street, Liverpool, tells us that in November, 1882, her brother, an engineer employed on a steamer, appeared to her in a dream, looking a good deal knocked about, and with some teeth out, and said, "It is all for the best"; and her husband testifies to her immediate mention of the dream. The brother had actually been wrecked at the time: "when he arrived home he had lost some of his teeth, and had been well knocked about." But everything depends on the detail of the teeth, which the husband does not mention. They were lost in reality; were they lost in the dream? In the absence of notes or corroborative testimony, we cannot be sure. This list could be easily extended.

must be reached, before we consider even a striking correspondence as worth attention ? And what proportion of striking correspondences are we to demand, before we consider that the hypothesis of chance is strained in accounting for them ?

In the first place, it is to be noted that there has, so far, been a complete lack of the statistics which alone could form the basis for an answer to these questions. It has never been known with any certainty what proportion of people habitually dream, what proportion of dreams are remembered at all, in what proportion of these remembered dreams the memory is evanescent, and in what proportion it is profound and durable. This latter point may be specially hard to establish satisfactorily in a particular case, as it is affected by the question whether a person's attention is habitually directed to his dreams, and also by the question whether he has happened to recount a particular dream to others, and so to stamp it on his own memory. By making inquiries on a large scale, however, a considerable approximation to certainty may be attained on these and various other points of importance. A good deal has been done in this way during the last three years ; and though I cannot say that the results are such as would allow us to base a theory of telepathy upon the facts of dreams alone, I think that they do much to diminish the *à priori* plausibility of the theory of chance, as a sufficient explanation of all cases of marked correspondence between a dream and an external event.

§ 3. The points to be considered have to do both with the *intensity* and with the *content* of the dream ; let us consider them in order.

First as to intensity. An exceedingly small proportion of dreams are remembered with distinctness several hours after waking. Even of the dreams which dwell in the memory, an exceedingly small proportion produce any appreciable amount of distress or excitement. And of these more impressive dreams, an exceedingly small proportion prove their intensity by being in any way acted on. What I have termed intensity may be indicated in another way, by the rapid repetition of a distinct dream two or three times on the same night; and this, too, when there is no apparent cause to prompt the dream, seems to be a comparatively rare occurrence (see p. 357). The dreams to be cited in this book will nearly all, I think, be distinguishable by one or other of these tests of exceptional intensity. And in proportion as the dreams which coincide with the event dreamed of are thus found to be in some other way exceptional—in proportion as the class to which they belong is found to form a small and sparse minority among the swarming multitude of unmarked dreams—in that proportion does it clearly become unreasonable to argue that the coincidences are sufficiently accounted for by the law of chances.   The argument which might seem effective so long as we had the whole multitude of dreams to range over—that multitude seeming sufficient to give the law of chances ample scope—assumes quite a different aspect when we find ourselves limited to the comparatively small group of *intense* dreams.

Next as to content. Before we can give weight to a dream-coincidence as pointing to anything beyond the operation of chance, we should inquire whether the event dreamed of is distinct, unexpected, and unusual. If it combine all three characteristics in a high degree, its evidential value may be very considerable ; in proportion as the degree falls short, or the combination fails, the evidential value sinks ; and none of the characteristics taken alone, even though present in a high degree, would lead us to include a dream in the present collection. Thus, the dream-content must be neither a vague impression of calamity nor of happiness ; nor a catastrophe on which the sleeper's mind is already fixed ; nor some such ordinary event as has frequently occurred in waking experience. It may, indeed, be not the less significant for being trivial ; but in that case it must be of a bizarre or unlikely kind.[1] Then again, amount of detail, and the number of connected events, are of immense importance, as each subsequently verified detail tells with ever-mounting strength against the hypothesis of accidental coincidence. Once more, dream-content must be considered to some extent in relation to the dream-habits of the particular dreamer. Before estimating the value of the fact that a person has dreamt of the sudden death of a friend on the night when the death took place, we should have to ascertain that that

---

[1] It is not easy to draw the line here.   How, for instance, ought the following case to be regarded ? We received the account through the kindness of Mr. James Sime ; the narrator is Mrs. Bell, of Windmill Road, Hamilton.

"July 21st, 1884.

" In the autumn of 1875, my father and I left home for Perthshire, giving the use of our Hamilton house to an uncle.   On Wednesday night previous to our return home, I dreamt that my cousin had broken the handle of a vegetable-dish, and said to her sister, ' Don't tell, for I see the soup-tureen handle has been mended, and I shall mend this too.' I told this dream to my father at breakfast on Thursday morning.   He laughed, and begged me not to speak of it to my cousins, lest they should say I had been thinking evil

person is not in the habit of dreaming of distressing or horrible events.[1] In respect of these various points, the instances to be cited, here and in the Supplement, are the sifted survival of many less definite coincidences in which the popular imagination would find a marvel. And in the case of this residue, where we have complete fulfilment of some of the above conditions, over and above the close proximity in time, or (it may be) absolute synchronism, of the event and the dream, the question as to a causal connection between the two is, at any rate, not to be swept out of court by a mere general appeal to the doctrine of chances.

But there is a further point in the content of the dreams that correspond with real events—true dreams, as we may for brevity call

of them. However, when we got home on Friday, just as my friends were leaving, I said in joke, ' Oh ! you didn't tell me you had broken the handle of the vegetable-dish.'
"My cousin at once turned to her sister, and said, ' Did you tell ?' I was amazed, and said, ' You don't mean to say you broke it.' She said, ' Yes, I did, on Wednesday, and I told my sister to say nothing about it to you, and I would mend it like the soup-tureen.'

"AGNES J. BELL."

In answer to inquiries, Mrs. Bell says :—
" I have to state that I am not a great dreamer, but the dream in question struck me as so exceptional that I repeated it in detail to my father in the morning."
Mrs. Bell's father corroborates as follows :—

"Auchingramont Road, Hamilton.
"August 2nd, 1884.
" I recollect, in the autumn of 1875, while at Comrie, my daughter telling me one morning of a dream she had about one of her cousins breaking a vegetable-dish.
" On returning to Hamilton we found the dream verified.

"DANIEL CLARKE."

Another informant tells us—and her statement is corroborated—how she announced to her family one morning, on the strength of a dream, that a cousin of theirs had been in bed with a quinsey, but would come to see them that day. He came, and said he had been kept away by a quinsey, a malady from which he had never suffered before. But on inquiry we find that quinsey was a familiar idea in the dreamer's family, as a governess had frequently had it ; and the coincidence thus seems too clearly within the range of chance.

[1] For example, we have not admitted the following case, which was sent to us by the Rev. T. C. Skeggs, of 14, Fitzwarren Street, Pendleton, Manchester.
"June 17th, 1884.
" In the year 1872 I was in China. I dreamed that a lady friend in England was in great trouble. For about two days I could not rid myself of the thought of her distress. The nature of her trouble was not at all defined to my own mind, only that she was prostrate with grief. About six weeks later the mail brought me news of her father's death, of whom she was passionately fond, and of course she was proportionately distressed. The painful impression caused by my dream led me to note the date at which it occurred, and when I compared it with the news contained in my letter, I found it tallied with the date of her father's death.
" The lady was an intimate friend, 12 years older than myself, and we had many interests in common with each other ; these formed a bond of sympathy.
"T. C. SKEGGS."
In another letter Mr. Skeggs adds:—" I do not often dream of personal friends. One point connected with that dream was exceptional, viz., the duration of the impression." The mere fact of the friend's distress, however, hardly affords a definite enough coincidence for the case materially to help the telepathic argument ; and inquiry brought out a "dream-habit" which still further lowers its value in this connection. " Am I a great dreamer ? I am. I frequently dream of horrors that are so vivid to my mind as to leave me quite exhausted in the morning."

them—which cannot but strike the attention as soon as we begin to examine actual specimens. It is that, among true dreams, by very far the largest class is the class where the truth is *death*—*i.e.*, where the event dreamt of as happening to another is of that most restricted kind which can only happen once in each individual's experience. Out of the 149 coincident dreams which are included in this book—as at least clearly finding in telepathy, if it exists, their most natural explanation—no less than 79 have represented or suggested death. This, it will be seen, is entirely in accordance with a theory of causal connection between event and dream, where the abnormal state of the person dreamt of is regarded as part of the cause ; but it is not at all in accordance with what we should expect accident to bring about. Nor could this argument well be met by the assumption that it is only in the case of a very grave event that the accidental correspondence attracts attention and gets recorded. For this would mean that the dreams of death which happen to correspond with reality are one specially-remembered class among the total number of accidentally-true dreams. Now it will be admitted that dreams of death constitute a minute proportion of *all* dreams ; it would follow, then, on the above assumption, that accidentally-true dreams of death constitute a similarly minute proportion of all accidentally-true dreams. But at this rate the total number of " true dreams"—in other words, the number of coincidences which the doctrine of chances will have to cover—swells to a most prodigious and unmanageable figure. It is just because a " true dream " is a very *exceptional* occurrence, that it was possible even to attempt to account for it as an accident ; if the " accident " is for ever " coming off," so much the worse for that attempt.

§ 4.   But the fact that a singular and marked event, such as death, is in so large a proportion of cases the central feature of the "true" dreams, supplies more than a general argument ; it supplies the means for an actual numerical estimate whereby the adequacy of the chance-hypothesis may be tested. For dreams of so definite a character, and which admit of being so clearly and briefly described, are quite a fit subject for statistics ; there is a possibility of finding out approximately what the actual frequency of a dream of this sort is ; and we shall then have the first necessary datum for deciding whether the frequency of the cases where it coincides with reality, is, or is not, greater than chance would fairly allow. If it turned out that all of us about once a week had a marked and distressing dream of the death of some friend or other, then, since people who are somebody's friends are perpetually dying, the coincidence of such a dream with the real event might be expected to occur by pure accident in a large number of cases. But if only a small minority of us could recall ever having had such a dream at all, the case would be reversed. The object, then, is to ascertain from a number of people, large enough and promiscuous enough to be accepted as a fair specimen of the whole population, what percentage of them have had the experience in question. With this view, efforts have been made, dating from the winter of 1883, to obtain a large number of answers to the following question :—

Since January 1st, 1874, have you ever had a dream of the death of some person known to you, which dream you marked as an exceptionally vivid one, and of which the distressing impression lasted for as long as an hour after you rose in the morning?

This question has been put to 5360 persons, as to whom it was not known beforehand whether their answer would be "Yes" or "No." Of these persons, 173 answered "Yes." Excluding 7 of these cases, in which the dreamer was at the time in a state of distinct anxiety as to the person whose death was dreamt of, we have a remainder of 166. These include a good many cases where it proved, on further inquiry, that the terms of the question had not been exactly met, as the impression had not endured in any vivid or distressing way. They also include 3 cases where the mind of the dreamer had been exceptionally directed to the person dreamt of; and 3 cases where the person dreamt of was in the same room as the dreamer, which may have had some tendency to produce the dream— one gentleman expressly stating his suspicion that his dream was caused by some sound made by his companion. We may, therefore, accept the 166 as a liberal estimate. But 18 of these persons professed to have had a dream of the sort inquired about more than once. It will be again a liberal estimate if we suppose each of these to have experienced 3 distinct examples within the specified time ; and the most convenient way of taking account of these repetitions will be to add 36 to the 166, making 202. With this substitution, $\frac{1}{26}$ of the whole number of persons asked may be taken to have given an affirmative answer. Now, the persons asked were a quite promiscuous body, and a body large enough to be safely regarded as a fair average sample of the population ; just as a similar number of persons, taken at random, would be accepted as a fair sample for purposes of statistics on short sight, or colour-blindness. We may conclude, then, that the number of persons who can recall having had—during the twelve years 1874-1885, and without special assignable cause— the experience named in the question, amount to about 1 in 26 of the population of this country.

The question next occurs, ought we, in making our calculation, to assign any limit to the area of acquaintances from whom the person dreamt of may be drawn, and of whom a certain proportion will, in the natural course of things, die within a period of 12 years ? On general grounds it may fairly be argued that the slightness of connection between two persons would diminish the chance that one would dream *accidentally*, no less than the chance that he would dream *telepathically*, of the death of the other ;[1] and that therefore a vivid dream of the death of a stranger, or of a slight acquaintance, when it coincides with the death, tells neither more nor less in favour of the action of something beyond chance than a similarly vivid and coincident dream of the death of a near relative. It will be seen, moreover, that, as far as the numerical estimate goes, it is unimportant how large or how small we take the area to be ; because whatever number of persons we include, on the average the same proportion of the number will die within any given time. Thus assuming this proportion who die to be one-fourth of the whole number, then, if we took a very large circle of acquaintances, say 400—the death of any of whom, if dreamt of when it occurred, would count as one of our coincidences—we should have to reckon that 100 of them actually die in the course of the time ; and if we took a very small circle of just the immediate relatives of the dreamer, say 4, we should have to reckon that 1 of them dies in the course of the time. And the chance of an accidental coincidence in the specified period between the single dream of death and the death itself is practically

---

[1] It is not always easy to find out, from a brief description, the strength of the bond that has existed between two persons. But I think I am safe in saying that the dreams of death in which the person dreamt of is not linked to the dreamer by a rather close tie of kinship or affection, do not amount to 10 per cent. of the whole number. In other respects the dreams do not seem to follow any line of *à priori* likelihood—*e.g.*, they concern the death of young persons quite as much as of old ones.

I may point out that a different estimate would have to be made for dreams dreamt by several dreamers about the *same* person : *e.g.*, an accidental coincidence of dream and death is less improbable than usual where the person dreamt of is a prominent public character, because he is (so to speak) within the dream-horizon of an immense number of people. But the proviso has no practical importance, as no cases of the kind occur in my statistics.

w

the same in both these cases. For though there will be, on the one hand, much less chance of its being the right individual that is dreamt of when the choice is among 400 than when it is among 4, on the other hand the 100 deaths will give 100 (or nearly 100) nights on which the coincident dream will have its chance of being dreamt, instead of only 1 night. Logically, therefore, there is no necessity for limiting the area in question. Let the number of any one's acquaintance be called x. Then, whether x be large or small, all that concerns us is the proportion of the x persons who die within the specified period of 12 years ; and this proportion, since the death-rate per year is about ·022, may be taken as ·264, or a little more than one-fourth.

The estimate from the above data is as follows. The probability that a person, taken at random, will have a vivid dream of death in the course of 12 years is $\frac{1}{26}$; the probability that any assigned member of the general population, and therefore that any particular dreamt-of person, will die within 12 hours of an assigned point of time is $\frac{22}{1000} \times \frac{1}{365}$; hence the probability that, in the course of 12 years, a vivid dream of death *and* the death of the person dreamt of will fall within 12 hours of one another is $\frac{1}{26} \times \frac{22}{1000} \times \frac{1}{365} = \frac{1}{431,363}$. (If x, the number of the dreamer's circle of friends, be taken into account, we then have, as the probability that *any* one of the dreamer's circle should die within the particular 24 hours defined by the dream, $x \times \frac{1}{27} \times \frac{22}{1000} \times \frac{1}{365}$; and as the probability that, if some one of the dreamer's circle dies within the particular 24 hours, it should be the *particular* one dreamt of, $\frac{1}{x}$; whence the probability of this double event $= \frac{1}{x} \times x \times \frac{1}{27} \times \frac{22}{1000} \times \frac{1}{365}$, *i.e.*, the result is unaltered.) That is to say, each group of 431,363 persons in the population of the United Kingdom will produce one such coincidence in the given time. Now let it be supposed for a moment that our appeal for evidence has effectively reached as large a section of the population as this : let it be supposed, that is to say, that the number of persons from whom we should, directly or indirectly, have received examples of such coincidences, if they had had them to communicate, amount to 431,363. In that case, then, the number of such coincidences which we ought, by the doctrine of chances, to have encountered is 1. The number which we have actually encountered, of vivid dreams of death, narrated to us at first-hand,[1] dreamt since January 1st, 1874, by persons free from anxiety, and falling within 12 hours of the death of the person dreamt

---

[1] In three cases the evidence, though not actually from the dreamer, is of the sort described in Vol. i., p. 148, as on a par with first-hand.

of [1]—is 24 : that is, a number 24 times larger than the doctrine of chances would have allowed us to expect.[2] And this number is very much below what we are justified in assuming. For while my colleagues and I are probably disposed rather to overrate than to underrate the extent to which the world is acquainted with our proceedings, we cannot suppose that the actual number of persons from whose collective experiences our examples are drawn really approaches half a million, as above supposed. (In Chap. XIII., I shall show grounds for thinking that a quarter of the number assumed would still probably be much above the mark.) Moreover, 7 of the 24 coincidences are represented as having been extremely close ; in 3 other cases the interval was at any rate not more than 4 hours, and in another was from 3 to 6 hours ; while in 9 more, where death and dream are merely stated to have fallen on the same night, the coincidence may have been exact, and is not likely to have been inexact to the extent of anything like 12 hours. Again, dreams are excluded where the actual *fact* of death was not in some way presented, even though the dying person was dreamt of in a remarkable way.[3] But most markedly have I understated the case in this respect, that I

---

[1] With 5 possible exceptions, where the 12 hours' limit may not have been nearly reached, but where it may have been exceeded. In 2 of these cases, the death took place in the afternoon and the dream followed the same night ; in the 3 others, the death was either on the night of the dream or on a day contiguous to that night, but its hour is not known. Two dreams are excluded which are known to have followed the death by a very little more than 12 hours, the death not having been heard of in the interval.

[2] Nos. 23, 114, 116, 118, 126, 127, 134, 141, 283, 309, 423, 426, 427, 428, 443, 448, 450, 452, 454, 455, 456, 458, 459, 702. No. 23 is included, though not literally a dream of death, on account of the very strong impression that it produced of the death of the person represented in it. No. 138 (p. 376) is excluded for the reason stated in " Additions and Corrections." I am excluding 6 cases where some ground for anxiety as to the condition of the person dreamed of existed, even though no special anxiety is remembered to have been felt ; the person who died, in one of these cases, was old and infirm ; in another was known to be slightly unwell ; and in two others was at sea. Another dream is excluded which was not literally of death, though interpreted as such by the dreamer ; and yet another where the fact of the coincidence of the dream with a sudden death was stated, but the witness found the subject too painful to give details. Of the 24 included dreams, 10 were of the deaths of near relatives ; and 4 or 5 concerned persons who were outside the circle of intimate acquaintance.

[3] I would draw special attention to this point. For when we come to deal with the *waking* cases, where a phantasm of a person is seen or heard at the time of his death, they may seem to present a marked difference from the *dreams* that will be quoted as having coincided with death,—these last being distinctly dreams *of death*, whereas it is only in a minority of the waking cases that any idea of death was conveyed. The waking percipient may have *surmised* the death, from the fact that he had seen or heard the phantasm ; but the phantasm itself, more often than not, was simply the natural-looking appearance or natural-sounding voice of the "agent." We must remember, then, that for aught we know, telepathically caused dreams of just this type may occur ; but unless they present specially remarkable features (as in case 23, p. 199 above,) we should not cite them as having even a *primâ facie* claim to be considered telepathic, just because of the immense scope for chance-coincidence that dreams afford. We demand *more* of a dream—that it shall suggest the right *event*, and not merely the right *person*—before we think it worth considering ; and the dreams to be quoted correspond with the *rarer* type of waking cases, where the phantasmal representation has in some way distinctly suggested death.

have introduced nothing but the bare fact of death, and have neglected the points of detail which in some instances add indefinitely to the difficulty of regarding the coincidence as a chance.

The above is a tolerably clear computation; and its validity could only be rebutted in two ways—(1) by impugning, on evidential grounds, the cases of coincidence that are alleged; (2) by impugning the approximate accuracy of the initial *datum*—that within the last 12 years not more than 1 person in 26 has, without clear cause, had a markedly distressing and haunting dream of the death of an acquaintance.

The evidential value of the alleged coincidences will be better estimated when we consider some of the actual specimens. But as regards the initial datum, on which the calculation depends, there are objections the force of which must be at once admitted. Dreams in general, it may be said, fade away from our memory because there is nothing to stamp them there; but if it happens that some real event recalls a recent dream, then, by the principle of association, this dream will obtain a more permanent lodgment in our mind. Now the death of relatives or friends is the sort of real event which it is practically certain that we shall hear of very soon after it occurs. A dream of such an occurrence is therefore practically certain to get stamped in the way described, if it has been at all synchronous with the fact. And it is thus allowable to suppose that a large number of such dreams may occur which lapse unnoted from the mind, but any one of which, had news of the real event been received immediately afterwards, would have been recalled and associated with it, and would have then added a case to the list of "remarkable coincidences."

This argument is to a considerable degree met by the terms of the question. What is asked is not merely whether people have had a dream of death; but whether they have had one which has haunted them for at least an hour after rising in the morning; and it will not be maintained that an experience of that sort is so likely to vanish utterly from the memory as an ordinary dream. But it might, no doubt, be rejoined that perhaps a good many of the *coincident* dreams were not marked at the time by any special vividness or impressiveness; and that the dreamer came to *imagine* this peculiarity of character in his dream, *after* it had come to assume importance in his eyes from the discovery that it had coincided with the reality. And I most fully recognise that when the argument begins to turn on such a point as the degree of vividness which a dreamer, looking back to a dream through the medium of subsequent impressions, can swear that it possessed, anything like positive proof becomes impossible. A dream so looked back to may get charged with an emotional character, just as we saw above that it might get filled in with a precision of detail, which it did not really possess. But I must here draw special attention to the safeguards already mentioned. Our collection includes a remarkably high proportion of cases where the coincident dream was marked as exceptional in character—*at the time*, and *before* the real event was known—by being immediately narrated as such, to someone else, (who, if accessible, has of course been questioned as to his memory of the fact); or by being noted in writing; or by being in some way acted on. Of the 107 dream-examples recorded in this book on the first-hand testimony of the dreamer, 72 are alleged to have been described, 11 more to have been recorded in writing (in one instance by a relative of the dreamer's), and 9 more to have been in some marked way acted on, before the corresponding event was known; and in 46 of the 72 cases where the dream was at once described, we have also the independent testimony of the person to whom it was described. In 18 other cases, we have the testimony of the person to whom the dream was described before the corresponding event was known, but not the dreamer's own account. Of the 24 dreams used in my numerical estimate, 3 were noted in writing, and 20 (including 2 of the previous 3) are alleged to have been mentioned, before the fact of the death was known; and in 15 of these 20 cases, we have independent testimony to this mention from the person to whom it was made. And I must further point out that, in order to explain away the result of the above computation in the way suggested, it would have to be assumed not only that *a great many* dreams of death pass unnoted and leave no impression, while still of such a nature that a vivid impression of them would revive if news corresponding to them were subsequently heard; it would have to be assumed that such an experience befalls *very nearly every adult in the country* at least once within the twelve years. For our conclusion was that coincident dreams of death in this country were 24 times as numerous as the law of chances—according to the *datum* which the census gave us—would allow. Therefore to make the law of chances applicable as an explanation, we must multiply our initial *datum* by 24; that is, instead of assuming 1 person out of every 26 to have had the required dream, we must assume 24 out of every 26—that is nearly every one—to have had it; nay, on the more probable estimate of our area of inquiry (p. 307), we must assume that on the average every one has had it as many as *four times* within the given period; though 96 per cent. of them forget all about it.[1] A good many of my readers will, I think, altogether repudiate such a supposition in their own case. I believe, indeed, that a perfectly impartial census would have given a decidedly smaller proportion than 1 in 26. For it is practically impossible to carry out a census of the sort required without getting an unfair proportion of *Yeses*. Persons who have only *No* to say in answer to such a question as was propounded, are apt to think that there is no good in saying it; and if they receive a printed form, instead of writing their answer on it and returning it, they are apt to consign it to the waste-paper basket—probably often with a vague notion that what was wanted was a *Yes*, and that sensible people, who do not have exceptional experiences, ought not to encourage the superstitions of those who do.[2]

§ 5. As pointed out above, it is only where the coincident dream exhibits some sort of *unique* event, such as death, that we can obtain the statistical basis necessary for an arithmetical estimate of chances. A very few remarks, however, seem worth making on dreams which offer less hope of a definite conclusion.

Certain other marked events, such as unexpected dangers and accidents, are comparable to death, though standing much below it, in the two main points—the *comparative* infrequency of their forming the subject of a markedly distressing dream, and the *comparatively* large proportion (though *absolutely*, of course, a very small proportion) of cases in which such a dream, when it does occur, coincides with reality. And even when we come down to unusual events of a more commonplace type, or to a detailed *nexus* of more or less familiar incidents—where it is, of course, out of the question to get any sort of numerical basis for computation—the same sort of argument may still be cautiously applied. It is true that the coincidences do not now occur among any comparatively small group of *dreamers*, such as the dreamers of death—the order of dream which is now in question being common to all who dream at all;

---

[1] If it be objected that such an extreme assumption would not be required, as persons who have the dream may have it repeatedly, I can reply that hardly any of the persons from whom we have received accounts of "coincidental" dreams of death recall having dreamt of death except on that one occasion; and it would be even odder that many of them should have completely forgotten a number of such vivid experiences than that they should have completely forgotten one.

[2] A further account of the census of which the above inquiry formed part will be ound in Chapter xiii.

but they still occur among a comparatively small group of *dreams*. In the cases which form a considerable proportion of our collection, where the dream was at. once narrated as an exceptionally odd or vivid one, the proof of its exceptional oddness or vividness is at once supplied. And further, an immensely large class, the purely fantastic dreams, to which no real event could possibly be recognised as corresponding, are excluded; as also are the commonest class of all where the dreamer is not the spectator but the hero of the dream, and no unusual incident or precise series of incidents is presented as occurring independently to *others*—who, if present, merely make a necessary background, or take their share of speech and action in conjunction with the dreamer. The distant event, or series of events, with which the dream corresponds, must both be possible (for it actually occurs), and must centre round some one other than the dreamer; and the consequent necessity that the marked point or points of the dream shall both be possible and shall centre round some one other than the dreamer, immensely reduces the list of dreams which come into the reckoning; and to the same extent reduces the *primâ facie* plausibility of the hypothesis that the coincidence is due to chance. No doubt, after all deductions, the number of dreams which remain to be taken into account, before we can decide as to the chances of accidental coincidences with reality, is here many times larger than our former restricted class, which was concerned with a single unique event: it may conceivably be many thousands of times larger. But, whatever the multiple, it is hard to believe that the number of events—even of more or less curious events—which it is *possible to dream of* as occurring to other people, does not bear an even larger ratio to the single event of death. For what limit can we so much as conceive to the sum of the details of circumstance which the whole dreaming population of the country can connect in imagination with the various members of their respective acquaintance?

Such considerations do not, of course, amount to an argument for telepathic correspondences on this wider ground—the *data* are far too indefinite for that. But they at least suggest that the adequacy of the chance-theory is not quite so obvious as is sometimes assumed.

This preliminary sketch of the evidential aspect of dreams may, perhaps, prevent misunderstanding. Among considerations so complex and data so uncertain, it is not easy to sum up a view in very precise terms; but our general position has been made sufficiently clear by my

statement that we should not, with our present evidence, have undertaken to make out a case for telepathy on the ground of dreams alone.
The question whether a case could be completely made out on that
ground, though it may be worth debating, seems incapable of
final settlement, until a very large section of the population takes to
keeping a daily record of their dream-experiences. A much larger
number of examples is needed for which, even taken in isolation, a
high evidential rank could be claimed—whether from the amount of
detail in the coincidence, as in cases 134, 138, and 142, or from some such
exceptional features as marked Mr. Wingfield's case (p. 199). But
meanwhile an argument of a quite different sort can be imported from
the department of evidence on which we mainly rely—the evidence of
telepathic impressions of distant events received in the waking state.
The probabilities of some real causal connection between event and
impression in the *less* conclusive cases cannot be fairly weighed
without regard to the existence of the *more* conclusive; and that
dreams form, on the whole, the less evidentially conclusive class can
be no ground for tabooing them, unless we can assign special reasons
why sleep should be a condition adverse to telepathic influence. In
the conception of telepathy which it is hoped that the reader will
by degrees come to share, no such reasons appear; while the
resemblances and the transition-cases, already referred to, between
the sleeping and the waking phenomena, make it practically impossible to reject in the one class an explanation which we admit in
the other. The examples which I shall proceed to give require no
further justification. They are not needed to prove our theory; but
many of them almost inevitably fall under it as soon as it is proved;
and we have no right to disregard any light which they may throw
on it.

PART II.—EXAMPLES OF DREAMS WHICH MAY BE REASONABLY
REGARDED AS TELEPATHIC.

§ 1. On surveying a large number of cases where a dream has
corresponded in time with the real occurrence of the event or events
which it represented, in such a way as strongly to suggest that it had
its source in a telepathic impulse, we find that they at once fall into
distinct classes. In the first class, the agent is in a normal state, or
is himself also dreaming : the external event here is simply the
occurrence to the agent of a particular thought or dream ; and the
percipient's impression is concerned simply with the content of that
thought or dream, not with the agent himself. In all other classes
the agent is in some condition or situation which is more or less
abnormal ; and the percipient has an impression of the agent as in
this situation, but an impression which may take various forms. Not
infrequently the central fact is dreamt of merely as a fact—as something the dreamer hears of, or becomes aware of, as having occurred,
without himself in any way coming into contact with it. In another
class of cases, he perceives the principal actor in the matter dreamt of
—the dying person, if death is the occasion—in such a manner as to
suggest the actual catastrophe ; this suggestion being often connected
with some special imagery or symbolism. And in yet another class, he
seems himself transported into the actual scene—to be an actual
spectator of the event.

I will begin then with some specimens of the first class, where
the dream has close relation to something that is in the agent's mind,
but the agent's own personality does not specially figure in it.[1] These
are, of course, the cases which come nearest to experimental thought-
transference ; and an additional point of resemblance is that they are
especially apt to occur when the agent and percipient are in tolerably
close proximity. One marked group of these cases is the simultaneous
occurrence of the same dream to two persons. Such an occurrence
would not be likely to be heard of except when the two dreamers

---

[1] We must insist on the fulfilment of at least one of two conditions : either the
thought, or the *personality*, of the agent must be distinctly represented in the dream.
This is, of course, a mere evidential rule ; but, owing to the immense scope for
accidental coincidences that dreams afford, it must be strictly applied. For example, Mrs.
Sidney Smith, of 7, The Terrace, Barnes, tells us of an extraordinary and indescribable
horror which she experienced in sleep, on the night of a brother's very tragic death ; but as
she did not connect the impression with her brother till she heard that he was missing, the
case cannot be even provisionally admitted.

were nearly related or were living in the same house ; indeed, unless the correspondence were extraordinarily close and detailed, it is only the fact of the dreamers' belonging to a narrowly restricted circle that could justify one in attaching the slightest importance to it. In a wider circle, coincidences of the sort might obviously happen, and perhaps often do happen, by pure accident. But relationship or habitual propinquity involves, of course, the chance that some item of joint waking experience has been the independent source of both dreams ; and no case would be admissible where any recent cause of this sort could be traced.[1]   One of the strongest evidential features would be the repetition of the occurrence with the same two persons ; as recorded, for instance, in a communication read to the Psychological Society on February 15th, 1877, Mr. Serjeant Cox presiding.

(88) " Mr. E. P. Toy stated that he and his wife were in the habit of dreaming upon the same subject at the same time ; this did not arise from mere coincidence, or in consequence of certain matters being naturally uppermost in their minds, for trifling things were dreamt of which had not been in their thoughts previously.   One night he dreamt that he had been charged by a bull, and so did she ; on another occasion he dreamt that he was at the funeral of a favourite child, and he did not grieve, although he liked the child very much ; his wife dreamt the same thing ; and they often had similar experiences."

Mr. Toy wrote to us, from Littlehampton, in November, 1883 :—

" The circumstances occurred some 8 or 10 years ago and the particulars have faded from my memory, as also from Mrs. Toy's.   I can only confirm the general facts as related in my note to Serjeant Cox.

" While writing, I may mention a still more extraordinary dream.   I dreamed that for some reason or other I had poisoned a woman, and the same night Mrs. Toy had a very vivid dream, in which she thought I was going to be tried for having committed a murder.   I do not think I am of a blood-thirsty disposition, and do not remember to have been reading anything to have suggested the dream, so the coincidence was, to say the least, very striking.

" EDMUND TOY."

[The force of these coincidences is diminished but not destroyed by the fact, which Mr. Podmore elicited in conversation, that both Mr. and Mrs. Toy have frequent and vivid dreams.]

---

[1] For example, we have a quite recent case where a brother and sister (Mr. and Miss Dawson, of Richmond Cottage, Worthing) dreamt, on the same night, and, apparently, at the same hour, 3 a.m., that their dog bit the brother in the foot.   The brother's dream was a very vivid one, as he woke with a scream, which was heard by his mother ; and both dreams were independently described next morning.   The dog had never bitten anyone before, and had been perfectly friendly with Mr. Dawson, and no mention had been made of any risk connected with him ; so that the coincidence seemed a striking one. But on making more precise inquiries, we found that soon afterwards he did actually bite Mr. Dawson, who had since been "unable to approach him." It is possible, therefore, to suppose that the idea of risk may have been latent in the family.

The following case is from the Rev. J. Page Hopps, of Lea Hurst, Leicester.

"September 15th, 1884.

(89) " Last week I dreamt of a 'dead' friend, and of this friend doing an exceedingly strange thing. It impressed me very much, but I said not a word concerning it to any one. Next morning, at breakfast, my wife hastened to tell me that she had dreamt a singular dream (a very unusual thing for her to say anything about), and then she staggered me by telling me what she had dreamt. It was the very thing that I had dreamed. We slept in different rooms, she having to attend to a sick child, and I not being very well. I do not care to tell you the dream ; but the special *action* in *both* dreams was something extremely curious and monstrously improbable. My wife ended her description by saying, ' Then she tried to say something, but I could not make it out.' I heard and remembered what was said, and that was the only difference in our dreams. We had not been in any way talking about our ' dead' friend.

"J. PAGE HOPPS.
"MARY HOPPS."

In answer to inquiries, Mr. Hopps says :—

" I would rather not go into details, especially in writing, though I think Mr. Gurney is right in wishing .for them. Some day I may give them, but what I told him in my first letter is *literally* true. The dream was an intensely improbable one. One curious thing about it was that, while looking at the appearance, I knew perfectly well I was lying in the particular bed I was in, and on the left-hand side, with my head towards the door. When I awoke, I was in precisely that position."

Mrs. Fielding, of Yarlington Rectory, near Bath, writes :—

"November 1885.

(90) " The other night my husband and I dreamt at the *same hour,* the same dream—a subject which neither of us had been thinking of for months. It was a dream of wandering about our first home, and in it looking at the same spot. "JANE E. FIELDING."

In answer to inquiries, Mrs. Fielding adds :—

" I do not remember anything more about the dream I spoke of. It was 17 years since we left Linacre Court, near Dover, the place my husband and I dreamt of at the *same* hour. We both dreamt of walking about the old place—and the old woodman—*just before* we awoke ; and we had not been either of us thinking of it in the least.

" My husband laughs at all such things as having any import, but to please me wrote the enclosed."

The enclosure was :—

" I remember awaking one morning about three weeks ago, and my wife telling me she had had a long dream about our first married home. I said ' How strange, as I have been dreaming the same just before I awoke.'

"J. M. FIELDING."

Asked as to the detail of the woodman, Mrs. Fielding replies, "We both saw the woodman in our dream."

Mr. Merrifield, of 24, Vernon Terrace, Brighton, tells us that, about 1865, he had a most distressing dream (with one exception totally unlike any other that he can recall), in which his death was foretold to him as about to happen within 24 hours. The impression was so painfully acute that he could not shake it off during the following day ; and he actually had an irrational feeling of relief when he woke on the second morning, and realised that the 24 hours were over. He then told the whole story to his wife.

(91) "She immediately said, 'I noticed that you woke up the night before last, and I had awakened from the same cause. I had dreamed most vividly that I was a widow, and the pillow was actually wet with tears. I never had such a vivid dream before, and it has troubled me ever since. I would not tell you, but it was a relief to me when I saw you coming home to dinner last night.'"

Mrs. Merrifield adds :—

"I saw myself dressed in weeds.—M. A. M."

In answer to inquiries, she says that she dreams a great deal, but that her dreams "are almost always of a pleasant nature. I never had any dream which was as vivid and the remembrance of which lasted as did that one. My pillow was quite wet with the tears I had shed."

The following example—from Mrs. Willmore, of 33, Castellain Road, Maida Hill, W.—is curiously similar, but depends on a single memory.

"1884.

(92) "The dream you ask me to narrate took place in 1856, at Neuilly, near Paris. I had a vivid impression that I was dying, and awoke with a start to hear my husband sobbing so painfully that I aroused him to ask what was the matter, upon which he said that he had dreamt that I was just on the point of dying. These two dreams must have occurred to both of us simultaneously, and seem to me to be a curious instance of thought-transference. I may add that there was such great sympathy between my husband and myself that; one day not long before his death, I well remember his saying that we should soon not need the communication of *speech*."

The next example is peculiar in that the percipient's impression seems due to a dream of the agent's of which the latter retained no memory. It will be seen that the amount of information conveyed exceeds what we can reasonably account for by the agent's having talked in his sleep. It is from our friend Mr. F. Corder, of 46, Charlwood Street, S.W., a gentleman of very high reputation in the musical world. He was at one time in the habit of hypnotising his wife for her health ; and "at the time," he says, "she gave me repeated proofs that she was able to ransack my mind and memory

far better than I myself could; but this was when desired to do so "—
whereas the case to be cited was spontaneous.

(93) Extract from Mr. Corder's diary, August 19th, 1882 :—

"Health symptoms much the same. Put her (Mrs. Corder) to sleep
before she got up, in order to know the exact hours at which restoratives
were to be given. She first said, 'I can't attend yet to those things ; I am
thinking out your thought.' I requested an explanation. 'About Jimmy
B. ; it is so strange, because I never saw him in my life; but you were
thinking about him.' I was ready to swear that I had not been thinking of
my old schoolfellow for many a long day, and was about to say so when
she went on : 'You were dreaming of him last night, and said, "Poor
Jimmy" in your sleep, so I was obliged to follow out your thought this
morning.' She then went on to remind me how the said Jimmy had gone
to a party with my brothers, sisters and self (this was at Christmas, 1865,
long before I knew her) ; how he drank too much, and was ill for several
days at our house, my mother nursing him. Not only had I absolutely no
remembrance of the dream (nor indeed of having dreamed at all), but the
incident itself had so completely faded from my mind that it was only by
the greatest effort of memory that I could recall it."

Mr. Corder further says :—

"On questioning my eldest sister some weeks later, all these details, which
I had absolutely forgotten, were corroborated. It is impossible, of course,
that my wife can, even in casual talk, have ever heard of this trivial
incident of my boyhood, any more than of other matters connected with the
same event which she also detailed. But more curious than anything is
the fact—for fact I suppose it is—that I could have dreamed of these
entirely forgotten matters, that they should again have passed away,
leaving no trace, and that yet she should read them in my mind the next
morning ! "

In another communication Mr. Corder adds :—

"March 19th, 1884.

" I may say that I was absolutely incredulous both as to the truth of
the dream-incident, and my having dreamed it ; but the moment I asked
my sister about J. B. having been ill in our house, she (whose memory for
youthful scenes is very strong) said unhesitatingly, 'Of course ; don't you
remember it was at the Mc——s' ball ? He drank too much wine and
came home in our cab. M. and C. carried him up to bed.' Those are
nearly my sister's very words. There was no discrepancy whatever between
her account of the matter and my wife's, but I cannot now remember
whether the latter related it with especial minuteness of detail. Certainly
the least discrepancy in the two accounts would have struck me, as—the
incident being so entirely forgotten by myself—I applied every word
uttered by both to my mind, to revive the dormant recollection."

Miss Corder corroborates as follows, in a letter to her brother :—

"The Rocks, East Bedfont, near Feltham, Middlesex.

" April 4th, 1885.

" As you ask me to give you an account of the incident so strangely

referred to by Pauline, I will put down what I remember. One night when
we were living either at Haddo or Canterbury Villas (the latter, I think)
the boys went to a party at the Mc——s', and there, it appeared, our young
friend Jimmy B. took too much refreshment. I forget if he was still with
the Rev. G. M. or in rooms ; but at all events they were afraid to take
him home, and brought him to our place. I and R. were awakened
by the noise the boys made in conveying J. up to C.'s room on the floor
above us ; so we listened, and became aware of the proceedings, which we
did not then fully understand. Next day J. had to keep in bed, and the
mother went up and waited on him. He was very unwell, and if I
remember rightly only got up at tea-time, when he took a cup of tea with
us, and then returned to his place. I have an impression that the mother
sent for Dr. Burton, who administered something. As to the notion that
I or R. could ever have told Pauline this story in any of our former talks,
I am *certain* that we have never done so. J. left England so long before
we met Pauline that he was only mentioned once or twice, as the chief
instigator of our dramatic performances in early days. Moreover, this
story is not at all what I should relate about a friend ; and I can safely
swear that it was never mentioned to anyone.

"This is all I remember, and it is quite distinct in my remembrance
now.   " CHARLOTTE CORDER."

[In spite of what Miss Corder says, it is, of course, within the range
of possibility that the incident had been described in Mrs. Corder's
presence ; but it would then be extremely odd that, on its recurring to
her, it should not have recurred as a thing previously heard of, but
should have seemed to her like entirely new information. We have,
moreover, in Mr. Corder's exclamation, " Poor Jimmy," a considerable
presumption that his dreaming thoughts did actually revert to his old
friend. The case, however, would hardly have been included, had we not
felt able to rely on Mr. Corder's statement as to the peculiar *rapport*
which at that time existed between himself and his wife.]

The next case is perhaps best regarded as one of simultaneous
dreams, though the one of the two parties who would most naturally
be regarded as the percipient feels positive that she was awake. It
belongs in one respect to a later class, since the agent's personality
and presence distinctly figured in the percipient's experience.

Miss Constance S. Bevan, of 74, Lancaster Gate, W., says :—

"February 18th, 1884.

(94) "On June 10th, 1883, I had the following dream. Someone told
me that Miss Elliott was dead. I instantly, in my dream, rushed to her room,
entered it, went to her bedside and pulled the clothes from off her face.
She was quite cold ; her eyes were wide open and staring at the ceiling.
This so frightened me that I dropped at the foot of her bed, and knew no
more until I was half out of bed in my own room and wide awake. The
time was 5 o'clock a.m. Before leaving my room I told this dream to my
sister, as it had been such an unpleasant one.

" CONSTANCE S. BEVAN."

Miss Elliott says :—

                                          " February, 1884.

"I awoke on the morning of June 10th, and was lying on my back with my eyes fixed on the ceiling, when I heard the door open and felt some one come in and bend over me, but not far enough to come between my eyes and the ceiling ; knowing it was only C., I did not move, but instead of kissing me she suddenly drew back, and going towards the foot of the bed, crouched down there. Thinking this very strange, I closed and opened my eyes several times, to convince myself that I was really awake, and then turned my head to see if she had left the door open, but found it still shut. Upon this a sort of horror came over me, and I dared not look towards the figure, which was crouching in the same position, gently moving the bed-clothes from my feet. I tried to call to the occupant of the next room, but my voice failed. At this moment she touched my bare foot, and a cold chill ran all over me and I knew nothing more till I found myself out of bed looking for C., who must, I felt, be still in the room. I never doubted that she had really been there until I saw both doors fastened on the inside. On looking at my watch it was a few minutes past 5.

                                          " E. ELLIOTT."

The following corroboration is from Miss C. S. Bevan's sisters :—

" Before leaving our room, my sister Constance told all about the dream she had had in the early morning.

                                          " C. ELSIE BEVAN."

" The first thing in the morning, Miss Elliott told me all about her unpleasant dream, before speaking to anyone else.

                                          " ANTONIA BEVAN."

In answer to inquiries, Miss C. S. Bevan says :—

" This is the first experience I have ever had of the kind, and I have not walked in my sleep more than three times in my life ; the last time was about a year ago ; on no occasion have I left the room. I do not have startling or vivid dreams as a rule. I did not look at my watch after waking, but the clock struck 5 o'clock."

In answer to inquiries, Miss Elliott says :—

" Although I am accustomed to have very vivid dreams, I have never had one of this kind before. When I found my friend was not in the room, and that the doors were securely fastened on the inside, I looked at my watch ; it was a few minutes past 5.

" I have never, I believe, walked in my sleep. There are two doors to my bedroom. One was locked on the inside ; the handle was broken off the other on the outside. Thus it was impossible for anyone to open it except from the inside."

[No one, probably, will regard this as an accidental coincidence ; but the hypothesis of sleep-walking had to be carefully considered. I have seen the rooms, and examined the door of which the handle is described as having been broken off. Miss Bevan had been (as was often the case) in

Miss Elliott's room over-night, and on her shutting the door at her departure, the outside handle fell off. She remembers its doing so ; and Miss Elliott heard it fall, and saw it on the floor outside when she left her room in the morning. Miss Elliott says that it remained unscrewed, and so liable to be shaken off every time the door closed, for about two months that summer. I unscrewed it, and tried to move the latch by turning the stump, but found it utterly impossible ; and to fit the handle on again without pushing the stump inwards, and so losing all chance of opening the door, was a work of very considerable care. But even on the violent supposition that Miss Bevan left her room noiselessly in her sleep, picked up the handle, deftly adjusted it, turned it, and entered—there remains an additional difficulty. For, in departing, she must have shut the door after her in such a way as to jerk the handle off again. This would make a loud sound ; yet it was not heard by Miss Elliott, who, on the hypothesis in question, was awake ; nor did it wake Miss Bevan herself, nor an aunt of hers who was sleeping in a room with which Miss Elliott's communicated. It seems almost incredible that she should have shut the door carefully after her, *taken off* the handle, and *deposited it on the floor*. Both the door of communication between Miss Elliott's and the aunt's rooms, and the free door of the latter room were locked, the former on Miss Elliott's side. Miss Bevan has *never left her room*, or anything like it, on the three occasions on which she has walked in her sleep. Moreover, she was sleeping in the same room as a sister who is a very light sleeper, and she considers that it is absolutely impossible that she should have left her room without waking this sister. Her room is separated from Miss Elliott's by a passage and a long staircase. Miss Bevan is not a " dreamer," and very rarely has a dream which she thinks it worth while to mention.]

Two points in this case deserve special notice. In the first place, whatever we call Miss Elliott's experience, it was wholly unlike an ordinary dream ; it was in itself as unusual in character as a " spectral illusion," or distinct waking hallucination of vision. Evidentially, this is very important ; for it at once renders irrelevant the theory of accidental coincidence, so far as that theory depends on the scope for accident which the vast *number* of dreams affords. The second point is the possibility, at any rate, that the two experiences were not only simultaneous but *reciprocal ;* that is to say, that Miss Bevan's dream may not have been simply the independent source of Miss Elliott's impression, but may have itself been modified by that impression.

§ 2. Passing now to examples where the supposed agent was awake, but in a perfectly ordinary and unexcited state, we must still, of course, reject cases where any normal cause for the dream can be plausibly assigned. Thus Mr. F. J. Jones, of Heath Bank,

Mossley Road, Ashton-under-Lyne, tells us how his little daughter astonished him by starting up from her sleep, saying, "Something has gone wrong with the ' Gogo's ' boilers." The " Gogo " belonged to a firm with which Mr. Jones was connected, and it was afterwards discovered that the boilers had at that very time suffered an accident in the Bay of Biscay. The coincidence remains, therefore, an odd one ; but we should certainly be inclined to refer the child's dream to some scrap of grown-up conversation that had been forgotten. Mr. E. W. P., of Barton End Grange, Nailsworth, describes how in a half-wakeful state he had been imagining himself to be reading "The Book of Days," till it seemed to become too dark to see—when all at once his wife said in her sleep, " You should not read in bed, it is so bad for the eyes." On inquiry, we find that Mrs. P. is not in the habit of talking in her sleep ; but we find also that Mr. P. has often read in bed, and that his wife has often remonstrated with him about it. The following cases seem free from such objections.

Mrs. Crellin, of 62, Hilldrop Crescent, N., says :—

"January, 1884.

(95) "My husband and I often find our thoughts occupied by the same subject, though there has been no apparent direction given to our thoughts by surrounding circumstances, and the subject of our thoughts may be distant in time and place. This rather curious incident occurred 12 years ago. In the middle of the night I awoke, and remaining awake I tried to recall one of Tennyson's poems, but was puzzled as to the first word. Was it ' *Home* they brought,' or ' *Back* they brought her warrior dead '? My husband had been soundly asleep, but suddenly turned round, and on my saying ' Are you awake ? ' he replied, ' Yes, and I awoke with the words on my lips, ' " Home they brought her warrior dead." ' As we had not been reading the poem together, it seemed a curious occurrence of sympathy. I am quite sure that I had not uttered a word of the poem aloud, for I was very anxious not to disturb my husband's rest in his then rather delicate state of health."

Mr. Crellin corroborates as follows :—

"January 19th, 1884.

"I have a distinct recollection of the incident, reported to you by my wife, referring to Tennyson's lines, ' Home they brought her warrior dead.'

"On my awaking from sleep she asked me, ' Are you awake? ' I replied, ' Yes, and with these words on my lips, " Home," ' &c. She said, ' Those are the very words I want to be sure about. I have been trying to recollect whether " Home " or " Back " is the word with which the poem begins.'

"I had not recently been reading Tennyson, and cannot account for what I have just narrated.

"PHILIP CRELLIN."

[It is, no doubt, possible to suppose that Mrs. Crellin unconsciously recited the line aloud ; but not only is she certain that she did not, but she had at the time a special reason for silence.]

The next incident concerns the same two persons; but here possibly it was the dreamer who was the agent. Mrs. Crellin says:—

"August, 1884.

(96) "I mentioned to you my husband's awaking from sleep and repeating the line from Tennyson which I had been trying to remember. That seemed to me a brain-wave, and it was immediate in its action; but what of a *deferred* brain-wave? Thus, three weeks ago, I was unable to sleep during the early hours of the night. I thought, amongst other things, of a rather comic piece of poetry which my husband used to repeat years ago. I stuck at one line and could not recall it. However, I fell asleep, and three or four hours after awoke, to find it was time to rise. My husband, after a good night's rest—undisturbed by poetry or prose—awoke also ; he stretched out his hand towards me, and repeated the line I had failed to remember in the night, and which did not occupy my thoughts when I awoke in the morning. This seemed a strange delay in giving the response." [1]

Mr. Crellin says :—

"62, Hilldrop Crescent, N.

"August 20th, 1884.

"My wife has told you of an incident which I am able to confirm. I awoke one morning recently, and immediately said to her, ' And his skin, like a lady's loose gown, hung about him '—this being a line of some humorous verses learnt by me when a youth, and which I have occasionally recited for the amusement of my friends, but which I had not repeated or thought of for a long period. My wife at once said that whilst lying awake during the night (I being asleep) she had been trying to recall this very line. I know of nothing that can have brought the line to my mind and lips at the moment.   "PHILIP CRELLIN."

§ 3. We come now to cases where the agent's mind was in a more or less disturbed state. The following account is from our friend Miss Mason, of Morton Hall, Retford, Notts. It was first printed in connection with a record of some thought-transference experiments, in *Macmillan's Magazine* for October, 1882.

(97) "The most remarkable case I have ever come across was an accidental one, where I had no intention of experimenting. During the summer of 1878 I happened to be staying at Oban, and on the 1st of August went to see the Falls of Lora, so well-known that I shall not

___
[1] We need not regard it as specially strange. See pp. 201-2.

undertake a long description of them. Loch Etive, which is a branch of the larger Loch Linnhe, is on a lower level. This difference in level occurs at its mouth, and is so abrupt that, when the tide is out, it leaves an irregular waterfall between the two. The mass of sea-water rushes from Loch Linnhe into Loch Etive, shaped into all kinds of cataracts and hollow whirlpools, and is approached either by standing on rocks of some height above the Falls, or on lower ones, almost on a level with the eddies below them.

"It is natural, on looking into such whirlpools and watching how irresistibly anything thrown into them is sucked down, to wonder whether anyone who fell in could possibly be saved. I was at the time in extreme anxiety about some friends of mine who were in great trouble, of which I alone knew, and might not tell ; and without intending it, I applied the picture metaphorically to the case, fancying my friends in the whirlpools and myself trying to save them. The picture impressed me so forcibly in this state of mind, that for the rest of the day I never got rid of it. Soon after I returned to a place where I had left my maid, more than 120 miles from Oban, and on the 7th of the same month something brought my anxiety and its accompanying picture before me even more vividly than before. I could think of nothing else the whole evening. To speak absurdly, I felt possessed by that scene to my fingers' ends. All night long I never closed my eyes, but lay awake, seeing my friends in the whirlpools and trying to pull them out. My maid, who slept in a room above mine, had undressed me as usual, but I hardly spoke to her, for I could not tell her of my anxiety, and had not another idea in my head to talk about. When she called me in the morning, she at once began to say that she had never passed so strange a night, for every time she fell asleep she awoke dreaming of the same place—'Water rushing over rocks, and the most dreadful whirlpools,' and that she was 'standing on high rocks, trying to save people out of them with ropes.' 'And,' she said, 'it was not a waterfall of a river, it was a *waterfall of the sea.*'

"This expression is remarkable, for there is perhaps hardly a place in the world, except the Falls of Lora, to which it would exactly apply. Without telling her why, I questioned her in detail as to all the features of the place she had dreamed of, and anyone who wishes for the full and minute description she gave me has only to look at that given by any local guide-book of the Falls of Lora. The only part of her dream which did not reflect my thoughts was that the persons whom she was trying to save from drowning were not the same that I was thinking of. It was not until she had told me all she could, that I gave her my reason for wishing to know so much about her dream, and said I had been thinking of the place she had described. Now she had never been to Oban, and had never heard or read anything about the Falls. I had never so much as mentioned them to her, and she had seen no one else at any time who had been there, nor had she ever seen a picture or a photograph of the place. Of this, both she and I were absolutely certain. If, therefore, the picture was not impressed by my mind directly upon hers, the only possible alternative is that of coincidence ; and the coincidence of her dreaming of such an unusual scene and circumstances at the same time that I was thinking of them so intently, would be doubly extraordinary, because it was not a single dream, but one repeated throughout the night, her anxiety to save the drowning persons waking her again and again. The maid is a matter-of-fact, middle-aged woman, who has lived nearly all her life in my family, and was my nurse. Though a Welshwoman, she has none of the imagination supposed to be an endowment of her race, and has displayed no talent for thought-reading; her position enables her to dispense with ceremonies, and she refuses to ' be bothered with such nonsense.' She still lives with us, is in the house at this moment, and wishes she did not remember the circumstances. I am not trusting to memory alone, for I not only entered the facts in my diary, but wrote a full account of them the next day in a letter to a friend, and, having told the story at the time, have other witnesses to prove that I do not exaggerate."

The dreamer says :—

" This account of the circumstances is correct. I had never heard Miss Mason mention her trouble. But I have forgotten many of the details of the dream.[1]

" MARGARET HERBERT."

Miss Mason's mother says :—

" I have heard both my daughter and my maid speak of the occurrence and describe it.

" M. MASON."

To pass from water to fire—the evidential force of the following case is not easy to estimate, without knowing how frequent dreams of conflagrations are ; but this particular dreamer, at any rate, can recall no similar experience, and has never in his life made a written note of a dream except on this occasion. Mr. D. B. W. Sladen, of 26, Campden Grove, Kensington, W., writes :—

" January 4th, 1886.

(98) " In December, 1881, we were living at 6, George Street, (East) Melbourne, Victoria. My father resided then, as he does now, at Phillimore Lodge, Kensington, W. In those days I always went to bed about midnight. I awoke suddenly, tremendously startled by a dream that my father's house was on fire. The dream impressed me so vividly that I felt convinced that a fire had actually happened there, and, striking a light, I walked across the room to the dressing-table, on which my diary lay (I used generally to jot down the events of the day just before turning in), and made a brief entry of it, there and then, first looking at my watch in order to be able to set down the time, which I found to be 1 a.m. I had, therefore, been in bed less than an hour, which of itself seems to add an extraordinary feature to the case (I refer to my sinking to sleep, dreaming,

---

[1] With regard to these words, Miss Mason says :—

" April 12th, 1885.

" My old nurse has such a dislike to the subject of thought-transference, which she considers ' nonsense,' that she would never have told me of her dream if she had known that it afforded an instance. And when I told her afterwards how her dream had answered to my thoughts, she was so angry at having unconsciously supplied me with an instance, that she always refused to talk of it again, though I have often tried to make her do so. It is, therefore, not surprising that she should have forgotten some of the details of a dream nearly 7 years ago."

and waking up, as after a long sleep, in so short a space of time).   The entry in my diary is, as it was likely to be when standing out of bed, very brief : ' *At night I dreamt that the kitchen in my father's house was on fire.   I awoke and found that it was* 1 *a.m.*' I kept my diary in a plain paper book ; and the entry comes below what I did up to midnight on December 22nd.   What I further still remember distinctly of the vision is this—that in it, the servants' bedrooms (which are really at the top of my father's house, while the kitchen, &c., are at the bottom) were adjoining the kitchen suite, all on one floor, and that the smoke and blaze seemed general.   Further, I remember distinctly, though I just made a bare entry in my diary and hurried back to bed, that two of my father's maids, named Coombes and Caroline respectively, were the only persons except myself present in the vision, and that I seemed to have no impulses and no power of moving, but was merely a spectator ; nor did the idea of any risk to myself form part of the impression.

"Six or seven weeks afterwards (mail contract between London and Melbourne is 42 days) I received a letter from my father, dated December 22nd, 1881.   He wrote, ' We had a fire on Sunday evening while we were at church.   Coombes went with a wax-taper to tidy her room, and, I suppose, blew it out and put it down with sparks.   Very soon after she left, a ring at the bell that the attic was on fire put Caroline on her mettle, while the other lost her head.   She dashed it out with water before the window-frame was burnt through, and subdued it. Fifteen pounds will repair the damage—two chests of drawers much burnt, wearing apparel, &c.   I gave her a sovereign for her pluck, as the roof would have been on fire in another five minutes.'

"Now I wish to draw your attention to what has attracted my attention most.   The Sunday before December 22nd, 1881, was December 18th.   I had the communication, therefore, in my sleep, not on the actual day of the fire, but on the day on which my father wrote the letter.   At Kensington, where my father was writing, Australian letters have to be posted in the branch offices about 5 p.m.   My dream was at 1 a.m.   Time in Victoria is 9½ hours ahead of English time.   When I was having the communication, therefore, it was about 3.30 p.m. in Kensington.   Now with the mail going out at 5 p.m., 3.30 would have been a very natural—I think I may say a most natural time for my father to be finishing a letter to me. [Mr. Sladen, sen., confirms this.] I, therefore, had my magnetic communication when he was at once focussing his mind on me, and focussing his mind on the fire, in order to tell me about it.

"I have asked my wife, and she remembers perfectly my waking her up, and telling her that I had dreamt that my father's house was on fire, and was so convinced of its betokening an actual occurrence that I should make a note of it in my diary there and then."

"DOUGLAS B. W. SLADEN."

[Mr. Sladen has kindly allowed me to inspect the diary and letter.]

In the next example the correspondence is of a more distinct kind.   Mrs. Walsh, of the Priory, Lincoln, writes :—

"February, 1884.

(99) " The gentleman who teaches music in my house tells me that

if anything sad or terrible happens to anyone he loves, he always has an intimation of it.

"I am very fond of him, and I know he looks on me as a very true old friend, and one of my sons, now in India, is the dearest friend he has.

"I went out one morning about 9 o'clock, carrying books for the library, and being very busy, took the short way to town. On some flags in a very steep part of the road, some boys had made a slide. Both my feet flew away at the same moment that the back of my head resounded on the flags. A policeman picked me up, saw I was hurt, and rang at the Nurses' Home close by, to get me looked to. My head was cut, and while they were washing the blood away, I was worrying myself that I should be ill, and how should I manage my school till the end of the term. I told no one in my house but my daughter, and no one but the policeman had seen me fall. I asked my daughter to tell no one. I had a miserable nervous feeling, but I pretended to her it was nothing. The next morning after a sleepless night, I could not get up. It was my habit to sit in the drawing-room while the music lessons were given, so my daughter went in to tell Mr. —— that I had had a bad night, and was not yet up. He said, 'I had a wretched night, too, and all through a most vivid dream.' 'What was it?' she asked. 'I dreamed I was walking by the Nurses' Home, and I came on a slide, both my feet slipped, and I fell on the back of my head. I was helped to the Home, and while my head was being bathed I was worrying myself how I should manage my lessons till the end of the term, and the worrying feeling would not go.'"

The percipient, Mr. T. J. Hoare, writes:—

"12, St. Nicholas Square, Lincoln.
"March 3rd, 1884.

"I shall be very pleased to relate the account of a dream, as described by Mrs. Walsh most accurately, which took place on a Tuesday evening early in November, 1882. The dream consisted of this: I supposed I was going down the Greystone Stairs, when I had a fall at the first flight, was picked up, and helped by a policeman to the Nurses' Institute, about 20 yards from the imaginary fall, being there attended by a nurse. I was much perplexed as to how I should manage to finish my work during the term. This was followed the next morning by a severe headache in the region of the imaginary blow.

"On seeing Miss Walsh the following morning, I was told by her that Mrs. Walsh was unwell, but not the cause. I replied I too felt unwell and accounted for it through the dream. Mrs. Walsh related to me the same evening her own adventure, which in every detail exactly coincided with my dream as happening to myself. I in no way knew of Mrs. Walsh's mishap till the evening after, when told by herself.

"In another instance, whilst staying in Devonshire, I received an impression, or felt a conviction, that something had happened to Mrs. Walsh. I think I wanted to write, so confident was I of something having taken place, but desisted because I had left Lincoln through an outbreak of small-pox in the house next my rooms, only the previous week, so was unwilling to correspond. On my return here, I found out that both my day [*i.e.*, the day of the impression] and the accident—a fall—were true.

" In many other instances have I received similar experiences, and so confident have I been always of their accuracy that I have written to the persons and places, and always received confirmation of my impressions. I have had, I think, 10 or 12 impressions. They are quite unlike fits of low spirits and indigestion, and I can easily distinguish them from such, as in every case I have been most conscious of outside action.

" T. J. HOARE."

In conversation Mr. Hoare stated that he undoubtedly had a positive pain at the back of his head, as if from a blow, on the day following this experience.

The following case is an interesting dream-parallel to the waking cases of the last chapter where the impression on the percipient's mind was of being wanted. (See especially Mr. Rowlands' case, p. 291.)   The account is from Mr. Joseph Albree, of 40, Wood Street, Pittsburgh, Pa., U.S.A.

"September 25th, 1884.

(100) " In the winter of 1863-4, a captain in the regular army of the United States came to P—— on recruiting service, accompanied by a second lieutenant. Very soon after his arrival the captain was taken sick with inflammation of the lungs. As I had known him intimately since his boyhood, he sent for me. I had him removed to a private house, and cared for him until he died, two days after. His companion, the lieutenant, remained in the city for 10 days after the captain's death, awaiting orders. He was a man of unusually reticent disposition ; and being an entire stranger in the city, and knowing no one but the person who had been at the death of his associate officer, he spent much time in my company. At length he received orders to proceed at once to a distant point. I bade him good-bye one evening, he intending to take an early train on the following morning, and I never expecting to see him again.

" Three nights after that, on Saturday, I awakened suddenly with the idea that some person was calling me, and that I was wanted immediately. I was conscious of having had a very vivid dream, but could not recall any part of it. There was present in my mind the very uncomfortable feeling that I was wanted at once. While sitting up in bed, endeavouring to collect my thoughts, the city bell struck midnight. After looking into the rooms where the children were, and finding them all asleep, I lay down again, striving unsuccessfully to recall a single incident of the dream. All Sunday and Monday I was impressed with a consciousness of some duty unperformed.

" On Tuesday evening, on my way home, an almost irresistible impulse came over me to turn aside from my direct way, down a little street leading in another direction. Standing a moment on the street corner at the parting of ways, I turned off, walked a few blocks, and came to the hotel where the lieutenant had lodged. I went into the office, and having no business or object in going there, I asked the clerk when Lieutenant O. left. The clerk said, 'There he sits, in the reading-room.' After a very brief greeting he asked me to go to his room. Following him up the stairway, the corner of a panel on the landing seemed to bring clearly to my mind the full details of my Saturday night's dream. From that point the stairs, hall ways, the room into which he led me, the furniture and general appearance, all were strangely familiar, although I had never been there before. The lieutenant's first words on closing the door were ' J., did you ever faint?' He then told me that his transportation order not having arrived, he had not been able to leave at the time fixed ; that on the preceding Saturday, while reading in the reading-room, he glanced at the clock, and noticing it was 5 minutes of 12 o'clock, took a light, went immediately to his room, placed the lamp on the table, fell on the bed, losing consciousness and knowing nothing until broad daylight on the Sunday winter morning, when he found himself dressed, lying across the bed, suffering intense pain in his forehead. His last conscious thought had been, ' If J. was here he could help me.' All that he told me was just what I had dreamed on the preceding Saturday night—the exact hour of the occurrence with the lieutenant, and the vivid dream with me, being fixed at midnight.

" I have seen or heard nothing of the lieutenant since that evening.
                                                  "JOSEPH ALBREE."

[As the details of the dream were not independently remembered, we should not be justified in attaching any importance to the apparent recognition of the scene when the percipient actually saw it.]

In reply to inquiries, Mr. Albree writes, on Oct. 20, 1884 :—

" In reply to your favour of the 7th inst., I can only say that my experience was such that no person could aid me, and I probably did not mention it to any one but my wife. While she fully recalls what I told her after my return from the hotel, she does not remember that I spoke to her *before* I saw the lieutenant. And yet I can scarcely think it probable that I did not, in the morning, speak of my troubled feelings, of my arising, turning up the gas, and going into the children's room. I have never seen or heard of the lieutenant since. The circumstances of our acquaintance were so peculiar and touching, and our relations so intimate for three weeks, that failing to hear from him I long since concluded that he fell in the active service to which he had been ordered.

" You ask if I have ever had an experience that was *not* similarly confirmed. Only once. I *very* seldom dream, but when I do the dreams are vivid. Once I dreamed that a lady friend had been murdered. The time, place, circumstances, and persons concerned were strongly marked. But the lady had been in no danger, and is still living."

The next example—from Mrs. Montgomery, of Beaulieu, Co. Louth —is remarkable in several ways.

                                                  "February, 1884.
(101) " Nearly 30 years ago I lost a sister. The place where she died being at some distance, my husband went to the funeral without me. I went to bed early, and had a frightful dream of the funeral ceremony. I saw my brother faint away at the service, and fall into the grave. I awoke with the horror of the dream, just as my husband entered the room on his return from the funeral, which had taken place at least eight hours before. I asked him to tell me if anything unusual had happened, as I had had a

terrible dream, and I related it.   He said, 'Who in the world told you that? I never intended telling you.' I said, 'I only dreamt it. Just as you were coming in I awoke.' "

[In this narrative a few words are taken from an account received from the Hon. Mrs. Montgomery Moore, as the letter received from Mrs. Montgomery herself, giving the greater part of the details, took this previous account for granted. The account, as it stands, was sent to Mrs. Montgomery, who then replied, "The paper is quite accurate"—making one trifling correction. Mr. Montgomery gave Mrs. Montgomery Moore a verbal confirmation of the occurrence, which had greatly impressed both him and his wife.]

Here the picture transferred to the percipient's dream was a precise and detailed one. It was of a sort which might at first sight seem more fitly to belong to a later class, where something of the nature of clairvoyance is suggested. Nor would the eight hours' interval between the event and the dream be an objection to this view; for I have already mentioned that the deferment or latency of telepathic impressions is specially frequent in dream and "border-land" cases; as though the idea or image had been unable to compete with the vivid sensations which external realities force on the mind, and only got its chance of emerging into consciousness when the senses were closed to these contending influences.[1] But seeing that at the moment of Mrs. Montgomery's dream her husband was just about to enter her room, with the shock of the burial-scene probably still fresh in his mind, it is at any rate conceivable that he then, and not the brother at the earlier time, transmitted the impression.

§ 4. We come now to the larger family of cases, in which the agent's personality, and not merely his particular thought, is reflected, and the dream conveys a true impression of his state, or of some event connected with him. I will first give a few examples where the fact which is a reality is presented or suggested without the agent's visible appearance in the dream, and without any distinct sense on the percipient's part of being present at the scene. The following narrative, from Mrs. Lincoln, now residing at 91, South Circular Road, Dublin, was sent to Professor Barrett in 1875.

(102) "On the morning of February 7th, 1855, at Mount Pleasant Square, Dublin, where I lived, I awakened from a troubled sleep and dream, exclaiming, 'John is dead.' My husband said, 'Go to sleep, you

---

[1] Telepathic dreams of the "clairvoyant" order seem capable of this deferment, just like any others: see for instance case 134 below.

are dreaming.' I did sleep, and again awoke repeating the same words, and asking him to look at the watch and tell me what o'clock it was then; he did so and said it was 2 o'clock. I was much impressed by this dream, and next day went to the city to inquire at the house of business; Mr. John C. being at Dundrum for the previous month. [He was not a relative, but a very intimate friend.] When I got to the house I saw the place closed up, and the man who answered the door told me the reason. 'Oh! ma'am, Mr. John C. is dead.' 'When did he die?' I said. 'At 2 this morning,' he said. I was so much shocked, he had to assist me to the waiting-room to give me water. I had not heard of Mr. C.'s illness, and was speaking to him a fortnight previously, when he was complaining of a slight cold, and expected the change of Dundrum would benefit him, so that he should return to town immediately. I never saw nor heard of him after, until I dreamt the foregoing.

"EMILY LINCOLN."

Mr. Lincoln says :—

" I certify to the correctness of the facts of my wife's awakening me at the date stated, asking me the time, &c., and to the further fact of the unexpected death of Mr. C. at the time.

"HENRY LINCOLN."

We find from the obituary of the *Freeman's Journal* that Mr. C. died on Feb. 7th, 1855.

[In conversation, Mr. Podmore learnt from Mr. Lincoln that his wife never talked in her sleep; and she, when asked whether her ordinary dreams were as vivid as this, replied in the negative. It appeared, however, that she had had several dreams which she regarded as premonitory, and as having been fulfilled.]

The next account was first given in *England*, April 1st, 1882, by its then editor, under the *nom de plume* "Coriolanus." He tells us that the publication of his name would deprive him of an actual benefit; but he allows us to say of him what is said above in connection with case 73 (p. 275). The experience here described is again his own.

(103) "In connection with the awfully sudden death of my friend, Mr. E. C. Barnes, the artist, I can vouch for the truth of the following extraordinary coincidence. At 6 o'clock last Sunday morning [*i.e.*, March 26th, 1882], the exact time of his decease, an intimate friend of the late artist, who was unaware of the fact that Barnes was ill, suddenly alarmed an entire household by sitting up in bed whilst fast asleep and shouting loudly twice, as if in intense agony. Three members of his family ran to his bedside to inquire if he were ill, when slowly awaking and rubbing his eyes, he said he was perfectly well, but supposed it was the storm which had affected him. At breakfast he was playfully rallied upon the occurrence, and more than once expressed the hope that nothing was amiss with his old friend Barnes. At dinner time a messenger arrived with the dreadful news. I have set this down for the

benefit of thinkers.   I know the facts to be as I have stated them.   Was there a mysterious cord of sympathy suddenly snapped when the artist breathed his last, and his friend was at that very moment so mysteriously convulsed?   Who knows?"

Writing to us on December 11th, 1884, the narrator adds :—

"The occurrence made the more impression on my family, as, on account of the great attachment they knew to exist between Mr. Barnes and me, they dreaded to tell the sad news, and in fact only gently broke it at breakfast time on the Monday morning.   They were much struck by my frequent references to Barnes during Sunday, after they had received the intelligence from his eldest son, who called at my house about 1 o'clock.   The deceased and I had known one another for many years."

Mr. Podmore called at the witness's house on September 1st, 1885, but found only his son and daughter at home.   Writing on the day of his call, he says : " I questioned the daughter on the Barnes incident.   She could at first remember no details at all ; but after reading through the extract from *England*, she told me that she had a distinct recollection of going to her father's room, when roused by his cry, to ascertain whether he or her brother were ill.   She did not remember his mentioning the name of Barnes at breakfast, or that the news of the death had been withheld from her father until the Monday morning.   But she told me that she remembered reading, a few days afterwards, the paragraph in *England* describing the occurrence ; and that, had any of the details been incorrect, the fact that her father had made a mistake would certainly have dwelt in her memory.   The son had been absent from home at the time."

It is worthy of note that such sudden startings from sleep, with the strong impression of a definite event, but without the memory of any dream leading up to the impression, seem by no means common occurrences, outside the cases which have coincided with some weighty reality.   For every fresh point (beyond the fact of coinciding with reality) that distinguishes the dreams that we are considering from ordinary dreams, goes, of course, to strengthen the argument against chance as the source of the coincidences, and to establish these cases as a distinct natural class.

The next case, in its absurdity and precision, is a great contrast to the last.   We received it from the Rev. A. B. McDougall, now of Hemel Hempsted, and at that time a scholar of Lincoln College, Oxford.

" November, 1882.

(104) " On the night of January 10th, 1882, I was sleeping in one of the suburbs of Manchester in the house of a friend, into which house several rats had been driven by the excessive cold.   I knew nothing about these rats, but during the night I was waked by feeling an unpleasantly cold something slithering down my right leg.   I immediately struck a light and

flung off the bed-clothes, and saw a rat run out of my bed under the fire-place. I told my friend the next morning, but he tried to persuade me I had been dreaming. However, a few days afterwards[1] a rat was caught in my room. On the morning of January 11th, a cousin of mine [Miss E. J. M. McDougall, since married], who happened to be staying in my own home on the south coast, and to be occupying my room, came down to breakfast, and recounted a marvellous dream, in which a rat appeared to be eating off the extremities of my unfortunate self. My family laughed the matter off. However, on the 13th, a letter was received from me giving an account of my unpleasant meeting with the rat and its subsequent capture. Then everyone present remembered the dream my cousin had told certainly 58 hours before, as having occurred on the night of January 10th. My mother wrote me an account of the dream, ending up with the remark, ' We always said E. was a witch : she always knew about everything almost before it took place.'   " A. B. McDOUGALL."

Here the point, of course, is that an exceedingly improbable incident is associated in the dream with the right person. It is worth noting that we have no exact parallel to such an incident as this among our *waking* cases. Thus, if the dream was telepathic, its very triviality may illustrate in a new way the favourable effect of sleep on the percipient faculty.

Dreams happening at times when the person dreamt of is known to be in peril are, as a rule, inadmissible as evidence. Thus we have a case where the mother of a lieutenant in the army dreamt, on the night of the storming of the Redan, that her son was wounded in the *left* arm. The subsequent newspaper account described him as having been severely injured in the *right* arm ; but his mother persisted in her view that the dream was correct, and it proved to have been so. But a dream concerning a wound is a very likely one for a mother to have under the circumstances ; and the detail is quite insufficient. In the same class we must include mothers' dreams of accidents to children, even apart from any special grounds of anxiety—the form of dream being not uncommon, and real accidents (if we include trivial ones) being frequent enough to make it certain that striking coincidences will every now and then occur by chance. Thus the wife of a rector in the West of England tells us how she once dreamt that one of her little girls, who was on a visit, had fallen down in the street and cut her forehead over the left eye, and how the morning's post

---

[1] There is a slight apparent discrepancy between these words and the date of the letter in which the capture is afterwards said to have been mentioned. The letters are destroyed ; and Mr. McDougall rightly prefers to leave the words as they stand. They, of course, in no way affect the central incident.

brought the news of that precise accident. The rector (who is sceptical on these matters) testifies to the fact that his wife mentioned to him her dream "that the child had fallen down and cut her forehead;" and also to the fact that "the next post brought the news." He says nothing about the *street* or the *left eye*—details which may have been read back into the dream afterwards. But in any case the accident is of a common type; the amount of correct detail is small; and moreover it came out in conversation with the lady that she dreams a good deal, and pays attention to her dreams. However completely telepathy were established, it might still be doubted whether such a coincidence as this ought to be referred to it.

As an interesting contrast, I may quote the following case, which is from Mrs. Hobbs, (wife of the Rev. W. A. Hobbs, formerly a missionary at Beerbhoom, Bengal,) now resident at Tenbury, in Worcestershire. The narrative was first written out for a friend, probably in 1877.

(105) " During our residence in India as missionaries, our children remained at home, either residing with my sister or at school, and about the years 1864 or 1865 our eldest boy was at school at Shireland Hall near to Birmingham. The principal was the Rev. T. H. Morgan, now Baptist minister at Harrow-on-the-Hill.

" One night, during the summer of one of the years I have mentioned, I was awakened from my sleep by my husband asking, 'What is the matter, J. ? Why are you weeping so? I could let you sleep no longer, you were crying so much.' I replied that I was dreaming, but could not tell the dream for some minutes. It had seemed so like a reality that I was still weeping bitterly.

" I dreamed that the sister (who acted as guardian to our boys in our absence) was reading to me a letter giving a detailed account of how our Harry died of choking, while eating his dinner one day at school.

" When sufficiently composed I again went to sleep ; but when I awoke in the morning, the effect of my dream was still upon me. My husband tried to rally me, saying, 'It is *only a dream*, think no more about it.' But my heart was sad, and I could not shake it off.

" In the course of the day I called on a friend, the only other European lady in the station. I told her why I felt troubled, and she advised me to make a note of the date, and then I should know how to understand my dream when a letter of that date came to hand. Our letters at that time came to us *viâ* Southampton, and nearly six weeks *must* elapse before I could hear if anything had transpired on that particular date, even if a letter could have been dispatched at once ; but it might not have been the 'mail day,' and that would give some additional days for me to wait. They were weary weeks, but at length the looked-for letter arrived, and it contained no reference to what I had anticipated. I felt truly ashamed that I had permitted a dream to influence me, and thought no more about it.

" A fortnight later another letter from my sister came in, bearing an apology for not having told me in her last what a narrow escape from death our Harry had experienced, and then went on to detail what I had dreamed, with the additional piece of intelligence that just as his head had dropped on the person supporting him, and he was supposed to be dead, the piece of meat passed down his throat, and he shortly after revived, and was quite well at the time of her writing.

" That boy is now a minister of the Gospel, and about a year ago I was talking with him about my strange dream, when a friend who was present said to him, ' Do you remember what you thought about when you were choking ? ' He replied, ' Yes, I distinctly remember thinking, I wonder what my mother will do when she hears I am dead.' "

In answer to our inquiries, Mrs. Hobbs says :—

"July 24th, 1884.

" I have not had any other dream of a like kind. I am not able to say how near in time the dream was to the event ; but that it was very near to the event is clear from the fact that I reckoned up the earliest time when I could get any information from England, supposing that the dream really pointed to anything ; and though no news came to the time expected, yet the *next* letter that came apologised for not having mentioned it in the *former* letter. So that the space between the event and the dream would be, at most, the space between the dream and the next mail leaving England for India."

Mr. Hobbs says :—

" So far as I am concerned in the above account, written by my wife, Jane Ann Hobbs, I declare it to be quite correct.

"WILLIAM AYERS HOBBS."

The following account is from the son, who is a Baptist minister at Tenbury.

"July 29th, 1884.

" I remember that I had a sharp, short struggle for breath, accompanied by a bursting sensation in the head and singing in the ears ; then I rolled over ; the pain in the head was succeeded by a drowsy, dreamy feeling ; a mist gathered before my eyes, and I was just on the point of losing consciousness, when the persistent thumps, which were being administered to my back by the anxious spectators, jerked the beef out of my throat, and I revived. I had no direct thought of my mother, as I imagine, for this reason : I was left in the care of an aunt, when my parents went to India ; and as the whole of my training since I was four years old had been undertaken by this aunt, prior to my going to Birmingham, it was to her that my thoughts reverted when I was choking ; and I distinctly remember that the thought flashed through my mind, ' How ever will Aunt Maria write to India about this.' I quite believed I was dying.

" H. V. HOBBS."

[In conversation, Mr. Podmore ascertained that the family are in no way given to real or supposed " psychical " experiences.]

Here the unusualness of the accident, and the uniqueness and emotional vividness of the dream may, we think, be safely accepted. The slight amount of discrepancy between the final sentences of the mother's and the son's account can hardly be held to affect the general trustworthiness of Mrs. Hobbs' narrative ; and it will be noticed that the agent's account of his own thoughts harmonises specially well with the actual nature of the percipient's impression, which was that the news was conveyed to her by her sister—the very person on whom her son imagined that sad duty as devolving.

The following case, though the dream was of an accident to a son, is strong of its kind—the form of the accident being uncommon, and the idea of it particularly strongly impressed. It is from Mrs. A. G. Sparrow, of Derwent Square, Liverpool.

"November, 1882.

(106) "Three or four years ago, I dreamt that my eldest son had broken his hand at football. Next day came a letter saying he had *sprained* his left hand. I was so impressed by my dream that I telegraphed to the head master, asking if the boy's hand was *broken.* I received a reassuring reply saying, 'Only a bad sprain, and doing well.' When he returned home at the holidays we at once saw that the hand had been broken and had joined without being properly set, and he will carry the ridge, caused by the join, to his grave."

[Mrs. Sparrow tells us that she has had no other dreams which impressed her similarly. The incident of the telegram is not likely to have been unconsciously invented.]

Perils by sea are another very common subject of dreams ; and where a large number of people are living a life of more than average risk, and a large number of relatives on land are living under a more or less constant sense of this risk, accidental coincidences between dreams and casualties are, of course, certain to occur. Especially will this be the case where the relatives live by the seaside, and where the very storm that destroys life on one element may disturb slumber on the other. We have quite a little collection of cases where wives or mothers of seafaring men have dreamt of fatal accidents which then proved to have actually occurred.[1] Such incidents have not usually

---

[1] To give one example—my friend, the Rev. R. B. F. Elrington, Vicar of Lower Brixham (who has met with several such cases), vouches for the fact that the following occurrence in his parish was described hours before the arrival of the news confirming the fears which it occasioned ; and he certifies to the good character of the witnesses.

"In the early spring of 1881, Mrs. Barnes, of Brixham, Devonshire, whose husband was at sea, dreamt that his fishing-vessel was run into by a steamer. Their boy was with him, and she called out in her dream, 'Save the boy!' At this moment another son sleeping in the next room rushed into hers, crying out, 'Where's father?' She asked

any claim to be considered as even *primâ facie* evidence for telepathy. Every now and then, however, " sea-dreams " present an amount of correct detail that prevents us from rejecting them.   Such a case is the following, from Mr. A. Ashby, of 34, Windmill Road, Croydon, Surrey.

"October 17th, 1882.

(107) "The following incident happened in about 1870.   I awoke in the morning and said to my wife, ' I have been with our son Alexander'(he was chief mate of a ship on a voyage to Port Natal, South Africa).   With great interest she listened to my dream.   ' Well,' I said, ' he is in anything but a comfortable position.   The captain is confined to his cabin, not able to come on deck ; the men, with the exception of one and a boy, likewise ill ; he has the whole duty of the ship to attend to, cook, navigator, and, in fact, everything to attend to ; nursing requires a considerable part of his time.'   The ship, if my memory is correct, was four or five hundred tons burden.   Well, sir, I dream but very little ; and on more than one occasion my dreams have been verified by coming events.

"We got a letter from my son in due course, and if I had been on board and seen, I could not have more accurately described the position of affairs on board ; fortunately, weather and wind were (as my dream indicated) favourable, or the result of this complication of adverse circumstances might have had a disastrous termination.

"A. ASHBY."

In answer to inquiries, Mr. Ashby says :—

"November 29th, 1882.

" I have nothing to add to the narrative of my dream.   I did not, as I should now do, make a minute of such a dream.   At the time, I thought, as of other dreams, it is only a dream.   Only on receipt of my son's letter, dated from Port Natal, South Africa, did the coincidence and singularity of the phenomena bring to my mind the dream, and how it exactly corresponded with the actual state of affairs on board the ship at the time it occurred.   I may mention my wife and daughter have reviewed the time and circumstance, and their memory is clear as to my relating the dream in the morning.   The scene is as fresh on mind and memory as if it had occurred yesterday."

In an interview with Mr. Podmore on October 8th, 1883, Mr. Ashby mentioned that he dreams very little.   At this interview his wife and daughter both stated that they recollected hearing of the dream

what he meant, when he said he had distinctly heard his father come upstairs and kick with his heavy boots against the door, as he was in the habit of doing when he returned from sea.   The boy's statement and her own dream so alarmed the woman that early next morning she told Mrs. Strong and other neighbours of her fears.   News afterwards came that her husband's vessel had been run into by a steamer, and that he and the boy were drowned."

This might seem at first sight, a favourable specimen, owing to the alleged *double* percipience.   But it is impossible to rely on a report from uneducated witnesses, of a confused scene in the middle of the night.   If the boy heard the sound which his father " was in the habit " of making, why should he have taken fright?   We cannot be sure that he did not imagine he had heard the sound *after* he had been infected with his mother's alarm ; for if this were so, the story might still easily have become just what it now is.

immediately after its occurrence and before its verification, but they could add nothing to the above narrative.

§ 5. This case forms a natural transition to the group where the reality is not only presented in a pictorial way, but the dream-scene corresponds (in whole or in part) with what the eyes of the supposed agent are actually beholding. The majority, perhaps, of the alleged dream-cases are of this pictorial sort; but most of them have to be set aside, on the ground either of inaccuracy of detail, or of the connection of the dream with matters that have been recently occupying the waking mind. Thus a widow whose husband was killed by an accident at sea gives us a circumstantial account of her coincident dream—" a vessel, like her husband's, wholly dismasted—the bare hull merely—being lowered by ropes down a beach, and all the crew assisting "; and declares that the scene of her dream was *exactly what was described* in the letter which afterwards brought her the news. It appears, however, that the narrator had never seen the actual ship; and inspection of the letter shows that, except the dismasting, the details of the dream had no counterpart whatever in reality. Thus all that remains is the simple coincidence of the dream and the death; and such coincidences, in the case of casualties at sea, must, as we have seen, be generally excluded. We apply this rule even where the date of the dream has been immediately noted in a diary, and where we have every assurance that it was unique in the dreamer's experience. Again, Mrs. Barter, of Careystown, Whitegate, Co. Cork, has kindly given us an account of a dream which she had at the time of the Indian Mutiny. She seemed to see her husband, then adjutant in the 75th Foot, wounded, and in the act of binding up his leg with his puggeree, when four men of his regiment lifted him up and took him into a battery. " I at once wrote it to him and, in reply to my letter, heard that such an event had actually taken place." The coincidence was extremely close, and Colonel Barter, C.B., has confirmed the account. He was carried into a battery by four sergeants; and he is nearly sure that his wife mentioned *sergeants* in her first account of her dream. But, on being specially asked as to the puggeree, he stated that he bound up his leg not with a puggeree, but with a black silk necktie. This defect, combined with the fact that Mrs. Barter was in a nervous state, and had another disturbing and quite unveridical dream about her husband during the same campaign,

Y

prevents us from allowing weight to the correspondence. So, again, Mrs. Powles, of Wadhurst, West Dulwich, has given us an account of a dream which her late husband narrated to her at the time, in which he saw his brother, Dr. Ralph Holden, who was exploring in the interior of Africa, lying under a large tree, supported by a man, and either dead or dying. They learnt from another explorer, Mr. Green, that Dr. Holden had died at just about that time, under a large tree, in the arms of his native servant ; and Mr. Holden recognised the scene of his dream in a sketch of the spot which Mr. Green had taken. But—to say nothing of the indefiniteness of the time-coincidence—the *entourage* is such as the idea of the death of an African traveller might readily enough suggest, quite apart from telepathy; and the sight of the sketch would be precisely calculated to give spurious retrospective definiteness to the dream-scene. And once more, a most vivid dream (with a remarkable amount of correct detail, as well as several important discrepancies,) in which a coachman, sleeping at a distance from his stables, saw a pony taken out, harnessed, and then after a time brought back, on the one single night on which this ever actually happened, has been dismissed, as too much connected with the dreamer's normal train of ideas ; though his master (Mr. J. S. Dismorr, of Thelcrest Lodge, Gravesend) and another witness both testify to the fact that the dream was described before the reality was known.

The following cases seem free from these objections, there having been no cause for anxiety on the percipient's part, and nothing to suggest the scene. The first is from the Rev. Canon Warburton.

"The Close, Winchester.
"July 16th, 1883.

(108) " Somewhere about the year 1848, I went up from Oxford to stay a day or two with my brother, Acton Warburton, then a barrister, living at 10, Fish Street, Lincoln's Inn. When I got to his chambers, I found a note on the table apologising for his absence, and saying that he had gone to a dance somewhere in the West End, and intended to be home soon after 1 o'clock. Instead of going to bed, I dozed in an arm-chair, but started up wide awake exactly at 1, ejaculating, ' By Jove ! he's down !' and seeing him coming out of a drawing-room into a brightly illuminated landing, catching his foot in the edge of the top stair, and falling headlong, just saving himself by his elbows and hands. (The house was one which I had never seen, nor did I know where it was.) Thinking very little of the matter, I fell a-doze again for half-an-hour, and was awakened by my brother suddenly coming in and saying, ' Oh, there you are ! I have just had as narrow an escape of breaking my neck as I ever had in my life.

Coming out of the ballroom, I caught my foot, and tumbled full length down the stairs.'

" That is all.   It may have been ' only a dream,' but I always thought it must have been something more.   " W. WARBURTON."

In a second letter Canon Warburton adds :—
                                                    " July 20th, 1883.

" My brother was hurrying home from his dance, with some little self-reproach in his mind for not having been at his chambers to receive his guest, so the chances are that he was thinking of me.   The whole scene was vividly present to me at the moment, but I did not note particulars any more than one would in real life.   The general impression was of a narrow landing brilliantly illuminated, and I remember verifying the correctness of this by questions at the time."

In conversation, however, Canon Warburton told me that the scene which he saw included a clock, and tables set round for refreshment, and that his brother confirmed the accuracy of these details.

Asked whether he had had similar vivid visions which had *not* corre-sponded with any real event, Canon Warburton replied, " This is my sole experience of the kind."

For the next case we are indebted to Mrs. Swithinbank, of Ormleigh, Mowbray Road, Upper Norwood, who is well acquainted with Mrs. Fleming, the narrator.

                                                    " October 17th, 1882.

(109) " Three years ago when staying at Ems for my health, one morn-ing after having my bath, I was resting on the sofa reading.   A slight drowsiness came over me and I distinctly saw the following :—

" My husband, who was then in England, appeared to me riding down the lane leading to my father's house.   Suddenly the horse grew restive, then plunged and kicked, and finally unseated his rider, throwing him violently to the ground.   I jumped up hastily, thinking I had been asleep; and on my going down to luncheon I related to a lady who was seated next to me what I had seen, and made the remark, ' I hope all is well at home.'   My friend, seeing I was anxious, laughed and told me not to be superstitious, and so I forgot the incident, until 2 days afterwards I received a letter from home saying my husband had been thrown from his horse and had dislocated his shoulder.   The time and place of the accident exactly agreed with my vision.   "LAURA FLEMING."

[Asked whether she can recall other dreams of a similarly vivid and realistic kind, Mrs. Fleming answers in the negative.]

The next account is from Mrs. Chambers Leete, of 28, Aberdeen Park Road, Highbury, N.   It may be compared with Mrs. Bettany's waking case (p. 194).

                                                    " September, 1884.

(110) " On the night of about the 12th of August, 1878, I had a dream which greatly troubled me, and caused me to feel quite ill, it seemed so real.   I distinctly saw my mother lying on a couch in a deathlike appear-ance, my father and brother by her side.   She looked at me, but could

                                                    Y 2

not speak ; the vividness awoke me. Falling asleep I dreamt the second time that she was dead.

"After writing home, I learned that on the night of my dream my mother had been seized with a prolonged fainting fit. I was in perfect health when I went to bed, but awoke with a terrible headache.

"ALICE E. LEETE."

In another communication, Mrs. Leete adds :—

"At the time of my dream I was companion to a lady in Dorsetshire. We had driven from a house called the Priory, Wareham, to the Grange, about 4 miles distant. It was on the night of our arrival this very vivid dream occurred to me. I mentioned it to her (and also to her housekeeper, who left soon after), she remarking first how ill I looked, and she told me not to let it worry me but write a letter to inquire if anything was the matter at home, which I did, but of course could not get an answer for two days, when I received a reply saying my mother had had, on the night I named, a dreadful fainting fit from which they thought she would not recover. I am afraid, if I wrote to her ladyship, she would not remember the circumstance, having so many things to occupy her mind, and as she thought so little about it at the time I feel sure it would not be any use troubling her.

"I can safely say that neither before nor since have I experienced a similar dream to the one of which I have sent you particulars."

In answer to an inquiry whether the details of the scene corresponded with her dream, Mrs. Leete says :—

"In reply to your inquiry I am unable to speak positively at this distance of time, but am under the impression that the scene did correspond."

Such incidents as these really belong to the class which may be described as *clairvoyant,* and which I am reserving for the end of the chapter ; but I have brought forward these few examples for the sake of a special observation. In all the earlier dream-cases of this chapter, the *rôle* of the percipient was purely *passive ;* the impression received by him was apparently a direct and literal reproduction in whole or in part, of what was, or had been, consciously in the agent's mind. But these last narratives have introduced the same difference as appeared in the concluding cases of Chapter VI. : though the scene which the dreamer pictured was the very one in which the agent was, the agent's own figure, with which his own attention was certainly not occupied, appeared in the dream. If, therefore, this part of the percept was transferred ready-made (so to speak) from the agent's mind, it must have been from a sub-conscious part of his mind. Such a view would present no serious difficulty ; for probably every one, after early childhood, retains at the background of his mind a dim realisation of his own personality in connection with his outer aspect ; and we have had proofs that a person may transmit an idea of which he is at the moment quite unaware.[1] At the same time, the cases where the agent's figure appears are equally suggestive of another explanation, and one which will prove of the highest importance in the sequel. They bring us to the point where we may suppose that the percipient is often *himself* the source of a great part of what he seems to perceive ; that he is no longer passively receptive of the impression which comes to him from without, but actively modifies and elaborates it. Thus, granted an idea of the agent to be transmitted, the appearance of the agent's figure in the telepathic picture will be no more remarkable than that, on reading a friend's name in a letter, I should be able instantly to project his image on my mental camera. It is only, however, in the next group of cases that this new *rôle* of the percipient becomes obvious.

§ 6. It will be useful at this juncture to recall the more familiar ways in which dreams are shaped. We all know that physical disturbances—whether of sound, or light, or cold, or touch—will excite dreams, in which the disturbance appears as an element, sometimes without undergoing any change, sometimes in some transfigured but still quite recognisable form. Now in such cases we of course trace the dream to the externally-produced impression ; but the impression is a mere nucleus, which the dreaming mind embodies, it may be, in a long and complicated series of self-spun fancies, and which twenty dreaming minds would embody in twenty different ways. So with mental disturbances ; a recent sorrow, or exciting work overnight, is as effective a nucleus as a knock at the door or an uncomfortable posture. The established idea works on, amid the floating crowd of images which are the potential material of dreams, and attracts a certain number of them into a more or less grotesque connection with itself.

There will thus be little difficulty in supposing that a percipient whom a strong " transferred impression " invades in his sleep may similarly combine it with his own dream-imagery. We have no reason to imagine his own activity to be suspended, or his mind made a *tabula rasa* for foreign images. We should not, therefore, demand of telepathic dreams any sober and literal transcription of actual events. We should rather expect to find the ordinary dream

---

[1] See pp. 78-9, 84, 103-9, 554-6.

elements, the medley of images, the impossibilities and incongruities, no less prominent here than elsewhere. The root idea being given by the " transferred impression," it may then become the sport of irresponsible fancy, which develops it either in some haphazard way, or in accordance with the dreamer's habitual lines of thought or emotion ; so that the real event is announced either in a manner typically dream-like and fantastic, or oftener, perhaps, in a manner which is to some extent symbolic.

I will begin with cases where the element thus supplied is of the slightest possible amount. In the following three examples the dreamer may be supposed simply to give the most obvious auditory form to the impression received ; though in the second and third it is, no doubt, equally possible to suppose a direct auditory transfer, as in some of the experimental cases.

The first case is from Miss Barr, of Apsley Town, East Grinstead, who has been mentioned above (p. 94, note).

" 1884.

(111) " In the early part of 1882, I had been working a good deal amongst the navvies employed on the new railroad, near East Grinstead, and had been particularly interested in the case of one man, ' Darkey,' as he was called by his fellow-workmen. I had become very intimate with the man, and he had told me all his previous history, and I had used my best endeavours to keep him from drink. On the night of Easter Tuesday, 1882, I dreamed that I heard the voice of the man calling me from the bottom of a well. I told my sister of it in the morning, and, during the course of the day, a messenger came to tell me that the man had actually fallen down a well overnight, from which, though in no danger, he had been extricated with some difficulty.   " L. BARR."

Miss Barr's sister, Miss Harriett A. L. Barr, has added her signature to this account, in attestation of having heard the dream narrated on the following morning.

[The idea of "the bottom of a well " is one that can be easily conceived to have been read back into the dream, after the reality was known. But the case does not depend on that detail.]

Here we may be practically certain that the man did not actually call on Miss Barr by name, as there could have been no chance of her hearing him.

The next case is from the late Mr. George Gouldrick, of 16, Union Street, Hereford.

" 1883.

(112) " In the month of April, 1876, I dreamt that an invalid, named Mary Scaffull, widow, an inmate of Johnson's Hospitals, Commercial Road, Hereford, (and whose husband had been an officer in the gaol of which I

was governor,) was crying out for water ; it appeared to have been a long dream, and the cry seemed to be kept up for some time.   When I was sitting at breakfast with my family next morning, I asked my wife when she had seen Mrs Scaffull last ; she replied, ' Some 9 days ago.   I took her a rice pudding ; I could not get into the house, the door being locked. I therefore had to leave it at her sister's, who was living in the neighbourhood, with a request that when she went to see her, she would take it to her ; the dish has been returned ,therefore I conclude she had the contents. Why, what is the matter, you seem troubled about her ? '   I then told her my dream, and said, ' I have determined to go after breakfast and see what state she is in.'   She answered, ' I am glad to hear you say so.'

"As I approached the house, I could hear a cry of distress proceeding from some one of the inmates of the hospitals.   I put my finger on the latch of the door occupied by Mrs. Scaffull, when I heard the following supplication proceed from her in the most distressing tone : ' Will some kind Christian friend give me some water ? '   I took a jug from her lower room, went to the pump and filled it, and then took it with all haste to her bedside.   When she saw me there with the water she said, ' Oh, Mr. Gouldrick, the Lord has sent you here, God Almighty bless you for bringing me this water.'   She then drank copiously of it, and said, ' It's the sweetest water I ever tasted all my life long.'   She died the same week, at the age of 77 years.   " GEO. GOULDRICK."

Mr. Gouldrick's daughter corroborates as follows :—

" December 11th, 1883.

" I was present at the breakfast-table when my father related his dream. I remember all that happened, and can therefore corroborate all he has written.   My mother has since died.   She was present also, and we expressed our astonishment when he returned home and told us what had happened.   The only reason I am aware of that the neighbours (who heard all) did not attend to her cry, was that she was in receipt of 7s. per week more than they were, and that caused an ill-feeling towards her.

" HANNAH GOULDRICK."

The next account is from Mrs. Morris Griffith, of 6, Menai View Terrace, Bangor.

" 1884.

(113) " On the night of Saturday, the 11th of March, 1871, I awoke in much alarm, having seen my eldest son, then at St. Paul de Loanda on the south-west coast of Africa, looking dreadfully ill and emaciated, and I heard his voice distinctly calling to me.   I was so disturbed I could not sleep again, but every time I closed my eyes the appearance recurred, and his voice sounded distinctly, calling me · Mamma.'   I felt greatly depressed all through the next day, which was Sunday, but I did not mention it to my husband, as he was an invalid, and I feared to disturb him.   We were in the habit of receiving weekly letters every Sunday from our youngest son, then in Ireland, and as none came that day, I attributed my great depression to that reason, glad to have some cause to assign to Mr. Griffith rather than the real one.   Strange to say, he also suffered from intense low spirits all day, and we were both unable to take dinner, he rising from the table saying, ' I don't care what it costs, I must have the boy back,' alluding to his eldest son.   I mentioned my dream and the bad night I had

had to two or three friends, but begged that they would say nothing of it to Mr. Griffith. The next day a letter arrived containing some photos of my son, saying he had had fever, but was better, and hoped immediately to leave for a much more healthy station, and written in good spirits. We heard no more till the 9th of May, when a letter arrived with the news of our son's death from a fresh attack of fever, on the night of the 11th of March, and adding that just before his death he kept calling repeatedly for me. I did not at first connect the date of my son's death with that of my dream until reminded of it by the friends, and also an old servant, to whom I had told it at the time. I append my signature in attestation of the report being a true and correct one, and also the signature of Kate Dew, who perfectly remembers the date and circumstances, and attests the truth of the above.   " MARY G. GRIFFITH.
                                           " KATE DEW."

In answer to inquiries, Mrs. Griffith says :—

" The experience came to me as a *dream*, but upon waking my distress was so great at the extreme reality of the impression of seeing my son looking so very ill and suffering, and the anguish of his voice in calling me by name, that although I tried for hours afterwards to sleep again, I was unable to do so from the haunting return of the scene and voice, whenever I closed my eyes. My husband had no dream, but all the next day he, like myself, became deeply depressed about our son, although I had said nothing to *him* on the subject. Towards evening some friends came in, and the impression faded, and the following morning on receiving my son's letter with photographs, I lost *all* feeling of anxiety about him."

In answer to further inquiries, Mrs. Griffith says :—

(1) " I have never in all my life, before or since, had any such distressing dream, nor am I ever discomposed in any way by uncomfortable dreams.

(2) " I never remember at any time having any dream from which I have had any difficulty in knowing at once, whilst awakening, that I had been dreaming, and never confuse the dream with reality.

(3) " I also unhesitatingly assure you that I have never had any hallucination of the senses as to sound or sight."

The following is part of a letter to Mr. Richard M. Griffith—dated Loanda, March 26th, 1871—which I have been allowed to copy.

" DEAR SIR,—It is my sorrowful duty to inform you that your son, Mr. R. M. Griffith, died in my house on the 11th inst. He was staying with me awaiting the arrival of machinery from England, but fell sick about the beginning of the month, and gradually sank, notwithstanding all our efforts to save him.—Yours very truly, ALEXANDER SMITH."

[It is to be regretted that no written note was made of the date of the dream ; but Mrs. Griffith is certain that the Saturday on which it occurred was afterwards rightly identified as March 11th by herself and her friends. Her reason for remembering the day of the week appears in the account.]

And now we come to the large and important group where the percipient forms a very distinct picture of the agent, whose figure and aspect (sometimes with the addition of speech) is not a mere element in a scene, but the one thing prominently represented. I will still keep for a time to simple cases, where the mental image that is conjured up corresponds pretty closely to the reality.

The following account is from the Rev. W. D. Wood Rees, Vicar of Barmby Moor, York.

"May, 1885.

(114) "In 1874, when reading for college, I frequently visited a man named William Edwards (of Llanrhidian, near Swansea), who was then seriously ill; he often professed pleasure at, and benefit from, my ministrations. He at length recovered so far as to resume work. I left the neighbourhood, and amid new scenes and hard work, I cannot say that I ever thought of him.

"I had been at college some 12 months, when one night, or rather early morning between 12 at midnight and 3 in the morning, I had a most vivid dream. I seemed to hear the voice of the above-named William Edwards calling me in earnest tones. In my dream I seemed to go to him, and saw him quite distinctly. I prayed with him and saw him die. When I awoke the dream seemed intensely real, so much that I remarked the time, 3 a.m. in the morning. I could not forget it and told some college friends all particulars. The next day I received a letter from my mother, with this P.S. : 'The bell is tolling ; I fear poor William Edwards is dead.' On inquiry I found that he did die between 12 and 3 ; that he frequently expressed the wish that I were with him. I. had no idea that he was ill.   "W. D. Wood Rees."

We find from the Register of Deaths that William Edwards died at Llanrhidian, on Oct. 14, 1875.

In answer to inquiries, Mr. Rees says :—

"My dream took place between midnight and 3 in the morning. William Edwards died *within that time.* My mother wrote her letter just after breakfast, when the death-bell was tolling for him—just at the time I mentioned my dream to some friends. I received the letter either the next night or the morning after. It was generally a two days' post. I was particular to inquire if the death took place the *night of my dream :* it did. I have not the date of the occurrence, but can get it, no doubt, from inquiring the date of the man's death. I had no object in making any note of them. The friends, I believe, were Rev. G. L. Rees, Howden, Rev. J. W. Roberts (dead), and I think, the Rev. T. S. Cunningham ; I will ask him. I have on other occasions dreamt of deaths, but have not taken any trouble to investigate them. I have sometimes dreamt I saw a person dying, and then heard they were ill. The vividness and reality of the case I mention caused me to take such notice of it."

The Rev. G. L. M. Rees corroborates as follows :—

"Howden, East Yorkshire.
"June 11th, 1885.

"The statement made by my brother, the Rev. W. D. W. Rees, relative to the death of William Edwards, is quite correct. I perfectly remember his relating to me a dream respecting his death, previous to the intelligence reaching us at college.   "G. L. M. Rees."

In conversation the Rev. W. D. Wood Rees informed me, without being asked, that he has never had any other dream that the least impressed him, or left any effect after waking. The man had got "quite well," and Mr. Rees had last seen him breaking stones on the road.

It would be tedious here to multiply cases where the mere fact of death has been vividly dreamt of, without more detail than this. Yet it is in their multiplication that the whole force of such cases consists, and a single coincidence of the sort might always be explained as accidental. Other examples, belonging to the important group which was used in my numerical calculation (pp. 304-7), will be found in the Supplement.

The next case is from Mrs. Fielding, of Yarlington Rectory, Bath, who was also the narrator of case 90, above.

"January, 1884.

(115) "I some time ago had rather a remarkable vision, but it was of the living. I have an only son, about 20, always in robust health, then in lodgings in London. Never were mother and son more to one another than we are. One night I awoke heartbroken by seeing him in bed very ill. I stood weeping by his bed, lifting his white face in my two hands, and saying he must be dying. On my husband waking I told him it all, and those at breakfast next morning, and said, ' Let us see if it's only a dream.' A week passed, and my usual letter did not come from my son. After a time one came saying he had been ill in bed a week, too ill to let me know, and the landlady had nursed him through it.

"JANE E. FIELDING."

In answer to inquiries, Mrs. Fielding adds :—

" I found my son's letter telling of the illness I spoke of, and find it was written on the 15th July, 1882, a Saturday, and my *vision-dream* —for it was too distinct for a common dream ; yet I was not wide awake, and could not vouch I had seen the picture *consciously*, yet it was most real—took place either on the night of 12th or 13th July, and I find both my husband and son-in-law remember my speaking of it, though the dates escape them. I now quote from my son's letter : ' I go back to the City on Monday, but I thought it was no use telling you, to make you anxious, of my attack of quinsey till I was better ; and the doctor and my landlady nursed me most carefully, and now I can swallow.' It has much pain, this complaint, and it was that look of pain I saw on his face in my vision that gave *me* such pain. I can swear to the vision having been before the letter came. Were I in the *least* dubious, I should be the first to say so, having a glimpse of the meaning of the word *science*. I can't recall any other such ' clear-seeing.' I never had a dream like this before."

I have seen Mrs. Fielding's letter to her son, dated Monday, July 24th, in which she says, " On Thursday morning [*i.e.*, July 13th] when I came down to breakfast, I said to Tom and Arthur [her son-in-law with whom she now lives], ' I hope Charlie is well ; for I had such a queer dream of finding him lying in bed on his face, and when I turned it round, it was ghastly pale and ill-looking—and I was so sighing all day after, and expected to hear, as I did, you were ill.' Now that's funny ! Shows how our souls are closely united. Arthur is just saying to me he 'quite remembers my telling him my dream.'"

[This practically proves that Mrs. Fielding is accurate in saying that her dream was described before the news was known. But the force of the coincidence is of course weakened by the fact that the illness extended over several days.]

In the next case the form of a vision—a figure at the bedside— suggests not so much a genuine dream as the sort of semi-waking hallucination which will be considered in the next chapter (compare also Mr. Wingfield's case, p. 199). The narrator is Mrs. L. H. Saunders, of St. Helen's, near Ryde, who was concerned in case 44.

"March 18th, 1885.

(116) "Towards morning of the 10th January, 1885, I was conscious of a young woman standing by my bedside clad in a grey dressing gown, holding in her arms, towards me, a child. The woman was weeping bitterly, and said, 'Oh ! Mrs. Saunders, I am in such trouble.' I instantly recognised her as Mrs. C. R. Seymour, and was about to interrogate her as to her trouble, when I was awakened by my husband asking me what was the matter, as I seemed so distressed. I told him I had had such a sad dream about poor Fanny Goodall (maiden name of Mrs. C. R. S.), but it really was to me more than a dream—so much so, that after rising I communicated it to the governess, Miss Monkman, also to the nurse and servant. I decided to send to her mother, Mrs. Goodall, to inquire if she had received any tidings of her daughter, who was resident in New Zealand with her husband and two children, but as on after consideration I felt I might cause her alarm, I altered my intention. This dream or vision made so deep and lasting an impression that I constantly alluded to it to members of our household, until circumstances occasioned my calling on Mrs. Goodall about the beginning of this month, March, 1885, when I made particular inquiries for her daughter ; and on being assured that she was well, according to letters by the most recent mail, I ventured to express my gratification, giving, as my reason for such, a narration of the 'vision' that had not even then ceased to haunt me ; which elicited from Mrs. Goodall and both of her daughters, who were present, fervent hopes that all was well with Mrs. Seymour.[1]

"On March 12th I again called on Mrs. Goodall, who on receiving me, with much emotion said, 'Oh, have you heard the bad news of Fanny? I have thought so much of what you told me ; her dear little Dottie has gone. I will read you her letters,' both of which, although coming by different mails, had only been received within the past 24 hours. I should mention that, although I have felt very interested in and thought much of Mrs. C. R. S. before and since her departure from this country, yet I have never corresponded with her ; but I now learn that she invariably mentioned me in her home correspondence, and felt much indebted to me for some trifling kindness I had been able to show her in the past. I am able to fix the date of my vision from circumstances which I need not here relate.

"BESSIE SAUNDERS."

[1] This has been completely confirmed by letters from Mrs. Goodall and her two daughters.

The force of the coincidence seems not much affected one way or the other by the following addition :—

"In reply to your question, I have had distressing dreams relating to death at intervals, which have not corresponded with reality ; but those you are already cognisant of [viz., this one and another which corresponded with reality [1]] are the only ones which impressed themselves sufficiently to induce me to take steps to discover if they did correspond with the reality, although I may have mentioned their purport casually at the time."

Mr. Latimer H. Saunders writes :—

"March 18th, 1885.

"I clearly remember on or about the 10th of January, 1885, early morning, suddenly awaking, and finding my wife leaning forward in bed. I asked her, ' What was the matter ?' She seemed agitated, and replied to the following effect : ' Oh, I have had such a horrid dream ! Fanny Goodall was standing here at my side, quite close, holding out the child in *such* distress, but I could not tell what she wanted ; it was so real, I could have touched her, but you awoke me.' Before rising, my wife repeated the incident in detail. Late on March 12th, she told me the sequel.

"Fortunately, I can safely fix the date as being the morning of either the 9th, 10th, or 11th of January, as during that month these were, owing to circumstances, the *only possible* occasions on which the incident, as related, could have occurred, while my mental impression, *independently* arrived at, strongly points to the 10th as the day.

"LATIMER H. SAUNDERS."

Miss E. A. Monkman, in a letter to Mrs. Saunders (dated 16, Castledine Road, Anerley, 16th March, 1885), of which I have seen a copy, gives exactly similar testimony as to Mrs. Saunders's description of her dream at the time, and adds that it must have been on the 9th or 10th of the month. And on March 20th, a servant in the house, unprompted (as Mrs. Saunders assures us), dictated the following statement :—

"I remember Saturday morning, the 10th of January last. The mistress came into the kitchen to speak about the flue. After doing so she told me of such a bad dream she had had of Mrs. Seymour, of New Zealand, coming to her bedside with her little child in her arms. Mrs. Seymour was crying so bitterly, and imploring her for help.—E. DAWSON."

The following is an extract from a letter received from Mrs. Seymour by Mrs. Goodall, dated January 15th, 1885.

"I do not know how to write it, mother. Dottie is dead ; a week ago this very Thursday evening she was taken ill, and on Saturday at 10 minutes to 10 in the evening she died."

[Allowing for longitude, the dream must have preceded the death by a few hours.]

---

[1] In this second case (as to which we again have Mr. Saunders's testimony to the fact that the dream was described before the reality was known) the dream was that a friend alighted from a hearse, and entered clad in deep mourning ; and it fell on the night on which that friend's mother, whom she was attending, unexpectedly died.

Very similar is the form of impression described in the next case, obtained (through the kindness of Mr. J. B. Johnston, of 17, Pilrig Street, Edinburgh) from Herr Heinrich von Struve, whose German account is here translated.

" 25, Pilrig Street, Edinburgh.

"July 10th, 1885.

(117) "In 1838, I was on terms of friendship with a captain of the 2nd Hussars, Herr von R., his company being quartered in a little town in Silesia, in the neighbourhood of which I was residing on my property. Early one morning I had ridden into the town, and visited Von R., whom I found taking coffee with his wife. While we were sitting chatting together, Von R. said to his wife, 'Lina, our friend Pogerell died last night.' 'What a thing to say, Albert!' his wife replied ; 'Pogerell was here only the day before yesterday, well and happy.' 'Very likely,' said Von R. ; 'but the fact is as I have said. Last night he stood by my bed, and said, "Farewell, R. ; I am departing to the great army. Greet my cousin G. from me, and ask him not to be angry that I have not mentioned him in my will, as he is well off, and my other relatives are poor and need support."' Some minutes after Von R. had told us this, a messenger was announced, who entered, bringing from the commanding officer of both of them in W., where the company of Captain von Pogerell was stationed, the announcement that 'Captain von Pogerell had a paralytic stroke last night, and died.' The town of W., where Von Pogerell was, was 4 German miles [about 12 English miles] distant from the place where we were ; the road was bad, and there was no ordinary means of communication. It was, therefore, inconceivable that any earlier news than that which this messenger brought could have reached Von R. He was a sober man, completely honest and truthful, who, except among very intimate friends, never spoke of his gift of seeing apparitions—a gift which he took no pride in. He would mention such experiences casually to his wife in the morning, or when his friends pressed him on the subject. "Von R. related to me some other highly interesting cases of the sort ; but I do not add them, not having been myself a party to them, as I was to the one which I have narrated.   "H. VON STRUVE."

In an English account which Herr von Struve has signed as correct, it appears that Pogerell was not an *intimate* friend, and that there had been no special reason for thinking of him.

[The case is one where the evidence of a person who was not the percipient is stronger than that of the percipient himself would have been (see p. 148). After an interval of 47 years, the mere memory of a coincident dream—for we must not assume that it was a *waking* vision[1]— would have very little force. But Herr von Struve himself would of course be awake, when sitting talking to his friends ; and the scene in its various stages—the statement of Von R., the conversation that ensued, and the arrival of the messenger—if really only imagined afterwards, would constitute an oddly distinct and detailed piece of retrospective hallucination.]

---

[1] In conversation Herr von Struve told me that Von R. certainly represented the vision as a waking experience. But on such a point second-hand evidence of a remote date can command but little confidence.

The next case, from a daughter of an officer of high position in the Austrian service, was procured through the kindness of Mr. W. E. H. Lecky, who is a friend of the narrator.

"Newbury, January, 1884.

(118) "One night, a few years ago, I had a very vivid dream about some one I had known as a boy in the Bedford Grammar School, but of whom I had not heard anything for a long time. I dreamt that he came to me draped in a long white garment, and that he said to me, 'I am so glad it is all over,' and putting his head on my shoulder, he sighed deeply, and said, 'I am so tired.' I woke from the fancied touch and did not go to sleep again for some time. It made such an impression on me that I told my sisters the next morning. A few days after, one of my sisters brought me a paper with the announcement of my friend's death in it, and, strange to say, he died the very night I dreamt about him.

"L. K. D."

In answer to inquiries Miss L. K. D. says :—

"February 29th, 1884.

"I have been trying to ascertain the exact date of my dream about my friend's death, but cannot remember anything nearer than that it was some time in the spring of 1878. I had not seen him for nearly four years, and *certainly* had not talked or even thought about him for some time, I might say years. I don't remember ever having such a vivid dream before or after."

The following corroboration is from Miss L. K. D.'s sister :—

"January 10th, 1884.

"With regard to my sister's dream about the person she knew as a boy in Bedford, I can remember distinctly that she told her dream to us all at breakfast, *before* we heard of the death.

"A. M. D."

Here the long white garment might be taken as representing the actual dress which the supposed agent was wearing ; for if a person's sub-conscious idea of his own aspect may be the source of a telepathic impression, that impression might very naturally include his garb at the time. But I should prefer to regard this particular investiture as supplied by the percipient's mind to its own dream-image.

In the following cases the dream contained the additional feature of conversation between the dreamer and the agent. This is, of course, a clear instance of something superadded by the dreamer's own creative activity.

Miss K. Gibson, of 3, Huntley Gardens, Glasgow, says :—

"November, 1883.

(119) "In August, 1867, my sister and I went to spend a few days with

a friend in the country. We were a very merry and youthful party ; and I do not think one grave or solemn thought crossed any of our minds. The brother of our hostess having been married the week previously, had sent a box of wedding cake, and according to the old custom we all determined ' to sleep on the wedding cake, and to tell our dreams in the morning.' Early on the morning of Thursday, I awoke, and when I fell asleep again, I dreamt I found myself in a very bare, cheerless room, in the corner of which stood a bed ; on it was lying a young man. I at once recognised him as a friend of my brother's, whom I had last seen (for only the second time in my life) the previous Christmas, a tall, strong, handsome young fellow, in apparently high health and spirits. I saw him now, a shadow of his former self, his face drawn and colourless, his eyes un-naturally large and bright ; his hand, which was lying outside the bedclothes, was thin and wasted, the great blue veins standing up like cords, and his fingers plucked restlessly at the coverlet. His hollow cough sounded incessantly through the room. I went up to him. ' Why, Mr. ——,' I said, ' how very ill you look ; what is the matter ? ' ' I am dying,' he said, ' I caught cold a month ago, and neglected it ; it has settled on my chest, and the doctors say I am dying of rapid consumption.'

" When I rose in the morning, I could hardly bear to tell my dream, but it had all been so painfully vivid, and haunted me so, that I told my sister before we went down to breakfast. I was much teased by my kind hostess, but I would not speak of the dream to any one. On the following Saturday evening we went home. I did not see my brother until the Sunday morning. When at breakfast he said, ' Did you hear, girls, of poor M.'s death ? ' ' No,' we said, ' when did it take place ? ' ' Early on Thursday morning ; he caught cold a month ago, neglected it, it settled on his chest, and he died of rapid consumption.'

" I may add that not only did I hardly know Mr. ——, having only seen him twice, but I do not think I had even heard his name mentioned from the time I saw him at Christmas, till the morning I dreamt of his death. I was only a child at the time.   " K. GIBSON."

Miss Gibson's sister corroborates as follows :—
                                        " November 17th, 1883.
" I quite remember my sister dreaming as she relates above. It made quite an impression on both of us when my brother mentioned Mr. ——'s death.   " M. H. MURRAY."

In answer to inquiries, Miss Gibson says :—

(1) " I have at various times had vivid dreams of deaths which have *not* come true, and whose origin I could trace." [This final clause prevents this statement from weakening the case as much as it would otherwise do.]

(2) " I do not know if Mr. M.'s room was ' bare and cheerless.' I *do* know that he died in lodgings.

(3) " The words in my dream and those of my brother exactly corresponded."

She believes that the death took place in Glasgow, where the young man certainly lived ; but no entry of it can be discovered in the Register for that place, and it is possible that he died away from home.

Professor Sidgwick, after an interview with Miss Gibson, April 20th, 1884, says : —

"She informed me that she did not take much interest in the subject of my inquiries. She was quite sure of the exact correspondence of the statements in her dream—'caught cold'—'month ago'—'neglected it'—'settled on chest'—'rapid consumption'—with the statements of her brother ; and her sister also noted the correspondence. She knew the young man was poor, so that the 'bare cheerless' room would be naturally suggested ; but she had never heard of him as consumptive: she could have had no other image of him from memory except that of a strong, healthy man. She was not interested in the young man, and believes that she had not thought of him between the Christmas when she saw him and the time of the dream and death. It was not remarkable that she told the dream, as she had rather a habit of dreaming and of telling curious dreams—not from any belief, but merely as curious. What *was* unusual was that she was reluctant to tell it, and only told it to her sister."

Supposing this dream to have been telepathically originated, it is difficult to know how much of its content was supplied to, and how much by, the dreamer. Given the idea of consumption, the development is, perhaps, not too detailed to have been independently imagined.

The following very similar case is from Mrs. Jarratt, of 96, Dalberg Road, S.W. I need hardly say that the mere recollection of a childish dream of a good many years back would not have been admitted as evidence : the evidence is the mother's attestation that the dream was described before the news of the death arrived.

"December 10th, 1883.

(120) "While I was a little girl, about 10 years old, an old friend of ours, particularly dear to me, a Danish gentleman (formerly tutor to the young Princes of Denmark, and afterwards teacher of languages in the High School, San Francisco), sought to improve his position by going to the city of Mexico. Some months after he left, I dreamed that I saw him sitting in my father's office, and immediately ran up to him, exclaiming, 'I'm so glad you've come back.' He put his hand up, as if to repulse me gently, and said gravely, 'You must not come near me. I am dying in Mexico of the sore throat, and I have come to tell your father.' I drew back, grieved and shocked, and woke. The next day I told everyone of my dream, and was well laughed at; but my father had not heard for some time past of our friend, nor did he till, three weeks after, I overheard a gentleman say to him, 'Well, doctor, have you heard about your friend H——?' My father having replied in the negative, the gentleman continued, 'I was told he died at Mexico, three weeks ago, of sore throat.'   "LITA JARRATT."

In answer to sbme questions, Mrs. Jarratt adds :—

(1) "My old friend's name was George J. Hansen. I remember my father remarking that my dream must have occurred at the same time as the death, or at any rate close upon it.

(2) "As the occurrence took place some 20 years ago, as well as I can remember, it would be a little difficult to find the people to whom I told my dream before its fulfilment, but I told it to everyone who would listen, which they were not all inclined to do, or if they did, they ridiculed me heartily."

Mrs. Jarratt's mother, Mrs. Farrar, corroborates as follows :—

"I beg to state that I perfectly remember my daughter telling me all about her dream within a few hours of its having occurred. It afterwards struck us all (her father as well as myself and several friends, most of whom unfortunately are since dead or have disappeared) as being very remarkable on account of its having occurred almost simultaneously, as far as we could learn, with Mr. Hansen's actual decease."

Miss H. Franconi wrote to us as follows from 1237, Stockton Street, San Francisco :—

"July 13th, 1884.

"In regard to the dream that my friend Mrs. Jarratt had, I only remember, as it is many years ago, that she dreamt of Mr. Hansen and told me all about it the following morning—but what the dream was about I cannot remember."

[In conversation, Mrs. Jarratt, who is a very clear-headed and sensible witness, gave me the additional detail that even in her dream "sore throat" struck her as an odd thing to die of. This is not a point as to which memory can at all be relied on ; but the mere fact that it *seems* to be remembered is some slight confirmation of the evidence that the actual disease was mentioned in the dream. The degree of exactitude in the coincidence does not, however, seem to have been established with certainty even at the time.]

The next case is uncorroborated ; but the style of the narrator does not suggest exaggeration. If the description is accurate, the dream was remarkably vivid, and included a minute point of correct detail. It is from Mr. E. J. Hector, of Valencia, Port Pirie, South Australia.

"July 5th, 1884.

(121) "On the night of my father's death, the 31st July, 1863, I went to bed as usual, about 11 p.m., in my usual good health, with a candle and matches on a chair at the side of my bed. I usually read for half-an-hour in bed, and did so on this occasion. I remember distinctly my last ponderings were on the very unsatisfactory scheme of life. Man learns gradually from childhood to mature age ; and just when he has acquired by experience and observation the knowledge how to make the best of life, he dies ; and his successor has to start at the same point as he started from. Whether I thought of my father in connection with this, I do not remember. In the night or morning I had a very vivid dream. I saw my father in bed at the Savings' Bank, in the room he usually occupied ; there was a sperm candle burning on a chair close to his bed. I was sitting in a chair close to his bed, and saw that he was dying and felt very distressed ; he was lying on his back and turned round and looked at me, saying, with

z

a smile, 'Never mind, my dear boy, I feel that I am going,' and seemed to be dying. The next thing was total darkness. I must have waked up, for I found the matches, and to reassure myself lighted the candle, glad to find it was a dream. It struck me as the most vivid I had ever had, but I confidently banished it at once, and slept soundly again till morning. I looked at my watch and noted the time ; it was 4 a.m.

"The dream never troubled me again, until I saw a man coming to me in the vineyard, at about 10 a.m., with the fatal telegram from a friend, that my father was dead ; but as soon as I saw a strange man hurrying down to me, a presentiment occurred to me that my dream had been true. I may say that I never believed in dreams, and do not since that event, which I think was only a most extraordinary coincidence, and was just the continuation of my train of thought, commenced during my waking moments and continued throughout my sleep, or perhaps, rather renewed, as it is not likely I should continue dreaming from, say 11.30 p.m. until 4 a.m. Strange to say, the same smile was on my father's face when I (at 6 p.m., or eight hours after he was found dead in his bed) saw him, and he lay in the room I dreamt he was in, and the wick of the sperm candle at his side was bent towards the door, precisely as I saw it in my dream, on the chair. The servant told us he went to bed as usual at 10 to 11 p.m., and not getting up as usual, she knocked at his door, but no answer being given, opened the door at 8 a.m., and found him dead.

" I had no cause of anxiety. My father was in excellent health. This was the first vivid dream I ever had, and I do not remember dreaming of others dying, or doing anything extraordinary. I am not much of a dreamer.

"Since then, however, I had a vivid dream of the death of my mother —not so clear or impressive as the other—but nothing happened, and I remember tracing this also to some kindred train of thought, just before dropping off to sleep. I am not a believer in any premonitory spiritual communication.   " E. J. HECTOR."

The *South Australian Register* for August 1, 1863, says that Mr. John Hector, manager of the Savings' Bank of S. Australia, having retired to rest in his usual good health on the night of July 30, was found dead in his bed next morning, and that the doctor pronounced death to have occurred from apoplexy about three hours previously.

[It is clearly by a slip that Mr. E. J. Hector has spoken of the night of the 31st of July instead of the 30th.]

The coincidence in this case, as in any other, may have been accidental, as the narrator supposes ; but he does not tell us what part of his previous train of thought found its " continuation " in the wick of the sperm candle—which, if rightly remembered, looks like a fragment of telepathic clairvoyance.

The next two cases are from Mrs. Freese, of Granite Lodge, Chislehurst. The occurrence of several such experiences to the same person is in itself a point of interest, provided that that person's recollection as to their having been of an exceptionally vivid and disturbing character can be relied on.

" March, 1884.

(122) " In July, 1871, my aunt Mary staying with me, and my husband not feeling at all well, it was decided he should go·to H. to spend a fortnight at the Vicarage with my married sister, Mrs. B. This place was specially chosen because he enjoyed so much riding with my brother-in-law or alone, as the case might be, and horse-exercise was so good for him.

" A few days after, I had a vivid dream about him, which I told to my aunt at breakfast time. I dreamed I was walking along the road to H., about midway between the N. station and the Vicarage, when I saw my husband sitting *on a gate* by the roadside. I was struck by his sad expression of countenance, and went up to him asking him if he was enjoying himself. ' Not at all,' said he, and added, ' I have just been thinking I will go on to the station and take the train home, and will you believe it, they wont let me ride either of the horses.' While expressing my astonishment I woke.

" I remarked to my aunt upon the absurdity of the part about the horses, as they were the chief inducement for him to pay this visit, and were always before at his disposal. I heard from my husband every day, but he wrote always cheerfully, and made no reference to the horses at all. A few days later he returned earlier than he was expected, and in the evening, when walking with him in the garden, he began to describe to me his visit, telling me he had not enjoyed it at all. He had been very wretched and lonely (for my sister had been unusually busy, also her husband), and that one day in a lonely walk towards N. he *sat on a gate* by the roadside to rest, and almost made up his mind to go on to N. and take the first train back to town, telegraphing to my sister some excuse, but, fearing to hurt their feelings, he desisted ; and, ' worse than that,' said he, ' what will you say when I tell you I have not been *once* on horseback. For some reason or another they would not let me ride either horse. One went down the other day, and in future, I believe, no one is to ride them.' I kept calling out, ' My dream ! my dream ! ' as he went on, and when I related it to my husband he could scarcely believe it. He would not write either about his depression or disappointment, as he did not wish to cloud me.

" OCTAVIA FREESE."

In answer to inquiries, Mrs. Freese adds :—

" I do not think I am given to vivid dreams. That about my husband was exceptionally vivid. I call exceptionally vivid a dream that takes hold of me, and that I cannot forget all the next day. The aunt to whom I told it has since died. I have no idea whether my husband sat on the gate before or after my dream, nor did I try to ascertain that at the time."

(123) " In September, 1881, I had another curious dream, so vivid that I seemed to *see* it.

" My two boys of 18 and 16 were staying in the Black Forest, under the care of a Dr. Fresenius. I must say here that I always supposed the boys would go everywhere together, and I never should have supposed that in that lonely country, so new to them, they would be out after dark.

My husband and I were staying at St Leonards, and on Saturday night I woke at about 12 o'clock (rather before, as I heard it strike), having just seen vividly a dark night on a mountain, and my eldest boy lying on his back at the bottom of some steep place, his eyes wide open and saying, 'Good-bye, mother and father, I shall never see you again.' I woke with a feeling of anxiety, and the next morning when I told it to my husband, though we both agreed it was absurd to be anxious, yet we would write and tell the boys we hoped they would never go out alone after dark. To my surprise my eldest boy, to whom I wrote the dream, wrote back expressing his great astonishment, for on that Saturday night he was coming home over the mountains, past 11 o'clock ; it was pitch dark, and he slipped and fell down some 12 feet or so, and landed on his back, looking up to the sky. However, he was not much hurt and soon picked himself up and got home all right. He did not say what thoughts passed through his mind as he fell.   " OCTAVIA FREESE."

In answer to inquiries, Mrs. Freese adds :—

" *Before* my son wrote about his fall in the Black Forest, I related my dream to my husband, and as he seemed a little moved by it, I wrote an account of it to my boy, saying his father did not wish them to be out after dark alone. I had not told my boy *when* it was, deeming that immaterial, but when in his letter, received days after, he said, 'Was it Saturday night ? because then so-and-so,' I remembered what I should not otherwise have noted, that it was Saturday night ; for on the Sunday morning my husband, being much worried about some business matter, elected to spend the morning with me in the fields instead of going to church, and as much to divert his mind as anything I related to him my dream of the night before."

Mrs. Freese sent us the letter from her son, which contained the following passage :—

" With regard to your dream : did you dream it on September 3rd ? if so it was on that night, coming home rather late, that I fell down a precipice of 8 feet, or perhaps more, in the dark, and might have broken my neck, but didn't. However, I don't think you will find me walking about after dark more than I can help, as the roads are very dark, and the fogs in the village awful.   " FRED. E. FREESE."

[September 3rd, 1881, was a Saturday.]

Mr. Freese writes :—

" March 17th, 1884.

" Mrs. Freese has read to me the paper she has sent you, and I feel bound to say that both the dreams she refers to concerning myself and our eldest son I well remember, and noted them at the time she described them, together with the circumstances that strangely accompanied them.

" J. W. FREESE."

In answer to the question whether he noted them *in writing*, Mr. Freese replies that he did not. " It *struck* me at the time as very remarkable, but life was then with me too busy to leave time to dwell upon the subject."

§ 7. In the foregoing examples the elements with which the dreamer may be supposed to have invested the telepathic impression have been few and simple. We now come to cases where definitely new elements have been introduced, and the impression which corresponds with reality acts as the germ of a quite imaginary dream-picture.

The following narrative was taken down in writing by Mrs. Saxby, of Mount Elton, Clevedon, at Tranent Lawn, Clevedon, on November 17th, 1883, and was read over to the narrator, Miss C. A., who certified that it was correct. Miss C. A. thinks that the occurrence took place in 1855.

(124) "When we were living at Leamington, I had a remarkable vision. I was sleeping with my sister Maria. Suddenly the curtains of our bed, at the side I slept, were undrawn, and Mr. L. appeared standing there. He said, addressing me by name, ' My mother is dead.' I tried to persuade myself I had been dreaming, and Maria said I had dreamt it ; but after a short time the same thing was done again, and the same announcement made. I was rather chaffed at breakfast because of the story I told. After breakfast I went into the drawing-room to practise. Presently I heard myself called, and I went out on the balcony to listen. It was the daughter of the man whom I had seen twice at night, and the granddaughter of the old lady whose death had been announced. She was riding on horseback. She said, ' Have you heard ?   My father is sent for, and my grandmother is dead ! ' "

The following corroboration is from the percipient's sister :—
"November 24th, 1883.
" I quite recollect my sister Charlotte telling me of the apparition or vision she saw of our friend appearing at her bedside and saying ' his mother was dead,' and its being corroborated the next morning by his daughter riding up to our house, and telling us her ' grannie was dead.' She was taken seriously ill the night before, her [*i.e.*, the narrator's] father was sent for, and she died soon after his arrival.   " A. M. A."

It seems safer to regard this experience as a dream than as that very much rarer phenomenon, a waking hallucination ; but we must not overlook the importance of the fact that the dream was almost immediately repeated. This feature has occurred before, and will occur again ;[1] and it is one which seems to be decidedly commoner in cases of coincident or (as we should say) *veridical* dreams than in dreams generally. Inquiries which have recently been made of more than 2000 persons, taken at random, have shown that less than 10 per cent. of them could recall having even on a single occasion dreamt the

---

[1] See, for instance, cases 102, 110, 113, 130, 141, 451, 457. Examples of recurrence not on the same night are No. 484 and Dr. Gibert's case, Vol. ii., p. 701.

same dream more than once on the same night—though it is of course by no means uncommon to have a fixed familiar dream which recurs again and again during long tracts of life.[1] No doubt memory cannot be entirely trusted on such a matter ; but it may be said with tolerable confidence that recurrences on the same night are decidedly rare ; and it is therefore most unlikely that this particular feature should *by accident* occur with noticeable frequency in the comparatively small group of dreams which have corresponded with a real external event.

In the next case, the details and images supplied are of a medical sort and have distinct reference to the dreamer's own profession. The first part of the account is from Mr. C. Burges, of 4, Lincoln's Inn Fields, and is given here by the kind permission of the Phasmatological Society of Oxford. Mr. Burges has revised it for publication.

"1879.

(125) "Although I am now a solicitor, I was for the first 8 years of my career a sailor, and on one of my voyages, I, being the second officer of an Indiaman, had a cabin common with the doctor of the ship. The doctor was named John Woolcott. As second officer, I, of course, had the middle watch, which meant my being on deck between 12 midnight and 4 a.m. every night. I went down to the cabin at the end of the watch, at about 4.30 one morning, and turned in as usual. Some time before I had to get up to relieve the deck at 8, the doctor called me up, and said that he had had a terrible dream. He thought that he saw his mother dying, and whilst she was lying in that state a cousin, a medical man, who was a surgeon in the Artillery, and whom he believed to be at that moment in China (it was the time of the Chinese war, in 1845), had suddenly appeared in the room, and when he saw his aunt, said, 'You are entirely wrong in supposing what is the matter with her ; she is not dying from what you say, but from such and such a complaint,' which he named. I do not at the present moment recollect what the diseases were, but the distinction was a well-defined one. He also said that another surgeon, who is still living, and whose name I do not like to give, was present, and insisted that the patient was dying of the complaint first named.

"From that time to the end of the voyage the doctor was so much impressed with this dream that he was quite a dispirited man, sufficiently so to occasion remark. When our ship arrived in the East India Docks, he came back to me, as he was just going ashore, I not being able to leave so soon, and said, 'It is all right, old fellow, the dream is all wrong ;

---

[1] Two cases have been reported to me of a dream of death occurring to the same person on three consecutive nights, without any correspondence whatever with any simultaneous reality. Another informant (the Rev. C. S. Taylor, of 1, Guinea Street, Redcliff, Bristol) reports a similar baseless experience on two consecutive nights ; and a fourth (Mrs. Bacon, of Much Hadham), on either two or three consecutive nights, the person dreamt of singularly enough dying suddenly a week afterwards. But I do not happen to have heard of any similar case where the recurrence was on the *same* night.

there is my brother Edward on shore, waiting for me, and he is not in mourning.'

"The fact, however, unfortunately proved to be that his mother had died, and that his cousin, the surgeon, had returned from China in charge of invalids, and was present at the death-bed, as dreamed. The brother, on coming down to meet the ship, had put on coloured clothes, so as not to give my friend a sudden shock.   "G. B."

Mr. Woolcott, F.R.C.S., consulting surgeon of the Kent County Ophthalmic Hospital, to whom the above was sent, says :—

"4, Elms Park Terrace, The Elms, Ramsgate.
                                   "December 20th, 1883.

"The statement about my mother's death and the dream at sea is correct. The dream and the death occurred at the same time, or within a few days of each other. I was on board the 'Plantagenet,' East Indiaman, and we had just left the Cape of Good Hope, on our homeward bound voyage, at which place I had received letters from home stating 'All well.' There was more in the dream, concerning a *post-mortem* examination, but it is of too painful a nature to mention, relating to the difference of opinion concerning the nature of the complaint my mother died of, and the medical men were of different opinions about it. I think a very remarkable point about my dream at sea, in 1845, was that I thought a cousin of mine, a surgeon in the Royal Artillery, was present at my mother's death. This proved to be the case. I had thought he was away in China, and had no idea of when he would return to England ; but he had unexpectedly come back, and had been summoned to her bedside in consultation, as stated in the narrative. My cousin was James E. T. Parrett, late surgeon Royal Artillery, now deceased. This dream haunted me frequently during the rest of the voyage home, and on several occasions awoke me in the night thinking about it. I could not shake it off."

In answer to inquiries, Mr. Woolcott says :—

"I have had startling dreams at other times, but they have not been concerning the *death* of any person.   "JOHN WOOLCOTT."

[Here the time-coincidence cannot be brought with certainty closer than a few days. On the other hand, the detail of the cousin's presence is a strong evidential point.]

In the next case, a definite scene is depicted, suggestive of death and appropriate to the person who had actually died ; but everything beyond the true impression of the death is supplied by the dreamer. The narrator is Mrs. Herbert Bolland (*née* Cary, granddaughter of the translator of Dante), of 7, Cranbury Terrace, Southampton. The experience was quite unique in her life, and exemplifies—what will be suggested by other cases—a possible effect of illness in heightening the percipient faculty.[1]

---

[1] See the list of cases in the Index under the heading *Illness.*

"July, 1884.

(126) "In September, 1879, I was in B——s, and laid up with a rather sharp attack of fever, kept to my room, and seeing no one. In the middle of one night I was awoke, as was my husband also, by a most piercing shriek ; he knew it was I who had cried aloud, whilst I had then no idea of it. But I began to tell him that I had been dreaming his sister was teasing me, and I looked up and saw (and as I came to that point I was again seized with horror) a tall man, dead, being carried, with his hair, which was very thick, falling back from his face. The figure impressed me with the idea of being upheld by four men, but I did not see any of them. I knew the figure at once, and kept saying, 'The Colonel's dead, the Colonel's dead,' and it was an hour or two before my husband could calm me, and I could go to sleep again. At last I did so, however, and the next sound we heard was the servant knocking at our door, and calling out, 'Get up, sir, the Colonel's dead ; you're wanted.'

"Colonel F. had died after a short illness, of which I knew nothing at all. My husband thought he had a cold, but had not named it to me or been anxious about it himself, and, as far as I was concerned, my acquaintance with him was of the slightest, so that if I had been told he had a cold, I should not have thought about it again.

"I may add that I have said many times, when asked to explain it, I believe it was caused by Major White, who was with the F.'s, thinking of us, and what a shock it would be, as my husband was the only other R.E. officer there, and would have to arrange for the funeral next day. That was what seemed to me likely, because I have noticed all my life that I frequently speak of the subjects which are in the thoughts of my friends and companions without any apparent cause, and have been accustomed to speak of it as the result of ' my sixth sense,' because I did not know what else to call it. It has often been a subject of annoyance to me in one way, which was that, with one very dear friend, our letters invariably crossed (though very infrequently written), so that we never felt as if we had an answer. She complained, and so did I, but we could not alter it.   "KATE E. BOLLAND."

We find from the Army List that Colonel F. died on September 7th, 1879.

The following is from Lieut.-Colonel Bolland, R.E. :—

"July 20th, 1884.

"With regard to Colonel F., I cannot say I remember that Mrs. Bolland mentioned his name, though she may have done so ; but having awoke me with a terrific scream at about 1 a.m., on the 8th September, 1879 (which I think was the date), she told me she had been dreaming of my sister, and when looking up to speak to her, she saw a tall man, dead, being carried by four other men, his head dropping, and long, thick hair falling back.

"She was terribly frightened, and it was some time before we again got to sleep. The next sound I heard was the servant knocking at my door, and calling out, 'Get up, sir, you are wanted ; the Colonel is dead !' I had known Colonel F. was ill, but had not thought seriously of it, nor had I named it to my wife, who had herself been ill some days with denzie fever. If I had thought of his illness at all, it would have been without any anxiety, as I had heard he was better, and able to lie on the sofa.   It is now some years since these things happened, and I may not be correct in my remembrance of all details; but as to both the waking [1] and the sleeping impressions being named to me before the events which they seemed to have indicated were known, or could be known to us in any ordinary way, I am positive.

"G. HERBERT BOLLAND."

In conversation with the present writer, Colonel Bolland spontaneously referred to the extraordinary character of the scream.

Colonel Bolland's account suggested some doubt in his mind as to whether his wife had actually *identified* the dead man before the news of the death was known, and this point was accordingly inquired about.   In his reply, Colonel Bolland mentioned that for some time past his hearing has been somewhat imperfect and uncertain, and he continues :—

"I can safely say that Mrs. Bolland, from the time of the event, has always said she said, 'It is the Colonel,' and I have never told her that I did not hear her, never doubting but that she said it. She, however, is much surprised that I never mentioned the fact of not having heard it. Her description at the time left no doubt in my own mind that it was Colonel F. She said she saw a long (or perhaps tall) man being carried, with his long hair falling back. Colonel F. wore his hair long for a military man of the present day, so the short description she gave me identified the man, as long hair is so rarely worn by military men. We may even have discussed whether it was he, but I don't remember her saying almost at once, 'It is the Colonel.' My wife has a very much better memory for conversations than I have, so that I will not undertake to say that we did not discuss, between 1 a.m. and 6 a.m., whether or not it was Colonel F. ; but I am certain I did not hear my wife say at once, immediately after her short description of the dream, 'It is the Colonel,' but she may have said it without my hearing it. Mrs. Bolland is so minutely accurate in repeating a conversation that I feel sure her version is much more to be relied on than my own."

And Mrs. Bolland adds :—

"July 27th, 1884.

"As regards my own opinion of what happened after my dream about Colonel F., I have not, nor ever had, any doubt that it was he I saw. I can see the whole scene before me now, as I saw it then, and I cannot get over my impression that I mentioned his name at once, or rather, as soon as I came upon the recollection of what had made me scream. I think I have told you that although my own scream awoke me, I did not at once know that I had been frightened, or that I had cried out. But in describing my dream to my husband, I suddenly came upon the picture again, and then I was so frightened it was some time before I could get over it."

[I received by pure accident a confirmation of the fact that Mrs. Bolland mentioned Colonel F. at the moment. I was sitting at tea with

---

[1] This refers to another case, No. 201, below.

Colonel and Mrs. Bolland; and the conversation turning on telepathy, but no mention having been made of the above case, a sister of Colonel Bolland's, who was present, suddenly said to Mrs. Bolland, " Do you remember about that time when you called out, ' There's the Colonel ?' " It turned out that she remembered these words as having occurred in a letter from Mrs. Bolland, which described the incident immediately after its occurrence; and neither of them could recall that the subject had been afterwards talked of between them.]

We come now to cases where a distinctly fantastic element appears; the reality is bodied forth in a dream-scene which has no relation to actual possibilities.

The following case is remarkable in that there were *two* percipients, for one of whom the distant event was embodied in a fantastic, and for the other in a more normal, manner. The doubling of the experience of course enormously increases the improbability that the coincidence was accidental; but it is open to us to suppose that only one of the dreams was directly connected with the absent friend, and that this dream produced the other, on the analogy of some of the cases of simultaneous dreaming already given.[1] Miss Varah, of 40, James Street, Cowley Road, Oxford, writes :—

" January, 1885.

(127) " A friend of mine, Mr. Adams, was seriously ill, and we were expecting his death. I had a dream that I saw the corpse of his wife laid out upon a bed, though we had no reason to suppose that she was even ill. A friend with whom I was staying also dreamed that she saw Mrs. Adams a corpse. [This is not accurate.] The morning's post brought news of her dangerous illness, and a telegram during the morning announced her death. My friend and I told each other our dreams in the morning at breakfast. My friend had called for her letters before coming down in the morning, fearing bad news. " MARIANNE VARAH."

In answer to inquiries, Miss Varah tells us that Mrs. Adams died between 11 and 1, on the night of February 25th, 1876, and we find the 25th given as the date in an obituary notice in the *Sheffield Daily Telegraph ;* but she does not know the exact hour of her dream. She adds, " The dream described is the only one I believe I ever had of the kind."

Miss Varah's friend, the late Mrs. Muller, wrote as follows :—

" 8, Bevington Road, Oxford.

" January, 1885.

" I dreamed that I was at Hastings, on the shore. I saw my friend, Miss Adams, running towards me. She passed me by, and then took off her hat and bent her head down into the sea. I tried to grasp her by her clothes, but she cried out, ' Don't stop me, for my mother is dying.'

---

[1] This alternative will be considered in Chap. xviii., on " Collective Cases."

In the morning I jumped out of bed on hearing the post, and said to Marianne Varah, 'Have you had a letter from Miss Adams? There must be something the matter with her mother.' Miss Varah answered, 'I have a letter, but have not opened it. I have had a very strange dream, but I thought nothing of it, because Mr. Adams is so ill.' Miss Varah then opened her letter, and called out, 'You are right.' There were a few lines, 'My mother is dangerously ill: doctors say no hope. We will send a telegram.' The telegram came during the morning of February 24th, [clearly a mistake for 26th,] 1876, saying she was dead. She had been in perfect health the day before.

"Neither Miss Varah nor myself are at all given to dreams, and had not till then believed in them at all.   "EMILY E. MULLER."

The next account is contained in a letter from Brigade-Surgeon Wright, Junior Army and Navy Club, St. James' Street, S.W., to his sister.

"October 18th, 1884.

(128) "You asked me to give you an account of the extraordinary dream I had in India, on the occasion of our mother's death. It was more vivid than an ordinary dream, and impressed itself so much on me that directly I awoke, which was at the conclusion of the dream, I looked at my watch, and, allowing for the difference of time between India and England, my mother was dying at the moment of my dream.

"I was out deer-stalking during the month of April, 1869, in the territory of our feudatory chief, the Maharajah of Gualior, who provided me with a guard of Sepoys, while in the jungle, to protect me from Dacoits. On the night of April 15th I slept outside the village of Kurkurree, under a large variety of fig-tree called in India a burgot tree. I dreamed that my father (who died in 1854) and mother appeared to me; the latter addressed and kissed me and asked me, 'Where is Maggie?' [the narrator's wife.] She then receded gradually and disappeared. I noted carefully the date and hour. When I returned from there to Theusie, where my regiment was stationed, I got a letter from my mother, written as if she was in excellent health and spirits; but soon after came two letters, one from my brother James, and one from my brother-in-law, Arthur Wright. I opened my brother's first, and, after the first paroxysms of grief had lessened, eagerly scanned it to see if the death corresponded with my dream, but no date was mentioned. Deeply have I often since regretted not having called somebody in before opening letter No. 2, in order to fully verify the circumstances. For really, now that the sad intelligence was known to me, Arthur's letter was opened by me more to see if it coincided as to the date of her death and my dream, and I then found that it coincided exactly.   "T. WRIGHT."

In a letter to us, Mr. Wright says :—

"October 24th, 1884.

"The dream took place about midnight, which, allowing for the difference of time between India and England, makes the coincidence very close. I did look at my watch directly I awoke, but regret very much not having taken written notes at the time. I awoke at the end of the dream. Death was suggested to my mind by seeing my mother accompanied by my father, who had predeceased her by 15 years.   I have not often dreamt of my relatives in a vivid way."

In answer to inquiries, he adds :—

" I was not awake.   The impression produced was that arising from a very vivid dream.   The date of my dream being April 15th, was far more than an inference, it was a certainty ; as when I got the two letters announcing my mother's death (one from my brother and one from my brother-in-law) I opened my brother's first, and after recovering somewhat from the shock of the sad intelligence, I eagerly re-perused it to see if the date of the death corresponded with that of my dream, but found that no date was mentioned.   I then hurriedly opened the second letter, with a view of seeing the date of her death, and then for the first time learned that she died on the 15th April, the date of my dream."

Miss Wright, Secretary of the Girls' Friendly Society, 3, Victoria Mansions, Victoria Street, Westminster, S.W., says :—

" October 18th, 1884.

" My mother died on April 15th, 1869, at 8 p.m.   Her death was sudden.   She was only 24 hours ill, and was quite unconscious for 4 hours before her death.[1]   " LUCY O. WRIGHT."

Here the dreamer's mind embodied the idea of death in the figure of a long deceased relative.   More commonly the imagery in such cases is drawn from the familiar earthly symbols of death—coffins, funeral processions, and graves.   A few examples may be given here ; others will be found in the Supplement (Vol. ii., pp. 417-26).   The following account is from the Rev. C. C. Wambey, of Paragon, Salisbury, who in conversation communicated the names of the persons concerned.

" April, 1884.

(129) " In my bachelor days I lived for two years at C., in the outskirts of London.   On a certain night I dreamed that Mr. W., with whom I was acquainted, and myself were walking in the cloisters of Westminster Abbey.

" He abruptly bade me ' Good-bye,' saying that he must go to a particular gravestone.   I—in my dream—entreated him not to go, but to come back with me out of the cloisters.   ' No, no,' he replied, ' I must go, I am *fated* to go '   With that he broke from me, hurried to the stone, and sank through the floor.   The next morning I mentioned the dream to my landlady, and told her it was my firm conviction that my friend was dead.

" The next morning's post brought me a letter from my brother, who stated that on the previous night Mr. W. had died suddenly from disease of the heart."

In answer to inquiries, Mr. Wambey says :—

---

[1] See on this subject Chap. v., § 10, and the list of cases in the Index under the heading *Unconsciousness.*

"May 17th, 1884.

"This occurred between June, 1855, and June, 1856; I forget the month and day.

"I mentioned the dream to my landlady next morning. The last time I saw Mr. W., he was in his usual health, and I had received no intimation whatever that he was ailing, before I had the dream.

"Just at this time I cannot recall any dream I may have had of a friend's death, but I have dreamt of a friend's *marriage*, which dream was fulfilled by the event, which took many by surprise; it appeared wholly improbable. Nothing had occurred to lead me to dream of Mr. W."

The next case is from Mr. N. T. Menneer, Principal of Torre College, Torquay.

"December 18th, 1883.

(130) "I thought you would be interested in the following account of a strange dream that came under my notice some 26 years ago.

"My wife, since deceased, had a brother residing at Sarawak, and at the time to which I refer, staying with the Raja, Sir James Brooke.

"The following is an extract from the second volume of *The Raja of Sarawak*, by Gertrude L. Jacob, p. 238. 'Mr. Wellington' (my wife's brother) 'was killed in a brave attempt to defend Mrs. Middleton and her children.' The Chinese, it appears, taking Mr. Wellington for the Raja's son, struck off his head.

"And now for the dream. I was awoke one night by my wife, who started from her sleep, terrified by the following dream. She saw her *headless* brother standing at the foot of the bed with his head lying on a coffin by his side. I did my best to console my wife, who continued to be much distressed for some considerable time. At length she fell asleep again, to be awoke by a similar dream. In the morning, and for several days after, she constantly referred to her dream, and anticipated sad news of her brother.

"And now comes the strangest part of the story. When the news reached England, I computed approximately the time, and found *it coincided with the memorable night to which I have referred.*

"N. T. MENNEER."

In reply to inquiries, Mr. Menneer adds:—

"My deceased wife never had, as far as I know, similar distressing dreams of death to which no real event corresponded.

"There is no doubt that the Chinese struck off his head. Particulars of his fate were sent to Mr. Wellington's father by the Raja himself.

"In saying I calculated the time and found it to correspond *approximately*, I probably gave you a wrong impression. I did not note down the date of the dream, but when the news reached England I calculated the usual time of such a voyage, and found it corresponded with the time I considered had elapsed since the night of the dream."

Professor Sidgwick, after an interview with Mr. Menneer, on September 17, 1884, wrote:—

"He said that Mrs. Menneer had no definite idea where her brother had gone ; they had not heard from him since his departure ; she had certainly no idea that he would be engaged in military operations at all, still less that he would be engaged with Chinese.   In fact she was in no state of alarm about him at all.   Mr. Menneer said that they did not put down the date of the dream at the time, and that when the news came he could not remember it exactly ; but he took pains to calculate it at the time, and satisfied himself that it was at the time of the death as nearly as he could reckon.   He had not been a believer in dreams previously.   He heard the particulars of the death from Mr. Wellington, the father."

This dream, if it is to be telepathically explained, must apparently have been due to the last flash of thought in the brother's consciousness.   It may seem strange that a definite picture of his mode of death should present itself to a man in the instant of receiving an unexpected and fatal blow ; but, as Hobbes said, " thought is quick." The coffin, at any rate, may be taken as an item of death-imagery supplied by the dreamer's mind.   The *repetition* of the dream should again be noted (p. 357).

In the following cases the imagery of death is still more elaborately developed.   Mrs. Hilton, a lady actively engaged in most practical work, and not in the least a " visionary," has given us the following accounts.

" 234, Burdett Road, E.

" April 10th, 1883.

(131) " The dream which I am about to relate occurred about 2 years ago.   I seemed to be walking in a country road, with high grassy banks on either side.   Suddenly I heard the tramp of many feet.   Feeling a strange sense of fear, I called out, 'Who are these people coming ?' A voice above me replied, 'A procession of the dead.' I then found myself on the bank, looking into the road where the people were walking, five or six abreast. Hundreds of them passed by me—neither looking aside nor looking at each other.   They were people of all conditions and in all ranks of life.   I saw no children amongst them.   I watched the long line of people go away into the far distance, but I felt no special interest in any of them, until I saw a middle-aged Friend, dressed as a gentleman farmer.   I pointed to him and called out, ' Who is that, please?' He turned round and said in a loud voice, ' I am John M., of Chelmsford.' Then my dream ended. Next day, when my husband returned from his office he told me that John M., of Chelmsford, had died the previous day.

"I may add that I only knew the Friend in question by sight and cannot recollect ever speaking to him."

We find from a newspaper obituary that J. M.'s death took place on January 14th, 1880.

(132) " About a year ago, I had a dream very similar to the preceding one.   The locality was the same.   The only difference was that I was standing in the road, trying to prevent a little girl from joining the pro-

cession. The lady, in whose charge the child was and who was standing by me in the road, said, 'I am giving her into the charge of Charles P., of Darlington,' mentioning the name of a well-known member of the Society of Friends. I replied, ' That is not Charles P.'   I called out as before, ' Who are you, please ? '   A young man in the procession turned round and said, 'I am J. G.'   Next morning I heard that J. G. had died rather suddenly in the night.   I knew this young man, but not intimately, and I had not seen him for months.

" Again, a third time, I found myself in the same place, but my terror was so extreme, that I kneeled on the bank and prayed that I might not witness the march of the dead.   Instantly I was removed, and the tramp of the terrible procession ceased.   I never discovered that anyone whom I knew died at the time of this last dream.

" In each of these three dreams I seemed to be under the influence and dread of some unseen power.   " MARIE HILTON."

In answer to inquiries as to the first of these cases, Mrs. Hilton says:—

" I did not know that John M. was ill, and had not even heard his name mentioned ; I could not trace any reason why he should have been in my thoughts."

In answer to inquiries as to the second case, she says :—

" I recognised the little girl as the child of a friend.   I had not heard anything about the child to make me dream of her.   Charles P. had been dead for some years at the date of the dream."

The absence of any ascertained coincidence on the third occasion might be represented as an argument for regarding the correspondence on the two previous occasions as accidental, but it would be a very weak one ; since even if the dream had recurred a thousand times, the chances against the accidental occurrence of two such coincidences would still remain enormous.   The tendency on the dreamer's part to symbolise death in one particular way is neither against nor in favour of the telepathic explanation.[1]

While on the subject of symbolic dreams, I may observe that many persons profess to have a particular recurrent dream, which in itself has no obvious relation to death, but which proves in fact to coincide more or less closely with deaths or other calamities that affect them.   I need hardly say that such statements have no evidential value, unless we can be sure that they are more than the loose assertions of persons who see no importance in noting misses as well as hits, and to whom it is no difficulty in the way of the supposed correspondence that the two events were separated perhaps by a month's interval.   In most of such cases, indeed, the dream

---

[1] It is worth noting that these dreams—for all their *bizarrerie*—seem to belong to a known type. Our friend, Mr. J. A. Symonds, has given us an account of a Swiss *Todten-Volk-Seher*, who sees a procession of the dead going along a path with a high bank on one side.

precedes the event and is professedly taken as a " warning " ; so that, however well attested, they could have no place in this book. Occasionally, however, a person who professes this remarkable gift can supply sufficiently circumstantial evidence to have some claim to attention ; and one rather striking instance of the sort will be found in the Supplement (case 460).

§ 8. I pass now to the final class of cases, where the dreamer seems, as it were, to be transported to the actual scene of the event. These cases, like the final cases of the 6th chapter, cannot but suggest certain phenomena of the waking state which are other than those of thought-transference—the phenomena of so-called *clairvoyance.* But I must again draw attention to the radical differences in the phenomena which that word may be made to cover. There are certain alleged facts of waking clairvoyance which, if true, would drive us to the conclusion that the percipient's powers of vision were independent of the thoughts, either actually passing or latent, in the minds of others. No doubt very many facts have been loosely ascribed to clairvoyance, which we should now regard as simple examples of thought-transference. This has been owing partly to the blindness of writers on clairvoyance to the enormous difficulties which the assumption of such a faculty involves ; but still more to the lack, until lately, of accurate experiments in thought-transference. But there remain facts which— if the testimony of Robert Houdin and other experts can be trusted— no possible extension of the theory of thought-transference will cover; and in which, though the particular result obtained depended in some manner on the particular person who sought to obtain it, the range of perception altogether transcended the past or present contents of that person's mind. Now with such cases as these we have nothing to do in the present work. Even should some of the examples to be adduced seem to take us beyond the confines of *thought-transference* in any literal sense, they will still not take us beyond the confines of *telepathy*—of a theory which implies *some* sort of influence of the mind of an agent on the mind of a percipient. The percipient may observe a scene, into the midst of which he finds himself mentally transported, with such completeness of detail, and for such a length of time, as at any rate to suggest some actual exercise on it of his own independent perceptional powers ; but it will still be a scene with some principal actor in which he is in some way linked. He may see a death-bed and the surrounding mourners ; but we have no sort of reason to suppose that he could similarly see *any* death-bed. There has, at any rate, been an *agent*, in the sense of a particular person whose *actual* presence in the scene has to be accepted as a condition of the percipient's *imagined* presence ; and however novel and exceptional the way in which the percipient's range of knowledge may seem to be extended, these further glimpses still take place apparently not in any chance direction, but in a direction marked out by his previous affinities with other minds. But in fact the process need not seem so exceptional, if we recall once more the right which experiment has given us to draw on parts of the agent's mind which are below the level of ostensible consciousness. For in none of the cases to be here cited do the percipient's impressions extend beyond what has been before the *mind*—though certainly beyond what has been before the *attention*—of persons actually present at the scene. We may perhaps be led sometimes to conceive *several* of these minds as contributing to the impression. But some of the experimental results have already introduced on a small scale the notion of joint agency,[1] and may thus enable us to maintain the analogy between experimental and spontaneous telepathy in a manner which least of all might have been expected.

I may cite at once the two cases which seem the furthest removed from any of the preceding, inasmuch as the " agency " in them is specially hard to conceive. They happen to be at the two extremes of the trivial and the tragic. The first is reported by a witness— Miss Busk, of 16, Montagu Street, W.—who is strongly adverse to the telepathic theory, and holds the view that all the alleged coincidences are accidental, and that the more numerous they are, the more clearly accidental must they be.

" 1884.

(133) " I dreamt that I was walking in a wood in my father's place in Kent, in a spot well known to me, where there was sand under the firs ; I stumbled over some objects, which proved to be the heads, left protruding, of some ducks buried in the sand. The idea impressed me as so comical that I fortunately mentioned it at breakfast next morning, and one or two persons remember that I did so. Only an hour later it happened that the old bailiff of the place came up for some instructions unexpectedly, and as he was leaving he said he must tell us a strange thing that had happened : there had been a robbery in the farmyard, and some stolen ducks had been found buried in the sand, with their heads protruding, in the very spot where I had seen the same. The farm was underlet, and I

---

[1] See Professor Lodge's experiment, p. 50 ; and the remarks on M. Richet's later results, p. 80.

2 A

had not even any interest in the ducks, to carry my thoughts towards them under the nefarious treatment they received.

"R. H. Busk."

Miss Busk's sister, Mrs. Pitt Byrne, who was present when this dream was told, corroborates as follows :—

"I distinctly remember, and have often since spoken of, the circumstance of Miss R. H. Busk's relating to me her dream of ducks buried in the wood; before the bailiff who reported the incident came up to town.

"J. PITT BYRNE."

The next case is remarkable for the number of points of correspondence, though the dream is typically fantastic and confused. The narrative is from Mrs. Storie, of 8, Gilmour Road, Edinburgh. It was written by her, she tells us, the day, or the day after, the news of the fatal accident arrived, merely as a relief to herself, and without an idea of any further use. She prepared an account for us in a more finished form ; but it seems preferable to give the original rough notes, which she has kindly allowed us to copy. The brother in this case was a twin with herself (see p. 279).

"Hobart Town.

"July, 1874.

(134) "On the evening of the 18th July, I felt unusually nervous. This seemed to begin [with the occurrence of a small domestic annoyance] about half-past 8 o'clock. When I went to my room I even felt as if someone was there. I fancied, as I stepped into bed, that someone *in thought* tried to stop me. At 2 o'clock I woke from the following dream. It seemed like in dissolving views. In a twinkle of light I saw a railway, and the puff of the engine. I thought, 'What's going on up there? Travelling? I wonder if any of us are travelling and I dreaming of it.' *Someone* unseen by me answered, 'No : something quite different—something wrong.' 'I don't like to look at these things,' I said. Then I saw behind and above my head William's upper half reclining, eyes and mouth half shut ; his chest moved forward convulsively, and he raised his right arm. Then he bent forward, saying, 'I suppose I should move out of this.' Then I saw him lying, eyes shut, on the ground, flat. The chimney of an engine at his head. I called in excitement, 'That will strike him!' The 'someone' answered 'Yes—well, here's what it was'; and immediately I saw William sitting in the open air—faint moonlight—on a raised place, sideways. He raised his right arm, shuddered, and said, 'I can't go on, or back, *No.*' Then he seemed lying flat. I cried out, 'Oh! Oh!' and others seemed to echo, 'Oh! Oh!' He seemed then upon his elbow, saying, 'Now it comes.' Then, as if struggling to rise, turned twice round quickly, saying, 'Is it the train? *the train, the train,*' his right shoulder reverberating as if struck from behind. He fell back like fainting ; his eyes rolled. A large dark object came between us like panelling of wood, and

rather in the dark something rolled over, and like an arm was thrown up, and the whole thing went away with a *swish*. Close beside me on the ground there seemed a long dark object. I called out, ' They've left something behind, it's like a man.' It then raised its shoulders and head and fell down again. The same *someone* answered, ' *Yes, sadly.*' [? ' *Yes,*' sadly.] After a moment I seemed called on to look up, and said, ' Is that *thing* not away yet?' Answered, ' *No.*' And in front, in light, there was a railway compartment in which sat Rev. Mr. Johnstone, of Echuce. I said, ' What's he doing there?' Answered, ' He's there.' A railway porter went up to the window asking, ' Have you seen any of —— ' I caught no more, but I *thought* he referred to the *thing* left behind. Mr. Johnstone seemed to answer, ' *No* '; and the man went quickly away—I thought to look for it. After all this the *someone* said close to me, ' Now I'm going.'   a tall dark figure at my head
I started, and at once saw William's back at my side. He put his right hand (in grief) over his face, and the other almost touching my shoulder, he crossed in front, looking stern and solemn. There was a flash from the eyes, and I caught a glimpse of a fine, pale face like ushering him along, and indistinctly another. I felt frightened, and called out, ' Is he angry?' ' O, no.' ' Is he going away?' Answered, ' *Yes,*' by the same *someone*, and I woke with a loud sigh, which woke my husband, who said, ' What is it?' I told him I had been dreaming ' something unpleasant '— named a ' railway,' and dismissed it all from my mind as a dream. As I fell asleep again I fancied the ' someone ' said, ' It's all gone,' and another answered, ' I'll come and remind her.'

"The news reached me one week afterwards. The accident had happened to my brother on the same night about half past 9 o'clock. Rev. Mr. Johnstone and his wife were actually in the train which struck him. He was walking along the line, which is raised 2 feet on a level country. He seemed to have gone 16 miles—must have been tired and sat down to take off his boot, which was beside him, dozed off and was very likely roused by the sound of the train ; 76 sheep-trucks had passed without touching him, but some wooden projection, likely the step, had touched the *right* side of his head, bruised his right shoulder, and killed him instantaneously. The night was very dark. I believe now that the *someone* was (from something in the *way* he spoke) William *himself.* The face with him was white as alabaster, and something like this [a small sketch pasted on] in profile. There were many other thoughts or words seemed to pass, but they are too many to write down here.

" The voice of the ' someone' unseen seemed *always above* the figure of William which I saw. And when I was shown the compartment of the carriage with Mr. Johnstone, the *someone* seemed on a line between me and it—*above* me."

In an account-book of Mrs. Storie's, on a page headed July, 1874, we find the 18th day marked, and the words, "Dear Willie died," and " Dreamed, dreamed of it all," appended.

The first letter, from the Rev. J. C. Johnstone to the Rev. John Storie, announcing the news of the accident, is lost. The following are extracts from his second and third letters on the subject :—

" Echuce, 10th August, 1874.

" The place where Hunter was killed is on an open plain, and there was consequently plenty of room for him to escape the train had he been conscious ; but I think Meldrum's theory is the correct one, that he had sat down to adjust some bandages on his leg and had thoughtlessly gone off to sleep. There is only one line of rails, and the ground is raised about 2 feet—the ground on which the rails rest. He had probably sat down on the edge, and lain down backwards so as to be within reach of some part of the train. It was not known at the time that an accident had occurred. Mrs. Johnstone and myself were in the train. Meldrum says he was not very much crushed. The top of the skull was struck off, and some ribs were broken, under the arm-pit on one side. His body was found on the Sunday morning by a herd-boy from the adjoining station."   " August 29th, 1874.

"The exact time at which the train struck poor Hunter must have been about 9.55 p.m., and his death must have been instantaneous."

The above corresponds with the account of the inquest in the *Riverine Herald* for July 22nd. The *Melbourne Argus* also describes the accident as having taken place on the night of Saturday, the 18th.

The following remarks are taken from notes made by Professor Sidgwick, during an interview with Mrs. Storie, in April, 1884, and by Mrs. Sidgwick, after another interview in September, 1885 :—

Mrs. Storie cannot regard the experience exactly as a dream, though she woke up from it.[1] She is sure that it did not grow more definite in recollection afterwards. She never had a series of scenes in a dream at any other time. They were introduced by a voice in a whisper, not recognised as her brother's. He had sat on the bank as he appeared in the dream. The engine she saw behind him had a chimney of peculiar shape, such as she had not at that time seen; and she remembers that Mr. Storie thought her foolish about insisting on the chimney—unlike (he said) any which existed ; but he informed her when he came back from Victoria, where her brother was, that engines of this kind had just been introduced there. She had no reason to think that any conversation between the porter and the clergyman actually occurred. The persons who seemed to lead her brother away were not recognised by her, and she only saw the face of one of them.

Mr. Storie confirms his wife having said to him at the time of the dream, " What is that light ? " Before writing the account first quoted, she had just mentioned the dream to her husband, but had not described it. She desired not to think of it, and also was unwilling to worry him about it because of his Sunday's work. This last point, it will be observed, is a confirmation of the fact that the dream took place on the Saturday night ; and " it came out clearly " (Mrs. Sidgwick says) " that her recollection about the Saturday night was an independent recollection, and not read back after the incident was known." The strongly nervous state that preceded the dream was quite unique in Mrs. Storie's experience.

[1] In conversation with the present writer, Mrs. Storie mentioned that on one other occasion in her life she had had a sort of "borderland" hallucination (see the following chapter) ; and that this had corresponded, certainly to within a few days, but she did not discover exactly how closely, with the death of another brother in America. She knew him to be delicate, but was not apprehending his death.

But as it appeared that, according to her recollection, it commenced at least an hour before the accident took place, it must be regarded as of no importance evidentially. The feeling of a presence in the room was also quite unique.

Here the difficulty of referring the true elements in the dream to the agent's mind exceeds that noted in Mr. Menneer's case (p. 365, but see pp. 230-1). For Mr. Hunter was asleep; and even if we can conceive that the image of the advancing engine may have had some place in his mind, the presence of Mr. Johnstone could not have been perceived by him. But it is possible, of course, to regard this last item of correspondence as accidental, even though the dream was telepathic. It will be observed that the dream followed the accident by about 4 hours; such *deferment* is, I think, a strong point in favour of telepathic, as opposed to independent, clairvoyance (see p. 329).

To come, however, to less abnormal cases—the following account is from Mr. J. T. Milward Pierce, who has a cattle-ranche in Nebraska.

"Blyville P.O., Knox County, Nebraska, U.S.A.
                                             "December 5th, 1885.

(135) "I have just, or rather a month ago, had a very unpleasant accident which has fortunately turned out all right and has given me the pleasure of forwarding to you a very complete and unmistakeable case of 'second sight.' I think it better to enclose the two letters you will find herein, as I received them to-day. They are in answer to two of mine dated about the 2nd or 3rd, about a week after the accident.

"The accident occurred at 7 o'clock in the morning of the 26th of October. I fainted from loss of blood, and was lying for a few moments on the ground. I was walking towards a pair of French windows, with my hands in my pockets, when I stumbled over a chair and fell right through the lowest pane of glass, face foremost, cutting my nose off on one side, and nearly taking an eye out—so you will see my sister's dream was pretty accurate. I also enclose a statement made by two residents here of this end of the case, which will, I hope, make it complete. I may say our time is 6½ hours ahead of [mistake for *behind*] England.
                                             "Jno. T. M. Pierce."

Mr. Pierce enclosed the following statement :—

"On Monday, October 26th, about 7 o'clock a.m., Mr. J. T. M. Pierce fell through a French window, cutting his face badly, and lay on the floor insensible for several minutes.   "J. Watson.
                                             "C. J. Hunt.

The enclosures, from Mr. Pierce's sister and mother, are dated respectively November 15th and 17th, 1885. Miss Pierce, after condolences as to the accident, writes :—

"Do you know it is the oddest thing, but on the 26th of October I dreamt that I saw you lying on the ground quite unconscious, your face bleeding and looking so dreadful. I woke up calling to you. I told Kate directly I came down, and we both marked the date. I told mother, too, I had had a bad dream about you, but I did not describe it for fear of frightening her. Was it not strange? It was such a vivid dream, it struck me very much, but I did not mention it in my last letter to you; I thought you would laugh about it. But it *is* strange—on the very day too."

In Mrs. Pierce's letter, the following sentence occurs :—

"Was not May's dream singular? She came down that morning you were hurt, and told Kate, every particular of it agreeing with the time you were hurt."

In answer to inquiries, Miss Pierce writes :—

"Frettons, Danbury, Chelmsford.
"December 31st, 1885.

"On the night of the 26th October (*i.e.*, 26-27), I dreamt I saw my brother lying on the ground, his face bleeding and dark; he was quite unconscious. I called to him, but he did not answer, and was stooping towards him, calling him by name, when I awoke. It was so vivid a dream that it produced a great impression upon me, and I felt as though some accident had befallen him. I cannot tell at all what time in the night it was. In the morning I told my sister, and put down the date, also mentioning it to one or two others; but to my sister I described it in the same words that I have now used.

"I am not at all accustomed to having bad dreams about friends; indeed, I never remember having had one before. Neither am I superstitious, but, nevertheless, I felt convinced that something untoward had occurred. So when the letter came, just three weeks after the accident, I knew it was the confirmation of my fears.

"M. PIERCE."

[The coincidence was not as close as Mrs. Pierce's words would imply; and she seems to have mistaken the morning on which the dream was mentioned. When Mr. Pierce was lying on the floor as described, the time of day at Chelmsford would be between 1.30 and 2 p.m. Therefore the dream on the following night must have been at least 8 hours, and may have been more than 12 hours, after the event. See the remark on deferment made in connection with the last case.]

The following narratives are from the Hon. Mrs. Montgomery Moore, now residing at Gipsy Lodge, Norwood.

"A. Adjutant-General's House, Royal Barracks, Dublin.
"December 5th, 1883.

(136) "I had driven my husband, then commanding the 4th Hussars, out in the carriage very early one morning, on his way to a shooting expedition. I returned home, rather tired and exhausted, about 8 o'clock a.m.; and after breakfasting, lay down on my bed before dressing for the day and fell asleep. I dreamed that a small blue three-cornered note was brought in to me, which contained these words :—

"'MY DEAR MRS. M. M.,—I know the Colonel is away; but would you look in his room for the rules of the " Kriegspiel " ? You will find them, I think, on his table. Yours sincerely,—GEORGE PHILIPS.'

" I awoke, and never having heard that there were ' Kriegspiel ' rules, I laughed at having dreamed of it. When I had finished dressing, I went into the drawing-room, and on the piano just outside my door, I saw the identical blue three-cornered note, which I found contained the exact . words written exactly as I had seen them in my dream. I mentioned it in my answer to Major Philips ; for going to my husband's room, I found the little book of rules on his table. This was, I believe, in March, 1877."

(137) "A thing of the same kind occurred in April or May just after. I was asleep in an armchair on a very hot day, about 4 p.m., when I dreamed of receiving a note from a lady, asking us to come to lawn-tennis. She was a person I was not intimate with, and to whose house I had never been. I woke and saw a note on the table by me, which a servant had put down noiselessly. On opening it I found it was an invitation to lawn tennis, from the lady of whom I had dreamed, and in the very words I had dreamed of reading. "JANE MONTGOMERY MOORE."

Asked whether she had had any similar experiences which had *not* corresponded with reality, Mrs. M. Moore replied, "No, I don't think I ever had."

In answer to further inquiries, Mrs. M. Moore says :—

" Probably both notes were written before I was asleep. Both places from which they came were very near to our house."

Here the immediate comparison of the reality with the dreams, and also the fact that the dreams contained apparently no extraneous features, make it especially unlikely that the correspondences were fictitiously " read back." And if not, the cases seem typical examples of telepathic clairvoyance ; for no one probably will suppose that the percipient could have obtained a similar vision of notes with whose writers, and in whose contents, she had no concern.

The next case was sent to us by Miss Richardson, of 47, Bedford Gardens, Kensington, W., who says :—

(138) "The writer is a very worthy wife of a shopkeeper at home, who told me the occurrence some years ago, then with more detail, as it was fresh in her memory ; and her husband can vouch for the facts told him at the time, and the strange ' uncanny ' effect of the dream on her mind for some time after."

From Mrs. Green to Miss Richardson.

" Newry, 21st First Month, 1885.

" DEAR FRIEND,—In compliance with thy request I give thee the particulars of my dream.

" I saw two respectably-dressed females driving alone in a vehicle like a mineral-water cart. Their horse stopped at a water to drink ; but as there was no footing, he lost his balance, and in trying to recover it he plunged right in. With the shock, the women stood up and shouted for help, and their hats rose off their heads, and as all were going down I turned away crying and saying, ' Was there no one at all to help them ?' upon which I awoke, and my husband asked me what was the matter. I related the above dream to him, and he asked me if I knew them. I said I did not, and thought I had never seen either of them. The impression of the dream and the trouble it brought was over me all day. I remarked to my son it was the anniversary of his birthday and my own also—the 10th of First Month, and this is why I remember the date.

" The following Third Month I got a letter and newspaper from my brother in Australia, named Allen, letting me know the sad trouble which had befallen him in the loss, by drowning, of one of his daughters and her companion. Thou wilt see by the description given of it in the paper how the event corresponded with my dream. My niece was born in Australia, and I never saw her.

" Please return the paper at thy convenience. Considering that our night is their day, I must have been in sympathy with the sufferers at the time of the accident, on the 10th of First Month, 1878.[1]

" It is referred to in two separate places in the newspaper."

The passage in the *Inglewood Advertiser* is as follows :—

" Friday evening, January 11th, 1878.

" A dreadful accident occurred in the neighbourhood of Wedderburn, on Wednesday last, resulting in the death of two women, named Lehey and Allen. It appears that the deceased were driving into Wedderburn in a spring cart from the direction of Kinypanial, when they attempted to water their horse at a dam on the boundary of Torpichen Station. The dam was 10 or 12 feet deep in one spot, and into this deep hole they must have inadvertently driven, for Mr. W. McKechnie, manager of Torpichen Station, upon going to the dam some hours afterwards, discovered the spring cart and horse under the water, and two women's hats floating on the surface . . . . The dam was searched, and the bodies of the two women, clasped in each other's arms, recovered."

The following is an extract from evidence given at the inquest :—

" Joseph John Allen, farmer, deposed :—' I identify one of the bodies as that of my sister. I saw her about 11 a.m. yesterday. . . . The horse had broken away and I caught it for her. Mrs. Lehey and my sister met me when I caught the horse. . . . They then took the horse and went to Mr. Clarke's. I did not see them afterwards alive.' William McKechnie deposed :—' About 4 p.m. yesterday, I was riding by the dam when I observed the legs of a horse and the chest above the water.' "

Mr. Green confirms as follows :—

" Newry, 15th Second Month, 1885.

" DEAR FRIEND EDITH RICHARDSON,—In reference to the dream that my wife had of seeing two women thrown out of a spring cart by their horse stopping to drink out of some deep water, I remember she was greatly

---

[1] The narrator has reckoned the difference of time the wrong way. The time in England which corresponded with the accident was the *early morning* of Jan. 9; and the dream which took place on the night of Jan. 9 must have followed the death by more than 12 hours. Thus, according to our arbitrary rule of limitation, the case ought not to have been included.

distressed about it, and seemed to feel great sympathy for them. It occurred on the night of the 9th of January.

" The reason I can remember the date so well is that the 10th was the anniversary of my wife and our son's birthday. As the day advanced she seemed to get worse, and I advised her to go out for a drive; when she returned she told me she was no better, and also said she had told the driver not to go near water, lest some accident should happen, as she had had such a dreadful dream the night before, at the same time telling him the nature of it. As my wife's niece did not live with her father, he was not told of it until the next morning, which would be our evening of the 10th, and which we think accounted for the increased trouble she felt in sympathy with him.   " THOS. GREEN."

Mrs. Green can recall no other dream of at all the same character.

[The amount of correspondence in detail here is considerable. The fact that the figures seen were merely recognised as "two females" diminishes, of course, the force of the coincidence ; though perhaps one would hardly expect identification of persons unknown to the percipient.]

In the next case the percipient withholds her name from publication, on the ground that she takes no interest in our work, and only wrote down the account at her aunt's request.

Mrs. P., of ―― Rectory, writes :―

"March 4th, 1885.

(139) " My niece has written down the dream. She adds to her plain account, in writing to me, that she thinks it rather more remarkable that she should have dreamt it, being a person who hardly ever dreams, unlike her mother and sister, who never sleep without dreaming. She also says she has often regretted not having written it down at the time, but can *safely sign all* she has stated.   " J. L. P."

"March 3rd, 1885.

" My aunt has asked me to try and recall a dream that I dreamt many years ago about an old man, the road-mender in our village, whom I had known and loved from my earliest childhood. He was naturally a bright cheerful old man, but was at the time I am speaking of in extremely low spirits, on account, as we supposed, of his wife, who was very ill and wretched, lying on what proved to be her death-bed. On the morning of my dream my sister and myself had both been awake at 6 o'clock, and I had fallen to sleep again before the servant came in, as usual, about 7 o'clock. On my waking from this sleep I told my sister that I had had a very painful dream about old William Thompson, whom I had seen in my dream running down the lane towards the Church fields in his grey stockings, looking very miserable, and I turned to her and said, ' I fear old William is going to make away with himself.' I hardly finished telling my sister the dream when our servant came in to call us, and said that our father (the rector of the parish) had been sent for in a great hurry to old William Thompson, who had just been found in the Church fields with his throat cut. He was without his shoes, and when my father got to him he was still alive. These are the circumstances as accurately related as I can recall them.

"I may add that I am not generally a dreamer, and have no recollection of any other dream about death.

"S. S. P."

We learn independently that the death took place on April 4, 1869. Miss S. S. P.'s sister writes :—

"I fear I cannot tell you more about my sister's dream than she has already stated, but as you wish to have what she has said confirmed by another person, I will add that I perfectly remember her telling me the dream before the servant came into the room and told us of the sad death of the old man.

"J. M. P."

The next case also has, unfortunately, to be given with initials only, as the writer fears that her friends would object to publicity. It belongs to a class which, as we have seen, must be treated with great caution—dreams occurring in seasons of anxiety. Still, judging from its effects, the experience must have been of a very unusual kind.

"January, 1885.

(140) "In the year 1857, I had a brother in the very centre of the Indian Mutiny. I had been ill in the spring, and taken from my lessons in the school-room. Consequently I heard more of what was going on from the newspapers than a girl of 13 ordinarily would in those days. We were in the habit of hearing regularly from my brother, but in the June and July of that year no letters came, and what arrived in August proved to have been written quite early in the spring, and were full of the disturbances around his station. He was in the service of the East India Company— an officer in the 8th Native Infantry. I had always been devoted to him, and I grieved and fretted far more than any of my elders knew at his danger. I cannot say I dreamt constantly of him, but when I did the impressions were vivid and abiding.

"On one occasion his personal appearance was being discussed, and I remarked, 'He is not like that now, he has no beard or whiskers,' and when asked why I said such a thing, I replied, 'I knew it, for I had seen him in my dreams,' and this brought a severe reprimand from my governess, who never allowed 'such nonsense' to be talked of.

"On the morning of the 25th September, quite early, I awoke from a dream to find my sister holding me, and much alarmed. I had screamed out, struggled, crying out, 'Is he really dead?' When I fully awoke I felt a burning sensation in my head. I could not speak for a moment or two; I knew my sister was there, but I neither felt nor saw her.

"In about a minute, during which she said my eyes were staring beyond her, I ceased struggling, cried out, 'Harry's dead, they have shot him,' and fainted. When I recovered, I found my sister had been sent away, and an aunt who had always looked after me sitting by my bed. In order to soothe my excitement she allowed me to tell her my dream, trying all the time to persuade me to regard it as a natural consequence of my anxiety. When in the narration I said he was riding with another officer, and mounted soldiers behind them, she exclaimed,

' My dear, that shows you it is only a dream, for you know dear Harry is in an infantry, not a cavalry, regiment.' Nothing, however, shook my feelings that I had seen a reality ; and she was so much struck by my persistence, that she privately made notes of the date, and of the incidents, even to the minutest details of my dream, and then for a few days the matter dropped, but I felt the truth was coming nearer and nearer to all. In a short time the news came in the papers—shot down on the morning of the 25th when on his way to Lucknow. A few days later came one of his missing letters, telling how his own regiment had mutinied, and that he had been transferred to a command in the 12th Irregular Cavalry, bound to join Havelock's force in the relief of Lucknow.

" Some eight years after, the officer who was riding by him when he fell, Captain or Major Grant, visited us, and when in compliance with my aunt's request he detailed the incidents of that sad hour, his narration tallied (even to the description of the buildings on their left) with the notes she had taken the morning of my dream. I should also add that we heard my brother had made an alteration in his beard and whiskers just about the time that I had spoken of him as wearing them differently.

In answer to inquiries Miss W. says :—   " L. A. W."

" As to date, the dream concerning my brother's death took place in the morning half of the night of the 25th of September ; and I think I noted in my MS. that an aunt to whom I related the dream at the time was so struck by the pertinacity with which I adhered to the various particulars, that she put down the date and also the details of the dream.

" I have *always* been a dreamer. I never had the same sort of dream of death."

Miss W. further tells us that her aunt is certain that she never destroyed her notes of the dream, but does not know where they are, and is too old to be worried. She adds : " My sister perfectly remembers all about it." The sister, however, will not write out her recollections—considering that attention to such matters is ridiculous.

[We cannot feel certain that Miss W. is correct in saying that her brother's death took place on the 25th. The *East India Register*, which ought to be the most correct authority, says that he was killed on the 26th ; and in that case his death may have exactly coincided with her vision. There was hard fighting on both days ; and in some accounts the names of the officers who fell on the two days are grouped without discrimination. *Allen's Indian Mail*, however, gives the 25th as the date of Lieutenant W.'s death. If that is right, then the coincidence could only have been exact on the supposition that the date of the vision given in Miss W.'s *first* account is the correct one.]

The next case is from Mrs. Hunter, of St. Catherine's, Linlithgow. It somewhat resembles Mrs. Storie's case, (p. 370) in the mixture of apparently true perception with foreign or symbolic elements—as though the vision were a scene which a painter or dramatist had framed on facts which he had only once heard hastily described.

                                                        " July 23rd, 1885.

(141) " I am almost afraid to give particulars about the dream I had, as

it is now some time ago, and I had not been remembering it much. I wrote to Mr. Hunter [her brother-in-law] at the time, and he has unfortunately not kept my letter, so I must trust to my memory.

"The date I do not recollect. The time was 2 o'clock, I think. I knew then, as I looked at my watch when I awoke, and Mr. Hunter told me it was just the hour at which the event took place.

"I thought I was at the Manse, Cockburnspath, where he lives, and I saw Mrs. Hunter evidently ill. She went to her room. I heard the doctor's trap pass the house, and every one was rushing to get him, but he was gone. My sister-in-law kept calling for me, but I could not reach her. By-and-bye a doctor arrived, and the nurse, a stranger to me, came to my room with an infant. She was putting white satin on the dress, and I remonstrated, saying that was only for dead infants. She replied, ' And isn't it right to do it to this one?' and I looked and saw the child was dead, and I knew it was a boy. I awoke, felt anxious, fell asleep, and again dreamt the same, except, I *think*, the first part, that of seeing Mrs. Hunter.

"When I awoke I just remarked to my husband I hoped nothing had gone wrong, and told him my dream during breakfast.

' Not hearing anything for two days I had almost dismissed all thought of it from my mind, but I was a little surprised to find I had been dreaming a fact.

"I knew quite well that my sister-in-law expected her confinement [not, however, for two months—see below], but had no misgivings, as she had been so strong before. I had engaged a nurse for her, and she was not the woman I saw in my dream. I knew the assistant who was with the doctor then, but I did not see him in my dream, only I knew it was not Dr. Black.

"I believe I never fall asleep for any time, however short, without dreaming something or other, consequently I seldom let my dreams trouble me. I am anxious to prevent undue importance being given to my dreams, and I don't think I ever had one of the kind before, and certainly not since. I *have* dreamt the same thing more than once, but very rarely, and *never* in the same night as I did this one.   "A. HUNTER."

In conversation Mrs. Hunter told me that in character and vividness this dream stood out distinctly from the general run of her dreams.

The following is Dr. Hunter's corroboration, written on July 30th, 1885 :—

"I have only now, while taking a brief holiday, found time to give you confirmation of the curious dream my wife had on the night of my sister-in-law's illness. When she awoke in the morning her first remark was ' I hope nothing serious has happened to Jessie. I have had such a horrid dream about her ; I dreamt she had miscarried, and the child was dead.' This she repeated more than once.   "GEORGE HUNTER, M.D."

The Rev. J. Hunter writes, from the Manse, Cockburnspath, N.B. :—

"July 24th, 1885.

"You ask if I can recall the fact of receiving a note from my sister-in-law making mention of her dream. We usually hear from her on the Monday evenings, and it is very possible that she might have mentioned it in such a note ; but I am sorry that I cannot definitely recall it. I find from my diary, however, that I met Mrs. Hunter, of Linlithgow, on the

Tuesday following, in Edinburgh, and went out with her to Linlithgow ; and I am perfectly positive that I heard of it on that Tuesday, if not on the night before. I have always regarded it as a strange occurrence, and have no manner of doubt that her dream corresponded, in a large measure, with the actual event. The event took place about 1 o'clock in the morning, December 17th, 1882, a Sunday. The baby lived only a minute or two. Mrs. Hunter tells me that she saw Dr. Black, our medical practitioner, drive past her window, and that he was not at home. True enough, Dr. Black was not at home at the time, but on a holiday. It was the assistant, Dr. Basil, who came after the confinement was about over. It was premature, and not expected for about two months. Mrs. Hunter of Linlithgow had arranged with my wife to come here during the confinement [she had attended her on a similar occasion in the previous year], but there was no expectation of it at the time."

[It is of course a point against the telepathic explanation, that the person dreamt of was to some extent on Mrs. Hunter's mind. On the other side we have the very exact coincidence of the dream with an event which was not regarded as imminent, and a considerable amount of correspondence in detail.]

The next account (which we owe to the kindness of Lieut.-Colonel J. D. Brockman) is from Dr. A. K. Young, J.P., F.R.C.S.I., of The Terrace Monaghan, Ireland. It is slightly abridged from the original, which we received in November, 1882.

(142) One Monday night in December, 1836, Dr. Young had the following dream, or, as he would prefer to call it, revelation. He found himself suddenly at the gate of Major N. M.'s avenue, many miles from his home. Close to him were a group of persons, one of them a woman with a basket on her arm, the rest men, four of whom were tenants of his own, while the others were unknown to him. Some of the strangers seemed to be murderously assaulting H. W., one of his tenants, and he interfered.

" I struck violently at the man on my left, and then with greater violence at the man's face to my right. Finding to my surprise that I did not knock him down either, I struck again and again, with all the violence of a man frenzied at the sight of my poor friend's murder. To my great amazement I saw that my arms, although visible to my eye, were without substance ; and the bodies of the men I struck at and my own came close together after each blow through the shadowy arms I struck with. My blows were delivered with more extreme violence than I think I ever exerted ; but I became painfully convinced of my incompetency. I have no consciousness of what happened, after this feeling of unsubstantiality came upon me."

Next morning Dr. Young experienced the stiffness and soreness of violent bodily exercise, and was informed by his wife that in the course of the night he had much alarmed her by striking out again and again with his arms in a terrific manner, ' as if fighting for his life.' He in turn informed her of his dream, and begged her to remember the names of those actors in it who were known to him. On the morning of the following day, Wednesday, he received a letter from his agent, who resided in the town close to the scene of the dream, informing him that his tenant, H. W., had been found on Tuesday morning at Major N. M.'s gate, speechless and apparently dying from a fracture of the skull, and that there was no trace of the murderers. That night Dr. Young started for the town, and arrived there on Thursday morning. On his way to a meeting of magistrates he met the senior magistrate of that part of the country, and requested him to give orders for the arrest of the three men whom, besides H. W., he had recognised in his dream, and to have them examined separately. [Dr. Young has given us in confidence the names of these four men ; and says that to the time of their deaths they never knew the grounds of their arrest.] This was at once done. The three men gave identical accounts of the occurrence, and all named the woman who was with them ; she was then arrested, and gave precisely similar testimony. They said that between 11 and 12 on the Monday night they had been walking homewards all together along the road, when they were overtaken by three strangers, two of whom savagely assaulted H. W., while the other prevented his friends from interfering.

H. W. did not die, but was never the same afterwards ; he subsequently emigrated. Of the other parties concerned, the only survivor (except Dr. Young himself) gave an account of the occurrence to the Archdeacon of the district in November, 1881, but varied from the true facts in stating that he had taken the wounded man home in his cart. Had this been the case, he would of course have been called on for his testimony at once.

The Archdeacon mentioned, now Bishop of Clogher, writes to us :—

"Knockballymore, Clones.
"Dec. 14, 1886.

"I saw Mr. Read [the survivor mentioned by Dr. Young, since deceased] and recollect a conversation with him. I cannot recollect the particulars, but am sure that his statement was confirmatory [of Dr. Young's account]. The late Mrs. Young often referred to the dream in conversation, and confirmed Mr. Young's relation.

"CHAS. W. CLOGHER."

An unsuccessful search has been made for some printed record of these facts. Dr. Young tells us that for many years he did not mention his experience except to his wife (now deceased) ; and in answer to an inquiry whether any independent record of the assault could be procured, he replied :—

"We had not at that time any local paper to record such an event ; and as the attack was not followed by destruction of life, and as there was not any clue to the intended assassins, the occurrence passed into oblivion. I pass the spot where I was conscious of the attack very frequently ; and I can point with my finger to within a foot or two of where I fought (shadowy), and the positions of all the parties present. Had not my wife been present and awake when I was so profoundly asleep, and witnessed the amazing and alarming violence of the blows I made, (a matter she spoke of afterwards to me more than once, with terror,) I never could have accounted for the very wretched feeling of weariness, prostration, and pain with which I got from my bed on the next morning."

In conversation Dr. Young mentioned that he did not dream much, and never remembered his dreams. This dream was quite unique in his experience.   His wife's testimony established the fact that it took place before or about midnight; when she saw him throwing his arms about, she had not herself been asleep.

We have a case singularly like this in detail, where a gamekeeper dreamt of taking part in an affray with four poachers at the very spot where such an event actually and simultaneously took place. The dream in this case is confirmed as having been described before the reality was known; but is too directly in the beaten track of the dreamer's waking ideas to be presented as a parallel to the foregoing narrative.

The following account is from Mrs. Manifold, of Barnaboy, Frankford, King's County, Ireland, and was obtained through the kindness of the Rev. J. B. Keene, of Navan.

"January, 1884.

(143) "I once dreamt that an uncle (Dr. Hobbs), whom I had not seen for some time, was driving with his wife in a gig, when he was attacked from behind, beaten, and left on the roadside.   The next morning I told my dream to my sister, who had been sleeping in the same room, and we thought no more of it till the afternoon, when a horse messenger came 30 miles to tell my father his brother had been beaten to death.   The circumstances were *exactly* as I had dreamt, but he did not die then, and is still alive in America."

In answer to inquiries, Mrs. Manifold writes on Feb. 5, 1884 :—

"I delayed answering yours of the 28th January, as I had written to ask a lady whom I thought might have remembered my having told my dream, relative to my uncle's accident, before we had heard of it, but she does not remember ; and my sister, to whom I alluded, has been dead some years.   I am not in the habit of dreaming of distressing things, but have on other occasions dreamt of persons and things I had not seen or thought of for a long time, and soon after have heard from or heard something particular of.   Dr. Hobbs was dragged from his gig, beaten on the road, and thrown into a bog hole, supposed to be dead, near the town of Borrisokane, Co. Tipperary, I think about the year 1846.   I was at the time unmarried, living at Green Hill, Frankford, 22 miles apart, and had no previous knowledge of any ill-feeling towards him, or anything to lead me to suppose such treatment would be likely to occur.   I wish I could have given you more satisfactory testimony, but under the circumstances am unable to do so.   "J. MANIFOLD."

Mrs. Hobbs, writing from London, Ontario, on Feb. 1, 1886, has sent us a description of the savage attack on her husband, which took place about 7 or 8 p.m. on April 12, 1845.

We find an account of the accident in the *Nenagh Guardian* for April 16th, 1845—which completely agrees with the above.   Two of Dr. Hobbs' assailants were identified, and sentenced to transportation.

In conversation Mrs. Manifold mentioned that, as soon as the news of the outrage arrived, her sister (since deceased) turned to her and exclaimed, "Your dream!"   The dream, she says, was of an unusually vivid and pictorial kind, as is shown by the fact that she gave a description of the road which she had seen to one of the men who went to her uncle's assistance, and was informed by him that it corresponded with the reality. But such assertion of correspondence, unless details are given, is of course not a point on which any stress can be laid.

The next account, which first appeared in a letter in the *Religio-Philosophical Journal*, is from Dr. Bruce, of Micanopy, Fla., U.S.A. The case might have been reserved as "collective," but for the fact that one of the dreams, though vivid and alarming, was probably not so distinctive as was afterwards imagined, and moreover was possibly dreamt on the night *preceding* that on which the tragic event took place (see p. 140).

"February 17th, 1884.

(144) "On Thursday, the 27th of December last, I returned from Gainesville (12 miles from here) to my orange grove, near Micanopy. I have only a small plank house of three rooms at my grove, where I spend most of my time when the grove is being cultivated. There was no one in the house but myself at the time, and being somewhat fatigued with my ride, I retired to my bed very early, probably 6 o'clock ; and, as I am frequently in the habit of doing, I lit my lamp on a stand by the bed for the purpose of reading. After reading a short time, I began to feel a little drowsy, put out the light, and soon fell asleep. Quite early in the night I was awakened. I could not have been asleep very long, I am sure. I felt as if I had been aroused intentionally, and at first thought someone was breaking into the house. I looked from where I lay into the other two rooms (the doors of both being open) and at once recognised where I was, and that there was no ground for the burglar theory ; there being nothing in the house to make it worth a burglar's time to come after.

"I then turned on my side to go to sleep again, and immediately felt a consciousness of a presence in the room, and singular to state, it was not the consciousness of a live person, but of a spiritual presence. This may provoke a smile, but I can only tell you the facts as they occurred to me. I do not know how to better describe my sensations than by simply stating that I felt a consciousness of a spiritual presence. This may have been a part of the dream, for I felt as if I were dozing off again to sleep ; but it was unlike any dream I ever had.[1] I felt also at the same time a strong feeling of superstitious dread, as if something strange and fearful were about to happen. I was soon asleep again or unconscious, at any rate, to my surroundings. Then I saw two men engaged in a slight scuffle ; one fell fatally wounded—the other immediately disappeared. I did not see the gash in the wounded man's throat, but knew that his throat was cut. I did not recognise him, either, as my brother-in-law. I saw him lying with his hands under him, his head turned slightly to the left, his feet close together. I could, from the position in which I stood, see but

---

[1] I have more than once pointed out (pp. 198-9, 301, 320) how irrelevant to cases where the dream is of a very exceptional or unique character is the ordinary argument that dreams, from their number, afford limitless scope for accidental coincidences of a striking kind.

a small portion of his face; his coat, collar, hair or something partly obscured it. I looked at him the second time a little closer to see if I could make out who it was. I was aware it was someone I knew, but still could not recognise him. I turned, and then saw my wife sitting not far from him. She told me she could not leave until he was attended to. (I had got a letter a few days previously from my wife, telling me she would leave in a day or two, and was expecting every day a letter or telegram, telling me when to meet her at the depôt.) My attention was struck by the surroundings of the dead man. He appeared to be lying on an elevated platform of some kind, surrounded by chairs, benches, and desks, reminding me somewhat of a school-room. Outside of the room in which he was lying was a crowd of people, mostly females some of whom I thought I knew. Here my dream terminated. I awoke again about midnight; got up and went to the door to see if there were any prospects of rain ; returned to my bed again, and lay there until nearly daylight before falling asleep again. I thought of my dream and was strongly impressed by it. All strange, superstitious feelings had passed off.

"It was not until a week or 10 days after this that I got a letter from my wife, giving me an account of her brother's death. Her letter, which was written the day after his death, was mis-sent. The account she gave me of his death tallies most remarkably with my dream. Her brother was with a wedding party at the depôt at Markham station, Fauquier Co., Va. He went into a store near by to see a young man who kept a bar-room near the depôt, with whom he had some words. He turned and left the man, and walked out of the store. The bar-room keeper followed him out, and without further words deliberately cut his throat. It was a most brutal and unprovoked murder. My brother-in-law had on his overcoat, with the collar turned up. The knife went through the collar and clear to the bone. He was carried into the store and laid on the counter, near a desk and show case. He swooned from loss of blood soon after being cut. The cutting occurred early Thursday night, December 27th. He did not die, however, until almost daylight, Saturday morning.

"I have not had a complete account of my sister-in-law's dream. She was visiting a young lady, a cousin, in Kentucky. They slept together Friday night, I think, the night of her brother's death. She dreamed of seeing a man with his throat cut, and awoke very much alarmed. She awoke her cousin, and they got up and lighted the lamp and sat up until daylight. That day she received a telegram announcing her brother's death.

"I cannot give you any certain explanation of these dreams. I do not believe that they are due to ordinary causes, but to causes of which science does not at present take cognisance.   "WALTER BRUCE."

In reply to inquiries, Dr. Bruce writes, on July 9th, 1884 :—

"I have never had another dream similar to the one related in the letter. I have at times had dreams that were vivid, or from some cause impressed themselves upon my mind for a time, such as anyone would be likely to have. I cannot call to mind, though, any of special importance, or with any bearing upon the dream in question.

2 B

"I did not mention the dream to any one before receiving the letter confirming it. I live in rather a retired place in the country, and if I saw any one during that time, to whom I would care to relate the dream, it did not occur to me to do so.

"You ask me how my wife knew of the circumstances of her brother's death. She was visiting her relatives in Va. at the time, and was present when her brother died."

The following account is from Dr. Bruce's sister-in-law, Mrs. Stubbing :—   "March 28th, 1885.

"Whilst in Kentucky on a visit, in the year 1883, I had a dream, in which I saw two persons—one with his throat cut. I could not tell who it was, though I knew it was somebody that I knew, and as soon as I heard of my brother's death, I said at once that I knew it was he that I had seen murdered in my dream ; and though I did not hear how my brother died, I told my cousin, whom I was staying with, that I knew he had been murdered. This dream took place on Thursday or Friday night, I do not remember which. I saw the exact spot where he was murdered, and just as it happened.   "ANNIE STUBBING."

("The Thursday and Friday night mentioned in this account are December 26th and 27th, [27th and 28th,] 1883. It was upon the Thursday night my dream occurred.—WALTER BRUCE.")

In reply to questions, Mrs. Stubbing says :—

"Yes, I saw one man cut the other. The wound was told to me to be just like what I had seen in my dream. I received a telegram announcing the death of my brother on Saturday morning. No, I never had any such dream as that before."

As a last example, I will quote in its entirety an account of a series of these quasi-clairvoyant impressions, occurring to a single percipient in connection with the same agent. The narrative is from Mrs. Vatas-Simpson, now residing at New Town, near Brisbane. Though parts of it may appear fanciful and subjective, cross-examination made it hard to doubt that these dreams, and others closely corresponding with facts, took place before the facts were known. But in the absence of written records, mere stray fragments have survived.

"82, Akerman Road, Brixton.
"September, 1884.

(145) "My eldest son and firstborn child left me to go to Australia in 1851. The compact between us was that at a certain time we were mutually to think of each other every day. He arranged the hours for himself, which arrangement caused my hours to be from 2 a.m. until 4 a.m. He did not appear to notice that it might interfere with my night's rest, nor did I say so, but most truly can I state *as a fact*, that during all these years there has not been one night that I have not been awake at the time specified ; in sickness, under the power of soporifics, or weary from exhausted activity, still I started up as the hour arrived. This may, perhaps, in some measure account for the close communion we have had

together, for not only have I seen him and been with him, but have heard the words he uttered.

(1) "I saw my son on his horse in a wild part of the country, and saw him dash into a foaming torrent. The horse could with difficulty stem the turbid river, and my son kept cheering him on by word and hand. After struggling on for some time I saw them land safely on the banks of the stream, and my son put his face against the neck of his horse for a few minutes, the noble creature returning the caress, panting and dripping as he was. Then my son looked round at me, and said, distinctly, 'Mother, mother, he has saved me.' That was all, but a letter coming in due course as usual, told me of this incident, and the exact words my son said when he felt himself once again on *terra firma.* So our spirits had held communion.

(2) "I saw my son on an open plain. He kept looking at me. He took from his baggage some articles of clothing, spread them out, shook his head, and put them down, then looked at me ; I mean by that, he looked up from the shirt or socks he had in his hands as though he gazed afar off. After disposing of these things in various ways, and seeming to be in deep thought, he slowly put them away again and started on his journey across country.

"The letter came saying, 'Oh ! mother dear, that I had your precious industrious fingers to mend my things for me, my socks and flannels, and sew on my buttons,' then narrating exactly what he had done on the wide plains, thus confirming in every particular my vision of him. He had travelled from Melbourne to Carpentaria, on foot and on horseback.

(3) "I saw my son nursing a little child, then dash over the plains on horseback without a hat, then dig a hole and place with much care, and very slowly, something in it, then kneel down and with his hands slowly fill the hole with earth. He had a book from which he appeared to be reading, which, by-the-bye, I thought very remarkable. He slowly and with much solemnity left the spot, book in hand, but did not turn to look at me.

"Then came the letter. On the wild sheep plains he was living with a man and his wife and little children. His pet was taken ill. He mounted horse to go 16 miles for doctor—too late ! his little favourite was dead. He dug the grave himself, and with his own hands put the little child into its last resting-place, and with prayer-book in hand read a portion at the grave.

(4) "I saw my son in a stream of flowing water. He now and then sank down out of view, but came to the surface again. It was a very distressing dream to me, because I saw two black objects near him and feared they were chasing him. I was much troubled.

"The letter from him gave me an account of the swimming across a river, accompanied by two blacks, who were travelling the same way.

"Then came a period of distress to me, because I felt that something had come between my son and me. At the usual time for dwelling upon his love for me, and his loving remembrance of all he had promised, I found an obstacle of some sort. It grieved me sadly. I could not understand it. Someone always stood between us ; a shadow was always hovering about. I saw him in a cloud, or a mist rose between us, or he passed from me looking back at me. There was no longer any communion. My daughters found something distressed me, and I told them that I feared for their brother Alfred. They tried to keep me contented, but I felt deserted. The letter came. He was married; and never since have I been blessed by having communion with him."

[Mrs. Simpson has explained in conversation that there was not the slightest breach of affection; only these peculiar communications ceased.]

In answer to inquiries, Mrs. Simpson adds :—

"I have never at any time made a secret of my constant communion with my loved son. All my family have heard my dreams, as they took place—often at the very time—and then have seen the corroboration of them when my letters arrived from Queensland. I have no letters in my possession, though they are only lately destroyed. Could I have foreseen the future, as it is now, I should most certainly have preserved a record of all events, with the dates.

"The dreams are purely matters of recollection. I fancy that I never wrote them, as I was very often suffering at the time. But they were always related to one or more of the family at the time they occurred.

"In my last to Ada [her daughter], I asked her as to my dreams, and she sends a few lines, which I copy from her letter :—

" 'With regard to your dreams I am not very clear, but I remember, when we were at Shanklin, you dreamt that something happened to Alfred, and there was water, and something dark kept close to him. That is all I remember of the dream. You told Mary and me about it, and you wrote it down, and said we should hear something more about it. In my heart I thought it *stuff*. However, by the next mail came a letter, saying that on such a day, giving the date and hour, Alfred was on horseback (I think), and something happened to the horse, and he would have been drowned but for some black men, who rescued and took care of him. It is years since I thought of it, but once set off, I daresay more would come to me.'

"Accept this at what it is worth. You see she has combined two of my dreams."

The following is an extract from the only letter of the son's bearing on these experiences that can be found; it refers to the third case.

"I arranged for the funeral this afternoon. My poor horse suffered, as you may suppose, hard riding. Twenty-third. Three times rode to Roma—18 miles and more before 1 p.m.; then we started to the burial ground. . . . . . I put Willy into his coffin, and into his grave. As a baby I nursed him to sleep, and into his cradle; now I went down into his grave, and drew the ropes from under, so that he was not shaken. A sad day's work."

This may conclude, for the present, the subject of dreams. If with respect to some of the cases cited I have used expressions implying that we may regard them as pretty certainly telepathic, this is on the understanding, as I have explained, that telepathy is established independently of them. But though this branch of evidence can scarcely be in itself conclusive, the study of it will materially assist our future progress.

CHAPTER IX.

"BORDERLAND" CASES.

§ 1. IN the cases of the last chapter, the percipient, at the moment of percipience, was distinctly asleep. But the passage from sleep to waking admits of many degrees; and a very interesting group of cases remain which cannot properly be classed as dreams, and yet which do not appertain to seasons of complete normal wakefulness. The discussion of these experiences, which occur on the borderland of sleeping and waking, will form the natural transition to the waking phenomena with which we shall be occupied during the remainder of our course. The whole set of cases in which telepathic impressions take a sensory form really belong to one large *genus*; whatever the state of the percipient may be, percepts or *quasi*-percepts which are not originated by anything within the normal range of his sense-organs are and must be *hallucinations*. For convenience, however, that term is confined to *waking* experiences, for which there is no other designation. Accordingly, as I have before spoken of *veridical dreams*, I shall in future have to speak of *veridical hallucinations*; and we are now to take the step which leads from the one class to the other.

There are certain reasons why this borderland might be expected to be rich in telepathic phenomena. An impression from a distant mind may or may not originate a sensory hallucination; but if it does so, this seems more specially likely to occur at any season, or in any state of the organism, which happens to be favourable to sensory hallucinations in general. Now the state between sleeping and waking has this character. Persons who have never had hallucinations of the senses at any other times, have experienced them in the moments which immediately precede, or immediately follow, actual sleep. And though neither form of experience is common, an examination of a number of instances seems to show that conditions which come nearest to those of sleep are more favourable than those of ordinary waking life, for the bodying forth of subjective phantasms.[1]

Of the hallucinations which precede sleep, the best-known class have received the name of "*illusions hypnagogiques.*" They have been carefully described by Müller, Maury, and other writers, who have themselves experienced them. For the most part they seem to begin with an appearance of bright points and streaks, which then form a more or less complicated pattern, or develop into a scene or landscape.[2] In these cases, it is probable that the origin of the phenomena is a slightly abnormal condition of the retina, and that elements of actual sensation from this peripheral source form the basis of the phantasmagoria which the mind elaborates. But there is another form, involving no peculiarity of the external organ, where some object that has been actually seen during the day seems to reappear before the eyes with all the vividness of reality. Maury gives a case of an "after-image" of the sort, which well exemplifies the stage between reality and dream. After a fatiguing day, his eyes had been gladdened by the sight of a beefsteak, which was to form his dinner. After dinner he became drowsy ; and in this state he had a distinct vision of this very steak, apparently as real and palpable as ever. Lapsing then into actual sleep, he had a vivid dream, in which the steak again reappeared. Here it is clear that the "*hypnagogic*" hallucination was as truly the projection of the percipient's own mind as the dream.

The hallucinations which immediately follow sleep are not infrequently the result of a previous dream, some feature of which is prolonged into waking moments, and becomes temporarily located among the objects that meet the eye. An Oxford undergraduate tells me that, having had a very vivid dream of being chased by a figure in green, he woke and saw the green figure in the middle of his room. "I had no doubt that I was awake, for I saw the light from the street lamp shining on my door. The figure was not in this light but nearer the bed, and the green tinge was very perceptible." The Rev. E. H. Sugden, of Bradford, writes to me : "Once I had a most

---

[1] The same seems to hold good in distinctly morbid cases. (See Dr. Pick's remarks in the Vienna *Jahrbuch für Psychiatrie* for 1880, Vol. ii., p. 50.) Dr. Maudsley says that, in recovery from chronic alcoholism, the hallucinations continue to occur between sleeping and waking, when they have ceased to occur at other times. (*The Pathology of Mind*, p. 485.)

[2] See some excellent examples in the next chapter, p. 474, note.

vivid dream about a man whom I knew well. On suddenly waking, I saw him, in the light of early morning, standing at my bedside in the very attitude of the dream. I looked at him for a second or two, and then putting my foot out, I kicked at him; as my foot reached him, he vanished." Another informant had a dream, in the train, of looking at her watch, and on waking saw the dial before her eyes "larger than the real one, and blue : after a few moments it flickered and went out like a candle." In these cases the impression was scarcely more than momentary; but other informants—among them Professor Balfour Stewart—have told me of similar experiences of their own which lasted a good many seconds; and in the stock example of the books, the dream-baboon remained grinning in a corner even while the percipient was sufficiently himself to walk across the room— a striking illustration of the psychological identity of the dreaming and the waking image.[1]

More striking are the cases where the images, though immediately following sleep, are not a continuance of a dream, or at any rate of a dream of which the slightest memory survives. Of course these experiences may not all have been hallucinations in the strict sense, but only misinterpretations of actual sensation—that is to say, some article of furniture or real object in the room may have served as the basis for the delusive image; and momentary illusions of this sort are perhaps not very uncommon.[2] But even so, the mind has imposed

---

[1] An attempt to ascertain the frequency of such experiences formed part of the statistical inquiry mentioned in the last chapter. But unfortunately, I cannot record an exact result. The question as first asked was—Have you experienced *dream-images which persist* into waking moments?—but on making further inquiry of a good many of the persons who answered "yes," I found that they had not understood *persist* to mean *persist as visible objects*. After these words were introduced, very few *yeses* were received; and I think it would be safe to say that the persons who can recall such a visible persistence do not amount to 1 per cent. of the population.

[2] For instance, Mr. Paul Bird, of 39, Strand, Calcutta, tells me that some years ago he woke, and saw a native standing against the wall, who on being regarded sank into a squatting posture. "I jumped out of bed, caught the intruder by the throat, and found he was a dirty linen bag, with the neck tied. Not till I actually clutched the neck was I convinced." Mr. Merrifield, of 24, Vernon Terrace, Brighton—with whom figures seen on waking last long enough for him "to reason that though I have been mistaken before, there can be no mistake this time, and to insist upon this to my wife, who remonstrates "– says, "If there is any light object in the room, or any dress or polished piece of furniture on which the light falls, my figure generally shapes itself about that." Even a persistent dream-image may attach itself to an external basis. Thus Miss I. Bidder, of Ravensbury Park, Mitcham, tells me of a nightmare from which a most distinct demon survived after she woke. She sat up to inspect its hand, which was clutching the bed-rail; but "it faded into the ornaments over the mantel-piece." We may regard as the lowest grade of such illusion the impression of waking among unknown surroundings. Thus one correspondent tells me that she has "watched the room gradually take its usual form, which on first waking had been some place quite different." And another informant writes : "The room I apparently woke in was a large room, with the chief space between the foot of the bed and the opposite boundary wall, which looked an immense way off, and the light did not appear to come in

its own creation from within on what met the eye from without ; and such cases, therefore, still bear out my point, that the tendency to externalise and objectify mental images is strongest at one special season of waking life. Of 302 cases of hallucinations of sight (exclusive of those given as telepathic evidence in this book), of which I have collected first-hand accounts during the last three years, as many as 43—that is, a seventh of the whole number— have taken place during the first few moments after waking. It is equally noteworthy that of the remainder, 66, making in all more than a third of the whole number, occurred to persons who were in bed—a proportion far in excess of that which the number of waking minutes spent in bed bears to the total number of waking minutes. Few of these cases, moreover, were of a character that would allow us to class them as *illusions hypnagogiques.* They did not visit persons who were familiar with such visions as sleep approached ; nor did they originate or develop in any way that suggests an unusual or fatigued condition of the retina. Nor again could by any means all of them be explained, like M. Maury's beefsteak, as " after-images "—revivals of past impressions ; for out of the 43 cases first mentioned only 23, out of the 66 other cases only 26, represented a face, form, or object that was recognised ; while in several even of these cases the person whose figure appeared was a deceased friend or relative who had not been actually seen for months or years. Similarly, of 187 first-hand cases of auditory hallu- cination in my collection, 63, or more than one third of the whole num- ber, took place in bed. Of these, 19 are described as either awakening the person, or occurring in the very first moment of waking, and in 10 of the 19 the sound was a recognised voice ; of the remaining 44, 17 were unrecognised voices, 11 were non-vocal sounds such as ringings and knocks, and only 16 represented recognised voices. It would seem, then, that the reasons which make bed a specially favourable place for such experiences are to be sought, not only in peculiarities of the sense-organs at the moments immediately contiguous to sleep, but in the more general conditions of quiet and passivity, of a comparatively anæmic brain, and of the partial lapse of the higher directive psychical activities. We cannot, I think, safely reckon

at the right place, though on the same side of the room as the window really was. I lay and pondered, feeling as if there was something inexplicable in the place, sure that I was wide awake. As I wondered, all the strangeness of the room and the added space vanished, and I found myself again in a small, narrow room, with the wall almost close to the bottom of the bed."

darkness as among these conditions, as a large proportion of the cases have occurred when the room was light—for instance, in the early hours of a summer morning.

§ 2. At any rate, bed being—from whatever causes—a place favourable to phantasms, it is reasonable to surmise that it may be a place favourable to the phenomena with which we are concerned in this book—the phantasms that coincide with reality. And such, in fact, it proves to be. Considering how small a portion of our waking life is included in the few moments after waking from sleep, or even in the short periods of wakefulness that normal healthy persons pass in bed, it is remarkable how large a proportion of our veridical examples (a number little less than the total of dreams, and amounting to about a fourth of the externalised waking cases,) fall within these seasons. And regarded as evidence of telepathy, it will be seen that these cases stand on an altogether different footing from the dream-cases proper with which they have seemed in one way so closely allied. Dreams, as we saw, are so frequent and various as to afford an immense scope for accidental coincidences ; it is far otherwise with these borderland impressions, or at any rate with those of them which the perceiver himself is able clearly to differentiate from dreams. If I have called them the *commonest* form of waking hallucination among sane and healthy people, this is not to be understood as meaning that they are absolutely common ; on the contrary, they are decidedly exceptional. Out of 5569 persons, taken at random, I find that only 18 are able to recall having within the last twelve years had a visual experience, and only 23 an auditory experience, of this kind.[1] If then we find a considerable number of cases where an experience of the sort has coincided with the death (or some distinct crisis in the life) of the person whose presence the hallucination suggested, the fact is at once noteworthy ; and the

[1] I may explain that the statistics about hallucinations, of which use was made on the preceding page, were not the result of inquiries addressed to a known and limited number of persons, but of testimony which has reached me in the more general course of psychological investigation. For the purpose then in view —namely, to ascertain the proportion which " borderland " hallucinations bear to hallucinations in general—statistics thus drawn from an unlimited circle are of course in place. But it is quite a different matter when we wish to discover how common the phenomena are, in the sense of discovering what proportion of people have had experience of them. The only way, then, is to make a definite inquiry on the subject, of a certain number of persons, large enough to be accepted as a fair sample of the population. This method of numerical inquiry was exemplified to some extent in the discussion on dreams ; but I am reserving for a separate chapter (Chap. xiii., at the beginning of Vol. ii.) the more detailed account of it, and of its bearing on the theory that the coincidences on which stress is laid in this book were due not to telepathy but to chance.

number of such coincidences that we can adduce forms a strong and independent proof—far stronger, at any rate, than was afforded by our list of coincident dreams—that telepathy and not accident is the explanation of them. Nor is the comparatively small number of persons who have experience of distinct "borderland" hallucinations the only point wherein this class is superior in evidential force to dreams. We can here, as a rule, be far more certain that the particular impression recorded was really of a sort unique or highly exceptional in the particular percipient's experience. This unique character is, no doubt, as we have seen, often asserted of dreams proper which afterwards prove to have coincided with reality. But there we lacked complete assurance that similar dreams which did not coincide with reality had not slipped out of memory. The impressions to be described in this chapter, on the other hand, have a character and an intensity which would ordinarily ensure their being remembered, even if no coincidence were established. Many of them, indeed, seem to have been distinctly waking impressions, belonging to a state of open eyes and alert senses, which was continued into normal waking life without any break or any feeling of change whatever. Still, as they occurred to persons who were in bed, and at seasons when the faculties are apt to be in an unstable condition, and when the stages of consciousness from moment to moment may be hard to define, it is safest to distinguish them from similar phenomena occurring during active waking hours, no less than from those of sleep.[1]

I may quote at once a case which illustrates the immense importance to the argument of distinguishing the experiences of the "borderland" from those of sleep. The following passage occurs in the *Life and Times of Lord Brougham*, written by himself (1871), pp. 201-3, and was originally an entry in his journal. The entry must apparently have been made very soon after the occurrence which it describes; as we can scarcely doubt that had the fact of his friend's death, which he learnt soon afterwards, been known to him at the time of writing, he would have included it in the account.

---

[1] Since we make so broad an evidential distinction between these "borderland" impressions and dreams, it is clearly incumbent on us to treat doubtful cases in the way least favourable to our argument, and to refer them to the dream-class. Thus in the well-known apparition-case recorded in Isaak Walton's *Life of Dr. Donne*, it is very probable that Dr. Donne, who had been left alone after dinner, was dozing. So, when the word *vision* is used, without special mention that the percipient was awake, we are bound to assume that he was asleep. This would exclude such a case as Ben Jonson's "vision" of his son, "with a bloodie cross upon his forehead," which synchronised with the child's death at a distance by the plague, as narrated by Drummond of Hawthornden. For taken as a *dream*, the experience, occurring at what was very possibly a time of anxiety, would not afford a sufficiently remarkable coincidence.

In December, 1799, Lord Brougham was travelling in Sweden with friends.

(146) "We set out for Gothenburg, [apparently on December 18th] determining to make for Norway. About 1 in the morning, arriving at a decent inn, we decided to stop for the night. Tired with the cold of yesterday, I was glad to take advantage of a hot bath before I turned in, and here a most remarkable thing happened to me—so remarkable that I must tell the story from the beginning.

"After I left the High School, I went with G., my most intimate friend, to attend the classes in the University. There was no divinity class, but we frequently in our walks discussed and speculated upon many grave subjects—among others, on the immortality of the soul, and on a future state. This question, and the possibility, I will not say of ghosts walking, but of the dead appearing to the living, were subjects of much speculation : and we actually committed the folly of drawing up an agreement, written with our blood, to the effect that whichever of us died the first should appear to the other, and thus solve any doubts we had entertained of the 'life after death.'[1] After we had finished our classes at the college, G. went to India, having got an appointment there in the Civil Service. He seldom wrote to me, and after the lapse of a few years I had almost forgotten him ; moreover, his family having little connection with Edinburgh, I seldom saw or heard anything of them, or of him through them, so that all his schoolboy intimacy had died out, and I had nearly forgotten his existence. I had taken, as I have said, a warm bath, and while lying in it and enjoying the comfort of the heat, after the late freezing I had undergone, I turned my head round, looking towards the chair on which I had deposited my clothes, as I was about to get out of the bath. On the chair sat G., looking calmly at me. How I got out of the bath I know not, but on recovering my senses I found myself sprawling on the floor. The apparition, or whatever it was, that had taken the likeness of G., had disappeared.

"This vision produced such a shock that I had no inclination to talk about it or to speak about it even to Stuart ; but the impression it made upon me was too vivid to be easily forgotten ; and so strongly was I affected by it that I have here written down the whole history, with the date, 19th December, and all the particulars, as they are now fresh before me. No doubt I had fallen asleep ; and that the appearance presented so distinctly to my eyes was a dream, I cannot for a moment doubt ; yet for years I had had no communication with G., nor had there been anything to recall him to my recollection ; nothing had taken place during our Swedish travels either connected with G. or with India, or with anything relating to him or to any member of his family. I recollected quickly enough our old discussion and the bargain we had made. I could not discharge from my mind the impression that G. must have died, and that his appearance to me was to be received by me as a proof of a future state, yet all the while I felt convinced that the whole was a dream ; and so painfully vivid, so

---

[1] As to compacts of this sort see Vol. ii., p. 66.

unfading was the impression, that I could not bring myself to talk of it, or to make the slightest allusion to it."

In October, 1862, Lord Brougham added as a postcript :—

"I have just been copying out from my journal the account of this strange dream : *Certissima mortis imago !* And now to finish the story, begun about 60 years since. Soon after my return to Edinburgh, there arrived a letter from India, announcing G.'s death, and stating that he had died on the 19th of December !

" Singular coincidence ! yet when one reflects on the vast numbers of dreams which night after night pass through our brains, the number of coincidences between the vision and the event are perhaps fewer and less remarkable than a fair calculation of chances would warrant us to expect. Nor is it surprising, considering the variety of our thoughts in sleep, and that they all bear some analogy to the affairs of life, that a dream should sometimes coincide with a contemporaneous or even with a future event. This is not much more wonderful than that a person, whom we had no reason to expect, should appear to us at the very moment we have been thinking or speaking of him. So common is this, that it has for ages grown into the proverb, ' Speak of the devil.' I believe every such seeming miracle is, like every ghost story, capable of explanation."

Lord Brougham's evidence in a matter of this kind cannot be fairly impugned on the ground that his character for public veracity was not always above suspicion. He clearly took no special pride or pleasure in the incident, and he advances a thoroughly rationalistic explanation of it. But of course the long interval which elapsed between his hearing of the date of the death and his recording it in writing greatly diminishes the evidential value of the case. I quote it rather for the sake of the important fallacy in the concluding remarks.

Lord Brougham, we see, rests his view that the coincidence in his case was accidental on the " vast number of dreams." But was his experience a dream ? This is no mere question of a name. Let us make the supposition that no death had occurred, and that the experience remained one which there is not even a *primâ facie* excuse for surmising to be anything but purely subjective : does it thereby subside at once into the general ruck of dream-experiences ? Is it indistinguishable in intensity and character from those countless multitudes, of which it would be true and relevant to say that the scope afforded by them for chance-coincidences is practically unlimited ? We can but accept what Lord Brougham himself has told us, and answer these questions by an emphatic negative. The complete consciousness of the real place and time, the intention to get out of the bath, the percipient's sense of his own actual posture when he caught sight of the figure, and the whole detail of the account, are all very unlike ordinary dreaming. But apart from such points as these, is it a well-known result of an ordinary dream that the dreamer, on recovering his senses, finds himself "sprawling on the floor"? On waking from an ordinary dream, are we wont to remark, as a point of interest, that "the apparition has disappeared"? Is it characteristic of an ordinary dream to be so painfully vivid and unfading that the dreamer cannot bring himself to make the slightest allusion to it? Call such an experience a dream, or call it (as we should do) a "borderland" hallucination—the only relevant question is, how often does its like occur? In Lord Brougham's own long life, at any rate, it was unique and unparalleled. In arguing, therefore, that the coincidence was not so very remarkable after all, because "dreams" are so numerous and various that one of them here and there is likely by chance to strike on truth, he makes himself the slave of a word. The instance is instructive, as showing the tendency of prepossessions, however legitimate and scientific in themselves, to lead on to illegitimacies of procedure. Lord Brougham is rightly certain that his experience is not supernatural—is "capable of explanation"; and then, as the only natural explanation that occurs to him is *chance*, he becomes equally certain that that must be the right one, wrests facts into conformity with it, and refers a very uncommon thing to a class of very common things.

§ 3. To come, however, to our own collection—before introducing the characteristic sensory cases, I will quote a couple of "borderland" examples of the more ideal type which has been prominent in the preceding chapters. In the first case, the transferred impression (if such it was) did not even suggest an idea to the percipient until it actually took shape in an exclamation of her own. The narrator's family dislike the subject, and her name is accordingly suppressed.

"December 22nd, 1883.

(147) "Two years ago my son was ill in Durban, Natal. I was told by his medical attendant, who is also my son-in-law, that the illness was *serious*, but I had no reason to suppose it was expected to end fatally. Of course, I, his mother, was anxious; but there came better accounts, and at last a letter from my son himself. He spoke of being really stronger, expressed regret at his enforced long silence, and added he hoped now to write regularly again. The load was lifted from my mind, and I remarked I felt happier than I had done for months. At this time I too was ill, and had a trained nurse with me. A few nights after the receipt of the letter, I *thought* I had been lying awake, and requiring to call my nurse who

was in my room, I sat up in bed and called loudly, 'Edward, Edward.' I
was roused by nurse answering, 'I fear, ma'am, your son will not be able
to come to you.' I tried to laugh it off, but a chill struck to my heart.
I noted the hour, 3.40 on Sunday morning. Without mentioning my
fears, I recounted the incident to my daughters, but I looked for the bad
news to come, and on Monday received the cable message, 'Edward died
last night.' Subsequently letters named the hour as being identical with
that in which I had involuntarily sent forth my cry for my loved son.
[This is not quite correct.] His sister, Mrs. C., in writing to me, said,
'O! mother, his one crave was for you, and to the last moment the
yearning he had for you seemed to dwell in his eyes.' I may add we were
more than even mother and son usually are to one another. I believe in
that one moment our souls were permitted to meet, and I thank God for
the memory of that hour.   "C. E. K."

In answer to inquiries, Mrs. K. says that her son had had delicate
health, and "for years I used to get up through the night and listen to
his breathing, and lived in the constant apprehension of learning sudden
bad news if he were out of my sight." She adds, "No doubt I was thinking
of him, but not painfully, for I had had his letter, and I thought he was
getting well. It certainly was not a dream—I sat up in bed to call my
nurse, when, to my surprise [1] and, for an instant, amusement, I uttered the
cry, 'Edward, Edward.' The great point is, of course, whether the hour
was *exactly* that of his death. My son died during the night, or rather,
early in the morning, of Sunday, August 28th, 1881. During that same
night I uttered my cry to him. It was the only time in my life that
anything of the kind took place. I never talked in my sleep, nor had any
experience the least like this before or since."

The following is from Mrs. K.'s daughter :—

"January 23rd, 1884.

"I remember that on the morning of the 29th August my mother
told me of the curious coincidence of which she has written to you. She
told me when I went into her room the first thing, and the nurse was
also in her room.   "E. E. K."

It having been pointed out to Mrs. K. that her daughter said the
29th, not the 28th, of August, she explains :—

"My daughter, E. E. K., says I told her of my cry in the morning of
the day after I uttered it; of course, it was therefore on the 28th that
everything occurred. In writing to you she did not realise that the death
and my cry were both *after midnight*, and simply writing from memory,
put the 29th, as being the day after the 28th. There is no doubt
Edward's death and my cry occurred during the night of the 27th, or
rather in the early morning of the 28th." [2]

---

[1] The reader who has studied the records of automatic phenomena in Chap ii., §§ 12
and 13, will not find it specially surprising that a telepathic impression should manifest
itself in an involuntary utterance of this sort.

[2] This is not very clearly expressed ; but there seems little doubt that the cry
took place on Sunday morning, August 28th, and was mentioned to E. E. K. a few
hours later.

Mrs. K. kindly wrote to another daughter at Durban, to make sure of the exact time of the death; and quotes the following passage from the reply :—

" Edward died at 20 minutes before 5 a.m.; his watch was just beside him, and as he drew his last breath, I looked at the time and said, 'Mother will be awake! how will she bear it?'" The writer adds that her husband's entry in his diary for August 28th, 1881, is, "Ned died 4.40 a.m."

Allowing for longitude the cry here followed the death by about an hour. Mrs. K.'s preoccupation with her son's condition is, of course, a weak point in the evidence : on the other hand she is very certain of the uniqueness of the experience. If the case was telepathic, its peculiar nature would strikingly support the view already advanced, that a telepathic impression may be produced below the threshold of consciousness. And on that view the slight deferment of the further effect by which the impression is plainly manifested becomes completely intelligible.

The next case is very similar to No. 103 (p. 330), but the effect on the percipient is even more unlike that of any ordinary dream. And from the evidential point of view, even those who most strongly realise the scope that the vast number of dreams affords for accidental coincidences, will hesitate to assume that a vast number of boys of 16 get up, dress, and wait for messengers in the middle of the night. The narrative is from a paper called " Man, Trans-Corporeal "—by Dr. C. B. Radcliffe, of 25, Cavendish Square, W.—which appeared in the *Contemporary Review* for December, 1874.

(148) " My grandmother, a lady considerably over 70 years of age, resided with my parents, and I was [at the time of the occurrence] staying at a place about 4 miles away from home. Everybody at home was, to all appearance, in good health, and had been so for a long time, and on that particular night I went to bed and fell asleep, without at all divining what was so soon to happen.

" I have no remembrance of having dreamt, and all I know is that, after having slept for a couple of hours, I woke with full conviction that my grandmother had been taken suddenly ill, that a messenger was on his way to fetch me, and that I should not reach home before all was over. A moment or two later I got up, lit a candle, looked at my watch, dressed, and waited at the window in the full belief that my grandmother was then dead and that I should have to go presently; and as I expected, so it was, the messenger arriving just as I was ready to return with him, and the death happening, as it proved afterwards, at the very moment I had looked at my watch. I had not any impression at the time that there was anything supernatural in the way in which the intelligence was thus conveyed to my mind. I remember nothing like a feeling of fear at the time, and I did not (I was a lad of

not more than 16 years of age) perplex myself with reasoning on the subject."
[We find that this incident took place in 1837, and no corroboration is now procurable. In deciding whether to include a case of this degree of remoteness, the intellectual status of the narrator must naturally be a chief consideration. Dr. Radcliffe tells us that it stands out very clearly in his memory, and that everybody who knew him at the time heard of it.]

§ 4. To pass now to definitely sensory cases, I will first quote one which is interesting as a perfect example of an "*illusion hypnagogique*," suggested apparently by the ideas in a neighbouring mind. Miss Deering, of Louisville, Kentucky, writes to us as follows:—

"October 18th, 1884.
(149) "I very distinctly remember that one day, a few years ago, my father lay down for a few minutes, as at that time usual before going to his office in the afternoon. Seated on a stool beside him, and with my left hand enfolded in one of his, I read the book in which I was at the time interested, for 5 or possibly 7 minutes. At the end of that time he turned his face towards me, and seeing that the room was shaded, remarked : 'Anna, you will injure your eyes reading in this dim light.' 'And I do not particularly like this book,' I responded. I held in my hand a historical novel, the name of which I am sorry I cannot recollect, but I remember vividly that the passage I had just read purported to be one of the last scenes in the life of Marie Antoinette, and I remember as distinctly that in that scene a tall man carried a coffin from a room in which Marie Antoinette and some attendant ladies were at the time standing. I remember that in the story that tall man stood prominently in the foreground, and that my mind was strained under the part he took in that scene almost to the verge of repugnance.

"In reply to my father's question why I did not like the book, I replied in substance as in the foregoing, and he immediately told me that he had just seen what I had described, and had opened his eyes and turned his face towards me to dissipate the scene, which for the moment he had looked upon as an isolated phantasm. [1]   "ANNA M. DEERING."

Mr. Deering writes :—
"Louisville, Kentucky, U.S.
"October 21st, 1884.
"While I lay with my daughter's hand in mine, as she relates in the accompanying memoir, I fell into the semi-slumber usual with me on lying down to rest for a few minutes after my luncheon, early in the afternoon. At these times I very seldom fall asleep, but simply into a species of slumber, in which I frequently find myself in a kind of rayless or moonless moonlight, looking, and this usually with serene pleasure, at nearby gardens, slopes, rivulets, and various little vistas, which more times than otherwise vanish at my bidding, and except I fall asleep, are immediately replaced by others. Sometimes these are peopled with

[1] A parallel case, where a dream seems to have been suggested by what someone else had been silently reading, is No. 407 in the Supplement.

apparently living figures, and frequently these also dissolve at my bidding and are replaced by others. There is, however, this difference ; any control I exercise for the purpose of a change seems to be more immediate and more absolute over a change of figures than over a change of scenes.

"I am quite sure that at these times I do not fall into any condition that fairly can be called pathological.

" Under the slumber now under consideration, my attention became fixed on a tall thin man, with head uncovered, beardless, and dressed in black. He came toward the foot of the bed on which I lay from the left ; and perhaps I should note that my daughter sat upon my left. Immediately I saw several other figures ; and though these stood outside the lines or field of my direct vision, I remember distinctly that they made on me an impression of sympathy with powerlessness. I might think that the sympathy touched me through the countenance of the man, were it not that he impressed me with also the opposite of powerlessness. His age seemed to be about 50, his face oblong, a little sallow, seriously thoughtful, and withal indicative of great but quiet firmness in action, whether from a sense of duty based on his own judgment, or duty under a sense of obedience, I cannot determine ; though, in the absence of any appearance of the vindictive, I think or at least am inclined to think that alike his presence and his action were based on simply an obedience to some rightful authority. This action was a reverent stepping forward, and a silent laying of his hands on a coffin that seemed to rest across the foot of the bed. The moment I saw the coffin I thought : I do not like this scene ; please go away and let something more agreeable come in. But the scene would not change, and again I thought : Please go away and let something more agreeable come in ; and again the scene would not change. He raised the coffin, it seemed as easily as though it had been that of an infant, and was in the act of stepping backward, as though withdrawing from a presence, when I thought : Then I will not prolong this slumber ; I will open my eyes and arouse myself. And, on immediately doing so, I spoke to my daughter as she narrates, and then, without anything like amazement, listened to her description from the book.

" I have been minute, as in the foregoing, because I wish to put every feature of and every impression given me by the scene carefully on record, against a search which I purpose to keep up for the book out of which my daughter at the time sat reading. She did not then or ever read to me what she had read, but simply and in her own language drew the scene ; and this in, perhaps, as few words as she has now written it, nor have we since that time in any particular way conversed about it. My impression is that the book she read was an octavo in paper covers, but its name or author, or whose it was or what became of it, neither of us can recollect ; nor do either of us at this time remember any of the scenes immediately preceding or attending the tragic death of Marie Antoinette, as these are, or may be, recorded in history.

"WILLIAM DEERING."

This incident was originally related in the Louisville *Medical News* by Professor Palmer, a letter from whom is appended.

"University of Louisville, Kentucky, U.S.A.
"September 26th, 1883.

"The article appearing on the other side is true in every particular. The gentleman, a resident of this city, a man of high nervous organisation, was born in Belfast, U.S.A. Between himself and his daughter exists a degree of attachment rarely seen in such kinship. I related the incident as he gave it to me.

"E. R. PALMER, M.D.,
"Professor of Physiology," &c.

It is obvious that the value of this narrative, as affording evidence of thought-transference, must be proportional to the degree of exactness with which the correspondence between the dream and the description in the book can be made out. It might, therefore, be considerably increased if the book could be discovered; but we have failed to find any historical novel, or any memoir or history, containing the incident. Even as it stands the coincidence is certainly remarkable; but as Miss Deering's description preceded her father's account of his vision, it is possible that its similarity to the description became unconsciously somewhat stronger in recollection than it was in reality.

This particular type is in any case unusual. Looking at the "borderland" impressions of the higher senses as a class, we at once observe the same important change as struck us in the course of our survey of dreams (pp. 341-2). The experience of the percipient is henceforth no longer (or only very rarely) a direct reproduction or embodiment of the idea or sensation of the agent; it is something in which his own creative faculties are at work. He is the author of his impression in the same sense as before he was the author of his dream. I merely note this in passing, reserving further discussion of this point till the subject of waking hallucinations can be treated as a whole.

§ 5. I will first take examples where a single sense only is concerned, and will begin with the sense of *hearing*. There is a group of cases where what has been heard has suddenly awakened the percipient—not, however, as the climax of a dream, but with the vivid and instantaneous impression of a sound externally caused. It may, no doubt, be suggested that in such cases the sound is the climax of a dream of which no memory survived. But if so, the immediate oblivion of the dream serves to set off the specially startling nature of the experience in the moment of waking; and such instantaneous startings from apparently dreamless sleep, with a definite sound in the ears which has no objective reality, are at any rate sufficiently rare to justify us in regarding them, for purposes of evidence, as *borderland* and not as *dream* experiences. The cases, however, differ considerably in their evidential force. In some which have most powerfully impressed the imagination of the percipients, the sound has been inarticulate and of the nature of a scream, not identified with the person afterwards assumed to have been the agent. Now this of course diminishes the improbability that its synchronism with an exceptional state of that person was accidental. And again, it is difficult in such circumstances to prove conclusively that the sound may not have been due to some normal cause which was not discovered; for odd sounds at night are not uncommon, and, till accounted for, may have a peculiarly exciting effect. As regards the first of these objections, it must be remembered, on the other hand, that screams are a very unusual form of purely subjective impression—my large collection of waking hallucinations of the sane does not include a single instance; while they do not seem an unlikely form to be taken by a hallucination which is the sensory embodiment of a sudden undefined idea of death or calamity.[1] As to the likelihood of a real external sound whose source was not discovered, the reader will be able to form his own judgment from the cases themselves.

The following account is from Viscount L., the very reverse of a credulous witness, and with no sort of leaning towards the marvellous.

"November 5th, 1884.

(150) "Thirty years ago and upwards [August 13th, 1849], I was staying with my father at our place in Ireland. I was then my father's second son, having an elder brother. I was awoke out of my sleep by violent screams, so much so that I got up and walked all over the house to endeavour to ascertain where the screams came from. All appeared, as far as I could judge, quite regular and quiet in the house (a very large one), and I went back to bed and thought no more about it. On inquiry in the morning, nobody had heard the screams except myself. But 2 days after, I received a letter, stating that my elder and only brother had died at Ramsgate after 6 hours' illness, of cholera, and died about the hour when I certainly heard screams."

In answer to inquiries, Lord L. says, "I never in my life experienced any sort of hallucination of the senses." In conversation, he informed me that his brother certainly died in the night. He had travelled to Ramsgate on the preceding day, and was taken ill after his arrival. Lord L.'s wife was sleeping in a room which opened into his, and heard nothing.

Now no doubt the wind sometimes plays odd tricks; and,

---

[1] See the discussion and examples of "rudimentary hallucinations," Chap. xiv., § 4, and Chap. xv., § 6.

moreover, it is possible to be awoke by a scream *of one's own* which seems to the bewildered sense to have been external.[1] But if a healthy man gets out of bed and walks all over a large house merely because the wind is high, he is, one would think, likely to remark that the wind is high—whereas Lord L. remarked (he tells me) that the night was calm ; and the sounds which so ring in his waking ears as to prompt this unusual course would at any rate be likely to be noticed by someone else. The use of the plural word "screams" is also worth noting, as opposed to the view that the sleeper woke himself by some shrill exclamation; indeed, his sex would alone make this explanation less plausible than in some other cases. But the case is remote in time, and depends on a single memory. This last objection does not apply to the following account, from Mrs. Purton, of Field House, Alcester.

"March 16th, 1884.

(151) "In the autumn of 1859, we were expecting my youngest brother home from Australia, after an absence of eight years. He was a passenger on board the ' Royal Charter.' The night, or rather in the early dawn of the fatal morning of the wreck of that unhappy vessel, I suddenly started out of my sleep and found myself seizing hold of my husband's arm, horrified at the most awful wail of agony, which appeared to me to fill the house. Finding my husband still asleep—he was a medical man, and had been out the whole of the previous night, so was unusually tired—I slipped out of bed and went round to look at all the children and to the servants' room, but found all quietly sleeping, so thinking it must have been the wind only which so disturbed me, I lay down again, but could not sleep. I noticed that day was just breaking. In the morning I asked different people if they had been disturbed by any unusual noise, but no one had heard it.

"The post brought a letter from a cousin in Liverpool, telling us the ' Royal Charter ' was telegraphed as having arrived at Queenstown, and we might expect to see Frank very shortly. We passed the day in most joyful anticipations of the meeting. My mother had his room prepared, a good fire burning, and his night-shirt and slippers laid out for use, and a nice supper ready. Wheels were heard, but, instead of Frank, my cousin appeared. She, as soon as the awful news of the wreck reached Liverpool, started off herself to bring us the melancholy tidings. Even then I did not connect the fearful sounds I heard with the wreck, but when the newspapers came and I read the accounts of the eye-witnesses of the wreck, and of the screams which rent the air as the ship broke her back and all on board were overwhelmed in the waves, I could only shudder and exclaim, ' *That* was what I heard.' It was months before I could forget the horror which thrilled my very soul at the remembrance of that awful night. "FRANCES A. PURTON."

---

[1] In proof of this, see case 126, p. 360, top.

In answer to inquiries, Mrs. Purton adds :—

" I never have had, at any other time than the one I mentioned to you, a vivid dream of death, or an auditory hallucination of any kind."

The following is an extract from a letter written to Mrs. Purton by her daughter, Miss Sarah Sophia Purton, who was about 12 years old at the time of the occurrence :—

" I distinctly remember your speaking of the cry of distress you heard when the ' Royal Charter' was lost. My remembrance of it is that you woke with this cry ringing in your ears, and got up at once, quietly, without disturbing my father, who had been out late somewhere to a patient. You found it was about 3 o'clock. You then went to the nursery and to each room where anyone was sleeping, but finding all was quiet and right you went back to bed. I fancy you inquired next morning if anyone had heard the sound which disturbed you, but could not swear to this."

Miss Purton writes to us :—

" April 7th, 1884.

"To the best of my recollection my mother spoke of the cry she heard the following morning. I distinctly remember her saying when she heard of the terrible cry as the vessel parted and went down, ' There, that was the cry I heard,' and the thrill it gave me at the time, but this must have been a day or two after the occurrence—either just before or after she had visited the scene of the wreck.   " S. S. PURTON."

Here, the vivid character of the impression, and the fact that it was unique in the percipient's experience, will probably be accepted without dispute. And if so, the coincidence—though easy enough to regard as accidental if it stood alone or nearly alone—seems fairly admissible as an item in a cumulative proof of telepathy.[1]

¹ We have received a similar case from Mr. D. H. Wilson, of Rosemont, Hyères, who was told by an intimate friend, Miss Maclean, that she was awakened one morning by an appalling shriek, and marked the hour ; and that at that exact time (allowing for longitude) her brother met with a violent death in Australia. But we have not been able to trace Miss Maclean ; and in this somewhat doubtful type, first-hand evidence is specially requisite.

The following case, though it is first-hand, and though the incident is unique in the narrator's experience, is open to objections of another kind. The account is from Miss Dora Kennedy, of Rockville, Rainhill, and was obtained through the kindness of the late Dr. Noble, of Manchester.

"September 29th, 1884.

" A young married sister of mine lived in the country, and was recovering from a long illness, through which I had nursed her. We went to Liverpool to consult her doctor, and to spend a few days with a relative. During the course of the visit, I had to leave her in the care of an aunt, whilst I went home for a short time to Manchester. In the middle of my first night at home, I was suddenly awakened by a piercing scream, and jumping out of bed, saw my mother coming into the room in great alarm. Having heard and been awakened by a scream, she thought something terrible had happened, and asked me what it was. I thought and said at once (as I felt quite sure) that something had happened to my sister in Liverpool. The next morning I returned to my sister, and on my arrival saw that they were greatly alarmed. My aunt told me that during the night she got up to give my sister her usual medicine, and by mistake took the wrong bottle containing laudanum, and gave a dose. Fortunately my sister only took a small portion before it was discovered. When my aunt knew what she had done, she gave a frantic scream, and said, ' Oh, I have killed her ! if only her mother and Dora ' (myself) ' were

To come now to cases where distinct words are heard—in the following example the voice heard was at once connected with a particular person; but still not with the person whom, if the incident be interpreted telepathically, we must regard as the agent. The account was obtained for us by Miss Fripp, of Lulworth House, Hampstead Hill Gardens, from her grandmother, Mrs. Roe.

(152) "Some years since, when in manifestly good health, I was aroused by what appeared to be some one at my bedroom door, calling ' Mary Anne, Mary Anne.' It seemed like my mother's voice, who had been dead two or three years. I roused my husband, but there was no one at the door or anywhere on the same floor. Going upstairs to my son's bedroom, it was so full of smoke that I was nearly suffocated, till I could open the window, when I found my son apparently asleep but quite insensible, till we got him into the air; and then when we aroused him, he remembered when he came up to bed he laid the pipe he had been smoking on a pile of handkerchiefs, which had been put on the dressing-table, and were completely burnt and the table injured, but no flames. Our medical man thought had I not gone in just in time, my son would have been dead.

" MARY ANNE ROE."

In answer to inquiries, Miss Fripp writes :—

"June 25th, 1884.

" I have asked Mrs. Roe the questions you sent me, and I find—

" (1) She has never had other dreams which impressed her in the same way as the two she wrote an account of. [The other dream was about the wreck of her son at sea.]

" (2) My mother was in the house when my grandmother had the warning about the fire. My grandfather told her in the morning that Mrs. Roe insisted on getting out of bed, as she fancied she had heard her mother's voice calling her outside the door.

" (3) There was no smell of smoke in the room ; Mrs. Roe's room was on a different landing, quite apart from her son's room.

" J. FRIPP."

Here again we have a case which might be variously described as an accident or as "special providence," if it stood alone, but which cannot be excluded from our cumulative argument. If telepathic, it

near.' My sister also told me how ardently she had longed for me. I never doubted (for we were deeply attached to each other) but that her longing for me had an influence over me, and that in some way we at home had been made aware of the scream. I was never troubled with morbid fancies."

Here the reference of the sound to a particular person was clearly not due to recognition, but merely to the fact that that person was at the time a special object of solicitude. But in what, it may be asked, is the case weaker than Lord L.'s or Mrs. Purton's, quoted above? The answer is that the fact of a second person's sharing in the experience is a strong (though not a conclusive) argument for supposing the sound to have been a real one, the source of which did not happen to be discovered. It will be seen readily how much more probable this hypothesis is in the present case than, *e.g.*, in the case given above (No. 36) as an example of collective telepathic percipience,—which happened also to be of the " borderland " type.

is a good instance of total unconsciousness on the part of the agent. (See p. 230.)

The next example—received in 1883 from the Rev. Andrew Jukes—resembles the last in that the voice, though recognised, was not that of the agent, but of a person some time deceased. In neither instance is there any reason to regard this feature as other than a purely subjective element supplied by the percipient's own brain—a piece of dream-like investiture in which the telepathic impression clad itself. (See above pp. 341-2, and below, Chap. XIII., § 5.) Mr. Jukes's case, however, differs from the preceding in the important evidential point that the words heard bore a distinct relation to the agent.

"Upper Eglinton Road, Woolwich.

(153) "On Monday, July 31st, 1854, I was at Worksop, staying in the house of Mr. Heming, the then agent there to the Duke of Newcastle. Just as I woke that morning—some would say I was dreaming—I heard the voice of an old schoolfellow (C. C.), who had been dead at least a year or two, saying, 'Your brother Mark and Harriet are both gone.' These words were echoing in my ears as I woke. I seemed to hear them. My brother then was in America; and both were well when I had last heard of them; but the words respecting him and his wife were so vividly impressed upon my mind that before I left my bedroom I wrote them down, then and there, on a scrap of an old newspaper, having no other paper in the bedroom. That same day I returned to Hull, mentioned the circumstance to my wife, and entered the incident, which had made a deep impression on me, in my diary, which I still have. I am as certain as I can well be of anything that the entry is a transcript of what I wrote on the bit of newspaper.

"On the 18th of August (it was before the Atlantic telegraph), I received a line from my brother's wife, Harriet, dated August 1st, saying that Mark had just breathed his last, of cholera; after preaching on Sunday, he had been taken ill with cholera on Monday, and had died on Tuesday morning; that she herself was ill, and that in the event of her death she wished their children should be brought to England. She died the second day after her husband, August 3rd. I immediately started for America, and brought the children home.

"The voice I seemed to hear, and which at first I thought must have been a kind of dream, had such an effect on me that, though the bell rang for breakfast, I did not go down for some time. And all that day, and for days after, I could not shake it off. I had the strongest impression, and indeed conviction, that my brother was gone.

"I ought perhaps to add that we had no knowledge of the cholera being in the neighbourhood of my brother's parish. My impression was that both he and his wife must, if the voice were true, have been taken away by some railway or steamboat accident. But you should notice that at the moment when I seemed to hear this voice my brother was *not* dead. He died early next morning, August 1st, and his wife nearly two days later, namely, August 3rd. I do not profess to explain it—I simply state the facts or the phenomena. But the impression made on me was profound, and the coincidence itself is remarkable.   " ANDREW JUKES."

Mr. Jukes has kindly allowed me to inspect the record in his diary. I had hoped to be able to incorporate this *verbatim* in the account ; but he has private reasons—quite unconnected with the present case—for desiring that this should not be done.

In conversation, I learnt from him that the words he heard formed, in fact, the continuation of a dream, but that the dream had not been about his brother and sister-in-law ; and he has dictated to me the words, " My impression is that the remark passed *while I was awake.*" He has never on any other occasion in his life made a written note of a dream. Asked if he could recall having experienced an auditory hallucination on any other occasion, he replied that he had "never experienced anything of the kind," except that on one occasion he had a subjective impression of hearing music.

Considering the uniqueness of the impression in this case, it is not evidentially important to decide at what exact stage of the waking process the auditory experience took place. That experience may fairly be assigned to the " borderland," on the ground partly of Mr. Jukes's conviction that he was more awake than asleep, and partly of the fact that the supposed agent or agents had not figured in the preceding dream. The time of its occurrence, however, was not that of either of the two critical moments of death in America. If it coincided with any special moment, it must probably have been with the first shock of alarm in the mind of Mrs. Jukes, at the idea of cholera in her household. But this is conjecture only ; we do not know how early on the Monday it was that the first symptoms of illness were apparent ; and the evidential force of the case is so far diminished.

The following example, where the voice was not recognised, presents the interesting point of immediate *repetition*, which we shall encounter in some of the visual cases (see p. 414). The narrator is Miss Thompson, now residing at 7, Place Vaugirard, Paris.

" 106, Boston Street, Hulme, Manchester.
" January 12th, 1884.
(154) " In the autumn of 1873 my cousin Harry, to whom I was engaged, suddenly came to spend a few days with my family, then staying in London. We made a bet for some gloves at parting After paying several visits in the country, he returned to his home in Yorkshire. During this time we had no letter from or news about him.

" On December 18th I awoke in the night, hearing someone earnestly calling me by name. I rose, and went down to my mother's room on the floor beneath, and asked her if she knew who had called me. She said I must have been dreaming, and told me to go back to bed. I did so, and again heard my name called distinctly.   I went again to my mother, who was a little vexed with me, as she feared I should disturb my father, who was sleeping in the room adjoining.   I therefore went back to bed, feeling ill at ease.   I don't think that I fell asleep again, but am not quite sure, but shortly after heard the voice distinctly calling me for the third time.   I was now thoroughly alarmed, and dared not stay upstairs alone, so went again to my mother, and stayed with her the rest of the night.

"The next day we heard that Harry Suddaby had died in the night, from a short attack of bronchitis.   I asked if Harry had called me really, but no one remembered his doing more than sending his love.

"CHRISTINE THOMPSON."

The Register of Deaths gives the date of the death as December 19th, 1873   It no doubt took place in the early hours of the morning.

In answer to inquiries, Miss Thompson writes on April 27, 1885 :—

"I have never had any experience similar to that of which I sent you an account, and am too practical a mortal to believe in anything at all resembling 'visions' or 'hallucinations.'   It was rather against my judgment that I was persuaded to send you the account."

[For Mrs. Thompson's corroboration, see the "Additions and Corrections," which precede Chap. I.]

In the next case—from Mr. Everitt, of Holders Hill, Hendon, and first published in *Light* for Jan., 1883—the voice was recognised. Though remote, the incident is of a sort that might well make a vivid impression.

(155)   "When quite a youth, I had a remarkable experience, in some respects not unlike that which the reprover of Job had.   In the silence and darkness of the night I was suddenly awakened from a deep sleep, and I heard a voice, and I have no doubt that I might have seen a spirit [1] if I had not been, like Eliphaz, so greatly frightened ; but I heard a voice, and that voice I recognised as the voice belonging to the dearest object I had in this world.   I had no reason at the time to believe otherwise than that the person to whom the voice belonged was in good health and many miles from where I was ; yet I heard and recognised the voice of my dear mother, who called me by the familiar name she always used, and strange to say she told me 'she was dead,' and the next post brought the too true and too sad news of her sudden departure from earth-life.

"I have always from a boy up to the present time locked my bedroom door on retiring for the night.   At the time there was no one sleeping in the room but myself.

"I was not in a drowsy state when I woke up, but all my senses were as clear and as vivid as they are now I am writing this ; they could not have been more so if any one shook me and shouted, 'Jump up, the house is on fire.'   Indeed, the feeling and belief was then, and still is, that I was suddenly awakened from a sound sleep by someone in the room, and I felt certain by a slight noise or movement which I heard that there was some-

---

[1] I must note here, as once before in relation to the word "supernatural," that we are in no way responsible for the expressions or views of our informants.

one bending over me ; which feeling was confirmed by the sound of my mother's soft and gentle voice which said 'Tommy' three times in a way as though she wanted or expected me to answer her, and she then said, 'Your mother is dead.'

"You can better imagine my feelings than I can describe them. I told my fellow apprentice in the morning what I had experienced, and said I was afraid that I should hear bad news from home. My father wrote to my eldest brother asking him to call and break the sad news to me, which he did. *I anticipated him by relating what I had heard the previous night.*   "THOMAS EVERITT."

The brother mentioned in this account is dead. In a letter written on the 5th of December, 1884, Mr. Everitt adds :—

"I showed my fellow-apprentice my night-shirt, which was wet with perspiration from covering my head over with the bedclothes; his evidence would be more valuable than my brother's but I have not the remotest knowledge as to where he is, not having seen or heard anything of him for nearly forty years. My wife, even before she was my wife, had often heard me speak of it ; the members of my family have on different occasions heard me refer to it, but all this, of course, would carry but little or no weight with it to the outside public. I only mention it now as showing how sure and certain the experience was."

In answer to further inquiries, Mr. Everitt says :—

"The date of my mother's death was the night of June 1st, 1841. It was the same night that she made me conscious of her presence, and also of her death." The Register of Deaths confirms the date given.

[Mr. Everitt has since had one other auditory hallucination, which also represented his mother's voice.]

The following account is from a gentleman residing at Tynemouth, who has at present a reason, which seems to me a sufficient one, for withholding his name from publication, but will withdraw this restriction after an interval of a few years.   "December, 1884.

(156) "On December 29th, or 30th, 1881, about 1 a.m., I awoke hearing my name called. Nobody was in the house, the servants being away for a holiday. I recognised the voice of my father.

"Next afternoon I received a telegram saying he was unwell, and on arriving I learnt from the doctor that my father had been unconscious, and had repeatedly called for me during the night in question. I had no idea of his illness at the time, and believed him to be perfectly well. The attack was very short and severe. He was in Dumfries, and I at Tynemouth, Northumberland."

In answer to inquiries our informant writes, on December 27, 1884 :—

" I paid no attention to the 'auditory experience,' although the thing came to my mind while dressing, and probably should never have given it further attention, if I had not been struck by the fact that apparently at or about the same time my father, although unconscious, had been calling for me. I had no means of comparing the exact times, as neither the doctor (whose name I forget, and who is now dead) nor I noted them.

This curious coincidence impressed the fact on my mind, the more so as I have never been able to find any reasonable explanation of the case ; and as the tendency of my education has been to believe nothing that can't be accounted for logically, I have almost come to doubt the fact, and in consequence have kept it to myself.[1]

" I never have had, either before or since the case I mentioned already, any hallucination of the senses. It may perhaps have some bearing on the case, so I add this postscript to say that at one time, when in sound health, my father was one of the most skilful amateur mesmerists I ever knew ; his power over some people being quite extraordinary, and sometimes it was exerted almost unconsciously by him."

In the next two cases, the words that the percipient heard seem actually to have been uttered (and, therefore, to have been heard) by the agent ; and we may, if we please, refer the examples to that rarer type where a sensation seems to have been quite literally transferred, as contrasted with the cases where the percipient supplies a sensory embodiment to a less definite telepathic impression.[2]

The first account was sent to us by the Rev. Augustus Field, Vicar of Pool Quay, Welshpool. He describes it as an " Extract of a letter received by me from my brother, Henry C. Field (Surveyor and Civil Engineer), resident at Tutatihika, Wanganni, New Zealand, in reply to letters we had written to him telling about our mother's death." A letter to us from Mr. H. C. Field himself, dated Wanganni, Sept. 25, 1886, gives a completely concordant account.

" March 7th, 1874.

(157) " I was deeply interested in the account of our mother's last illness, and was particularly struck by the circumstance of my name being called, because I heard it. I am not accustomed to dream, and am sure I speak far within the mark when I say that I have not dreamed a dozen times since my marriage, 23 years since. Dreams, too, are supposed to arise from something affecting one's mind, and producing some temporary strong impression, and in this case there was nothing which could affect me in *that* direction, but some quite the reverse.

" Our first horticultural show of the season took place on November 27th. I won several prizes ; and after the show closed at 10 p.m., I had to take home some of my smaller exhibits, and arrange for getting the others home next morning. It was thus near midnight when I reached home, and the only things talked about by —— and myself afterwards were the show and matters of local interest. If anything, therefore, were likely to be on my mind when I fell asleep, it would probably be one or other of the above matters. I do not know how long I slept, but my first

---

[1] A person may very naturally be disposed to keep to himself, and even after a time to doubt, an experience which he cannot fit into any natural scheme ; and this cause has probably prevented many telepathic incidents from becoming known. The presentation of a large collection of cases, and the vindication of their purely natural character, may perhaps do something towards removing this difficulty.

[2] Compare the dream-cases Nos. 112 and 113 ; and several examples in Chapters xiv. and xv.

sleep was over and I was lying in a sort of half-awake, half-asleep state, when I distinctly heard our mother's voice say faintly, 'Harry, Harry!' and when daylight came and I thought the matter over, I wondered what could have possessed me to fancy such a thing.   Our Uncle C. and his family called me Harry, and Uncle B. sometimes did so, and the D.'s also called me Harry, but with these exceptions I was called Henry by all our relations.   It is possible our mother may have called me 'Harry' during my very early childhood, but so long as I can remember she always called our father 'Papa' and me 'Henry.'   It seemed to me, therefore, so utterly absurd that I should fancy her calling me by a name that I never recollected to have heard her use, that I mentally laughed at the idea and wondered how such a thing should have entered my head.   Still the circumstance struck me as so strange that I underlined the date on the margin of my working diary, in order that if anything should occur to corroborate it I might be certain as to the time.   Directly, therefore, after I reached home with S.'s and your letters, I turned to the diary and found the underlined date was November 28th.   It was evidently during the afternoon of November 27th that our mother uttered my name (this would have been so, A. F.); and allowing for the difference of longitude, the time would be early morning of the 28th with us, so that I don't think there can be any question that the call actually reached my ear.   I am only sorry that I was not sufficiently awake to note the *exact* time, but should fancy it to have been between 2 and 3 o'clock in the morning, which would represent a few minutes later on the previous afternoon with you."

The Rev. A. Field adds that in a subsequent portion of the letter his brother refers to a letter written a few weeks earlier, in which he had offered his sister a home, " and says that he believes he was led to do this partly in consequence of the idea which the circumstance he had described had left on his mind, viz., the probable death of our mother."

In his letter to us, Mr. H. C. Field says, " The voice, though not loud, was so distinct that, as I had not time to collect my senses, I started up in bed, expecting to see my mother beside it."   His wife was aroused by this movement, and Mr. Field at once told her of his experience.   He adds that he " is not superstitious," and " hardly knows what it is to dream," which he attributes to his active out-door life.

Miss Field wrote to us in October, 1885 :—

" On 26th November, 1873, while sitting by my mother's bed, I heard her say most plainly, 'Harry, Harry.'   On the following day she died. In course of time we heard from my brother in New Zealand that at a corresponding time (their night) he distinctly heard the same in his mother's voice, and noted the fact in his diary.

"SOPHIA HUGHES FIELD."

Later, the Rev. A. Field sent us the following extract from his diary :—

"November, 1873.

"' Thursday, 27th, arrived in London at 5.30 a.m., by train, to 70, Bassington Road.   Found mother conscious, &c. ; read, &c., with her at frequent intervals through the day.   K. and A. (my brother and sister) arrived.   Gradually weaker, and at last, 5.45 p.m., she passed away.'

" You will understand my object in giving you these full particulars. I myself heard (as I thought) my mother mention my brother's name, and spoke of it to my sister and my aunt. I think they told me that she had mentioned his name several times during her last brief illness. She was seized with paralysis on Wednesday, 26th, and her speech became more and more affected. It was this that made me feel uncertain whether my brother's name was really mentioned in my hearing by my mother or not. In consequence of what my aunt and sister said, I could have no longer any doubt."

[It will be seen that the percipient's impression probably coincided closely with the death, but that Miss Field's written recollections do not confirm (though they do not contradict) her brothers' idea that the name was uttered on the same afternoon.]

The next account is from Mrs. Stent, living at 14, Singapore Road, Ealing Dean, a former valued servant of Miss Craigie, of 8, McGill College Avenue, Montreal. I cite the account which she gave to Miss Craigie, rather than a later one (completely agreeing with it except in one detail) which she wrote for us on June 1, 1885.

(158) " On the 18th of Oct., 1881, I was awakened by hearing myself called twice by an old servant, who was ill in an infirmary in Chelsea. I then heard ' Reggy ' (one of the young gentlemen of the house we had lived together in) called once. It was half-past 4, but I could not sleep so got up and dressed. [Here the later account adds, " I told the housemaid, E. Morris, and we wondered what it meant."] It was impossible for me to go that day to the infirmary, for my present mistress had company ; but I went the next day.   .   .   . She *had* called twice for me and once for ' Reggy,' (so the patient in the next bed informed me,) and *had* died at the hour, half-past 4 the morning before—the precise time I had heard myself called. [The later account adds, " I was not dreaming. I never had anything of the kind happen to me before, and she called us so plain."]   " E. STENT."

In reply to inquiries, Mrs. Stent says that she has lost sight of E. Morris, and adds :—

" Elizabeth Membrey.[the deceased] was my dearest friend, and was more to me than a sister, but was no relation to me—only my dear friend. I think the bond of sympathy was very strong between us; only death could break it. We told our troubles to one another ; for years past we did not do anything without talking about it first. Mr. Reggy was the son of the lady where we lived in service together, and she was very fond of him, and he went to the infirmary to see her as often às he could find time."

The medical superintendent of the Chelsea Infirmary writes to us :—
" I find that Elizabeth Membrey was in this Infirmary from July 15th until October 18th, 1881, when she died."

In conversation, Mrs. Stent (a sensible and sober-minded witness) said that she marked the time of her experience as 4.30, as she heard the half-hour strike just after she got up, and did not sleep again. In her later written account she said that the porter told her the time of death was 20 minutes to 4. But this seems to have been a slip ; as she has found and handed to us a post-card, written to her by Mr. R. W. Craigie (the " Reggy " of the narrative) on the day of the death, as shown by the post-mark—which gives the time as 4.30. Mrs. Stent further mentioned that she was not expecting the death—that her friend had seemed cheerful, and it was thought that she would leave the hospital. She was suffering from an old injury to the base of the skull.

§ 6. I pass now to the cases where the sense of *sight* alone was concerned. The first instance was thus narrated by the Bishop of Carlisle, in the *Contemporary Review* for January, 1884.

(159) " A Cambridge student, my informant, had arranged, some years ago, with a fellow student that they should meet together in Cambridge at a certain time for the purpose of reading. A short time before going up to keep his appointment, my informant was in the South of England. Waking in the night, he saw, as he imagined, his friend sitting at the foot of his bed. He was surprised at the sight, the more so as his friend was dripping with water. He spoke, but the apparition (for so it seems to have been) only shook its head and disappeared. This appearance of the absent friend occurred twice during the night. Information was soon received that shortly before the time of the apparition being seen by the young student, his friend had been drowned whilst bathing."

Having learned that the Bishop's informant was Archdeacon Farler, we applied to this gentleman, who wrote to us on Jan. 9, 1884 :—

" Pampisford Vicarage, Cambridge.

" The fact of having witnessed the vision was mentioned the next morning at breakfast, several days before I received the news of my friend's death, to my tutor, John Kempe, Esq., his wife, and family. Mr. and Mrs. Kempe are now dead, but it is probable his family might remember the circumstance, although they were but children at the time. I was staying at Long Ashton, in Somersetshire ; my friend died in Kent.[1] As I did not feel frightened at the time of the vision, I have always spoken of it rather as a singular dream than an apparition.

" The date of my vision was either the 2nd or 3rd of September, 1878,[2] but I have not my memoranda with me to be quite sure. I also saw the vision again about the 17th of the month. These are my sole experiences of an apparition. I have never experienced any sort of sensory hallucination.   " J. P. FARLER."

We find from the Register of Deaths that the narrator's friend was drowned in the river Crouch, on Sept. 2, 1868.

Mr. W. J. Kempe writes to us, from Long Ashton School, (1885), that Archdeacon Farler certainly told him of the occurrence, but he does not remember exactly when. Other members of the family, who have been applied to, were either away from home at the time, or too young to be told of the matter.

[1] This is clearly a slip ; in another letter Archdeacon Farler gives the name of a village in Essex as the place where the death occurred.
[2] This is an error. The year was first written 1888, and then, by an obvious slip, the second 8 was altered to a 7, instead of to a 6. Mr. J. Kempe died in 1874.

Here the repetition during the night reminds us of several of the dream-examples, and of case 154 above. The feature in waking cases is of special interest. For repetition after a short interval is an occasional feature of *purely subjective* hallucinations ;[1] and this point may be added to many others which will occupy us hereafter, showing the fundamental identity, in relation to the percipient's senses, of subjective and telepathic phantasms. The subsequent vision on the 17th may be attributed to the emotional excitement of the recent bereavement.[2]

The feature of repetition occurs again in the next case. The percipient, Major A. P. Scott Moncrieff, is dead ; but his widow, who describes his experience, was cognisant of it before the news of the death arrived. She wrote on May 20, 1885 :—

"14, Gilmore Place, Edinburgh.

(160) "The circumstances of the dream or vision, as far as I can remember at this distance of time, were these. A. awoke me one night, and said, 'I have had a strange dream about S., and I fancied I saw her standing at the foot of the bed ; indeed, I had to rub my eyes to convince myself that she was not really there.' He fell asleep, and again dreamt the same, and this made a powerful impression upon his mind, with almost a depressing effect. He was in perfect health at the time, and of a thoroughly practical nature ; not at all given to sentimentality. He had also no reason to believe that S. was in frail health. Some weeks after, the news came of her death, and by comparing dates, and allowing for the difference of time between India and Scotland, the event must have taken place during the period of these dreams ; but whether at the time of the first or the second, I cannot remember. This happened on the 7th September, 1852.   "ELIZABETH H. S. MONCRIEFF."

Mr. R. Scott Moncrieff, of 4, Mardale Crescent, Edinburgh, writes to us :—

"I very well remember my brother, the late Major A. P. Scott Moncrieff (whose widow has written the preceding narrative) telling me of this apparition, as he believed it to have been, of our sister Susan, after the news reached us of her death in Edinburgh, on September 7th, 1852. I was living in Calcutta at that date ; my brother was with his regiment at Dinapore. In the month of November, I was on a visit to his house in Hazareebagh, where he was then living with his wife ; and it was then that he told me of the apparition. As he was a man of a very unromantic, practical character, always ready to ridicule a ghost story, I was the more struck with the depth of the impression left on his mind by the vividness of the apparition, as he believed it to have been, which had led to his taking a note of the date in writing.

---

[1] See Chapter xii., § 10. In Dr. Jessopp's experience (*Athenæum* for Jan. 10, 1880), the figure which he saw disappeared suddenly, and reappeared after about five minutes ; and my own collection includes a very similar case. See Vol. ii., p. 237, note.

[2] See Chapter xi., § 6 ; but see also the remarks on Mr. Keulemans' case, p. 445.

"He told me that after having been asleep for a time, during the night of that date (which must have been the 7th September), he awoke, feeling the heat rather trying; that he saw, by a light burning in the room, the punkah swinging above the bed, and then saw our sister Susan standing at the foot of the bed, gazing at him very earnestly; that he was so surprised, he sat up, rubbed his eyes, and looked again, seeing her still there, that he exclaimed, 'O, Susan!' (I think he added, 'what are you doing here?' but I am not certain that these were his words; though I am certain that he did utter some such words after saying, 'O, Susan!'); that his wife awoke on hearing him speak, and said, 'What is it, Alick?' or words of similar import; but that he, fearing lest, in the state of health she was then in, it might prove injurious to her to be told what he believed he had seen, said he had awakened from a dream, but did not tell her how fully he was convinced he had been awake when he saw the apparition of his sister, which had disappeared before his wife had spoken to him.   "R. SCOTT MONCRIEFF."

Miss Scott Moncrieff, of 44, Shooter's Hill Road, S.E., writes :—

"I heard the same account from my brother, Major Scott Moncrieff, on his return from India.   "MARY ANNE SCOTT MONCRIEFF."

[As a matter of form, we have verified the date of death, in the obituary of the *Scotsman.* But such verification of course adds nothing unless the date of the percipient's experience is *independently* remembered.]

The next example is from Miss Barr, of East Grinstead, who has been already mentioned (p. 342).

"1884.

(161) "On the night of January —, 1871, I awoke up with the idea that someone was moving by the bedside. I was a little frightened, and I saw the curtain at the side of the bed slightly pulled aside, and a hand, with the back turned towards me, appearing round the curtain. I recognised the ring on the hand as that of my cousin and dear friend [Captain C. M.]. I told my sister in the morning that I had seen a hand,[1] wearing a ring, but did not tell her that I had recognised the ring, as I did not care to make too much of the incident. On that day, as we learnt from a letter received a few days afterwards, my cousin died in Canada, from the effect of an accident.   "L. BARR."

Mrs. and Miss Harriet Barr also attest with their signatures the fact that the vision was narrated before the news of the death was received.

Miss L. Barr afterwards stated that she thought the death "must have been on or about the 6th of January, 1870;" and we find from the *Indian Army List,* and from the *Times* obituary, that it took place on that day, at Halifax, Nova Scotia. She tells us that she has experienced in her life only one other hallucination, which occurred in close connection with a bereavement (see p. 510).

We have received the following account from our friend Mr. J. A. Symonds.

---

[1] On this fragmentary form of apparition, see Chap. xi., § 4, and Vol. ii., p. 33, note.

"Davos, 1882.

(162) " I was a boy in the Sixth Form at Harrow ; and, as head of Mr.
Rendall's house, had a room to myself. It was in the summer of 1858. I
woke about dawn, and felt for my books upon a chair between the bed
and the window ; when I knew that I must turn my head the other way,
and there, between me and the door, stood Dr. Macleane, dressed in a
clergyman's black clothes. He bent his sallow face a little towards me
and said, ' I am going a long way—take care of my son.' While I was
attending to him, I suddenly saw the door in the place where Dr. Macleane
had been. Dr. Macleane died that night (at what hour I cannot precisely
say) at Clifton. My father, who was a great friend of his, was with him.
I was not aware that he was more than usually ill. He was a chronic
invalid. "JOHN ADDINGTON SYMONDS."

We learn from the Rev. D. Macleane, of Codford St. Peter, Bath, that
his father, Dr. Macleane, " died at Clifton at a quarter before 6 a.m., on
May 14th, 1858."

[Mr. Symonds has had one or two purely subjective visions when in a
waking state.]

The following case is from the Rev. W. J. Ball, of 6, Pemberton
Terrace, Cambridge. It is apparently a good example of the vivid
survival of a dream-image into waking moments—an experience
which Mr. Ball tells us he cannot recollect to have occurred to him
on any other occasion.

"1884.

(163) " During my college days I had a very dear and intimate chum,
R. F. Dombrain. We used to walk together, read together, pray together,
and would have thought it wrong to keep any secret from each other. We
hoped to go together into the foreign mission-field ; but my friend was
ready to go before I was, and it was while he was in London making
arrangements about going abroad, that he was seized with a very bad fever,
and his life for some time despaired of. At last he recovered and returned
to Dublin, where I saw him several times. He was not quite restored to
health, but I hoped he would soon be so. This was the state of things
when I went down to the County Limerick, in the spring of 1853. I
received a few letters from my friend which told me of gradually improving
health. I was busily occupied about my mission work at the village of
Doon, and felt perfectly at ease about my dear friend's recovery.

" A few days had elapsed without any tidings reaching me, when on
the morning of the 14th of April I had the most vivid dream I remember
ever to have seen. I seemed to be walking with young Dombrain, amidst
some beautiful scenery, when suddenly I was brought to a waking condition
by a sort of light appearing before me. I started up in my bed, and saw
before me, in his ordinary dress and appearance, my friend, who seemed to
be passing from earth towards the light above. He seemed to give me
one loving smile, and I felt that his look contained an expression of
affectionate separation and farewell. Then I leaped out of bed, and
cried with a loud voice, ' Robert, Robert,' and the vision was gone.

2 D

"In the house there was sleeping a young servant boy, whose name was also Robert. He came running into my room, saying that my loud cry had awakened him from sound sleep, and that he thought I was ill. The whole scene was so impressed upon my mind that I felt the death of my friend just as really as if I had been by his bedside, and seen him pass away. I had looked at my watch and found the time 3 minutes past 5. I knew that at that moment my friend's spirit had passed from his body. I could think of nothing else. A class of Scripture readers came to me at 10 o'clock that morning. I told them I could not speak to them of the appointed subject, but must tell them what had occurred, and for a long time I lectured them entirely on the subject of the future state, and the separation of the soul from the body. During the whole of the day the same sad gloom weighed down my mind which I should have felt had I been with my friend at his death-bed. I wrote to my sister asking for particulars, and I wished to know the exact time the death had taken place. Never once did the slightest doubt cross my mind that my friend had died.

"The following morning I received a letter from my sister, stating that for a few days Mr. Dombrain had not been so well, and that at 3 minutes past 5 in the morning he had quietly passed away from this world. Since then I have very often mentioned the circumstance to friends, and the deep impression made by the event can never pass from my mind."

Mr. Ball wrote to ask his sister for her recollections. Her reply contained the following passage, the original of which was sent to us :—

"12, Upper Leeson Street, Dublin.

"July 17th, 1884.

"I have not a distinct remembrance of the dream. I have heard you allude to it from time to time, and feel *quite confident* of its reality.

"S. P. BALL."

We find from the obituary in the *Gentleman's Magazine* that Mr. Dombrain's death took place at Dublin, on April 14th, 1853.

The appearance of *light* in this case is to be noted (see cases 178 and 184 below).

The next account is from the Rev. C. C. Wambey, of Salisbury, the narrator of case 129.

"April, 1884.

(164) "Mr. B., with whom I was intimately acquainted before he left England, was appointed to the mathematical mastership in Elizabeth College, Guernsey. Some 10 years after his appointment, I accepted a temporary sole charge in the island, and renewed my acquaintance with my quondam friend; indeed, I was with him some portion of nearly each day during my stay in Guernsey. After my return to England, we maintained a regular correspondence. In the last letter I had from him, he described himself as being in unusually good health and spirits.

"One morning I surprised my wife by telling her that poor B. was dead—that he had appeared to me in the night. She endeavoured to assuage my grief, suggesting that the apparition, whatever it may have been, was due to my indisposition. I had been ailing for some time. I answered that I had received too certain intelligence of my friend's death.

"A few days subsequently, I had a letter in a black-edged envelope, bearing the Guernsey postmark. In that letter Mrs. B. told me that her husband had died after a few hours' illness, and that during that illness he *frequently spoke of me*."

In answer to inquiries, Mr. Wambey says :—

"I have seen other forms than that I have mentioned. My grandfather appeared to me on the night in which he died; but I was in the house at the time, and he had been sinking for many hours. [The only other case—the subjective vision of an unrecognised figure—took place when Mr. Wambey was reading late at night, at a time when he was seriously overtaxed by work.]

"From his widow's letter I ascertained that Mr. B. died the night in which he appeared to me. I was awake—I could hardly have been deluded on this point—when my friend appeared to me. I did not notice his dress, I was so engrossed with his face—his look. Mrs. Wambey endorses the statement that I told her next morning I had seen my friend, and that I was sure he was dead. I think it was in 1870."

We learn from a son of Mr. B.'s that the date of his father's death was October 27th, 1870.

Mrs. Wambey, writing on May 17, 1884, corroborates as follows :—

"My husband, the Rev. C. C. Wambey, the morning after he had seen Mr. B., mentioned the circumstance to me, and with much grief expressed his firm conviction that his friend was dead.   "M. B. WAMBEY."

Our informant in the next case, Captain P., withholds his name from publication, as the percipient would object to its appearance. It will be seen that she admits the occurrence.

"December, 1884.

(165) "Some time at the end of 1868, I was discussing with a lady of my acquaintance the question of making compacts to appear after death. I doubted whether such compacts could be fulfilled ; she stoutly maintained that they could be. Finally we agreed to make such a compact ourselves —that whichever of us first died should appear after death to the other.[1]

"At the beginning of the next year I went on a voyage in the merchant ship 'Edmund Graham,' of Greenock, to Australia, and on the 22nd of June, when we were between the Cape of Good Hope and Australia (lat. 40° S., long. 22 E.), and the ship running before a heavy gale of wind, the sea swept over the deck and washed 7 of us, myself among the number, overboard. I gave myself up for lost, and I remember well that I thought of the panorama of their past lives which drowning men are said to see, and hoped that the show would commence. Then I regretted I was without my oilskin, as the water would have time to wet me through before death, and I expected to find it very cold ; as far as I can recollect, this was all that passed through my mind. The next moment I caught hold of a loose rope that was hanging from the ship, and hauled myself on deck. The others were drowned. This took place between 3 and 4 a.m.

[1] See Vol. ii., p. 66.

on June 22nd.[1] A few months afterwards I had a letter at Bombay, from my friend, in which she mentioned that on the night of the 22nd June she had seen me in her room.

"When I saw her again, I received from her a full account of the circumstances. She told me that she woke up suddenly in the night, and saw me at the other end of the room, and that I advanced towards her. Whether she noticed the dress which I was wearing I cannot say. I have often since heard her describe the incident. As far as I can recollect, she told me the precise time of the appearance ; and my belief is that it coincided in time with my being washed overboard. Though I cannot recollect calculating the difference of time, by reference to the longitude, I think it most likely that I did do so and found the times to correspond. I was certainly, at that time, quite alive to the fact that 22° of longitude would make a sensible difference in the apparent time.   "M. P."

The following is a portion of a letter from the percipient to Captain P. :—

"I enclose the papers you gave me to look at the other night, and in looking over the printed notes of the Society, I see (as a Catholic) I can have nothing to do with it.

"You can tell your friend the reason I decline saying anything about it is because I am a Papist, and that I consider those sort of things much too sacred to make the topic of conversation at any modern scientific meeting."

These last remarks exemplify what was said above (p. 130) as to a particular class of obstacles which our investigation has to encounter, and which we can only trust to time to remove.

The next case is one of the very few which is here quoted from a previous collection. It was first published by Mr. Dale Owen, in his *Footfalls on the Boundary of Another World,* pp. 299-303. One of us has seen the percipient, Mrs. Wheatcroft, who, however, finds herself precluded by family reasons from giving any further account.

(166) "For the following narrative I am indebted to the kindness of London friends. Of the good faith of the narrators there cannot be a doubt.

"In the month of September, 1857, Captain G. W., of the 6th Dragoon Guards, went out to India to join his regiment. His wife remained in England, residing at Cambridge. On the night between the 14th and 15th of November, 1857, towards morning, she dreamed that she saw her husband, looking anxious and ill, upon which she immediately awoke, much agitated. It was bright moonlight ; and looking up, she perceived the same figure standing by her bedside. He appeared in his uniform, the hands pressed across the breast, the hair dishevelled, the face very pale. His large dark eyes were fixed full upon her ; their expression was that of great excitement, and there was a peculiar contraction of the mouth, habitual to him when agitated. She saw him, even to each minute particular of his dress, as distinctly as she

---

[1] By this the narrator undoubtedly meant "on the night of June 22-23," as he believes the coincidence to have been exact.

had ever done in her life ; and she remembers to have noticed between his hands the white of the shirt-bosom, unstained, however, with blood. The figure seemed to bend forward, as if in pain, and to make an effort to speak ; but there was no sound. It remained visible, the wife thinks, as long as a minute, and then disappeared.

"Her first idea was to ascertain if she was actually awake. She rubbed her eyes with the sheet, and felt that the touch was real. Her little nephew was in bed with her : she bent over the sleeping child, and listened to its breathing ; the sound was distinct ; and she became convinced that what she had seen was no dream. It need hardly be added that she did not again go to sleep that night.

"Next morning she related all this to her mother, expressing her conviction, though she had noticed no marks of blood on his dress, that Captain W. was either killed or grievously wounded. So fully impressed was she with the reality of that apparition that she thenceforth refused all invitations. A young friend urged her, soon afterwards, to go with her to a fashionable concert, reminding her that she had received from Malta, sent by her husband, a handsome dress cloak, which she had never yet worn. But she positively declined, declaring that, uncertain as she was whether she was not already a widow, she would never enter a place of amusement until she had letters from her husband (if, indeed, he still lived) of later date than the 14th of November.

"It was on a Tuesday, in the month of December, 1857, that the telegram regarding the actual fate of Captain W. was published in London. It was to the effect that he was killed before Lucknow on the *fifteenth* of November.

"This news, given in the morning paper, attracted the attention of Mr. Wilkinson, a London solicitor, who had in charge Captain W.'s affairs. When, at a later period, this gentleman met the widow, she informed him that she had been quite prepared for the melancholy news, but that she felt sure her husband could not have been killed on the 15th of November, inasmuch as it was during the night between the 14th and 15th that he appeared to herself.[1]

"The certificate from the War Office, however, which it became Mr. Wilkinson's duty to obtain, confirmed the date given in the telegram, its tenor being as follows :—

· No. 9,579.   ' War Office.

'January 30th, 1858.

'These are to certify that it appears, by the records in this office, that Captain G. W., of the 6th Dragoon Guards [a mistake, as Mr. Dale Owen points out, for 6th (Inniskilling) Dragoons], was killed in action on the 15th November, 1857.   (Signed)   ' B. Hawes.'

"While Mr. Wilkinson's mind remained in uncertainty as to the exact date, a remarkable incident occurred, which seemed to cast further suspicion on the accuracy of the telegram and of the certificate. That

---

[1] The difference of longitude between London and Lucknow being about 5 hours, 3 or 4 o'clock a.m. in London would be 8 or 9 o'clock a.m. at Lucknow. But it was in the *afternoon*, not in the morning, as will be seen in the sequel, that Captain W. was killed. Had he fallen on the 15th, therefore, the apparition to his wife would have appeared several hours before the engagement in which he fell, and while he was yet alive and well. —[R.D.O.]

gentleman was visiting a friend, whose lady has all her life had perception of apparitions, while her husband is what is usually called an
impressible medium; facts which are known, however, only to their
intimate friends. Though personally acquainted with them, I am not at
liberty to give their names. Let us call them Mr. and Mrs. N.

"Mr. Wilkinson related to them, as a wonderful circumstance, the
vision of the Captain's widow in connection with his death, and described
the figure as it had appeared to her. Mrs. N. turning to her
husband, instantly said :—

"'That must be the very person I saw the evening we were talking
of India, and you drew an elephant with a howdah on his back. Mr.
Wilkinson has described his exact position and appearance; the uniform
of a British officer, his hands pressed across his breast, his form bent
forward as if in pain. The figure,' she added to Mr. W., 'appeared
just behind my husband, and seemed looking over his left shoulder.'"

[Mr. and Mrs. N., who were Spiritualists, then obtained what purported to be a message from their strange visitant, saying that he had
been killed that afternoon by a wound in the breast; but the message
may perfectly well have been the automatic result of their own ideas, as it
contained nothing beyond what they might have guessed from the
nature of the apparition. This occurred at 9 in the evening; and the
date was fixed as the *fourteenth* of November, by the date on a bill which
was receipted, as it was remembered, on the same evening.]

"This confirmation of the widow's conviction as to the day of her
husband's death produced so much impression on Mr. Wilkinson that he
called at the office of Messrs. Cox and Greenwood, the army agents, to
ascertain if there was no mistake in the certificate. But nothing there
appeared to confirm any surmise of inaccuracy. Captain W.'s death was
mentioned in two separate despatches of Sir Colin Campbell; and in both
the date corresponded with that given in the telegram.

"So matters rested, until, in the month of March, 1858, the family of
Captain W. received from Captain G. C., then of the Military Train, a
letter dated near Lucknow, on the 19th December, 1857. This letter
informed them that Captain W. had been killed before Lucknow, while
gallantly leading on the squadron, not on the 15th of November, as
reported in Sir Colin Campbell's despatches, but on the *fourteenth in the
afternoon*. Captain C. was riding close by his side at the time he saw him
fall. He was struck by a fragment of shell in the breast, and never spoke
after he was hit. He was buried at the Dilkoosha; and on a wooden
cross erected by his friend, Lieutenant R., of the 9th Lancers, at the head
of his grave, are cut the initials G. W., and the date of his death, the 14th
of November, 1857.[1]

"The War Office finally made the correction as to the date of death,
but not until more than a year after the event occurred. Mr. Wilkinson,
having occasion to apply for an additional copy of the certificate in
April, 1859, found it in exactly the same words as that which I have

[1] It was not in his own regiment, which was then at Meerut, that Captain W. was
serving at the time of his death. Immediately on arriving from England at Cawnpore, he
had offered his services to Colonel Wilson, of the 64th. They were at first declined, but
finally accepted, and he joined the Military Train, then starting for Lucknow. It was in
their ranks that he fell. [R. D. O.]

given, only that the 14th of November had been substituted for the 15th.[1]

" This extraordinary narrative was obtained by me directly from the parties themselves. The widow of Captain W. kindly consented to examine and correct the manuscript, and allowed me to inspect a copy of Captain C.'s letter, giving the particulars of her husband's death. To Mr. Wilkinson also the manuscript was submitted, and he assented to its accuracy so far as he is concerned. That portion which relates to Mrs. N. I had from that lady herself. I have neglected no precaution, therefore, to obtain for it the warrant of authenticity.

" It is especially valuable, as furnishing an example of a double apparition. Nor can it be alleged (even if the allegation had weight) that the recital of one lady caused the apparition of the same figure to the other. Mrs. W. was at the time in Cambridge, and Mrs. N. in London ; and it was not till weeks after the occurrence that either knew what the other had seen.

" Those who would explain the whole on the principle of chance coincidence have a treble event to take into account ; the apparition to Mrs. N., that to Mrs. W., and the actual time of Captain W.'s death, each tallying exactly with the other."

Mr. Wilkinson, of Winton House, Ealing, W., writes to us :—

"November 5th, 1884.

" Mr. Robert Dale Owen personally investigated the case, and submitted the messages to Captain Wheatcroft's widow. I revised the part belonging to me, and that part which referred to the appearance to Mrs. Nenner was revised by her and her husband, Professor Nenner. I gave the original certificates of death by the War Office to Mr. Owen.

" W. M. WILKINSON."

[The Mr. N. mentioned was the Rev. Maurice Nenner, Professor of Hebrew at the Nonconformist College, St. John's Wood. Both Mr. and Mrs. Nenner are dead.

It should be observed that there was no provable recognition of Captain Wheatcroft by Mrs. Nenner. We only know of the following points to connect her vision with Captain Wheatcroft's death :—Similarity of attitude ; uniform of a British officer ; wound in the breast ; date ; and, apart from Mrs. Wheatcroft's vision, there is nothing remarkable in this combination. But it is certainly curious that on that day she should have had a vision which corresponded, at least up to a certain point, with what Mrs. Wheatcroft saw.[2]

We do not know the hour of Captain Wheatcroft's death, as he may

---

[1] The originals of both these certificates are in my possession ; the first bearing date 30th January, 1858, and certifying, as already shown, to the 15th ; the second dated 5th April, 1859, and testifying to the 14th. [R. D. O.]

[2] There is another curious incident, connected with this case. In a letter written on July 28th, 1876, to the Rev. B. Wrey Savile, and kindly sent by him to me, a clergyman of the Midland counties gives permission to use his wife's testimony to the fact that Captain Wheatcroft "appeared, on the date named, to an old playfellow and friend of his "— herself. I have corresponded with the clergyman in question, but further details cannot now be procured.

not have died the moment that he was struck. If the death was immediate, it must have preceded Mrs. Wheatcroft's vision by at least 12 hours. See p. 140, note.]

The next account was received, in 1883, from M. de Guérin, now residing at 98, Sandgate Road, Folkestone. It is impossible to be certain that the coincidence was as close as the narrator imagines; but the presumption is to some extent favoured by the fact that he was the percipient in a similar but more remarkable case, which will be cited in a later chapter (No. 315).

(167) "My brother Henry died in Exeter in July, 1855. I was then on a voyage home [from Shanghai]. I was very ill at the time. We were within one or two degrees of the line, fearfully hot. I had been in bed about a couple of hours and was wide awake, when I saw an almost exactly similar vision [*i.e.*, similar to the other case referred to] of Henry. I immediately called out to my fellow passenger : 'Frank, my brother Henry is dead, I have just seen him.' I wrote to this gentleman [Mr. Francis L. Brine, Finsbury Distillery, Finsbury Square] to ask if he remembered anything about it. He replies : 'Too many years have rolled by since to enable me to recall the details to which you refer, but I believe every word of it. When my father died, I wrote to my sister in India, and she wrote back to say, "I knew of our sad loss at the time it occurred ; dear father came to wish me good-bye also."'[1] "WM. C. L. DE GUERIN."

In conversation, Mr. de Guérin told the present writer that he believes his brother to have died on the day of the vision. We find from the Registrar of Deaths that the death took place on July 19th, 1855 ; but the day of the vision cannot now be independently fixed. It occurred at about 11 p.m., near the island of Ranbon, which is almost exactly antipodal to England ; and the death took place at 3 p.m.; so that, if the day was the same, the vision preceded his death by some 4 hours. Mr. de Guérin knew his brother to have been suffering from a lingering illness, but had no immediate apprehension of the end. He had last heard of him in April.

---

[1] Mr. Brine has kindly sent us a letter from his sister (who is too much out of health to be questioned in detail) in which the following passage occurs :—

"You remember my seeing poor father when he was dying. And you must have heard our poor mother speak of her brother, when at Bishop's Waltham school, seeing his father (our grandfather) when dying. When he was sent for his remark was, ' I know what I have to go home for ; my father is dead ; I saw him pull the bed-curtain aside in the night.' " Another sister of Mr. Brine's mentions a still more striking experience of her own, which should have been a good case, as she at once wrote down the date of her seeing the phantasm ; but she declines further correspondence.

As bearing on this family susceptibility to telepathic influences, I may mention that a sister of Mr. de Guérin's was a joint percipient with him in the case which is to be cited later ; and also that Mr. de Guerin told me that there had been similar instances in their mother's (the Read) family ; one of whom (Mr. de Guérin's grandfather) had seen a phantasmal hearse drive up to his father's door on the morning that the father died—he himself not knowing of the death or of its imminence, as he was not staying at the house and was approaching it as a visitor. This incident does not now admit of verification ; but we shall find further on that quite as *bizarre* experiences can be telepathically explained (see Chap. xii., § 7).

The next narrative is of a more uncommon character. There are reasonable grounds, in this instance, for withholding the name of the narrator, Mrs. T., from publicity.

"1883.

(168) "On November 18th, 1863, I was living near Adelaide, and not long recovered from a severe illness at the birth of an infant, who was then 5 months old. My husband had also suffered from neuralgia, and had gone to stay with friends at the seaside for the benefit of bathing. One night during his absence the child woke me about midnight; having hushed him off to sleep, I said, 'Now, sir, I hope you will let me rest!' I lay down, and instantly became conscious of two figures standing at the door of my room. One, M. N. [these are not the real initials], whom I recognised at once, was that of a former lover, whose misconduct and neglect had compelled me to renounce him. Of this I am sure, that if ever I saw him in my life, it was then. I was not in the least frightened; but said to myself, as it were, 'You never used to wear that kind of waistcoat.' The door close to where he stood was in a deep recess close to the fireplace, for there was no grate; we burnt logs only. In that recess stood a man in a tweed suit. I saw the whole figure distinctly, but not the face, and for this reason : on the edge of the mantelshelf always stood a morocco leather medicine chest, which concealed the face from me. (On this being stated to our friends, the Singletons, they asked to go into the room and judge for themselves. They expressed themselves satisfied that would be the case to anyone on the bed where I was.) I had an impression that this other was a cousin of M. N.'s, who had been the means of leading him astray while in the North of England. I never saw him in my life; he died in India.

"M. N. was in deep mourning; he had a look of unutterable sorrow upon his face, and was deadly pale. He never opened his lips, but I read his heart as if it were an open book, and it said, 'My father is dead, and I have come into his property.' I answered, 'How much you have grown like your father!' Then in a moment, *without appearing to walk*, he stood at the foot of the child's cot, and I saw *distinctly* the blueness of his eyes as he gazed on my boy, and then raised them to Heaven as if in prayer.

"All vanished. I looked round and remarked a trivial circumstance, viz., that the brass handles of my chest of drawers had been rubbed very bright. Not till then was I conscious of having seen a spirit,[1] but a feeling of awe (not fear) came over me, and I prayed to be kept from harm, although there was no reason to dread it. I slept tranquilly, and in the morning I went across to the parsonage and told the clergyman's wife what I had seen. She, of course, thought it was merely a dream. But no—if it were a dream, should I not have seen him *as I had known him*, a young man of 22, without beard or whiskers?[2] But there was all the difference that 16 years would make in a man's aspect.

"On Saturday my husband returned, and my brother having ridden out to see us on Sunday afternoon, I told them both my vision as we sat together on the verandah. They treated it so lightly that I determined

---

[1] See p. 409, note.
[2] *Cf.* cases 194, 449, 515.

to write it down in my diary and see if the news were verified. And from that diary I am now quoting. Also I mentioned it to at least 12 or 14 other people, and bid them wait the result.

"And surely enough, at the end of several weeks, my sister-in-law wrote that M. N.'s father died at C—— Common on November 18th, 1863, which exactly tallied with the date of the vision. He left £45,000 to be divided between his son and daughter, but the son has never been found.

"Many people in Adelaide heard the story before the confirmation came, and I wrote and told M. N.'s mother. She was much distressed about it, fearing he was unhappy. She is now dead. My husband was profoundly struck when he saw my diary corresponding *exactly* to the news in the letter I had that moment received in his presence."

Mrs. T. states that she has never experienced a hallucination of vision on any other occasion.

Mr. T. has confirmed to us the accuracy of this narrative; and Mrs. T. has shown to one of us a memorandum of the appearance of two figures under date November 18th, in her diary of the year 1863; and a newspaper obituary confirms this as the date of the death. We learn from a gentleman who is a near relative of M. N.'s, that M. N., though long lost sight of, was afterwards heard of, and outlived his father.

If we regard this vision as telepathic, the agent can apparently only have been the dying man; and the case would then seem to be an extreme instance of the very rare type where the agent's personality does not appear, but some idea or picture in his mind is reproduced in the percipient's mind with a force that leads to an actual percept. For, as the narrator herself suggests, had she bodied forth the idea of M. N. from her own unaided resources, she would almost certainly have pictured him with the aspect that had been familiar to her. But though we have to draw on the father's mind for the unfamiliar features, we must not forget the possibilities of agency below the threshold of consciousness (pp. 78-9, 230). And it is at least worth suggesting that the percipient's mind brought its own affinities to bear—exercised, so to speak, a selective influence; and that thus it was rather owing to her special interest in the son than to the conscious occupation of his father's mind with him, that the telepathic impulse which was able to affect her took this particular form. As to the appearance of the *second figure*, it may possibly have been also telepathically produced; but I prefer to lay stress on it simply as one of the numerous indications that these waking percepts are really dream-creations, not objective presences.

We obtained the next case through the kindness of Miss Beale, Principal of the Ladies' College, Cheltenham, to whom it was sent some years ago by the narrator, Miss T. J. C.

(169) " When I was between 13 and 14, I went to spend a few days at the house of some friends, where I shared a room with a companion a year older. Happening to awake one night, I saw distinctly the figure of a man (in what might have been a loose dressing-gown) standing before the dressing-table with his back towards the bed, and holding out one hand as if feeling his way. I remember rubbing my eyes to convince myself I was not dreaming, and on my looking up a minute after, the figure was gone. This startled me, and I awoke my companion. She, however, tried to persuade me it must have been her brother (the only man in the house), and that he had probably come in to look what o'clock it was by an old watch which always stood on the dressing-table, and was considered a great authority in the house. (I forgot to say there was bright moonlight shining into the room.) Only half convinced I fell asleep again, and at breakfast next morning asked C. (my companion's brother) what he had been doing in our room the previous night. He said he had certainly not been there, but asked what I had seen, and on my telling him, looked so startled and pained that I did not pursue the subject.

" A few days after this, his mother told me that C. had seen the figure in his room the same night on which I had seen it in mine, and had recognised it as that of a very great friend and old shipmate of his own. When C. left the navy on account of ill-health, this friend got leave to spend a few days on shore with him, and on parting with him, said, ' Well, whoever dies first will come and see the other.' On the day on which Mrs. B. spoke to me of the occurrence, C. had heard of the death of his old shipmate. It had taken place on board ship, off the coast of Spain, on the night on which the apparition was seen by C. and myself.

" T. J. C."

Miss C. writes to us :—

" 1, Clarendon Place, Stirling.
" February 28th, 1884.

" The above story was sent by me to Miss Beale some years ago. The ' C.' mentioned in it has been dead for many years, and his mother's memory is so much impaired by age and infirmity as to make her evidence of no value. I do not know that I can add anything to what I have already written. The occurrence is as fresh in my memory as when it happened. I was almost a child at the time, and no idea of my having seen a spirit ever entered my head, until Mrs. B. spoke to me of the death of her son's friend. The two rooms (the one in which ' C.' slept and that in which my companion and I slept) were on the same floor, and near each other."

In conversation, Miss C. told me that she had never experienced a hallucination of vision on any other occasion. The figure which she saw corresponded with " C." 's description of what he saw, except that she did not see the face.

This case, if correctly reported, contains the remarkable feature of double percipience ; which, however, will be more conveniently discussed at a later stage (Chap. XVIII.). Evidentially, I may observe, the narrator's recollection of what she learnt about " C." 's experience makes it more probable that she is accurate as to the coincidence, than if she were merely recalling a childish experience of her own.

We owe the following case to the Rev. T. Williams, Rector of Aston-Clinton, Tring. The first note, written down by Mr. Williams from his sister's account of the occurrence, was copied from his diary by the present writer.

(170) "Mrs. Stewart, sister-in-law of Jane, my sister's servant, came up to ask if any news from home. She said, with her husband in bed—moonlight—chest of drawers between window—saw her mother standing—felt perfectly awake—she hid her face—a third time looked up—heard [? saw] nothing, but heard men calling up—knew exact time. She came up to my sister's and related this the same day—said dreading to hear knock at door all day—fearing to hear of something having happened to her mother. Her friends, who lived at Church Stretton, came a month after to christening of her baby ; in mourning—said mother's sister, who exact image of her mother, had died at the very time of her vision—but friends did not tell Mrs. Stewart, because of her condition. This written from my sister's account, who saw Mrs. Stewart on the day of the vision, and heard account of what seen from herself." The date 1880 is added.

The following account is from the husband of the percipient, who is herself dead. His mother's name is also appended to the statement.

"April, 1885.

"Mrs. Stewart, the wife of a carpenter, living in Abergavenny, Monmouthshire, and who [Mrs. S.] is since dead, was, in the year 1874, in bed, and early one morning, being sure she was awake (for she had just heard the railway men being called to their work by the call boy), she looked up to see the time, and in one corner of her room she saw distinctly what she thought was her mother, intently looking at her. She was startled, and hid her face. On looking again the vision was still there, but on looking up a third time it had disappeared. Mrs. Stewart came up that day to see a sister-in-law who was in service near the town, to ask if she had had any tidings from her home (the impression the vision had made was so great), but nothing had been heard. Time passed on, and all seemed forgotten, when some of her friends came up to Abergavenny, to the christening of a little baby, born in the meantime. They were in mourning, and inquiries were made as to the friend mourned for, when it was told that on the night Mrs. Stewart thought she saw her mother, a sister of the mother's, to whom she bore a great likeness, had died about the hour named, at some distance off ; but they did not tell Mrs. Stewart of the death until some weeks after it happened, as Mrs. Stewart was in delicate health and much attached to her aunt.   "JOHN STEWART."

Miss Williams, of Abergavenny, writes on July 1, 1885 :—

"Mrs. Stewart was not an excitable woman, had never had any hallucination of the senses, and was a quiet, somewhat silent person. Her mother-in-law is now living in Abergavenny, and is a very sensible, respectable, practical woman. She probably heard Mrs. Stewart speak of the occurrence soon afterwards, and was anxious to add her testimony to the statement. I probably mentioned the statement to my brother in 1880, and he set it down in his notebook."

In reference to this last sentence, Mr. Williams says :—" I am more inclined to think that I heard of it within a day or two after it happened, and that if I added the date 1880, it must have been the date of my copying it into my notebook from some loose memoranda."

Here we have a singular feature—an appearance which suggested not the agent but a person closely resembling her. The case thus stands in a sort of midway position between the more normal cases and the class of unrecognised phantasms, of which several specimens have already been given (pp. 218, 384, 409, 427). The same peculiarity occurs in the next case. The narrator, Miss R., was willing to have her name and address published ; but her family disliked the idea, and we have acted in accordance with their wishes.

"May 8th, 1879.

(171) " In the year 1861 my parents were living in Soho Square, and I and my brother Alfred, aged 24, were living with them. On the 15th October my brother went to spend the evening at the house of an old schoolfellow, where it was not unusual for him to remain for the night, in order to avoid coming home at a late hour. It was customary for him, if he happened to come home after my parents had gone to bed, to go quietly to my mother's bedside and to give her a kiss if she were awake, and if not, to leave his hat upon the dressing-table as a sign that he had been there.

"She went to bed on October 15th without expecting his return that night, but after her first sleep she awoke up suddenly and saw him, as she thought, standing at the foot of the bed ; she said softly, ' I am not asleep, my dear,' but he went away instead of going to kiss her ; and this surprised her.

"On the morning of the 16th October, at breakfast time, she said to me : ' Where is Alfred?' I replied, ' He did not come home last night, mamma.' She answered, ' Oh, yes, he did ; and he came into my room when he was partly undressed, but he did not speak to me as usual.' In the course of an hour my brother came in, and my mother asked him if he had been into her room during the night. He assured her he had not been home. She said, ' It is very strange, for I am quite convinced that someone was standing at the foot of my bed when I awoke in the night.'

"At about mid-day a letter arrived to inform us that our cousin, Frank, only a few years older than my brother Alfred, had died at 1 o'clock that morning in London. My mother instantly exclaimed, ' It was Frank whom I saw ! I can recall him to mind distinctly as I saw him, and though at the time I thought I was looking at Alfred, yet I thought there was something strange in his appearance, and I could not understand why he came in to see me without his coat on.' "

We find the date of death, October 16th, 1861, confirmed by the obituary in the *Times*.

On March 20th, 1884, the narrator informed Mr. Podmore as follows:—

" Before writing this account, I wrote a letter to my cousin's family to confirm my recollection of the time at which he died, and received an answer to the effect that he died at 1 a.m. There was no very great likeness between my brother and my cousin ; merely a general family resemblance. Both were fair : but Frank was taller than Alfred, and had a fine beard, whilst Alfred had but a slight one.   " M. E. R."

Miss R.'s brother says :—   " March 20th, 1884.

"I remember this circumstance, but attach no importance to it, and detect nothing of the marvellous in the narrative.   " G. A. R."

The next case is from Mrs. Duthie, housekeeper to the Rev. J. C. Macphail, of Pilrig Manse, Edinburgh, who writes :—

"December 8th, 1885.

(172) "My son has shown me the paper signed by our housekeeper, Mrs. Elizabeth Duthie, and has told me of your desire to be assured of her reliability. Mrs. Duthie has been with me for more than 30 years, and I know her to be one on whose statement the fullest reliance may be placed.   " J. CALDER MACPHAIL."

Mrs. Duthie writes :—

" Pilrig Manse, Edinburgh, August 22nd, 1885.

" In August, 1883, the family of the Rev. J. C. Macphail had all gone to the country, leaving me alone in the house. An intimate friend of mine, a Miss Grant, who lived in Aberdeen, had been for some time seriously ill, and I was anxious about her, though I did not know that death was near. On Sunday night, the 26th of August, about 8 o'clock, I retired to my room, which is separated from the rest of the house, with a flight of stairs leading up to the door. I got into bed, and was lying half-asleep, with my face to the wall, when I felt that someone was bending over me, looking into my face. I opened my eyes, and looked up into the face of my friend Miss Grant. I started up in bed, and, looking round, saw Miss Grant's figure leaving the room. I then got out of bed, and going to the door, looked down stairs, but no one was to be seen. I went down the stairs into the kitchen, but no one was there, nor was there a trace of anyone. I looked at the clock, and saw it was a few minutes past 9, and then went back to bed, feeling very uncomfortable, and certain something had happened to my friend. All next day (Monday) I felt unhappy about it, and waited anxiously to hear of my friend ; but, as there was no one else in the house, I did not mention my experience of the previous night to anyone. That night I received information from Aberdeen that my friend had died at 9 o'clock on the previous night—at the very time I had seen her form in Edinburgh.

" I have never had a hallucination of the senses on any other occasion.
                                        " ELIZABETH DUTHIE."

Mrs. Duthie's *vivâ voce* account, given to the present writer a year later, exactly corresponded with the above. She is quite certain that her eyes were open when she saw the face.

In answer to inquiries Mrs. Duthie says :—

" I am *quite certain* that this experience fell on a *Sunday,* though I forget the exact day of the month ; and I could not have imagined that it fell on the Sunday *after* I got the news, for I heard of the death the very next day."

She has sent us a printed notice which she received, to this effect :—

"22, Thistle Street, Aberdeen.
"27th August, 1883.
"Helen Grant died here last night at 9 o'clock.
(Signed) "WM. GRANT."

Mr. G. W. Macphail writes :—

"Mrs. Duthie told my mother of her strange experience less than a month after the event, and I learnt it shortly after from Mrs. Duthie."

The next case is a deposition made by Mrs. Still, (known in her professional capacity as Mrs. Byrne), who was introduced to Mr. Myers by Mrs. Longe, of Coddenham Lodge, Cheltenham.

"Cheltenham, December 27th, 1882.

(173) "Mrs Byrne was stewardess on the steamer 'Lyra,' Captain Gilpin, in the River Plata line of steamers. One morning—probably between 6 and 7, but she had no watch—she was lying in her berth. She awoke, and saw Captain Gilpin's head passing slowly along her berth and looking at her. This was a familiar gesture on his part, as he used to be friendly with Mrs. Byrne, and ask her to sit on a seat outside his cabin, and used to look through his window in this way when he thought she was sitting there. Mrs. Byrne got up at once, and went into the pantry, and there heard that Captain Gilpin had been killed (though not instantaneously) by the fall of a spar at 6 that morning."

An extract from the official log-book, obtained by us from the General Register and Record Office of Shipping and Seamen, shows that the accident to Captain Prince Gilpin took place at 5.30 a.m., February 19th, 1878, on the "Laplace," not the "Lyra." He was crushed against the engine-room skylight by a heavy sea ; and his death was due to fracture of the ribs and injuries to the lungs. This would quite correspond with Mrs. Byrne's statement that his death was not instantaneous.

[The coincidence here must have been very close ; as there cannot have been more than a short interval between Captain Gilpin's death and Mrs. Byrne's natural time for rising, and in this interval, apparently, the vision occurred. The short period within which the whole contents of the narrative are comprised is further of importance as making the case an easy one to carry correctly in the memory ; and it seems very unlikely that the percipient should have come to imagine that she got up immediately after her vision and ascertained what had occurred, if the vision really took place on some other morning. Mrs. Byrne had been on two previous voyages with Captain Gilpin. She has experienced one other visual hallucination, which may have been purely subjective.]

The lady who narrates the following case desires that her name may not be published.

"May, 1885.

(174) "An attack of rheumatism and nervous prostration left me far from well for some weeks last spring, and one night I had a strange

unaccountable vision which has left a vivid impression upon my. memory. I had gone to bed early and was lying awake alone, with a night-light burning in order in some degree to dispel the gloom. Suddenly across the lower end of the room passed Major G.'s figure, dressed in his usual every-day costume, neither his features nor his figure any whit altered. It was no dream, nor was I in the least delirious or wandering, therefore a conviction seized me that something must have occurred; in consequence I particularly marked the hour, when the clock struck 11 shortly afterwards. The next morning I was not the least surprised when my sister handed me a note from Miss G. announcing her brother's death, and was fully prepared before reading it to find that he had passed away before 11 the previous evening—which presentiment, strange to say, was fully verified; Major G. having died at a quarter to 11. Major G. had returned in a bad state of health from Egypt, where he had been serving in the campaign of 1883. For some time he appeared to recover and was able to go about and enter into society during the winter, but during the last month the old symptoms had returned, and gradually he grew worse and worse, until no hopes of his recovery were entertained. Though not personally intimate with him, we were well acquainted with his family, and naturally his case formed a topic of conversation among us. We had also received bad accounts a few days before and were aware that he was in a critical condition; nevertheless at the time of his death he had been quite out of my thoughts and mind. I had never before had any apparition of any description whatsoever, nor has this one been followed by any other.

"C. P."

Miss Scott Moncrieff, of 44, Shooter's Hill Road, Blackheath, says :—
" As I was at [the town where Miss P. lives] at the time, I can myself so far confirm the story as to mention that, on the day after it occurred, we heard that the young lady had been so shaken in her nerves by her illness that she had been seeing what you would call a 'hallucination,' and was going to Malvern for change of air."

She adds that Miss P. was staying with her when the above account was written, and that as to the date, "both she and I remembered that it was on a Thursday near the end of March or beginning of April."

We find from an obituary notice that Major G. died on *Thursday*, April 3rd, 1884.

In an interview with Mr. Myers, December 26th, 1885, Miss P. added the following details :—

" Major G.'s phantom was in his ordinary walking costume—hat and ulster—in which Miss P. was accustomed to see him. The figure passed quickly across the end of the room without turning its head, but the face as well as the figure were distinctly recognisable. The figure made no noise, and disappeared as it reached the wall.[1] Miss P. at once conjectured that Major G. must be passing away; but she felt no fear. Although

---

[1] The mode of movement and of disappearance here described are not infrequent in visual hallucinations. In my collection (p. 392), besides about a dozen cases where the disappearance was through a door, behind a curtain, into a corner, and so on, I find four where it was respectively through the wall, into the wall, through the window, and into a bookcase. Movement of some sort, as will be seen later, is an extremely frequent feature of both subjective and telepathic phantoms.

Major G. was known to be fatally ill, there was no expectation of his death from day to day. He was not prominently before Miss P.'s mind. Miss P. was somewhat out of health at the time, but never suffered from any kind of hallucination of sight or hearing. She did not mention the incident to her family for fear of ridicule. Miss P.'s sister (to whom the incident was first told) said that she remembered receiving next morning the letter as to Major G.'s death ; and also remembered that some time later Miss P. told her of the incident. [Here the knowledge of the percipient that Major G. was in a critical state is, of course, an element of weakness ; but it remains a remarkable coincidence that she should have had her one experience of a sensory hallucination at the exact hour of his death.]

The next account is from Mr. Runciman, of Oak Villa, Geraldine Road, Wandsworth.

"May 5th, 1884.

(175) "On the morning of December 2nd, 1883, at about 7 o'clock in the morning, I had a dream which merged into a waking hallucination as follows :—I dreamt Mr. J. H. Haggit was lying on my bed, beside me, outside of the bedclothes. I dreamt I saw him there, and I also thought I saw him there *after* dreaming. I arose and rested on my right elbow, looking at him in the dusky light. There was a very small jet of gas burning in the room. I reflected, 'Am I awake, or is this a dream ?' I cannot yet answer this question to my own satisfaction ; I cannot tell when my dream merged in my waking thoughts. I only am sure that as the figure disappeared I was as wide awake as I am now. He was dressed in grey tweed, as I had been used to see him actually dressed.[1] He was turned from me so that I could only partially see his face. Yet I was certain it was he. I was alarmed and shocked to find my dream a reality —as I then thought it. I was about to speak when, in a twinkling, the image of Mr. H. was gone. I was leaning on my right arm and half raised from the bed. It was only half light, our gas burning but turned low. I mentioned the matter on that day to Mr. G. Aynsley, of No. 3, Glover Terrace, South Shields. I was oppressed during the whole day by the unusual experience of the morning, and hence spoke to the above and another twice about the incident.

"I had a note, next day I think, saying that Mr. H. died about 6 hours after his fancied presence in my bed.

"I knew that Mr. H. was afflicted, as he had been for 8 years or so, by bronchial asthma. As he had lived so long in spite of great suffering, I quite thought he would live longer. I had no idea he was near death.

"I believe this was a merely natural occurrence. I am not orthodox in religion.   "THOMAS RUNCIMAN."

We find the date of the death confirmed by the obituary of the *Darlington and Stockton Times.*

Mr. Aynsley corroborates as follows, on May 20, 1884 :—

"3, Glover Terrace, South Shields.

"I remember hearing Mr. Thomas Runciman speak of a vivid dream

[1] See pp. 539-40.

2 E

and hallucination which he had had on the day that Mr. Haggit died. He told me that he dreamt that he saw him lying on the bed beside him, in his ordinary dress, but very pale and haggard. He was so impressed that he awoke, and saw him quite plainly there. I ascertained afterwards that he had died about 6 hours after, on the day that Mr. Runciman related the circumstance. "GEORGE AYNSLEY."

In answer to inquiries, Mr. Runciman writes :—

" With regard to my having had any other hallucination, I have had others, but lapse of time and inattention have quite dimmed the remem brance of them. They were of a different kind to this last case. They were, I should say, simply 'nightmare' or 'daymare.' That is, they were such, that I quite believe I was *asleep* while experiencing them. In the last case I had not a peculiar sense of breaking out of sleep at once, and with a snap, as it were. I render my idea but imperfectly in the preceding sentence—perhaps I would more truly describe myself as breaking free, not from what was sleep, but from a tyrannous mistake as to my circumstances at the time. This sense was absent in the last case. I believe I might be awake, I even *think* I was awake, with the image of a dream still strongly on my mind. But in the earlier cases I concluded long ago that I was asleep and vividly dreaming till the image disappeared. Briefly, I cannot be sure in the latter case that I was asleep, although all experience would go to say I was. In the earlier cases many years ago I concluded that *waking* had caused what looked real to disappear. But do not think for one moment that I consider the last case any less a delusion than the former. I only try to describe my experience and belief at the moment of hallucination. It is difficult to define the difference in these cases."

In conversation with our colleague, Mr. R. Hodgson, Mr. Runciman mentioned that he found afterwards from the servant that at the time of his hallucination Mr. Haggit was apparently suffering intense agony. The figure was not part of his dream at all ; he saw it when he woke. It appeared to be lying almost on its right side, between Mr. Runciman and his wife, with the left side-face exposed and eye open, but the body was motionless, though it seemed to Mr. Runciman to be alive. In addition to the low gaslight, the dusky light of the morning was coming through the window, the blind of which was up. The light was sufficient for Mr. Runciman to see the time by his watch. He tells us that he made a written note of the experience, but does not remember whether this was done before he heard of the death. He has searched for the note, but cannot find it, and thinks that it must have been lost at the time of a removal.

§ 7. I will now give some examples where two senses were concerned. The following, from Mr. D. H. Wilson, of Rosemont, Hyères, includes an impression of weight as well as of sight. The case belongs to the group where the agent is comatose (pp. 230, 406).

" 1876.

(176) "My mother told me one morning, when I went to see her, that in the previous night she had had a startling experience. She was awakened by feeling a heavy weight on her feet, and on sitting up saw the form of her

husband (my father was then thousands of miles away) seated on the bed, in his nightshirt, and having the appearance of a corpse. After a few moments the form vanished. I recommended my mother to record this experience in her diary, and she did so. In due course she was informed by her husband that on that particular night he was in a state of coma, having been delirious for some days, and his life was quite despaired of by the doctors.   "D. H. WILSON."

In answer to our inquiries, Mr. Wilson wrote in February, 1884 :—

"My mother (who is no longer alive) had never seen anything of the kind previously, to the best of my knowledge." He thinks that the occurrence was in the winter of 1862.

Mr. Wilson's sister, Mrs. Kimber, of 3, Roland Gardens, S.W., has given us a completely concordant account, but cannot recall how long after the incident it was that her mother told her of it. She says, "At the time of the apparition, all hope of his [her father's] life had ceased."

In the following cases the sense of touch becomes more definite ; and in the first of them, if memory can be trusted, even the sense of smell was concerned—projected, as we may suppose, like the other sensory features, from the percipient's own mind.[1] Mrs. Brooke, of Woodlands, Kenford, Exeter, narrates :—

"June 29th, 1884.

(177) "I have a very vivid recollection that, towards dawn (?) on the morning of August 3rd, 1867, I was roused from my sleep to find my brother, an officer in the 16th Lancers, then quartered in Madras, standing by the bed. My impression is that he bent over me, kissed me, and passed quietly from the room, making signs to me not to speak, and that I was full of joy, thinking he had returned home unexpectedly, and lay awake till the maid called me, when my first words to her were that my brother had come home and I had seen him. I remember my bitter disappointment when at last made to believe that this was not so, and that it was quite impossible I could have seen him ; also that I was scolded and silenced for holding to my story.

"I cannot remember how much time elapsed before the news came by telegram that my brother died suddenly of jungle fever on August 2nd ; full particulars did not reach us for weeks later, and it was not till long afterwards that I put two and two together, as the saying is, and, found that, as I then and now firmly believe, my favourite brother came to me at the hour of his death.

"The date I fixed by reference to a childish diary I then kept, long since destroyed, but I cannot give you the exact hours. I know by letters that my brother died soon after 10 o'clock p.m. on August 2nd, and I

---

[1] This feature occurred in case 18, p. 191, which, however, differed in the point that the smell represented what was occupying the agent's mind. I may remark that, except in disease, subjective hallucinations of smell—or at any rate cases that can be clearly identified as such—seem very rare ; I have only two first-hand specimens in my large collection—besides one or two where a hallucination of smell has survived as the consequence of a dream. In one case of this latter sort (which I cannot obtain first-hand for publication), a distinct smell of death followed on a dream which is alleged to have coincided with the unexpected death of the person dreamt of.

know that my room was not quite dark when I saw him, and that I did not fall asleep again before morning on August 3rd. "M. A. BROOKE."

The *Army List* confirms Aug. 2, 1867, as the date of death. The vision seems to have followed the death by 9 or 10 hours.

In answer to inquiries, Mrs. Brooke says :—

"I fear that at this distance of time, 17 years, I shall not be able to find anyone who remembers my mentioning my vision of my brother, unless it might be the maid, who was with me for more than 15 years, and I will write to her and find out if she recollects it.

"I have never had any 'hallucination of the senses,' on any other occasion than that you know of."

[In this other case what seemed to be seen was the unaccountable opening of a locked door—which, as I have before remarked, is a known form of hallucination. See p. 102, note.]

In a personal interview with Mrs. Brooke, Professor Sidgwick obtained the following additional details :—

She was 13 years old. She was quite sure it was not a dream. It was quite impossible that it could have been some one else, mistaken for her brother. The room seemed to be full of a peculiar scent which her brother was fond of. She had written to the maid who, however, said, in reply, that she had only a vague recollection of the incident.

We must not forget that "borderland" impressions, or rather, perhaps I should say, dreams which the dreamer mistakes for waking percepts, are probably commoner in early youth than in later years : and in such a case as Mrs. Brooke's, therefore, the evidential superiority which I have pointed out as distinguishing waking from sleeping experiences could not rightly be insisted on. At the same time, whatever name we give them, we have no grounds for thinking that imaginary percepts so vivid and convincing as those here described fall to the lot of any considerable proportion of children.

In the next case the imagery supplied by the percipient's mind is very marked, and reminds us of some of the former dream-cases. The narrator is Miss Schmidt, of Ducklington Rectory, near Witney.

"June, 1884.

(178) "On New Year's Eve, 1852, I awoke about 12.40 a.m. and found my room so brilliantly illuminated that I imagined I had forgotten to put out my candle, and that something must have caught fire. I got up and, on looking round, saw at the foot of the bed a coffin resting on chairs, on each of which was a silver candlestick with a large wax taper alight; in the coffin was a figure of my father. I put out my hand and touched him, when it became quite dark. I felt for my matchbox and lighted a candle, looked at my watch and wrote down the time. The next morning I told my friend, with whom I was staying in Paris at the time, and on the morning of the 2nd of January we received a letter from Marseilles, saying that my father had died suddenly at 12.40 on New Year's Eve, and

that he had expressed such a strong wish to see his youngest child (*i.e.*, myself) again just before his death.   " E. A. SCHMIDT."

On one, and only one other occasion in her life, Miss Schmidt has seen an appearance of an unusual kind ; this, however, was seen on different occasions by several persons, and, whatever it was, can scarcely be taken to prove any special liability to hallucinations. She was requested to put us in the way of procuring the corroboration of her friend, who is a Russian. On March 12th, 1885, she writes :—

"I have taken all the steps I feel I can justifiably take with regard to securing for you the testimony of the Princess D. [name given]. It has already given me a great deal of awkward unpleasantness when inquiring at the Russian Embassy, &c., as the Prince and Princess are much mixed up in politics, and Russians are, as perhaps you know, not a little suspicious of the inquiries of strangers."

The most remarkable feature in this case is the light. The appearance of a dark room as being filled with light is a form of hallucination (or of hyperæsthesia) which is occasionally experienced on waking, apart from any further abnormality. I have received at least five well marked instances of the sort, not including those where there has been a further development of the hallucination—a luminous figure, or a figure in addition to the light.[1] The full interest of this point will appear later. (See Chap. XII., § 7.)

The next case was first printed in the *Spiritual Magazine* for February, 1863. The narrator is the late Mr. George Barth, of 6, Highfield Villas, Camden Road, N.

(179) "On the 14th of May, 1861, our son George, a most excellent and religious youth of 19 years, was removed from this to the spirit-world. Perceiving that the time of his departure was near, his mother and I alone watched by his bedside. When the last breath had been taken in and expired, I quietly remarked, 'He is now gone.' His mother inquired the time, and then observing the rising sun just shining over the blind of the room, which had an aspect to the east, she said, 'See ! the natural sun is just rising as our dear boy is rising to his Heavenly home.' I have an object in noting the rising of the sun at the moment of his departure.

"Mr. Williams, of Romford and Bishopsgate Without, a highly intelligent and worthy man, is united to our eldest daughter. At this time he was staying at his house in the City, his wife having been only a few days previously confined. He was sleeping in a room, the window of which faced the east. He states that he was soundly asleep, his hands outside the bedclothes, when he was suddenly aroused by feeling each of his hands firmly grasped and pressed. He instantly sat up, and by the

---

[1] It is recorded by Despine père, *De l'Emploi du Magnétisme Animal* (Paris, 1840), p. 240, that his patient, Estelle, saw all the objects in a perfectly dark room. A friend tells me that she has on several occasions, when feverish, had a "borderland " hallucination of a cat, which she has actually pursued about the room. On all these occasions the room, which was in reality dark, has appeared light—the light fading out as the hallucination vanished.

bedside stood George, holding his hands and smiling in his face with a look of peculiar sweetness and kindness. George was attired (seemingly) in his nightdress. Mr. Williams was not at all alarmed ; he knew it was George in the spirit, and his presence filled his brother-in-law with a calm feeling of peace and happiness, which remained for many hours. They thus held hands and looked on one another for a minute or longer; then the grasp relaxed, and George's spirit [1] faded away.

"Mr. Williams noticed that the rising sun was shining into his room over the blind. His impression was, and still is, that he saw George by this light and not by any other. At 8 o'clock Mr. Williams went to his wife's room and told her, in the presence of his mother and the nurse, that George was dead. 'Have you heard from father?' was the natural query. 'No ; but I have seen George—he came for a minute this morning at sunrise.' 'Oh, nonsense ! you have been dreaming, James.' 'Dreaming ! I never was more awake in my life. I not only saw him, but I felt his hands pressing mine.' 'Nonsense, James ; I know, poor boy, how ill he is, but father does not expect him to go yet. I still hope to be up and able to see him.' Mr. Williams quietly rejoined, 'You will see, dear. Mind, we shall presently have a letter or messenger from papa, telling us.' In an hour later Mr. Williams received the letter which he expected.

"Mr. Williams and George were mutually much attached ; in all his boyhood anxieties his brother James was George's confidant and friend. Hence a parting visit and a parting smile, and last friendly grasp of the hands was that which a departing spirit might be glad to give to his friend and brother ; but he could not go in the body, nor give it while his body kept him. "GEORGE BARTH."

The *Times* obituary confirms the date of the death.

Two daughters of Mr. Barth write to us as follows :—

"Delmar Villa, 520, Caledonian Road.
"April 20th, 1882.

"The extract you send from the *Spiritual Magazine* was written by my dear father, in order to give a correct account of my brother George's appearance to my brother-in-law, Mr. James Williams. The incident was spoken of at the time it occurred amongst us all in my father's house ; likewise I visited my sister and brother-in-law the day following George's death, and heard the account from himself.

"My father's reason for sending the notice to the magazine arose from some friend having published an incorrect statement.
"CHARLOTTE WALENN."

"3, Park Place West, Gloucester Gate, N.W.
"July 29th, 1884.

"I was a very young child at the time of my brother George's death. The only confirmation I can give you is the fact of hearing my father speak of the occurrence to friends interested in such matters, on several occasions, just as it is stated in his narrative. My eldest sister, Mrs. Williams, has been dead some years, but my brother-in-law is still alive, and will, no doubt, give you any help in the matter.
"ALICE BARTH (Mrs. Frederick Usher)."

The account was sent to Mr. Williams, who resides at Fern Bank,

[1] See p. 409, note.

Crowborough, Tunbridge Wells. He made no corrections in it, and referred to it in a manner which implied its substantial accuracy ; but he declined any further correspondence on the subject.

The following account is from Mr. George J. Coombs, Sheriff's Officer for the County of Nottingham. He tells me that he enjoys singularly robust health, and he is certainly as free from superstitious fancies as can well be conceived.

" Journal Chambers, Pelham Street, Nottingham.
"December 28th, 1883.

(180) " In the middle of the month of June, 1880, my aunt left Salisbury and went to the Washington Hotel, Liverpool, where I joined her from Nottingham, for the purpose of seeing her off to America, on board the Allan Line steamer, *Circassian*, the following day.

" Her business was to realise some property. She was getting into years, and very much pressed me to accompany her, but I was unable to leave my business for so long a time. She, however, made me promise to meet her on her return, and said it was her intention to spend the winter at Nottingham before returning to Salisbury.

" About the 25th July following, at 4 o'clock in the morning, while in bed, I suddenly awoke and said to my wife, ' Someone has taken hold of my hand ; the hand was quite cold. I believe it was my aunt ; I saw her rush out of the room.' The door was open on chain, and I immediately jumped out of bed to see, and the chain was still on. I said to my wife, ' My aunt is dead, and she has come again over the water,' to which she replied, ' You are dreaming ; you had too much supper last night ' ; to which I said, ' No, I am positive of the impression.'

"I received a letter from a solicitor in Hamilton, about a fortnight afterwards, announcing my aunt's decease, and a reference to the dates convinced my wife that she died at the very time I had the visitation. When I left my aunt in the steam tug which accompanied the *Circassian* down the Mersey, her farewell words were, ' I shall see you first when I come back.'
"GEORGE J. COOMBS."

In answer to inquiries, Mr. Coombs adds that the vision was not distinct, but that the hallucination is unique in his experience. In conversation, he described the impression as extremely striking and startling. The door was so chained that it was impossible for anyone to enter the room.

Mrs. Coombs corroborates as follows :—   "July 25th, 1884.

" I very well remember the morning when my husband awoke early, and said he saw his aunt rush out of the bedroom, and that she had taken hold of his hand ; also that, when the news of Mrs. Rumbold's death came from Hamilton, the remark was made that it was the very date my husband narrated his dream. I cannot fix the date without an Almanac of 1880, but it was our Village Feast Monday morning, which is, I believe, the third week in July.   "S. A. COOMBS."

We asked if it was possible to obtain corroboration as to the date of the death. Mr. Coombs sent us the solicitor's letter ; but this letter assumes

knowledge of the death, and was not written till September 27th. The
letter received by Mr. Coombs " about a fortnight " after the death, and
which must be the one by which the coincidence was fixed, is the
following. It is undated, but the postmarks are Hamilton, July 21st, and
Nottingham, August 5th, 1880.

" 188, King Street East, Hamilton, Canada.

" DEAR SIR,—I am sorry to have the painful task to inform you of
the death of your aunt, Mrs. Rumbold. She came to me on a visit on
July 3rd, feeling very poorly. I thought it must be over-fatigue, and
probably after a rest she would be better. She continued getting worse
and lingered on till the 19th.—Yours truly,   " A. JARVIS."

[Monday in the third week of July, 1880, fell on the 19th, which
is so far in favour of the accuracy of Mrs. Coombs' memory. It seems
practically beyond doubt that at the time that the news arrived, Mr.
Coombs, as well as his wife, fixed the date of the dream as Monday the
19th ; and the fact that in his letter to us, written more than 3 years
afterwards without reference to documents, he says " about the 25th," is,
therefore, unimportant.

We learn, however, from Mrs. Jarvis that Mrs. Rumbold died at
4 p.m. ; so that the impression, though falling, of course, within a time of
most serious illness altogether unknown to the percipient, preceded the
actual death by about 16 hours.]

In the next case, the sense of touch was associated with that of
hearing. Though the evidence is that of an uneducated witness, the
facts are well-evidenced ; and it is at any rate a *primâ facie* mark of
accuracy that the want of exact coincidence of time is expressly noted.
The first part of the account was written down by a careful assistant
at Bangor.

" December, 1883.

(181) " My present housemaid's mother, Ellen Williams, one night in
1872, distinctly and suddenly felt the pressure, as of some one's hand upon
her breast, at the same time heard the voice of her son, ' Ffoulk,' then a lad
at sea, saying, twice ' Mother, mother.' She was not asleep, and she
told her husband at once that she was sure it was her boy's voice, and
that she feared there was something the matter with him. When they
saw notice of the arrival of the ship in Liverpool, they wrote at once. A
reply came from the captain that the boy had died of yellow fever, six
days out from Rio de Janeiro, giving the date, which corresponded
exactly with the mother's note of the occurrence. She is still living in
the same place, near Port Dinorwic, in Carnarvonshire. She never had
any similar experience before or since, and has no objection to the mention
of her name."

In answer to inquiries our informant writes :—

" I fear Mrs. Williams could not write the details herself, but she
might dictate to another. Her daughter tells me she was then a child at
home, and remembers that her father, who has since died, did all he could
to convince his wife that her fears were groundless, and would not let

her dwell on the subject. They did not hear of the death till some months after, and the captain sent the date, which was copied into the family Bible."

And later she adds :—

"I have had an interview with Mrs. Ellen Williams, in the presence of her daughter, and have translated exactly what she said in Welsh. She insisted upon the night of the *4th* being the time of her impression. The captain's statement that the *6th* was the date of death makes a material difference. I copied the spelling of Pernambuco as it was written on the fly-leaf of the Bible."

The following is the percipient's testimony :—

"January 9th, 1884.

"I hereby declare that on the night of the 4th of February, 1872, about 1 o'clock, I distinctly saw my son Ffoulk, looking very weak and ill, and felt the pressure of his hands and heard his voice, saying, 'Mother! mother!' I did not know if I was asleep. I believed not. I mentioned it at once to my husband, who did not understand my feelings.

"We did not hear till the following Good Friday of his death, which the captain said took place on the *6th* of February, I do not know at what hour.

"Witness my mark, ELLEN WILLIAMS her + mark.

"In the presence of my daughter, who also testifies that I spoke of it at once, and commonly, and remained in great anxiety until the news reached us.   "MARY WILLIAMS."

The record in the family Bible stands :—

"Ffoulk died at sea, 6th of February, 1872, in lat. 5.51 S., long. 34.35 W., of the yellow fever, on board the barque 'Barbadoes,' on his passage from Pernabucca to Liverpool."

Our original informant adds :—   "June 25th, 1884.

"I recollect pressing the question at the time as to whether Ellen Williams had ever had any impression or hallucination of any kind, and she positively denied ever having experienced such, except on that one occasion."

[The two days' interval between the impression and the death, if correctly remembered, of course weakens the case for evidential purposes. Still, the impression almost certainly corresponded with a time of unforeseen and desperate illness.]

§ 8. Lastly, we have a group where the two higher senses of sight and hearing were both concerned. The following account is from Miss Kate Jenour, of 23, Belsize Square, South Hampstead, N.W.

"November, 1884.

(182) "On the 4th of May, 1883, when on board H. M. S. *Spartan*, on my way to Capetown, I was awoke by hearing someone in my cabin, which I alone occupied, when to my surprise I saw the figure of a friend of mine standing by my berth. It then disappeared, and by the first mail after my arrival at Capetown, I received the news of my friend's death,

which took place at 10.30 p.m. on that night. I told 2 or 3 passengers on board, who made a note of it."

In answer to inquiries, Miss Jenour says :—

"I was certainly awake; I had no sense of awaking *afterwards*, but the sense of waking *before* I saw the figure, my first impression having been that the steward had come in to shut the port-hole. I had a light burning in my cabin. The figure looked quite solid and natural, and was in day-dress. I knew the girl to be consumptive, but had not thought of her as likely to die, and indeed had not been thinking about her at all; she was an acquaintance and neighbour, but not an intimate friend.

"I think the vessel was about half-way to the Cape. Next day I described what I had seen to my cousin, Mr. Jenour, Captain Wait, Mr. Frames, who is now a lawyer in Grahamstown, and Mr. Hope Hall. I was so impressed that I could not help speaking of it, in spite of expecting to be laughed at : had it been a *dream*, I should have thought nothing of it.

"I am certain I mentioned the date of my vision in my first letter to my father, written when I got to the Cape, and before the news of the death reached me; and I am also certain that when I received the news of the death, I noted, and my cousin noted, that the dates were the same. I cannot now be sure of the exact day.

"I have had no other such waking vision except once, soon after, at Capetown; when I saw the figure of a dressmaker whom I knew in England, and who (as I learnt on my return to England) had died about the same time; but the date was not fixed.   "K. J."

We find from the obituary in the *Times* that the death took place on May 2, 1883.

Miss Jenour's cousin is unfortunately at a distance, and his address cannot at present be ascertained. Captain Wait writes, in April, 1886, that he does not recall Miss Jenour's mention of the incident. The fact of the coincident death not being then known, such a narration might naturally make very little impression. I wrote to ask Mr. Frames if he remembered any singular announcement made by Miss Jenour during the voyage; but he replied in the negative.

Miss Jenour's father writes on Nov. 1, 1885 :—

"I can positively state that by the next mail to the Cape, after the death of a young friend of ours, I wrote to my daughter; but before my letter can have reached her, she, on arriving at Capetown, wrote to me to say that the lady in question had appeared to her in her cabin, at sea, between Madeira and the Cape, and that she mentioned the fact the following morning to her relatives and friends on board. On comparing dates, it was certain that the appearance was on the same day that the lady died. Since then my relatives have confirmed this in every particular.
                                              "H. J. JENOUR."

Mr. Jenour is certain that his daughter's letter contained the date of her vision, and he has kindly searched for the letter. He writes, on Dec. 1, 1885 :—

"The letter I most wanted I cannot find, but have one dated June 5th, in which my daughter again refers to Miss B.'s death, and adds, 'On the

2nd of May,[1] in the night, or rather morning,[2] I awoke up and saw Edith standing by my bed. I told about it at the time.' The lady died at half-past 10 o'clock at night."

Mr. Jenour tells me that it was the close coincidence of time that specially struck him, and he mentioned the circumstance to others. Miss Jenour is equally confident that the coincidence of time was noted in Capetown ; though, as she has mentioned, her memory does not retain the exact date. We find from the *Times* that the *Spartan* left Plymouth on the 20th of April, and arrived at Capetown on the 10th of May; therefore her recollection that "the vessel was about half-way" is not far wrong.

The next case is from Mrs. Richardson, of Combe Down, Bath.

"August 26th, 1882.

(183) "On September 9th, 1848, at the siege of Mooltan, my husband, Major-General Richardson, C.B., then adjutant of his regiment, was most severely and dangerously wounded, and supposing himself dying, asked one of the officers with him to take the ring off his finger and send it to his wife, who at that time was fully 150 miles distant, at Ferozepore. On the night of September 9th, 1848, I was lying on my bed, between sleeping and waking, when I distinctly saw my husband being carried off the field, seriously wounded, and heard his voice saying, 'Take this ring off my finger, and send it to my wife.' All the next day I could not get the sight or the voice out of my mind. In due time I heard of General Richardson having been severely wounded in the assault on Mooltan. He survived, however, and is still living. It was not for some time after the siege that I heard from Colonel L., the officer who helped to carry General Richardson off the field, that the request as to the ring was actually made to him, just as I had heard it at Ferozepore at that very time.

"M. A. RICHARDSON."

The following questions were addressed by us to General Richardson, whose answers are appended.

(1) Does General R. remember saying, when he was wounded at Mooltan, 'Take this ring off my finger, and send it to my wife,' or words to this effect ?

"Most distinctly ; I made the request to my commanding officer, Major E. S. Lloyd, who was supporting me while my man had gone for assistance. Major Lloyd, I am sorry to say, is dead."

(2) Can he remember the *time* of this incident ? Was it morning, noon, or night ?

"As far as memory serves, I was wounded about 9 p.m. on Sunday, the 9th September, 1848."

(3) Had General R., before he left home, promised or said anything to Mrs. R. as to sending his ring to her, in case he should be wounded ?

"To the best of my recollection, never. Nor had I any kind of presentiment on the subject. I naturally felt that with such a fire as we were exposed to I might get hurt."

---

[1] The date of the dream in the first account, the 4th of May, was given from memory only, under the impression that the death had occurred on that day—not from any independent record.

[2] The vision took place soon after midnight—which of course would make its actual date May 3.

Four years after the above was written, Mrs. Richardson gave me *vivâ voce* a precisely accordant account. She described herself as a matter-of-fact person, and does not have frequent or vivid dreams.

The details as to the ring seem fairly to raise this case out of the category of mere visions of absent persons who are known to be in danger, and with whom the percipient's thoughts have been anxiously engaged.

The next case was received towards the end of 1882, from Mr. J. G. Keulemans, who has already been mentioned more than once (pp. 196, 235, 255).

(184) In December, 1880, he was living with his family in Paris. The outbreak of an epidemic of small-pox caused him to remove three of his children, including a favourite little boy of 5, to London, whence he received, in the course of the ensuing month, several letters giving an excellent account of their health.

" On the 24th of January, 1881, at half-past 7 in the morning, I was suddenly awoke by hearing his voice, as I fancied, very near me. I saw a bright, opaque, white mass before my eyes, and in the centre of this light I saw the face of my little darling, his eyes bright, his mouth smiling.[1] The apparition, accompanied by the sound of his voice, was too short and too sudden to be called a dream : it was too clear, too decided, to be called an effect of imagination. So distinctly did I hear his voice that I looked round the room, to see whether he was actually there. The sound I heard was that of extreme delight, such as only a happy child can utter. I thought it was the moment he woke up in London, happy and thinking of me. I said to myself, ' Thank God, little Isidore is happy as always.' "

Mr. Keulemans describes the ensuing day as one of peculiar brightness and cheerfulness. He took a long walk with a friend, with whom he dined ; and was afterwards playing a game of billiards, when he again saw the apparition of his child. This made him seriously uneasy, and in spite of having received within 3 days the assurance of the child's perfect health, he expressed to his wife a conviction that he was dead. Next day a letter arrived saying that the child was ill ; but the father was convinced that this was only an attempt to break the news ; and, in fact, the child had died, after a few hours' illness, at the exact time of the first apparition.

Mrs. Keulemans says :—   " May 29th, 1885.

" I remember that, the day when little Isidore died, my husband said that he felt strongly impressed that there was something wrong

---

[1] Mrs. Luther, of Adelaide Crescent, Brighton, has supplied us with a very close parallel to this form of impression, in a case which we do not include in our evidence, since the vision, though coinciding with the death of the person seen, may have been due to the percipient's state of anxiety about him. The incident was related to Mrs. Luther by her friend, Miss D. Brooke (since dead), within a year of its occurrence. "Suddenly her attention was called from the thoughts of her young friend, which filled her mind at the time, by a bright light shining in the looking-glass. She thought some one must have entered the room, but on looking at the glass, she saw in the midst of the bright light which therein appeared, her young friend, with a peaceful, happy smile upon his face. As she looked, it and the light gradually disappeared, and she was left again in comparative darkness." See also cases 163 and 178 above, and compare the disc of light in case 220.

with the little boy in London. It was in the evening that he asked me whether I had received any news from my mother about Isidore. I replied that no letter had come, and asked him why he wanted to know. He made the same remark as before, but would not further explain himself. I tried to expel his gloomy forbodings by referring to a letter we had from my mother, stating that Isidore was very happy, and was singing all day long. My husband did not seem pacified. When the letter mentioning his illness came, my husband was very much dejected, and told me that it was no use trying to make a secret of it, as he knew the worst had happened. He said afterwards that he had seen a vision.

"A. KEULEMANS."

The second apparition in this case may be regarded as a sort of recrudescence of the first. (See, however, Chap. XII., § 6.) With respect to this feature of repetition after a good many hours or days, I may mention that I have but one example of it in my collection of purely subjective hallucinations, and, except in very markedly pathological cases, it seems to be extremely rare—rarer than the more immediate repetition of which I spoke in connection with case 159, above. It is perhaps allowable to surmise its connection with a special character of intensity in some of these telepathically produced impressions. Other telepathic examples are Nos. 213 and 240.

In the next example the repetition was of the more immediate sort, recalling cases 159 and 160, above. The account is from Mrs. Sherman, of Muskegon, Michigan, and was received through the kindness of Mr. F. A. Nims, solicitor, of that city, who has known Mrs. Sherman and her family for years.

"Muskegon, Michigan.
"November 18th, 1885.

(185) "On the 4th of July, 1868, my sister Lizzie and myself left Detroit and went to Saginaw, for the purpose of making a short visit with friends there. Our train was due in Saginaw about 7 p.m., but through detention did not arrive there until between 10 and 11. Owing to the lateness of the hour of arrival, we did not go to the residence of our friends, but to the Bancroft House, then the principal hotel in that city. The weather was very warm, our ride had been very dusty, and we were very tired. We had supper, and soon after retired. My sister and I occupied the same room and bed. It was nearly or quite 12 o'clock when we retired. As I now recollect, I went immediately to sleep. I was awakened by feeling what seemed to be a hand on my shoulder. I saw my brother Stewart standing by the bedside, and I had an impression at the same time that my brother-in-law Phillip Howard was also in the room. My brother said to me : 'Kate, mother wants you! get up and go home.' I at once became very much excited and awakened my sister, and told her that I had seen Stewart and what he had said, and that I felt sure that mother was sick or in trouble, or that something unusual had happened to her. We got up, and immediately after heard the clock strike one. There

was bright moonlight that night, and all objects in the room and outside the windows were plainly visible. There had been a menagerie in town that day, and it was yet in the neighbourhood, and we could hear the noises of the animals, and talked about them. My sister did not share in my alarm or anxiety, and ridiculed what she called my 'Ghost Story,' and we soon retired again. My mind was somewhat troubled with what had occurred, and I did not go to sleep quite so soon as my sister did, but I did go to sleep again, and the air being somewhat cooler, before going to sleep I had pulled the sheet up over my neck. While asleep I was again awakened by feeling the sheet pulled down off me,[1] and I again saw my brother Stewart, and he repeated the same language as on the first occasion. At this time his appearance was very much more persistent than before, but his face seemed to retire and gradually fade away.[2] He looked pale and ill, but at that time my concern and anxiety was on account of my mother. I supposed that she was threatened with some serious illness, and that the appearance had relation to that. I again aroused my sister and told her what had occurred, and we both got up and dressed, and did not retire again that night. I am not sure that I mentioned the circumstance to any of our friends that day. If I did, I am not in a position now to obtain the verification of it.

"We returned home on the afternoon of Monday, the 6th of July, arriving there between 6 and 7 o'clock. We found our father and mother very much disturbed in consequence of a telegram which they had received to the effect that Stewart was dying. When my mother communicated the news to us, I answered 'He is dead'; for then the significance of what had occurred at Saginaw first flashed upon me. It was but a very short time after this, the same evening, that we received another telegram giving the tidings of his death. My sister Lizzie had received a letter from him but a day or two before we went to Saginaw, in which he promised to make us a visit in the following October, and there was nothing to afford any ground for anxiety on his account in the letter. As I have been since informed, he died about a quarter before 1 o'clock on the morning of the 5th of July, about the time of his first appearance to me, as near as I can ascertain.

"I have a letter from my sister Lucy, the wife of Phillip Howard, at whose house he died, giving full particulars of his death, from which it seems that he was taken suddenly and violently ill on the 3rd or 4th of July, of what was supposed to be yellow fever.

"During his illness he talked a great deal about our mother, and seemed in his delirium to be watching for her and to think that she was coming to see him. He died, as stated, that Sunday morning, and was buried by order of the authorities on the afternoon of the same day.

"You inquire if I have ever had any previous hallucination of that kind. I have never had but one; that occurred when I was 7 years old At that time a young girl, a relative and playmate of mine, was ill with some form of fever. I had not been allowed to see her for two or three days. On waking one morning, I saw or dreamed she came and kissed me and bade me good-bye. This was before I had arisen. My mother

---

[1] I need hardly point out that this sensation is no more a proof of an objective presence than any other feature of the hallucination.
[2] Compare p. 444, note ; and see Chap. xii., § 10, and Vol. ii., p. 97, first note.

soon afterwards came into the room, and I told her that —— had come and kissed me and bid me good-bye. Within a few minutes after this some one of the family came from the house where the little girl resided, and said that she was dying. My mother immediately went over to the house, which was not far off, and when she arrived there the little girl was already dead.

"These are the only cases of what you call 'hallucination' that have occurred in my experience.

"The occurrences at Saginaw were real, and I have never had a doubt about my brother, in some way or form, appearing to and communicating with me.   "KATE SHERMAN."

Mrs. Sherman's sister, Mrs. Park, corroborates as follows :—

"Muskegon, Michigan.

"I have read the foregoing statement signed by my sister, Mrs. S., and am able from my own recollection to confirm the same, except, of course, that I did not myself see my brother, Stewart Paris, or his apparition, at the same time that my sister did.

"At the time of the occurrences at Saginaw, I supposed what my sister said that she saw to be a dream, or something of that character, and gave the matter no serious thought or consideration until our return home the next day, when we learned of our brother's illness and death.

"I remember, however, that what my sister said she saw made a very strong impression upon her, and that she said, and seemed to believe, that some serious illness or misfortune had occurred or was about to occur to our mother.   "ELIZABETH O. PARK."

Mr. Nims adds that he had hoped to get a statement from Mrs. Paris, mother of Mrs. Sherman and Mrs. Park ; but "while she remembers hearing about the vision on her daughters' return from Saginaw, she is unable to say whether it was before or after the news of the death."

The next case is from Miss Bibby, of Chaceley Lodge, Tewkesbury.

"1883.

(186) "In the early autumn of 1860, when I was between 19 and 20, I was staying with friends who lived near Rugby. I had gone to bed and fallen asleep, and was awakened by a consciousness of some one being in the room. I saw, as I imagined, my grandfather standing at the foot of the bed. He was then, as far as I knew, at his own house a few miles out of Liverpool. Immediately the figure moved to the side of the bed, the curtains of which had not been drawn. The figure did not, so far as I remember, touch either the bed or the curtains. The only remark he made was 'Good-night, Miss Nellie, Ma'am'—he was always in the habit of calling me 'Nellie' and sometimes in fun, 'Miss Nellie, Ma'am,' quoting the way in which Irish servants used to address my grandmother, after whom I was christened. He was the only person who ever called me 'Miss Nellie' or 'Nellie,' my father having a great objection to all pet names.

"I soon fell asleep again, and next day mentioned the circumstance to my friends, and the day after received from my father the news of my grandfather's sudden death, about the time when he had appeared to me

So little did I anticipate such news that before I broke the black seal on my father's letter I exclaimed, 'Dear me, I fear poor Edward has gone,' alluding to my youngest brother who had been ailing for some time.

" ELLEN BIBBY."

[The corroboration of the friends with whom Miss Bibby was staying cannot unfortunately be obtained, as she has lost sight of them.]

The next account is from Miss Hosmer, the celebrated sculptor.

(187) " An Italian girl named Rosa was in my employ for some time, but was finally obliged to return home to her sister on account of confirmed ill-health.   When I took my customary exercise on horseback I frequently called to see her.   On one of these occasions I called about 6 o'clock p.m., and found her brighter than I had seen her for some time past. I had long relinquished hopes of her recovery, but there was nothing in her appearance that gave me the impression of immediate danger.   I left her with the expectation of calling to see her again many times.   She expressed a wish to have a bottle of a certain kind of wine, which I promised to bring her myself next morning.

" During the remainder of the evening I do not recollect that Rosa was in my thoughts after I parted from her.   I retired to rest in good health and in a quiet frame of mind.   But I woke from a sound sleep with an oppressive feeling that someone was in the room.   I reflected that no one could get in except my maid, who had the key of one of the two doors of my room—both of which doors were locked.   I was able dimly to distinguish the furniture in the room.   My bed was in the middle of the room with a screen round the foot of it.   Thinking someone might be behind the screen I said, ' Who's there ? ' but got no answer.   Just then the clock in the adjoining room struck 5 ; and at that moment I saw the figure of Rosa standing by my bedside ; and in some way, though I could not venture to say it was through the medium of speech, the impression was conveyed to me from her of these words : ' Adesso son felice, son contenta.'   And with that the figure vanished.

" At the breakfast table I said to the friend who shared the apartment with me, ' Rosa is dead.'   ' What do you mean by that ? ' she inquired ; ' You told me she seemed better than common when you called to see her yesterday.'   I related the occurrence of the morning, and told her I had a strong impression Rosa was dead.   She laughed, and said I had dreamed it all.   I assured her I was thoroughly awake.   She continued to jest on the subject, and slightly annoyed me by her persistence in believing it a dream, when I was perfectly sure of having been wide awake.   To settle the question I summoned a messenger, and sent him to inquire how Rosa did.   He returned with the answer that she died that morning at 5 o'clock.

" I was living in the Via Babuino at the time.

" The above has been written out by Miss Balfour, from the account given by Lydia Maria Child [to whom Miss Hosmer had narrated the facts] in the *Spiritual Magazine* for September 1st, 1870, with corrections [of a trifling kind] dictated by me, July 15th, 1885.

" H. G. HOSMER."

The account given by Miss Child, which Miss Hosmer pronounced correct at the time, gives a few more details, tending to show that she was quite awake for an appreciable time before her vision. "I heard in the apartments below familiar noises of servants opening windows and doors. An old clock, with ringing vibrations, proclaimed the hour. I counted one, two, three, four, five, and resolved to rise immediately. As I raised my head from the pillow, Rosa looked inside the curtain and smiled at me. I was simply surprised, &c."

[Miss Hosmer does not remember the exact date of the occurrence, but says it must have been about 1856 or 1857. The old lady with whom she was residing is dead.]

We received the following account from the Rev. J. Barmby, of Pittington Vicarage, Durham, who writes :—

"December 29th, 1884.

(188) " What follows was communicated orally to the Rev. J. T. Fowler, Librarian and Hebrew Lecturer in the University of Durham, by Mr. Clarke, one of the principal tradesmen in Hull, on the 9th of October, 1872. Mr. Fowler took notes in writing of what Mr. Clarke told him at the time, which notes he handed to me in the same month of October. I put them into the following form after receiving them, and have no doubt of their substance and details being exactly given. The events related had occurred about four years previously to Mr. Fowler's interview with Mr. Clarke."

"Mr. Clarke, of Hull, had known for twenty years a Mrs. Palliser, of the same place. She had an only child, a son called Matthew, who was a sailor. Being of the age of 22, he had sailed from Hull to New York. About a month after his departure, Mrs. Palliser came to Mr. Clarke in tears, and said, 'Oh, Mr. Clarke, poor Mat's drowned.' Mr. C. said, 'How have you got to know ?' She replied, 'He was drowned last night going on board the ship, in crossing the plank, and it slipped ; I saw him, and heard him say, "Oh, mother."' She stated that she had been in bed at the time, but was sure she was wide awake : and that she had seen also her own mother, who had been dead many years, at the bedfoot crying, and making some reference to the event. Mr. C. said to her, ' Oh, it's all nonsense, I don't believe anything of the sort.' She earnestly persisted in her conviction, and called on Mr. C. perhaps half-a-dozen times during the ensuing week. In order to pacify her, he undertook to write to the agent of her son's ship at New York. This she had wished him to do, thinking that he, as a business man, would know better how to write than herself. After the despatch of the letter, Mrs. P. kept calling on Mr. C. about every week, to ask if he had heard anything. In about a month's time a letter arrived from New York, addressed to ' Mrs. Palliser, care of Mr. Clarke.' It was opened by Mr. Clarke's son, in the presence of Mrs. Palliser, who, before it was opened, said, ' Aye, that'll contain the news of his being drowned.' The letter conveyed the intelligence that Matthew Palliser, of such a ship, had been drowned on such a night, through the upsetting of a plank, as he was going aboard the ship. The night specified was that of Mrs. P.'s vision.

" Mr. Clarke described Mrs. Palliser as ' a well-educated woman, a very respectable old lady who had seen better days,' about 65 years of age. She had, he said, been a widow for some years before her son was drowned. She was then living in a passage leading out of Blackfriars Gate, in Hull. He had seen her 'the day before yesterday.' She had told the story 'thousands of times,' and it was well-known in Hull."

The Rev. J. T. Fowler, of Bishop Hatfield's Hall, Durham, writes :—

"November 26th, 1884.

"I know nothing about the case I mentioned to Mr. Barmby beyond what I gave him in writing.

"Mr. Clarke, a tradesman in Hull, told me of the case of Mrs. Palliser, and got her to come to his office, in Queen Street, Hull, for me to take down from her own lips the notes I gave to Mr. Barmby. I took great pains to get the whole of the story correctly.   "J. T. FOWLER."

Mr. Clarke writes :—   "Winterton Hall, Doncaster.

"January 20th, 1885.

"Widow Palliser was a woman who had seen better days, and worked for my firm, Clarke and Son, Clothiers, Queen Street, Hull. She had an only son, Matthew. I assisted her in getting him to sea. One morning she came to me with tears rolling down her cheeks and said, 'Mat's dead ; I saw him drowned ! Poor Mat, the last words he said were, "Oh ! my dear mother." He threw up his hands and sank to rise no more.' I asked how she knew. She said, 'I saw him going on board his ship, and the plank that he walked upon slipped on one side, and he fell overboard between the quay and the ship, and was drowned. My own mother, who had been dead many years, came to the foot of my bed and said, "Poor Mat's gone ; he's drowned." '[1] I then said, 'Why, Mat's in New York' (I always felt interested in this woman and her son). 'Yes,' she said, 'he was drowned last night at New York ; I saw him.'

"Mrs. P.'s object in coming to me was to ask if I would write to the agent in New York, to ascertain the facts. I said I would, and wrote stating that a poor widow had an only son on board such a ship, and she had a vision that an accident (I said nothing about drowning) had happened to her son, and I would take it as a great favour if he would ascertain and tell me all particulars. In about 3 to 5 weeks (she came day by day to ask if we had received a reply, always saying that she knew what the answer would be), at length, the letter arrived. We sent for Mrs. P., and before the letter was opened by my son, I said to her, 'What will be its contents ?' She at once and decidedly said that 'Mat was drowned on the very night that she saw him, and in going on board the ship the plank slipped, and he fell overboard between the quay and the ship.' So it was. Mrs. P. was then wearing mourning for Mat.

"My son and half-a-dozen young men can verify this if needful.[2]

"Mrs. P. died soon after.   "M. W. CLARKE.

"Reproduction of the letter received from the agent of the ship, as nearly as I and my son can remember :—

"'New York, date unknown.

"'I have made inquiries of Matthew Palliser, age about 20, and learn

---

[1] Mr. Clarke is quite confident that Mrs. Palliser spoke of her experience as a waking one.

[2] In conversation, Mr. Clarke's son has completely confirmed the account.

that he fell off a plank in going on board his ship, and got drowned on......' The date was the same as Mrs. Palliser said.

" 'The mate has charge of his chest, and will give it to his mother when the ship arrives in Liverpool.' "

In answer to inquiries, Mr. Clarke adds :—   "April 6th, 1885.

" We have no copy of the agent's letter, but both my son and myself and others are certain that Mrs. P.'s vision and the agent's account of the accident *were the same*, both as to the time and cause, viz., that Mrs. P. saw her son slip off the plank in going on board his ship, and that he was drowned between the quay and the ship ; agent's account that he fell off the plank and was drowned, *at the time* mentioned, between the ship and the quay. Mrs. P. died soon after the event, which in my opinion shortened her life."

[In the absence of a written note, we cannot of course be perfectly certain that Mrs. Palliser did not read back the details of the plank and the quay into her vision *after* the arrival of the news, and that Mr. Clarke is right in his recollection of having heard these details from the first. But there can hardly be a doubt that the vision was described as a very impressive one *before* the arrival of the news ; and Mr. Clarke's interest in the matter may fairly be supposed to have made him careful in his scrutiny of the dates.]

If correctly reported, this case curiously combines a sort of clair-voyant vision [1] with a more ordinary apparition, the figure at the foot of the bed—the latter being of an eminently " borderland " type. Such dream-like combinations (see pp. 425-6) have a very special bearing on the connection which I am seeking to establish between sleeping and waking telepathic percepts.[2]

The next account—from Mrs. Woodham, of 5, Royal Naval Cottages, Penge—was obtained through the kindness of the Hon. Roden Noel.

"June 26th, 1884.

(189) " I had in my service a charwoman, of about 60 years of age, who had served me faithfully for more than 20 years. Her husband had been one of my husband's coastguardmen, and on his death the poor woman had to work to support herself and four children, two of whom turned out badly.   I had helped her as much as I could besides employing her, and found her very valuable in being trustworthy.   She regarded me with great affection, and used to say to my daughters that there was no one to her like ' the mistress,' as she always called me.

" In August [a mistake for October] of last summer I had agreed to visit my sister, who resides in Edinburgh, and having fixed the day, a Wednesday, had arranged for Mrs. Halahan to come as usual.   My son, who was going with me, persuaded me to set out on the day previous. Mrs. H. arrived, expecting to see me.   Strange to say, she was very much taken aback and moved, and exclaimed, ' The mistress gone without seeing

---

[1] See pp. 266, and 368-9.
[2] For a purely subjective waking hallucination which represented a living and a dead person, see p. 499, note.

me!' She went to my house as usual during my absence (about a month). One day, while working at my married daughter's house, she was taken suddenly ill, about 6 o'clock in the evening—was conveyed home in a cab, and died next morning.

"Meanwhile my daughters did not mention to me the death of my dear servant, but only that she was ill, knowing it would grieve me; but just at the time of her death (10 days before I returned home) I was sleeping in the room with my sister in Edinburgh, when, in the dusk of the morning, I was awakened by a loud knock, and saw the figure of a woman in a loose dress, standing at the side of the bed, looking towards me. I sat up, and said emphatically, 'Who are you, and what do you want?' I repeated the question twice, which awoke my sister, who asked who I was speaking to? I replied, 'To the woman standing there.' Immediately the figure melted away like a shadow. I was so impressed with what I had seen that I went up to the room on several successive evenings, wondering whether that shadow-like form would again appear, but it never came. On returning home, the first question I asked my daughter was about my old servant, as, thinking she was ill, I wished to go to see her. I was astonished and grieved at the news of her death. All at once the truth flashed across my mind, and I exclaimed, 'Why, I saw her myself,' and then related to my son and daughter the above facts. My description was so clear and vivid that they were equally impressed as to its truth, and feel as sure as I do of the occurrence being a fact.

"I never saw anything of the sort before, nor have I or my family ever believed in ghosts; but they implicitly believe this, knowing that I am in no way fanciful. I feel sure that my dear servant (who was, I find, speechless for some hours before her death) had me on her mind. I can only think that the dusk of the morning and the darkness of the room (between 5 and 6 in the morning, the hour at which she died) prevented my recognising the features, but I can truly vouch for the above facts.

"ELEANOR E. WOODHAM."

The account of the narrator's sister (March 5, 1886) is that Mrs. Woodham awoke her in the dusk of the morning by saying twice, "Who are you?" and when asked to whom she was speaking, replied, "Don't you see that woman standing there?" pointing to the side of the bed; then, on her sister's remarking, "You must have been dreaming," she replied, "I have been awake for some time, and distinctly saw her there."

In conversation, Mrs. Woodham assured the present writer that she has never had any other visual hallucination. The dress of the phantasm, so far as observed, sufficiently corresponded with Mrs. Halahan's usual aspect; but the only at all distinctive point was the covering of the head—not a cap but a loose wrap or shawl. Mrs. Woodham was once, when a girl, woke in the same way by a loud knock which could not be traced to any objective source; and this experience, she says, precisely coincided with the death of a relative in the house. It is noteworthy that though her sister is a very light sleeper, and though it was very near her usual hour of waking, the loud knock did not wake her; this is at any rate some proof that it was hallucinatory. Mrs. Woodham is able to fix the hour of her experience, as she did not go to sleep again, and the work of the household began soon after. Her son and daughter personally confirmed the narrative as to the points in which they were concerned ; and Miss Woodham remembered that the hour of the death was stated to her to have been 6 a.m. At my request she went to see Mrs. Halahan's daughter, who confirmed the fact that this was the hour. Thus, supposing the *days* to have been the same, the coincidence was extremely close. Mrs. Woodham is not certain of the exact number of days which elapsed between her experience and her return home, but thinks they did not exceed a fortnight ; and she did her best at the time, by going over the events of these intervening days, to fix the date of her vision ; but all that could be fixed with certainty was a very close approximation with the death ; which an *In Memoriam* card, copied by Miss Woodham, fixes as October 23, 1883.

The evidential weight of this case is of course reduced, not only by the uncertainty as to the day of the vision, but by the fact that the figure was not recognised. But theoretically, as I have pointed out above (p. 221), the mere lack of recognition would not be a serious difficulty. If, as we have seen reason to think, a telepathic disturbance may take place below the threshold of consciousness, if its manifestation may be delayed for hours, if it may first reveal itself in semi-automatic movements, or in an idealess cry (as in case 147)—there seems no reason why, when it takes more distinct sensory form, this form should not be itself an imperfect development, an embodiment of an idea that has only partially been apprehended. This, however, will become clearer in connection with the whole subject of the development of telepathic hallucinations (Chap. XII.).

The next and concluding case is from Mrs. Lightfoot, a lady who is none the worse witness because she takes not the slightest interest in our work. The names and dates were filled in by the present writer, immediately after a personal interview, January 30, 1884.

"51, Shaftesbury Road, Ravenscourt Park, W.

"January 11th, 1884.

(190) "In giving the following experience, I may premise that as a child, and since, I have comparatively had but little knowledge (as a personal experience) of fear ; and in the existence of ghosts I have always disbelieved. Did I ever see or hear sights or sounds for which, on examination, I could not account, I have always come to the conclusion that they arose from natural causes which were beyond my reach of inquiry —hence I always refused to accept anything, without proof, and I may add, that I have rarely been convinced.

"Some 10 years ago, when in India, I contracted a great friendship, which was reciprocated, for a lady, Mrs. Reed, the wife of an officer. She had not been very strong, but when I parted from her with the intention of returning to England, no danger (the word had not even been mentioned) was anticipated, and for some few months after my return I heard from her, bright and cheerful letters enough. In them she certainly spoke of her health not being good, but nothing more. Then after a time her letters ceased, but I heard very regularly from others at the same place, and they mentioned that her health was gradually getting worse, and that she would probably be ordered to England for a thorough change, but still I heard no sound of fatal ending, and I was looking forward to her return with a great degree of pleasure.

" It was my practice not only to go to bed very late, but also for the last half-hour to pick up a book, the most uninteresting and dry that it was possible to find, and so try to soothe the mind. The moment I commenced to really feel sleepy, I would lower the gas to almost a pin's point (for I did not care to extinguish it, as I had a child of 3 sleeping in the same room), and then I could always compose myself comfortably to a sleep into which I could then fall in a very few minutes.

" On the night of September 21st, 1874, I had followed this exact routine. I had put aside my book, lowered the gas, and at a little after midnight I was sound asleep. As I knew afterwards, I must have slept about 3 hours, when I was suddenly aroused (and was, so far as I know, *perfectly wide awake*) by a violent noise at my door, which was locked. I have some recollection of feeling astonished (of fear I then had none) at seeing or rather hearing within the instant my door thrown violently open, as though by someone in great anger, and I was instantly conscious that someone, something—what shall I call *it ?*—was in the room. For the hundredth part of a second it seemed to pause just within the room, and then by a movement, which it is impossible for me to describe—but it seemed to move with a rapid push—*it* was at the foot of my bed. Again a pause ; for again the hundredth part of a second, and the figure-shape rose. I *heard* it, but as it got higher its movements quieted, and presently *it* was above my bed, lying horizontally, its face downwards, parallel with my face, its feet to my feet, but with a distance of some 3 or 4 feet between us.[1] This for a moment, whilst I waited simply in astonishment and curiosity (for I had not the very faintest idea of either who or what it was), but no fear, and then it spoke. In an instant I recognised the voice, the old familiar imperious way of speaking, as my Christian name sounded clear and full through the room. ' Frances,' it repeated, ' I want you ; come with me. Come at once.' *My* voice responded as instantaneously, ' Yes, I'll come. What need for such a hurry ? ' and then came a quick imperative reply, ' But you *must* come *at once ;* come instantly, and without a moment's pause or hesitation.' I seemed to be drawn upwards by some extraordinary magnetic influence, and then just as suddenly and violently thrown down again.

" In one second of time the room was in a deathly stillness, and the words, ' She is dead,' were simply burnt into my mind. I sat up in bed dazed, and *now*, for the first time, frightened beyond measure. I sat very still for a few moments, gradually making out the different forms in the room, then I turned the gas, which was just above my head, full on, only

[1] This rather bizarre form of impression has a close parallel in the case of a purely subjective experience, described to me by Mrs. Pirkis, of the High Elms, Nutfield, Surrey, who has never had any other hallucination. She was one night sleeping with her sister— both being in perfect health—when, suddenly waking, she saw a figure kneeling over her sister, "a foot or something less above her, in reversed position, face towards the foot of the bed. It was a beautiful picture. I lay watching it, I should say, for about 4 or 5 minutes, till it melted away as I looked."

to see that the room was totally unchanged.   At the foot of my bed, at some distance from it, was the child's iron cot.   I got up and looked at him ; he was sleeping quite peacefully, and had evidently been totally undisturbed.   I went to the door, to find it *fast locked.*   I opened it, and gazed into the passage—total silence and stillness everywhere.   I went into the next room, where there were sleeping two other children and their nurse, to find equal quietness there.   Then I returned to my room, and I must confess it, with an awful fear oppressing me.   She had come once— might she not come again ?   I wrote down the date and the hour, and then opening shutter and window only looked out for the welcome dawn.

"I went down to breakfast that morning, but said nothing of the details of my dream,[1] only mentioning that I had had a very bad and a very vivid one.   Afterwards I found I could settle to nothing, and at last was becoming positively so ill that I was obliged to go back to bed.   That same afternoon, curiously enough, a sister came to see me, who had been abroad with me, and whilst there had known and liked this same friend. She saw I was much upset about something of which I did not care to speak, and, by way of cheering me up, began telling me news of various mutual friends.   At last, during a slight pause, she said, ' By-the-way, have you heard anything lately of Mrs. Reed ?' when last I heard she was not very well.'   *Instantly* came my reply, ' Oh, she is dead,' and it was only my sister's look of blank horror and astonishment that recalled me to myself.   ' What do you mean, when did you hear ? ' came from her in rapid utterance, and then I bethought me, *how* indeed did I hear—*who* had told me ?   But tell her the dream I *could* not, so I merely answered, ' You will see that I am right when you look in the newspapers—*how* I have heard of it I will tell you some other time,' and directly I changed the conversation.   The visit did good, however, for I got up and went out with her, and I can only say that the impression my manner and words made upon her was so deep that, the moment she arrived home, she sat down and wrote to a lady in the West of England—one who knew us *all*, and who heard by every mail from her husband, who was in the same place as our friend.   My sister told her exactly what I had said, and begged that she would at once send her particulars, since I had not done so.   By return came the reply :—

"'I cannot, dear Lady B., in the least understand your letter, nor what your sister can possibly mean.   The last foreign mail only came in *this* morning' (after the date, of course, of my dream), ' and so far from being "dead" my husband tells me Mrs. Reed is much better ; therefore, where Mrs. L. (myself) can have obtained her news is beyond my comprehension, for it is *quite impossible* that she can have had later news than mine, in fact, not so late, since my foreign letter arrived after your visit to her.'   [This is not a *copy* but a *reminiscence* of the letter.]

"And so the matter rested, but within a month from the date of my dream came the news of Mrs. Reed's death, on September 21st.

"I have but little now to add.   The bereaved husband returned to England and called upon me.   He gave me some details of the last days, and on my asking whether he remembered her last words, he turned to me

---

[1] Though the narrator twice uses this word, she certainly did not regard her experience as a dream.

with quite a look of surprise, and said, 'Why, Mrs. Lightfoot, I believe *your* name was the last she mentioned.' Further, it was *many* months afterwards before my sister again broached the subject, but at last one day she said, 'I do wish you would tell me *how* you knew of Mrs. Reed's death.' Of course I then told her, and, I may add, that so deep was the impression produced upon her that even in her last illness, which occurred 7 or 8 years afterwards, she spoke of it. For myself I never really recovered the shock for a long time, and even now the impression is as vivid as though it only happened yesterday.

"Frances W. Lightfoot."

Both the *Calcutta Englishman* and the *Pioneer Mail* (Allahabad) give September 20th, 1874, as the date of Mrs. Reed's death. Mrs. Lightfoot has unfortunately not kept her note of the day and hour. As she has now no *independent* recollection of the date of her experience, but only remembers the fact of the *coincidence*, and as it is practically certain that she heard the *correct* date of the death, the 20th, which has since become converted in her memory to the 21st, it seems tolerably safe to assume that her experience fell on the night of the 20th, that is, on the early morning of the 21st—not on the *night* of the 21st, as stated in the account.

In answer to the question whether this was the only occasion on which she has had a sensory hallucination of this kind, Mrs. Lightfoot answered "Yes." She adds that her sister, Lady B., "mentioned the matter at once to several friends and relatives." The sister has since died.

[In conversation, Mrs. Lightfoot confirmed again the fact of having had no sort of visual hallucination on any other occasion. She once, and once only, has had another remarkable *auditory* experience, when the sudden hearing of her Christian name saved her from a terrible fall in the dark. The origin of the sound was carefully inquired into and could not be ascertained.

As a proof of the absolute conviction produced in her that her friend was dead, she told me that she had prepared a birthday present to send her, and the box was actually soldered up, and had been going by the next mail; but she found it impossible to send it.

She had been under the impression that the time of death exactly coincided with her vision; but she had reckoned difference of longitude the wrong way. Mrs. Reed's husband informed her, on her inquiry, that the death took place at 11, that is 11 p.m. (as she thinks of September 21st, but no doubt of September 20th); and the vision was probably, therefore, 8 or 9 hours *after* it.

My impression of Mrs. Lightfoot entirely corresponds with her own description of herself—that she is a practical person, and without any sort of predisposition to frights or visions. The present one gave her a most severe shock, the effects of which lasted for some time.]

In this chapter, various points of interest or difficulty have been passed over with very inadequate comment. It seemed better, however, not to forestall the more complete discussion of the relation of telepathy to sensory impressions, which will shortly follow.

CHAPTER X.

HALLUCINATIONS : GENERAL SKETCH.

§ 1. WE are now approaching the most important division of our subject. So far the impressions, possibly or probably telepathic, that we have considered, have been (1) the *non-externalised* sort (chiefly ideal or emotional, but sometimes with a physical element) occurring during the hours of normal waking life ; and (2) this sort, and also the *externalised* sort, occurring either in sleep or in a bodily and mental state which, though not that of sleep, is yet to some extent distinguishable from that of ordinary waking life. The class, then, that remains to be considered is the externalised sort—impressions of sight, hearing, or touch—occurring to persons who are quite clearly wide awake. The reader will not now need to be told to what family of natural phenomena I am about to refer this class. Something is presented to the percipient as apparently an independent object (or as due to an independent object) in his material environment ; but no such object is really there, and what is presented is a phantasm. Whatever peculiarities such an experience may present, there can be no mistake as to its generic characteristics : it is a *hallucination.*

It is naturally only with one particular species of the great family of hallucinations—the *veridical* species which psychology has so far not recognised—that I am here directly concerned. But it is not easy to treat the single species satisfactorily, without either assuming or supplying a certain amount of information with regard to the family to which it belongs. To assume this information would hardly be safe ; for though most educated persons may have a general idea what hallucinations are, the idea is not always the result of very close or critical study. It seems better then, to err, if at all, on the side of excess, and to devote one chapter to a brief general sketch of the subject ; in attempting which I shall endeavour to avoid side issues, and to confine myself to points that will aid comprehension in the sequel.

Is it possible to treat Hallucinations as a single class of phenomena, marked out by definite characteristics ? The popular answer would no doubt be Yes—that the distinguishing characteristic is some sort of false belief. But this is an error : in many of the best known cases of hallucination—that of Nicolai, for instance—the percipient has held, with respect to the figures that he saw or the voices that he heard, not a false but a true belief; to wit, that they did not correspond to any external reality. The only sort of hallucination which is necessarily characterised by false belief is the purely non-sensory sort—as where a person has a fixed idea that everyone is plotting against him, or that he is being secretly mesmerised from a distance. Of hallucinations of the *senses*, belief in their reality, though a frequent, is by no means an essential feature ; a *tendency* to deceive is all that we can safely predicate of them.

If we seek for some further quality which shall be distinctive of both sensory and non-sensory hallucinations, the most hopeful suggestion would seem to be that both sorts are *idiosyncratic and unshared.* However false a belief may be, we do not call it a hallucination if it has " been in the air," and has arisen in a natural way in a plurality of minds. This is just what an *idée fixe* of the kind above mentioned never does : A may imagine that the world is plotting against him ; but B, if he spontaneously evolves a similar notion, will imagine that the world is plotting not against A, but against himself. Instances, however, are not wanting where the *idée fixe* of an insane person has gradually infected an associate ;[1] and as contact between mind and mind is, after all, the " natural way " of spreading ideas, we can make no scientific distinction between these cases and those where, *e.g.,* the leader of a sect has instilled delusive notions into a number of (technically) sane followers. But again, hallucinations of the *senses* are also occasionally shared by several persons. Most of the alleged instances of this phenomenon are, no doubt, merely cases of *collective illusion*—an agreement in the misinterpretation of sensory signs produced by a real external object ; but wide inquiries have brought to light a certain number of

---

[1] A distinct description of *folie à deux* seems to have been first given in 1860, by Baillarger, in the *Gazette des Hôpitaux.* The subject was developed in 1873 by Lasègue and Falret, in an essay reprinted in Lasègue's *Etudes Médicales.* See also E. C. Seguin in the *Archives of Medicine* (New York, 1879), i., p. 334 ; Dr. Marandon de Montyel, in the *Annales Médico-psychologiques,* 6th series, Vol. v., p. 28 ; and G. Lehmann in the *Archiv für Psychiatrie* (Berlin), Vol. xiv., p. 145.

instances which I regard as genuine *collective hallucinations,* neither externally caused nor communicated by suggestion from one spectator to another. If then sensory and non-sensory hallucinations agree in being as a rule unshared, they agree also in presenting marked exceptions to the rule—exceptions easy to account for in the latter class, and peculiarly difficult in the former. The conclusion does not seem favourable to our chance of obtaining a neat general definition which will embrace the two ; and in abandoning the search for one, I can only point, with envy, to the convenient way in which French writers are enabled not to combine but to keep them apart, by appropriating to the non-sensory species the words *délire* and *conception délirante.*

Let us then try to fix the character of *hallucinations of the senses* independently. The most comprehensive view is that *all* our instinctive judgments of visual, auditory and tactile phenomena are hallucinations, inasmuch as what is really nothing more than an affection of ourselves is instantly interpreted by us as an external object. In immediate perception, what we thus objectify is present sensation ; in mental pictures, what we objectify · is remembered or represented sensation. This is the view which has been worked out very ingeniously, and for psychological purposes very effectively, by M. Taine ;[1] but it is better adapted to a general theory of sensation than to a theory of hallucinations as such. To adopt it here would drive us to describe the diseased Nicolai—when he saw phantoms in the room, but had his mind specially directed to the fact that they were internally caused—as *less* hallucinated than a healthy person in the unreflective exercise of normal vision. I prefer to keep to the ordinary language which would describe Nicolai's phantoms as the real specific case of hallucination. And I should consider their distinctive characteristic to be something quite apart from the question whether or not they were actually mistaken for real figures —namely, their marked resemblance to real figures, and the consequent necessity for the exercise of memory and reflection to prevent so mistaking them. The definition of a sensory hallucination would thus be *a percept which lacks, but which can only by distinct reflection be recognised as lacking, the objective basis which it suggests.*[2]

---

[1] *De l'Intelligence,* Vol. i., p. 408, &c.

[2] *Objective basis* is to be taken as a short way of naming the possibility of being shared by all persons with normal senses. But in that case, how far will the definition fairly allow for *collective* hallucinations ? This question will be considered in Chap. xviii. I may mention that, owing to the special difficulties which collective hallucinations present, I have not included them in the statistics given above, pp. 392-3, and below, pp. 503, 510.

It may be objected that this definition would include illusions. The objection could be obviated at the cost of a little clumsiness; but it seems sufficient to observe that illusions are merely the sprinkling of fragments of genuine hallucination on a background of true perception. And the definition seems otherwise satisfactory. For while it clearly separates hallucinations from *true perceptions*, it equally clearly separates them from the phenomena with which they have been frequently identified—the remembered images or *mental pictures* which are not perceptions at all. It serves, for instance, to distinguish, on the lines of common sense and common language, between the images of " day-dreams " and those of night-dreams. In both cases vivid images arise, to which no objective reality corresponds; and in neither case is any distinct process of reflection applied to the discovery of this fact. But the self-evoked waking-vision is excluded from the class of hallucinations, as above defined, by the point that its lack of objective basis can be and is recognised *without* any such process of reflection. We have not, like Nicolai, to consider and remember, before we can decide that the friends whose faces we picture are not really in the room. We *feel* that our mind is active and not merely receptive—that it is the mind's eye and not the bodily sense which is at work, and that the mind can evoke, transfigure, and banish its own creatures; without attending to this fact, we have it as part of our whole conscious state. Dreams of the sensory sort on the other hand are pure cases of hallucination, forcing themselves on us whether we will or no, and with an impression of objective reality which is uncontradicted by any knowledge, reflective or instinctive, that they are the creatures of our brain.

But, though the definition may be sufficient for mere purposes of classification, it takes us but a very little way towards understanding the real nature of the phenomena. It says nothing of their origin; and, though it distinguishes them from mere normal acts of imagination or memory, it leaves quite undetermined the faculty or faculties actually concerned in them. And when we pass on to these further points, we find ourselves in a most perplexed field, where doctors seem to be as much at variance as philosophers. The debate, most ardently carried on in France, has produced a multitude of views; but not one of the rival theorists seems ever to have convinced any of the others. The contradictions might even seem to lie in the facts themselves; for what single guiding clue shall be found to phenomena of which some occur only in the light, others only in the

dark ; some are connected with hyperæsthesia of the senses, others
with blindness and deafness ; some are developed, others dispersed,
by fixity of gaze ; some are promoted by silence and solitude, others
by the stir of the streets ; some are clearly relevant, others as clearly
irrelevant, to the percipient's mental and moral characteristics ? Still
progress has been made, to this extent at any rate, that it is now
comparatively easy to see where the disputed points lie, and to attack
them with precision.

§ 2. It was, of course, evident from the first that there was a
certain *duality* of nature in hallucinations. In popular language,
the *mind* and the *sense* were both plainly involved ; the hallucinated person not only *imagined* such and such a thing, but
imagined that he *saw* such and such a thing. But the attempts
at analysing the *ideational* and the *sensory* elements have too
often been of a very crude sort ; the state of hallucination has been
represented as one in which ideas and memories—while remaining
ideas and memories and not sensations—owing to exceptional
vividness took on the character of sensations. By the older writers,
especially, it was not realised or remembered that sensations have
no existence except as *mental* facts ; and that, so far as a mental
fact takes on the *character* of a sensation, it *is* a sensation. This was
clearly stated, as a matter of personal experience, by Burdach and
Müller ; in the French discussions, the merit of bringing out the point
with new force and emphasis belongs to Baillarger.[1] He showed

---

[1] In the long and rather barren debates which took place in the *Société Médico-
psychologique* during 1855 and 1856, Baillarger, no doubt, insisted too strongly on an
absolute gulf between percepts (true or false) and the ordinary images of fancy or memory.
But his opponents made a far more serious mistake in so far identifying the two as not to
perceive a difference of *kind*, at the point where the sensory element in the mental fact
reaches such abnormal strength as to suggest the real presence of the object.   Griesinger's
statement (*Die Pathologie und Therapie der Psychischen Krankheiten,* p. 91), and Wundt's
(*Grundzüge der Physiologischen Psychologie,* Vol. ii., p. 353) seem too unguarded in the same
respect. In a case which I have received, a child of four stopped in her play, looked intently
at the wall, then "ran to it, crying out 'My mother,' threw her little arms as if it were
round a person, saying again, 'My mother,' and seemed wonderfully surprised at the
fact that there was no substance to clasp." A child of four does not throw its arms
round a memory.   Nicolai's case is here very instructive. He experimented on himself,
and found that however vividly he pictured in his mind the persons of his acquaintance,
he could never succeed in *externalising* them in such a way as to make them the
least comparable to his phantoms ; and his testimony on this point is the stronger
in that his particular phantoms cannot have been of the most vivid sort, since he
was always able to distinguish them from *realities.* Even more distinct mental
images—the result of a rarer visualising power—may fall far short of hallucination.
Raphael, who saw his "Transfiguration" in the air, Talma, who asserted that he worked
himself into the necessary state of excitement on the stage by peopling the theatre with
skeletons, are not recorded to have ever really localised their images as objects that
concealed the walls and the furniture. It is worth noting that probably no recollected
visual image was ever so absolutely and flawlessly correct as a good musician's silent
evocation of music, either by memory or by reading of the noted symbols ; but even *he*
is far from mistaking his vivid silent impression for actual sonority. I may add that as

that when the hallucinated person says " I see so and so," " I hear so and so," the words are literally true. If the person goes on to say " *You* ought also to see or hear it," he is of course wrong ; but when he says that *he* sees or hears it, his statement is to be taken without reserve. To *him,* the experience is not something like or related to the experience of perceiving a real external object: it is *identical* with that experience.[1] To the psychology of our day this may seem a tolerably evident truth. Still it is easy to realise the difficulty that was long felt in admitting that any experience which was dissociated from the normal functions of the sense-organs could be completely sensory in character. Popular thought fails to see that the physical question which for practical purposes is all-important—whether the object is or is not really there—is psychically irrelevant; and a man who has been staring at the sun will, as a rule, think it less accurate to say that he *sees* a luminous disc wherever he looks than to say that he *fancies* it. The best corrective to such a prejudice is the following experiment of Fechner's.

Two small slits are made in a shutter, and one of them is filled with a piece of red glass. The opposite wall is therefore lit by a mixture of white and red light. A stick is now placed across the red slit ; its shadow is of course cast on the wall ; and the part of the wall occupied by the shadow, though illuminated only by *white* rays from the other slit, appears—owing to the optical law of contrast—a bright green. Let this shadow now be looked at through a narrow tube, which prevents any part of the wall external to the shadow from being seen. Nothing red is now in the spectator's view, so that there can be no effect of contrast : the red glass may even be removed ; none but white rays are passing to his eye from the shadow ; yet its colour remains green. And in this case the chances are that, unless previously warned, he will tell the exact truth ; he will admit, and even persist, that what he sees is green. He will scout the idea that the green is a mere memory of what he saw before he applied the tube ; he will assert that it is presented to him as an immediate fact.

long ago as 1832 the late Dr. Symonds, of Bristol, drew exactly the right distinction between images and hallucinations. (Lecture reprinted in *Miscellanies,* p. 241.) It is curious to find the same line drawn in the earliest really scientific attempt to deal with the subject that I have met with—the dissertation against Hobbes and Spinoza in Falck's *De Dæmonologiâ recentiorum Autorum* (1692) ; but Falck still thinks that hallucinations are a mode in which dæmons sometimes manifest their presence.

[1] It may even be *superior* in distinctness to the percept of a real object ; as when a short-sighted person who, during the hypnotic trance, had been impressed with a hallucination representing horsemen at some distance, saw them *clearly,* and remarked on this peculiarity. (Richet, *L'Homme et l'Intelligence,* p. 234.) See also Mr. Schofield's case, and the remarks on it, Vol. ii., p. 72.

And such is assuredly the state of the case; but it is a state which, from the moment that he has put the tube to his eye, is kept up purely as a hallucination, and without regard to the facts of the external world. The delusion is of course instantly dispelled by the removal of the tube—when he perceives that the only light in the room is white, and that the shadow is grey; but for all that, he will probably never doubt again that a genuine hallucination of the senses is something more than "mere fancy."

It is impossible to be too particular on this point; for high authorities, even in the present day, are found to contest it. When a person who habitually speaks the truth, and who is not colour-blind, looks at an object and says, "My sensation is green," they contradict him, and tell him that however much he *sees* green, his sensation is *grey*. Whether this be a mere misuse of language, or (as it seems to me) a misconception of facts, it at any rate renders impossible any agreement as to the theory of hallucinations. For it ignores the very point of Baillarger's contention—that images sufficiently vivid to be confounded with sensory percepts *have become* sensory percepts.

When once the truth of this contention is perceived, it is also perceived that the previous speculations had been largely directed to a wrong issue; and that the *dual* character of a false perception is after all no other than that of a true perception. A hallucination, like an ordinary percept, is composed of present sensations, and of images which are the relics of past sensations. If I see the figure of a man, then—alike if there be a man there and if there be no man there—my experience consists of certain visual sensations, compounded with a variety of muscular and tactile images, which represent to me properties of resistance, weight, and distance; and also with more remote and complex images, which enable me to refer the object to the class *man*, and to compare this specimen of the class with others whose appearance I can recall. If Baillarger did not carry out his view of hallucinations to this length, the whole development exists by implication in the term by which he described them—*psycho-sensorial*. The particular word was perhaps an unfortunate one; since it suggests (as M. Binet has recently pointed out[1]) that the psychical element is related to the sensorial somewhat as the soul to the body; and so, either that psychical events are independent of physical conditions, or that sensations are not psychical

---

[1] *Revue Philosophique* for April, 1884, p. 393.

events. *Ideo-sensational* would avoid this difficulty; but the obverse term which M. Binet proposes—*cerebro-sensorial*—is on the whole to be preferred. For this brings us at once to the *physical* ground where alone the next part of the inquiry can be profitably pursued—the inquiry into *origin.* From the standpoint of to-day, one readily perceives how much more definite and tangible the problems were certain to become, as soon as they were translated into physiological terms. So far as the controversy had been conducted on a purely psychological basis, it had been singularly barren. In the vague unlocalised use, "the senses" and other ever-recurring terms become sources of dread to the reader. But as soon as it is asked, Where is the local seat of the abnormal occurrence? and on what particular physical conditions does it depend?—lines of experiment and observation at once suggest themselves, and the phenomena fall into distinct groups.

§ 3.   In its first form, the question is one between *central* and *peripheral* origin. Do hallucinations originate in the brain—in the central mechanism of perception? or in some immediate condition of the eye, or of the ear, or of other parts? or is there possibly some joint mode of origin?

For a long time the hypothesis of an exclusively central origin was much in the ascendant. But this was greatly because—as already noted—Esquirol and the older writers did not recognise the sensory element as truly and literally sensation, but regarded the whole experience as simply a very vivid idea or memory. If the central origin is to be established, it must be by something better than arbitrary psychological distinctions. Hibbert and Ferriar, going to the other extreme, contended that the memory was a *retinal* one ; if a man *sees* what is not there, they held, it can only be by a direct recrudescence of past feeling in his retina. " But," urged Esquirol, "the *blind* can have hallucinations of vision ; the *deaf* can have hallucinations of hearing ; how can these originate in the peripheral organs?" The obvious answer, that this did not necessarily thrust the point of origin back as far as the cerebrum, does not seem to have been forthcoming ; and the opposite party preferred to fall back on definite experiment. They pointed out, for instance, that visual hallucinations often vanish when the eyes are closed ; or that they may be doubled by pressing one eyeball. There was not enough here, however, to show that the external organs so much as *participated* in the process, much less that they *originated* it, even in these particular cases; while for other cases the observations did not hold. The fact that external objects are hidden from view by the interposition of our own eyelids or any other opaque obstacle, has become to us a piece of absolutely instinctive knowledge; and we should surely expect that an object which was but the spontaneous projection of a morbid brain, might still be suppressed by movements and sensations which had for a lifetime been intimately associated with the suppression of objects. And as for the doubling by pressure of one eyeball, it might fairly have been represented as telling *against* the theory of retinal origin. For the impression—not coming from without—would cover the same retinal spot after the displacement of the eyeball as before; and the natural hypothesis seems certainly to be that retinal identity would, in its mental effect, overpower the sensation of the moved eyeball's position.[1]

An immense advance was made by Baillarger, who maintained the central origin by really scientific arguments. He pointed out (1) that the external organ may often be affected by local irritants— inflammation, blows, pressure, galvanism—without the production of any more pronounced form of hallucination than flashes, or hummings; that is to say, the peripheral stimulation sometimes fails to develop hallucination, even under the most favourable conditions; (2) that there is a frequent correspondence of hallucinations of different senses—a man who sees the devil also hears his voice, and smells sulphur—and that it is impossible to refer this correspondence to abnormalities of the eye, ear and nose, occurring by accident at the same moment; (3) that hallucinations often refer to dominant ideas— a religious monomaniac will see imaginary saints and angels, not imaginary trees and houses. Hence, argued Baillarger, "the point of departure of hallucinations" is always "the intelligence"—the imagination and memory—which sets the sensory machinery in motion.[2] He naïvely admitted that how this action of an immaterial principle on the physical apparatus takes place passes all conception; but it might be forgiven to a medical man, writing forty years ago, if

---

[1] The obliteration by closure of the eyes is certainly not invariable. See, *e.g.*, Dr. Voisin, *Leçons Cliniques sur les Maladies Mentales*, p. 72. Sir J. F. W. Herschel, in his *Familiar Lectures on Scientific Subjects*, p. 406, has described some hallucinations of his own, of which "the impression was very strong—equally so with the eyes open or closed." As regards the failure of lateral pressure to double the image, I do not know whether any clear case has been recorded. Brewster, indeed, speaks of the immobility of the image when the eyeball is displaced; but he made no sufficient distinction between actual hallucinations and mental pictures; while he had an odd notion that even the latter were "painted" on the retina. (*Letters on Natural Magic*, 1868, p. 131.)

[2] Baillarger, *Des Hallucinations*, pp. 426, 469, 470.

2 G

he had not fully realised "brain as an organ of mind," and so did not see that what he took for a special puzzle in the theory of hallucinations, is simply the fundamental puzzle involved in every mental act. Passing him this, we may say that his treatment of the question entitles him to the credit of the *second* great discovery about hallucinations. He had already made clear their genuinely sensory quality; he now made equally clear the fact that the mind (or its physical correlate) is their creator—that they are brain-products projected from within outwards.

This is a most important truth; but it is very far from being the whole truth. Baillarger saw no *via media* between the theory which he rejected—that the nerves of sense convey to the brain impressions which are there perceived as the phantasmal object—and the theory which he propounded, that "the intelligence" (*i.e.*, for us, the brain, as the seat of memories and images), of its own accord and without any impulse from the periphery, excites the sensory apparatus. It seems never to have struck him that there may be cases where the sense-organ supplies the *excitant*, though the brain supplies the *construction*—that irritation passing from without inwards may be a means of setting in motion the constructive activity. He took into account certain states of the organ—*e.g.*, fatigue produced by previous exercise—as increasing the susceptibility to excitation from "the intelligence," and so as conditions favourable to hallucination; but he got no further.

The facts of hallucination absolutely refuse to lend themselves to this indiscriminate treatment. Following the path of experiment, we are almost immediately confronted with *two* classes of phenomena, and *two* modes of excitation. We need not go, indeed, beyond the elementary . instances already mentioned. Fechner's experiment, where green was seen by an eye on which only white rays were falling, fairly illustrates Baillarger's doctrine—the green being produced not by an outer affection of the eye, but by an inner affection of the brain. But in the case of a person who has been staring at the sun, the "after-image" or hallucination can be clearly traced to a continuing local effect in that small area of the retina which has just been abnormally excited; and it will continue to present itself wherever the eye may turn, until rest has restored this area to its normal condition. A still simpler form of change in the external organ is a blow on the eye; and the resulting "sparks" are genuine though embryonic hallucinations.

Such cases as these last are, however, hardly typical ; for in them the brain is not truly creative ; it merely gives the inevitable response to the stimuli that reach it from below. They are, moreover, *normal* experiences, in the sense that they would occur similarly to all persons with normal eyes. Let us then take another instance, where the mind's creative *rôle* is fully apparent, while at the same time the primary excitation is clearly not central. Certain hallucinations—as is well-known—are *unilateral, i.e.*, are perceived when (say) the right eye or ear is acting, but cease when that action is obstructed, though the left eye or ear is still free. Now this in itself could not be taken, as some take it,[1] for a proof that the exciting cause was not central ; it might be a lesion affecting one side of the brain. But very commonly, in these cases, a distinct lesion is found in the particular eye or ear on whose activity the hallucination depends.[2] It is then natural to conclude that the hallucination was the result of the lesion, and that the one-sidedness of the one depended on the one-sidedness of the other ; and the justice of the conclusion has been proved in many cases by the fact that the hallucination has ceased when the local lesion has been cured. Other cases which strongly suggest a morbid condition of the external organ are those where the imaginary figure moves in accordance with the movements of the eye. The visual hallucinations of the blind, and the auditory hallucinations of the deaf, would also reasonably be referred to the same class—the seat of excitation being then, not necessarily the external organ itself, but some point on the nervous path from the organ to the brain. In the case, for instance, of a partly-atrophied nerve, the morbid excitation would be at the most external point where vital function continued.[3] It should be noted, in passing, that a distinct lesion, *e.g.*, atrophy of the globe, of one eye may give rise to hallucinations of the *sound* eye [4]—the sight of which then receives,

---

[1] Dr. Régis in *L'Encéphale*, 1881, p. 51 ; Prof. Ball in *L'Encéphale*, 1882, p. 5.

[2] Dr. Régis in *L'Encéphale*, 1881, p. 46 ; Dr. Voisin in the *Bulletin Général de Thérapeutique*, December 15, 1868, and *Op. cit.*, p. 68, &c. ; Dr. Despine, *Psychologie Naturelle*, Vol. ii., p. 29 ; Krafft-Ebing, *Die Sinnesdelirien*, p. 25 ; Dr. Köppe's paper on "Gehörsstörungen und Psychosen," in the *Allgemeine Zeitschrift für Psychiatrie*, Vol. xxiv., pp. 18-28 and 39-46.

[3] Delusions due to visceral disturbances are often quoted as cases of hallucination excited from parts below the brain. Thus a woman dying of peritonitis declares that an ecclesiastical conclave is being held inside her (Esquirol, *Maladies Mentales*, Vol. i., p. 211). But here there is a prior and independent basis of distinct sensation ; so that the experience would at most be an illusion. And it is hardly even that ; for one cannot say that the false object is sensorially presented at all ; no one knows what a conclave in such a locality would actually feel like ; the conclave is merely a *délire*—an imagination suggested by sensation, but which does not itself take a sensory form.

[4] *Vienna Asylum Report*, 1858, cited by Griesinger, *Op. cit.*, p. 88.

so to speak, the rebound of the central disturbance initiated by its fellow.

§ 4. But we may now proceed a step further. The excitation may be external not only in the sense of coming from the external *organ,* but in the sense of coming from the external *world.* It may be due not to any abnormality of the eye or the nerve, but to the ordinary stimulus of light-rays from real objects. Some interesting evidence on this point has been lately described by M. Binet.[1] His experiments were conducted on five hysterical young women at the Salpêtrière, who, when hypnotised, could be made to see anything that was suggested to them ; and also on an insane patient at St. Anne, who had a standing visual hallucination of her own. The results confirmed the rule first enunciated by M. Féré—that "the imaginary object is perceived under the same conditions as a real one " ; and to this M. Binet adds the further conclusion, that a sensation derived from a *real* external source, occupying the same position in space as the imaginary object seemed to occupy, was an indispensable factor of the hallucination. Space fails me to describe the results in detail. It is enough to say that a prism applied to one eye doubled the imaginary object ;[2] that a spy-glass removed or approximated it, according as the object-glass or eye-piece was applied to the patient's eye ; that a mirror reflected the object and gave a symmetrical image of it ; and that the optical effect, as regards angles of deviation and reflexion and all the details of the deception, was in every case precisely what it would have been had the object been real instead of imaginary. Here then we seem fairly driven outside the patient's own organism ; the conclusion is almost irresistible that some point of external space at or near the seat of the imagined object plays a real part in the phenomenon. To this point M. Binet gives the name of *point de repère ;* and he regards it as producing a nucleus of sensation to which the hallucination accretes itself. When the *point de repère* is in such a position as to be reflected by the mirror, then the imaginary object is reflected, and not otherwise ; the object is, so to speak, attached to its *point de repère,* and will follow the course of any optical mutations to which its external nucleus is subjected.[3]

---

[1] In the *Revue Philosophique,* April and May, 1884.

[2] This observation was first made by M. Féré ; see *Le Progrès Médical,* 1881, p. 1041.

[3] The full explanation of these phenomena seems to be as follows. If the *point de repère* is not at, but close to, the spot where the imaginary object appears (as seems to

In these cases, it will be seen, the experience was really a sort of monstrous *illusion*—totally different, however, from ordinary misinterpretations of sensory impressions; for we must beware of confounding the excitation that comes from the *point de repère* with the sensory element of the hallucination itself. The former is an unnoticed peg for the percept; the latter is its very fulness and substance, and is entirely imposed or evoked *by* the brain, not supplied *to* it. The type is too interesting to pass over: at the same time, I am bound to say that it seems to be extremely rare. I have made many endeavours to obtain the prism-effects with hypnotised (but not hysterical) "subjects"; but I have never succeeded, except when some conspicuous real object had first been put under the instrument, and the idea of doubling had thus been prominently suggested.[1]   Professor Bernheim, of Nancy, tells me

have been the case in some of the experiments), there is no difficulty. The *point de repère* is then itself part of what is all along perceived; and in any effects produced on it by optical apparatus, it will carry the neighbouring object with it by *association*. If, however, the actual area covered by the object is sufficiently distinguished from its surroundings to act itself as *point de repère*, and no other possible *points de repère* exist in the field of vision, the case is different, but can still be explained. It will not be disputed that a slightly longer time is necessary for the formation of the image of a suggested object and the conversion of this image into a percept, than for the experience of sensation from an object actually before the eyes. When, therefore, the operator points to a particular place on the white table-cloth, and says, "There is a brown butterfly," we may suppose that in the patient's consciousness a real sensation of white precedes by an instant the imposed sensation of ·brown. So when the card-board on which a non-existent portrait has just been seen is again brought before the patient's eyes, it is almost certain that the recognition of it as the same piece of white card-board (known by its *points de repère*) precedes by an instant the hallucinatory process and the re-imposition of the portrait. That there is this instant of true sensation seems to be shown, indeed, by one of M. Binet's experiments. The patient having been made to see an imaginary portrait on a blank piece of card-board, this was suddenly covered by a sheet of paper. The patient said that the portrait *disappeared for a moment*, but then reappeared on the paper with complete distinctness. We may thus fairly conclude that an area which was actually seen before the hallucination was induced in the first instance, will also be actually seen for a moment when vision is redirected to it (or its reflection), after the optical apparatus has been brought into play. During that moment, it will, of course, be seen under the newly-introduced optical conditions; and *association* may again cause the object which supplants it to follow suit. It is quite possible, however, to suppose that the supplanted area continues further to *provoke* the hallucination, in the same sense that the white rays provoked the green percept in Fechner's experiment. The rays which are lost to consciousness continue to excite the sensorium physically; and this physical excitation will have definite peculiarities, corresponding to the distinguishing marks of the area whence it comes. Double this excitation by a prism, or reflect it from another quarter, and the percept which it provokes may naturally be doubled or seen in the new direction. So, if both eyes were employed in Fechner's experiment (p. 462), might the green percept be artificially doubled.

[1] In this connection, I may quote the following spontaneous case—where the imagination of the percipient may probably have been adequate to conjure up the reflected figure. The account is from Mr. Adrian Stokes, M.R.C.S., of 16, Howell Road, St. David's, Exeter.

" When I was living in Bedford Street North, Liverpool, in the year 1857 (I think), my wife roused me from sleep suddenly and said, 'Oh! Adrian, there's Agnes!' I started up, crying, 'Where? Where?' but, of course, there was no Agnes. My wife then told me that she had awoke, and had seen the form of her only sister, Agnes, sitting on the ottoman at the foot of the bed. On seeing this form she felt frightened; but then, recalling her courage, she thought if the figure were real she would be able to see it

that he has also made repeated trials, and has never confirmed the results of the Salpêtrière. And one further reservation must be made. It is just conceivable that the changes wrought on the imaginary percept were due, not to the optical instruments, but to *thought-transference.* For M. Binet and his assistants of course knew themselves, in each case, the particular optical effect to be expected. An experimenter who has not expressly recognised the reality of thought-transference would never think of so arranging his experiment that he himself should not know, till after the result, which instrument was in use or what was its position; nor indeed is it easy to imagine how such a condition could in practice be carried out. We have reason, moreover, to think that the hypnotic *rapport,* which enables the operator to impose a hallucination on the " subject," is a condition decidedly favourable to telepathic influence. The point seems worth suggesting, if only because thought-transference is a possibility which will assuredly need to be taken into account at many points, in that wide investigation of hysterical conditions which is assuming so much prominence in France. It would be most interesting if a state of hallucination turned out to be one in which the " subject " is specially susceptible to " transferred impressions."

§ 5.   But in any case, imaginary objects which are projected on a convenient flat surface form a very outlying class. For the common run of visual hallucinations, even of those seen in good light, we cannot assume the necessity of any objective *points de repère,* or any definite external stimulation of the retina.[1] On the contrary,

---

reflected in the mirror of the wardrobe, which she had in full view as she lay in bed. Directing her eyes, therefore, to the mirror, there she saw, by the light of the fire that was burning brightly in the grate, the full reflection of the form seated on the ottoman, looking at a bunch of keys which she appeared to hold in her hand.   Under the startling effect caused by this sight, she called me to look at it, but, before I was awake, the form and its reflection had vanished.   It was not a dream, my wife is certain.

" 'When my wife saw her sister sitting at the foot of our bed looking at the bunch of keys, she (the sister) was clad in the ordinary indoor dress of the time.   I remember the start of surprise with which I awoke and exclaimed.   My wife has never, that I know of, experienced any hallucination or delirium ; and is a woman of excellent sense and judgment.   She never saw any other vision but that one. '

[1] It should be observed that light may favour, and darkness hinder, the projection of a phantasm, owing to the different effect of the one and the other on the *general* physiological state.   The presence of light might thus be a necessity, quite apart from any distinguishable *points de repère ;* and this may apply not only to a crucial case—as, *e.g.,* where Professor Bernheim made a hypnotic "subject " see a phantom-balloon in a cloudless blue sky—but to the common type of hallucinations which cease when the room is darkened.   In the same way the presence of light is occasionally found to be a condition of *auditory* hallucinations.   (Ball, *Leçons sur les Maladies Mentales,* p. 116.)   See also the very interesting case given by Professor F. Jolly in the

they have every appearance of being *centrally initiated,* as well as centrally constructed. For instance, it is quite as easy to make the patient see objects in free space—say, out in the middle of the room; and such is the common form of spontaneous hallucination, both of sane and insane persons, where human figures are seen. The eyes are then focussed, not on the real objects from which *points de repère* would have to be supplied, but on the figure itself; which may be much nearer than the wall behind it, and may thus require a very different adjustment of the eyes. For eyes adjusted to the imaginary object, the real objects behind, though in the line of sight, may be quite outside the range of clear vision; and we can scarcely suppose *points de repère* to excite a percept whose position is such that, for *it* to be visible, they themselves must cease to be so. And the difficulty of regarding external points of excitation as a necessary condition becomes even greater when the hallucination is a *moving* one. I refer not to the cases where the imaginary figure follows the movements of the eye, owing to some morbid affection of that organ which acts as a real moving substratum for it, but to those where the eye follows the figure in its seemingly independent course. Here we should have to assume that the *point de repère* keeps changing; that is, as the imaginary figure passes along the side of the room, in front of a multitude of different objects—pictures, paper, furniture, &c.—the very various excitations from these several objects act in turn as the basis of the same delusive image. There seem no grounds for such an assumption. What is there to produce or to guide the selection of ever-new *points de repère* ? To what external cause could we ascribe the perpetual substitution of one of them for another ? On the view that the figure may be centrally initiated, no less than centrally constructed, none of these difficulties occur. Such a figure may just as well appear in the empty centre of the room as on a piece of card-board, and may just as well move as stand still. Stronger still are cases where the hallucination is not in the line of vision. Dr. Charcot has noted a curious form of unilateral hallucination, which occurs sometimes to hysterical patients with

---

Archiv für Psychiatrie, Vol. iv., p. 495. His paper is on the production of auditory hallucinations by the application of an electric current in the neighbourhood of the ear. In one case, he shows good reason for attributing the hallucination, not to a stimulation of the *auditory* nerve, but to a transference to the auditory centre of the stimulus given to fibres of the *fifth* nerve. For the subjective sounds did not, as in all the other cases, correspond in a regular way to the opening and closing of the current, but appeared under all conditions in which *pain* was produced. See also Köppe (*Op. cit.,* p. 54) on the same subject.

normal eyes, on the side on which they are hemianæsthetic—animals passing rapidly in a row from behind forwards, which usually *disappear* when the eyes are turned directly to them.[1] Another type where the hallucination passes out of the range of direct vision is presented by Bayle's case, where a spider used first to appear life-size, and then gradually to expand till it filled the whole room.[2] Sir J. F. W. Herschel describes an analogous experience of his own. The same sort of argument applies to hallucinations where a figure appears repeatedly, but only in one place, while still not an illusion due to any real feature in the place—as in the case of a patient of Morel's,[3] who always saw a headless man at the bottom of the garden, or of an informant of my own whose phantasmal visitant confined itself to a particular bed; and also where the percipient is haunted by a figure which can be seen only in one direction, as in Baillarger's case of a doctor who could not turn without finding a little black cow at his side.[4] The mind may locate its puppet according to its own vagaries; and this last experience is very like a sensory embodiment of the well-known delusion that somebody is always behind one.

We find, however, our clearest examples of the central initiation of hallucinations, when we turn to cases where excitation from the outer world is plainly absent. This class includes phantasms seen in complete darkness,[5] and also hallucinations of pain, and probably the large majority of auditory hallucinations, which have so far been

[1] *Le Progrès Médical,* 1878, p. 38. It is probable that an attentive regard is a condition for the establishment of *points de repère.* In the case of M. Binet's "subjects," a certain peculiarity in the fixed regard, which might act in this way, is strongly suggested by the following fact. In some cases, after a screen had been interposed between the patient's eyes and the imaginary object, she continued to see not only that object (say, a mouse), but a *real object* (say, a hat) on which it had been placed. Thus the hat assumed the property—shared by the imaginary mouse, but unshared by any other real objects—of remaining as a percept in spite of an opaque barrier. Kahlbaum describes a patient who saw the form of his deceased child *only* when he fixed his eyes steadily on a point. ("Die Sinnesdelirien" in the *Allgemeine Zeitschrift für Psychiatrie,* Vol. xxiii.,p.7; and see also below, p. 493, second sentence.) But in the general run of spontaneous hallucinations, there is no reason for supposing that the regard has any of this exceptional intentness.

[2] *Revue Médicale,* 1825, Vol. i., p. 34.

[3] *Traité des Maladies Mentales,* p. 357.

[4] Baillarger, *Des Hallucinations,* p. 312; Ball, *Leçons sur les Maladies Mentales,* p. 73.

[5] Sir J. F. W. Herschel mentions that some of his own hallucinations could be seen with open eyes *only* if the darkness was complete. (*Op. cit.,* p. 407.) Some of Nicolai's visions could only be seen when the eyes were shut; and this was also a feature of a very interesting case recorded by Dr. Pick (in the Vienna *Jahrbuch für Psychiatrie* for 1880, Vol. ii., p. 50), where nevertheless the figures seen gave an impression of complete externality, and were often addressed by the patient. Schüle records a similar instance. (*Handbuch der Geisteskrankheiten,* p. 128.) In the *Gazette Médicale de Paris* for March 21, 1885, Professors Bernheim and Charpentier describe some experiments made in a dark room, where—*points de repère* being necessarily absent—the visual hallucinations of hypnotic "subjects" proved not to be modifiable by optical instruments in the way above described.

disregarded. Here the alternative is simple. The initiation must either occur in the brain, or be due to some morbid or abnormal condition of the outer sensory apparatus. We have already duly noted the latter mode as a frequent one. But the fact that certain hallucinations have been undoubtedly due to injury of the external organ does not establish, or even strongly suggest, the existence of a similar condition in cases where it defies detection.[1] As a rule, where the abnormal condition has been made out, hallucinations have not been its only result. The ulceration of the cornea which initiates visual hallucinations has begun by affecting the vision of real objects. Illusions, or false perceptions of colour, usually precede the appearance of more distinct phantasms.[2] So, in cases of more transient abnormality—such as the *illusions hypnagogiques* mentioned in the last chapter—other signs precede the hallucination. The observer, whose eyes are heavy with sleep, begins by seeing luminous points and streaks, which shift and change in remarkable ways ; and it is from these as nuclei that the subsequent pictures develop. Mr. James Britten, of Isleworth, tells me that, as a boy, he often saw in the dark a distant, tiny point of light, which approached and became an eye, then turned into a face, and then, coming nearer, " developed into a mass of very horrible faces," quite unlike any that he had ever seen or imagined. Similarly one of the seers of "Faces in the Dark" (*St. James's Gazette*, February 10th, 15th, and 20th, 1882) described the frequent vision of a shower of golden spangles, which changed into a flock of sheep. Now, since our physiological knowledge leaves no doubt that the points, streaks and spangles are due to the condition of the retina, it is safe in such cases to conclude that this condition has initiated the hallucination. But it is not equally safe to conclude that the process must be the same for cases where the points, streaks and spangles are absent. I do not forget that even a normal eye is subject to affections which escape attention until a special effort is made to realise them. But wherever the hallucination can be gradually traced in its development from more rudimentary sensations, these last seem to be very distinct and exceptional things, unknown in ordinary experience. Moreover, the vision itself is commonly of a changing kind—the features developing rapidly out of one another ;

---

[1] For statements of the opposite view see (as well as M. Binet's papers above referred to) Professor Ball, in *L'Encéphale*, 1882, p. 6., and *Maladies Mentales*, p. 111, &c. ; and the classical paper of Dr. Régis on unilateral hallucinations, *L'Encéphale*, 1881, p. 44.

[2] Dr. Max Simon in the *Lyon Médical*, Vol. xxxv., p. 439 ; Voisin, *Op. cit.*, p. 70.

often also of a swarming kind—detailed landscapes, elaborate kaleido-scopic patterns, showers of flowers, lines of writing on a luminous ground, and so on.[1] Now, compare such experiences with ordinary cases of "ghost-seeing" in the dark. A man wakes in the night, and sees a luminous figure at the foot of his bed. Here the hallucination comes suddenly, single and complete, to a person whose eyes are open and unfatigued; it is not preceded by any peculiar affection of vision, is not developed out of anything, and does not move, or swarm, or develop fresh features; nor does it fulfil the test of hallucinations due to the state of the external organ, by moving as the eye moves.[2]

[1] Galton, *Inquiries into Human Faculty*, pp. 159-63 ; Maury, *Le Sommeil et les Rêves*, p. 331. Probably the first clear description of these phenomena is that given by Vair, Bishop of Pozzuolo, *De Fascino Libri tres* (Venice, 1589), p 112. The following cases—the first from Mrs. Willert, of Headington Hill, Oxford, the second sent to me by the Rev. J. A. Macdonald, of Manchester, in the words of his wife—are as good specimens as could be found. Mrs. Willert wrote on Dec. 20, 1883 :—
"The pictures I see generally appear at night before going to sleep, always in complete darkness, and I believe usually when I am rather tired. I can see them with my eyes open, but the colours are much less brilliant than when my eyes are shut. I am quite conscious at the time of the unreality of the scenes—indeed, they seem to be very much like the constantly changing slides of a magic lantern, and I should say of the same size ; when they disappear everything is black again. I see all kinds of things, generally in quick succession ; never, however, blending into one another. I can never recall the same picture however much I try. I see landscapes, interiors and exteriors of houses, &c., and single objects, such as ,flowers, books, boots, feathers, pots, &c., &c., and sometimes figures—of which, however, I can never distinguish the faces. Once or twice I have seen a little scene enacted. I remember one distinctly. I saw a man in the dress of the last century riding down a lane. As he came forward, two men, also on horseback, rushed out on him from behind some trees and knocked him down. I longed to know the end of this little story, but it disappeared. I am never conscious that the things I see have any connection with what I have been thinking of, nor do I ever remember to have recognised a place I know amongst the many landscapes I see."
Mr. Willert tells me that his wife can always narrate these visions as they pass, and is certainly wide awake at the time.
Mrs. Macdonald says :—
"For many years I have been accustomed to see multitudes of faces as I lie awake in bed, generally before falling asleep at night, after waking up in the morning, or if I should wake in the middle of the night. They seem to come up out of the darkness, as a mist, and rapidly develop into sharp delineation, assuming roundness, vividness, and living reality. Then they fade off only to give place to others, which succeed with surprising rapidity and in enormous multitudes. Formerly the faces were wonderfully ugly. They were human, but resembling animals, yet such animals as have no fellows in the creation, diabolical-looking things. So curiously and monstrously frightful were they that I cannot conceive whence they could have come if not from the infernal world. I could not, certainly, at other times, by any voluntary effort of imagination, conjure up anything even remotely approaching their frightfulness. Latterly the faces have become exquisitely beautiful. Forms and features of faultless perfection now succeed each other in infinite variety and number."
I will add one more experience, which would, I think, be specially hard to refer to the *Licht-staub* of the eye, inasmuch as it had an obvious cause of another sort. A friend wrote to me on Sept. 29, 1885 :—
"Between sleeping and waking this morning, I perceived a dog running about in a field (an ideal white-and-tan sporting dog, 'bred out of the Spartan kind,' &c.), and the next moment I heard a dog barking outside the window. Keeping my closed eyes on the vision, I found that *it came and went with the barking of the dog outside;* getting fainter, however, each time."
[2] M. Binet treats all "ghost-seers" as so paralysed with terror that they do not move their eyes from the figure—which leaves it open to him to guess that the figure would move if their eyes moved. Brewster (*Natural Magic,* p. 130) had the same idea. To Wundt, also, stationary hallucinations that can be looked away from seem unknown as a distinct and fairly common type, and he inclines to regard them as mere illusions.

Such visions are commonly explained—and often, no doubt, with justice—as due to nervousness or expectancy. But nervousness and expectancy act by exciting the mind, not by congesting the retina ; they work on the imagination, and their physical seat is not in the eye, but in the brain. We should conclude, then, that the brain initiates the hallucination ; and that nocturnal visions, which vary so greatly both in themselves and in the general conditions of their appearance, vary also in their seat of origin.

The auditory cases are even plainer. For here the hypothesis of *points de repère* seems quite out of the question. It has never been observed that the hallucinations occur when the attention is being fixed on particular external sounds, or begin or cease synchronously with the beginning or cessation of such sounds : in fact silence seems to be a specially favourable condition for them. The only alternative, therefore, to supposing them to be centrally initiated, is to suppose some abnormality in the external organ itself. Such an abnormality has often been detected ; and even when not absolutely detected, it may sometimes be inferred from other symptoms. Thus, an enlarged carotid canal, or a stoppage which produces an unwonted pressure on the vessels, will first make itself felt by hummings and buzzings; hallucination then sets in, and imaginary voices are heard which we should naturally trace to the local irritation that produced the former sounds.[1] But the analogy is not obvious between these

Brewster's own case of Mrs. A., and the well-known cases given by Paterson (*Edinburgh Medical and Surgical Journal*, January, 1843) would alone suffice, I think, to refute this view. See also Kandinsky's and Schröder van der Kolk's experiences (*Archiv für Psychiatrie*, 1881, p. 461, and *De Pathologie en Therapie der Krankzinnigheid*, p. 27). I have in my possession a good many examples where the imaginary figure has been looked away from and back to again. (See for instance, Mr. Turner's case, quoted below, p. 491.) The Rev. P. H. Newnham tells us of three occasions, during the autumn of 1883, on which he saw and recognised in church the figures of persons who proved not to have been there. In two of the three cases the figure thus seen had peculiarities which made it quite unmistakeable, and was observed in the same place more than once during the service, just as any real member of the congregation might have been. The third case is this :—

"I went, as usual, to the school, about a quarter-of-an-hour before service, and either spoke or nodded to all the teachers present. I particularly noticed one in whom I am much interested, sitting with her class, nodded to her, and she smiled back again. Subsequently, in church, I noticed her again, and counted her (I always count my congregations) *twice over* ; once when I counted the entire number present ; once when I counted children and adults separately. It turned out, however, that the girl had not been present. I think I was never so surprised in my life. I made several inquiries, but there was no mistake. She had been detained at home, much to her vexation and annoyance, during the whole afternoon on which I had seen her in two different places, and had had my eye upon her, practically, the whole time."

[1] The abnormality may be of the most transient kind. Thus on one occasion I myself distinctly traced the illusion of hearing steps accompanying my own to the recurrent variations in the blood-flow of the ear, caused by the very act of stepping. But I may add that hummings are sometimes experienced where no cause whatever can be discovered in the condition of the ear ; and thus may possibly themselves be centrally initiated. (See Köppe, *Op. cit.*, p. 50.)

cases and those where there are no hummings and buzzings, and no grounds for supposing that there is a stoppage or lesion of any sort. Among a numerous, though much neglected, class of phenomena— the casual hallucinations of the sane—the commonest form by very far is for persons to hear their name called when no one is by. The experience is often remarkably distinct, causing the hearer to start and turn round. It is not at all connected with conditions that produce blood-pressure, such as lying with one ear closely pressed on the pillow; it comes in a sudden and detached way, and apparently at quite accidental moments. Another experience, which I have myself occasionally had when going to sleep, but without any external pressure on the ear, is for sentences which are floating in one's head to take on a slightly externalised form—a *central* " illusion hypnagogique," in contrast to the visual sort which are due to the *Licht-staub* of the retina. And when we come to insane cases, we find a more positive refutation of peripheral origin. A well-known form of hallucination occurs in the form of dialogue; the patient returns answers to the voices that haunt him, and is answered in turn. He can regulate the course of his own delusion. Dr. V. Parant has recently reported the case of an asylum-patient who, when thwarted or annoyed, would go to special spots to consult imaginary advisers; the replies that she received—it need hardly be said—always corresponded with her own desires and prejudices. Another insane woman used to play " odd and even " with an imaginary prefect of police, whose guesses were always wrong.[1] We clearly cannot suppose here an *intermittent* abnormality of the ear, which always sets in by chance at the very moment when the imaginary speaker's replies fall due. It may be added that even where a distinct morbid cause can be traced, it is as often as not a *central* cause. After a long course of alcohol a man begins to hear voices; but alcohol, while admittedly affecting brain-tissue, has no recognised tendency to affect the ear.

Again, we have to remember the clear relation which often exists between sensory hallucinations and more general ideas and delusions.[2] This remark, which is a common-place of alienists, applies far beyond the limits of insanity. One of the commonest

---

[1] *Ann. Médico-psych.*, 6th series, Vol. vii., p. 379; Ball, *Maladies Mentales*, p. 98. See also Kahlbaum, *Op. cit.*, p. 10; the cases described by Michéa in the *Ann. Medico-psych.* for 1856, p. 389; and M. Sandras' own experience in the same journal for 1855, p. 542.

[2] Lélut, *L'Amulette de Pascal*, p. 101; Krafft-Ebing, *Op. cit.*, p. 19; Griesinger, *Op. cit.*, pp. 97-8; Wundt, *Op. cit*, Vol. ii., p. 356; Dagonet, *Les Maladies Mentales*, p. 94.

incidents of the witch-cases is the apparition of the supposed witch to the victim. The explanation of this phenomenon must surely be sought in the pre-occupation of feeble and excitable minds with a particular terrifying subject. And these cases present a further feature, the importance of which has, I think, escaped notice, and which points still more decisively to a purely cerebral origin. They comprise the most remarkable examples on record of hallucinations of *pain.* The verdict of the victims' senses often was that the witch was not only visibly present, but was torturing them.[1] The pains were often distinctly localised, and were specifically described—as beating, scratching, pinching, biting; while the parts affected were, of course, not being externally excited more than any other part of the body.

A further argument for the central initiation of many hallucinations of the distinctly morbid sort may be drawn from the *course* which the morbid process takes. The first stage is often not a sensory hallucination at all ; it is a mere delusion ; the patient thinks that plots are being concocted against him. After a time his secret enemies begin to reveal themselves, and he hears their abusive and threatening language. We surely cannot ascribe the sensory experience here to a lesion of the ear which happens to occur independently, but regularly, at this particular stage ; it follows, on the other hand, in the most natural way, if we regard it as imposed from within, as soon as the disease has gone far enough for the mind to clothe its imaginary fears in a more vivid form. Specially conclusive in this respect are the cases where voices begin to address the patient in the most internal way, without sound, and only after a time take on a distinctly audible character.[2] But of all the cases in point the most interesting are those where one type of hallucination assails one side of the body and another the other.[3] They confirm what was said above—that the mere fact of a hallucination being *unilateral,* or peculiar to one side of the body, though suggesting a defect in the external organ, is by no means a

---

[1] Mather, *Wonders of the Invisible World* (Boston, 1693), p. 105; *Magnalia Christi Americana* (London, 1702), pp. 68, 69, 72, 75; Deodat Lawson, *Further Account of Tryals of the New England Witches* (London, 1693), p. 2 ; *Sadducismus Triumphatus* (London, 1689), p. 375 ; *Sadducismus Debellatus* (London, 1698), p. 3 ; Boulton, *Complete History of Magick* (London, 1715), Vol. ii., p. 31 ; Durbin, *A Narrative of Some Extraordinary Things* (Bristol, 1800), p. 17 ; *Zwei Hexenprocesse in Ballenstedt* (Quedlinburg, 1863), p. 56.

[2] Griesinger, *Op. cit.*, p. 91. The bearing of this fact on the theory of central origin has been noted by Mr. Sully, *Illusions*, p. 119.

[3] See Dr. Magnan's account in the *Archives de Neurologie*, Vol. vi., p. 336.

proof of it.[1] The double sensory experience follows with exactness the course of the delusions. The patient first suffers from melancholy and discouragement ; this develops into a belief that he is surrounded by enemies : and he then hears insulting voices on the right side. To this unhappy stage succeeds in due course one of exaltation and self-esteem ; the patient believes himself to be some royal personage. And now encouraging and eulogistic voices present themselves on the left side. " The good and the evil genii form a sort of Manicheism which governs him." Here the imagination, as its operations become more complex and establish an opposition of character between its creatures, takes advantage (so to speak) of the fact that the body has two opposite sides ; it locates friends and foes just as they might be located in a picture or a play which represented an impending contest. It will scarcely be maintained that by accident the left ear began to be locally affected just at the time when the development of the plot necessitated the entrance of the friendly power upon the scene. Another case involves the sense of touch. A man, after praying for a year that his actions might be Divinely guided, heard a voice say, " I will save thy soul "; and from that time forward he felt his left or his right ear touched by an invisible attendant, according as he was doing right or wrong.[2] Did the auditory hallucination coincide by chance with the commencement of local irritation in the *pinna ?* Dr. Magnan adds three examples of alcoholism, where abuse and threats were heard on one side, praise and consolation on the other. In these cases there were crises of fury, in which hallucinations of all the senses took place, involving both sides alike, and masking the more ordinary condition. On the decline of these crises, the opposed auditory hallucinations recommenced. It seems impossible to resist Dr. Magnan's view, that the poison, distributed through the whole brain, provokes at times a general crisis; but that when this subsides, it localises its action at the weakest spot. Should this happen to be the auditory centre on one side, a single

---

[1] *Cf.* Dr. A. Robertson in the *Report of the International Medical Congress*, 1881, Vol. iii., pp. 632-3. A gentleman who writes to me from the Junior United Service Club, and who describes himself as " a military physician of long foreign service and not of superstitious tendencies," says that as a youth he was once transported with passion during an argument. "There was a large knife lying on the table, and I distinctly heard a voice whisper *into my right ear*, 'Take up that knife and use it.' I glanced over my shoulder involuntarily for the speaker "—who of course was not visible. There was no question of lesion here, either of the sense-organ or of the brain ; for my informant has never had any other hallucination in his life. That a *whisper* should thus be located in one ear is specially natural ; since it corresponds with our usual way of receiving real whispers.

[2] *Démonomanie des Sorciers*, Paris, 1582, pp. 11-12. For a wonder (see p. 177) Bodin gives the case at first-hand ; and there is no reason to doubt its truth.

unilateral hallucination would be the result; but if both centres remain affected the projection may assume the complex two-sided form.

But perhaps the strongest cases of all in favour of a purely central initiation yet remain—the cases of hallucination *voluntarily originated.*[1] Wigan's instance has often been quoted, of the painter who, after carefully studying a sitter's appearance, could project it visibly into space, and paint the portrait not from the original but from the phantasm.[2] He ended by confounding the phantasmal figures with real ones, and became insane. Baillarger reports another painter, Martin, as having similarly projected pictures, which so interested him that he requested anyone who took up a position in front of them to move.[3] And I may add that in one of the cases of *persistent dream-images* mentioned in the last chapter, my informant, Lieut.-Colonel Hartley, of Hartley, near Dartford, remarks, "I can always produce this phenomenon, if I know that I am dreaming, by opening my eyes, which wakes me, but the dream-image persists." I confess that I should have been tempted to regard the voluntary cases as conclusive evidence of central initiation, had I not found so high an authority as Professor Ball explicitly claiming them as hallucinations provoked by an " abnormal sensation."[4] He does not tell us what the abnormal sensation is, or what causes it. He contents himself with pointing out that hallucinations are very like dreams; that some dreams are (and, therefore, apparently, all

---

[1] It is odd to find *involuntariness* not infrequently taken as the distinctive abnormality in hallucinations (Falret, *Op. cit.*, p. 281; Buchez and De Castelnau in the French debates of 1855-6); and the odder, inasmuch as not only may hallucinations be voluntary, but the mental pictures and memories, from which they are to be distinguished, are often of course involuntary.

[2] *The Duality of the Mind*, p. 124.

[3] See also Cardan, *De Varietate Rerum*, (Basle, 1557) p. 314, who says he has always been shy of mentioning the peculiarity—" Cum volo, video quæ volo, oculis, non vi mentis." Kahlbaum (*Op. cit.*, p. 33), and Maisonneuve (*Recherches et Observations sur l'Epilepsie*, Paris, 1803, p. 295), give each an instance; and Sir H. Holland (*Chapters on Mental Physiology*, p. 47) says that he has met with several cases. One of the seers of "Faces in the Dark" reported that he could produce the vision of the spangles and sheep at will. His case differs, however, from those given in the text. For, in the first place, his vision was one of old standing; and, in the second place, his retina must have been pretty constantly in the abnormal state. I should thus ascribe the phenomenon to a concentration of attention on actual visual sensations, which fell by habit into the familiar lines. It would be interesting to know whether, after the spangles had appeared, it was possible to *check* their development into sheep.

[4] *Op. cit.*, p. 122. This error (as it seems to me) depends on what has become a very common misreading of the term " psycho-sensorial." The theory so designated is often described as "théorie mixte"—the " mixture " being of the "imagination" and of some prior " abnormal sensation," which sets the imagination to work. But hallucinations (as we have seen) are psycho-*sensorial* in virtue not of their *antecedents*, but of their *content*—because they are things actually *seen* and actually *heard*. The " sensorial " element in them is not the incentive or the raw material of the abnormal activity, but its product.

dreams must be) provoked by external stimulation—say a knock at the door; and that we can sometimes direct the course of a dream at will: *ergo*, it is easy to see how some people may start a hallucination at will. It would be more to the purpose if he would introduce us to a dreamer who can designedly start a pre-arranged dream by knocking at his own door.

§ 6. There is only one other point, in relation to the question of origin, that needs special attention; and that concerns hallucinations of what may be called the lowest or most rudimentary grade. There is a class of experience which all the writers who describe it [1] agree to treat as a quite unique type, and of which frequent examples have been observed among religious mystics, and persons who believe themselves to be in direct communication with spiritual guides. They describe a voice which is yet soundless, which utters the "language of the soul" inside them, and which they hear by means of a "sixth sense," and without any apparent participation of the ear. "I should hear the voice just as well if I were stone deaf," such a person will say; "my ear has nothing to do with it." [2] Owing to the absence of a definable sensory quality, Baillarger distinguished this class as *psychic* [3] hallucinations, in opposition to *psycho-sensorial*; and M. Binet himself, who insists on an external or peripheral basis for all other hallucinations, is inclined to treat these as exceptional, and to grant them an origin from within. As one who holds that that is equally the origin of a large number of the undoubted *psycho-sensorial* hallucinations, I cannot recognise this exception; and to me the class in question is of interest, not as *distinguished* from the psycho-sensorial family, but as a true species of that genus, presenting the sensorial element reduced to its very lowest terms. I regard it as the first stage of a graduated series—the embryonic instance of the investiture of an image or representation with a sensory or presentative character. In proportion as the sensorial element in hallucination is attenuated and dim, or full and distinct, will the perception appear internal or external; and these cases are simply the most internal sort, between which and the most

---

[1] I find that I must except Dr. Dagonet (*Op. cit.*, p. 92); who, however, is certainly wrong in regarding the phenomena in question as necessarily indicative of insanity.

[2] Köppe, *Op. cit.*, p. 34.

[3] The term must, of course, not be confounded with our special sense of the word "psychical," explained on p. 5, note.

external sort there exists various degrees of *partial* externalisation.
This view has surely everything to recommend it. We can but take
the perceiver's own account—that he has a distinct impression of
words; and that this impression has an actuality which clearly
separates it from the mere image or memory of words. How can
this separation be conceived, except by recognising the presence of a
genuine, though faint, sensorial element?[1] The question is of
importance to my argument; for to admit a genuine sensory
element in the most "internal" species of hallucination—which all
agree to be centrally initiated—will practically be to admit a similar
initiation for *other* psycho-sensorial hallucinations.

The Rev. P. H. Newnham, of Maker Vicarage, Devonport, already
so often mentioned, has supplied me with some examples which are
eminently in point. He has had on several occasions "psychic"
hallucinations in the ordinary sense—an impression of words which
"seem to be formed and spoken within the chest.", But he has also
experienced and clearly distinguished another type of hallucination—
a *soundless* voice, which yet seems to speak *into his right ear* (he is
deaf of the left ear), and which thus produces the sense of externality,
though not of actual sound. We must surely recognise this as the
stage just above that of "psychic" hallucination.[2] And we meet with

---

[1] Of what exactly this element may consist is another question. Dr. Max Simon
(in the *Lyon Médical*, Vol. xxxv., pp. 435, 486) has made the suggestion that what is
felt is a muscular impulse to form the words, rather than the sound of them—an impulse
exhibited in its extreme form in the irrepressible continuous vociferation of mania ; and on
this account he even refuses to regard the experience as hallucination at all. It is quite
possible that the constitution of the phantasmal words may be a complex one, and may
include an embryonic sense of muscular impulse. But it seems certain that the patient's
sensation is of something other and more than this. For him the words are not suggested
or initiated, but actually and completely impressed. The impression is not recognised as
impulse any more than as sound ; but it is an impression of objective reality. Here, then,
we surely trace the characteristic hallucinatory element. The close connection between
the auditory and speech centres is well illustrated in the following case of undoubted hallucination, recorded by Holland (*Medical Notes and Reflections*, 1840, p. 232). A slight
concussion of the brain having produced a temporary inability to find the right words and
to speak coherently, the patient was some days later amused by hearing, as it seemed
close to his ear, a dialogue in which the phrases exhibited precisely similar defects. (See
Dr. A. Pick's remarks in the *Prager Medicinische Wochenschrift* for October 31, 1883.)

[2] The most interesting case known to me of the speaking "within the chest" forms
another instructive link, since the *internal* voice is expressly described as *audible*, and as
producing a strong impression of a second person's presence. A Yorkshire vicar, whose
name I may mention but not print, writes to me :—

"In the autumn of the year 1858, I was staying at Invercargill, the most southern
part of New Zealand. There was only one hotel there in those days, kept by a Dane.
There was no village of any kind ; the place was as wild as could be. When I had been
about two days at this inn, I heard myself addressed by name, and found that the speaker
was one of the sailors who had worked the vessel in which I had sailed from England to
New Zealand. He was a man I knew well, because he was on one occasion put in irons
for mutinous language, on our passage, and I had often spoken with him both before and
since that event. When the ship reached the Heads, as the entrance to Port Chalmers is

2 H

exactly parallel degrees of *visual* externalisation. I have received
several accounts from persons who profess to see with the " spiritual
eye," and whose language betrays the struggle to describe something

called, this man, with five or six others of the crew, deserted, taking the ship's whale-boat
in the darkness of the night, and leaving it on the beach.

" In the evening I went into the large kitchen of the hotel, where this man and several
others were sitting round the fire, smoking and drinking. The landlord was there, and we
were all very friendly together. I found that three or four of the men were also some of
the men who had deserted, though I did not remember them at first. They told me they
were going in the morning to the Island of Ruapuke, where there was a missionary, as
one of the party wished to be married, and there was no minister on the mainland in that
neighbourhood. I said I should rather like to see the mission-station, and they said they
meant to stay there a day or two before returning, as there were a great many wild boars
in the island, and would have some hunting, sleeping in their boat at night. They told
me they had plenty of provisions—meat, fish, bread, and so on, besides beer and spirits,
and one or two bottles of champagne for the wedding breakfast. They said it would be
necessary to start about 4, as it was high water on the bar about 5, and the bar was a
very shallow one at the point they desired to cross it. They were all most eager for me
to join them, and I had thoroughly entered into the spirit of the thing, and promised to
go if they would call me. I remember rising up to go to bed, and saying, ' Well, as I
shall have to be up before 4, I won't sit up any longer.' It was then about 11. They
said they were all going to ' turn in ' directly, and would rouse me up, never fear ; ' Don't
you be afraid, we won't go without you,' or words to that effect.

" I left them with the fullest intention of going with them I ever had of doing anything in my life. The thing was settled. That was why I was going to bed, otherwise I
should have stayed another hour at least. I had no candle on the way, but usually struck
a match when I reached the bedroom, and lit the candle in the room. When I left the
kitchen I walked through a good-sized room, or second kitchen, and into the front part of
the inn, and came to the staircase. I had got up about four or five stairs, when someone
or something said, ' *Don't go with those men.*' There was certainly no one on the stairs,
and I stood still and said, ' Why not ? ' The voice. which seemed as if some other person
spoke audibly inside my chest (not to the ear), said in a low tone, but with commanding
emphasis, ' You are *not* to go.' ' But,' said I, ' I have promised to go.' The answer came
again, or rather I should say the warning, ' You are *not* to go.' ' How can I help it ? ' I
expostulated, ' they will call me up.' Then most distinctly and emphatically the same
internal voice, which was no part of my own consciousness, said, ' You must bolt your
door.' All this time I had stood still on the staircase. I did not even remember there
was a bolt to the door, for I recollect just for a moment thinking I must and *would* go, and
then such a strange feeling of mysterious peril that I wondered how I should secure the
door in case there was no lock or bolt. On reaching the room I lit the candle, and felt
very queer, as if some supernatural presence was very near me. There was a strong common
iron bolt to the door, I discovered on examination. As a proof that there had been no
mere revulsion of feeling, I may mention that even now I hesitated whether to secure the
door or not, so anxious was I to go, and so accustomed in those days (I was only 19 years
old) to doing my own will at all hazards. At the very last moment (it was quite a ' toss
up ' which it should be) I bolted the door and got into bed. A great calm succeeded the
past agitation, and I soon fell asleep.

" The next thing I heard was about 3 in the morning (I suppose) a hammering at
the door, as I had expected. I was wide awake, but gave no reply. Then I heard voices,
and the door violently shaken and kicked at. I did not speak, for I knew I should have
been over persuaded if I had called out. I did not mean to go. At last, after a thunder-
ing noise, I heard them cursing and swearing, as well as shouting. But I lay still as a
mouse. So at last they gave it up and went away. I lay awake some little time wondering
whether, after all, I had not been foolish, and then fell into a sound sleep.

" About 9 o'clock I went down into the breakfast-room, where a military gentleman,
a captain or a colonel, was at his breakfast. As I entered the room, he said, ' Have you
heard what has happened ?' ' No,' said I, ' I am just down.' ' Why,' he said, ' it seems
that a party left this hotel this morning for Ruapuke, and their boat has been capsized
on the bar, and they are *every one of them drowned.*' I said, 'Why, I was to have gone
with them, and very nearly did.' ' Then,' said he, ' you've had a lucky escape.' I told
him I had had a kind of warning not to go, and had bolted my door, &c. ; but I did not
tell him all the details.

" Two or three of the men's bodies were washed up on the beach that day, and
the rest in a few days more. Not one of them was saved, and if I had been with
them I must have perished without a doubt."

that is indescribable—seeing that is *not* seeing, a perception of objects which yet are not perceived as in the external world.   And just higher in the scale we have the stage of Blake's visionary experiences. He constantly saw slightly-objectified figures with which he was on such familiar terms as to take their likenesses ; but on only one occasion in his life did he see a " ghost "—*i.e.*, have a completely objectified hallucination—which so terrified him that he rushed out of the house.[1]

In the same connection, it is of interest to observe that below even the lowest stage of sensory hallucination there is a type of delusion which may take a very distinct form, and which looks like *potential* hallucination—namely, the sense of a *presence*, felt not merely in the general way which probably every one has experienced, but as the presence of a particular person.   It is well exemplified in the following account, from Mr. W. de V. Wade, of The Downs, Dunmow :—

"About 4 years ago I awoke about 2 o'clock in the morning, with a curious feeling that a great friend of mine, who is in India, was in my room.   I do not think I had been dreaming about him.   I felt an irresistible impulse to call out his name, and, although I was wide awake, it took me some moments to realise that he could not be in the room.   It was quite dark, and as soon as I had satisfied myself that it was merely a delusion, I went off to sleep again.   Some time in 1882, I was thinking about my brother, who is in America, before I went to sleep.   In the middle of the night I suddenly woke up, with the feeling that he was in the room and had spoken to me.   I actually listened for a second or two, in the anticipation that he would speak again.   Hearing nothing, I controlled a great inclination to call out his name, and then, after arguing to myself that it must be all nonsense, I went to sleep."

Another of my correspondents has had a similar impression with respect to a sister.   " On one or two occasions the feeling has been so strong that I have got up and left the room."   The close connection between a vivid sense of presence and actual hallucination is further shown by examples where the one developes into the other.   Thus, Mr. Joseph Kirk, of the Audit Office, Royal Arsenal, Woolwich, informs me that a niece of his had, one night, an overwhelming sense of an unseen visitant, which lasted some time before it culminated in a clear auditory impression, the words, " I must go now—good-night." Another informant—a lady of vigorous practical intelligence— experienced lately a similar subjective conviction of a particular friend's presence (probably due to the fact that she was apprehending

---

[1] For further examples of different degrees of externalisation, see Chap. xiv., § 1.

news of this friend's death), and then saw her form, "standing in a natural attitude and looking straight at my face. The colour of her dress and cap, and the fashion of both, were absolutely familiar to me." In such a process as this, we seem to see the central origin absolutely laid bare.

§ 7. The general conclusion from the foregoing paragraphs is plain—that hallucinations of the senses may be spontaneously initiated by the brain ; that they are often a pure projection of the brain from within outwards. The hypnotic "subject" will smack his lips over the sweetness of sugar when there is nothing in his mouth—will sniff with delight at a piece of wood when told it is a rose. When the brain does for sight and hearing what it there does for taste and smell, we have a percept which differs from an ordinary external percept only in lacking the objective basis which it suggests. And looking back from this point, we can completely account for the fact noticed in the preceding chapter, that hallucinations occur with disproportionate frequency to people who are in bed. For it is only natural that images should assume the unwonted vividness of sensations especially at those moments when the external organs of sense are not occupied with *other* sensations. We know that the sort of day-dream which comes nearest to hallucinations is favoured by *repose* of the sense-organs ; that when we want to call up the vivid image of a scene, to make it as real—as sensorial— as possible, we close our eyes. One step farther, and we realise the complete continuity of the waking and the sleeping phenomena. Dreams are by far the most familiar instances of the projection by the mind of images that are mistaken for realities : indeed, it is just because they are *so* familiar, and waking hallucinations comparatively so rare, that there is a danger of overlooking the psychological identity of the two classes. We might call dreams the normal form of hallucination, or waking hallucinations the pathological form of dreaming ; and we might present the waking- dreams of haschisch-poisoning and of starvation[1] as a sort of intermediate link. The normal dream disappears when sleep departs ; having been able to impose its images as realities only because in sleep our sensory faculties are to a great extent benumbed, and

---

[1] See the interesting case of Mr. Everts, in *Scribner's Magazine* for November, 1871. Dagonet considers that fasting, meditation, and solitude favour hallucinations by " diminishing the impressionability of the senses " to external stimuli. (*Op. cit.*, p. 93.)

images cannot therefore be compared with actual presentations. Thus the normal dream cannot survive the corrective which the contact of the waking-senses with the external world supplies; it fades like a candle at sunrise; and its images, if they survive, survive as images and nothing more, memories of a vanished world. . The hallucination, or pathological dream, on the other hand, does not require to be thus guarded from comparison with real presentations ; its "images" are able to resist the normal corrective, for they are often as fully charged with sensory quality as the external realities which compete with them.

§ 8. I may now proceed to an altogether different question— namely, at what part or parts of the brain the *constructive* process takes place, and in what it can be conceived to consist. The distinction that has so long occupied us, between central and peripheral initiation, may henceforth be dismissed ; for wherever *initiated,* hallucinations are assuredly *constructed* by the brain from its own resources. An initiating stimulus may probably come from any point on the line from the external organ to the central terminus, along which a nervous current passes in our normal perception of objects. But that stimulus will clearly not determine what the imaginary object shall be, or invest it with any of its qualities : it will merely set the constructive machinery in motion ; and the same stimulus—the same inflammation of the eye or ear—may set the machinery in motion a hundred times, and each time evoke a different hallucination. Where then, and what, is this constructive machinery ? It would be out of place here to attempt any minute account of the various theories, which have for the most part rested on anatomical observation ; and the more so, that their details are still *sub judice.* But in a more general way the problem can be stated, and even I think to some extent determined.

There can be no doubt that certain sensory centres are connected in a special way with hallucinations. This follows, as soon as the full sensory character of the phenomena is recognised ; for that character can only be the psychical expression of physical changes at the " sensory centres "—the spots where (in the ordinary crude but convenient language) impressions are transformed into sensations. As to the exact locality of these spots, there is a conflict of views which may be to some extent reconciled if we regard the process as taking place in several stages. Some (Luys, Ritti, Fournié) believe the principal scene of action to be the large mid-way masses called the optic thalami; others (Schröder van der Kolk, Meynert, Kahl-baum, Kandinsky) would place it lower down—the centre for vision, for instance, in the corpora quadrigemina; while others again (Hitzig, Ferrier, Tamburini) locate it higher up, in the cortex itself. But the authorities are generally agreed in connecting the several forms of sense with several limited areas, distinct from the larger tracts associated with the most highly developed phenomena of intelligence.

A diagram may make the relation of the parts clearer.

Let A represent the retina of the eye, which in itself has no more power of seeing than a mirror has. Let B represent the group of cells in the brain which constitutes the sensory centre—say the "visual-ising centre"—and which is excited into activity whenever sight takes place. And let C represent the cortical or exterior substance of the hemispheres of the brain, part of which is excited into activity whenever any of the higher psychical faculties—intelligent perception, imagination, comparison, memory, volition—are called into play. A is connected with B by the fibres of the optic nerve, and B is connected with C by other nerve-fibres. Now *any* disturbance of the cells at B which reaches a certain intensity will be accompanied by the sensation of sight; and when this disturbance is propagated onwards in the natural course from B to C, this sensation will develop into a complete percept—an object for the mind—which can be reflected on, compared with other objects, and remem-bered. But the indispensable event—the disturbance or discharge at B—may itself originate in several different ways. It may be excited (1) normally, from A, by the stimulus of external rays of light, which makes us see surrounding objects; (2) accidentally, from A, by the stimulus of a blow on the eye, which makes us see sparks; (3) pathologically, or by morbid irritation at A, or on the line of nerve A B; and (4) pathologically or abnormally, but spontaneously, at B itself.

Now for *one* view of the construction of hallucinations these data are sufficient. We have only to suppose that in cases (3) and (4) the agitation at the sensory centre falls readily into certain lines and combinations, so as not only to produce a large variety of sensations—colours, if it be the visual centre, sounds, if it be the auditory one—but to arrange these elements in various definite groups. Everything will now proceed precisely as if these effects had been due to the presence of a real object. The excitation will pursue its ordinary upward course to the highest parts of the brain, and will lead to intelligent perception of the sensory group as an object; while, in the most complete or " external " form of hallucinations, it is possible that by a yet further process a refluent current passes downwards to the external organ,[1] to which the perception is referred, just as though its object were really acting on the eye or ear from outside. There then is the full-fledged hallucination; and its creative machinery, according to this view, lies wholly in the sensory centre.

But there is another view. I have noted *four* ways in which the machinery may be set in motion; but there is a *fifth* possible way. The excitation may come *downwards* from C—from the seats of ideation and memory. And clearly this sort of excitation will have a dominance of its own. It will have *its own* psychical counterpart— an idea or a memory; and when it sets the sensory machinery in motion, that machinery will not now produce or combine a group of sensations determined by its own activity; but will merely embody, or as we might say *execute*, the idea or memory imposed on it. Here, then, the only machinery which is in any sense *constructive* is situated in the higher ideational tracts. But as long as the nervous activity is confined to the ideational tracts, though there is construction, there is no hallucination. That word is never used to describe the mere image or memory of an object; and in serving as a basis to such an image or memory, however vivid, the cells at C are merely performing their normal functions. It is only when the activity escapes downwards, with such force as strongly to stimulate the cells at the lower centre, that sensation floods

---

[1] Krafft-Ebing, *Op. cit.*, p. 11; Despine, *Etude Scientifique sur le Somnambulisme*, p. 328; Tamburini in the *Revue Scientifique*, 1881, p. 139; Wundt, *Op. cit.*, Vol. ii., p. 356. This point, however, can hardly be said to be established. The mere subjective fact of the reference to the external organ would not prove (as Tamburini seems to assume) that the organ had been actually excited by a refluent current. Nor (for the reason given on p. 465) can a proof be found in the fact that pressure on the side of one eyeball doubles the phantom—a result which must be attributed either to the doubling of some *point de repère*, or to the association of the sense of lateral pressure with the doubling of real objects. Nor does the fact that "hypnagogic illusions," hallucinations which consist in the surviving of dream-images into waking moments, and hypnotic hallucinations, can give rise to *after-images* (as noted by H. Meyer, Gruithuisen, and MM. Binet and Féré, respectively), imply more than the brief continuance of excitation at the *central* cells. A stronger case, at first sight, is that described by Dr. Pick, of Prague, where only the upper halves of imaginary figures were seen with the right eye; and where it was ascertained that the field of vision was defective over nearly the whole of the upper half of the right retina, to which, of course, the lower half of the figure would have corresponded, but in which the ophthalmoscope revealed no abnormality. But even this is not conclusive as to a refluent current; for Dr. Pick may be right in supposing that some lesion of the nerve-fibres connected with this portion of the retina had led to functional inactivity of the corre-sponding part of the centre itself. I may add, for what it is worth, an observation of Sir J. F. W. Herschel on his own hallucinations seen in the dark, that " the forms were not modified by slight pressure [of the eye], but their degree of visibility was much and capriciously varied by that cause."

the image, and we get the delusive percept or hallucination. The
force of this downward current may exhibit all degrees. It is
probable that even for the barest idea or memory of an object
there is some slight downward escape, causing a slight reverberation at B; and where, as in rare morbid cases,[1] the escape is
wholly barred, all power of calling up visual images is lost. With
every increase in the force of the escape, there will be a rise of
sensory quality, and a nearer approach to absolute hallucination;
and every stage will thus be accounted for, from the picture "in
the mind's eye" to the phantom completely externalised in space.
On this view, the *provenance* of the phenomenon clearly cannot be
assigned to a single locality: the hallucination is *constructed* at one
place, but it only becomes *hallucination* at another. We do not
dispute whether a photograph comes into existence in the camera or
in the developing-room.

§ 9.   Here, then, are the two possibilities: (1) that hallucinations
are produced by an independent activity of the specific sensory
cells—the sensations which arise there being perceived as objects
when the nervous current passes upwards to the higher parts of the
brain; (2) that the part played by the specific sensory cells is only
a response to what may be called *ideational* excitation, propagated
downwards from the higher tracts where the image has been formed.

In attempting to decide between these possibilities, not much
assistance is to be had from direct pathological and physiological
observations.   These have been mainly directed to an end rather
the converse of mine—to utilising the facts of hallucination for
fixing the locality of the centres, by inspection of the brains of
persons who have been in life markedly hallucinated; and even
so not very successfully; for cerebral pathology, as Ball trenchantly
remarks, has a way of lending itself to the demonstration of
whatever one wants.[2]   We are thus thrown back on less direct

---

[1] In the *Archives de Neurologie*, Vol. vi., p. 352, there is cited "un cas de
suppression brusque et isolée de la vision mentale des signes et des objets," where
the suppression extended to dreams.   "Je rêve seulement paroles, tandis que je
possédais auparavant dans mes rêvers la perception visuelle."

[2] Lesions rarely confine themselves neatly to specific areas.   We find Dr. Luys,
the chief advocate of the optic thalami as the primary seat of hallucinations, admitting
the constant spread of lesions from the thalami to the cortex (*Gazette des Hôpitaux*,
December, 1880, p. 46); and Dr. W. J. Mickle (*Journal of Mental Science*, October, 1881,
p. 382,) considers—as the result of a number of very careful necropsies—that in cases
of hallucination "thalamic disease plays a less important part than cortical."   But on
the other hand, he did not find that the lesions were definitely associated with the
spots on the cortex which Ferrier and the advocates of restricted cortical localisation

arguments, derived from the nature of the hallucinations themselves. And I think the mistake has again been in imagining that one or other of two alternatives must be exclusively adopted—that either the lower or the higher origin of hallucinations is the universal one. All, I think, that can be fairly said is that, while the first mode of origin is a *probable* one for some cases, the second mode is a *certain* one for others.

For simple and recurrent forms of hallucination, much may be said in favour of the lower origin. It is in accordance with all that we know or conjecture as to nerve-tissue, that certain cell-modifications and radiations of discharge would be rendered easy by exercise ; and thus the changes to which any morbid excitement gives rise might naturally be the same as have often before been brought about by normal stimulation from the retina or the ear. The elements would fall readily, so to speak, into the accustomed pattern. An object which has been frequently or recently before the eyes, a word or phrase that has been perpetually in the ear—these may certainly be held capable of leaving organic traces of their presence, and so of establishing a sort of lower memory ; as markedly shown, for instance, in cases where uneducated persons have in delirium recited passages of some strange language, of which the sound but not the sense has at some past time been familiar to them. That this lower memory should act automatically seems natural enough when we remember how large a part even of the higher memory is also automatic : an unsought word, suddenly reverberating in the

---

mark out as the visual and the auditory centres ; while lesions at these spots—the angular gyrus and the first temporo-sphenoidal convolution—seem to be found in cases where no hallucination has been observed. (*Journal of Mental Science*, October, 1881, p. 381, and January, 1882, p. 29.) This want of correspondence will seem less surprising, if we remember that in the vast number of casual hallucinations nothing that could be called a lesion exists ; that for the delusions of sleep, of the delirium of fever, of fasting, of the early stages at any rate of haschish and opium-eating, only the general physiological explanation can be given that they are due to some change in the constitution or distribution of the blood ; and also that the more persistent hallucinations of the insane belong, as a rule, to the *earlier* period of *irritation*, rather than to the *later* one when marked lesion has supervened, and dementia is creeping on. Even if we take subsequent cortical lesion as a sign that the weak spot existed from the first in the highest part of the brain, this would be no proof that the specific sensory centre is cortical. If lesions are not bound to be locally restricted, much less are irritations ; and there is nothing to refute the supposition above made, that, when the hallucination occurs, a current has passed downwards to the lower centre—the mischief in the cortex having been primarily an excitant of ideational activities only, and the hallucination being due (as Dr. Mickle well expresses it) to " a tumultuous disorderly reaction of disturbed ideational centres upon sensorial." The same may be said of the *artificial* irritation of the "cortical centres " during life. Ferrier regards the movements which result when an electrical stimulus is applied to these areas, as an indication that visual or auditory sensations (*i.e.*, hallucinations) have been evoked. We may quite accept this interpretation, but still suppose that the primary seat of the sensation was not the spot where the stimulus was applied, but a lower centre on the path along which the irritation passed.

sensorium, is on a par with the images that emerge into consciousness without our being able to connect them with our previous train of ideas. Now it is remarkable how large a number of hallucinations are of this primitive type. I mentioned above that, among the sane, the commonest of all cases is to hear the name called ; and even with the insane, the vocabulary of the imaginary voices often consists of only a few words, usually threatening or abusive, but sometimes quite neutral in character.[1] So of optical hallucinations. With the sane, a large number consist in the casual vision—an *after-image,*[2] as we might say—of a near relative or familiar associate. A friend, who has had considerable experience of the persistence of a dream-image into the first few moments of waking, tells me that "sometimes these images return during the day, or continue appearing, always suddenly, for several days after." The Rev. Robertson Wilson, writing from the United Presbyterian Manse, Strath Devon House, Dollar, tells me that at a time when he was in disordered health owing to overwork, he used to take long excursions, and especially interested himself in the inscriptions in country churchyards.

"One day, after having spent a considerable time in inspecting a village churchyard, what was my horror and consternation to find, on leaving it, that wherever my eyes rested I could descry nothing but monumental inscriptions. The dust on the roadside somehow seemed to form itself into letters. The macadamised highway seemed written all over with mourning, lamentation, and woe : and even when I turned my gaze to the stone dykes on either side of the way, it was only to find that, by some subtle chemistry of my brain, the weather-stains and cracks shaped themselves into words which I could plainly decipher, and found to be of the same nature as those which I had recently been reading in the churchyard. Every time that autumn and winter that I paid a visit to a churchyard, the experience recurred ; and on more than one occasion also without that exciting cause."

The Rev. G. Lyon Turner, Professor of Philosophy at the Lancashire Independent College, Manchester, tells me that he saw one night suspended from the ceiling of the room, which he knew to be plain,

"A large chandelier with some 10 scroll-shaped branches, and the jets shining brightly through the ground-glass globes at the end of each. I at once recognised the chandelier as a duplicate of the chandelier which hung

---

[1] On this subject see Dr. V. Parant in the *Ann. Médico-psych.*, 6th series, Vol. vii., p. 384 ; Kahlbaum, *Op. cit.*, p. 5; and Kraepelin's paper, "Ueber Trugwahrnehmungen," in the *Vierteljahrschrift für Wissenschaftliche Philosophie* for 1881, p. 225. These embryonic hallucinations often develop into more complex form ; Ball, *Op. cit.*, p. 67.
[2] This is a convenient description ; but it must not be held to imply any *retinal* affection, of the sort that Hibbert, Ferrier, and Brewster supposed. See p. 487, note.

in the college chapel connected with the Countess of Huntingdon's college at Cheshunt, where I received my training for the ministry. I moved my head, to see whether the phantom moved too. But no, it remained fixed ; and the objects behind and beyond it became more or less completely visible as I moved, exactly as would have been the case had it been a real chandelier." Mr. Turner woke his wife, who naturally saw nothing.

Another correspondent saw a spectral figure enter his room and stand at the foot of his bed. " Of course I put my head under the bed-clothes, and yet I saw it." It seems so unlikely that the imagination would attract its visitor " under the bed-clothes," that one prefers to suppose a mechanical continuance of reverberation at the lower centre ; and the more so that the spectre was a sort of after-image, based on the memory of a picture. More persistent cases are still frequently of a single object. I have mentioned the doctor and the black cow, and the headless man at the bottom of the garden ; similarly a lady, when in bad health, always saw a cat on the staircase ; and among the insane, a single imaginary attendant is tolerably common.[1] Wherever such simple cases are not connected with any special *délire* or any fixed set of ideas, they may, I think, be fairly (though of course not certainly) attributed to an activity following the lines of certain established tracts in the sensorium. We might compare this locality to a kaleidoscope, which when shaken is capable of turning out a certain limited number of combinations.

On the other hand, hallucinations produced *at the will* of the percipient *must* first take shape above the sensory centres. For it is indisputable that the *idea* of the object to be projected—the picture, face, sentence, or whatever it may be—must precede its sensory embodiment as a thing actually seen or heard ; and the idea, as well as the volition, is an affair of the higher tracts. And apart from these rare voluntary specimens, the astonishing variety and complexity of more common cases—whether visual appearances or verbal sequences—seem absolutely to drive us to a higher seat of manufacture ; for they demand a countless store of elements, and limitless powers of ideal combination. The patient listens to long discourses, or holds conversations with his invisible friends ; and what is heard is no echo of former phrases, but is in every way a piece of new experience. So, too, the number and variety of visual hallucinations which may occur to a single person, sometimes even within the space of a few minutes, is astonishing. The physiologist Bostock, who had many hallucinations ,

---

[1] Blandford, *Insanity and its Treatment*, p. 155 ; Kahlbaum, *Op. cit.*, p. 3 ; Binet in the *Revue Philosophique* for May, 1884, p. 500.

at a time when he was suffering from nervous exhaustion, says that he did not in a single instance see any object with which he had been previously acquainted. Nicolai, who was never otherwise than perfectly sane, and who eventually recovered, continually saw troops of phantoms, most of them of an aspect quite new to him ; and in insanity such a phenomenon is common enough. So, too, the seers of *Faces in the Dark* (p. 473), who had in the course of their lives seen many thousands of phantasmal faces, had never seen one that they recognised. Mrs. Macdonald, quoted above, has only occasionally recognised a face ; and another of my correspondents, who has been similarly troubled, says, "The faces I have seen have always been unknown faces." Even in the perfectly casual hallucinations of the sane and healthy, what is seen is less commonly a mere revival of an object which the eyes have previously encountered than an unrecognised person.[1] A lady of my acquaint-

---

[1] The following case is of special interest ; being the most marked instance of a *mere revival* that I have encountered ; while at the same time clearly due to a train of thought and memory involving the highest cerebral tracts. The account is from the Rev. P. H. Newnham.

"One of my parishioners is an old woman, now in her 85th year. Though poor and in receipt of parish relief, her education has been good. She retains her faculties in almost undiminished power. She is always bright and cheerful, and I never saw any very aged person at all her equal for a wholesome common-sense. I am very much attached to her ; and for some years past have always sent her a little present on her birthday(January 5th), and have visited her either on the day itself, or as soon after it as possible.

"This year [1885] I visited her on January 6th, and after I had offered the usual congratulations, she said, with a little air of injured innocence, 'It's 2 years since you came to me on my birthday,' or words to that effect. I felt quite sure she was mistaken, and told her so ; but she was confident she was right ; and I did not contest the point ; but when I said good-bye, added as a last word, 'Mind, I can't believe about those 2 years.' On returning home I referred to my parish books, and found that her birthday in 1884 fell on Saturday, and that being unable to go down and see her myself, I had sent my curate to her, with a message and our little gifts.

"On April 14th, being down in the village where she lives, she called on me in my class-room, and begged me to come and see her, as she had something particular to tell me. On my going to see her, she reminded me of our conversation on January 6th, and of my parting words ; and said that she now knew she had 'told me a great story,' and wanted to beg my forgiveness. And how she had found out her mistake was as follows :—

"On the night of March 24th she went to bed early, but could not sleep. This was unusual with her. She lay awake over 3 hours, with no desire to sleep. She could not understand it ; but lay very quiet and happy, thinking of nothing particular. All at once my late curate passed into the room, and stood at the foot of her bed. (This gentleman had left me on January 8th, having obtained an appointment as Naval Chaplain.) As she lay in the bed, the curtains shut off the view of the door, so that she cannot say whether he entered the door or not. He stood at the foot of the bed, with a little basket under his arm, and told her that I could not come to see her myself, but would come as soon as I could, and meantime had sent her a present, which he had in the little basket. Having delivered this message, he disappeared.

"And then it flashed upon her memory that this was the exact reproduction of an actual scene which had taken place on January 5th, 1884. Everything was the same : position, manner, words, exactly as it had been on that day. And my poor old friend was almost broken-hearted to think how she had forgotten, and said what was untrue about me.

"I simply give the narrative as she told it to me. I visited her again a week later and made her repeat the story. She did so without the slightest alteration of facts. I cross-questioned her thoroughly as to details, the mode of entry of the figure, the appearance of

ance, who has been occasionally subject to seeing figures on awakening from sleep, and who tells me that the experience has had no perceptible connection with health, says that on no single occasion has the face been a known face, though the faces are often so clearly seen that, if subsequently met, they would be at once recognised. Another informant, who says that she can evoke figures at any time by looking intently before her, adds that she "cannot tell beforehand what kind they will be, though able after a minute or two to describe the features and dress to anyone that is by." Here, then, we have an immense amount of high creative work—of what in psychical terms we should call *par excellence* the work of the imagination; and this is work which we have good grounds for supposing that the highest cortical tracts, and they alone, are capable of performing. From our experience of the number and mobility of the ideas and images that the mind in a normal state can summon up and combine, we know that the cells of the highest cerebral areas are practically unlimited in their possible groupings and lines of discharge; but we have no right to assume the same inexhaustible possibilities as existing independently in any specific sensory centre —we might almost as well expect a kaleidoscope to present us with an ever-fresh series of elaborate landscapes. The very common implication of two or more senses must also surely be accounted for by supposing a simultaneous excitation of the several centres involved, from a common higher point; for the difficulty, pointed out by Baillarger, of referring the correspondence to simultaneous but independent abnormalities of the external organs applies equally to the specific centres. And over and above all this, there is the connection so frequently observed between the delusions, the *conceptions délirantes*, of the insane and their sensory hallucinations, which makes it almost impossible not to regard the latter as a

---

it, &c., &c. She simply said that everything was as natural as life ; that she was wide awake ; that it was no dream or anything of the kind. I pressed her as to the words spoken ; whether they were soundless or internally spoken words ; but here again she was perfectly clear ; the words were spoken aloud, just as they were in the actual occurrence. She was perfectly aware all the time that it was a vision ; and never for a moment thought it either the real man, or his 'ghost.' She is not in the slightest degree superstitious."

I may add the following parallel though much less elaborate instance. Mr. Alfred Wedgwood, of 20, Shorncliffe Road, Folkestone, describes how, having been trying unsuccessfully in the course of the day to recall the French for "It does not matter," he saw, just as he was stepping into bed, a sheet of paper a foot broad between him and the sheets, with *N'IMPORTE* in large letters stretching all across it. He could have sworn that the object was really there, and immediately told his wife of the experience, as she testifies. We must, of course, attribute this hallucination to the previous gropings after the word.

particular effect of the more widely diffused cerebral disturbance; while even with sane persons of low mental development, we may note in a more general way the prevalence of a particular form of hallucination during the prevalence of a particular superstition—as in the witch-cases above mentioned. The conclusion seems to be that for many hallucinations the mode of origin can be no other than the *centrifugal*—i.e., a process in the direction from higher to lower centres.[1]

§ 10. I have throughout tried to express what I have called the centrifugal theory in such terms that it might be accepted even by those who locate the sensory centres themselves not below, but in, the cortex. According to these physiologists, the whole *double* transformation, of physical impressions into visual or auditory sensations, and of these sensations into complete perceptions and mnemonic images, would be practically referred to one place. It must be admitted that this view seems at times connected with the want of a due psychological distinction between sensation and perception. But even supposing a specific centre of sensation to be thus equally the seat of psychic functions higher than sensation, it would still be none the less liable to be stimulated by parts of the cortex external to itself; and the nature of many hallucinations would still indicate that they depend on this stimulation, and not on a mere spontaneous quickening of morbid activity in the centre itself. For instance, a girl is violently distressed by seeing her home in flames, and for days afterwards sees fire wherever she looks.[2] One must surely trace the hallucination to the *distress*, and so to an " escape of current " from the seat of ideas and images other than visual ones. Again, in the conditions described above, where the hallucinations faithfully reflect the changes of the whole moral and intellectual bias, the local excitement in the sensory centre would still be traceable to an abnormally strong irradiation from the regions where the highest co-ordinations take place—these regions being themselves, *ex hypothesi*, already in a state of pathological activity. The other hypothesis would be that the mere hyper-excitability at the centre

---

[1] The view has been maintained that this process consists merely in the *removal of an inhibition* normally exercised on the sensory centres from above. (See, *e.g.*, Kandinsky in the *Archiv für Psychiatrie* for 1881.) But this seems to ignore the whole of the facts which support the theory of "ideational excitation."

[2] Griesinger, *Op. cit.*, p. 99. For an auditory case, see the account, in the *Lyon Médical*, Vol. xxxv., p. 437, of a young Frenchman who was rendered insane by the German invasion, and who was then haunted by the sound of guns firing.

itself made it impossible for images to arise without getting hurried on, so to speak, into sensations by the violence of the nervous vibrations.[1] But then, what should cause images belonging to one particular order of ideas—the order which happens to be diseased—to be picked out for this fate in preference to any others? The hyperexcitable centre in itself, as an arena of images, could have no ground for such a partial selection among the crowd of them which emerge during every hour of waking life. Among the endless and multiform vibrations involved, why should the excessive amplitude that corresponds to sensation be confined to a particular set? A reason must exist. The unique agreement between the sensory hallucinations and the more general moral and intellectual disorder must have its particular physical counterpart; and for this "a strong downward escape of current" is at any rate a sufficiently comprehensible metaphor.

---

[1] This seems to be what Wundt has in view when he speaks of hallucinations as originating, not in an actual *irritation*, but in a heightened *irritability*, of the sensory centres (*Op. cit.*, Vol ii., p. 357); and such a state may doubtless contribute to the effect, even where the disturbance is plainly propagated from above. There are even special cases of "ideational excitation" of which an abnormal strain or instability at the lower place seems a more prominent condition than an abnormal pressure at the higher. We might thus explain the *echoing* hallucinations, where a person finds that what he is reading to himself repeats itself audibly—the occasion for the discharge being here no doubt the slight reverberation which the mere idea of words may be supposed to set up at the auditory centre. (See Kraepelin, *Op. cit,*, p. 356.) Very comparable are the hallucinations which present themselves only when a certain amount of external stimulation is supplied. For example, a man finds an old hallucination of hearing recur when people are talking in his neighbourhood, though able at the same time to distinguish what they are saying (Kahlbaum, *Op. cit.*, pp. 7, 8, 27); another is troubled by insulting voices at night only when the patients in adjoining rooms are audibly speaking or moving (Köppe, *Op. cit.*, p. 49). And with these may perhaps be classed the hallucinations, primarily due to lesions of the eye, which are found to be greatly favoured by a multiplication of external impressions, as by a visit to a busy city (Voisin, *Op. cit.*, p. 71).

CHAPTER XI.

§ 1. We have briefly surveyed hallucinations in their more general aspects. But before concentrating our view exclusively on the peculiar telepathic species, we shall do well to pause for a little at an important sub-genus to which that species belongs, but of which it forms numerically only a small part—namely, transient hallucinations of the sane.

These hallucinations, of course, like all others, are the creation of a mind in an abnormal state ; but the abnormality may arise in two very different ways. In the large majority of cases it is purely subjective and in some sense pathologic ; and the percepts have no objective basis at all outside the perceiving organism. In a comparatively small residue of cases the abnormality is not pathologic or subjective, but consists (it is maintained) in an impression or impulse transferred from another mind. The percepts still conform perfectly to my definition of a sensory hallucination, in lacking the objective basis *which they suggest ;* for that basis would be the actual physical presence of some human body, with its weight, its power of setting the air in vibration by the breath and vocal cords, and all its other attributes. But *an* objective basis of another sort they have—namely, the exceptional condition of the person whom they recall or represent. Now, having regard to these facts of origin, we might fairly expect that a careful comparison of the purely subjective and the telepathic experiences would reveal a large amount of *resemblance,* but also a certain amount of *difference,* between them. And in no way can we better approach the telepathic or " veridical " class than by following out this comparison.

The available material for the task is, unfortunately, far from abundant ; for the purely subjective hallucinations of the sane have met with singularly little attention from psychologists. Here and there a medical man, or a writer of repute, has been led to make some observations by finding a "subject " in himself; a few cases of very marked abnormality, where the phenomena have been recurrent and distressful, have become celebrated—students of the literature get to dread the very names of Nicolai and "Mrs. A."; and the hypnotic cases have an interest of their own, owing to the important place which hypnotism is fast taking in mental science. But no attempt, so far as I know, has been made to obtain wide statistics of perfectly casual cases—of hallucinations in which, if they are still technically pathologic, the abnormality has been of the slightest and most transient kind. The collection which I have formed during the last few years, numbering more than 500 cases, is at any rate large enough to support certain general conclusions.

§ 2. And first, as regards the bodily and mental condition of the percipient. Probably the common view of hallucinations of the sane, so far as they are recognised at all, is that they are in all cases due to disease or morbid excitement, or at the very least to indigestion. Ask the first twenty rational men you meet how they would account for a phantasmal visitant if they themselves saw one : as many as ten perhaps will answer, "I should conclude that I had dined or supped too well." "Lobster-salad" is an explanation which I have personally heard suggested many times. It may be at once noted, then, as a point of interest—one, moreover, in which the casual and the telepathic classes completely agree—that in not a single instance known to me has the hallucinated person, according to his own account, been suffering at the time from indigestion. Lobster-salad is the parent of nightmares, of massive impressions of discomfort and horror; not, however, as a rule, even in dreamland, of the distinct and minute visualisation, and the clear-cut audition, which constitute the more specific hallucinations of sleep; and certainly not of waking hallucinations. Nor is morbid excitement of a more general sort a frequent, though it is an occasional, condition; and the same may be said of the ordinary nervous exhaustion that follows hard work. We have only to recall that the commonest occasions of all for delusions of the waking senses are the moments or minutes that immediately follow a night's rest (p. 392). For the majority of cases, the only rule that can be laid down as to the nature of the peculiar disturbance involved is a negative one—that it is not observably connected with any morbid state.

2 I

Thus the one of my informants who has had perhaps the most interesting experiences of subjective hallucinations, says, " It is when I am at my best physically, and when my mental faculties are keenly interested in something, that the pictures are most frequent and vivid. They are mostly quite the antipodes of my mental occupation." A gentleman who has repeatedly had the hallucination of hearing his name called, tells me that this has always occurred during his holidays, when he was specially well and taking much exercise. And out of 489 visual and auditory cases (waking and " borderland "), I find that only 24 occurred to persons who were in a decidedly abnormal physical state—ill, or fainting, or overtired, or under anæsthetics. Certain exceptional though slight derangement there must undoubtedly be ; but the hallucination itself is usually the only symptom of it ; and as little in the purely subjective as in the telepathic class can we lay our finger on any special predisposing condition.

The puzzle is the greater in that the phenomenon of waking hallucination in a sane and healthy subject (as the numbers to be presently given will show), is a rare one—rare not merely in the sense of occurring to only a small percentage of the population, but in the sense of occurring to most of these only once or twice in a life-time. One would have expected that any state of the brain which was liable to occur at all without assignable provocation, would be liable to occur repeatedly. We should account it, for instance, a very odd fact if a person had had one or two extremely distinct dreams in his life, and had had no other experience whatever of dreaming. But we can only take the statistics as we find them. And this peculiar rarity of purely subjective hallucinations of the senses at any rate helps to explain a similar peculiarity in the telepathic class. Our telepathic evidence will show that the hallucination which the percipient describes is as a rule the single and unique instance in his experience. Now at first sight this seems strange, inasmuch as many percipients have been in quite as intimate connection with other persons as with the "agent" of their one phantasmal visitation ; and some of these persons have died or have passed through a crisis similar to that to which we trace the visitation in the one instance; why then has it never been repeated ? The only answer would seem to be that hallucinations, even when telepathic in origin, depend further on some exceptional condition of the percipient himself. And this answer can now be supported by the analogy of the non-telepathic class ; where the conditions, unnoticed and innocuous to health as they so often are, are yet so exceptional that they may occur only once in a life-time. The same observation will further tend, I think, to remove a certain vague prejudice which the telepathic evidence encounters in the minds of persons who have never met with an instance of hallucination of any sort. Such persons can often hardly bring themselves to conceive that a sane, healthy, waking mind can really get momentarily off the rails, and can feign voices where there is silence, and figures where there is vacancy, though ear and eye are both alert and discharging their normal functions. Even supposing transferred impressions possible, they will say, why under their influence should sound and sober senses exhibit a perfectly isolated piece of eccentricity, and just for a minute, once in a life-time, fall victims to delusions such as we commonly associate with sick-beds and madhouses? This vague *à priori* objection will disappear when the statistics of transient hallucinations are better known; seeing that the isolated piece of eccentricity does undoubtedly occur—how or why we cánnot say—in numbers of instances with which telepathy has nothing whatever to do.[1]

---

[1] This difficulty in believing that isolated cases of distinct sensory hallucination may occur to persons who are in sound bodily and mental health, was shown in some of the comments which followed Dr. Jessopp's account of his own experience ("An Antiquary's Ghost-story," in the *Athenæum* for January 10th, 1880) ; for it seemed to be thought that his narrative, as it stood, was incredible, and that he must have been dreaming. I could parallel that case with scores of others, but select the two following as of special interest. The first is from a distinguished Indian officer.

"I had been taking luncheon with some friends, and after it was over, my host proposed that I and my fellow guest should accompany him to see some alterations he was making in his grounds. After we had been out some little time, looking at these changes a native servant approached me with a message from my hostess, asking me to go into the house to speak to her. I at once left my friends, and accompanied the man back to the house, following him through the verandah into the room where the luncheon had been laid. There he left me, and I waited for my hostess to come, but no one appeared ; so after a few minutes, I called her by name, thinking that she might not be aware that I had come in. Receiving no answer, after once again repeating her name, I walked back into the verandah, where, on entering, I had observed a durzee (or tailor) at work, and asked him where the man was who came in with me. The durzee replied, 'Your Excellency, no one came with you.' 'But,' I said, 'the man lifted the chik ' (the outside verandah blind) ' for me.' 'No, your Excellency, you lifted it yourself, the durzee answered. Much puzzled, I returned to my friends in the grounds, exclaiming, ' Here's a good joke ;' and then, telling them what had happened, and what the durzee had said, I asked them if they had not seen the servant who called for me shortly before. They both said they had seen no one. ' Why, you don't mean to say I have not been in the house?' I said. ' Oh, yes ; you were in the midst of saying something about the alterations, when you suddenly stopped, and walked back to the house ; we could not tell why,' they both said. I was in perfect health at the time of the occurrence, and continued to be so after it."

The next account is from Dr. Charles M. Smith, of Franklin, St. Mary's Parish, Louisiana, He narrates that a lady of his acquaintance, Mrs. P., lost her life at Last Island, in the terrible hurricane of August, 1856. "Nearly two months afterwards, on my way to visit a patient in the country, I met Mr. Weeks, a brother of Mrs. P., and in the buggy with him a lady so wonderfully like Mrs. P. that, but for my knowledge of her death, I would have declared it to be herself. The carriage and horses used by Mr. Weeks were easily distinguished by certain well-marked peculiarities from any other in the parish, and I saw these as distinctly as the occupants themselves." Dr. Smith bowed, and called Mr. Weeks by name, but no notice was taken, and the buggy passed on. Returning home

§ 3. These characteristics, then—(1) the general absence of any obvious predisposing cause, of any assignable abnormality of mind or body, in the person affected, (2) the comparatively small number of persons affected, and (3) the very frequent uniqueness of the affection in the respective experiences of these persons—may be reckoned as distinct grounds of resemblance between the purely subjective and the telepathic classes. Another marked characteristic that they have in common is (4) the usually very brief duration of the phantasm : both sorts of affection are emphatically *transient* hallucinations of the sane—the majority of cases being almost momentary, and very few probably extending to half a minute. And again (5) the disproportionate number of " borderland " experiences in both classes is a fifth important common point. These five heads of resemblance are those which a broad view of the phenomena at once reveals. Our next step would naturally be to see if more detailed resemblances exist between special groups of cases in the two classes ; and every common feature that we find will of course go to strengthen the conclusion that the telepathic phantasms are indeed hallucinations, and not (as some have held) quasi-material appearances. At this point, however, we find ourselves confronted by a problem of considerable difficulty as well as interest, which requires to be carefully considered.

The difficulty is this. If the characteristics of the two classes of hallucination are to be discussed and compared, it is obviously assumed that we know on inspection which cases ought to be referred to the one class, and which to the other. Now, though the elements of a telepathic case have been made tolerably plain, and in the main the grounds of distinction may be clear enough, the attempt actually to draw a dividing line will very soon show us that at present no such line can be drawn. With the discovery that one person's senses can be affected by something that is happening to another person at a distance, our point of view is, in fact, altered in relation to the whole subject of transient hallucinations of the sane. Ever since the abandonment of the idea, once widely held, that delusions of the senses were the direct and (in a manner) objective productions of the devil,[1] the universal assumption has been that they are *all*

an hour later, he made particular inquiry, and found that no persons in the least resembling those he had seen had arrived in the village ; and he afterwards learnt that Mr. Weeks had been at his home 30 miles away at the time. " The conclusion seemed inevitable," he adds, " that the whole affair was an optical delusion."

[1] See above, p. 179.

purely subjective phenomena—even the belief in "ghosts" having been really no exception to the rule, since the believers have not regarded these as hallucinations at all, but as independent entities. Now when telepathy of the externalised type is admitted, the first effect, of course, is to destroy the generality of the old assumption by driving it quite decisively off a certain part of the field : it is involved in the new doctrine that a certain number of sensory hallucinations —the majority, namely, of those which have markedly corresponded to real and unforeseen events—can no longer possibly be regarded as purely subjective.[1] But the effect does not stop short here. The new *vera causa*, which has decisively occupied one corner of the field, throws, so to speak, a shadow of doubt over the rest; for while we perceive its reality, we have as yet neither probed its conditions nor measured its range. I have already pointed out (p. 97) that the action of telepathy cannot be dogmatically limited to those most conclusive cases on which our evidential proof of it must depend; and if its reality in the world renders the old doctrine of the subjectivity of hallucinations definitely *untenable* in some cases, we need not be surprised if in others it renders it *doubtful*, and doubtful, moreover, in various degrees. Thus, between the hallucinations which are clearly subjective and those which are clearly telepathic, there will be a neutral region, where neither explanation can be adopted with certainty. Now, on all accounts it is important that this neutral region should be recognised and defined. It is important theoretically, because in time we may learn more of the conditions of the phenomena, and may be able to assign them with confidence to this class or that ; but even more is it important evidentially, because, till the grounds of doubt are understood, there is always a risk that purely subjective cases will be misinterpreted, and will be reckoned into the cumulative proof of telepathy, or in some other way laid to the account of supernormal influences. It seems advisable, therefore, to take a glance along the whole line of transient hallucinations of the sane, up to the point at which the action of telepathy may appear to be clearly assured. I will make my survey as rapid as possible, being loth to detain the reader among these subjective and dubious cases,

[1] At this point, the truth of the doctrine is of course not assumed to have been proved ; the proof is a long cumulative process, which will be carried on to the end of the book. But it would have been intolerably inconvenient, both to writer and reader, to defer all attempts at logical treatment and analysis until the whole of the cases had been presented *en masse*. I may take leave therefore, by anticipation, to describe as telepathic the incidents which every reader who, in the end, agrees that telepathy is a true fact in Nature, will agree in regarding as almost certainly true examples of it.

while the main body of the telepathic evidence is perforce kept
waiting.

§ 4. In the first group, the cause of the phenomena is, by exception, quite clear. The hallucination is an *after-image*—the direct
reproduction of some object or sound with which the senses of the
percipient have been particularly occupied ; and though we may not
always be able to say why the reproduction takes place at such and
such a moment, the purely subjective character of the experience
is obvious. It is sometimes due to mere fatigue of the retina ; it
occurs, for instance, after long gazing at objects through a microscope.
Some examples due to a more central cause have been given in the
preceding chapters ; *e.g.*, M. Maury's hypnagogic vision of the beefsteak (p. 390), Mr. Wilson's visions of the tombstones, and Mr. Turner's
phantom-chandelier (p. 490),—the latter case being remarkable for the
length of time which had elapsed since the real object had been seen.
Another type is where the original impression has been of a distressing kind. Thus, Dr. Andral reports [1] that, having received a shock from
the condition of a child's body in the dissecting-room, he was startled
next morning, on waking, by a vivid repetition of the spectacle. I
have a similar first-hand case from a friend, who in girlhood suffered for
several nights from a hallucination caused by the unaccustomed sight
of death ; and another where a lady had a vivid waking vision of a
servant who had startled her some hours before. The transcript
is not always quite literal. Thus, a gentleman tells me that the
figure of a deceased friend, whom he had just been seeing in his
coffin, appeared to him, but in his living aspect and carrying a port-
folio ; and another informant—the Rev. J. M. Blacker, of 121, St.
George's Road, S.W.—who one morning had a vision of the upper
parts of three cooks in white caps, and was able to trace the impression
unmistakeably to a recently seen placard, but noticed nevertheless
that the resemblance was only of a general kind. As good auditory
examples, I may mention the hallucination of hearing the bells of
the Town Hall at Manchester play " Auld Lang Syne," experienced
more than once by a lady when sleeping in a room where she had on
former occasions heard the actual performance ; and a case where a
young lady, who had suffered considerably from the manners of
young schoolboy brothers,. was afterwards startled, when alone, by
such remarks as " Shut up," and " Get out of the way."

[1] Kraft-Ebing, *Die Sinnesdelirien*, p. 16.

Under the same head may fairly be reckoned such cases as Mr. A. Wedgwood's (p. 493, note), where the phantasmal object, though not reproducing anything that had recently been before the eyes, was the immediate and indisputable result of a very special train of thought. Comparable, again, are representations of an object or a sound which depend on the fact, not that it *has been* seen or heard, but that it is *about to be* seen or heard—that the percipient is *expecting* it ; but as in almost all the visual experiences of this sort the object has been a living human form, the cases will fall more conveniently into a later group.

In the next group the object seen, or the sound heard, is non-human in character, but is no longer traceable to any special previous occupation of the mind or the senses.   Such cases are common in insanity and in disease, and the hallucination is then often of a grotesque or horrible sort.   They also occur, though forming a decided minority, among the waking hallucinations of sane and healthy persons ; but seem then to be rarely, if ever, grotesque or horrible.   The most grotesque case that I have received is a vision of dwarfish gnomes dancing on the wall ; but this was seen by a young child.   A star, a firework bursting into stars, a firefly, a crown, landscape-vignettes, a statue, the end of a draped coffin coming in through the door, a bright oval surrounding the words, " Wednesday, October 15, Death "—these are the principal phantasms of inanimate objects in my collection.   Another known type, described by Sir J. F. W. Herschel, is a geometrical pattern, which sometimes takes very complicated forms.   I have also three cases where the hallucination was of a dog, and another where it was of running cats, indefinite in colour and form (this last, however, occurring only when the brain was exhausted).   Out of my 302 visual cases (p. 392), only 20 belong to this non-human type.   The non-vocal auditory cases are also comparatively few in number—41 out of the total of 187.   They comprise tappings, tickings, knocks, and crashes ;[1] the sound of footsteps or of a door opening ; 7 cases of the ringing of bells, 2 of the striking of clocks, and 7 of music.   Such types seem, on the very face of them, to be altogether remote from telepathy ; and though we shall find further on that this is not quite universally the case—that there are instances of strong and unique

---

[1] Some of these may possibly have been real noises whose cause was not ascertained. But I have included no case where my informant did not himself hold this explanation to be excluded.

hallucinations of light or noise which have too markedly coincided with some external crisis for the hypothesis of telepathic origin to be ignored—the vast majority of these non-human phantasms may be safely pronounced purely subjective affections.

The same may be said of another smaller group of visual hallucinations which represent fragments of human forms. Thus, two of my informants on waking from sleep, and a third when awake and up, have distinctly seen an imaginary hand and arm;[1] another sometimes sees a little finger in the air; another when recovering from illness, had a vision of decapitated heads; another has suffered at times from an appearance of eyes and part of a face floating by; and with these may be classed, as auditory parallels, cases where what has been heard has been a sound of groaning, or indistinguishable sounds of talking, or short meaningless sentences —a class of which I have some half-dozen specimens.

We must regard as a separate type the cases where faces or forms appear either in rapid succession or in a multitudinous way. Several varieties of this experience were described in the last chapter (pp. 473-4). I have one other example, where crowds of people and animals made their appearance every night for months; but the percipient in this case was in weak health. We have seen that this type is probably connected with the *Licht-staub* of the retina, and its subjectivity will not be questioned. It scarcely belongs to the family of *transient* hallucinations at all, since— alone among the waking hallucinations of persons in apparently normal health—these swarming and changing visions are liable to last for a considerable time.

And finally we come to the visual cases representing complete and (more often than not), quite natural-looking human forms, usually alone but occasionally in company, and occasionally also with the addition of some independent object, such as a carriage or a coffin; and to the parallel auditory cases where distinct and intelligible words are heard, which are not (as in the first group) mere echoes of vividly-impressed phrases. These phenomena—which comprise the great majority of the whole number of transient hallucinations of the sane—fall at once into two great classes; that where the figure or voice is *recognised*, and that where it is *unrecognised*. Of both these classes, as of the previous ones, it

---

[1] We have had, however, a *telepathic* example of this type, in case 161, p. 416.

may at once be said that the majority of the instances included in
them are in no way available to prove influence from another mind.
Where the figure or voice has been recognised, the absent person
whose presence was suggested has generally been in a quite normal
state at the time ; and where the figure or voice has been unrecognised, no crisis affecting any person nearly connected with the
percipient has coincided with the hallucination. The *recognised*
phantasms have, moreover, usually represented persons whom the
percipient was habitually seeing in real life—often a relative or a
servant living in the same house—so that the delusion may
still be explained by the analogy of after-images ; or else they
have represented dead persons whose memory was dear to the
percipient, and whose images might readily be evoked by memory.[1]
Of the *unrecognised* phantasms we have no reason to suppose that
they represented any one at all, even in those cases—the majority of
the whole number—where the non-recognition was not due to any
indistinctness in the phantasm, but was of the same kind as when
in real life we see a face or hear a voice which we perceive at once
to be strange to us. But while as a rule so clearly subjective,
these human and well-developed forms of hallucination include also
nearly the whole of the instances which will be presented in the
following chapters as telepathic. It is naturally among them,
therefore, that the *ambiguous* cases to which I have referred are
principally to be found.

The main grounds of ambiguity (apart from mere uncertainties as
to matters of fact, which are not now in question,) are, I think, four in
number, and are summed up in the following types[2] :—

(1) Coincidentally with a " recognised " hallucination, the person
whose presence it suggested has been in a condition more or less
unusual ; but we may fairly doubt whether it was unusual *enough* to
justify even a provisional supposition that it affected the percipient.

(2) At the time of a " recognised " hallucination, the person whose
presence it suggested has been apparently in a perfectly normal
condition ; but the same hallucination has been *repeated*, and
repeated to *different* percipients ; and the improbability that the
independent hallucinations of several persons should by accident

---

[1] See above, p. 490. The term "after-image" in connection with the apparitions of
dead people was suggested in a paper privately communicated to me by Mr. J. Jacobs.

[2] To be quite complete, this list ought perhaps to include the ambiguity which is
involved in the percipient's failure to connect his impression, at the time, with the supposed
agent ; but this point is sufficiently noticed elsewhere (pp. 221, 452-3, and Chap. xii., § 5).

represent the same person suggests some special power of influence in the latter.[1]

(3) The person whose presence the hallucination presented has been in a decidedly abnormal condition at a time sufficiently near the time of the hallucination for the correspondence to be observed; but the correspondence has not been exact; and the doubt is whether the amount of discrepancy is such as to admit, or such as to preclude, the hypothesis of a causal connection. The question here is the one which was early raised, when we were considering the elements of a telepathic case (pp. 138-9), and was then left undecided.

(4) The case is so far suggestive of telepathy that, at or very near the time of the hallucination, some absent person has been in circumstances which might seem to identify him as the agent; but there is also evidence of a *condition in the percipient's own mind* which might be regarded as the independent cause of his experience.

Let us begin with this last head, and inquire of what nature an independent subjective cause of the phenomena now in question is likely to be.

Though for the most part, as I have said, the predisposing conditions of these rare and transient delusions entirely elude us, just three emotional states can be named which are present often enough to warrant a suspicion that they may be truly efficacious. These are special forms of *anxiety;* of *awe;* and of *expectancy.* We will consider them in order.

§ 5. First, then, as to *anxiety.* A person who has been brooding over the state of some absent friend or relative suddenly has a hallucination which suggests that person's presence. Now suppose that the crisis which was apprehended—say the death of the person whose serious illness was the cause of the anxiety—turns out afterwards to have occurred at the same time as the hallucination. Let us take a couple of cases—one auditory, the other visual.

The following account is from Mr. Timothy Cooper, late of 21, Cadogan Terrace, Victoria Park, E.

"January, 1882.

"My father was a Baptist minister at Soham, Cambridgeshire. In the year 1849, being one of a large family, I went from home to begin the battle of life. There was great love between my mother and me. When I had been away about a year, I was sent for in a hurry to see my dear

---

[1] For illustrations of this very rare and isolated type, see Chap. xiv. § 5.

mother, who was thought to be dying. I got leave of absence for a week and went home, and the last day before returning to business, while sitting by my mother's side, I said, ' Mother, if it is possible, when you pass away will you come and tell me ? ' She said, ' I will if I possibly can.' On the morning of October 7th, 1850, I awoke and felt like a soft hand touch me, and heard the well-known voice say, 'I am gone,' and something seemed to glide away from my side. I awoke the young man who was sleeping with me, and said, ' My mother is gone. She has just been here and told me so ; ' and just as I said it the clock standing on the stairs struck 3. The news came to hand that my mother had died at five minutes to 3.   " TIMOTHY COOPER."

We have verified the date of death in the *Baptist Reporter*.

The next account is from Miss Summerbell, of 140 Kensington Park Road, W., who has had no other hallucination of vision. This one was mentioned at once to the friend with whom she was staying.

                                                      " November, 1882.

" I do not know how far the following story will be considered significant, as I was in much anxiety about the gentleman whom it concerns at the time. I have been for many years on terms of close intimacy with the family of a Dutch nobleman [Jonkheer Huÿdecoper], who reside in Holland. Early in July last, I received a letter from the eldest daughter of the house, saying that her father was seriously ill. From that time I received news of his condition every day. On the 27th July, I received a post-card, saying that he was slightly better. I was staying at the time at the Spa, Tunbridge Wells, and suffering much from neuralgia. On the night of the 27th, I was lying unable to sleep from pain ; no doubt I dozed now and then, but I firmly believe that I was awake when what I am about to relate occurred. It was beginning to be light, and I distinctly saw every object in the room. I do not know whether it is necessary to say that in Holland, when a person of distinction dies, a ' prieur d'enterrement ' is employed. This man is dressed in black, with dress coat, knee-breeches, and cocked-hat, with bands of crape hanging from the corners. It is his office to go to all the houses where the deceased was known, and announce the death. On the morning of which I speak, I saw the door of my room open, and a ' prieur d'enterrement ' enter. He said nothing, but stood with a long paper in his hand. I remember distinctly wondering whether I had fallen asleep and was dreaming ; I looked round and saw the furniture, and the window, with the dim light coming through the closed blind. I looked at my watch ; it was nearly 5 o'clock. I looked towards the man, but he was gone. It is nearly 6 years since I lived for any time in Holland, and I had forgotten the custom of announcing deaths ; or at least, I had not thought of it for years." Miss Summerbell's friend, as it proved, had died about an hour and a half before her vision.

[We may note here how curiously the idea of death, in working itself out, availed itself of materials that had long been dormant—the slumbering memories which associated Dutch customs with Dutch friends in the percipient's mind.]

Supposing these incidents to be correctly reported, which we have no reason to doubt, what is the most probable interpretation of them ? Is the state of mind in which the percipients were a sufficient cause for what they respectively heard and saw ? If so, the coincidence between the death and the hallucination would be accounted for by the fact that the very conditions which led to the death were also indirectly (through the anxiety connected with them) the cause of the hallucination. But to answer the question,[1] we need some independent evidence of the power of simple anxiety about an absent person to produce a distinct delusion of the waking senses. Anxiety is readily enough assumed as a *vera causa* of such delusions, just as lobster-salad is ; but can the assumption be supported ? Not very completely, it must be admitted. The cases are nearly all of the same indecisive type ; for the condition of an absent person which is sufficiently exceptional to create grave anxiety about him is, as a rule, also sufficiently exceptional to afford a conceivable occasion for telepathic influence, supposing telepathic influences to be facts in Nature; and the hallucination can, there-fore, only be assumed to be certainly due to anxiety by rejecting *à priori* the other explanation. Thus, in the collection of hallucinations which I have mentioned, I find none of such a type as this—that a mother, in great anxiety for a sailor son, seems to see his figure in the room, though really the weather at sea has been calm and he has met with no mishap. Still, evidence pointing in this direction does exist. For instance, the records of witchcraft contain many cases, which there is no reason to call in question, of apparitions of the supposed witch to the supposed victim—indeed Bernard[2] mentions this form of hallucination as one of the signs of "possession"; the experience seems, however, to have been invariably connected with a thoroughly morbid and hysterical condition of the percipient.

[1] A caution may not be out of place against the common habit of deciding such questions off-hand, from a single instance, by mere bias. Some informants have sent us cases of the sort expressly as subjective experiences ; others as proofs that the dying person's thoughts turned to them at the last. But if the proof of telepathy itself requires an accumulated mass of evidence, much more must the decision in these doubtful instances.

[2] *Guide to Grand Jurymen*, 1627. As typical instances I may refer to the *History of the Witches of Renfrewshire*, pp. 74-5 ; the report of the *Tryal of Witches at Bury St. Edmunds on the Tenth Day of March, 1664* (published in 1682), where some of the victims who saw the form of Amy Duny saw apparitions of cats and mice as well ; and the *Tryals, Examination, and Condemnation of Four Notorious Witches* at a Worcester assizes, where the child who had the hallucination had apparently been previously unhinged by fright, and shortly died. As a rule, it is expressly stated that the apparitions took place during "*fits*"—*i.e.*, hysteric or epileptic seizures ; but this seems not to have been invariable. See Deodat Lawson's *Further Account of the Tryals of the New England Witches*, (London, 1693,) p. 9.

Again, an unusually absorbing possession of the mind with the person whose form appears, at the very moment when the appearance takes place, may make even an "ambiguous" experience seem almost beyond question subjective. Thus a lady writes to us:—

"Rather more than 10 years ago a person with whom I had had much to do was lying dangerously ill. In the evening of a certain day I was standing in my own room, thinking of her case, and reproaching myself for one or two things in connection with my conduct to her, when I turned suddenly round, and saw her gazing steadily, very steadily, and reproachfully at me. She died that night. She was not a near relative, or an intimate friend."

In the case of auditory hallucinations, the evidence is clearer: some of these, occurring in circumstances of anxiety, bear the conclusive mark of a purely subjective experience. A sister in trouble about her brother, who has had an accident, hears the words, "Your brother is dead." A mother nursing her son in a dangerous crisis hears an imaginary voice say, "You can't save him." In impressions corresponding so closely to the hearer's state of mind, and *not* corresponding to the actual facts, there can be no question of telepathy. On the whole, then, it seems reasonable to conclude that anxiety has a certain independent tendency to promote hallucinations. Even so, we might fairly enough argue that it is as likely to *facilitate* telepathic hallucinations as to *produce* purely subjective ones. But when the question is of admitting cases to the present collection, the assumption ought always to be made against the telepathic hypothesis; and our principle has been to regard anxiety which has reached a certain pitch as distinctly weakening the evidential value of a coincidence, though great perfection in other points—as, for instance, a complete identity of time—might more than outweigh the objection. The fact that the anxiety may not have been actually dominating consciousness at the moment of the hallucination cannot be held to remove the probability (such as it is) that the hallucination was subjectively caused; for it is the rule rather than the exception for hallucinations which can be at all connected with previous experience to be developed from ideas that are quite latent.[1]

[1] The following are instances in point, which we certainly should not feel justified in presenting in the cumulative proof of telepathy.
Miss Emma Schau, of 4, Clifton Road, Camden Square, N.W., writing in April, 1883, records that, at the time of the Danish-German war, she was woke by the sound of a heavy tread slowly approaching her; and then, when completely awake, saw a shadowy form stand by her, and recognised the presence of her favourite brother, who was in the field, and who, as it proved, had been killed on that morning.
"From the last letters that we had received from my brothers, complaining of their

§ 6. The next predisposing condition of hallucinations that we
have to consider is *awe*, in that special form which is connected
with the near sense of death, and with which elements of grief
and regret are often mingled. It is remarkable how large a
proportion of phantasms of the recognised sort represent friends
or relatives whose recent death is being mourned. Out of 231
cases, I find that 28 are of this type; of which 6 took place on the
day or the morrow, 4 within a very few days, and the rest within
a very few weeks, of the death.[1] Now the reader may ask
how an emotional condition due to a death can affect the interpretation of any phantasms that could possibly be regarded as
telepathic; for telepathy, as treated in this book, is an action
between the minds of *living* persons. But it must be remembered
that we have already assumed the possibility of a certain period of
latency in telepathic impressions. That a certain period has followed
a death before the occurrence of the hallucination representing the
person who has died, is not, therefore, fatal to a telepathic explanation
of the case ; and the question how far the percipient's own emotional
state is to be preferred as an explanation will depend, to some
extent, on the length of this intervening period. We are, therefore,
led on to the wider question—by how large an interval must two
experiences be separated before the possibility that they may be
telepathically connected is excluded? This, it will be seen, is the
very question involved in No. 3 of the four grounds of ambiguity
above set forth.

Putting aside for the moment any special theory, it will be seen
that the argument for a causal connection between an event of one
class, A, and an event of another class, B, arising from the frequency
with which such events approximate to one another in time, is not an

inactivity, I had reason to believe that they would not be in this engagement [the battle
of Midsunde], and I went to bed with my mind free from anxiety on their account."

The next narrative was sent to us in German by Fräulein Wilhelmine Ivens, of Allée
152, Altona, Holstein, who has had no other hallucination. The incident was mentioned
to our friend, Miss Porter, almost immediately after its occurrence.

"Aug. 31, 1884.

"In the summer of the year 1873, I was staying for some weeks at my home. My
father became ill, and shortly before my return to England he went to the country to
recruit. At the beginning of September I returned to London. I was anxious about my
father ; but a letter which I received in the middle of September reassured me. On
September 23rd, while in the house, I heard my mother call me twice ; and in the garden
I heard my name distinctly called once, in my mother's voice. On the night of September
23-24, my father died. On the 25th I received the news that he had reached home very
ill, and the 26th brought me the intelligence of his death."

[1] I am excluding some cases where the interval is known to have been as great as 2
months ; but including some which are stated to have occurred "soon" or "very soon"
after the death, without specification of time.

argument whose force stops suddenly at any predictable point. It is an argument whose force gradually diminishes in proportion as the correspondences of time throughout a series of cases get less and less precise, and only becomes inappreciable when marked gaps begin to occur in the series. Thus the fact that certain psychical phenomena form a cluster, comparatively thick at first and gradually becoming more and more sparse, in the few days that follow deaths, would strongly indicate some common bond of connection between the phenomena and the deaths, even if such a thing as telepathy in connection with living persons had never been observed. But as a matter of fact, we find the cluster of cases as thick just *before* life has ceased as just *after.* Hence the presumption of a single common cause for the whole group.

Now not only is telepathy the only common cause which it seems possible to name ; and not only is it the cause which is, so to speak, in possession of the field : it is a cause with which, up to a certain point after death, the theory of an emotional origin cannot even come into competition. For however efficacious grief, or the general awe which death inspires, may be to provoke hallucinations representing the dead person, the grief and awe cannot operate till the fact of his death is known ; and for any one at a distance from him, this knowledge must necessarily follow the death at a very appreciable interval. Up to that point, then, we must hold that there is an appreciable chance that the hallucination is telepathic in character, and that an impression, received from the agent before or at death, has lain latent for a while in the percipient's mind. At the same time this theory of latency is one that ought not to be strained. The fact that in the majority of our cases there seems to be no latency at all, and that in another large group the period of latency is short, establishes a sort of presumption that it is not likely ever to be very long ; and while admitting that any limitation that we can make is arbitrary, we prefer—for evidential purposes—to draw the line early, and (as explained in Chap. IV.) we have drawn it at 12 hours after death.

The cases, however, where knowledge of the death, and the emotion caused by it, have preceded the hallucination, stand on very different ground. A new element is now introduced, which has seemed to many weighty authorities a full and sufficient explanation of all *post-mortem* phantasms. I am not aware, indeed, that any crucial instance has ever been forthcoming—that anyone, believing a friend to be dead who was really in a perfectly normal state, has seen his " ghost." Moreover, most of those who have attributed *post-mortem* phantasms to the percipient's emotional condition have done so under an *à priori* conviction that with physical death all possibility of affecting others must necessarily cease—a conviction which my colleagues and I do not share.[1]   At the same time, death is so wholly unique a fact in human experience that it seems reasonable to believe the ideas and emotions connected with it capable of producing very unique effects ; and personally I am disposed to regard such ideas and emotions as probably the sufficient cause of any hallucinations that occur while they are present, as long as such hallucinations present no features which the percipient's mind would have been unable to supply.   The presumption is at any rate so strong, that no experiences of any sort—even though otherwise admissible, as following within the 12 hours' limit—have been included in our telepathic evidence, if the fact of the death was already known to the percipient, and if his experience was unshared by any one else ; and this principle is the easier to justify in that the day immediately succeeding a death seems the most likely of all periods for abnormal subjective impressions connected with the death to occur.

§ 7.   The remaining head that we have to consider is *expectancy.* The evidence as to the power of this condition of mind to produce waking hallucinations is rather more definite than in the case of anxiety.   Braid describes a lady who, as soon as the idea was suggested to her, saw coruscating flames issue from the poles of a magnet, or wherever she believed the influence of the magnet to extend ; and

---

[1] As our telepathic theory is a psychical one, and makes no physical assumptions, it would be perfectly applicable (though the *name* perhaps would be inappropriate) to the conditions of disembodied existence.   And it may be quite fairly asked why this possibility was not taken account of above, in connection with the phantasms that have shortly followed deaths.   What need is there, it may be said, to trace these phenomena to a state of the agent preceding or exactly synchronising with his physical decease, when his psychical life may be supposed to be continuing after the great change?   The answer is that the point is not one of theoretic possibilities, but of *evidence ;* and that the *evidence* for *post-mortem* communications seems to us inconclusive.   In all the evidential cases cited in this book, the very keystone of the argument is the *coincidence*—more or less close, but always close enough to be remarked—with death or some other external fact.   That— and often that alone—is the obstacle to regarding the cases as purely subjective : failing that, very special and peculiar features must be present, to establish even a presumption of some exciting cause external to the percipient's own mind.   For example, the same hallucination might affect several persons independently and at different times ; or the phantasm might convey information, afterwards discovered to be true, of something which the percipient had never known—this last condition being probably the only one which could prove an *intelligent* external cause.   A certain amount of evidence of both these types exists, of a quality which makes it imperative on us to keep our minds open for more ; but at present it will bear no sort of comparison with the evidence for telepathy. For a sketch and criticism of the present state of the question, see Mrs. Sidgwick's paper "On the Evidence, collected by the S.P.R., for Phantasms of the Dead," in Vol. iii. of the *Proceedings.*

in the dark, liability to this form of delusion seems not very uncommon. Crucial examples of a more developed type—except in crises
of epidemic excitement (see Vol. II., pp. 187-8)—are less easy to find.
I have one daylight case where a man who was searching for a
tennis-ball had a distinct apparition of the missing object in a spot
where it was not. And expectancy may probably be answerable for
a good many apparitions seen in rooms believed to be "haunted." I
select the following example, however, as free from all superstitious
associations, and as almost certainly a hallucination, and not a mere
illusion. A barrister—whose name I am at liberty to mention, but
not to print—writes to me :—

"December 21st, 1885.

"In October, 1885, I was stopping for the night at the Swan Hotel at
B., on circuit. My bedroom was No. 17. My friend K., a brother
barrister, occupied No. 16. Between No. 17 (my room) and No. 18 there
was a communicating door, and before retiring to rest I was under the
impression that the door was between my room and my friend K.'s. I had
told my friend K. so, when bidding him good-night, and he had jokingly
remarked that he would come in and frighten me during the night. I discovered before going to bed that our rooms did *not* communicate. I must
have been asleep some hours, when I woke up with a sensation that someone was close to my bed, and feeling about the other side of the chintz
curtain at the head of the bed. I could hear the rustling and crackling
of the curtain close to my face. I felt perfectly unable to move, or
protect myself—not through any fear, but from a want of power of
movement.[1] After a few seconds this powerlessness went off, and I sprang
out of bed, and saw the figure of my friend K. retreating towards the foot
of the bed. He kept his face averted, his head a little bent, but I could
see the wire and one of the glasses of his spectacles as he turned from
me ; he was dressed in his night-shirt. And what made me believe in the
reality of the appearance was the 'solidity' of the white nightdress, and
the light on the spectacles. The room was in dim light, owing to gas-
lamps in street, and a fanlight over door admitting light from gas in
passage. I grasped at my friend with both hands and supposed I had
missed him as my hands met in the grasp. I attempted again to grasp
him, when he disappeared as if through the floor under the washing-stand.
I then realised, with some interest, that it was a hallucination, and I
sat on the bed, wide awake, interested in thinking it over. I told K. of
it next morning. I am uncertain whether there was a fan-light over the
door, but such was my impression at the time ; anyway, the room was
light.   "T. H. L."

"K." sent me a completely concordant account a month earlier. He
says that he never walked in his sleep, and adds :—

"I had no notion where L.'s room was that night, but afterwards

---

[1] I have two other cases where a subjective hallucination seen on waking was accompanied by inability to speak or move. See also the telepathic case No. 210, below.

found that it was separated from mine by a passage. I don't think the sleep-walking theory is possible ; and he is quite clear as to my vanishing."

The auditory examples are commoner and clearer. As might be expected, they are specially connected with sounds which occur in an isolated way, such as those of bells and clocks. Thus a lady tells me that more than once, in her student days, when wondering what time it was, she distinctly heard the college clock strike, and then ascertained that the impression had been a delusion. She has also heard an imaginary "Come in," after knocking at a door. Another lady not unfrequently had a similar clock-hallucination when she was afraid of being late in the morning. A gentleman tells me that he has had the hallucination of hearing billiard-balls, when in bed near a billiard-room. That the habit of half-unconsciously looking out for any particular sound has a tendency to produce a phantasm of it is also shown by the experience of domestic servants. I have cases from two members of this class who occasionally, when at their household work, have heard the voice of their mistress calling them in tones as unmistakeable as if they were real. And another informant tells me that she distinctly heard her father's voice call to her one morning, " Come, Sissy, it's past 8, you're late," and ascertained that he had said nothing. No one will doubt that such experiences as these are purely subjective.

Cases occur, however, where the other explanation seems less clearly excluded. Mr. Charles Ede, of Wonersh Lodge, Guildford, a doctor by profession, who describes himself as a very unlikely person to be " deceived by morbid fancies," sends us the following example. Some ladies who lived about half-a-mile from him had a large alarm-bell outside their house, and one night he seemed distinctly to hear the sound of this bell. He learnt afterwards that there had been an alarm of thieves that night, and that at the very time, 1.30 a.m., when he was startled by the sound, his friends had been on the point of ringing the bell in the hope that it would bring him ; but they had not actually rung it. The hallucination may have been due to the sub-conscious idea of a possible summons in Mr. Ede's mind ; and the coincidence may probably have been accidental ; but if such a thing as telepathy exists, the probability does not amount to certainty. Again, a clergyman is awakened at 7.30 one morning by the sound of his name, ascertains that no one has called him, and learns in less than an hour that a friend, for whom he was fulfilling a trust, had unexpectedly died at 7.30 that morning. He has never on any other occasion heard an imaginary voice. Still, an experience of this sort, coming in sleep, and at the very time when the organism would be, so to speak, preparing itself for the sudden change and the summons to activity which waking involves, must be classed as ambiguous.

A type of case which often makes a great impression on those who experience it is where the expectation is of some one's *arrival*. The following auditory specimen is from the Hon. Mrs. Fox Powys, already mentioned (p. 271).

"July, 1882.

"I was expecting my husband home, and shortly after the time he ought to have arrived (about 10 p.m.) I heard a cab drive up to the door, the bell ring, my husband's voice talking with the cabman, the front door open, and his step come up the stairs. I went to the drawing-room, opened it, and to my astonishment saw no one. I could hardly believe he was not there, the whole thing was so vivid, and the street was particularly quiet at the time. About 20 minutes or so after this my husband *really* arrived, though nothing sounded to me more real than it did the first time. The train was late, and he had been thinking I might be anxious.

"AMY C. POWYS."

In answer to inquiries, Mrs. Powys adds :—

"To me the whole thing was very noisy and real, but no one else can have heard anything, for the bell I heard ring was not answered. It was a quiet street in town, and there was no vehicle of any kind passing at the time; and on finding no one on the landing as I expected, I went at once to the window, and there was nothing to be seen, and no *sound* to be heard, which would have been the case had the cab been driven off."

Now the hearing of a bell, and the hearing of a carriage driving up, are both known forms of subjective impression, even apart from expectancy, nor is there anything odd in their combination; and if, as I suspect, slight hallucinations of such non-vocal sounds are tolerably common, it is natural to suppose that expectancy might exaggerate them. The recognised voice was, no doubt, a more distinctive feature ; but in the percipient's circumstances, and after the other sounds heard, this seems too natural an addition to warrant us in connecting it with the fact that her husband's thoughts happened to be directed to her at the time. And if this case may be dismissed, *à fortiori* may others of a less prolonged and complicated kind—especially those lacking the distinct *timbre*-element of bell and voice, and so more easily accounted for as mere misinterpretations of real sounds whose source was not evident.

In the parallel visual cases, the impression is, at any rate, often of the most distinctive and unmistakeable kind ; and it is impossible not to be struck by the number of instances in which this startling

2 K 2

experience—the single visual hallucination of a person's life—has
represented the figure of a friend or relative who was on his way to
the place where his figure appeared, and whose mind was probably to
some extent picturing his own arrival.[1] None the less, I think, if
expectancy existed on the percipient's part, must it be assumed to
have been the sufficient cause of the hallucination. Such a case as
the following, sent to us by the Rev. F. R. Harbaugh (Pastor of the
Presbyterian Church), Red Bank, Monmouth Co., New Jersey, U.S.A.,
is very instructive.

"February 7th, 1884.

"While a resident of the city of Philadelphia, I made an appointment to meet a personal friend. At the appointed hour I was at the
designated place. My friend was tardy in his appearing. After a while,
however, I saw him approaching (or thought I did). So assured was I of
his advance that I advanced to meet him, when presently he disappeared
entirely.

"The locality where I thought I saw his approach was open, and
unobstructed by any object behind which he could have disappeared.
Only by leaping a high brick wall (an enclosure of a burying-ground)
could he have secreted himself. The hallucination was complete—so
distinct as to lead me to advance to meet him without a thought of optical
illusion.

"I immediately went to the office of my friend, and there learned from
him that he had not been away from his desk for several hours.

"F. R. HARBAUGH."

In answer to an inquiry, Mr. Harbaugh adds :—

"The appointment was *forgotten* by my friend, as he stated in his
apology when I entered his office."

Telepathy from an unconscious region of the defaulter's mind
would scarcely be a plausible explanation of this occurrence.

At first sight it may perhaps seem strange that the ordinary
every-day sort of expectancy which existed in these cases should be a
sufficient cause for so rare and startling a delusion. But remembering
that in the majority of startling delusions of the sort there is no

---

[1] The following case, from Mrs. Smith, of 9, Morden Road, Blackheath, is a typical
one.

"My father and mother lived, when young, near St. Albans, in a house separated
by three fields from the high road. My father had been staying in Warwickshire, and
was returning by the night mail coach. My mother had risen early to be ready for his
return, and after seeing that breakfast and a bright fire were ready for his reception, she
took her work to the window and sat there awaiting my father's return. She presently
looked up and saw him approaching ; she watched him until close to the house, when she
went to the house door intending to meet him, but he had vanished. Half an hour afterwards he really arrived. My mother was a Quakeress of exceeding truthfulness, and
possessing to the full the perfect self-command and self-repression inculcated by her sect.
I have often heard her say that she never had seen my father more distinctly than on that
occasion."

assignable cause at all, and that a person may therefore be on the very verge of hallucination without knowing it, we may not unreasonably suppose that a very slight ostensible cause might give the final impulse. It must be noticed, moreover, that in these arrival-cases the alternative to the hypothesis of the subjective origin of the hallucination is by no means clear. For what would the telepathic explanation involve? That on the agent's part the mere sense of being about to arrive, with thoughts perhaps affectionately turning to the percipient, is adequate to generate a telepathic impulse. Now have we any right to make such an assumption?

§ 8. This question, it will be seen, brings us round to the head of ambiguity numbered 1 in the above list;—where the doubt was whether a supposed agent's condition is abnormal enough for a synchronous hallucination of the percipient to form with it a coincidence deserving of attention. And it happens that it is only in the *arrival*-cases that this question has practically been difficult to decide. Many individual incidents of other types have, of course, been excluded from our evidence, on the ground that the abnormality of the alleged agent's condition was only slight, or that it was prolonged over a considerable time;[1] but these arrival-cases seem to

---

[1] I give the following case as an interesting puzzle : the reader must decide whether or not it affords evidence for telepathy. The narrator, Mr. W. A. S., is an unexceptionable witness, and has never had any other visual hallucination.

"January 14th, 1883.

"In the month of April, 1871, about 2 o'clock in the afternoon, I was sitting in the drawing-room of my father's house, in Pall Mall. The window of the room fronted south ; and the sun was shining brightly in at the window. I was sitting between the fire-place and the window, with my back to the light ; my niece was sitting on the opposite side of the fire-place ; and opposite me, at the further corner of the room, was a door partly open, leading directly to the staircase. I saw what I supposed at the first moment to be dirty soapy water running in at the door ; and I was in the act of jumping up to scold the housemaid for upsetting the water, when I saw that the supposed water was the tail or train of a lady's dress. The lady glided in backwards, as if she had been slid in on a slide, each part of her dress keeping its place without disturbance. She glided in till I could see the whole of her, *except the tip of her nose, her lips, and the tip of her chin, which were hidden by the edge of the door.* Her head was slightly turned over her shoulder, and her eye also turned, so that it appeared fixed upon me. She held her arm, which was a very fine one, in a peculiar way, as if she were proud of it. She was dressed in a pale blue evening dress, worked with white lace. I instantly recognised the figure as a lady whom I had known some 25 years or more before ; and with whom I had frequently danced. She was a bright, dashing girl, a good dancer, and we were good friends, but nothing more. She had afterwards married, and I had occasionally heard of her, but do not think I had seen her for certainly more than 20 or 25 years. She looked much as I used to see her— with long curls and bright eyes, but perhaps something stouter and more matronly.

"I said to myself, 'This is one of those strange apparitions I have often heard of. I will watch it as carefully as I can.' My niece, who did not see the figure, in the course of a minute or two exclaimed, '.Uncle A., what is the matter with you? you look as if you saw a ghost!' I motioned her to be quiet, as I wished to observe the thing carefully ; and an impression came upon me that if I moved, the thing would disappear. I tried to find out whether there was anything in the ornaments on the walls, or anything else which could suggest the figure : but I found that all the lines close to her cut the outline of her

form a distinct little class of their own. It happens also that some of them have presented features which tell rather strongly in favour of a telepathic origin. For instance, the vision representing the coming person has included some detail of dress or appearance which the percipient's mind would have been most unlikely to supply; or again, though the person whom the vision represented was actually about to arrive, his arrival was improbable and unexpected, and therefore the vision could not be connected with the percipient's attitude of mind. Such instances—though forming too small a group to be conclusive—do not seem any longer to be *ambiguous* in at all the same degree as those before considered, and they may fairly take their place among the positive evidence in a later chapter.[1] On the other hand—in view of the fact that in the vast majority of the cases where the evidence for telepathy reaches a certain strength, the agent is doing or suffering something much more remarkable than merely returning home—we do not feel that the telepathic explanation can claim any high degree of probability in any arrival-case where the hallucination has not presented some exceptional evidential feature; and accordingly no such case has been admitted in the sequel.

The discussion of these ambiguous cases has not, I hope, been altogether without positive instruction; but it was necessary, if only to clear the way for further examination of the telepathic phantasms. For if the question whether, or in what sense, those phantasms are *hallucinations* requires us to compare them with other hallucinations of the sane, the comparison must clearly be confined to cases which are *certainly* subjective, to the exclusion of cases which may conceivably themselves be telepathic.

figure at all sorts of angles, and none of these coincided with the outline of her figure, and the colour of everything around her strongly contrasted with her colour. In the course of a few minutes, I heard the door-bell ring, and I heard my brother's voice in the hall. He came upstairs, and walked right through the figure into the room. The figure then began to fade away rather quickly, at first losing the colours and then the form ; and though I tried, I could in no way recall it.

"I frequently told the story in society, treating it always as something internal rather than external, and supposing that the lady was still alive ; and rather making a joke of it than otherwise. Some years afterwards I was staying with some friends in Suffolk and told the story at the dinner table, saying that it was no ghost, as the lady was still alive. The lady of the house said, 'She is not alive as you suppose, but she has been dead some years.' We looked at the peerage, and we found she had died in 1871. (I afterwards found out that she had died in November, whereas the apparition was in April.) The conversation continued about her, and I said, 'Poor thing, I am sorry she is dead. I have had many a merry dance with her. What did she die of ?' The lady of the house said, 'Poor thing, indeed, she died a wretched death ; she died of cancer in the face.' She never showed me the front of her face ; it was always concealed by the edge of the door."

[1] See Chap. xiv., § 7. In § 6 will be found a few cases where even the condition of arrival was lacking, and the coincidence that suggests telepathy depended simply on a peculiarity of dress or aspect.

CHAPTER XII.

THE DEVELOPMENT OF TELEPATHIC HALLUCINATIONS.

§ 1. THE main points which I shall illustrate in the present chapter
are two: (1) the *gradual development* of many telepathic hallucinations; and (2) the frequent embodiment of the idea which is at the
root of them in an *original, improbable, or fantastic* manner—its
clothing upon (so to speak) with images that indicate a distinct
process of mental activity. Both of these points present themselves
also in hallucinations of the sane of the purely subjective class; and
the consideration of them will, I think, sufficiently establish the
parallelism—as phenomena for the senses—of subjective and telepathic
phantasms.

As regards gradual development,—one form of it might be found
in that *deferment* of the percipient's experience, which is as frequent
a feature in the phantasmal group as we have found it to be in
other groups of telepathic cases.[1] We should scarcely look for any
very precise analogy to this deferment in the purely *subjective* class;
inasmuch as the connection of a purely subjective hallucination with
an idea which has previously obtained *unconscious* lodgment in the
mind must, from the very nature of the case, be hard to establish. I
may, however, refer once more to the *N'IMPORTE* incident, and to
the other case described at p. 492, note, where an idea which was so
far latent that even a deliberate search for it failed to evoke it,
projected itself in sensory form at what appeared to be a quite casual
moment. I will add an experience which has been described to me
by a naval Captain, who has never in his life had any other hallucination of the senses. During his first important command, he twice
in one night had a distinct auditory impression of the words,
"Captain F., come on deck"—the reality of the impression being

[1] See, *e.g.*, pp. 201, 265, 329.

shown by the fact that he obeyed the imaginary summons. He does
not recall any preceding knowledge of danger. But it turned out
that the course which the ship was running was in fact a dangerous
one; and it is natural, therefore, to conclude that some sub-conscious
idea that his presence might be needed shaped itself in this outward
form.[1]

But the development of which I wish here to speak is that
which occurs after the abnormal experience has actually commenced.
Such development may take various forms. Thus, (1) the phantasm
may be recognised only some moments after it has been perceived,
or even after it has ceased to be perceived; or (2) a visible figure
may take shape gradually ; or (3) the process of illusion may include several distinct stages. In all these cases we may suppose that
the idea, at first but dimly conceived and vaguely apprehended, is
working itself into definiteness (as so often occurs in the processes of
abstract reasoning), and that the character of the projection under-
goes a corresponding change. Nowhere do we more clearly see the
affinity of the waking hallucinations to dreams, which often, of course,
exhibit the working out of an idea in a prolonged and elaborate
form.

§ 2. And first very briefly to exhibit these types among purely
subjective experiences—the following case, which most of my readers
will probably refer to that class, is one where the phantasm was only
recognised in the instant of or after disappearance. The narrator is
Mr. R. Gibson, of Mulgrave Cottage, Limerick.

"February 25th, 1884.

"As well as I can remember, it was in the year 1862. I know it was
in the early part of my courting days, so that it must have been 1862 or
1863. I was walking home one night about 10 p.m.—the night was not
dark, I could see clearly for many yards ahead—when I met face to face
a man in the bye-road which leads from the high road to my father's house.
I felt that sort of start one does when you feel you are coming against
something in the dark, without actually striking against it. Then the
thought came, 'Confound his impudence, why does he not move out of my
way?' and I stepped straight forward, intending to walk bang into him,
but as I stepped right up to him, with my chest up to him, he was gone,
and the instant as he vanished I thought, 'Oh, Lord, that is my Grandfather Gibson.' I felt rather queer, I can tell you, but I looked well
round, and there was no one near. I carefully went to that place night
after night again, and watched the spot often other nights over our wall,

---

[1] The more striking case quoted in the note on pp. 481-2, may without improbability
be attributed to a similar latent idea of danger.

and I could never either see or think I saw anything again. My grandfather was dead about 11 years at the time, and was never much in my
thoughts, as I had never been much with him; and at the time I was
thinking only of the events of the evening, as I suppose most young men
madly in love, as I was, would have been. I was about as happy and as
full of health and life as I suppose any fellow could possibly be. It was
quite a puzzle to me for many years what it could have been for; but I
think I know now." [This last sentence merely refers to the fact that
Mr. Gibson was at that time becoming involved in an affair that turned
out unfortunately.]

The *gradual formation* of the phantasm is a decidedly rare
phenomenon. M. Marillier, in one of the most interesting accounts of
subjective hallucination ever published,[1] says of his own experiences,
" C'est un fait intéressant à noter que les hallucinations n'apparaissent
pas d'ordinaire d'emblée, mais qu'elles se développent et grandissent,
se rapprochent peu à peu, tandis qu'elles disparaissent toujours
brusquement." On the whole, I think that it is less uncommon for
the *disappearance* to be gradual—a fading away, occasionally accompanied by an expansion of the figure.[2] Other cases do not get beyond
the stage of indefinite cloudy forms. But I have very few subjective
cases where a definite object took shape out of a vague mass. One of
these belongs to the " swarming " class—the faces, sometimes hideous
and sometimes beautiful, being described by my informant as developing out of mist. Another informant tells me that during fainting-fits,
to which in boyhood he was rather liable, he always saw white cloudy
masses pass in front of him, which gradually assumed a general
resemblance to human forms. A third case is from Mr. Robert
Collings, of 118, Earl's Court Road, S.W. When a boy, he awoke one
night, and found the moon brightly illuminating the side of the room
facing the bed.

"While gazing, I distinctly saw—rising in the moonlit space between
the curtains at the foot of the bed—what appeared to be vapour or
cloud, and as this grew higher, it gradually assumed the shape of a draped
female figure, holding towards me in one hand a lamp and in the other a
basin, from which steam seemed to rise. The form vanished slowly, and
I afterwards fell asleep without experiencing either fear or horror."
Mr. Collings' brother, who was sharing his room at the time, writes,
from the Royal Naval Club, Portsmouth, that he distinctly remembers
hearing of this vision immediately afterwards.

[1] *Revue Philosophique* for February, 1886, p. 212.

[2] For example, Mr. I. Nicholl, of 32, Lancaster Gate, W., describes to me a waking
hallucination representing a child of his, whom he " saw in his night-gown, coming from
the window. It increased in size and gradually vanished."

This experience may probably be accounted for as a recrudescence of what the boy's eyes had shortly before beheld on several occasions during a trifling illness. The case, however, ought strictly to rank as ambiguous, because the relative who had tended him in this illness had just died (see p. 512). It will be seen that the disappearance, as well as the appearance, was gradual.

The occurrence of subjective hallucinations *in several stages* is, on the other hand, common enough. I have mentioned the occasional development of an undefined impression of a presence into definite visible or audible form (p. 483, and see Vol. II., p. 201). In another case, as to the subjective character of which I myself entertain little doubt, my informant describes seeing an unusual light on the staircase, looking up, and then perceiving a deceased relative standing with a candle on the stairs. Dr. Jessopp (p. 499, note) saw a large white hand, before he turned round and beheld the complete form of his nocturnal visitor. But the more usual type is where two or more senses are concerned. So marked an instance as the incident of the servant and the message, quoted above (p. 499, note), is no doubt exceptional ; but a figure which speaks, or which shakes the percipient's arm ; the sound of footsteps or of an opening door, followed by an entrance ; a voice and a kiss—such incidents, though far less frequent than hallucinations of the single senses, are yet well represented among the subjective delusions of the sane.

§ 3. I turn now to the telepathic cases. The most striking case of delayed recognition in our collection is perhaps that of Mr. Marchant above (p. 207). A case where the phantasmal figure was taken first for one person and then for another, the latter being the one who died at the time, will be found in Vol. II., p. 71.[1] In the

---

[1] See also case 501, and compare the very parallel dream-case, No. 455. There is a curious case in the Supplement, No. 572, where a phantasm was not recognised at the first moment, owing to its appearing *too near* the face of the percipient.

As it happens, we have only one simple auditory example of delayed recognition ; and that one cannot be presented as a numbered item in the telepathic evidence, since the 12 hours' limit (p. 139) is known to have been slightly exceeded. The account was written down, a few months after the occurrence, from the dictation of the percipient— Sister Bertha, Superior of the House of Mercy at Bovey Tracy, Newton Abbot—who read it through on December 29th, 1885, pronounced it correct, and signed it.

" On the night of the 10th of November, 1861 (I do not know the exact hour), I was up in my bed watching, because there was a person not quite well in the next room. I heard a voice, which I recognised at once as familiar to me, and at first thought of my sister. It said, in the brightest and most cheerful tone, 'I am here with you.' I answered, looking and seeing nothing, ' Who are you ?' The voice said, ' You mustn't know yet.' I heard nothing more, and saw nothing, and am certain that the door was not opened or shut. I was not in the least frightened, and felt convinced that it was Lucy's [Miss Lucy Gambier Parry's] voice. I have never doubted it from that moment. I had not heard of her being worse ; the last account had been good, and I was expecting to hear

two following examples, the face of the apparition seemed familiar, though the percipient could not at the time identify it. The first is from Mr. T. W. Goodyear, now of Avoca Villa, Park Road, Bevois Hill, Southampton.

"Highfield Villa, Winchester.

"February 9th, 1884.

(191) " I may remark first of all I am considered by my friends as possessing iron nerves, am passionately fond of athletics, and certainly not given to letting imagination or fear run off with my senses. But although I can without boasting say I hardly know what fear is, I am peculiarly susceptible to mental impressions ; that is, I can often tell what is passing in the minds of others (especially my wife) when out walking with them— so much so that I have almost frightened one or two people by offering to tell them the subject on which they were thinking, and in some cases exactly what they were thinking about that subject. However, I daresay that is common enough, but what I am particularly writing you on is to tell you two facts, one of which occurred 10¼ years ago and the other 7 years ago nearly. [For the second case see Vol. II., p. 115.] It seems a long time ago to be reproduced, but to me the scenes are fresh as if they only happened yesterday.

"The first was this. I was going from the house I lived at to a shop kept by my brother, and when about half way, it came on to rain very fast. I called in at the house of a lady friend and waited some time, but it did not clear, and as I was afraid my brother would be leaving, I said I must go. I rose to do so, and went into the hall, and my friend rushed away upstairs to get an umbrella, leaving me in the dark. In the higher part of the door was a glass window, and I all at once, in the darkness, saw a face looking through that window. The face was very well known to me, though for the instant I did not associate it with the original, as she was 300 miles away. I instantly opened the door, found nobody there, and then searched the ivy with which the porch and house are covered. Finding nothing, and knowing it was impossible anyone could have got away, I then for the first time inquired of myself whose was the face I had seen. I at once knew the face was that of a married sister-in-law of my wife's. I told all our family of the circumstance directly I got home, and judge of our dismay when we had a letter to say she died at the very hour I saw her. Monday was the evening I saw the face, and on Wednesday, when we were at dinner, the letter came.

"T. W. Goodyear."

In answer to the usual question, Mr. Goodyear replies that he has had no other experience of a visual hallucination.

that she was at Torquay. In the course of the next day (the 11th), mother told me that she had died on the morning of the 10th, rather more than 12 hours before I heard her voice."

The narrator informs us that she has never in her life experienced any other hallucination of the senses.

Mrs. Gambier Parry, of Highnam Court, Gloucester, step-mother and cousin of the "Lucy" of the narrative, writes :—

"Sister Bertha (her name is Bertha Foertsch) had been living for many years as German governess to Lucy Anna Gambier Parry, and was her dearest friend. She came to us at once on hearing of Lucy's death, and told me of the mysterious occurrence of the night before."

Miss Goodyear corrobrates as follows :—

" Hartley Wintney, Winchfield.

"March 12th, 1884.

" My brother (Mr. Goodyear, of Winchester) says you wish confirmation of a statement he made as to seeing the face of a friend—who lived some 300 miles off—the evening she died. We are none of us likely to forget the assertion he made as to seeing the face, one evening some 12 years or so ago ; still less the great astonishment when two days after (midday of second day) we had a letter to say she had died on that particular evening. My other brother, who was away from home, was written to on the intervening day, and mention was made of the strange affair, so that he, too, could corroborate the statement, as his letter would reach him before the one announcing the death reached us.

" MARY APPLETON GOODYEAR."

A brother of Mr. T. W. Goodyear writes :—

"March 19th, 1884.

" I recollect my brother mentioning the strange occurrence of seeing the face of a friend a day before her death, though he was in Hampshire and she in Yorkshire. I have not kept my letter, or would forward it to you, but can vouch for the accuracy of the account.

" G. A. GOODYEAR."

We find from the Register of Deaths that the death took place on November 3, 1872 ; consequently $12\frac{1}{4}$, not $10\frac{1}{4}$, years before Mr. Goodyear wrote to us. Mr. Goodyear seems also to have made an error as to the day of the week ; for Nov. 3 was a Sunday. But it seems very unlikely that at the time both he and his sister should have been wrong in their identification of the evening of the vision as that of the death. Mr. G. A. Goodyear's words " a day before her death," if more than a slip of writing, can hardly weigh against the evidence of the other two witnesses ; and so far as they had any weight, it would tell against the supposition that the vision was as late as Monday.

In the next case our informant is unwilling to have her name published, as relatives might object ; but says that " the narrative can be verified by private communication."

" Belgravia Institute for Trained Nurses.

" December, 1884.

(192) "On the afternoon of Sunday, December 18th, 1864, my father-in-law, Mr. B., my husband, and I were sitting in the dining-room at D. Hall. The room was a large one, about 26ft. by 30ft. ; on one side was the fireplace, with a door at each side ; opposite the fireplace were three windows ; standing with your back to the fireplace, at the end of the room on your right were two more windows, and on your left a blank wall. These windows were some height from the ground, probably 7ft. or more, so that no one could look in unless standing on a chair. It was dark, and we were sitting round the fire, the shutters not having been closed. Mr. B. faced the two windows, I sat on the other side of the fireplace, with my back to the said windows, my husband being in the

middle facing the fire. Suddenly Mr. B. said, ' Who is that looking in at the window ?' pointing to the furthest of the two windows. We laughed, knowing that no one could look in, as there was nothing there for them to .stand on. Mr. B. persisted in his assertion, saying that it was a woman with a pale face and black hair ; that the face was familiar to him, but he could not remember her name : and he insisted on my husband going round the outside of the house one way, whilst he went the other. They, however, saw no one. As they went out, I looked at the clock. The time was 5.45 p.m.

"On the following Tuesday I heard of the death of my mother, Mrs. Ranking, who had died at St. Peter's Port, Guernsey, *exactly at* 5.45 *p.m. on Sunday, December* 18*th*, the hour at which the face appeared at the window. She had been delirious before her death, and calling piteously for me. Directly Mr. B. heard of her death he exclaimed, ' It was Mrs. Ranking's face I saw in the window on Sunday ' (he had only seen my mother two or three times). We were not aware that my mother was seriously ill. I do not presume to offer any scientific explanation of these facts, but I firmly believe that my mother's last thoughts were of me, her eldest child. I had only been married two months, and she had not seen me since my wedding-day.　　　　　　　　　　　　　　　　" E. A. B."

In answer to inquiries, Mrs. B. says :—

"Both my father-in-law and my husband are dead. I know of no independent way in which I can fix the date of the apparition, but I know that my husband and I had been to church that afternoon, and if you look at any almanack for 1864, you will see that December 18th in that year was on a Sunday, and that was the day on which my mother died."

We find from the *Times* obituary that Mrs. Ranking died on Sunday, December 18, 1864, "after a short illness."

I have had a thoroughly satisfactory interview with Mrs. B., who is anything but a sentimental witness. She showed me a photograph of D. Hall, which made it evident that the face at the window cannot have belonged to a real person. Even a tall man's head could not have been visible from inside the room where the party were sitting, the ledge being more than 6 feet from the ground ; and there was nothing under the window to climb up by: Still, the father-in-law would not be persuaded but that it was a real face, though of course totally unable to account for it. He was certain he knew the face, though unable to put a name to it. He had seen Mrs. Ranking only twice. It is practically certain that he had never had any other hallucination ; and he was most unwilling to regard this as one. The death was very sudden, from dysentery. Mrs. B. distinctly remembers noting the time, 5.45, while her husband and father-in-law were searching. The light was bright firelight.

In the next two cases we have the feature of gradual formation, as well as delayed recognition. The following account appeared in the *Church Quarterly Review* for April, 1877, pp. 210-11.

(193) "In the house in which these pages were written, a tall and wide staircase window, with a northern aspect, throws a strong side-light on the entrance into the chief living room, which stands at the end of a

passage running nearly the length of the house. It was after mid-day, in mid-winter, many years since, that the writer left his study, which opens into the passage just mentioned, on his way to his early dinner. The day was rather foggy, but there was no density of vapour, yet the door at the end of the passage seemed obscured by mist. As he advanced, the mist, so to call it, gathered into one spot, deepened, and formed itself into the outline of a human figure, the head and shoulders becoming more and more distinct, while the rest of the body seemed enveloped in a gauzy, cloak-like vestment of many folds, reaching downwards so as to hide the feet, and from its width, as it rested on the flagged passage, giving a pyramidal outline.[1] The full light of the window fell on the object, which was so thin and tenuous in its consistency that the light on the panels of a highly varnished door was visible through the lower part of the dress.[2] It was altogether colourless, a statue carved in mist. The writer was so startled that he is uncertain whether he moved forward or stood still. He was rather astonished than terrified, for his first notion was that he was witnessing some hitherto unnoticed effect of light and shade. He had no thought of anything supernatural [3] till, as he gazed, the head was turned towards him, and he at once recognised the features of a very dear friend. The expression of his countenance was that of holy, peaceful repose, and the gentle, kindly aspect that it wore in daily life was intensified (so the writer, in recalling the sight, has ever since felt,) into a parting glance of deep affection. And then, in an instant, all passed away. The writer can only compare the manner of the evanescence to the way in which a jet of steam is dissipated on exposure to cold air. Hardly, till then, did he realise that he had been brought into close communion with the super-natural. The result was great awe, but no terror, so that instead of retreating to his study, he went forward and opened the door close to which the apparition had stood.

"Of course, he could not doubt the import of what he had seen ; and the morrow's or the next day's post brought the tidings that his friend had tranquilly passed out of this world, at the time when he was seen by the writer. It must be stated that it was a sudden summons, that the writer had heard nothing of him for some weeks previously, and that nothing had brought him to his thoughts on the day of his decease."

The widow of the narrator writes to us :—

"Pozzoforte, Bordighera.
"December 18th, 1883.

"The article in the *Church Quarterly* to which you refer was written by my husband, but I regret to say that I can add no particulars relating to the experience he therein relates. He never could talk of it—could scarcely bear to refer to it even.[4] I do not think that he ever had any other experience of the same kind."

[1] For this sort of formation, compare cases 311, 315, 485. The appearance of mist is described in other cases which do not present the same gradual development ; see, *e.g.*, No. 210 below ; No. 555, where the figure seemed to have a cloudy fringe ; No. 518, where it remained cloud-like throughout ; and compare the appearance of "massed and dis-ordered drapery," in case 252.

[2] This peculiarity has been observed in purely subjective hallucinations ; see Vol. ii., p. 38, note.

[3] I must again point out that this unfortunate word is quite opposed to our own view of the phenomena.

[4] This being so, it would not be justifiable to publish his name.

The next account is from a lady known to the present writer, whose only reason for withholding her name and address is her fear that a near relative might object to their publication. The description seems to warrant us in regarding the visual experience, at any rate, as a waking and not a mere " borderland " specimen.

" December 17th, 1883.

(194) "Years ago, a friend and myself made the time-worn arrangement that whichever died first would endeavour to return to visit the other. Some years after, I asked this man's sister to remember me to him and say, did he remember his promise, and having received for answer ' Perfectly, and I hope I shall appear to ——, and not she to me,' the whole matter passed out of my mind. My friend was in New Zealand, his sister I don't know where. One night I awoke with a feeling some one was in the room. I must tell you that I always have a bright light burning on a table, not far from my bed. I looked about, and presently saw something behind the little table ; felt myself grow perfectly cold ;[1] was not in the least frightened, rubbed my eyes to be sure I was quite awake, and looked at it steadfastly. Gradually a man's head and shoulders were perfectly formed, but in a sort of misty material, if I may use such a word. The head and features were distinct, but the whole appearance was not substantial and plain ; in fact it was like a cloud, formed as a man's head and shoulders. At first I gazed and thought, who is it, some one must be here, but who ? Then the formation of the head and forehead (which are most marked in my friend) made me exclaim to myself ' Captain W——.' The appearance faded away.

" I got up and put the date down ; and waited until news from New Zealand was possible. I made inquiries about my friend, never doubting but that he was dead. The answer always came ' No news.' At last this also, ' We are so anxious ; it is so long since we have heard. We shall again wait another mail, and write to so-and-so.' And then came the news, a mere scrap, ' Have had a severe fall off the coach ; can't write ; head all wrong still.' That was all, and pretty much the exact words as far as I can remember. In due time we heard more. He had fallen off the coach, and was insensible for some time, and then, as he had said, his head was not clear for a while. I have never had the slightest doubt but that, while insensible, his spirit came here. The appearance to me was coincident with the time of his insensibility. I have never had but this one experience of an apparition. " E. W. R."

In a subsequent letter, Miss R. adds :—

"January 1st, 1884.

" I put the date down in a book I use daily ; there is a page for every day in the month. I mentioned it to several people—quite 3 or 4. One was extremely amused because my friend had not died ; which she always used to assure me was—she was sure—a cause of sincere regret to me."

The present writer has seen the book, which is one containing reading

---

[1] As to this sensation see Vol. ii., p. 37, note.

for every day of the month. The words written in pencil, on the page of the 15th day, are: "Night of this day, March, '74."

In answer to further inquiries, Miss R. adds :—

"I saw his sister, I should say fully a year and a-half before I saw him myself, but as this is not to be substantiated in any possible way—and is only a thought—I cannot verify it. I certainly did not write to him or hear from him between the time of my sending the message and receiving the answer, and his appearing. I am not aware that I had had anything to recall him to me particularly.

"My sister has written the note on the other sheet. She feels as sure as I do that I told her very soon afterwards, but does not like to write more positively."

The following is the sister's note :—

"Ditchingham.
"May 1st, 1884.

"As far as I can remember, my sister told me of her vision soon after it occurred, and before the news of her friend's accident arrived. It is so many years ago that I cannot speak more positively.

"Mother C."

In conversation, Miss R. especially, and unasked, confirmed the fact that the feeling of a presence in the room preceded the vision. She described the formation of the figure as like a cloud taking a definite shape. She further said that the hair of the head which appeared was distinctly *grey*, and that this was the chief reason why she did not sooner recognise the face. Her friend had *black* hair when she last saw him, and she had never thought of him otherwise; but she found out afterwards that he had become grey, and was so at the time of his accident.[1] She also stated that she had ascertained beyond a doubt that her vision fell during the period of her friend's insensibility; and her memory on this point may reasonably be trusted, since, when the news of the accident arrived, she had in her written entry the means of fixing with certainty the date of her experience.

The previous compact in this case is to be specially noted. It is a feature which we have already encountered (cases 146, 165, 169) and shall encounter again (see Vol. II., p. 66). In the next two examples, again, a feeling of a presence preceded the visual hallucination.[2] Miss Rogers, of 56, Berners Street, W., narrates as follows :—

"October, 1884.

(195) "I was on a visit at Colnbrook, in Buckinghamshire, in 1878, and one night when I went to bed, and while yet fully awake, I felt an influence

---

[1] As to this point see the beginning of § 8 below; and compare cases 449 and 515 where a still more marked change in the aspect of the agent's hair reappears in the vision.

[2] *Cf.* the "borderland" case, No. 172, where the apparition was preceded by a feeling as of "someone bending over." In such cases one may suspect that what is described as a sense of presence (as sometimes in ordinary life) is really a faint auditory impression, not noticed as such, and here of course hallucinatory like the visual impression which it introduces. *Cf.* cases 182, 201.

as if some one was in the room.   I sat up to see what it was, and saw my grandmother, in the plaid cloak she usually wore, leaning upon my mother's arm.[1] I looked round the room to see whether the vision could have arisen from any reflection from the mirrors in the room, and while doing so I saw the figures walk slowly round the room and disappear. I afterwards ascertained that my grandmother died in London about the time I had seen the apparition in Buckinghamshire.   "KATE ROGERS."

In conversation, Miss Rogers told Mr. Podmore that she was not absolutely certain as to the year in which this incident occurred. Subsequently she found from the *Times* obituary (as we had meanwhile discovered from the Register of Deaths) that her grandmother, Mrs. Macdonald, died on March 14, 1877.

In answer to inquiries, Miss Rogers says that she has had no other hallucination.   She adds that the phantasm was seen "soon after getting to bed, about 10 p.m."; and that "on my return home, I heard that my grandmother had passed away just about the time of my vision."

Appended is a letter from Mrs. Rogers, (a sister of our valued helper, the Rev. J. A. Macdonald,) who was herself nursing her mother at the time.   "October 30th, 1884.

"On receipt of your letter relative to the hour of my mother's death, I made inquiries of those who remembered the time, and I find she died nearer to 12 o'clock p.m.   The reason my daughter mentioned 10 as the time of the vision only depended upon the usage of the family she was visiting, who generally retired at 10.   Her memory could not serve her to fix the time exactly ; besides, in cases of visitors being in the house, the family remained up later.   The exact time of the appearance cannot be noted now, only that on reflection my daughter thinks it would be later than 10.   Besides, she would, perhaps, have remained up a long time in her room, conversing with the lady of the house, before going to bed, as was often the habit.   It was between 7 and 8 years ago that this experience occurred, and my daughter cannot fix exact times and hours ; but, at the time, she thinks her vision corresponded with the time of the death.   My daughter is very sorry that a more definite account cannot be given of the circumstances.   The facts can be depended upon, but the hours and times have entirely slipped our memories.

"My daughter suggests that she was so greatly attached to her grandmother that, in so continually thinking of her, the vision might have come through the influence of strong imagination ; but it impressed itself upon her mind at the time as a real presence, and she told me about it on her return to town.   She did not expect her grandmother's death just then, as she had been ailing for years, and the death occurred rather suddenly.   "JANE M. ROGERS."

In conversation, Mrs. Rogers explained to Mr. Podmore that Miss Rogers, being absent from home, did not know of any change in her grandmother's condition.

The following is a letter from Miss R.'s friend, Mrs. F.   She is not

---

[1] As to the appearance of the second figure, see p. 545 below.

explicit as to the vision having been mentioned *before* the news of the death arrived. But we presume she means to imply that it was, as the question was definitely asked ; and in a previous short note she uses the words, " Kate certainly seemed to know her grandmother was dead, before the news reached us."   "April 8th, 1885.

" Mrs. R. has sent your note to me, asking me to reply to it ; but it is really little I can tell you in reference to the matter, beyond that Miss R. felt convinced that her grandmother was dead before the news reached us, from a dream or vision[1] (whichever you like to call it) that she had had. I cannot give you her words as she told it to me. The fact that Miss R. had a vivid dream in reference to the death of her grandmother did not strike me as anything but natural. She was always deeply attached to her, and doubtless had gone to bed with an anxious mind, knowing that her grandmother was ill.   " C. B. F."

The next account is from Mr. J. G. F. Russell, of Aden, Aberdeenshire.

"32, Upper Brook Street, W.
"January 3rd, 1886.

(196) " Early in October, 1872, whilst at H. M. Embassy, at Constantinople, to which I belonged, when crossing a garden (which separated the secretary's house, where I lived, from the Ambassador's palace), on my way to dine there, about 8 o'clock in the evening (it was about dusk), I felt some irresistible, magnetic sort of influence compel me to turn round and look behind me.[2] I saw an indistinct white form, about the height of a human being, gazing at me, as if it were trying to attract my attention. It was only a very few yards off. I at once walked towards it, and spoke, but it vanished.[3] So convinced was I that *something* had got within the precincts of the Embassy walls and gates (all being well secured and watched), that I returned to my own quarters, examined the closed gate, and questioned the guard on duty as to whether any stranger could have entered. ' Impossible,' he said ; and our sporting dogs, none of which were white, were sleeping peacefully on the doorsteps. I then returned, through the same garden, to the Embassy Palace, to dinner, and back again at night. I saw nothing. Again I made inquiry whether any intruder had entered the gates, but it was proved to me to be materially impossible ; nor could any one have scaled the high wall, or disappeared as quickly as did the white figure when I advanced towards it.

" Very soon after, I learnt that a married aunt of mine, to whom my family and myself were much attached, had died in my father's house, in the North of Scotland, during the afternoon of the same day on which I saw the figure.   " J. G. F. Russell."

Mr. Russell adds, in reply to inquiries :—

"I have no recollection of mentioning, at the time I saw the ' white figure ' in question at Constantinople, to any one but the guard at the gate that I *had* seen anything ; I may have done so, but anyhow I could now get no corroborative testimony from my then colleagues. I have no

---

[1] As to the great injustice done to the telepathic argument by confounding dreams and waking visions, see above, pp. 394-7, and Vol. ii. pp., 2, 3.
[2] Compare case 162, where Mr. Symonds says, " I knew that I must turn my head."
[3] As regards the vanishing of hallucinations on sudden speech or movement, see Vol. ii., p. 91, second note.

record in my book as to the evening when I saw the white figure. I simply recollect that, on hearing of her death, I found it was on the same day, and making allowance for distance at the same hour, as when I saw the said apparition. When I heard of my aunt's death from my wife, I replied that on that night I had seen a strange white apparition."

We learn from Mr. Russell that he has had no other experience of the sort, with the exception of a single faint impression of a shadowy figure at a time when he was out of health, and the very palpable "apparitions" that may be seen at séances.

His diary, though it contains no mention of the incident above described, affords a means of confirming the coincidence. He finds from it that he dined at the Embassy on September 26th, September 28th, and October 1st. On the two latter occasions he visited elsewhere after dinner, and returned home by the quay ; but on September 26th, when the party was a large and gay one, he returned home by the route through the garden ; and on passing through the scene of his odd experience, he distinctly remembers saying to himself, " Well, that apparition has not spoilt my evening ; let us see if it will come to me again." It was on the 26th of September, 1872—as we find from an obituary notice in two Aberdeen papers—that his aunt died. Mr. Russell says, " As far as my wife can recollect, the hour of my aunt's death was between 4 and 5 p.m." —which would be between 6 and 7 at Constantinople ; thus the vision followed the death by between 1 and 2 hours.

In the following case a visual phantasm first appears, and then words are heard which, in the mind of both agent and percipient, were probably of all others the most significative of the bond between them. The narrator is Mrs. Bishop, formerly Miss Bird, the well-known traveller and authoress. The account, received in March, 1886, is almost identical with a second-hand version which was given to us in March, 1883. When travelling in the Rocky Mountains, Miss Bird had made the acquaintance of a half-caste Indian, Mr. Nugent, known as " Mountain Jim," over whom she established a considerable influence.[1]

(197) " On the day in which I parted with Mountain Jim, he was much moved and much excited. I had a long conversation with him about mortal life and immortality, and closed it with some words from the Bible. He was greatly impressed, but very excited, and exclaimed, ' I may not see you again in this life, but I shall when I die.' I rebuked him gently for his vehemence, but he repeated it with still greater energy, adding, ' And these words you have said to me, I shall never forget, and dying I swear that I will see you again.'[2]

" We parted then, and for a time I heard that he was doing better, then that he had relapsed into wild ways, then that he was very ill after being wounded in a wild quarrel, then lastly that he was well, and planning revenge. The last news I got when I was at the Hotel

---

[1] See *A Lady's Life in the Rocky Mountains*, Letters vi-ix. and xiii-xvii.
[2] As to this promise, see Vol. ii., p. 66.

Interlaken, Interlaken, Switzerland, with Miss Clayton and the Kers. Shortly after getting it, in September, 1874, I was lying on my bed about 6 a.m., writing to my sister, when, looking up, I saw Mountain Jim standing with his eyes fixed on me, and when I looked at him he very slowly but very distinctly said, ' I have come, as I promised ' ; then waved his hands towards me, and said, ' Farewell.'

"When Miss Bessie Ker came into the room with my breakfast, we recorded the event, with the date and hour of its occurrence. In due time news arrived of his death, and its date, allowing for the difference of longitude, coincided with that of his appearance to me.   " I. B."

In answer to inquiries, Mrs. Bishop says that she has never had any other hallucination of the senses ; that she had last seen Mountain Jim at St. Louis, Colorado, on December 11th, 1873 ; and that he died at Fort Collins, Colorado. She hopes to be able to show us the diaries in which the date was recorded ; but she wrote from abroad, and under very great pressure.

We have procured a copy of some of the testimony given at the inquest at Fort Collins, from which it appears that the death took place on Sept. 7, 1874, between 2 and 3 p.m.—which would correspond with about 10 p.m. at Interlaken. The coincidence therefore cannot have been as close as Mrs. Bishop imagines. If the vision took place on the 8th of September, it followed the death by 8 hours ; but if it took place on the 7th, then the 12 hours' limit was exceeded by some 4 hours.

In the next two cases there is a distinct hallucination of sound, suggestive of some one entering or approaching the room (compare the " borderland " cases 182 and 190) ; and in the second of the two, a short interval elapses before the visual percept is developed.

Mrs. Stella, of Chieri, Italy, writes, on January 14th, 1884 :—

(198) "When I was about 15, I was staying on a visit to Dr. J. G., of Twyford, Hants, and I formed a friendship with my host's cousin, a boy of 17. We became inseparable, boating and riding together and sharing all our fun, just like brother and sister. He was very delicate, and I took care of him, and looked after him, until we never passed an hour away from each other. I tell you this to show there was not a particle of morbid sentiment between us ; we were like two boys together.

"One night Mr. G. was sent for to see his cousin, who had been taken suddenly very ill with inflammation of the lungs, and the poor boy died the next night. They did not tell me how ill he was, so I was quite unaware of his danger, and therefore not anxious in any way. The night he died, Mr. G. and his sister went round to their aunt's house, leaving me alone in the drawing-room. There was a bright fire, and like many girls I delighted to sit by the fender, reading by firelight. Not knowing of my friend's danger I was not uneasy, only vexed that he could not come and spend the evening with me, so I felt lonely. I was reading quietly when the door opened,[1] and Bertie (my friend) walked in. I jumped up to get him an arm-chair near the fire, as he looked cold, and he had no greatcoat on, and as it was snowing, I began to scold him for

---

[1] See p. 102, note.

coming out without his wraps. He did not speak but put up his hand to his chest and shook his head, which I mistook to mean his cold was on his chest, and that he had lost his voice, to which he was subject. So I reproached him again for his imprudence. While speaking, Mr. G. came in and asked me to whom I was speaking. I said, 'There's that tiresome boy without his coat, and such a bad cold he can't speak; lend him a coat and send him home.' I shall never forget the horror and amazement on the good doctor's face, as he knew *(what I did not)* that the poor boy had died half-an-hour ago, and he was coming to break the news to me. His first impression was that I had already heard it, and that I had lost my senses. I could not understand either why he made me leave the room, and spoke to me as if I were a small child. For a few moments we were at cross purposes, and then he explained to me that I had had an optical illusion ; he did not deny that I had seen Bertie with my eyes, but explained it all most scientifically, as he was anxious not to frighten me or leave a distressing impression. I have never spoken of it to anyone before now, partly as it is a most distressing remembrance, and partly in the fear of being thought fanciful and being disbelieved. My mother said I was dreaming, and forbad me ever to mention it. I was not dreaming, but reading a book called ' Mr. Verdant Green,' not at all a book to send one to sleep, and I well remember at the time the door opened I was laughing heartily over some of its absurdities.   "I. S."

Asked if she has ever had any other visual hallucination, Mrs. Stella answers in the negative ; and adds that she is "not at all imaginative or nervous." She has had an auditory hallucination which was veridical, and is described in Vol. II., p. 109. She cannot recall the exact date ; but we find from the *Medical Register* that Dr. J. G. was only at Twyford from 1864 to 1873—within which period the occurrence must have fallen.

In answer to further inquiries, Mrs. Stella writes :—

"Their house must have been a quarter-of-an-hour's walk from Mr. G.'s, and Bertie died about 20 minutes before he [*i.e.*, Mr. G.] left the house. The apparition had been in the room about 5 minutes when Mr. G. came in. What to me has always been so strange is, that I *heard* the handle of the door turn and the door open ; in fact, it was the noise of the lock turning which caused me to look up from my book. The figure walked across the room to the opposite side of the fireplace, and sat down while I lighted the candles. It was all so real and natural that I can hardly realise even now that it was not so."

Later she adds :—

"With regard to the 5 minutes, I daresay the time was not quite so long, although some minutes may have elapsed between the entrance of the apparition and that of Mr. G. The only light in the room was that of the fire, and as, of course, I had no idea but what it was the real ' *Bertie*,' I did not take much notice of him. I purposely did not ask him any questions on account of his apparent inability to talk, and I myself went on speaking in order to give him time to regain breath, which, on account of his delicate chest, often occurred, and his silence for 5 minutes or even longer would not have astonished me, as the cold outside was intense, and great cold often oppressed his breathing. There was nothing in his appearance that struck me as different from usual, except his paleness and silence, and to both I was accustomed.

"I am sorry to say that Mr. G. died about 10 years ago. Unfortunately the circumstance was never mentioned to any members of my family ; partly because Mr. G. advised me to say nothing, and partly from my own fear of being laughed at, as I was very young at the time."

[Here, as in so many other cases, the central fact of the coincidence is independent of the details, and is far more likely than they to have been correctly retained in memory.]

The second case is from Mr. B., confidential clerk to a firm with a principal of which we are well acquainted. He withholds his name from publication, having a strong dislike to the subject. The account is in the words of Mr. D. H. Wilson, of Rosemont, Hyères, but has been read over and corrected by Mr. B. The fact that the percipient had just got up and opened his door 'may be taken as a proof that he was awake when the visual experience took place.

                                        "October 24th, 1883.

(199) "Mr. B. is a gentleman whom I have known for more than 15 years. He is practical, shrewd, and very trustworthy. I am indebted to him for the following narration : One morning, a few months ago, at 5 o'clock, he was awakened by a noise outside his room, but near his room door. Opening the door he saw no person. He returned to bed, and had scarcely composed himself when he was very disconcerted by seeing the form of a lady friend of his glide or flit across the room. He thereupon woke Mrs. B. and informed her of the fact. This was Saturday, and at the end of the next week Mr. B. called at the house of his friend, the subject of his vision, and was informed that the lady had thrown herself out of the window the previous Saturday at about 5 o'clock in the morning, and was instantaneously killed."

We learn from Mr. B. that the hallucination of the senses here described is the only one that he has ever experienced.

In this example we observe a failure to co-ordinate the elements into a completely natural-seeming incident. A feature in Mr. Keulemans' case (No. 184) has been reserved for mention here as illustrating the same point. He says :—

"The sound [of the child's voice] did not proceed from the locality where the vision [of the child] was seen, nor did it seem to be in any way produced by the organs of speech belonging to the apparition ; for the mouth did not move. I heard the voice at a short distance, and on my right side, simultaneously with the vision, which appeared at a greater distance, on my left, or rather in front of me."

§ 4. So much, then, for gradual development. I proceed to my second main point—the embodiment of the idea which is at the root of the hallucination in a manner that is to some extent original, and implies a creative process carried out by the percipient's own mind.

There is no need to illustrate this process at any length in the purely subjective class. A certain amount of it is, in fact, involved in every sensory hallucination which is anything more than a mere momentary revival of familiar images, due, as I have suggested, to a disturbance at the sensory centre, unprompted by any agitation in the higher tracts of the brain (pp. 489-90). Wherever the higher tracts of the brain are the first in action, and the hallucination represents an object which the senses have never actually encountered, there clearly the mind has more or less created its object ; and of the transient hallucinations of the sane the majority seem to belong to this class. A special type that is worth noting is where the hallucination is in part mere reminiscence and in part a new creation. For example, a gentleman tells me that, having been compelled to kill a favourite dog, he very soon afterwards had the subjective vision of a dog running across the lawn, and pursued by a man in a white flannel jacket ; and my friend Mrs. Hunter, of 2, Victoria Crescent, St. Helier's, describes how, having just dismissed for the night a young daughter under 15 years of age, heard her lock her door, locked her own, and resumed her own train of thought, she looked up, and there the child " stood smiling, in dressing-gown and hair floating down her back, just as she had left me, but *with a baby in her arms* "—the apparition lasting for a few seconds.[1] A good example of a subjective hallucination whose development from the root-idea is obvious, is a visionary crown, clearly seen by a lady hovering near the head of a preacher to whom she was listening (as she implies) with sympathy and admiration. As more or less fantastic instances, I may mention the apparition, out of doors, of a tall female figure, which went on in front of the percipient, and whose head then left its body ; a man in parti-coloured Oriental garb, about as wide as high, and with a face like a king on a card ; and some curious appearances of " flats," human-looking figures without any apparent depth, by which a gentleman tells me that he has been more than once visited. Peculiarities in costume and appurtenances are very common ; a woman in grave-clothes, a woman in brocaded silk with a small book in her hand, a black man with a knife in his hand, a sweet-looking creature in a low black dress and mantilla, a tall man with dark curly hair and in antique dress, a woman with a crown and a child, recalling a statuette of the Virgin—such are among the visual hallucinations in my collection which there is no reason to suppose other than purely

---

[1] *Cf*. Mr. Blacker's case, p. 502.

subjective affections. Of auditory cases, some that have been already
given show the construction from a root-idea in the percipient's mind
very plainly—*e.g.*, the words, "You can't save him," "Your brother
is dead," "Take up that knife and use it " (pp. 509, 478, note). Another
good example is that of a clergyman's wife, who tells me that she
was once startled by the remark, " Those ladies will borrow money
from George to-day," while she was sitting alone, and picturing a call
which her husband was paying to some impecunious parishioners
whom she mistrusted—unless, indeed, the fact that the loan was
actually requested be held to make the case "ambiguous." The
hearing of long, original discourses could, of course, not be reckoned
as a *transient* hallucination, and is a type which scarcely occurs at
all among hallucinations of the sane ; but occasionally a very few
words may be quite sufficient to show independence of mental
action—as where a lady who was expecting to be called by her sister
in the morning, distinctly heard, in fictitious tones, not the expected
message, but the much more agreeable one, " Not five ; don't get up
yet."

§ 5. And now to turn to the parallel features of original or
fantastic construction in the telepathic class of hallucinations. The
question as to the existence and interpretation of these features is
of such special importance to my general argument that, at the risk
of wearying the reader, I must make its bearings plain.

I must recur for a moment to the breach which has been more
than once noted (pp. 111-12, 190, and 234) as dividing telepathic
phantasms from the less concrete forms of telepathy, and especially
from the results of experiments in thought-transference. To resume
the two marked points of difference :—in the experiments, (1) the
" subject " never perceives the transferred image as an actual sight or
sound—there is never an external hallucination ; and (2) the image
always represents the precise object which is consciously occupying
the agent's mind ; whereas in the case of the spontaneous phantasms
the percept (1) appears to be external, and (2) represents something
which is certainly not consciously occupying the agent's mind—to
wit, his own form or voice.[1] Here is an undoubted *crux*. When the

---

[1] I am here speaking of the common type of spontaneous cases. There are other cases,
both visual and auditory, which conform more nearly to the experimental type, in so far
as something that is occupying the senses or the mind of the agent is distinctly represented
in the phantasmal appearance (see, *e.g.*, cases 151, 157, 158, 220, 221, 267, 268, 269, 270, 288,
291). But such representation is decidedly exceptional, and in visual cases applies usually
to only a single feature in the appearance ; *e.g.*, in case 210 below we might trace the perception of the wound, and in case 213 the perception of the checked shawl, to the agent's
conscious thought, but not the perception of his or her complete figure.

agent is painfully concentrating his attention on a card, with the object
of getting the impression of it transferred to the percipient, one might
have imagined that he was in a stronger and more hopeful condition for
producing a telepathic effect than when his thoughts are wandering
at random, and are perhaps not occupied with the percipient at all ;
and yet the effect on the percipient seems often to be of a far more
dominant and startling kind in the latter case than in the former.
We may observe further that just the two forms of telepathic impression which, in the ordinary course of experiment, do occasionally reach
the pitch of *hallucination*—the transferences of pains and of tastes—
are conspicuous by their absence from the records of spontaneous
cases, the latter being totally unrepresented and the former very rare :
while, on the other hand, the spontaneous class abounds in specimens
where the psychical condition of the agent—whether sleeping,
swooning, or dying—has apparently lapsed to the very verge of
nothingness.   Spontaneous telepathy would thus seem to depend as
little on the agent's intensity of feeling (for what can be more
intensely felt than acute physical pain ?) as on his intensity of
concentration ; or, if some actual intensity of experience be imagined
for him even at moments when it is least apparent (Chap. V., § 10),
it will at any rate not be imagined as abnormal preoccupation with
his own physical attributes.

Now it is manifest that these differences may be reduced, in
proportion as the extent of the impression actually transferred from
the agent to the percipient in the phantasmal cases can be conceived to be small, and the part which the percipient's own creative
energy supplies can be conceived to be large.   If we are at liberty
to assume that even a dim and shadowy idea, when once it obtains
a lodgment in the mind, may body itself forth as a sensory phantasm,
clearly all that we shall have to suppose transferred from the one
mind to the other is a dim and shadowy idea.   We shall thus shift,
so to speak, the responsibility for the hallucination to the *percipient's*
mind ; which we shall conceive as actively generating and projecting it
under a peculiar form of impulse, instead of passively receiving a full-
fledged percept from the *agent's* mind, where nothing in the least
resembling such a percept had any conscious place.

An unknown quantity—the peculiar form of impulse—has, no
doubt, here to be assumed ; for unless the transferred idea involves a
certain impulsive force which causes the mind to react on it, and to
project it as a hallucination, why does it not remain as a mere idea ?

It might, indeed, be not unreasonably replied that it *does* remain as a mere idea in many cases, as we saw in the 6th chapter; and that there may be many other cases where it never reaches the stage of even a conscious idea—never forces itself on the attention at all,— and where, therefore, we never hear anything about it (see p. 97). We have already had numerous experimental instances of what may be called "underground telepathy": in Mr. Newnham's cases, for instance, (pp. 64-70,) no one would ever have known that there had been a transference of ideas, but for the fact—which was not in any way vital to the transference—that Mrs. Newnham had her hand on a planchette at the time. And if we could conceive that a great deal of *spontaneous* telepathy takes place similarly underground and unnoticed, then we might regard the sensory phantasms as a sort of accidental group—as just the cases which here and there get above ground, owing to some exceptional favouring condition in the percipient. The question why an idea that has been telepathically transferred should give rise to a hallucination, might thus be answered by saying that it does so only in the proportion in which purely subjective ideas develop purely subjective hallucinations—the specific cause being as unknown in the one case as in the other. All this, however, is highly hypothetical; and we need not shrink from the provisional hypothesis that a telepathically-conveyed idea which is to some extent charged with emotion, really has a certain peculiar tendency to develop into hallucination. Our very ignorance in some measure justifies this assumption; for unable as for the most part we are to connect transient hallucinations of the sane with any antecedent condition at all, we need the less scruple to admit a novel condition when we find one. And in connection with such an onward passage of the impression, it is very pertinent to recall the particular impulsive quality which we found to attach to some of the *experimental* transferences—where the impulse took effect not in sensory but in muscular disturbances, (see pp. 74-9, and 84.)[1]

To return, however, to the actual content of the percepts, and

---

[1] I may note further how the very fact of an *unrecognised* telepathic phantasm bears witness to the suggested specific tendency of telepathic impressions to pass into hallucinations. We have had instances, in former chapters, of vague but strong impressions, not connected by the percipient at the time with any particular person, which afterwards seemed to have been due to the condition of a particular person. Now one would have supposed, if an undistinctive telepathic idea was to assume more definiteness, that it must be by becoming a *distinctive idea*, an idea of the particular agent. But what we find is that the undistinctive telepathic idea sometimes becomes more definite in a quite different way —namely, by becoming an *undistinctive percept*, an *unrecognised form*. It is hurried on into hallucination, so to speak, without having first declared itself as an idea; it assumes the definiteness of visible shape, while yet its content or message remains indefinite.

XII.]   *TELEPATHIC HALLUCINATIONS.*   539

their relation to the ideas from which they spring. If once it be granted that the telepathic phantasm need not be the literal embodiment of any clearly-defined idea or image, but may be worked out from a suggestion of a vague kind, we should certainly be prepared for variety and independence in the working out. The mind is no mere collection of separate compartments, into which new ideas will fit and then rest in a passive way; but an organism of interacting parts, where any change or any intruding element may set in motion whole trains of images and associations. We know what small and dim suggestions will sometimes set large tracts of mental machinery to work; we may therefore well credit the vaguer or sub-conscious order of telepathic impressions with such a power. What more natural, then, than that these further images and associations should be embodied in the sensory projection? We have already noted the process in dreams; we found the telepathic impression operating not to suspend or fetter, but simply to invoke and inform, the spontaneous activities of the dreaming condition. We have since caught the percipient mind at work, so to speak, in the gradual stages which waking hallucinations often present; and we have noted the originative activity which often goes to the shaping of purely subjective specimens. What is now suggested is that the waking mind may unconsciously react, as in a dream, on the nucleus of a " transferred impression," and, in the act of externalising the percept, may invest it with its own atmosphere and imagery.[1] We shall thus have a ready explanation for many degrees of distinctness and individualisation, and many diversities of character, in what is perceived. Suppose the same kind of real event—say the peaceful death of an aged parent—to occur in twenty cases, and in each of them to produce a real and unique sort of disturbance in some absent person's mind; then, if that disturbance clothed itself in some sensory form—or, as I should say, if it reached the point of causing *hallucination*—the hallucination might take twenty different forms. One percipient may hear his parent's voice; another may imagine the touch of his hand upon his head; a third may see him in his wonted dress and aspect; a fourth may see him as he might appear when dying; a fifth

---

[1] The psychological identity of hallucinations and dreams—alike in subjective and in telepathic cases—is a point which I am the more anxious to enforce in that there seems sometimes to be a difficulty in catching it. For example, a leading daily paper contrasts members of the Society for Psychical Research with the sensible people "who believe that all those apparitions and stories of second-sight which engage the curiosity of that Society may be relegated to the limbo of waking dreams." With the substitution of "class" for "limbo," this "relegation" is precisely what the present argument seeks to effect.

may see him in some transfigured aspect; a sixth may see a figure
or hear a voice resembling his, but not recognise it, or recognise it
only in recollection ; and others may invest the disturbing idea with
every sort of visible symbolism, derived from their minds' habitual
furniture and their wonted trains of thought.

§ 6. This frequent activity of the percipient's mind in the
elaboration and projection of his percept forms a ready key to much
of the evidence that follows.   How, for instance, on any theory of
merely passive affection of the percipient's mind or senses, could we
account for the appearance of a dying friend, attired in the style of
dress which was habitual to him at the time when the percipient
associated with him, but which has been discontinued, or, at any rate,
is not that in which he would be pictured in his own mind ?   The
"ghosts of clothes" in general—a stock bugbear—are the simplest
things in the world to explain on a theory of telepathic impressions ;
but the ghosts of *old* clothes—how could they be impressed *ab extra* ?
What, on the other hand, is more natural, when once the percipient's
active share in the phenomenon is recognised, than that he should do
what we saw Mr. W. A. S. do in the neutral case quoted above (p. 517,
note)—that he should invest the idea of his friend with the visual
traits that memory supplies, and should project the figure into space
in its most familiar aspect ?

A few instances of this sort may be quoted.   The first is from
Miss Cressy, of Riverhead, near Sevenoaks.

"December 18th, 1883.

(200) "My younger brother was in Australia, and had not written to his
family for some four or five months, from which my mother had concluded he
must be dead. I was sitting with her and my sister in our dining-room one
morning, about 11 o'clock, engaged with my sister in writing a German
exercise.   Being at a loss for the right declension, I looked up, repeating
the declension, when I saw my brother standing on the lawn in front of
the window apparently looking at us.   I jumped up, saying to my mother,
'Don't be frightened, mother, but there is T. come back all right.'   (My
mother had heart disease, and I feared the sudden shock.) 'Where?' said
my mother and sister, 'I don't see him.'   'He is there,' I answered, 'for
I saw him ; he is gone to the front door,' and we all ran to the door.   My
father, who was in his library, heard the commotion, and opened his door
to ask the cause.   I had by this time opened the front door, and not
seeing my brother, I thought he was hiding for fun among the shrubs, so
I called out, 'Come, T., come in, do not play the fool or you will kill
dear mother.'   No one answered, and then my mother exclaimed, 'Oh,
you did not see him really, he is dead, I know he is dead.'   I was
mystified, but it did not seem to me the right solution of the mystery.   I

could not think he was dead, he looked so honestly alive. To tell the truth, I believed for some time that he was in the garden. However, he was not, nor was he dead. About a year afterwards he returned home, and when recounting his troubles, he told us that he had been very ill, and that while he was delirious he had constantly requested his comrades to lay him under the great cedar tree on his father's lawn, and turning to my father he went on, ' Yes, father, and do you know I seemed to see the dear old place as plain as I do now.' 'When was that?' said my father. He gave the date, and my mother, who had written it down, looked and said, ' Why, that was the very time when your sister declared she saw you on the lawn.' 'Yes,' said my father, 'and your mother at once killed you,' and there was a good laugh at my expense.

"I have often thought over it, but have never been able to account for it. This brother was not a particular favourite. Had it been my sister, I could have supposed that, as she was rarely absent from my mind, I might have conjured up her form in my imagination. Then I would have bitten my tongue out rather than have startled my mother. But I never doubted for a moment that my brother was there. I was about 25 years of age, and had no theory as to ghosts or spirits in general. I was at that time far too much occupied with the cares and anxieties of the family to have time to dwell on such fancies, and was also too matter-of-fact to think much about such phenomena. I remember at the time, that I saw my brother dressed as he usually was when he came home from London, not as he was when he left home, nor as he could be in Australia, nor as I had ever seen him when walking in the garden. He had on a tall hat and a black cloth suit, neither of which he had taken with him. Of course, at the moment none of these thoughts occurred to me, but when, in consequence of the jokes and ridicule at my expense, I tried to follow up the ideas that had been floating through my mind, to see whether they had any connection with my absent brother, I could make nothing of it.   "A. CRESSY."

In answer to inquiries, Miss Cressy adds :—

"I have delayed answering your last communication in the hope of recalling the name of some person still living to whom I had mentioned the vision about which I wrote to you, but I am sorry to say there is no one. I only am left of all the party. You ask when it occurred. As nearly as I can remember it was at the beginning of 1854. My brother left England for Melbourne in September or October, 1852. As nearly as I can remember, I got his first letter at the beginning or middle of May, 1853. We got three or four letters in succession, the last saying that he and his companions were going to Fryers Creek diggings. Then we heard nothing more for eight months. During those eight months it was that I saw him as I have described. I believe it was February, 1854.

"I have never before or since had any apparition, and that was the reason I wrote you the account of it, because it seemed to me to prove that it was no hallucination,[1] but simple fact. I was then young and vigorous ; I had no superstitions, never having experienced any exceptional sorrows : those I had gone through were common enough, and more calculated to develop the matter-of-fact side of my character than to induce a morbid or dreamy imagination. That brother was always said to

---

[1] The word is of course used here in its common sense of *purely subjective* hallucination.

be very like me, and it is a singular fact that in matter of health we suffered very much alike. He always leant on me when in any trouble, and his thoughts during that illness might almost unconsciously have wandered to me."

Miss Cressy tells me that her recollection of her mother's entry of the date in her pocket-book, and of the reference to this date after her brother's return, is quite distinct ; and it is a confirmation of this that, unprompted by me, she had made a search for the book, which, however, could not be found. She considers that the dress and rapid disappearance of the figure would alone exclude the hypothesis of mistaken identity ; but, in fact, the figure was close to the window ; and had not the recognition been absolute and startling, she would never, she says, have exclaimed as she did, since the importance of not causing any shock to her mother was much on her mind.

The next case (which again exemplifies the development of a feeling of presence into distinct hallucination) is from Mrs. Bolland, of 7, Cranbury Terrace, Southampton, the narrator of case 126 above.

"July, 1884.

(201) "About March, 1875, the circumstances hereafter detailed happened to me at Gibraltar. I wrote an account of them from memory in 1878. It was published in *All the Year Round*, of August, I think, that year, but I have not since seen it, so I can only give the story as far as I remember it now.

"I was lying down in my drawing-room on a bright sunshiny afternoon, reading a chapter on Chalk Streams in 'Kingsley's Miscellanies,' when I suddenly felt that some one was waiting to speak to me. I looked up from my book and saw a man standing beside an arm-chair, which was about 6 feet from me. He was looking most intently at me, with an extraordinary earnest expression in his eyes, but as I walked forward to speak to him, he disappeared.[1]

"The room was about 18 feet long, and at the further end of it I saw our servant [Pearson], holding open the door as if he had admitted a visitor. Thinking that perhaps he too was but a delusion, I spoke to him, asking if anyone had called. To which he replied, ' No one, ma'am,' and walked away. I then tested myself as to whether I had been sleeping, seeing that it was 10 minutes since I lay down. I said to myself what I thought I had read, began my chapter again, and in 10 minutes had reached the same point.

"1 then thought it over again. I knew the face quite well, but could not say whose it was, but the suit of clothes impressed me strongly as being exactly like one which my husband had given to a servant named Ramsay the previous year. This man was a discharged soldier whom I had found in a dying state in Inverness, and who had been taken into our service after leaving the infirmary. He turned out badly and I had to send him away before we went to Gibraltar [in February, 1875], but he was taken on as waiter at the Inverness Club, and I had no cause to be anxious about him, as I thought he was well and doing well, and would probably profit by his past experience and keep that situation.

---

[1] *Cf.* case 196, and see Vol. ii., p. 91, second note.

" I told my husband when he came in what I had seen, and also told his colonel's wife (now Lady Laffan), but did not put down the date. But almost as soon, I believe, as a letter could have come from Inverness, my husband received one from his late sergeant, to say that Ramsay was dead, but giving no particulars. To this my husband wrote that he was sorry, and would like to hear 'any particulars of his illness and death.' This was the answer : ' Ramsay died in hospital, raving, and calling incessantly for Mrs. Bolland.'

" I will only add that I believe the face of the man I saw was that of Ramsay as I had known him at first, when I visited him as a dying man in the infirmary. But seeing him every day as my servant, and in health, it had passed from my mind, or rather did not connect itself with this man in my memory.

" I may add that I had been in ill-health for some years, but at that time was stronger than I ever was in my life, the warm climate suiting me —so well that I felt a strength and enjoyment of life for its own sake, which was a delight to me.   " KATE E. BOLLAND."

In reply to inquiries, Mrs. Bolland adds, " This is the only instance in which I have ever experienced a hallucination of the sense of sight."

The following corroboration is from Lieut.-Colonel Bolland, R.E. :—
     " July 20th, 1884.
" With regard to the apparition at Gibraltar, Mrs. Bolland mentioned it to me an hour or two after she saw it, which would be about 4 or 5 o'clock in the afternoon. She said she knew the face, but she could not say whose it was, but distinctly recognised the clothes worn as being like a suit I had given to Ramsay when in Inverness.

" The news of his death was a shock, coming shortly afterwards ; and I wrote to my late sergeant on the Ordnance Survey at Inverness (Sergeant Dedman, R.E.), for particulars, with the result which Mrs. Bolland has told you.   " G. HERBERT BOLLAND."

We learn from Mr. J. Wilson Black, house-surgeon at the Northern Infirmary, Inverness, who has kindly referred to the books, that Archibald Ramsay was admitted to that institution on Feb. 24, 1875, suffering from tumour of the brain, and died on March 9. Mr. Black adds :—" None of the officials at present in the house were in it at the time ; and I am consequently unable to say at what hour he died." Mrs. Bolland has kindly endeavoured to find out, from the Library at Gibraltar, on what day she took out the book that she was reading ; but without success.

We find that the above account completely agrees with the fuller one in *All the Year Round*. That account, however, contains a more complete explanation of the non-recognition of the face. As regards the momentary mistaking of the man for a visitor, these words occur : " I will only remind you that, as far as appearances went, the man was a gentleman. He had gentle birth on one side, was always refined in his manners, and, moreover, was dressed in a suit of clothes of which no gentleman need have been ashamed." The paper ends with the following additional incident :—

" There is one odd fact as a pendant to this little story. The man Pearson, whom we had just brought all the way from the Ultima Thule of the ancients, at great expense, gave warning that day, because, he said,

' the house was haunted.' He gave no explanation, and I said nothing, as the reason of his sudden wish to leave only reached me through my maid. You will remember that he stood at the door, having apparently shown in my mysterious visitor. Had his notice to quit come a day later, I should have said he heard other servants speaking of the circumstance in houses where I had mentioned it. But he gave it that day and before I had spoken of it at all. Nor have I heard up to this moment what he meant. Puzzled but not alarmed myself, I would not risk frightening my household, so when my maid told me what he had said, I only replied, 'Nonsense!' and that was the end of it. He left us, and the news of Ramsay's death came after he had gone, or I think I should have felt inclined then to question him."

The narrator in the following case, Miss S., fears that publication of her name might be disadvantageous to her.

"March 11th, 1884.

(202) "In August, 1881, I had been ordered by my doctor to take absolute rest, not even to read at all, and to do no work whatever. I therefore took lodgings in a cottage near London for a few weeks. During the last 6 or 7 years, I had been rather intimate with a lady (Mrs. A.), whose daughter I had instructed during that period. This lady had gone to the sea-side with her family during the summer holidays, but had sent me a message, before she left town, that the suddenness of her departure had prevented her from coming to see me, but that she would certainly do so on her return. In the meantime I had heard, through mutual friends, that she and her family were in good health, and would probably return about the middle of September.

"About 3 weeks after Mrs. A.'s departure, I was expecting a friend to come and see me, and had ordered a carriage, to take her a drive. The morning proved wet, and she did not come, and after waiting some time, I went out alone, in an open landau, at about 3.30 or perhaps as late as 4 p.m. I had not left the house more than 20 minutes, when, in an open lane, I saw coming towards me Mrs. A. with one of her younger children. She was sitting in her own victoria, which I knew well. As she sat I saw only the three-quarter face; but I recognised the bonnet, and also the sealskin jacket, which she was wearing, as one that she generally wore in winter. I remember them particularly, because it struck me, as the carriage approached, that it was very odd of her to be wearing a sealskin jacket in August. Just as the carriage came up to me, and was passing me, so near that if I had put out my arm I could have touched it, I sat up, and called out, 'Oh, Mrs. A.' She did not move or turn her form towards me, but seemed to be half-turned towards the child, who sat on the further side of me. I was very much astonished at this, and then I turned round to look after the victoria, and, as far as my recollection serves me, I saw it slowly drive away. I am perfectly sure that I could not have been mistaken; I was never more certain of anything in my life than that I had actually seen my friend and her little child.

"For the next 10 minutes or so, I was puzzling to think what could have brought her back to London, and was very vexed with myself for not having at once told the coachman to turn and drive after the carriage. I did, however, as soon as I could collect my senses, tell him to drive home as quickly as possible ; and as soon as I reached the cottage I said to my landlady, ' There is a lady and a little girl waiting for me upstairs, I suppose ? ' When she assured me that there was not, I at once sent the servant over to my sister's house, about 10 minutes' walk off, to see if Mrs. A. had perhaps gone there. When the servant came back with no tidings of her, I was very much astonished, and couldn't help wondering over it for the rest of the evening.

"Two or three days afterwards, I asked the landlady to get me a daily paper, feeling a longing to read *something ;* and, at my landlady's urgent entreaty not to tire myself, I said that I would only look at the births, deaths and marriages. There I saw the announcement of the death of Mrs. A. at the sea-side, on the very day when, as I thought, I had passed her in her carriage, near London.

" I afterwards learned from her relations that she had died after a very short illness, at 6 p.m. on that day, and that she had lain in a state of unconsciousness for some hours before her death. It could not have been much less than two hours before her death—that is during the time when she lay unconscious—that I saw her.   " E. L. S. "

We find the announcement of the death in three London daily papers for August 30th, 1881.

In conversation, Miss S. stated that she had never been the subject of any hallucination. She is short-sighted, but wears suitable glasses, and was wearing them on this occasion. No corroborative testimony can be obtained. The landlady was very old, and very unlikely, even if now alive, to remember so trifling an incident as Miss S.'s question about the supposed callers ; and Miss S.'s sister was absent from home when the inquiry was made at her house.

This might conceivably have been a case of mistaken identity. But it would have been an extraordinary one ; and the sealskin jacket in August would have been as odd a costume for any real person as Miss S. conceived it to be for her friend. It is worth mentioning that visions of horses and carriages are a known species of purely subjective hallucination ;[1] and it is therefore not as strange as it might appear that a telepathic hallucination should assume this elaborate form. But more important is the appearance of a second human figure—that of the dying friend's child. I have already (p.426) pointed to a similar feature in one of the " borderland " cases as an indication that telepathic percepts, in their sensory character,

---

[1] *Cf.* Dr. C. M. Smith's case, p. 499, note ; and see also some collective hallucinations in Chap. xviii., § 5, and the apparently telepathic case, No. 264. Occasionally a subjective experience takes a still more elaborate form. Thus an informant who at one time had a slight tendency to visual hallucination, describes seeing, when quite awake, the details of a complete funeral procession. A somewhat similar telepathic case will be quoted in the Supplement, No. 586 ; see also case 207 below. But the more elaborate scenes, so far as I can judge, are generally of the less externalised sort which were treated in Chap. vi. as vivid mental pictures, not sensory hallucinations.

are really projections from within. I may now point out, as a fresh instance of parallelism between telepathic and casual subjective phantasms, the extreme *rarity* of the cases in which a second figure thus appears. In my large collection of subjective hallucinations of vision—putting out of the question the peculiar *illusions hypnagogiques* (pp. 473-4)—I find only seven cases, that is, less than 3 per cent., presenting more than one human figure;[1] three of which occurred to percipients who were in bed, while in two others the percipients were extremely young. And among the telepathic examples in this book, I find almost exactly the same proportion.

As further illustrating the construction of the phantasm from material which the percipient's mind supplies, I may mention a point in case 184. On the day when little Isidore left Paris for London, his hair was cut very short; and the long "fringe," which was removed, could not (the narrator says) have grown to its customary length in the month which followed before the death. But, as he adds, "In my memory his image still preserved the usual features, with the fringe over his forehead ; and on the morning when the vision awoke me, I saw him with the fringe over his forehead."[2] In another " borderland " case, No. 495, where the phantasm of a dying female relative appeared, the dress—" out-door walking costume, the bonnet being a prominent part of it "—was that in which the percipient had last seen her, nine years previously ; in a waking case, No. 555, where the phantasm represented the percipient's mother, " the attire was the same in which I had last seen her several

---

[1] See Dr. Smith's case, p. 499, note, and Mrs. Hunter's case described in § 4, above. ther telepathic instances are Nos. 188, 195, 492, 511, 519, 568, 673 ; besides the cases in which a complete scene with several figures has been represented, as Nos. 299, 505, 548. In case 185 there was the sense of a second person's presence, but the hallucination was of one figure only. The dream-case, No. 128, is also worth comparing, as illustrating the identity of the process by which the sleeping and the waking mind may react upon and embody a telepathic impression.

[2] It may be remembered that Mr. Keulemans had in the evening a *second* vision of his child, which was treated above as a mere recrudescence of the morning's hallucination. Mr. Keulemans himself, however, is inclined to explain it otherwise. His grounds are that this second vision, which took place in the bright gaslight of the billiard-room, represented the boy's figure, in an attitude suggestive of death, enclosed as it were in a dark cellar or vault, with a little window in it ; and he afterwards found that at that hour the dead body had been taken to a mortuary, which he afterwards saw, and which vividly recalled the visionary scene. (I attach more importance to these details than I should otherwise do, on account of the care which Mr. Keulemans has brought to bear on the study of his own visual impressions, and of his training in habits of accurate observation.) He suggests that this second vision was due to a telepathic impulse from his wife's mother, who had the body conveyed to the mortuary and whose thoughts were naturally directed to him. Now on this view of the "agency" the experience none the less involves an *independent* contribution on the part of the percipient. For he saw the child's figure, though as if dead, *in his little blue sailor suit*; which was familiar to him, but which we can hardly conceive to have been present, in association with the ideas of death and burial, in his mother-in-law's mind.

years before;" and in another waking case, No. 645, the phantasm appeared in a dress which the agent had not worn or seen for nine months, but which she had been wearing during the weeks when the percipient had last been in her company. (See also case 552.)

§ 7. The examination of these precise points may lead us on to more general ground. If we admit a power in the percipient to evolve a waking dream from the nucleus of a "transferred impression," we at once get rid of what has been a very real obstacle to the recognition of the telepathic evidence. Phantasms having often been conceived as in some way objective and independent presences, it has seemed to the sceptic that all idea of reality about them was sufficiently refuted, if they possessed features which were a clear reflection of the percipient's beliefs and ideas. Students of folklore and of comparative thaumatology have observed that such phenomena, in various times and countries, have borne a perceptible relation to prevalent habits and opinions; and if specimens which have coincided with, and so seemed to announce and typify, unusual events, have borne a similar relation, it has been easy to argue for their purely subjective character from this *subordinate* point, and to ignore the *essential* point—the fact of the coincidence. This wrong issue is precluded as soon as the analogy of dream is boldly insisted on, and the phenomena are described as hallucinations, not presences, and as veridical, not objective. Any presumption against them, as sentimental, or superstitious, or fantastic, then loses its basis. The naked fact of coincidence can no more be sentimental or superstitious than stoical or sceptical; but subjective colourings may attach to waking hallucinations as easily as to dreams; and it cannot seem surprising that the same mental habits and traditions which give a particular character to so many of the hallucinations which are illusory through and through—hallucinations and nothing more—should give a similar character to some of the hallucinations which are not illusory through and through, but are projected under the stimulus of a true impression from the mind of some absent person. The same cast of ideas through the dominance of which a *dévote* may receive a false impression that she has met the Virgin in a wood, may very naturally lead her, or one like her, on the receipt of a true impression that some beloved relative is dying, to body forth the figure as robed in white and with a radiant face; and much more *bizarre* apparitions than this might, on the same principle, be accepted as having a causal

2 M 2

connection with a real event.[1] The opportunity for observing such phenomena in telepathic cases is, no doubt, limited by the fact that cases of any evidential weight are almost confined to quite modern days, and for the present to the more advanced nations; but it is possible that as interest in the subject increases, a wider area will be covered. Meanwhile we have quite enough cases to illustrate the point.

As examples of phantasmal appearances presenting features which would in reality be impossible, the following three accounts may serve. The first is from Mrs. Allom, of 18, Batoum Gardens, West Kensington Park, W.

"June 28th, 1885.

(203) "I have not the least objection to giving an account of the apparition I had of my mother, which appeared to me at the time of her death, although it is a subject I have very rarely mentioned, partly that it is an occurrence I hold very sacred, and partly that I do not care to have my story doubted or laughed at.

"I went to school in Alsace in October, 1852, when I was 17, leaving my mother in England in delicate health. About Christmas, 1853, 14 months after I left home, I heard that my mother's health was worse, but I had no idea that she was in any danger. It was the last Sunday in February, 1854, between 1 and 2 o'clock, I was seated in a large school-room reading, when suddenly the figure of my mother appeared to me at the far end of the room. She was reclining as if in bed, in her night-dress. Her face was turned towards me with a sweet smile, and one hand was raised and pointing upwards.

"Gently the figure moved across the room, ascending as it went until it disappeared. Both the face and figure were wasted as if by sickness, as I never had seen her in life, and deadly pale.

"From the moment I saw the apparition I felt convinced my mother was dead. So impressed was I that I was unable to attend to my studies; and it was positive pain to me to see my younger sister playing and amusing herself with her companions.

"Two or three days after, my governess, after prayers, called me to her private room. As soon as we entered I said, 'You need not tell me. I know my mother is dead!' She asked me how I could possibly know. I gave no explanation, but told her I had known it for three days. I afterwards heard my mother died on that Sunday, at the time I had seen her, and that she had passed away in an unconscious state, having been unconscious for some day or two before her death.

"I am by no means an imaginative, sensitive woman, and never before or since have I experienced anything similar.   "ISABEL ALLOM."

Mrs. Allom's mother was Mrs. Carrick, wife of Mr. Thomas Carrick, the well-known miniature-painter. Mrs. Allom has kindly procured a

---

[1] See for instance, the narrative of the apparition of the Gwrach y Rhibyn, in Sikes's *British Goblins*, p. 217, which was related to the author at first-hand, in 1878. This extraordinary phantasm, a dreaded local celebrity, seems on the occasion described to have supplied the embodiment for a real telepathic impression.

copy of an entry inscribed by her father in an old family Bible, which states that Mrs. Carrick died on January 30th, 1854 ; and we have verified the date in the *Times*. This day, we find, was a Monday, not a Sunday.

Mrs. Allom is sure that she has never had a hallucination on any other occasion. She once, however, had a rather marked *illusion*, when a Christmas-tree assumed momentarily, to her eyes, the aspect of her mother's form. She is a practical person, and assures me that she has all her life been free from fancies and superstitions. Her sister was delicate and nervous, and on that account Mrs. Allom did not tell her of the vision above described. If she is correct in her recollection that her experience was on a Sunday, and is not merely inferring that, by combining her recollection of the closeness of the coincidence with her idea that the death was on a Sunday, the hallucination must still have fallen at a time of most critical illness. That she has said February, instead of January, seems to be an obvious slip either of writing or memory ; as that the vision should have followed the death by a month, or even by a week, is wholly inconsistent with the rest of the statement.

The next case is from Mrs. C., the narrator of case 80 above, to which the following sentence was appended :—

(204) "At another time I saw a figure of a friend pass before me, ascending. I received a letter to say she had died that night."

In answer to inquiries, the narrator added :—

"February 19th, 1884.

"As to your question relating to the vision of my friend, I was saying my prayers, and immediately mentioned it to my husband [since deceased], and have subsequently mentioned it to others. She was in Cheltenham, and I had left her shortly before, she promising to come to town to consult a doctor on a painful but not dangerous complaint. It appears she had eaten a pork chop, and was very sick. Her husband not apprehending any danger, asked a friend to see to her and stay with her, while he went to business. She was sick all day, and to their horror, died that night.

"E. C."

Mrs. C. further mentions that she has a ring which gives Sept. 25, 1852, as the date of her friend's death.

In conversation, Mrs. C., who is a practical person with no leaning to superstitious fancies, told me that she was not thinking of her friend when the vision was seen. It was completely external, but in the air, so to speak, and high up. It is the only hallucination that Mrs. C. has ever experienced.

The next case is from the *Memoirs of Georgiana, Lady Chatterton* (1878), by E. H. Dering, the second husband of Lady Chatterton, pp. 185-186. The author says :—

(205) "In March, 1869, while we were at Malvern Wells, an event occurred, which the reader will, of course, take for what he thinks it is worth, but which I cannot see my way to explain as a coincidence.[1] She (*i.e.*, Lady Chatterton) had a great regard for Father Hewitt, O.S.B. ; and he had

[1] This word is often, but very unfortunately, used as equivalent to *chance-coincidence*.

always shown a very marked sympathy for her in her difficulties. One afternoon she said, 'I am sure that dear Father Hewitt is dead. I saw him just now, when I went upstairs, as clearly as possible, dressed in the Benedictine habit, only it was of dazzling whiteness. He seemed high above me in the air,[1] and he looked at me. I knew then that he was dead.' It was about 2 o'clock in the afternoon. The next morning's post brought us the news that he died at the time when she saw him."

In reference to this incident, Lady Chatterton's niece, Mrs. Ferrers, of Baddesley Clinton, Knowle, writes to us as follows :—

"March 24th, 1885.

" I was with her at Malvern Wells at the time, in some lodgings that we hired for a few weeks ; and Father Hewitt was then at Woolton, a village in Warwickshire, my aunt and Mr. Dering renting Woolton Hall that year. I cannot give you the exact date, but I remember that it was one day in Easter week of that year (1869). I was in the drawing-room of those lodgings after luncheon, about a quarter past 2 o'clock, when my aunt came downstairs from her bedroom and told me that she was quite sure Father Hewitt was dead for she had seen him, &c. We all knew that he was ill of one of his usual severe attacks of gall-stones, but that complaint is not considered a fatal one, and so we were full of hopes that we should find him better on our return home. He was one of the best and dearest of our friends, and his death, corroborated the next morning by hearing his name given out at Mass,[2] to be prayed for among the dead, was a heavy blow to us all. We afterwards heard that he had died at 2 o'clock on the day my aunt saw him.   "REBECCA H. FERRERS."

[We learn from the Provincial of Canterbury, the Rev. H. E. Moore, that the date of the Rev. Peter Joseph Hewitt's death was March 11th, 1869. Easter Sunday in that year fell on March 28th ; Mrs. Ferrers is therefore mistaken in supposing the occurrence to have taken place in Easter week ; but this is not material. The coincidence was probably exact to a quarter-of-an-hour.]

The luminous appearance of the figure here should be specially remarked. For luminosity is a sufficiently frequent feature both in purely subjective and in telepathic hallucinations, to be included as a fresh point of resemblance between the two classes. It is possibly to definite hallucinations of this character that we should trace the widely-diffused superstition which finds in a mysterious light the sign of a supernatural presence;[3] but considering how natural the

---

[1] Other examples of a figure seen above the percipient, or ascending, are Nos. 163, 352, and 512.

[2] In this detail there is an apparent, though perhaps not a real, discrepancy from Mr. Dering's account.

[3] See Mr. Andrew Lang's remarks in the *Nineteenth Century* for April, 1885, p. 629. The following passage occurs in Rink's *Tales and Traditions of the Eskimo* (1875), p. 43. "The Supernatural Rulers, or Inue, as far as they may be perceived by the natural senses, generally have the appearance of a fire or bright light ; and to see them is in every case very dangerous, partly by causing *tantamingnek*—viz., frightening to death—partly as foreshadowing the death of a relative (*nâsârnek*)." Superstitions of this sort are likely enough to produce the very experiences on which they feed ; but the hallucinations of light described in the present work are certainly not suggestive of anything like *tantamingnek*.

symbolism of light is in connection with supernatural ideas, such a hypothesis is perhaps superfluous. It is at any rate not possible to reverse the process, and to trace the hallucinations to the superstition ; for they go on occurring in the present day, as my collection alone would show, to persons who have no previous acquaintance with or belief in the superstition. The light occurs in various forms and degrees. One form already mentioned (p. 437) is the impression of a dark room as illuminated, which is sometimes experienced on waking. In the group of non-human phantasms described above, we found a star, a firework, a firefly, a bright oval, a chandelier (p. 503, and see also Vol. II., pp. 193-4). Among the subjective human phantasms, seven appeared with a candle in the hand. In a considerable number of the nocturnal cases, though no special radiance is mentioned, the aspect of the figure seems to have been far more distinct and detailed than that of a real person would have been,[1]—*e.g.*, the grotesque appearance mentioned in Vol. II., p. 237, note, which was remarkable for brilliance of costume, " disappeared, leaving the room in darkness " ; and in other cases the figure has appeared as radiant.[2]

The position in which the phantasm was projected in the last two cases quoted may have been the result of some dim idea of departure or transition. In other cases there is the distinct symbolism of death. Two such cases, of the " borderland " class, have been already given (Nos. 178 and 190). The following example belongs to a season of active waking life. The percipient, Lieut.-Colonel Jones, of 8, Sussex Place, N.W., is a man as free from superstition as can well be imagined, who has never experienced any other hallucination whatever. He has shown us a letter, written at the time, in which his father alludes to the apparition.

" 1883.

(206) " In 1845 I was stationed with my regiment at Moulmein, in Burmah. In those days there was no direct mail, and we were dependent upon the arrival of sailing vessels for our letters, which sometimes arrived in batches, and occasionally we were months without any news from home.

" On the evening of the 24th of March, 1845, I was, with others, dining at a friend's house, and when sitting in the verandah after dinner, with the other guests, in the middle of a conversation on some local affairs, I all at once *distinctly* saw before me the form of an open coffin, with a favourite sister of mine, then at home, lying in it apparently dead. I

---

[1] See p. 462, note, and Vol. ii., p. 72, note.

[2] As telepathic cases which present the same points, I may refer to Nos. 163, 178, 184, 210, 213, 220, 230, 250, 253, 311, 314, 315, 323, 332, 491, 494, 498, 512, 513 (2), 515, 550, 553, 567, 658, 673, 702. Luminosity is also a marked feature of some of the dream-cases, *e.g.*, Nos. 449, 460, 464.

naturally ceased talking, and everyone looked at me in astonishment, and asked what was the matter. I mentioned, in a laughing manner, what I had seen, and it was looked upon as a joke. I walked home later with an officer very much my senior (the late Major-General George Briggs, retired, Madras Artillery, then Captain Briggs), who renewed the subject, and asked whether I had received any news as to my sister's illness. I said no, and that my last letters from home were dated some three months prior. He asked me to make a note of the circumstance, as he had before heard of such occurrences. I did so, and showed him the entry I made opposite the day of the month in an almanack. On the 17th of May following, I received a letter from home announcing my sister's death as having taken place on that very day—viz., the 24th of March, 1845.

"R. WALLER JONES."

As to the coincidence of hour, Colonel Jones only learnt that the death occurred in the morning of the 24th. His vision was seen after an early dinner, so that, allowing for longitude, the correspondence of time was certainly near, and may have been exact. There had been a very close attachment between sister and brother.

We may regard the next two cases—one visual and one auditory —as exemplifying the religious investiture of a telepathic impression. The first, in which the accuracy of the description " waking dream " is specially well shown, is from Mrs. Larcombe, of 8, Runton Street, Hornsey Rise, N., a sensible and superior person who has seen a good deal of the world. She has had no other hallucination, unless an unexplained appearance seen by her in early childhood, and by others as well as herself, was of that character.

"July 17th, 1882.

(207) " When I was about 18 or 19, I went to stay in Guernsey. This would be about 30 years ago. About 10 a.m., one day, I was sitting in the kitchen, blowing up the fire with the bellows. I heard some very beautiful music, and stopped to listen, at the same time looking up. I saw above me thousands of angels, as tight as they could be packed, seeming to rise far above and beyond me. They were only visible as far as the head and shoulders. In front of them all I saw my friend, Anne Cox. As I looked and listened, the music seemed to die away in the distance, and at the same time, the angels seemed to pass away into the distance, and vanish like smoke.

" I ran up to Miss White, the young lady staying in the house, and told her what I had seen. She said, ' You may be sure your friend, Anne Cox, has gone to Heaven.' I wrote home at once, to Lyme Regis, and found that Anne Cox had died that very day.

" Anne Cox and I had been very close friends. She was just my own age, and was almost like a sister to me.

" M. A. LARCOMBE."

Mrs. Larcombe states positively that she was in no anxiety about her friend, and had no knowledge of her illness. She cannot recall where the death occurred, and it has therefore been impossible to discover its exact date.

The next case is from Mrs. Udny, of 61, Westbourne Park Villas, W.

"July, 1883.

(208) "This family story fell within my own recollection, and I can vouch for the accuracy of the facts. The dates put it beyond any question of being imagined *after* the circumstances had occurred.

"In January, 1850, my husband (George Udny, of the Bengal Civil Service) was in Calcutta, and I was living in London. His sister Emily (Mrs. Ryan) was living near me in London, and her husband, Edmund Ryan, was in Calcutta.

"On the 20th February, 1850, I received a letter from my husband, saying poor Edmund was very ill. Owing to some political news of importance my letter of the 9th had come with a Government dispatch a day later than the ordinary mail of the 8th, the regular mail-day.

"Soon after receiving my letter, on the same day, my sister-in-law, Emily Ryan, came to me in great anxiety to know if I had any later news of her husband than the 9th, as she also had heard he was very ill. I explained to her how impossible it was that there should be any *later* news, as the 9th itself was later than I had ever known the mail leave before. She then explained the reason for her extreme anxiety for news to the 10th January, and told me the following curious circumstance :—

"On the 10th January, she had been engaged in her devotions between 11 a.m. and noon, according to her custom ; for she was in the habit of rising late, and did not make her appearance in the family circle till the middle of the day. While thus engaged on her knees, and making her husband the special subject of her prayers, she thought some one spoke quite distinctly close to her ear, ' Pray not for him, he is in Eternity. Be still and know that I am God.'

"She was so much astonished, she thought some one must have come into the room unperceived by her, and rose from her knees and looked around her, but could see no one. She was, however, so much impressed by the circumstance that she wrote it down at once, with the date of day and hour, and sealing up the paper, carried it downstairs and gave it to the care of a young niece living in the house (Tempè Raikes), telling her to keep the seal unbroken till she asked for it.

"On the morning she came to me, 20th February, hearing of her husband's serious illness on the 8th January, she had asked for her sealed note and had broken the seal and read in the presence of her mother and aunt the above circumstance, and finding the date, which she had forgotten, only two days later than her news from Calcutta, came off to me to inquire for later news, but only heard my letter of the 9th.

"She had, therefore, to await the arrival of another mail—a fortnight after—when the letters of the 23rd January, arriving on the 8th March, told her that her poor husband had died on the *10th January*, between 5 and 6 p.m.—the exact time, allowing for the difference of longitude, that she had been forbidden to pray for him in London.

'· A. L. UDNY."

We find from notices in the *Gentleman's Magazine* and the *Annual Register* that Mr. E. B. Ryan died at Calcutta, on Jan. 10, 1850.

Mrs. Udny showed Mr. Podmore the notes (committed to paper on April 27, 1861, in order to preserve the memory of the occurrence) from which this account was taken. Mrs. Ryan, now Mrs. Hermon, cannot be questioned on the subject.

In a second letter, Mrs. Udny adds :—

"I have just received the enclosed from my niece—the Tempè Raikes of my family story. I think you will find it very satisfactory as to the main facts of the story. I think you will find my dates are more accurate than my niece's; she has got a little confused as to the hours— perhaps not allowing for the difference of longitude. I distinctly remember Mrs. Ryan's telling me that she was praying between 11 and 12 a.m., and I think I mentioned in my mem. to you that her husband died about 5 o'clock p.m., because my husband wrote that to me from Calcutta. And the singular thing which struck me at the time was that the difference would be exactly that of the longitude."

The enclosure was as follows :—

"25, Victoria Square, Clifton.

"September 16th, 1883.

"About the story of Aunt Hermon [formerly Ryan], the facts, as far as I can recollect, are that she wrote out what had happened one morning at her private prayers, and gave me the sealed letter about it, and said in a few weeks she would either ask me for it to burn it, or to read it out. Six weeks after, when she heard of Uncle Ryan's death, she asked for it and gave it to her mother ; and in it she had written that, while praying for her husband (from whom she had heard nothing for 6 months), a voice came to her ears, 'He is in Eternity.' She went on, thinking it a silly fancy, and again it said, 'It is too late, he is in Eternity.' She was so convinced of its truth she left off, and was sure she would hear something had happened. He had died that very morning at 4 o'clock, for she had dated her letter, and, moreover, she was quite prepared when his death was announced to her. The overland mail in those days took six weeks coming.   "TEMPE S. BRIGHT (*née* Raikes)."

§ 8. To return, however, to the details of the phantasmal appearance—the theory which I have advanced as to the projection of the percept has received illustration in cases where all its features could be, and in my view have been, supplied by the percipient's mind. But it must now be added that there is a converse type, where the dress or aspect includes features which equally clearly could *not* be supplied by the percipient's mind ; and here the former explanation will, of course, not apply. In cases of this type, the actual aspect of the agent, at the time of the occurrence, has included some marked variation from any- thing that the percipient would naturally picture. If, then, the phantasmal appearance includes this same feature, it must be an element that the *impressing* mind has contributed, and not the *impressed ;* in other words, we must here admit that a ready-made concrete image, and not a mere idea, has been transferred from one to the other. There is no reason to doubt that such an image occupies a certain place in the agent's mind ; and when a peculiarity of aspect is temporary and accidental, it is sometimes a very prominent part of consciousness. Even when the peculiarity (as it appears to the percipient) is one to which the agent himself has become accustomed —as a change in the growth or colour of the hair—the fact remains that a certain sense of one's own aspect probably always exists at the background of consciousness. This it is which sometimes, at the season when latent ideas are apt to assume arbitrary prominence, creates for the scantily-clad dreamer such embarrassing situations ; this it is which, in rare but well-attested cases, projects the apparition (purely hallucinatory, as I should hold) of a person's own self or "double " ;[1] and I may again recall the experimental indications that even ideas which cannot be recognised as part of consciousness at all may be susceptible of telepathic transference (pp. 78-9, 84). I do not indeed pretend that the analogy here can give entire satisfaction ; or that the translation of a vague sub-conscious image in one mind into a sharply-defined, and at the same time a perfectly correct, percept in another, is a fact for which the rest of our evidence, whether of experimental or of spontaneous transferences, would have ever prepared us. All that I would claim is that it is a fact which the conception of psychical transferences is not inadequate to embrace. Another conception no doubt there is—that of some *independent* exercise of the percipient's own faculties—which suggests itself in respect of this type of experience, as before in the cases where the percipient's point of observation seemed transferred to a distant scene (pp. 266, 340, 368-9). But in the absence of more distinct

---

[1] These experiences seem to be of two sorts. Sometimes the percipient's impression is that his own point of observation has been transferred to a point outside his body, whence he sees his body in the place where it really is. An instance is given in Vol. ii., p. 85, note ; and my collection of hallucinations includes two other cases of the kind, in one of which the "subject" was under chloroform, and in the other was recovering from fever. Another correspondent has had impressions of the same sort, which seem to have stopped short of actual hallucination. He writes : " I have occasionally felt as though I knew that the body was lying in the bed, but that the spirit was hovering about it, and contemplating it. When this is the case I am apt to feel some difficulty in waking, and even feel a little unwell through the following morning." With these experiences should be compared the less marked cases where the impression is simply of " going out of oneself "—a well-known feature of various abnormal conditions ; see for instance Mr. Varley's description above referred to (p. 288, note) ; case 215, below ; and Cardan, *De Varietate Rerum* (Basle, 1557), p. 314. But in another class of cases the percipient retains his normal point of observation, and simply sees a phantasm representing himself at a place which is really vacant. An instance of this is case 333 (Vol. ii., p. 217) ; and I have another chloroform-case in which the patient, a medical man, seemed to see his own "double " contemplating him.

contemporary evidence for such exercise, I think that we should avoid even provisionally resorting to a theory which introduces problems as formidable as any that it can be employed to explain. And in the present cases, as in the former ones, since nothing is perceived that is definitely outside the agent's range of knowledge, the extension of the percipient's faculties—his *clairvoyance,* if we like to call it so—may still be perfectly well regarded as a *telepathic* extension, an abnormally increased power of receiving impressions from another mind, or rather a power of receiving impressions from the more withdrawn strata of another mind, under conditions of crisis or excitement.

To come now to the evidence—as to which one preliminary remark is needed. Some of the cases to be quoted are, I think, clearly of the type described; others are also instances of it, if quite correctly recorded. But we must remember that a narrative which is completely correct as to the central facts which go to prove the telepathic origin of the phantasm, may yet be inexact in the particulars which now become important. A *striking coincidence* is rather apt to suggest to the imagination a *detailed correspondence;* and the percipient, in looking back to his experience after hearing of certain features which belonged to the aspect of his dying friend, may come to imagine that they were represented in the phantasm. Every example, therefore, must be weighed with this possibility in view.

A genuine instance of the type, I believe, was the one already quoted (No. 194) where the *grey* hair was a detail of appearance which Miss R. had never imagined, and was very unlikely to conjure up. Another is the following, received in 1882 from Captain G. F. Russell Colt, of Gartsherrie, Coatbridge, N.B.

(210) "I was at home for my holidays, and residing with my father and mother, not here, but at another old family place in Mid-Lothian, built by an ancestor in Mary Queen of Scots' time, called Inveresk House. My bedroom was a curious old room, long and narrow, with a window at one end of the room and a door at the other. My bed was on the left of the window, looking towards the door. I had a very dear brother (my eldest brother), Oliver, lieutenant in the 7th Royal Fusiliers. He was about 19 years old, and had at that time been some months before Sebastopol. I corresponded frequently with him ; and once when he wrote in low spirits, not being well, I said in answer that he was to cheer up, but that if anything did happen to him, he must let me know by appearing to me in my room, where we had often as boys together sat at night and indulged in a surreptitious pipe and chat. This letter (I found subsequently) he received as he was starting to receive the Sacrament from a clergyman who

has since related the fact to me. Having done this, he went to the entrenchments and never returned, as in a few hours afterwards the storming of the Redan commenced. He, on the captain of his company falling, took his place, and led his men bravely on. He had just led them within the walls, though already wounded in several places, when a bullet struck him on the right temple and he fell amongst heaps of others, where he was found in a sort of kneeling posture (being propped up by other dead bodies) 36 hours afterwards. His death took place, or rather he fell, though he may not have died immediately, on the 8th September, 1855.

" That night I awoke suddenly, and saw facing the window of my room, by my bedside, surrounded by a light sort of phosphorescent mist, as it were, my brother kneeling. I tried to speak, but could not. I buried my head in the bedclothes, not at all afraid (because we had all been brought up not to believe in ghosts or apparitions), but simply to collect my ideas, because I had not been thinking or dreaming of him, and, indeed, had forgotten all about what I had written to him a fortnight before. I decided that it must be fancy, and the moonlight playing on a towel, or something out of place. But on looking up, there he was again, looking lovingly, imploringly, and sadly at me. I tried again to speak, but found myself tongue-tied. I could not utter a sound.[1] I sprang out of bed, glanced through the window, and saw that there was no moon, but it was very dark and raining hard, by the sound against the panes. I turned, and still saw poor Oliver. I shut my eyes, walked through it,[2] and reached the door of the room. As I turned the handle, before leaving the room, I looked once more back. The apparition turned round his head slowly and again looked anxiously and lovingly at me, and I saw then for the first time a wound on the right temple with a red stream from it. His face was of a waxy pale tint, but transparent-looking, and so was the reddish mark. But it is almost impossible to describe his appearance. I only know I shall never forget it. I left the room and went into a friend's room, and lay on the sofa the rest of the night. I told him why. I told others in the house, but when I told my father, he ordered me not to repeat such nonsense, and especially not to let my mother know.

" On the Monday following,[3] he received a note from Sir Alexander Milne to say that the Redan was stormed, but no particulars. I told my friend to let me know if he saw the name among the killed and wounded before me. About a fortnight later he came to my bedroom in his mother's house in Athole Crescent, in Edinburgh, with a very grave face. I said, ' I suppose it is to tell me the sad news I expect ; ' and he said, ' Yes.' Both the colonel of the regiment and one or two officers who saw the body confirmed the fact that the appearance was much according to my description, and the death-wound was exactly where I had seen it. But none could say whether he actually died at the moment. His appearance, if so, must have been some hours after death, as he appeared to me a few minutes after 2 in the morning. Months later, a small prayer-book *and the letter I had written to him* were returned to Inveresk, found

---

[1] See p. 513, note.

[2] In my collection of purely subjective hallucinations there is a case where this very expression is used. It occurs also in the " ambiguous " case, p. 517, note.

[3] Communication with the Crimea was then conducted by telegraph for only part of the way.

in the inner breast pocket of the tunic which he wore at his death. I have them now."

The account in the *London Gazette Extraordinary* of September 22nd, 1855, shows that the storming of the Redan began shortly after noon on September 8th, and lasted upwards of an hour and a-half. We learn from Russell's account that "the dead, the dying, and the uninjured, were all lying in piles together"; and it would seem that the search for the wounded was still continuing on the morning of the 9th. The exact time of Lieut. Oliver Colt's death is uncertain.

In a further communication, Captain Colt says :—

"My father received Admiral Milne's message just as we were starting in the drag—a large party—on a visit to some ruins, several miles off. He was driving, and I was sitting next to him, and he remarked, 'It was well I told you not to say anything about having seen your brother Oliver to your mother. I hope you will forbid it to be mentioned by any one whom you told, as it might doubly alarm her now, since this news."

Captain Colt told me in conversation that he has never on any other occasion experienced a hallucination of the senses.

He mentioned several persons who would be able to corroborate this narrative. We received the following letter from his sister, Mrs. Hope, of Fermoy.

"December 12th, 1882.

"On the morning of September 8th, 1855, my brother, Mr. Colt, told myself, Captain Ferguson of the 42nd Regiment, since dead, and Major Borthwick of the Rifle Brigade (who is living), and others, that he had during the night awakened from sleep and seen, as he thought, my eldest brother, Lieut. Oliver Colt of the Royal Fusiliers (who was in the Crimea), standing between his bed and the door ; that he saw that he was wounded in more than one place—I remember he named the temple as one place— by bullet-wounds ; that he aroused himself, rushed to the door with closed eyes and looked back at the apparition, which stood between him and the bed. My father enjoined silence, lest my mother should be made uneasy ; but shortly afterwards came the news of the fall of the Redan and my brother's death. Two years afterwards, my husband, Colonel Hope, invited my brother to dine with him ; the former being still a lieutenant in the Royal Fusiliers, the latter an ensign in the Royal Welsh Fusiliers. While dining, they were talking of my eldest brother. My husband was about to describe his appearance when found, when my brother described what he had seen, and to the astonishment of all present, the description of the wounds tallied with the facts. My husband was my eldest brother's greatest friend, and was among those who saw the body as soon as it was found."

[It will be seen that this corroboration varies from the previous account in two points, which, however, do not greatly affect its value. The date was really September 9th, not the 8th—but it is very natural that the vision should have become associated with the *memorable* date, which was of course the 8th ; and the figure was kneeling, not standing.]

For present purposes, the detail to be noticed here is, of course, the position of the wound : stress can hardly be laid on the correspondence in the kneeling posture. But the appearance of " phosphorescent mist " [1] is another point of interest (see p. 526, first note) ; as is also the percipient's previous request to his brother to appear to him, which assimilates the case to the one where a distinct compact to this effect had been made (Vol. II., p. 66).

The next account, which we owe to the kindness of Major Taylor, of the Royal Military College, Farnborough, is from a lady, Miss L., who withholds her name from publication, in deference to the views of a near relative.

"Jan. 4th, 1886.

(211) "On one of the last days of July, about the year 1860, at 3 o'clock p.m., I was sitting in the drawing-room at the Rectory, reading, and my thoughts entirely occupied. I suddenly looked up, and saw most distinctly a tall, thin old gentleman enter the room and walk to the table. He wore a peculiar old-fashioned cloak, which I recognised as belonging to my great-uncle. I then looked at him closely, and remembered his features and appearance perfectly, although I had not seen him since I was quite a child. In his hand was a roll of paper, and he appeared to be very agitated. I was not in the least alarmed, as I firmly believed he was my uncle, not knowing then of his serious illness. I asked him if he wanted my father, who, I said, was not at home. He then appeared still more agitated and distressed, but made no remark. He then left the room, passing through the half-open door. I noticed that, although it was a very wet day, there was no appearance of his having walked in mud or rain. He had no umbrella, but a thick walking-stick, which I recognised at once when my father brought it home after the funeral. On questioning the servants they declared that no one had rung the bell, neither did they see anyone enter. My father had a letter by the next post, asking him to go at once to my uncle, who was very ill in Leicestershire. He started at once, but on his arrival was told that he had died exactly at 3 o'clock that afternoon, and had asked for him by name several times in an anxious and troubled manner, and a roll of paper was found under his pillow.

" I may mention that my father was his only nephew, and, having no son, he always led him to think that he would have a considerable legacy. Such, however, was not the case, and it is supposed that, as they were always good friends, he was influenced in his last illness, and probably, when too late, he wished to alter his will.   "E. F. L."

In answer to inquiries, Miss L. adds :—

" I told my mother and an uncle at once about the strange appearance *before* the news arrived, and also to my father directly he returned, all of whom are now dead. They advised me to try to dismiss it from my memory, but agreed that it could not be imagination, as I described my uncle so exactly ; and they did not consider me to be either of a nervous or superstitious temperament.

[1] In conversation, Captain Colt applied almost the same words to the appearance of tenuous blue mist as Mr. J. Russell Lowell used (see Vol II., p. xxii.) in describing his purely subjective phantasms.

"I am quite sure that I stated the facts truthfully and correctly to Major Taylor. The facts are as fresh in my memory as if they only happened yesterday, although so many years have passed away.

"I can assure you that nothing of the kind ever occurred to me before or since. [This is in answer to the question whether Miss L. had ever had a hallucination of the senses on any other occasion.] Neither have I been subject to nervous or imaginative fancies. This strange apparition was in broad daylight, and, as I was only reading the *Illustrated Newspaper*, there was nothing to excite my imagination."

A notice in the *Leicester Chronicle* shows that the death occurred on August 4, 1855, and the incident is therefore more remote than Miss L. imagined.

The next account is from Dr. Bowstead, of Caistor. Though remote in date, the main incident does not seem likely to have been greatly modified in memory ; and it has been regarded by the narrator as simply a most striking fact, for which he had no theory to account.

"July, 1883.

(212) "In September, 1847, I was playing in a cricket match, and took the place of long-field. A ball was driven in my direction, which I ought to have caught, but missed it, and it rolled towards a low hedge; I and another lad ran after it. When I got near the hedge, I saw the apparition of my half-brother, who was much endeared to me, over the hedge, dressed in a shooting suit with a gun on his arm ; he smiled and waved his hand at me. I called the attention of the other boy to the same, but when we looked again, the figure had vanished. I, feeling very sad at the time, went up to my uncle, and told him of what I had seen; he took out his watch and noted the time, just 10 minutes to 1 o'clock.

"Two days after, I received a letter from my father, informing me of the death of my half-brother, John Mounsey, which took place [at Lincoln] at 10 minutes to 1. His death was singular, for on that morning he said he was much better, and thought he should be able to shoot again. Taking up his gun, he turned round to my father, asking him if he had sent for me, as he particularly wished to see me. I was a great favourite of his. My father replied the distance was too far and expense too great to send for me, it being over 100 miles. At this he put himself into a passion, and said he would see me in spite of them all, for he did not care for expense or distance. Suddenly a blood vessel on his lungs burst, and he died at once. He was at the time dressed in a shooting-suit, and had his gun on his arm. I knew he was ill, but a letter from my father previous to the time I saw him told me he was improving, and that he might get through the winter; but his disease was consumption, and he had bleeding from the lungs three months before his death.

"ROWLAND BOWSTEAD, M.D."

We find from the Register of Deaths that Mr. John Mounsey died on September 23, 1847.

In answer to inquiries, Dr. Bowstead says :—

"No note was taken at the time, only my uncle, at whose school I was at the time, looked at his watch and noted the time, but never thought anything about the occurrence. He himself had once a similar thing happen to himself when an uncle died ; but not so vividly as mine. There is not a soul now living to get any information from, for the lad who was with me and who did not see anything, although he looked in the same direction, is now dead; but the announcement of the death two days afterwards told of my brother's death at the time I saw him. All the family connection are dead ; his son died in 1853, and his wife in 1854. I have had no hallucinations since."

In conversation, Dr. Bowstead told me that he was not in the least expecting his brother's death. He has a very vivid remembrance of his uncle's look, and of his pulling out his watch. The boy who was near him in the cricket-field, Fred Court by name, afterwards went to Australia, where he died.

Here, it will be seen, the dress of the apparition did not contain any features that were new to the percipient—to whom the sporting aspect of his brother was (as I learnt from him in conversation) both familiar and interesting ; still, the correspondence, if accurately remembered, is remarkable. This case deserves consideration from those who would attribute "phantasms of the living" to a diseased state of body or mind in the percipient. A cricketing school-boy, in full exercise, is rarely a prey to physical ills : and though his mental condition after just missing a catch may be a pitiable one enough, it is not one that we commonly associate with hysteria or superstition.

The next case is from Mr. John Hernaman, F.S.A., Head Master of the Lambeth Boys' School, Hercules Buildings, London, S.E. He tells us that this account (which we received in 1884) was written within two years of the occurrence ; and that he has had no other experience of hallucination.

(213) "When I lived in Bishopsgate, my rooms were at Salvador House. It was a grand old house. Formerly the home of a Spanish Ambassador, it had undergone strange vicissitudes. . . . My apartments consisted of a suite of five rooms, which I occupied with my housekeeper, a middle-aged woman, and her son, a youth of 18, who waited on me. I gave up three of the suite for their use, reserving only two very large rooms, which communicated with each other, for my own.

"Well, one night as I lay asleep, I all at once woke to perfect consciousness, as wide awake as I am now ; and there, in the embrasure made by the thickness of the wall, stood a little old woman in her night-dress and cap, with a small black and white checked shawl, as far as I could make out, like a duster-pattern, over her shoulders. I want you particularly to remember the shawl. I knew her well, and, as I lay, remarked to myself on the beauty and transparency of her complexion, while a soft lambent light seemed to play over the whole figure, such as you would see on your fingers when you rub a match, or the liquid gleaming phos-

2 N

phorescence[1] one sometimes finds ridging the wavelets at sea. On noting this, the work of an instant, an intense and indescribable feeling took possession of me, beginning somewhere in the region of the feet, and, passing up my spine,[2] reached my head, where 'each particular hair did stand on end.' Vexed and annoyed with myself, I turned away from the sight, as the chime of St. Botolph's struck the quarter to 2. When the sounds had died, and after the clock had struck the hour, I fell asleep again, and rested undisturbed till morning.

"On going downstairs, I met one of our clergy, the Rev. George Wrench, the greatest friend I had in Bishopsgate, [since deceased] and said, 'Laugh at me! Here am I, a man supposed to be educated, of average intelligence, at least, living in the very centre of the centre of civilisation, an utter disbeliever in ghosts, and yet last night I saw one.' 'Nonsense!' said he. ''Tis true!' I repeated. 'Well, come, who was it?' 'Mrs. P.,' I answered. 'You don't say so! Do you know she is very ill?' 'Not I.' 'But she is though,' rejoined he, and we chaffed each other about the strange visitant.

"Well, all that day I went about my work and never gave my ghost a thought, retired to bed as usual, slept well and woke exactly at the same time as on the night previous. This I know by the jingle of the chimes immediately after waking, and the clock striking the succeeding hour of 2. The same intense, indescribable feeling passed over me—that horrid, creepy dread, but I resolutely turned from the side on which the embrasure lay, and reproached myself for being a fool. Nor would I look, and yet I felt assured of her presence.

"When I got up, I found that she had sent a message, wishing to see me. She was the attendant on the pews at my side of the church, a poor widow woman of quiet, gentle manners, a friend of my housekeeper's, who sometimes came in to help if we had any extra company. Often when I have gone round to the kitchen, she has risen up respectfully, while I used to say, 'How much you remind me of my dear old mother,' and have more than once caressingly stroked her hair. I went to see her. There she lay in her little bed—so clean and tidy—so peaceably passing away in a trance-like calm. She at once recognised my voice, when a pleased smile of restful satisfaction seemed to play over her face. [Mr. Hernaman then read a passage of the Bible to the patient.] As I was leaving the room, on turning to look at her, I noticed how striking were the points of resemblance to the figure in the embrasure, but it was incomplete—the shawl was wanting. So I said to her sister who was nursing her, 'Have you ever during her illness had thrown about her a little black-and-white checked shawl?' I gave no reason for my question. 'No, sir!' was the answer, 'No! We haven't such a thing in the house!' Then suddenly she exclaimed, 'Oh! do you mean a little brown-and-white plaid, like this?' making a sudden dive behind a box near the bed's head, from which she brought up the identical shawl, *a brown-and-white checked*, which she at once placed round the shoulders of the invalid, and the picture was complete.

[Next night, a friend of Mr. Hernaman's, Mr. James F. Maule, now residing at 61, Rouel Road, Bermondsey, spent the night with him.]

---

[1] *Cf.* the "phosphorescent mist" in case 210.
[2] See Vol. ii., p. 37, note.

" My rest was sound and undisturbed till the morning when George my housekeeper's son, came rushing into the bedroom, after a hasty knock, with a face full of fright, and said, 'If you please, sir, Mrs. P wants you again!' While I dressed, my friend laughed at me and joked immoderately. George brought me in a cup of coffee, which I hastily swallowed while dressing; but before I could get to her house, which was hard by, she had passed away.

" All I have said with regard to myself is true as it occurred to me and yet my judgment refuses to believe it. I consulted a medical friend, I was so annoyed with myself for thinking the thing possible for a moment. He too laughed at me, but wished George to occupy the spare bed till my holidays came, which were close at hand.

" I did learn some months later that she had saved a little money—not much, about £90, I believe—and was very anxious indeed that I should have charge of it for her two children, who were living at home with her.

" JOHN HERNAMAN."

In answer to inquiries, Mr. Hernaman adds, on March 7th, 1885 :—

" The matter to which you refer occurred some 14 years ago."

We applied to Mr. Francis Tee, of Finsbury Street, E.C., a brother of the Mrs. P. of the narrative, and he sent us a mourning card which showed that Mrs. P. died on Dec. 14th, 1871, aged 53 years.

Mr. Maule, writing to us on Dec. 19, 1886, says that he well recollects the incident, and " never saw anyone in such a state of mind as Mr. Hernaman was about the affair."

Here the shawl is the important detail. Other noteworthy points are the light (pp. 550-1), and the sort of attempt at a repetition on the second night, which may or may not have been a mere recrudescence of the previous impression (see p. 445).

The next account is from Mr. J. H. Redfern, of 20, Great Ancoats Street, Manchester, who has been carefully cross-examined *vivâ voce*.

" January, 1883.

(214) " My wife died in December, 1874. While apparently in her usual health, and without any premonitory symptoms, she was suddenly seized with an illness (effusion of serum on the brain), which in a few days terminated in death. For something like 36 hours previous to death she was in a comatose state,[1] and thus she passed away. She had an aunt, a widow, to whom she was much attached. Her aunt resided 4 or 5 miles away from us, but twice or thrice a year she came to see us, and usually stayed a few days or a week, and one of these visits was always at New Year's time. My wife died a few days before Christmas Day, and in due course the funeral took place. The day after, having obtained the address of her aunt—for I did not before know it—I sent her a 'memorial card,' thinking it might prevent the shock she might probably experience if she came, and only then learned the death of her niece.

" The New Year came, but she came not. We wondered and talked about her for nearly 3 months, but heard nothing. One Sunday afternoon,

---

[1] See Chap. v., § 10, and compare cases 128, 152, 176, 202, 203, 217, 277, 452, 561.

at tea my daughter sprang up from the table exclaiming, 'There's aunt coming up the garden;' and surely it was her indeed. We ran to meet her, and brought her into the house. Overcome with emotion she sank into a chair, and wept for some time. At length, becoming calmer, we learned that she had been seriously ill for some time. Her account of the matter was this :—

"On the day of my wife's death she was—in the evening—engaged in the kitchen in the performance of some domestic duties. Turning round from a table at which she had been engaged, she saw my wife coming out of a lobby into the kitchen, and approaching her with a smile upon her face, her arms extended as if to greet her (her usual manner of welcoming anyone). She herself advanced to meet her niece, and expecting to embrace her, when suddenly 'she was gone,' and she herself was alone. Confused and wondering, she looked about her, and noticed the time, 8.30 p.m. by the clock.

"I asked her if she had been thinking about her or talking of her. She said she had not thought of her for days. I asked her if there was any other woman in the house with herself. She replied, 'Yes, one, who, feeling unwell, had gone to lie down some hours before.' Shortly afterwards this person came downstairs. She asked her 'had she been down before?' Her reply was 'No, I fell asleep.' 'I said nothing to her,' said she, 'for I knew she had not; besides I could never have mistaken her for Sarah' (my wife). 'She was much older, and had dark hair, while Sarah's was light and golden. I could have mistaken no one for Sarah, but,' she added, 'I saw her as plainly as I see you now.'

"My wife died at 8.40 p.m. There might be a difference in the clocks.

"In answer to a question, she said that her niece was not in her usual dress. She had on a long white robe or night-dress, with frillings at the neck and wrists. Her hair was not gathered up and arranged as usual, but was drawn from the fore part of her head and fell down her back. That described her appearance exactly. The doctors had directed her hair to be loosed and drawn back from the forehead, and it hung down her shoulders and back.

"She said that she had no idea that my wife was in any but her usual health, not thinking of any evil. A few days afterwards she went to spend a few days with a friend whom she had promised to stay with for a short time at Christmas. Returning home, the letter was handed her, and she was jokingly told that it had been waiting for her a week. Opening it, she saw the name and the date. The whole thing—forgotten for the time—flashed upon her mind, and she fell off from the chair, remembering no more until days afterwards she found herself in bed, where she remained until within a few days of her coming again to see us.

"The letter was afterwards discovered upon the floor. She had said nothing of the appearance to any in the house. They did not understand the thing at all. The medical man called in to attend her, said that she had received some great mental shock, and for some time he feared that she would not recover from it.

"I give you these facts just as they are, making no comments upon them, simply vouching for their accuracy.   "J. H. REDFERN."

We find from a notice in the *Manchester Guardian* that Mrs. Redfern died on December 18th, 1874. Mr. Redfern tells us that the aunt died about a year before he sent us the account.

In answer to inquiries, Mr. Redfern adds, on March 19th, 1883 :—

" I never knew who the medical man was ; doubtless someone in the neighbourhood called in in a hurry., The woman in the house with my wife's aunt at the time, of whom she inquired as to whether she had before come downstairs, confirmed the fact that she had not; this woman has since left the place. The old lady was clear-headed and truthful, and repeated the story often, and in the same manner, to the last. I think upon referring to the MS. you will see that she had no knowledge or idea of her niece's illness ; she said that the thought of her death never entered her mind. She noted the day and the hour. She had arranged to visit some friends, and to stay with them for a short time. She went a day or two after. I had not her address, [*i.e.*, at Gorton, where she lived,] but in a few days obtained it, and sent per post a memorial card. It appears that during the time of her absence upon this visit, this card (of course in an envelope) was delivered. Upon her return it was handed to her. Not thinking anything about it she opened it, read it, let it drop, and swooned. She was, I believe, unconscious for a long time, and a long illness followed We wondered that we never saw or heard from her."

Mr. John Robert Redfern, of 41, Bickley Street, Moss Side, Manchester (a cashier, and foreign and corresponding clerk in a firm of shippers), says :—   " June 28th, 1883.

" With reference to the appearance at the time of her death of my mother to her aunt, Nancy Juison, I can state that the account furnished by my father as given by her is a correct one. I have heard the statement from herself, and have not the slightest doubt of her veracity, or as to her convictions on the subject. I knew her intimately all my life up to her death."

Mrs. Hannah Lees, of Clifton Crescent, Rotherham, says :—
                                                        " June 5th, 1883.

" The account of my sister's death (Mrs. Redfern) and her appearance to my Aunt Nancy, as given by Mr. J. H. Redfern, is just as narrated by my aunt, and I am satisfied as to the truth of aunt's statement, and her belief in the matter."

[The testimony here is not first-hand. Had the aunt been alive we should, of course, have obtained her account from herself. But since we reckon as on a par with first-hand evidence the testimony of persons who have been made aware of the percipient's experience *before* the percipient has learnt the event that has befallen the agent (p. 148), we may regard as practically on the same level a case where the percipient's experience, though not described to the witnesses before the news was known, produced an effect—her prolonged absence through illness--which they remarked on and wondered at.]

The next case, from Mr. Rouse, of Jarvis Road, Croydon (agent for Cockerells, coal merchants), is another marked instance of deferred recognition (see § 3). As regards the special point of dress, it is inconclusive ; as though the aspect of the agent was at the time actually as represented in the phantasm, it was also probably an aspect familiar to the percipient. Writing to us on the 11th of June, 1883, Mr. Rouse explains that in the early part of 1873 he had been a member of a circle which met to investigate spiritualistic phenomena. At each of the séances, which were held in a private house, he sat next to the same lady, Mrs. W., between whom and himself a strong sympathy existed. On one occasion Mr. Rouse had to go to Norwich on the day when the sitting was usually held. Late on the evening of that day he went out for a walk in the outskirts of the town.

(215) "It was in the brightest moonlight, about full moon, I should think, with hardly a cloud in the sky ; yet there was a thick white haze overhanging the fields. After walking a little distance I found myself on the top of a small hill, which enabled me to see a considerable distance along the road in front of me, the only living object apparently in view being a human form in the middle of the road, yet so far off that I could not tell if it was a woman or a man, and did not take much notice of it. However, in walking on, I soon made it out to be a woman, and concluded it was a country woman walking into Norwich. The next moment I began to fear that, the time and place being so lonely, the woman would be afraid to pass me. I, therefore, under this feeling, got as near as possible to one side of the road, thus giving her all the width on the other side to pass ; but, to my astonishment, she also left the middle of the road, and took the same side as myself, as if determined to meet me face to face. I then walked into the middle of the road, thinking I would avoid her, but, to my surprise, the woman did the same, so I then concluded to walk on as we were.

"I had not advanced many more steps, however, before instead of a country woman, as I imagined, with eggs and poultry for next day's market, I could plainly see that the figure before me was a well-dressed lady in evening dress, without bonnet or shawl. I could see some ornament or flower in her hair, gold bracelets on her bare arms, rings on her fingers, and could hear the rustle of her dress. She now seemed to approach me more rapidly, and I noticed that, if I stepped in the least degree out of the direct line between us, she did the same.[1] In the next minute I felt certain that I had seen the lady before, and immediately afterwards I recognised her as Mrs. W. I had not the least fear, for she was so real that I thought she had, like myself, unexpectedly and suddenly got to Norwich. I, therefore, met her without the least shake or tremble, delighted to see my friend. We approached within about 5 feet of each other ; she gazed at me very intently as I thought ; she held out her hand to me, and I could see her face and lips move as if about to speak to me. I was in the act of taking her hand to greet her, but had not touched her, when some iron hurdles which formed the fencing of the cattle market, rang as if they were being struck with an iron bar. This startled me, and unconsciously I turned round to see what made the noise. I could see nothing, and instantly turned again to Mrs. W. but she was gone.

"Now it was that I began to tremble, and for some time I felt that she

---

[1] It is not specially remarkable that a hallucinatory object should persist in appearing in the direct line of vision. See p. 472.

was still near me, although I could not see her. But I soon pulled myself together and walked back to Norwich and my bedroom, but not to sleep, for I could not get rid of the feeling that perhaps my friend had suddenly died or met with some serious accident. I, therefore, wrote to a gentleman in London—a mutual friend—telling him what I had seen and what my fears were, asking him to be very careful, but to make inquiries about Mrs. W., as to her welfare, and what and where she was on that night and time. The next day's post brought me the welcome tidings that Mrs. W. was quite well and in good health, that at the very time I saw her, about 11 p.m., she was sitting in her usual place in the circle in London, and that there, for the first time in her life, she had fallen into a trance which frightened the other sitters very much, and they had great difficulty in bringing her back to ordinary life.   "JOHN ROUSE."

Mrs. W. has read through the above account, and writes to us as follows, in June, 1883 :—

"It is perfectly correct. I quite remember the séances and the particular occasion to which Mr. Rouse refers, when I became unconscious one night, at about 11 o'clock, and on recovery had no recollection of anything but that I had *gone suddenly out of myself*.[1] My dress at the time of the occurrence is stated quite correctly. I also remember one of our circle calling with Mr. Rouse's letter, to ascertain, at his request, whether I was still in earthly form. Talking over the matter with him, and afterwards with the others, all agreed as to the time of my becoming oblivious. I have never had the same experience before nor since then.

"L. E. W."

[The evidence here will, of course, suffer in the eyes of many, from the fact that both agent and percipient were at the time attending séances. It must also be mentioned that on such occasions Mr. Rouse has seen or imagined vague appearances. He has, however, only on one other occasion (when again there were singular points of correspondence with reality) had anything like a distinct hallucination ; and he is a sensible and clear-headed man.]

The next case is from Mrs. Peek, of 3, Fairfax Place, Dartmouth. The fact narrated has remained in the mind of a practical and unvisionary person, quite free from superstitious fancies, as simply the oddest thing she ever experienced.

"October, 1884.

(216) "On the 25th of April, 1867, at about 11 o'clock at night, I was alone in the lower part of the house, to see if the doors were securely fastened, and the dogs housed and fed. Having satisfied myself upon these points, I had lifted my hand to turn out the gas in the kitchen, when something drew my eyes towards the doorway, and I saw for the space of a few seconds a figure standing there, dressed in lightish coloured clothes, with long boots on, as if for riding ; the face was shadowy, yet I thought I could recognise the contour of my brother, who lives in Natal. When it was

[1] It occasionally happens at séances—whether owing to the attitude of expectancy or to some other condition—that a sitter falls into an odd unconscious, or semi-conscious state; which would have nothing alarming in it to any one familiar with the phenomena of hypnotism. As to the subjective sense of "going out of oneself" see above, p. 555, note.

gone, I hurried up the stairs to the dining-room, where others of the household were sitting; they noticed how frightened I seemed, and when I told them about it tried to laugh me out of my fear, but I felt convinced in my own mind as to the reality of my experience, and noted the day of the month.

"About six weeks afterwards, I received a letter from my brother telling me that his wife was taken very ill on the 25th of April, while he was away on a journey, from which he returned that same day, only in time to start at once for his mother-in-law, leaving his wife without anyone to care for her except two Kaffir girls, for their farm was many miles from any other dwelling. He spoke in his letter of the great distress of mind he suffered during his long ride of 30 miles, at the thought of leaving his apparently dying wife, and how often he wished I had been near to help him in his trouble.   "ANNA W. PEEK."

In answer to inquiries, Mrs. Peek says :—

"I can assure you that the vision you received an account of from me is the only one I have ever witnessed.

"My brother returned late at night from a journey, and started again on a ride of 30 or more miles over a rough road in the Little Tugela district, so he would certainly be on his journey at 2 o'clock a.m. [which, however, would correspond with midnight, not 11 p.m., in England.]

"I will get my husband and another gentleman, who was staying with us, to sign their names in testimony that I spoke of it to them directly I came into the room where they were, after seeing the vision. The day following, I mentioned it to my uncle, who advised me to take a note of the date."

"We hereby bear testimony to the foregoing statement.
                   "ROBERT PEEK.
                   "G. H. COLLINS."

In conversation, Mrs. Peek told me that the full gas-light was on the figure; but it seemed tenuous and half transparent.[1] The dress was quite distinctly marked, but the face was indistinct. She wrote down the date at her aunt's suggestion, and compared it, when the letter came, with the one there mentioned.

[The coincidence here is not, of course, as striking as in many other cases, as the condition of the agent was not of an extremely abnormal sort; but the special direction of his thought to the percipient, if correctly recorded, may fairly be taken into account.]

Here again the dress seen was not so unusual that one might not conceive it to have been independently supplied by the percipient's brain in the act of projecting the phantasm; but the other hypothesis would at any rate be in place.

The next case is also a doubtful one as regards the dress; since when a man is telepathically impressed to conjure up his father's image, it is undeniably possible for him, out of his own mental

[1] See p. 526, first note, and Vol. ii., p. 38, note.

resources, to conjure it up in a night-cap. Still such an aspect was
very much out of keeping with the scene in which the phantasm was
located. The account is from Mr. Timothy Cooper,[1] mentioned above
(p. 506), and appeared in *Light* for January, 1882.

(217) "In the year 1871, I was living at Seaview, Seaton Carew, going
daily to Stockton-on-Tees to business. It was race week in August, and
so a busy time. I was going down into the cellar to fetch butter for a
customer, and as I was on the top step, I saw my father standing at the
bottom of the cellar steps in his shirt and night-cap, and he seemed to
walk into the cellar. I went down and fetched the butter, and looked
for my father, who was nowhere to be seen. I went up and said to my
employer's wife, 'I must go home now, for my father will not last long,
and wants to see me.' So on the last day of the races I started, and arrived
at Amersham, my father's residence, a journey of about 250 miles. On
the Saturday afternoon I inquired of my sister how my father was at the
time I had seen him at Stockton. She said he lay as if dead for more
than half-an-hour ; in fact, they held a looking-glass to see if he breathed.
He died November 23rd, 1871.   "TIMOTHY COOPER."

We have verified the date of death in the *Nonconformist.*

[The impression in this case seems to have prompted the percipient to
take a long journey ; but we do not know in what degree previous anxiety
may have contributed to it.]

Sufficient illustrations have now been given of the two types
of case, where special features of dress and aspect may lead us pretty
confidently to refer the detailed form which the hallucination takes
to the percipient and to the agent respectively. But the majority
of visual telepathic phantasms, as we shall find later, present no such
special features ; the aspect of the figure is free from striking
peculiarities, and the dress little noticed, and such as either of the
two persons concerned might readily picture as natural and familiar.
In all such cases, and alike whether the agent is or is not so habited
at the moment, it seems to me reasonable to refer the details of the
appearance to the percipient's mind. As compared with our total
ignorance concerning the prior process of *transference,* our view of the
immediate process in the percipient which issues in sensory hallucination may be said to be knowledge ; in it we at any rate have the
analogy of subjective hallucinations to go by. Inasmuch, then, as
a member of a civilised community has been impelled to project a
phantasm—for there it stands, projected—it is in accordance with
analogy, and we may almost say inevitable, that he should project
it in *some* dress ; and it is surely simpler (as I have suggested

[1] Mr. Cooper unfortunately went to reside in America before it was possible for us
to make his personal acquaintance ; but we have had a satisfactory account of him. His
father was the Rev. James Cooper, for many years pastor of the Baptist Church at
Amersham.

above, to suppose that he does this wholly from his own resources, which are adequate for the purpose, than to suppose that a detailed image is supplied to him, clean-cut and complete, from indefinite unconscious or sub-conscious strata of the agent's mind. The point becomes clearest when there is a clear *choice* of familiar dresses. For instance, a son sees the phantasm of his mother "dressed in a peculiar silver-grey dress, which she had originally got for a fancy-ball" (Vol. II., p. 81). That *he* should so *project* her image, under a sudden telepathic influence received from her (p. 538), no more needs explanation than that any other item of past experience should present itself unsought in memory or dream; but that *she* should so *transmit* her image would decidedly need explanation; for even if she was conscious at the time—which she most likely was not—unless her mind was consciously engaged with this particular dress, what disturbance can we assume of the quite impartial state of latency in which her ideas of her various dresses would be? There being no sudden call on her—as there is on her son—to represent her image, there would be no impulse to the selection (whether conscious or casual) of one particular form of representation. And the same argument will apply wherever the phantasmal costume, or any part of it, is such as would not form an almost necessary element in the agent's consciousness at the time. In most cases where costume is noticed at all, it includes particulars the choice of which presents no difficulty if we leave the *percipient* to make it, among the various familiar aspects of the friend whose image he is *ex hypothesi* impelled to construct; but any precedence of which over others on the *agent's* side would imply a detailed activity of construction, occurring not only without consciousness, but apparently *without cause;* since there is no ground for connecting the construction (least of all the unconscious construction) of highly elaborated visual images with the conditions of spontaneous telepathic agency.[1]

---

[1] Any hypothesis that the condition of agency *in itself* (*i.e.*, apart from that reaction of the percipient on the impression to which I have attributed its projection in sensory form) tends to elicit and transmit out of the recesses of the agent's mind some definite image of his own aspect, would seem open to this objection—that there are a large number of telepathic phantasms—notably the *auditory* class—in which nothing connected with the agent's aspect appears. Apart from literal representations of some conscious thought or sensation of the agent (p. 536, note), it has seemed an adequate hypothesis that the particular form of sensory development is determined on the *percipient's* side; and it would be very difficult to combine with this the hypothesis that *sometimes* the form is *compelled* to be visual by the preponderating force in the *agent's* mind of a latent image of his own aspect. For if the image is *latent*, and has no particular relevance to the circumstances of the moment, such an image has had just the same amount of presence in the agent's mind, and just as much (or little) chance of telepathically asserting itself, in the *non-visual* cases.

§ 9. Before quitting the subject of the development of telepathic phantasms, I may be allowed to point out its relation to the physiological sketch at the close of the 10th chapter ; for it happens to supply substantial confirmation to the views of centrifugal origin there maintained. The whole idea of morbid excitation from the more external parts of the sensory apparatus becomes here irrelevant. All that has been said in this chapter as to the development of the hallucination from the nucleus of a transferred impression marks out the higher part of the brain—the part which is concerned with ideas or general images of persons and things, and not with immediate perception of them—as the place where the abnormal process starts ; the hallucination itself being due to the downward promulgation of the disturbance from these higher tracts to the specific sensory centre concerned. Especially must this origin commend itself in respect of the phantasms which are bodied forth in a more or less fanciful form, with elements which are clearly the percipient's own contribution, but which he would never have contributed had not telepathy supplied an idea for him to clothe. But perhaps the cases where the hypothesis is most helpful are those of which Mr. Marchant's (p. 207) is the type, where no obvious *rapport* exists between the two parties concerned. How—we naturally ask— could the idea of Kelsey be impressed on Mr. Marchant's mind with such force as to embody itself in a visible phantom, when Kelsey's mind was presumably not occupied either with Mr. Marchant or with himself in relation to him ? From a physiological point of view the fact becomes less startling if we suppose the primary change in Mr. Marchant's brain to take place at the part which is the great store-house of old impressions ; at the part, moreover, where an appropriate physical basis may be found not only for distinct and recognisable images, but for sub-conscious ideas and memories, and for the most distant and intangible associations. In the register of the brain it is seldom that a record, once made, is so utterly obliterated that, under suitable conditions, it may not be revived. And if once a relation be established between two persons, and the records of it registered in their two brains, it may be possible for the same harmony occasionally to manifest itself between those records—even though they be long sunk below the level of conscious attention—as between the *immediate* impressions of the moment ; and, this once granted, we have seen how the physiological process may lead on to the projection of the visible phantom.[1] In psychical terms, I see no reason why sub-conscious ideas and memories which are in no distinct way present to consciousness, such as Kelsey's sense of his old relationship to Mr. Marchant, should not evoke similar blind movements in Mr. Marchant's mind, which, gathering strength, might lead him to body forth the vision of his old acquaintance. A hallucination which is thus initiated by the quickening of long-buried memories, and of dim tracts of emotional association, is the most conspicuous example of the projection of an idea from within outwards; and the tremor to which the sensorium reverberates will presumably start in the inmost penetralia of cerebral process.

§ 10. The parallelism between telepathic and purely subjective hallucinations has now been traced out in the most essential particulars. To the five heads of resemblance enumerated in the last chapter (p. 500), the present chapter has added the various modes of gradual development, and of original or fantastic embodiment; the special point with respect to luminosity (pp. 550-1); and the general but not invariable limitation of the percept to a single human figure (pp.545-6). I may note further the interesting negative characteristic that (with very rare exceptions) neither subjective disturbances nor transferred impressions seem to produce visual hallucinations representing a person who is actually present with the percipient at the time.[2] One fails at first sight to see why this should be. If pre-occupation of the percipient's mind with the person seen is to go for anything in the subjective cases, is not the mind often completely pre-occupied with a person who is present? and if *rapport* is to go for anything in the telepathic cases, is not *rapport* often at its maximum of strength with a person who is present? I suppose the explanation must be analogous to the reason why the stars are not visible by day; and that vision of friends who are absent depends on a vague sense of remoteness and abstraction in relation to them, the possibility of

---

[1] I have sufficiently emphasised the difficulty of expressing the *transmission* of telepathic impressions in physical terms (pp. 110-13). And though I here suggest that the difficulty is lessened if we may draw on unconscious parts of the mind, and old records in the brain, my physiological point is independent of this suggestion, and is limited to the percipient's own organism. There certain nervous changes do undoubtedly take place, in correspondence with the psychical fact of the hallucination; and my object is to show that what we observe as to the psychical fact may be best accounted for on a particular view of the physical process.

[2] I have encountered only seven instances of the kind, two of which are described later (Vol. ii., p. 24, note, and p. 218). The negative fact is worth pointing out; but positive instances (unless perchance "collective," like case 333), would, of course, be more naturally interpreted as purely subjective, on the analogy of after-images (p. 505), than as telepathic.

which is swamped by their presence. The possibility seems, indeed, to be to some extent affected by the presence of *any* companion—a large majority of hallucinations, alike of purely subjective and of telepathic origin, taking place when the percipient is alone. Various other points of frequent or occasional resemblance between the two classes remain, which have been noted or will be noted as they occur in the examples, and need here only be briefly summarised. Such are the various degrees of externalisation, and of apparent solidity or tenuity;[1] rudimentary appearances;[2] fragmentary appearances;[3] rapid repetitions;[4] movement in the figures seen;[5] gradual disappearance;[6] special modes of disappearance;[7] disappearance on sudden speech or gesture;[8] response of the phantasmal voice to words of the hallucinated person;[9] the fact that the hallucination is unshared by other persons who may be in the hallucinated person's company or vicinity;[10] and the fact that every now and then the liability to either type of hallucination seems hereditary.[11]

Of still greater importance are the *contrasts* that exist between the phenomena of the two classes; *e.g.*, the great superiority in number of visual over auditory cases in the telepathic class, which is the reverse of what obtains in the purely subjective; and the large proportion, in the purely subjective class, of *unrecognised* phantasms, which are decidedly exceptional in the telepathic. But these points of contrast are chiefly interesting as bearing on a larger question which I can now no longer defer—the question whether the cases presented as telepathic can reasonably be regarded as more than merely accidental coincidences; and they will find their appropriate place in the next chapter.

[1] Pp. 480-3, 488, 526, 568 ; Vol. ii., pp. 29-38, 120, 137.
[2] Chap. xiv., §§ 4 and 6.
[3] P. 504 ; Vol. ii., p. 33, note ; and see cases 116, 240, 553, 572.
[4] P. 414 ; Vol. ii., pp. 105, 237, note.
[5] This feature is so common, in both classes, that I need hardly call special attention to it where it occurs. In this chapter alone, for instance, we have encountered it in 7 cases—Nos. 198, 199, 202, 203, 204, 211, 215.
[6] See above, p. 521, and Vol. ii., p. 97.
[7] See p. 432, note, and, *e.g.*, case 211, above.
[8] See Vol. ii., p. 91, second note ; and add cases 499 and 540 to the list.
[9] P. 476 ; and see cases 498, 547, 568, 639, 654.
[10] See above, p. 223, and Vol. ii., p. 105, second note. The cases where the experience affects more than one person will be discussed in Chap. xviii., and may perhaps be found to supply a fresh point of resemblance between hallucinations of subjective and of telepathic origin.
[11] Vol. ii., p. 132, note.

END OF VOLUME I.

PRINTED BY THE NATIONAL PRESS AGENCY, LIMITED, WHITEFRIARS STREET, LONDON, E.C.

Lightning Source UK Ltd.
Milton Keynes UK
UKOW04f0944121115

262504UK00001B/2/P